The Making of Samuel Beckett's *Not I / Pas moi, That Ti*

BECKETT
DIGITAL
MANUSCRIPT
PROJECT

VOLUME 10

The Making of Samuel Beckett's *Not I / Pas moi*, *That Time / Cette fois* and *Footfalls / Pas*

JAMES LITTLE

UPA
University Press Antwerp

BLOOMSBURY

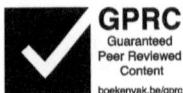

The GPRC label (Guaranteed Peer Review Content) was developed by the Flemish organization Boek.be and is assigned to publications which are in compliance with the academic standards required by the VABB (Vlaams Academisch Bibliografisch Bestand).

The research leading to these results has received funding from the European Research Council under the European Union's Seventh Framework Programme (FP7/2007–2013) / ERC grant agreement n° 313609.

Published with the support of the Belgian University Foundation
Uitgegeven met steun van de Universitaire stichting van België.

UPA is an imprint of ASP nv
(Academic and Scientific Publishers nv)
Keizerslaan 34 · B-1000 Brussels
T +32 (0)2 289 26 50 · F +32 (0)2 289 26 59
info@aspeditions.be · www.aspeditions.be

—

ISBN of the Bloomsbury edition: 978 13 5026 905 7
ISBN of the UPA edition: 978 94 6117 439 0
NUR 632
Legal deposit D/2023/11.161/032

—

Book design and typesetting: Stéphane de Schrevel

Distribution for the Benelux:
ASP / University Press Antwerp
34 Keizerslaan, B-1000 Brussels
www.aspeditions.be

Distribution for the rest of the world:
Bloomsbury
50 Bedford Square, London, WC1B 3DP
www.bloomsbury.com

My I's are nothing and my mes are nothing and
my my's are nothing and so for all the other persons
in the quartet or quintet as may be. (Beckett, 'Kilcool')

Table of Contents

The Beckett Digital Manuscript Project 10
Acknowledgements 12
List of Abbreviations 14
Note on the Transcriptions 23
List of Illustrations 24

Introduction: Staging the Subject–Object Breakdown 26

Part I The Making of *Not I / Pas moi*

1 Documents 48
1.1 Autograph Manuscripts 49
1.1.1 English 49
1.1.2 French 66
1.2 Typescripts 68
1.2.1 English 68
1.2.2 French 77
1.3 Setting Copies, Galleys, Proofs and Annotated Copies 82
1.3.1 English 82
1.4 Pre-book Publications 87
1.4.1 French 87
1.5. Editions 88
1.5.1 English (UK) 88
1.5.2 English (US) 91
1.5.3 French 95
1.5.4 Multilingual 97
1.6 Playscripts and Production Notes 100
1.6.1 English 100
1.7 Genetic Map 110

2 The Genesis of *Not I / Pas moi* 114
2.1 Before *Not I / Pas moi* 115
2.1.1 'Kilcool' 115
2.1.2 'Petit Odéon' Fragments 127
2.2 The Genesis of *Not I* 141
2.2.1 Chronology 141
2.2.2 Genesis 154
2.3 The Genesis of *Pas moi* 204
2.3.1 Chronology 204
2.3.2 Genesis 208

Part II The Making of *That Time / Cette fois*

3 Documents 224
3.1 Autograph Manuscripts 225
3.1.1 English 225
3.1.2 French 233
3.2 Typescripts 234
3.2.1 English 234
3.2.2 French 254
3.3 Setting Copies and Galleys 257
3.3.1 English 257
3.3.2 French 259
3.4 Editions 260
3.4.1 English (UK) 260
3.4.2 English (US) 262
3.4.3 French 263
3.4.4 Multilingual 265
3.5 Playscripts and Production Notes 267
3.5.1 English 267
3.5.2 Multilingual 269
3.6 Genetic Map 274

4 The Genesis of *That Time / Cette fois* 278
4.1 The Genesis of *That Time* 279
4.1.1 Chronology 279
4.1.2 Genesis 288
4.2 The Genesis of *Cette fois* 329
4.2.1 Chronology 329
4.2.2 Genesis 335

Part III The Making of *Footfalls / Pas*

5 Documents 350

5.1 Autograph Manuscripts 351

5.1.1 English 351

5.2 Typescripts 355

5.2.1 English 355

5.2.2 French 359

5.3 Setting Copies, Galleys and Proofs 361

5.3.1 English 361

5.3.2 French 365

5.4 Pre-book Publications 368

5.4.1 French 368

5.5 Editions 370

5.5.1 English (UK) 370

5.5.2 English (US) 378

5.5.3 French 381

5.5.4 Multilingual 382

5.6 Playscripts, Production Notes and Annotated Copies 384

5.6.1 English 384

5.6.2 Multilingual 394

5.7 Genetic Map 396

6 The Genesis of *Footfalls / Pas* 400

6.1 The Genesis of *Footfalls* 401

6.1.1 Chronology 401

6.1.2 Genesis 411

6.2 The Genesis of *Pas* 456

6.2.1 Chronology 456

6.2.2 Genesis 461

Conclusion: Beckett's 'dark matter' 477

Works Cited 488

Works by Beckett 488

Other Works Cited or Consulted 491

Index 510

The Beckett Digital Manuscript Project

Series Preface

This volume is part of the Beckett Digital Manuscript Project, a collaboration between the Centre for Manuscript Genetics (University of Antwerp), the Beckett International Foundation (University of Reading) and the Harry Ransom Humanities Research Center (University of Texas at Austin). The development of this project started from two initiatives: (1) the 'inhouse' genetic edition of four works by Samuel Beckett (a cooperation between the Universities of Antwerp and Reading), and (2) the series of Variorum Editions of Samuel Beckett's Bilingual Works, initiated in 1986 by Charles Krance, with the permission and support of Samuel Beckett. With the kind permission of the Estate of Samuel Beckett, these initiatives were developed into the Beckett Digital Manuscript Project, which combines genetic criticism with electronic scholarly editing, applied to the study of Beckett's manuscripts.

The Beckett Digital Manuscript Project consists of two parts:

a A digital archive of Samuel Beckett's manuscripts (www.beckettarchive.org), organized into 26 research modules. Each of these modules comprises digital facsimiles and transcriptions of all the extant manuscripts pertaining to an individual text, or in the case of shorter texts, a group of texts.
b A series of 26 volumes, analysing the genesis of the texts contained in the corresponding modules.

The Beckett Digital Manuscript Project aims to contribute to the study of Beckett's works in various ways: by enabling readers to discover new documents and see how the dispersed manuscripts of different holding libraries interrelate within the context of a work's genesis in its entirety; by increasing the accessibility of the manuscripts with searchable transcriptions in an updatable digital archive; and by highlighting the interpretive relevance of intertextual references that can be found in the manuscripts. The Project may also enhance the preservation of the physical documents as users will be able to work with digital facsimiles.

The purpose of the Beckett Digital Manuscript Project is to reunite the manuscripts of Samuel Beckett's works in a digital way, and to facilitate genetic research: the project brings together digital facsimiles of documents that are now preserved in different holding libraries, and adds transcriptions of Beckett's manuscripts, tools for bilingual and genetic version comparison, a search engine, and an analysis of the textual genesis of his works, published in print with a selection of facsimile images, as in the present volume. Due to an agreement with the Estate of Samuel Beckett and the publishers of Beckett's work, the digital editions only contain draft versions leading up to the publication of the text (the so-called 'avant-texte'), including page proofs. They therefore exclude epigenetic material such as later annotated editions.

Dirk Van Hulle
Mark Nixon

Acknowledgements

Firstly, I would like to express my gratitude to Edward Beckett for his continual support of the Beckett Digital Manuscript Project, which makes this volume possible.

I am also very grateful to the holding libraries preserving Beckett's manuscripts, especially Stephen Enniss and Elizabeth L. Garver (Harry Ransom Humanities Research Center, The University of Texas at Austin); the University of Reading's Beckett International Foundation and the Institut Mémoires de l'édition contemporaine, Caen; Corinne Gibello-Bernette, Pascale Guillemin and Maria Serrano (Bibliothèque nationale de France); Claire Boreham and Katie Ankers (British Broadcasting Corporation Written Archives Centre, Caversham, Reading); Andrew Isidoro and Kathleen Monahan (John J. Burns Library, Boston College); the Rare Book and Manuscript Library, Columbia University, New York and the Deutsches Literaturarchiv Marbach; the Special Collections Research Center, Syracuse University Libraries and the Tophoven-Archiv, Straelen; Heather Smedberg, Special Collections & Archives, University of California, San Diego); Estelle Gittins, Aisling Lockhart, Jane Maxwell and Sharon Sutton (Manuscripts and Archives and Digital Collections, The Library of Trinity College Dublin); Tim Hodgdon and Ashley Werlinich (Manuscripts Department, Wilson Library, University of North Carolina, Chapel Hill); Joel Minor (Julian Edison Department of Special Collections, Washington University Libraries, Saint Louis) for their help with the location and bibliographic description of the documents. A special thank-you to Breon Mitchell (The Lilly Library, Indiana University, Bloomington), who generously shared his bibliographic research and was most helpful with my queries.

I am fortunate to have written this book as part of the Centre for Manuscript Genetics (University of Antwerp), where Dirk Van Hulle and Pim Verhulst, in addition to the inspiring example of their own work, gave generous advice and support for my research. The Antwerp team, especially Ellen Vanderstraeten, were tireless in responding to my numerous requests. During research trips, the warm hospitality of Olga Beloborodova and her family was most appreciated. I wish to thank Ruth Burleigh, Burç İdem Dinçel, Wei Feng, Matthew Feldman, Sam Gilchrist Hall, S. E. Gontarski, Gabriel Heaton, Barry Houlihan, Andrew Key, James Knowlson, Matthew

McFrederick, Anna McMullan, Lois More Overbeck, Mark Nixon, Georgina Nugent-Folan, John Pilling, Martina Pranić, Martin Procházka, John Ptacek, Hannah Simpson, Daniela Theinová and Feargal Whelan for their valuable help with and responses to my research. Special thanks to Olga Beloborodova, Vanessa Joosen, Emilie Morin and Shane Weller for their feedback on an earlier version of this book in manuscript form. I would also like to thank Gérard Kahn, Francisca Rojas del Canto and Michiel Willems for their assistance with the encoding, proofreading, dating and collation of the textual versions. I am grateful to Brian Moore for proofreading the book and to Jonathan McAllister for creating its index. As co-editor of the digital edition which accompanies this book, Vincent Neyt has been a pleasure to work with and learn from. Myriam Jeantroux kindly shared her transcriptions of the 'Petit Odéon' Fragments.

A 'Postdoc2MUNI' fellowship at Masaryk University, Brno gave me time to finish the book for which I am very grateful. My colleagues at the Centre for Irish Studies, Charles University have been a constant source of encouragement. This book is derived in part from an article entitled '"Not there": "dark matter" in Samuel Beckett's *Footfalls*', published in the *International Journal of Performance Arts and Digital Media* (2021), copyright Taylor & Francis, available online: http://www.tandfonline.com/10.1080/14794713.2021.1874162 and an article I co-authored with Olga Beloborodova for the *Contemporary Theatre Review* entitled 'Staging Beckettian Minds: *Umwelt* and Cartesian Stage Space in Beckett's Plays', copyright Taylor & Francis, available online: https://www.tandfonline.com/10.1080/10486801.2021.1969559. Parts of the description of 'Kilcool' are based on chapter 7 of *Samuel Beckett in Confinement: The Politics of Closed Space* (Bloomsbury Academic, 2020). I am grateful to the publishers for permission to reproduce this material. The correspondence of Barney Rosset is reproduced with the kind permission of Astrid Myers Rosset, executor of the Barney Rosset Estate.

My family – Mary, Joe, Conor and Úna; Wanda, Jarek, Kasia and Gosia – provided rock-solid support as I wrote the book. It is dedicated, with love, to Magda.

List of Abbreviations

Holding Libraries and archives

BBCWAC	British Broadcasting Corporation Written Archives Centre, Caversham, Reading
BC	John J. Burns Library, Boston College
BnF	Bibliothèque nationale de France, Paris
CU	Rare Book and Manuscript Library, Columbia University, New York
DLA	Deutsches Literaturarchiv Marbach
HRC	Harry Ransom Humanities Research Center, Austin, Texas
IMEC	Institut Mémoires de l'édition contemporaine, Caen
IU	The Lilly Library, Indiana University, Bloomington
SU	Special Collections Research Center, Syracuse University Libraries
TA	Tophoven-Archiv, Straelen
TCD	Manuscripts and Archives, The Library of Trinity College Dublin
UCSD	Special Collections and Archives, University of California, San Diego
UoR	Beckett International Foundation, University of Reading
WL	Manuscripts Department, Wilson Library, University of North Carolina, Chapel Hill
WU	Julian Edison Department of Special Collections, Washington University Libraries, Saint Louis

Manuscripts relating to *Not I / Pas moi*

Abandoned sections:

AS1	English manuscript of 'Kilcool' (MS-TCD-4664).
AS2	French manuscript of the 'Petit Odéon' Fragments (MS-UoR-2927).
AS3	French typescript of the 'Petit Odéon' Fragments (MS-UoR-1227-7-16-3).

Manuscripts on loose sheets:

EM1	English Manuscript 1 of *Not I* (MS-UoR-1227-7-12-1).
EM2	English Manuscript 2 of *Not I* (MS-UoR-1227-7-12-1-analysis).
FM1	French Manuscript 1 of *Not I* (MS-UoR-1396-4-25).
FM2	French Manuscript 2 of *Not I* (MS-UoR-1396-4-26).

Typescripts:

ET1	English Typescript 1 of *Not I* (MS-UoR-1227-7-12-2).
ET2	English Typescript 2 of *Not I* (MS-UoR-1227-7-12-3).
ET3	English Typescript 3 of *Not I* (MS-UoR-1227-7-12-4).
ET4	English Typescript 4 of *Not I* (MS-UoR-1227-7-12-5).
ET5	English Typescript 5 of *Not I* (MS-UoR-1227-7-12-6).
DLA TS	English Typescript 5 (copy) of *Not I* (DLA, SUA: Suhrkamp/03 Lektorate/Theaterverlag).
ET5'	English Typescript 5 (copy) of *Not I* (*Not I* folder, TA).
ET6	English Typescript 6 of *Not I* (MS-UoR-1227-7-12-7).
ET7	English Typescript 7 of *Not I* (MS-UoR-1227-7-12-8).
ET8	English Typescript 8 of *Not I* (MS-UoR-1227-7-12-10-synopsis).
CPG	Corrected playscript of *Not I* for Grove Press (MS-BC-1991001-43-10).
FT1	French Typescript 1 of *Pas moi* (MS-UoR-1396-4-27).
FT2	French Typescript 2 of *Pas moi* (MS-BnF-4-COL-344-27).
FT3	French Typescript 3 of *Pas moi* (MS-BnF-4-COL-178-970).

Setting copies, galleys and proofs:

FSC	Setting copy of *Not I* for Faber and Faber (MS-HRC-SB-5-3).
GSC	Setting copy of *Not I* for Grove Press (SU, Grove Press Records, box 91).
GG	Galleys of *Not I* for Grove Press (SU, Grove Press Records, box 91).
PPG	Page proofs of *Not I* for Grove Press (IU, Mitchell/Beckett mss., 1937–1992).

Pre-book publications:

1975a	Complete text of *Pas moi*, published under the title 'Pas moi', *Minuit* 12 (January), 2–9.

Playscripts and production notes:

RC playscript	Royal Court playscript of *Not I* (MS-HRC-SB-5-4).
RC notes.A	Production notes for Royal Court *Not I* (MS-UoR-1227-7-12-11).
RC notes.B	Production notes for Royal Court *Not I* (MS-UoR-BW-A-2-3).
BW playscript	Royal Court playscript of *Not I* (MS-UoR-BW-A-2-1).

Manuscripts relating to *That Time / Cette fois*

Manuscripts on loose sheets:

EM	English Manuscript of *That Time* (MS-UoR-1477-1).
EN	English Notes on *That Time* (MS-UoR-1639, 02r).
FM	French Manuscript of *Cette fois* (MS-UoR-1657-1).

Typescripts:

ET1	English Typescript 1 of *That Time* (MS-UoR-1477-2).
ET2	English Typescript 2 of *That Time* (MS-UoR-1477-3).
ET3	English Typescript 3 of *That Time* (MS-UoR-1477-4).
ET4	English Typescript 4 of *That Time* (MS-UoR-1477-5).
ET5	English Typescript 5 of *That Time* (MS-UoR-1477-6).
ET5'	English Typescript 5 (copy) of *That Time* (WU-MSS008-II-3-68).
ET6	English Typescript 6 of *That Time* (MS-UoR-1477-10).
ET7	English Typescript 7 of *That Time* (MS-UoR-1477-9).
ET8	English Typescript 8 of *That Time* (MS-UoR-1477-7).
ET9	English Typescript 9 of *That Time* (MS-UoR-1477-8).
FT1	French Typescript 1 of *Cette fois* (MS-UoR-1657-2).
FT2	French Typescript 2 of *Cette fois* (MS-UoR-1657-3).

Setting copies, galleys and proofs:

SSC	Setting copy of *That Time* for Suhrkamp Verlag (DLA, SUA: Suhrkamp/03 Lektorate/Theaterverlag).
GSC	Setting copy of *That Time* for Grove Press (SU, Grove Press Records, box 91).
GG	Galleys of *That Time* for Grove Press (SU, Grove Press Records, box 91).
PPM	Proofs of *Cette fois* for Les Éditions de Minuit (MS-UoR-3628).

Playscripts and production notes:

RC playscript	Royal Court playscript of *That Time* (MS-BC-1991001-13-4).
RC ms	Production notes for Royal Court *That Time* (MS-UoR-1639, 01r).
German Nb	Production notes for Schiller-Theater *Damals* (MS-UoR-1976, 01r–06r).

Manuscripts relating to *Footfalls / Pas*

Manuscripts on loose sheets:

EM	English Manuscript of *Footfalls* (MS-UoR-1552-1).

Typescripts:

ET1	English typescript 1 of *Footfalls* (MS-UoR-1552-2).
ET2	English typescript 2 of *Footfalls* (MS-UoR-1552-3).
ET3	English typescript 3 of *Footfalls* (MS-UoR-1552-4).
ET4	English typescript 4 of *Footfalls* (MS-UoR-1552-5).
FT1	French typescript 1 of *Pas* (MS-BC-1991001-12-24-1).
FT2	French typescript 2 of *Pas* (MS-BC-1991001-12-24-2).

Setting copies, galleys and proofs:

PPF	Page proofs of *Footfalls* for Faber and Faber (MS-UoR-1552-7).
Footfalls(SB)	Setting copy of *Footfalls* for Faber and Faber (MS-UoR-2828).
GSC	Setting copy of *Footfalls* for Grove Press (SU, Grove Press Records, box 91).
GG	Galleys of *Footfalls* for Grove Press (SU, Grove Press Records, box 91).
NRFSC	Setting copy of *Pas* for *La Nouvelle Revue Française* (MS-BC-1991001-18-11).

Pre-book publications:

1977b	Complete text of *Pas*, published under the title 'Pas', *La Nouvelle Revue Française* 296 (September), 9–14.

Playscripts, production notes and annotated copies:

RC playscript.A	Royal Court playscript of *Footfalls* (MS-HRC-SB-3-7).
RC Nb	Production notes for Royal Court *Footfalls* (MS-UoR-1976, loose sheets).
RC playscript.B	Royal Court playscript of *Footfalls* (MS-BC-1991001-12-11).
RC playscript.C	Royal Court playscript of *Footfalls* (MS-UoR-1552-6).
WU playscript	Royal Court playscript of *Footfalls* (WU-MSS008-II-2-42).
Footfalls(CI)	Corrected copy of Faber and Faber *Footfalls* (MS-UoR-2461).
German Nb	Production notes for Schiller-Theater *Tritte* (MS-UoR-1976, 82v–90v).

Editions of *Not I / Pas moi, That Time / Cette fois* and *Footfalls / Pas*

1973a	*Not I*. London: Faber and Faber. 16 pp.
1974	*First Love and Other Shorts*. New York: Grove Press. *Not I*, 73–87.
1975b	*Pas moi*. Paris: Les Éditions de Minuit. 24 pp.
1975c	*Oh les beaux jours suivi de Pas moi*. Paris: Les Éditions de Minuit. *Pas moi*, 79–95.
1976a	*That Time*. London: Faber and Faber. 16 pp.
1976b	*That Time / Damals*. Frankfurt am Main: Suhrkamp Verlag. 81 pp.
1976c	*Footfalls*. London: Faber and Faber. 13 pp.
1976d [1977]	*Ends and Odds: Eight New Dramatic Pieces*. First Evergreen edition. New York: Grove Press. *Not I*, 11–23; *That Time*, 25–37; *Footfalls*, 39–49.
1977a	*Ends and Odds: Plays and Sketches*. London: Faber and Faber. *Not I*, 11–20; *That Time*, 21–30; *Footfalls*, 31–7.
1977c	*Pas*. Paris: Les Éditions de Minuit. 18 pp.
1978a	*Pas suivi de quatre esquisses*. Paris: Les Éditions de Minuit. *Pas*, 7–17.
1978b	*Stücke und Bruchstücke*. Frankfurt am Main: Suhrkamp Verlag. *Not I*, 10–28 (only on the verso pages); *Pas moi*, 31–40; *That Time*, 42–60 (only on the verso pages); *Footfalls*, 64–74 (only on the verso pages); *Pas*, 77–82.
1978c	*Cette fois*. Paris: Les Éditions de Minuit. 25 pp.
1981	*Ends and Odds: Nine Dramatic Pieces*. First enlarged edition. New York: Grove Press. *Not I*, 11–23; *That Time*, 25–37; *Footfalls*, 39–49.
1982	*Catastrophe et autres dramaticules: Cette fois, Solo, Berceuse, Impromptu d'Ohio*. Paris: Les Éditions de Minuit. *Cette fois*, 7–25.
1984a	*Collected Shorter Plays*. London and Boston: Faber and Faber. *Not I*, 213–23; *That Time*, 225–35; *Footfalls*, 237–43.
1984b	*Collected Shorter Plays*. New York: Grove Press. *Not I*, 213–23; *That Time*, 225–35; *Footfalls*, 237–43.
1986a	*Catastrophe et autres dramaticules: Cette fois, Solo, Berceuse, Impromptu d'Ohio, Quoi où*. Paris: Les Éditions de Minuit. *Cette fois*, 7–25.
1986b	*The Complete Dramatic Works*. London and Boston: Faber and Faber. *Not I*, 373–83; *That Time*, 385–95; *Footfalls*, 397–403.

In the digital edition of the Beckett Digital Manuscript Project, the sentences of all the versions of *Not I / Pas moi*, *That Time / Cette fois* and *Footfalls / Pas* are numbered (see 'Compare Sentences' in the top banner above the transcription on every page). This numbering system serves as a tool to make the electronic texts citable. The base texts that were used for the numbering are the Faber and Faber editions of *Not I* (1973a), *That Time* (1976a) and *Footfalls* (1976c). The sentences of the 'Abandoned Sections' of *Not I*'s genesis have not been numbered.

Other works by Beckett

ATF	*All That Fall and Other Plays for Radio and Screen*, pref. by Everett Frost (London: Faber and Faber, 2009).
BDL	*Beckett Digital Library: a digital genetic edition*, ed. by Dirk Van Hulle, Mark Nixon, Vincent Neyt and Veronica Bălă (Brussels: University Press Antwerp, 2016). The Beckett Digital Manuscript Project, http://www.beckettarchive.org.
BDMP1	*Samuel Beckett's 'Stirrings Still' / 'Soubresauts' and 'Comment dire' / 'what is the word': a digital genetic edition*, ed. by Dirk Van Hulle and Vincent Neyt (Brussels: University Press Antwerp, 2011). The Beckett Digital Manuscript Project; module 1, http://www.beckettarchive.org.
BDMP2	*Samuel Beckett's 'L'Innommable' / 'The Unnamable': a digital genetic edition*, ed. by Dirk Van Hulle, Shane Weller and Vincent Neyt (Brussels: University Press Antwerp, 2013). The Beckett Digital Manuscript Project; module 2, http://www.beckettarchive.org.
BDMP3	*Samuel Beckett's 'Krapp's Last Tape' / 'La Dernière Bande': a digital genetic edition*, ed. by Dirk Van Hulle and Vincent Neyt (Brussels: University Press Antwerp, 2015). The Beckett Digital Manuscript Project; module 3, http://www.beckettarchive.org.
BDMP7	*Samuel Beckett's 'Fin de partie' / 'Endgame': a digital genetic edition*, ed. by Dirk Van Hulle, Shane Weller and Vincent Neyt (Brussels: University Press Antwerp, 2018). The Beckett Digital Manuscript Project; module 7, http://www.beckettarchive.org.

BDMP8	*Samuel Beckett's 'Play' / 'Comédie' and 'Film': a digital genetic edition*, ed. by Vincent Neyt and Olga Beloborodova (Brussels: University Press Antwerp, forthcoming). The Beckett Digital Manuscript Project; module 8, http://www.beckettarchive.org.
CIWS	*Company / Ill Seen Ill Said / Worstward Ho / Stirrings Still*, ed. by Dirk Van Hulle (London: Faber and Faber, 2009).
CP	*The Collected Poems of Samuel Beckett*, ed. by Seán Lawlor and John Pilling (London: Faber and Faber, 2012).
D	*Dream of Fair to Middling Women*, ed. by Eoin O'Brien and Edith Fournier (Dublin: Black Cat Press, 1992).
Dis	*Disjecta: Miscellaneous Writings and a Dramatic Fragment*, ed. by Ruby Cohn (London: Calder Publications, 2001).
E	*Endgame*, pref. by Rónán McDonald (London: Faber and Faber, 2009).
EB	*Echo's Bones*, ed. by Mark Nixon (London: Faber and Faber, 2014).
ECEF	*The Expelled / The Calmative / The End / First Love*, ed. by Christopher Ricks (London: Faber and Faber, 2009).
HD	*Happy Days: A Play in Two Acts*, pref. by James Knowlson (London: Faber and Faber, 2010).
HII	*How It Is*, ed. by Édouard Magessa O'Reilly (London: Faber and Faber, 2009).
KLT	*Krapp's Last Tape and Other Shorter Plays*, pref. by S. E. Gontarski (London: Faber and Faber, 2009).
LSB I	*The Letters of Samuel Beckett, vol. I, 1929–1940*, ed. by George Craig, Martha Dow Fehsenfeld, Dan Gunn and Lois More Overbeck (Cambridge: Cambridge University Press, 2009).
LSB II	*The Letters of Samuel Beckett, vol. II, 1941–1956*, ed. by George Craig, Martha Dow Fehsenfeld, Dan Gunn and Lois More Overbeck (Cambridge: Cambridge University Press, 2011).
LSB III	*The Letters of Samuel Beckett, vol. III, 1957–1965*, ed. by George Craig, Martha Dow Fehsenfeld, Dan Gunn and Lois More Overbeck (Cambridge: Cambridge University Press, 2014).

LSB IV	*The Letters of Samuel Beckett, vol. IV, 1966–1989*, ed. by George Craig, Martha Dow Fehsenfeld, Dan Gunn and Lois More Overbeck (Cambridge: Cambridge University Press, 2016).
M&C	*Mercier and Camier*, ed. by Seán Kennedy (London: Faber and Faber, 2010).
MD	*Malone Dies*, ed. by Peter Boxall (London: Faber and Faber, 2010).
Mo	*Molloy*, ed. by Shane Weller (London: Faber and Faber, 2009).
MPTK	*More Pricks than Kicks*, ed. by Cassandra Nelson (London: Faber and Faber, 2010).
Mu	*Murphy*, ed. by J. C. C. Mays (London: Faber and Faber, 2009).
NABS	(with Alan Schneider) *No Author Better Served: The Correspondence of Samuel Beckett & Alan Schneider*, ed. by Maurice Harmon (Cambridge, MA and London: Harvard University Press, 1998).
PTD	*Proust and Three Dialogues with Georges Duthuit* (London: John Calder, 1976).
SP	*Selected Poems, 1930–1989*, ed. by David Wheatley (London: Faber and Faber, 2009).
TFN	*Texts for Nothing and Other Shorter Prose, 1950–1976*, ed. by Mark Nixon (London: Faber and Faber, 2010).
TN4	*The Theatrical Notebooks of Samuel Beckett, vol. IV, The Shorter Plays*, ed. by S. E. Gontarski (London and New York: Faber and Faber; Grove Press, 1999).
Un	*The Unnamable*, ed. by Steven Connor (London: Faber and Faber, 2010).
W	*Watt*, ed. by C. J. Ackerley (London: Faber and Faber, 2009).
WfG	*Waiting for Godot*, pref. by Mary Bryden (London: Faber and Faber, 2010).

Reference works

*OED*a	*Oxford English Dictionary*, Apple ed. (Oxford: Oxford University Press, 2017).

*OED*b	*Oxford English Dictionary*, online ed. (Oxford: Oxford University Press, 2020).
PR	*Le Petit Robert*, iPad application, version 3.1 (Paris: Dictionnaires Le Robert / Sejer, 2016).

Books of prayer

BCP 1926	*The Book of Common Prayer and Administration of the Sacraments and Other Rites and Ceremonies of the Church According to the Use of the Church of Ireland* (Dublin: Association for Promoting Christian Knowledge, 1926).
BCP 1928	*The Book of Common Prayer, with the Additions and Deviations Proposed in 1928* (London: Society for Promoting Christian Knowledge, 1928).

Note on the Transcriptions

The transcription method applied in this study attempts to represent Beckett's drafts with as few diacritical signs as possible, crossing out deletions and using superscript for additions. No special symbol is used for facing-leaf additions on the verso pages of notebooks, but they are identified as such in the discussion. Bold typeface is used to highlight words in quotations from Beckett's manuscripts and published work. Uncertain readings are in grey. Alternative transcriptions are welcome on www.beckettarchive.org through the 'Your Comments' function.

Since Beckett does not use the conventions of French punctuation in his manuscripts and typescripts, I do not follow them for French passages cited from these documents, only for citations taken from printed sources in French, with the exception of double spaces after full stops and angled quotation marks (« guillemets »), which have been normalized to single spaces and single quotation marks.

List of Illustrations

1 The first page of Beckett's 'J. M. Mime' (AS1, 01v).
2 Pountney's model of the 'Kilcool' drafts in AS1.
3 My model of the 'Kilcool' drafts in AS1.
4 Beckett's 'Analysis' of *Not I* (EM2).
5 Beckett's two lists on the fifth typescript of *Not I* (ET5, 06v).
6 Beckett's torn synopsis of *Pas moi* (FT2, 02r).
7 Beckett's and Whitelaw's notes on RC notes.B (01r).
8 Beckett's stage sketch in the 'Kilcool' drafts (AS1, 17r).
9 Caravaggio, *The Beheading of St John the Baptist*.
10 Beckett's 'synopsis' of *Not I* (ET8).
11 The first manuscript of *Not I*, with stage directions squeezed into the margins (EM1, 01r).
12 Beckett's edits to the chevron markings in the left margin of his first *That Time* typescript show red-pen indentations taking priority over those in black (ET1, 02r).
13 Beckett's edits to the final page of his first *That Time* typescript (ET1, 06r).
14 Beckett's second typescript of *That Time*, with the text divided into columns (ET2, 06r).
15 Sellotape markings on Beckett's third typescript of *That Time* (ET3, 01v).
16 Beckett's revised 'Continuity' typescript of *That Time* (ET7, 01r).
17 Beckett's first page of his *Footfalls* manuscript, featuring three diagrams of Mary's pacing (EM, 01r).
18 Beckett's pasted diagram of May's steps in the Faber setting copy of *Footfalls* (*Footfalls*(SB), 8).
19 In the same setting copy, Beckett extends May's number of steps to nine in the stage directions but not in the dialogue that follows (*Footfalls*(SB), 9).
20 Differences from the published text in Beckett's setting copy for Faber (*Footfalls*(SB), 12).
21 Beckett's handwritten version of lines which appear in none of the published editions of *Footfalls* (RC playscript.B, 04r).
22 Beckett's typed version of the lines which appear in no published edition (RC playscript.C, 04r).
23 Beckett's edits on *Footfalls*(CI) (9).
24 Beckett's two sketches of dialogue and pacing on an annotated Royal Court playscript of *Footfalls* (RC playscript.C, 06r).
25 A page of Beckett's notes on Freud's 'Anatomy of the Mental Personality' (TCD MS 10971/7/6).

Introduction: Staging the Subject–Object Breakdown

In the summer of 1979, Beckett read Lawrence Shainberg's *Brain Surgeon: An Intimate View of His World*. The book gives an account of Shainberg's period of research on a neurosurgery ward, where he interviewed patients and staff and observed the process of brain surgery as it took place in the operating theatre. 'It impressed me strongly', Beckett wrote to the author:

> I read it too fast & shall read it again. Mere decay is a paltry affair beside the calamities you describe. It is all I can speak of. And the ever acuter awareness of it. And the preposterous conviction, formed long ago, that here in the end is the last & by far best chance for the writer. Gaping into his synaptic chasms. (15 July 1979, *LSB IV* 506)

As shown by Matthew Feldman (2006), Beckett's deep interest in the human mind can be traced back as 'long ago' as his intensive period of research into psychology and psychoanalysis, carried out while he was undergoing psychotherapy with Wilfred Bion in 1934–5. Resulting in 54 pages of notes on eight books on psychoanalysis and one overview of contemporary psychology, this research gave Beckett a terminology for his budding aesthetics.[1] For instance, in a 1934 review of Thomas MacGreevy's poetry, Beckett describes it as having 'endopsychic clarity' (*Dis* 69), using an adjective repeated throughout the writing of Ernest Jones and noted down by Beckett when reading his *Papers on Psycho-analysis* (TCD MS 10971/8/3; see Feldman 2006, 79). But this research was more than just

1 Here are the texts from which Beckett took his Psychology Notes: Karin Stephen, *Psychoanalysis & Medicine: A Study of The Wish to Fall Ill*; Sigmund Freud, 'The Anatomy of the Mental Personality', in: *New Introductory Lectures on Psycho-analysis*; Robert S. Woodworth, *Contemporary Schools of Psychology*; Ernest Jones, *Papers on Psycho-analysis*; Ernest Jones, *Treatment of the Neuroses*; Wilhelm Stekel, *Psychoanalysis and Suggestion Therapy*; Alfred Adler, *The Neurotic Constitution: Outlines of a Comparative Individualistic Psychology and Psychotherapy*; Alfred Adler, *The Practice and Theory of Individual Psychology*; and Otto Rank, *The Trauma of Birth*. Pointing to the fact that Beckett took notes on only one psychology book (as opposed to eight texts on psychoanalysis), Matthew Feldman states that Beckett's notetaking from Woodworth's *Contemporary Schools of Psychology* 'is responsible for our understanding of this corpus of material as the "Psychology Notes" rather than the "Psychoanalysis Notes"' (2006, 102).

'notesnatching' (Beckett to MacGreevy, early August 1931, qtd. in Nixon 2011, 103). In his systematic investigation of contemporary theories of mind, Beckett also found an intellectual framework for exploring the breakdown between subject and object that was to become such an important part of his work.

Take the 1934 essay 'Recent Irish Poetry', in which the importance of the subject–object breakdown for Beckett's own aesthetics is clearly stated. The essay opens by distinguishing between those few Irish poets – such as MacGreevy – whom Beckett saw as creating something innovative in the long shadow cast by the work of W. B. Yeats and those Yeats disciples whose poetry – in Beckett's view – was dead as a doornail, as suggested by the initialism found in the essay's title (R. I. P.):

> I propose, as rough principle of individuation in this essay, the degree in which the younger Irish poets evince awareness of the new thing that has happened, or the old thing that has happened again, namely the breakdown of the object, whether current, historical, mythical or spook. The thermolaters – and they pullulate in Ireland – adoring the stuff of song as incorruptible, uninjurable and unchangeable, never at a loss to know when they are in the Presence, would no doubt like this amended to breakdown of the subject. It comes to the same thing – rupture of the lines of communication. (*Dis* 70)

Whether it is object or subject breaking down, the key point here is that communication between the two is ruptured. Beckett goes on to outline the different ways of giving aesthetic shape to this rupture once you are aware of it:

> The artist who is aware of this may state the space that intervenes between him and the world of objects; he may state it as no-man's-land, Hellespont or vacuum, according as he happens to be feeling resentful, nostalgic or merely depressed. (70)

As Mark Nixon has pointed out, Beckett typically used the verb 'to state' – or the corresponding noun 'statement' – in his 1930s writings on aesthetics when signalling an aversion to mere description (2011, 179–80), and we can consider the above passage as part of a move against representationalist poetics which would gather force in his later work. What is more, Beckett's closing words directly link aesthetic form to the psychological state of the artist. His focus on the psychological aspects of the breakdown between subject and object is evident again in a diary entry of 19 November 1936 on the writings of expressionist painter Franz Marc:

> Interesting notes in Marc re subject, predicate, object relations in painting. He says: paint the predicate of the living, Picasso has that of the inanimate. By that he appears to mean not the relation between subject & object, but the alienation (my nomansland).[2]

Note Beckett's psychoanalytic terminology: 'alienation', used by psychoanalysts when describing social estrangement (see Freud 1933, 168), is here deployed to outline an aesthetic territory which the artist should explore – the 'no-man's-land' of 'Recent Irish Poetry'. As Beckett noted when reading about Existentialism in Woodworth's *Contemporary Schools of Psychology*, 'physics relates facts to one another, psychology relates them to the subject' (TCD MS 10971/7/7; see Woodworth 1931, 38). Psychology and psychoanalysis thus provided schools of thought that helped the Irish author work through aesthetic questions such as the subject–object breakdown. As the present genetic study aims to show, this breakdown is staged in the three late plays *Not I / Pas moi*, *That Time / Cette fois* and *Footfalls / Pas*.

It is important to note that Beckett's Psychology Notes are not without a fair degree of 'detached intellectual irony' with regard to psychoanalysis and its forms of treatment (Nixon 2011, 41). For instance, he calls Freud acolyte Ernest Jones 'Erogenous Jones' when noting the name of the author of *Papers on Psycho-analysis* (TCD MS 10971/8/1). This is more than just a crude joke. In an early footnote, Jones admits that he has not always been completely accurate with his use of terminology: 'In earlier writings I had

2 I would like to thank Mark Nixon for his help with this passage from Beckett's German Diaries.

thoughtlessly used the word "erogenous". A moment's reflection, however, shews that "erotogenic" is a more correct form' (1923, 32n1). So, Beckett is not only making fun of Jones, he is also undermining the authority of the analyst by pointing to his mistake. To emphasize the creative – and often subversive – deployment of psychoanalytic material in Beckett's plays, I will adopt (and adapt) Anthony Uhlmann's concept of the 'philosophical image' which he uses to describe material Beckett borrows from philosophy:

> Images can pass between literary and philosophical discourse, no doubt being transformed in the process of translation, but also carrying with them something in common, a translatable component which inheres in the image which is put into circulation. (Uhlmann 2006, 3)

In a similar way, Beckett uses psychological concepts as 'psychological images' in his writing.

Staging the Breakdown

The recent availability of Beckett's Psychology Notes has enriched scholarly debate on his staging of the human mind.[3] For instance, Shane Weller argues that having drawn on psychoanalytic terminology relating to schizophrenia and hysteria in his earlier work (*Murphy*, *Eleutheria*, *All That Fall*), Beckett 'appears to go on to actualise a condition of hysteria in later plays such as *Not I* (1972), *Footfalls* (1976) and *Rockaby* (1981)' (2008, 36). Weller quotes a passage dealing with hysteria from Jones's *Treatment of the Neuroses*, on which Beckett took the following notes:

3 Beckett's Psychology Notes were acquired by Trinity College Dublin in 1997 (Frost and Maxwell 2006, 19). For other readings of Beckett's work which draw on these notes, see Barry (2008), Maude (2015) and Barry, Maude and Salisbury (2016).

> An important characteristic of hysterical disorder is the excessive development of fantasy at the expense of adjustment to reality. Thus it becomes practically irrelevant whether a given traumatic memory recovered from the unconscious corresponds with a fact or not, the effect on the patient is the same. (TCD MS 10971/8/21; see Jones 1920, 108–9)

In *Not I*, *Footfalls* and *Rockaby*, according to Weller, 'a female figure exhibits precisely those functional derangements of speech identified by Freud as symptomatic of hysteria' (2008, 36). As in Jones's definition, he contends, 'the distinction between recollection and imagination is submitted to disintegration' in these plays (Weller 2008, 36), something which is also a feature of *That Time*.[4] At the end of his article, Weller revises this slightly, identifying *Not I* and *Footfalls* as being marked by 'an attempt to complicate (without simply effacing) the distinction between schizophrenia and hysteria' (2008, 46). With regard to *Footfalls*, Beckett's use of psychological images is complicated by the play's epigenesis – defined as 'the continuation of the genesis after publication' (Van Hulle 2019a, 47) – which reveals multiple models of the mind in his theatre text.

In the first edition of *Footfalls*, V comments on May as she paces wordlessly up and down the narrow strip of light: '**My voice is in her mind.** [...] She has not been out since girlhood. (*Pause.*) **She hears in her poor mind, She has not been out since girlhood.** (*Pause.*) Not out since girlhood' (1976c, 11). In this version of the text, we are told clearly by V that her maternal voice is part of May's imagination. Therefore, May cannot tell the difference between 'imagined experience' and 'real experience'. However, in a playscript edited in view of the Royal Court premiere in May 1976, Beckett deleted the text marked in bold above (RC playscript.B, 03r). This deletion was carried over into subsequent published versions, including Faber's collected volume *Ends and Odds*: 'She has not been out since girlhood. (*Pause.*) Not out since girlhood' (1977a, 35). This gives us two versions of May's mind in different versions of Beckett's play: in the first edition, V is a figment of her imagination; in post-performance versions of the text, the

4 Weller also identifies in *Not I*, *Footfalls*, *Rockaby*, *That Time* and *A Piece of Monologue* instances of 'splitting', which is linked to hysteria in the work of Pierre Janet as well as that of Freud and Josef Breuer (Weller 2008, 36–7).

inability to distinguish reality from fantasy is shifted from being an aspect of the storyworld to being part of the interpretive process. Such revisions make it hard to give May a diagnosis of hysteria, which presumes some kind of normative background against which we can judge the reality of what we see in front of us. And the same applies to *Not I* and *That Time*, where an obscure background provides us with insufficient context to see the stage characters as representations of a specific psychological disorder.

Enacting the Mind

Rather than thinking of May's mind as an actualized version of a psychological condition, it may be useful to think of Beckett's stage minds as 'enacted', particularly due to their performative nature. In a paradigm of enactivist cognition, the mind is constituted by its interactions with the material world in which it operates. This builds on Andy Clark and David Chalmers' theory of the extended mind, which they define as follows:

> If, as we confront some task, a part of the world functions as a process which, *were it done in the head*, we would have no hesitation in recognizing as part of the cognitive process, then that part of the world *is* (so we claim) part of the cognitive process. (2010, 29; emphasis in original)

In radical enactivism, however, the mind is not simply sometimes extended by an artefact outside the cranium. While the extended mind thesis still rests on the default assumption that the mind is internal, radical enactivists argue that the mind should be viewed as 'extensive, not merely as sometimes extended' (Hutto and Myin 2013, 137). In this version of cognition, the most basic model of the mind is 'fundamentally, constitutively already world-involving' (Hutto and Myin 2013, 137). Thus, 'basic cognition is literally constituted by, and to be understood in terms of, concrete patterns of environmental situated organismic activity, nothing more or less' (Hutto and Myin 2013, 11).[5]

Archaeologist Lambros Malafouris draws on the model of enactive cognition to argue that the knapped stone tools of early Palaeolithic humans

5 For more, see Hutto and Myin (2017).

are not signs of an internal mental intention, but 'enactive cognitive prostheses' (2013, 163). Malafouris uses such examples to show that 'the material physical qualities of artifacts do not depend on mental states but rather constitute those states' (2013, 164). Olga Beloborodova's research demonstrates that we can consider the aesthetic artefact in the same terms. In a genetic analysis of Beckett's *Play*, Beloborodova focuses on the sixth English typescript, which was subject to a large number of handwritten revisions as Beckett holidayed in the Austrian Alps in August 1962, far from his typewriter (as he repeatedly remarked in letters to his friends). This heavily scored document, with autograph revisions in 'at least five different inks' and arrows moving chunks of text around, is an excellent example of how Beckett's manuscripts are part of 'a hybrid cognitive system' where 'what seems like a suffocating deadlock yields a number of crucial insights' in the compositional process (Beloborodova 2018, 291–2).[6] If Beckett had an 'enactive way of thinking on paper' (Van Hulle 2015, 206), then he also had an enactive way of thinking in space. Just like the compositional spaces on which Beckett's plays were written, the spaces for which these performance texts were composed, and in which their author directed his work, were a crucial part of his materially constituted cognitive system. Moreover, these spaces were shared by the audiences who interpreted his plays. Since Beckett wrote his plays to be enacted in particular kinds of theatre spaces, an enactivist paradigm can help us understand Beckett's stagings of the human mind.

Beckett's Cartesian Theatres

Teemu Paavolainen has pointed to the importance of theatrical metaphors in contemporary theories of cognition (2016). A well-known example is Daniel Dennett's materialist critique of the Cartesian model of mind as a Cartesian Theatre, in which one spectator nests inside another. As Dennett sees it, the problem with Descartes's dualist system is that each spectator would themselves need to have a brain (with a corresponding 'theatre' inside their head), so the theatre would need to multiply infinitely to sustain just one being's conscious states. This idea of an internal Cartesian Theatre

6 For images of the typescript, see *BDMP8*. I would like to thank Olga Beloborodova for sharing her unpublished thesis with me.

as 'a place where "it all comes together" and consciousness happens' is 'an illusion', according to Dennett (1991, 39). And the theatre is an important metaphor in outlining what he sees as the absurdity of the separation between the mind and the material world.

For their part, theatre historians have outlined the impact that Cartesian geometry had on the design of actual stages, with David Wiles using 'Cartesian' as a synonym for 'perspectival' viewing (2007, 14):

> The corollary of Cartesian space was, eventually, the retreat of the actor into a frame. If the authentic homuncular *ego* is already peering out at the action through the cornea, then it makes sense to gaze in at the stage performance through another focalizing lens created by a proscenium arch. (2007, 7; emphasis in original)

The manuscripts of *Not I*, *That Time* and *Footfalls* suggest that Beckett's stage image is designed so as to be viewed through just such a focalizing lens. This much is evident in the mention of a stage curtain on the first page of the first draft of each play, which implies a proscenium covered by that curtain. Indeed, such a framing of the stage image is the norm in Beckett's theatre: on the first page of his first compositional notebook for his first completed play, *Eleutheria*, he sketched a diagram of a rectangular proscenium end stage (HRC SB MS 3/2, 01r), a performance space that played an ever-present role in Beckett's theatrical imagination, showing up in his manuscripts and the theatres he directed in.[7]

For Bruce McConachie, the Cartesian model of seeing associated with the proscenium stage enforces a particular relation between viewing subject and aesthetic object: 'Following from its foundation in the concepts of containment, center–periphery, and near–far, Cartesian thinking organized a world in which people believed they could gaze objectively at passive objects' (2001, 587). Historically, this relationship between audience

7 While more research is needed on the theatres Beckett directed in, it is notable that of those analysed in this book, the Royal Court, the Odéon-Théâtre de France, the Théâtre d'Orsay and the Schiller-Theater all allowed for end-stage performance, framed by a proscenium. For more on Beckett's use of the proscenium, see Little (2020c); Beloborodova and Little (forthcoming).

and stage 'developed from the perspectivism of Renaissance painting' (McConachie 2001, 587). In his analysis of the development of theatre optics in eighteenth-century France, Pannill Camp compares the proscenium arch to the '"window frame" that conventionally opened onto the unified and rendered space of perspective painting' (2007, 631). This was a visual paradigm of which Beckett was highly critical. In a letter to art critic Georges Duthuit, he forcefully rejects the concept of the artist as 'he-who-is-always-*in-front-of* the work of art (9 March 1949, *LSB II* 139). Instead, in the work of painter Bram van Velde, Beckett praised the breakdown of relations between viewing subject and aesthetic object:

> For me Bram's painting owes nothing to these feeble consolations. It is new because it is the first to repudiate relation in all these forms. It is not the relation with this or that order of opposite that it refuses, but the state of being in relation as such, the state of being in front of. We have waited a long time for an artist who is brave enough, is at ease enough with the great tornadoes of intuition, to grasp that the break with the outside world entails the break with the inside world, that there are no replacement relations for naive relations, that what are called outside and inside are one and the same. (*LSB II* 140)

In describing 'outside and inside' as 'one and the same', Beckett uses concepts very similar to anti-dualist theories of enactive cognition developed later in the century. However, in spite of his rejection of perspective painting, it is precisely the perspectival framework of the proscenium stage that is used repeatedly in his plays. It would appear that Beckett needed the physical setup of an actual Cartesian Theatre in order to enact the breakdown of subject and object in *Not I*, *That Time* and *Footfalls*. Writing of the Royal Court main auditorium – where Beckett directed *Not I*, *That Time* and *Footfalls* – Iain Mackintosh suggests ways in which a proscenium stage can simultaneously enforce a divide between audience and actor while also allowing for a bridging of that divide:

> The magic of the Royal Court lies in that it is both conventional in form and little in size so that it can present itself as either a two-space theatre, with the actors' world revealed as the curtain rises, or as a single room, which we the audience share with the actors, and it can do this without any architectural or theatrical flexible devices other than the ambivalence achievable in such a well-proportioned small space. (2005, 51)

One of the disorienting effects of viewing Beckett's late plays in a proscenium theatre is the disruption of such spatial relationships: Is Listener lying on a bed or floating in space? Is Mouth 'back in the field' or in some kind of afterlife (1973a, 15)? Are we sharing in May's thoughts or spectating on a conversation from without? In this way, Beckett plays with the limits of proscenium theatre and those of the human mind. This book contends that the Cartesian Theatre of a proscenium end-stage allowed Beckett to enact the breakdown of subject and object by – on the one hand – suggesting a contextual background to these stage images, while – on the other – shrouding that background in the stage darkness that pervades his later works.

Mind ... Gap

Beckett had long admired playwrights who used background not to explain their art, but who created specific theatrical effects with it. In early 1931, he gave a series of lectures on 'Racine and the Modern Novel' in Trinity College Dublin, comparing Racine's use of background favourably to the novels of Honoré de Balzac: Racine used a 'graded depth of background', Beckett's student Rachel Burrows recorded, 'All to create atmosphere, not explicating background of Balzac' (TCD MIC 60/69). For Beckett, Racine's plays were 'Withdrawn from social scale to mind' (TCD MIC 60/75), creating hermetic characters who are 'each trying to get into the other's state of mind' (TCD MIC 60/81). Beckett admired Racine's ability to state the complexity of psychological processes without explaining them to his audience. Thus, in *Andromaque*, Beckett saw 'Tragic conflicts associated without being unified' (TCD MIC 60/57). Nevertheless, as recorded in the notes of another student, Beckett did identify the play's dramatic catastrophe: 'the play ends when the minds become depolarised, when it becomes a oneness of consciousness, an awareness' (McKinley 2006, 310). Such psychological unity is not a feature of Beckett's late plays. But they do provide just enough perspective to keep the interpretive process going. In *Not I*, the dimly lit figure of the Auditor, standing downstage in a black djellaba, gives a visual counterpoint to the image of Mouth suspended eight feet above stage level, suggesting a minimal visual perspective. In *That Time*, it is aural perspective which is meant to help us situate the voices of the spotlit Listener, '*coming to him from both sides and above*' (*KLT* 99), the three sonic sources representing different points of his life. In *Footfalls*, the combined visual and aural perspective suggested by the pacing May and the invisible voice of her mother drives our interpretation of the play. This is in line with Beckett's lectures on Racine, in which he told his students: 'Only interesting use of background is perspective' (TCD MIC 60/70).

Beckett's use of the darkened proscenium stage as interpretive catalyst is reminiscent of the work of Gestalt psychologists, who believe that a natural function of the brain 'is to close up gaps', as Beckett recorded in his Psychology Notes (TCD MS 10971/7/12; see Woodworth 1931, 109). According to Wolfgang Iser, writers often use similar strategies: 'the deliberate gaps in the narrative are the means by which the reader is enabled to bring both scenes and characters to life' (1980, 38–9). Beckett's work is the subject of the final chapter in Iser's *Implied Reader*, which analyses the ways in which writers use gaps to provoke their audiences into active interpretation. Writing of *Imagination Dead Imagine*, Iser argues that Beckett's writing 'is not a sterile monologue, it is an invitation to participation' (1980, 270). Beckett certainly makes use of 'deliberate gaps' in his work. The wartime novel *Watt* is presented as a manuscript featuring gaps marked 'Hiatus in MS' and important informational gaps regarding its main characters (*W* 207). In later prose works such as *The Unnamable*, these informational gaps become so vast that it is impossible to interpret the text according to any narratological schema which depends upon 'realistic story parameters' (Fludernik 2005, 237).[8] Instead, Beckett's work comes

8 Central to Monika Fludernik's model of 'natural' narratology is the concept of 'narrativization', through which texts are '*made to conform* to real-life parameters' (2005, 238; emphasis in original). Though she does not deal with *The Unnamable* specifically, it would, according to her model, be subject to a narrativization which 'makes much of Beckett's work readable as the vagaries of a deranged mind' (2005, 237–8). As she states: 'Narrativization relies on

to be increasingly dominated by what H. Porter Abbott terms 'egregious gaps' – narrative gaps that we want to fill but cannot (2013, 105–39).[9] In the darkened prosceniums of Beckett's later plays, these gaps become part of the stage space, which on the one hand encourages interpretation by framing minimalist images in the familiar paradigm of the picture-frame stage while also denying the interpretive stability that the Cartesian space associated with representationalist theatre would seek to guarantee. This is not a question of *representing* epistemological uncertainty but of *producing* it. In *Not I*, *That Time* and *Footfalls*, each time we try (and fail) to fix the image of the human mind onstage, we enact the breakdown of subject and object that Beckett was so keen to explore across his career.[10]

Documents, Chronology and Genesis

This book is divided into three parts, each focussing on a given play.[11] Within each part, there is a section detailing the extant compositional documents relating to the genesis in English and French ('Documents') and another tracking this genesis in both languages ('Genesis'). A 'Genetic Map' at the end of each 'Documents' section allows the reader to see the relationships between documents. Readers primarily interested in the genesis of individual plays may wish to start with the 'Genesis' section and refer back to 'Documents' as required. My analyses of the English-language geneses each follow a textual structure derived from Beckett's own compositional process: I base my analysis of *Not I* on a typescript 'synopsis' that he made of the play (ET8); for *That Time*, I draw on the paragraph divisions of

realistic story parameters. Within my model the concept of realism, even if of a decidedly constructivist kind, therefore plays a crucial, if not central, role. Narrativization reaches its limits precisely where realist modes of understanding cease to be applicable' (2005, 237).

9 Extending Iser's theory to argue that gaps are widespread throughout narrative – rather than just appearing at strategic points – Abbott considers narrative, 'like the universe', to be 'comprised largely of "dark" matter and energy' (2013, 109). I will return to this metaphor in my Conclusion.

10 In this sense, I regard interpreting theatre as a form of '*participatory sense-making*', a phrase which defines 'social understanding as something that is enacted' (Di Paolo, Rohde, and De Jaegher 2010, 71–2; emphasis in original).

11 The best way to read this book is in tandem with the digital genetic edition of the plays, which is available on the BDMP website (www.beckettarchive.org).

the published text; in the case of *Footfalls*, I follow the scenic divisions of the piece. The analyses of the French texts focus on key aspects of a given translation process. While my main focus will be on the genetic changes which highlight Beckett's staging of the subject–object breakdown, I also discuss other key intertexts in his creative process, in the hope that this will encourage future work on these manuscripts. Since the focus of the BDMP is on Beckett's French and English texts, his involvement in the production of German-language editions is not analysed in detail, though his directorial notes for *Damals* and *Tritte* (published as part of Beckett's *Theatrical Notebooks*) are dealt with in the relevant 'Documents' section. The genetic dossier of *Not I* contains two abandoned works – the 'Kilcool' drafts and the 'Petit Odéon' Fragments – which are discussed in chapter 2.1 ('Before *Not I / Pas moi*').[12]

Each genetic analysis is preceded by a 'Chronology', which sets the genesis in the context of other works Beckett was involved in creating at the time. In an article on genetic criticism and the sociology of writing, Dirk Van Hulle has used the term 'creative concurrence' to describe this interaction of 'works that populated the author's writing desk at any given moment' (2021, 51). The 'diachronic counterpart' of this concept is 'creative recurrence' (Van Hulle, 2021, 47), which takes into account elements of a writer's oeuvre that returned at different stages in their career. This latter term is a helpful way to conceptualize Beckett's creative (re-)use of elements from his Psychology Notes, which 'recur' most frequently in his composition of *Not I* (see chapter 2.2.2). In his analysis of the Psychology Notes in *The Unnamable*, Reza Habibi has noted multiple instances where Beckett used these notes in the novel's English translation but not in the French original, which he puts down to their being 'more readily available as a source of allusion in that language' (2018, 225). We will see the same pattern in the genesis of *Not I*,

12 I use Almuth Grésillon's definition of the genetic dossier as a 'set of all the preserved written genetic witnesses of a work or of a project of writing, classed according to successive stages of their chronology. Synonym: "avant-texte"' ['ensemble de tous les témoins génétiques écrits conservés d'une œuvre ou d'un projet d'écriture, et classés en fonction de leur chronologie des étapes successives. Synonyme: "avant-texte"']. Grésillon suggests this term as an alternative to 'avant-texte' to allow for the genetic analysis of written evidence of the creative process for which a textual model is not suitable (Grésillon 1994, 242, 109).

with concepts from psychology and psychoanalysis also echoing through *That Time* and *Footfalls*.

In order for creative material to be (re-)used, it has to be remembered, a cognitive process that Beckett thematizes in *That Time / Cette fois*. This work can be regarded as a 'memory play', which Attilio Favorini defines as a play

> in which the intention to remember and/or forget comes prominently to the fore, with or without the aid of a remembering narrator; in which the phenomenon of memory is a distinct and central area of the drama's attention; in which memory is presented as a way of knowing the past different from, though not necessarily opposed to, history; or in which memory or forgetting serves as a crucial factor in self-formation and/or self-deconstruction. (2008, 138)

One might object that such a wide-ranging definition is too broad to be useful. But in the case of *That Time*, we can identify specific ways in which memory is deployed. For instance, Beckett seems particularly interested in staging the process of memory in a state of breakdown, focussing as much on his character 'forgetting it all' (1976a, 15; *KLT* 105) – a counterpoint to May's obsessive 'revolving it all' in *Footfalls* (*KLT* 110, 114) – as the process of successful recollection (see chapter 4.1.2).

Perhaps paradoxically, in order to stage the mind in a state of mnemonic breakdown, *That Time* draws heavily on Marcel Proust's 'livre mémoire' *À la recherche du temps perdu* (de Compagnon 1997). With regard to his creative use of canonical texts, studying Beckett's manuscripts raises the question of where and how he got his source material. This is especially relevant in the case of Shakespeare, whose work Beckett learned by heart as a schoolboy. Later in his writing life, he often used versions of Shakespeare's texts which I have not been able to trace in published editions, possibly because he recalled them without recourse to the printed page (see chapter 2.2.2). Another key text in this regard is the Bible, as well as its associated liturgies, which echo through the three plays studied in this volume. In English, Beckett most often used the King James Version, but the question of biblical intertextuality becomes more varied in the French translations *Pas moi* and *Pas* (see chapters 2.3.2 and 6.2.2). With the publication of *Beckett's Digital*

Library, we know which French Bibles he owned at his death.[13] But *Pas moi* and *Pas* feature biblical intertexts not found in the author's library, with Beckett even going so far as to create what seems to be his own translation of a prayer from *The Book of Common Prayer* in *Pas* (see chapter 6.2.2). If, as Iain Bailey argues in his study of Beckett, the Bible and intertextuality, extant 'documentation represents only a portion of the author's activity' (2010, 92), then Beckett's use of canonical texts shows simultaneously the difficulty of identifying every intertext in a 'manière sûre' (Grésillon 1994, 216, qtd. in Bailey 2010, 90) as well as the importance of specific social and cultural influences on the genesis of his work.

One of the major questions in the study of Beckett's poetics has been to what extent his work, including its cultural and social aspects, was subject to processes of 'vaguening' and 'undoing'. Having been introduced to the field over three decades ago by two influential monographs – S. E. Gontarski's *Intent of 'Undoing'* (1985) and Rosemary Pountney's *Theatre of Shadows* (1988) – such terms have taken on a renewed importance in recent years as more of Beckett's 'grey canon' becomes available for study.[14] Gontarski's model of 'undoing' describes concrete details being erased progressively in the drafts of Beckett's playtexts:

> the plays most often emerge from and rest on a realistic and traditional substructure, against which the final work develops dialectically. While Beckett labors to undo that traditional structure and realistic content, he never wholly does so. The final work retains those originary tracings and is virtually a palimpsest. (1985, 2)

13 Copies of David Martin's and Louis Segond's translations are preserved in Beckett's library (https://www.beckettarchive.org/library/SAI-BIB.html and https://www.beckettarchive.org/library/SEG-SAI.html).

14 Gontarski coined the term 'grey canon' to denote Beckett's 'letters, notebooks, manuscripts' and other written material which falls outside the published 'white canon' (2006, 143).

Though authorial addition and subtraction are implied in Gontarski's dialectical model, it is the latter that has received much greater focus in Beckett scholarship. For her part, Pountney characterized Beckett's dramaturgy in terms of 'vaguening', based on the manuscript note 'vaguen' she found on a typescript of *Happy Days*. This she saw as 'explicit testimony to Beckett's policy of "vaguening" the later drafts of his plays' (1988, 149). Indeed, Pountney applies the term to Beckett's entire body of work, with the emphasis firmly on reduction: 'The process of drafting each play [...] may be seen as a microcosm of the development of Beckett's oeuvre as a whole, *a refining and scaling down of the text*' (1988, 195; emphasis added). Discussing Gontarski's analysis of the genesis of *Play* in terms of increased formalism (1985, 94) and Pountney's identification of textual reduction as a key part of the making of *Come and Go* (1988, 84), Erik Tonning warns that while their 'conclusions are sound and indeed indisputable, the trajectories mapped out – from realist detail and plotting to formalism and ambiguity – may [...] be overly linear' (2007, 74).

More recently, scholars have proposed alternatives to Pountney's and Gontarski's terms, such as 'redoing' (Little 2017, 176–85; Van Hulle and Weller 2018, 243) and 'pentimenti' (McNaughton 2018, 19–20; Van Hulle 2019a), the latter borrowed from the world of art criticism, where it describes the layers of a painting that the artist later painted over, but which still 'contribute to the colour and texture of the final result' (Van Hulle 2019a, 39).[15] Both 'redoing' and 'pentimenti' will be used in this volume, which provides evidence that composition for Beckett was a delicate balancing act rather than a one-way process of reduction (see Tonning 2007, 74). For instance, *Not I* presents many examples in which 'undoing' is balanced by 'redoing', as when Beckett's deleted manuscript note on pronunciation was given an epigenetic afterlife in performance, with Billie Whitelaw using his suggested 'babby', for 'baby', in the BBC television adaptation of the play (Beckett 2008b, 08:04–08:05; see chapter 2.2.2). He also added detail to the text of *Pas moi* in translation, outlining context which is left implicit in the English version by rendering the phrase 'just hand in the list ...' (1973a, 10; *KLT* 88) as '**tout inscrit sur un bout de papier...** plus qu'à le donner...' (1975b, 14) (see chapter 2.3.2). While not proposing to replace Gontarski's

15 Van Hulle outlines a six-part model of conceptual, structural, biographical, textual, translational and intertextual pentimenti (2019a, 40).

and Pountney's very useful concepts, this study of *Not I / Pas moi*, *That Time / Cette fois* and *Footfalls / Pas* will further enhance our understanding of Beckett's poetics by providing a more detailed picture of his methods of authorial revision. For instance, in the chapters on *Not I* and *Pas moi* (2.2.2, 2.3.2), we will see 'verbal' and 'syllabic undoing' used to pare down the text, increasing the sense of a 'steady stream' of words for Beckett's audiences (1973a, 10; *KLT* 88). Sometimes, however, Beckett goes against this subtractive practice, adding detail in order to make his text more vague, as when he made an important insertion regarding *Not I*'s Auditor: 'sex undeterminable' (ET5, 01r; see chapter 2.2.2.). In my genetic analysis of *Footfalls*, I elaborate on the epigenetic transformation of May's mind as an instance of 'structural undoing', with Beckett removing text that clarified the psychological background of the play (see chapter 6.1.2). Yet he also reintroduces elements deleted from earlier drafts, like the pillow which is removed in the genesis of *That Time*, but returns as an '*oreiller*' in *Cette fois* (1978c, 7), suggesting a more realist background to the reader of the French text (see chapter 4.2.2). Throughout, we will see Beckett varying his compositional strategies, with the performance of these texts in the theatre constantly informing his writing process.

Texts in Performance: 'an effort towards completion'

In a seminal article on Beckett's theatre practice, Gontarski emphasizes the extent to which Beckett's work in the theatre changed his relationship to performance texts: 'what Beckett began to understand about theatre [...] was that *text is performance*' (1998, 141; emphasis added). Offering an alternative perspective, Anne Ubersfeld contends that 'a refusal to accept the text–performance distinction will lead to all kinds of confusion since the same tools are not used for the analysis of both' (1999, 5). How, then, are we to make sense of the relationship between text and performance in the obscure worlds of Beckett's late theatre? In their BDMP volume on *Godot*, Van Hulle and Pim Verhulst make the following distinction between textual and performance variants: 'Textual variants are changes that Beckett made either in draft documents leading to a published text or in revised editions. Performance variants are changes that Beckett made for a particular production' (2017a, 38). Though the difference between changes made for performance and those made for a publication can be difficult to define in Beckett's late theatre writing, the methodological distinction between text and performance is maintained in this volume. Since *Not I* and *Footfalls* were revised when being adapted for TV performance, these recordings are also regarded as versions of the published text, with the emphasis laid on the degree of Beckett's involvement in a given change. The performance history of each text is discussed in the 'Chronology' subchapter which precedes the genetic analysis proper; changes to the text made in view of a given performance are also discussed in the 'Documents' section.[16] The book thus gives a better picture of Beckett's work as a playwright in a period he was fully active as a professional theatre practitioner, drawing on Bruno Latour's Actor–Network Theory to outline the dynamic relationships between Beckett and his 'actors', whether these be humans, stage spaces or manuscripts (see chapter 2.3.1).

Analysing Beckett's edits to the stage directions of *Footfalls*, Gontarski contends that such changes 'certainly should be part of any English text or production': 'Without these final revisions, the only accurate text of *Footfalls* – that closest to Beckett's final conception of the work – is the French text, *Pas*' (1998, 140). But as Gontarski himself notes, adjectives such as 'final' and 'definitive' are problematic when dealing with Beckett's theatre texts (1998, 136). Because of its status as a blueprint for performance, a playtext is particularly difficult to define in terms of completion, as noted by Jean-Loup Rivière: 'L'inachèvement n'est [...] pas seulement un critère du texte dramatique, c'est plus précisément sa *définition*' [incompletion is [...] not only a criterion of the dramatic text, it is more precisely its definition] (2005, 11; emphasis in original). Beckett seemed to recognize this when describing *Not I* and *That Time* to Faber's Charles Monteith, contrasting them with his *Rough for Theatre* (*I* and *II*) and *Rough for Radio* (*I* and *II*): 'The former are no doubt Roughs too, but they are an effort towards completion, whereas the other 4 were dropped as having no future' (4 October 1975, *LSB IV* 410). Note Beckett's noun phrase here – not 'finished' or 'completed' texts but 'an effort *towards* completion'. Due to his role as director and translator of his

16 Annotated copies of *Footfalls* are discussed alongside playscripts and production notes, due to these copies' close relation to performance (see chapter 5.6.1). *Not I*'s annotated copies are grouped with setting copies and galleys, as these annotated copies do not appear to have been used for a stage production (see chapter 1.3.1).

own plays, Beckett's staging of the subject–object breakdown was a process – not a one-off event. What follows is the story of that process.

Part I

The Making of *Not I / Pas moi*

1 Documents

1.1 Autograph Manuscripts

1.1.1 English

Abandoned sections (AS)

AS1 (MS-TCD-4664)

The notebook containing the 'Kilcool' drafts is a 'HÉRAKLÈS' school copybook 'with stiff yellow cover and black spine, stitched', measuring '271 × 209 mm' (Maxwell 2006, 188). The cover features the image of Hercules the Archer 'd'apres [*sic*] BOURDELLE' [after sculptor Émile-Antoine Bourdelle].

Attached to the flyleaf is a stapled note on card, written in blue ink:

> Fragments of theatre
> –
> Beginning of French
> translation of
> Words & Music (AS1, front flyleaf)

This card has been foliated 'i' in pencil by an archivist.

In addition to the card, the notebook features 23 folios with writing, followed by 20 blank folios. At the back of the notebook, there is some damage to the inside of the spine and a strip of a page is still attached, indicating that further pages have been ripped out. On the back flyleaf, an archivist has marked in pencil: 'Foliated 1 July 1969 / folios i + 23'. This indicates that Beckett did not have this notebook in his possession when he started work on *Not I* in 1972.

The pages are squared throughout, with writing in red, black, blue-black and blue ink. The same blue pen is used for 'J. M. Mime' and the 'Kilcool' drafts (see 06r and 10r).

01v–09r: 'J. M. Mime'

Folio 01r is blank, while folios 01v–09r contain material for 'J. M. Mime', which Beckett tried to write for his friend the actor Jack MacGowran in 1963 (Pilling 2006, 161; see Beckett to Alan Schneider, 15 and 23 March 1963, *NABS* 136–7). As Anna McMullan describes it,

> the manuscript is in several sections, or stages, only the first of which can be classified as 'mime': three leaves of diagrams, calculations and stage directions, marking out a square with paths leading to and from the centre. The aim for the two 'players' is to complete a circuit by the longest possible route. Folios 4–5 contain dialogue, initially between She and He, and then, after a line drawn by Beckett, between M (Mother) and S (Son). Folios 6 to 8 consist of three densely written pages of monologue by S (Son) with comments and additions on the leaves opposite. A last paragraph on f.8(v.) is heavily scored out, and the final folio, f.9, shows a reprise of the diagram on f.2, and the word 'Abandoned' in Beckett's hand. (2006, 333)[17]

01v

The draft starts with notes in black pen, followed by a diagram of a square with four corners labelled A, B, D, C (clockwise from top left; see Fig. 1). The centre is marked O, and is intersected by diagonal lines leading from A to D and from C to B. The result is a precursor of the diagram Beckett drew on an undated manuscript of the TV play *Quad* (UoR MS 2198, 02r; first broadcast 1981).[18] Gontarski links the geneses of the two plays (1985, 180), while McMullan explores the differences between them (2006, 336, 339).

The bottom half of the page features permutations for possible paths along the lines in the diagram according to the rubric: 'Starting from O return to O by greatest number of paths (one way)' (01v). There is then a more complex diagram of paths in the square at the bottom of the page.

17 'J. M. Mime' is published in facsimile by Gontarski (1985, 199–208).

18 I would like to thank Mark Nixon for his help with my research on this manuscript.

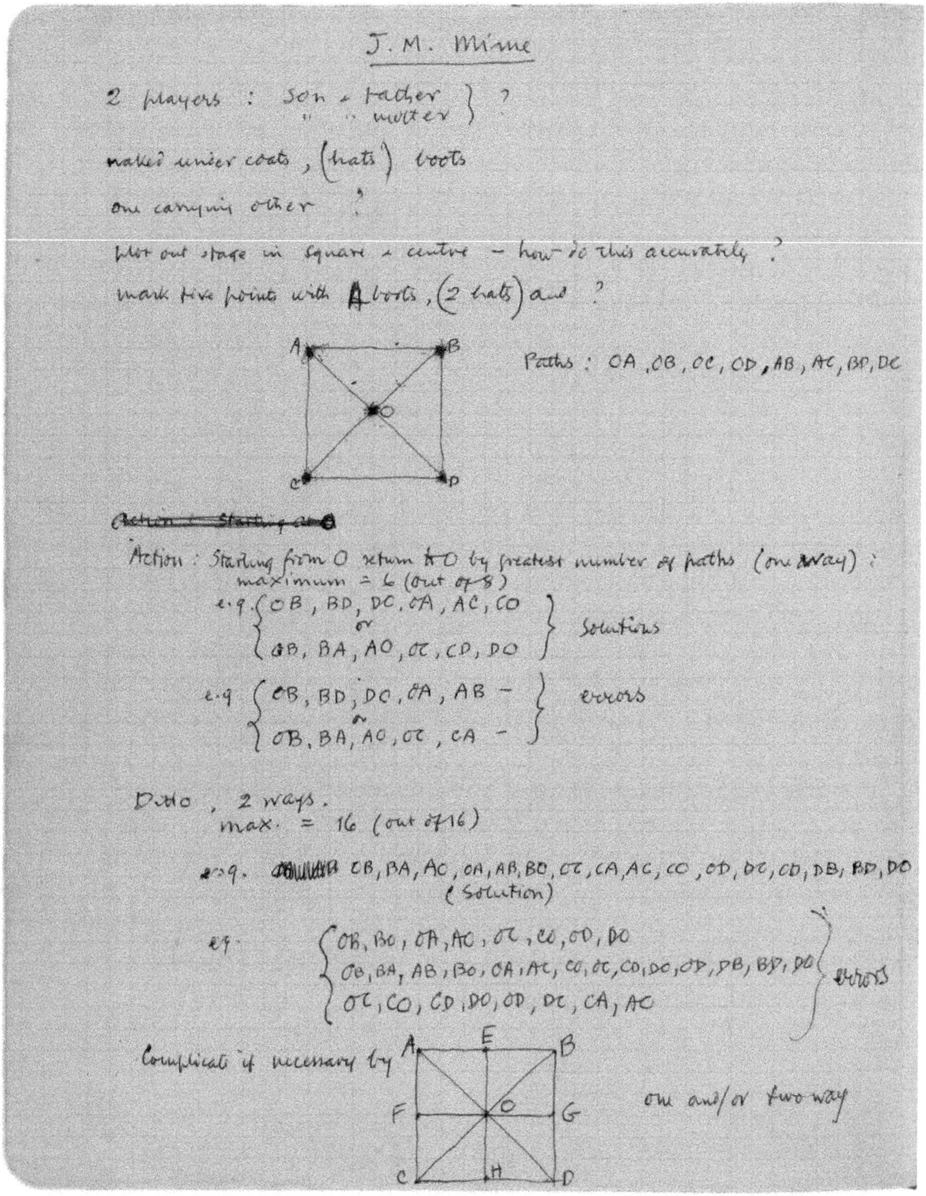

J. M. Mime

2 players : son + father } ?
" " mother

naked under coats, (hats) boots

one carrying other ?

plot out stage in square + centre – how do this accurately ?

mark five points with A boots, (2 hats) and ?

Paths : OA, OB, OC, OD, AB, AC, BD, DC

~~Action : Starting at O~~

Action : Starting from O return to O by greatest number of paths (one way) :
maximum = 6 (out of 8)

e.g. { OB, BD, DC, CA, AC, CO
or
OB, BA, AO, OC, CD, DO } Solutions

e.g. { OB, BD, DC, CA, AB –
or
OB, BA, AO, OC, CA – } errors

Ditto, 2 ways.
max. = 16 (out of 16)

e.g. OB, BA, AC, OA, AB, BO, OC, CA, AC, CO, OD, DC, CD, DB, BD, DO
(Solution)

e.g. { OB, BO, OA, AC, OC, CO, OD, DO
OB, BA, AB, BO, OA, AC, CO, OC, CD, DO, OD, DB, BD, DO
OC, CO, CD, DO, OD, DC, CA, AC } errors

Complicate if necessary by

one and/or two way

Fig. 1: The first page of Beckett's 'J. M. Mime' (AS1, 01v).

02r–03r

Folio 02r contains multiple lists of permutations in red, black and blue ink. These permutations are categorized as either 'Errors' or 'Solutions' (02r). Some conceptual notes are added in red ink and there is a more complex version of the square diagram at the top of the page.

Folio 03r is divided by page-width lines into three main sections: section one contains another version of the diagram from 01v, together with a list of paths geometrically labelled; section two lists a series of solutions and errors to the paths in the square, heavily deleted; section three redrafts these lists and includes notes on them.

04r–05r

Folio 04r contains a dialogue between She and He which McMullan describes as follows: 'A major motif in the dialogue section is the attempt of the players to follow instructions given in a book, from which She is reading, and which repeats the stage directions at the top of f.4' (2006, 336). The stage directions in question read: 'Set up a five ounces[19] facing south, all ~~points joined~~ pips connected' (04r). There then follows an antagonistic conversation in which He repeatedly interrupts She's efforts to read these instructions aloud.

The dialogue continues for a few lines on folio 05r, but a page-wide dividing line near the top of the page signals a greater specification of the characters' identities, which change from She and He to become M. [Mother] and S. [Son]. In spite of this change of identities, the earlier antagonism continues and the dialogue ends halfway down the page with the Son pushing the Mother onto the ground, thwarting her efforts to rise: 'Stay down a little, it will do you good' (05r).

19 As McMullan points out, 'five ounces' is the literal English translation of 'quincunx', the shape sketched in the earlier diagrams (2006, 336).

06r–08r

The Son starts a long monologue at the top of folio 06r which fills the next three tightly spaced rectos. He starts by speaking about the stones which are 'up stage right' (06r), the coat (under which he is naked) and his mother and father. Some themes in this monologue foreshadow those of plays in this module:

- childhood loneliness, as in *Not I*, *That Time* and *Footfalls*: 'When I was a boy there were other boys. To talk to. To play with. I talked & played alone' (06r; see McMullan 2006, 341).
- a woman's search for flowers, as in *Not I*: 'She lags behind looking for flowers' (06r).
- a combination of long silence and talking to oneself, as in *Not I* and *That Time*: 'This talking keeps me up. Mother was like me for many years. Many many years. Talking I mean. To herself. The miles, the miles, sometimes hand in hand, talking to ourselves. Then she stopped. Not a word now. Unless when spoken to. Then she ~~answers~~ may answer' (06r).
- the division of the speaking self, as in *Not I*, *That Time* and *Footfalls*: 'When I say talking to myself I mean there are two of me, one talking, the other listening' (06r).
- a lack of parental love, as in *Not I*: 'Mother never kissed us. Turn her head away and hold us off when we tried' (07r).

The monologue becomes progressively less coherent and 08r features a long stream of prose reminiscent of *The Unnamable*, with short phrases separated by commas (a style reworked in *Not I*). This speech is, however, punctuated by stage directions, which eventually have the Son taking a book from his pocket and reading the instructions: '"Set up quink [quincunx]"' (08r). He then revisits the rule from earlier in the draft, reading it aloud from his book: '"Starting from centre return to centre ~~using all eight by longest one way~~ using all eight ways or paths one way only, that is to say omitting none & retracing none."' He finishes: '"Not for beginners"' (08r).

The versos of the 'J. M. Mime' draft are used for doodles, notes, insertions onto the facing rectos and diagrams. The final recto of this draft features yet another version of the square diagram, followed by the word 'Abandoned' in blue ink (09r).

09v–19r: 'Kilcool'

The 'Kilcool' manuscript contains various attempts at getting the composition of what Beckett called his 'lit face' play underway (Beckett to Barbara Bray, 26 August 1963, *LSB III* 567).[20] The earliest date is hard to decipher, but it is most likely 'Paris 24 8 63' (10r), which would be in line with the dates of the letters to Schneider and Bray mentioning the piece (see chapter 2.2.1). The other two dates on the manuscript are from later in the year: 'USSY 23.12.63' (12r) and 'Ussy 29 12 63' (15r).

Rosemary Pountney identifies three separate 'fragment[s]' in the notebook and, like S. E. Gontarski, only studies seven of the pages (Pountney 1988, 92; see Fig. 2).

In his analysis of the document, Gontarski discounts the draft beginning on 17r as belonging to a 'different play, with three or four characters', though elsewhere he admits that the draft material of 'Kilcool' goes 'perhaps as far as leaf 19' (1985, 141, 135). Certainly, elements in this fourth draft point to other late works: the lover who turns up at night both prefigures the situation narrated in ... *but the clouds* ... (1977) and echoes the title of Beckett's short prose piece 'Horn Came Always at Night' ('Horn venait la nuit', 1973); the relationship between the main female protagonist described in the monologue and the older Mrs Frost prefigures that between Amy and

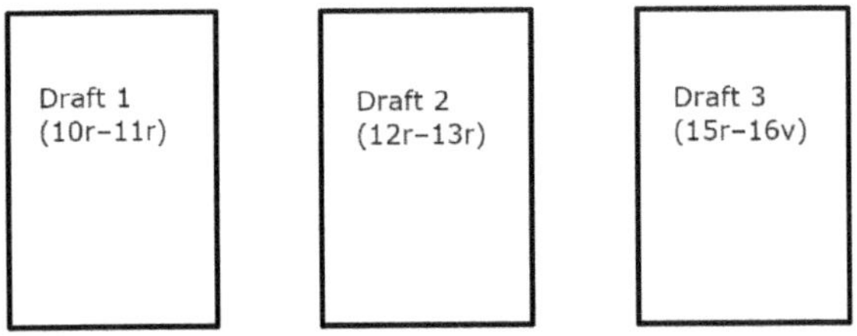

Fig. 2: Pountney's model of the 'Kilcool' drafts in AS1.

20 As Olga Beloborodova and Pim Verhulst argue, Beckett's interest in the 'lit face' motif is by no means restricted to 'Kilcool' and *Not I* (2019).

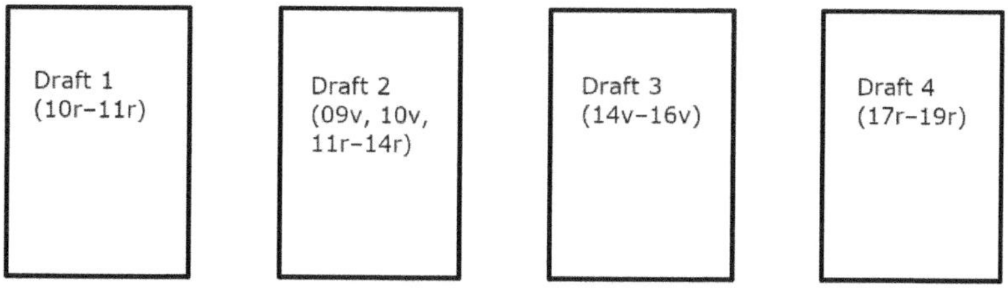

Fig. 3: My model of the 'Kilcool' drafts in AS1.

her mother Mrs Winter in the story recounted in *Footfalls*.[21] However, as well as its material proximity to the other drafts, textual elements which relate this fourth draft to the preceding three – the interruption of speech by 'tears', the presence of a 'Lover', and mention of 'Age' and the 'Voice', all of which are elements listed in an early outline – suggest that it too should be seen as part of the 'Kilcool' drafts (AS1, 18r–19r, 11v; see Fig. 3).

The 'Kilcool' drafts are almost entirely in blue ink, with a small amount of black ink used for doodles and notes on the versos. The versos also contain calculations, insertions for the facing rectos, as well as the note: 'A.F. 813 $17^{\underline{th}}$ Sat.' (11v). This may be an address, with A.F. the abbreviation of a place name. The only Saturday in 1963 which fell on the 17th was in August, just before the earliest date on the 'Kilcool' drafts.

20r–23r: *Paroles et musique* Fragment

The final folios contain a partial translation of *Paroles et musique* (*Words and Music*) in black ink. This translation starts at the beginning of the play and in total corresponds to just under half the published text. It begins with the opening stage directions:

> Musique[22] (20r) <u>Petit orchestre en train de s'accorder doucement</u>
>
> [MUSIC: *Small orchestra softly tuning up.*] (*CDW*, 287)

21 The date of composition of 'Horn venait la nuit' is uncertain. Beckett told John Calder he composed it circa 1960 (Nixon 2010, xvii).

22 An underlining of 'Musique' is deleted with a wavy line.

Paroles addresses Croak as 'Seigneur' (20r–21r) rather than the 'Milord' of the published text. Croak's 'masse' (Beckett 2014a, 65) is still a 'bâton' (21r) and there are other variants throughout.[23]

The translation breaks off at the lines:

> Paroles (hésitant). Age est ... âge est quand ... vieillesse s'entend ... si c'est bien ce qu'entend mon Seigneur ... est quand (23r)
>
> [WORDS: [*Faltering.*] Age is ... age is when ... old age means ... if that is what my Lord means ... is when] (trans. based on *CDW*, 289)

On 21 December 1962, Beckett wrote to Barbara Bray: 'Trying to translate "age is when"' (TCD MS 10948/1/214). He then put the translation of *Words and Music* aside for more than a year. This allows us to date this draft of the translation to December 1962; it also corresponds to the slightly later dating elsewhere in the notebook (specifically the 1963 dating of the 'J. M. Mime' and 'Kilcool' drafts).

AS2 (MS-UoR-2927)

The copybook containing the 'Petit Odéon' Fragments is described in the catalogue of Beckett's manuscripts at the Beckett International Foundation, University of Reading, Special Collections:

> Notebook containing original holograph manuscript notes for an unpublished, abandoned play in French. Dated Ussy, February 1967 on f. 1, also Ussy, April 1968 on f. 16. Squared-paper exercise book, 20 × 15 cm [...]. Notebook in Italian 'La vita degli animali' series, with a colour photograph of a beaver

23 For a genetic analysis of *Words and Music*, see Pim Verhulst, *The Making of Samuel Beckett's Radio Plays* (Brussels and London: University Press Antwerp and Bloomsbury, forthcoming).

on the front cover, a fawn on the back. Inscribed by Beckett on front cover 'PETIT ODÉON FRAGMENTS' in blue ball-pen. No pagination. (Bryden, Garforth and Mills 1998, 72)

In her description of this notebook, Myriam Jeantroux divides the 'Petit Odéon' Fragments in ten, using the title's concept of 'FRAGMENTS' as a structuring principle (AS2, cover; see Jeantroux 2004, 197–200). The outline below follows Jeantroux's divisions. For the most part, Beckett drafted on the rectos, sketching loose jottings and edits to the text on the facing versos. Doodles are predominantly found on the versos.

flyleafverso: Fragment 1 (blue ink)[24]

Draft synopsis of a theatre scenario involving a man and a woman, headed 'A [*for* À] tantôt cauchemar' (AS2, flyleafverso).

01r–05r: Fragment 2 (blue ink)

Dialogue between two women, F1 and F2, ending with a black felt-tip horizontal line about halfway down folio 05r.

05r–06r: Fragment 3 (blue ink)

Monologue spoken by F1, starting with stage directions: 'Réduction de l'espace par draps très légers' (05r). Two black felt-tip notes on folio 05v.

06v–07v: Fragment 4 (blue ink)

Dialogue between two characters, A and B. One loose jotting on folio 06v relates to Fragment 5.

24 Each subheading is followed by a given fragment's main writing tool. Any additional inks used are discussed in the paragraph below.

07v–11r: Fragment 5 (blue ink)

Monologue spoken by an unnamed woman. Folio 08v features calculations regarding the number of medicinal doses given to a male and a female character.

11v: Fragment 6 (black ink)

Dialogue between two characters, E1 and E2, headed '<u>Répliques</u>' (AS2, 11v).

12r: Fragment 7 (black ink)

Draft synopsis; a version of the material found on flyleafverso.

12v–15r, 16r: Fragment 8 (black ink)

Monologue of a female protagonist, preceded by a paragraph of monologue by a lone figure of indeterminate sex. A large doodle on folio 13r divides these two monologues. Ends with a line across the page in blue ink and the date 'Ussy Avril 68', also in blue ink (16r).

15v: Fragment 9 (blue ink)

The top margin features a draft version of the first paragraph of the synopsis on flyleafverso. The rest of the page is filled with notes on medicinal doses.

17r: Fragment 10 (black ink)

A short paragraph headed '<u>jeu du caillou</u>' [stone game] (17r), followed by seven lines of calculations and a quote on physics from an unidentified source.

35v: *Plafond* (black ink)

Folios 17v–35r are blank, but the final squared verso of the notebook features a draft of *Plafond* (1985), Beckett's translation of his prose piece *Ceiling* (1985). The draft does not feature the fifth paragraph of the published text, which starts: 'Vague conscience seule d'abord' (Beckett 2014d, 74). It is edited substantially throughout, notably the repeated paragraph: '~~Plus loin~~ Allez' (35v).

Given that *Plafond* was published in 1985, we may assume that Beckett returned to this notebook in the 1980s, a fact supported by James Knowlson's covering note on the typescript drafts of the 'Petit Odéon' Fragments, AS3.

AS3 (MS-UoR-1227-7-16-3)

> Untitled typescript, with manuscript additions and corrections by Samuel Beckett, of an unpublished play in French [...]. 27 × 21 cm. 4 leaves. Inscribed 'for Reading University Library. Sam. Beckett' and 'Petit Odéon' on f. 1 and f. 3. Pagination found only on f. 2, in type. (Bryden, Garforth and Mills 1998, 71)

The 'Petit Odéon' typescript features handwritten edits in blue and black ink. The final page has the following note in the bottom margin:

> ↳ Grégoire de
> Tours
> Ode 67.73 (04r)

The last line may be a phone number. The rightwards arrow possibly indicates Paris street directions from rue Grégoire de Tours to rue de l'Odéon, which leads to the Odéon Théâtre for which Beckett tried to write his piece.[25]

A covering note by James Knowlson details the acquisition history of the document:

25 I owe a debt of gratitude to Vincent Neyt for deciphering this note.

> [I believe this is the same abandoned play as that in MS. notebook [67-68] lent for S.B. Exhibition R.U.L. 1971. [...] But at present this is surmise, April '73. JKnowlson*][26]
>
> Gift to R.U.L. & signed by S.B. Given to J.K. April 19/1973

Knowlson later returned to this document, linking a new note with an asterisk to the text above:

> *Indeed, this is the case. The typescript covers 2 extracts from the holograph contained in MS 2927 notebook.
> JK. 1988

So, having lent the notebook to Reading for their Samuel Beckett Exhibition in 1971, Beckett then gifted the university his typescript in 1973. Given his use of the notebook in the 1980s and the dating of Knowlson's final note, it would then appear that Reading acquired the notebook in the later part of that decade.

The document contains two drafts, each of which is a revised version of a fragment in AS2. Draft 1 (AS3, 03r–04r) is a revised version of Fragment 5 (AS2, 07v–11r) which ends 'frotter à côté' (AS3, 04r), the same words which finish a long paragraph on AS2 (10r). It seems Beckett then continued his draft in the notebook before breaking off on the next page (AS2, 11r). The same blue pen is used in the notebook as for the holograph edits to Draft 1 of the typescript. Draft 2 (AS3, 01r–02v) is a revised version of the monologue in Fragment 8 (AS2, 12v–15r, 16r). The few edits to Draft 2 are in black ink.

English manuscripts (EM)

EM1 (MS-UoR-1227-7-12-1)

The earliest extant draft of *Not I* is described in *Beckett at Reading* as follows:

26 All square brackets in original, except for those around ellipsis.

> Untitled original manuscript of *Not I*. Black ink pen [...]. Dated 20 March 1972–21 April 1972. 27 × 21 cm. 6 leaves. (Bryden, Garforth and Mills 1998, 65)

The BDMP catalogue separates the draft material on the first five folios of EM1 from the analysis on folio 06r (see EM2 below). The rectos of folios 1–5 contain a draft of the stage speech and stage directions. Folios 05v and 04v are both headed 'Addenda'.

The rectos of folios 1–5 are numbered by hand. On folio 05v, numbered '6' by hand, there are three additional sections labelled A–C; folio 04v is numbered '7' and contains the Addenda D–H as well as a note on the movement of the Auditor. The start of the stage speech on folio 01r is dated '20.3.1972', the end of the stage speech on folio 05r is dated '1.4.72' and the end of the Addenda on folio 04v seems to be dated '21.4.'72', strongly supporting the hypothesis that Beckett drafted the speech first and added the Addenda at a later stage (see Gontarski 1985, 142). All three dates are labelled 'Paris' and folio 05r is inscribed: 'For Reading University / Library – / Sam. Beckett'.

There are regular additions and deletions across EM1 and the entire manuscript is written in black ink. About three quarters of folio 01r is taken up by an initial draft of the opening lines of monologue; this is then struck through with a large St Andrew's Cross and further deleted with squiggles from a black felt-tip pen. In the left margin of folio 01r, Beckett composed the first part of the stage directions; these are continued in the top margin. The top left corner of folio 01r contains the document's only doodle.

The left margin of folio 01r contains the encircled note 'KLE / 12.32', which may be a Paris phone number.

EM2 (MS-UoR-1227-7-12-1-analysis)

The sixth page in MS-UoR-1227-7-12-1 is undated and consists of an 'Analysis' of what was already written. According to Gontarski, 'The Addenda items are [...] the elaborations Beckett called for in the Analysis' and 'The Analysis and at least the first part of the Addenda were evidently written after the completion of [ET2]' (1985, 144). Indeed, it does appear

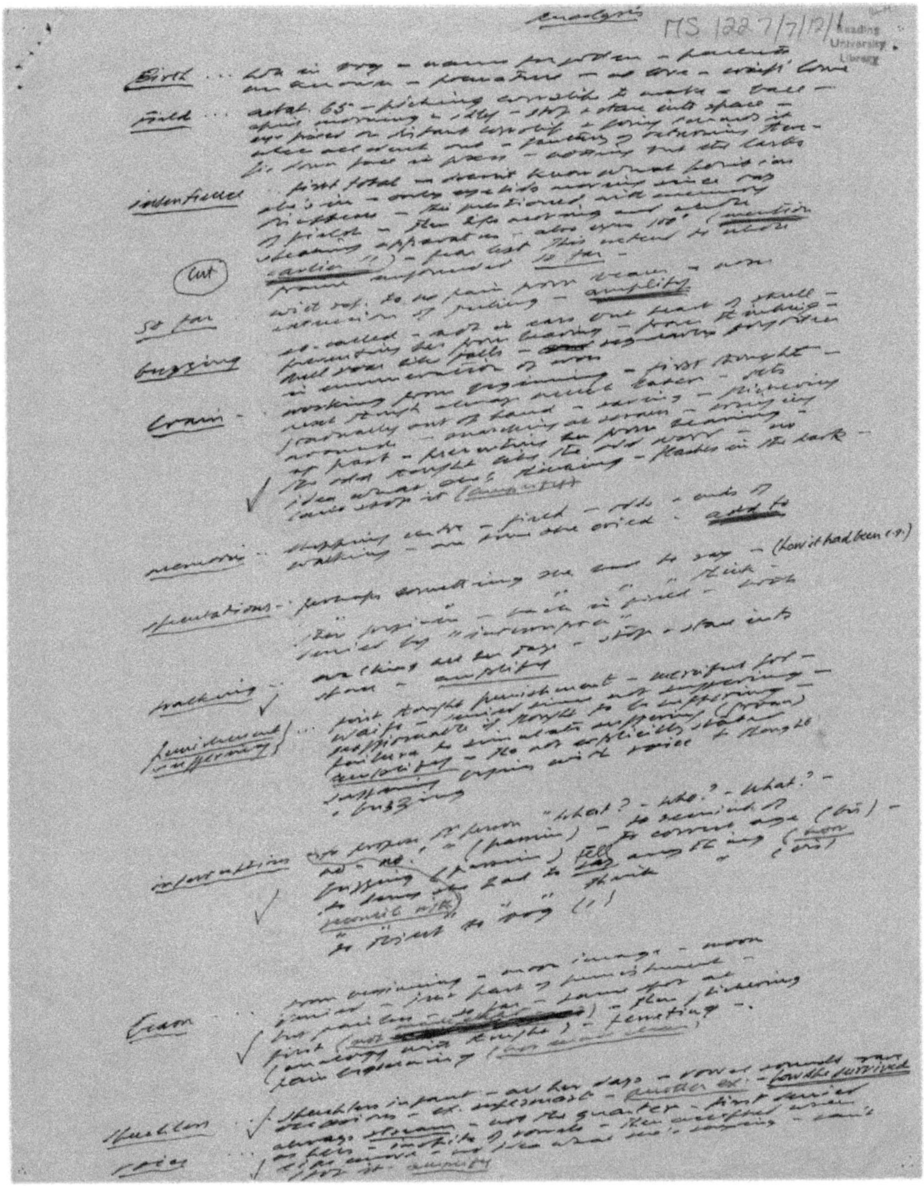

Fig. 4: Beckett's 'Analysis' of *Not I* (EM2).

that the Analysis was written after ET2 was typed up, but not after it was edited by hand (see ET2, chapter 1.2.1).

The Analysis is divided into fourteen sections based on different themes (see Fig. 4). Many of the terms in the Analysis are found in the Addenda, before being integrated into later typescripts. Under each heading in the transcription of themes below, terms used in the Analysis which are found in ET2, ET3 or the Addenda are discussed in square brackets:

<u>Birth</u> [...]

['waifs' a supralinear addition in ET2 (01r–02r)]

<u>Field</u> [...]

<u>insentience</u> [...]

['hundred degrees' mentioned in Addendum A (EM1, 05v), which is typed up in ET2 (05r)]

<u>So far</u> [...]

<u>buzzing</u> [...]

['dull roar like falls' found in Addendum A (EM1, 05v), which is typed up in ET2 (05r)]
['heart of skull' is found on ET2 as 'in the heart of the skull' (02r), before being changed to 'dull roar in the skull' (ET3, 02r)]

<u>brain</u> [...] **[✓]**

['can't stop' appears in Addendum F (EM1, 04v)]
['raving' appears in Addendum A (EM1, 05v), which is typed up in ET2 (05r)]
[Brain described as 'flickering' in Addenda A and H (EM1, 05v, 04v); also in ET2 (05r)]

memories [...]

['the one time she cried' appears in Addendum A (EM1, 05v), which is typed up in ET2 (05r)]

speculations [...]

walking [...] **[✓]**

['walking all her [...] days' found in Addendum A (EM1, 05v), which is typed up in ET2 (05r)]

punishment
suffering[27] [...]

interruptions [...] **[✓]**

[Interruption as it appears on ET2 – '... what?...~~I?~~ who?...what? ...no...~~no~~ NO!' (01r) – corresponds to how it is outlined on the Analysis: 'what? – who? – what? – no – no!']

beam [...] **[✓]**

['the ray ... **flickering** on & off' appears in Addendum A (EM1, 05v), which is typed up in ET2, with 'and' replacing '&' (05r)]

speechless [...] **[✓]**

[Addendum B is entitled 'Example of "rare ~~occurrence~~ occasion"' and elaborates on this theme (EM1, 05v)]

27 These two themes are grouped as one by means of a wavy line running down the right hand side of the two words.

[Addendum C is entitled 'Ex. 2 of speechlessness' and also elaborates on this theme (EM1, 05v)]
['Another ex. how she survived' becomes the court scene, appearing on ET3 (04r)]

voice [...] (EM2, 01r) **[✓]**

['no idea what she's saying!' appears in Addendum A (EM1, 05v), which is typed up in ET2 (05r).]

The above evidence supports Gontarski's assertions that the Addenda are elaborations of the items in the Analysis and that 'Beckett [...] most likely made his Analysis from [ET2]' (Gontarski 1985, 144). The fact that the interruptions to Mouth's monologue are edited by hand on ET2 to bring them into line with the text of the Analysis suggests that Beckett first typed up ET2, then wrote the main text of the Analysis before finally editing ET2 by hand. The concentration on Addendum A in EM2, as well as the fact that ideas on EM2 are developed further in Addenda B and C, suggests that Beckett finished his Analysis before finishing his Addenda on EM1 (see Genetic Map).

Additions in red and black ink suggest multiple campaigns of revision to EM2, at least one of which seems to have taken place after Beckett completed the handwritten annotations on ET2 (see chapter 2.2.2). The Analysis contains instructions to 'amplify' certain parts of the text, to 'cut' others, and features six tick marks in the left margin (marked in bold above). The fact that some of these revisions are integrated into ET3 suggests that the Analysis was revised before Beckett typed up this document. For instance, the open variant 'to deny she had to say tell anything' (EM2) appears on ET2 as 'had to say' (03r) and on ET3 as 'had to tell' (04r).

1.1.2 French

French manuscripts (FM)

FM1 (MS-UoR-1396-4-25)

> Untitled original manuscript of Samuel Beckett's translation of *Not I* into French. 27 × 21 cm. 5 leaves. [...] Written and corrected in black ink. Pagination by Beckett in black ink, ff. 2–5. Corrections in text and, infrequently, margin. (Bryden, Garforth and Mills 1998, 68)

The manuscript is dated 'Paris / 1.3.73' (01r) and 'El Jadida 13.3.73' (04r) and contains a partial translation of Beckett's play. In addition to the black ink used throughout the manuscript, there is a blue-ink squiggle in the top left corner of folio 01r. The number '50' is written in pencil in the top margin of the same page. Since its size and writing tool are the same as the archival markings in the top right margin, this number was almost certainly added by an archivist, not Beckett himself.

There are doodles in the top left and bottom right corner of folio 02r, the same page on which the translation temporarily breaks down, marked by a gap in the text. The translation continues up to the passage where the protagonist recalls sitting in Croker's Acres, crying into her hand, whereupon the words cease (05r). The text on each recto is crossed out with large St Andrew's Crosses. There are two boxed additions on folio 01v: 'bourdon' and 'illumination éclair'.

FM2 (MS-UoR-1396-4-26)

> Untitled original manuscript of Samuel Beckett's translation of *Not I* into French. [...] 27 × 21 cm. 8 leaves. (Bryden, Garforth and Mills 1998, 68)

This manuscript is dated 'Paris / 2.5.74' (01r), 'Ussy / 10.5.74' (05r), 'Ussy 12.5.74' (07r) and 'Ussy / 19.5.74'. It contains a translation of the playtext including stage directions. The text and corrections are written in black ink.

On folio 08r, Beckett drafted the opening stage directions, which he labelled 'A', as well as the closing stage directions and note on the Auditeur's gestures, which he labelled 'B'. On folios 01r and 07r, he added the letters 'A' and 'B' to indicate that the stage directions should be added there. In the left margin, in neat handwriting, Beckett added references for the biblical passages from which Bouche quotes (06r, 07r). These will be discussed in more detail in chapter 2.3.2.

1.2 Typescripts

1.2.1 English

English typescripts (ET)

ET1 (MS-UoR-1227-7-12-2)

> Untitled typescript, with manuscript additions and corrections in black ink, of a revised fragment of MS 1227/7/12/1. F.1 labelled 'I' and inscribed 'for Reading University Library, Sam. Beckett'. 27 × 21 cm. 2 leaves. (Bryden, Garforth and Mills 1998, 66)

This undated typescript is a typed-up version of EM1. There are additions and corrections in black ink in the left margin. Having reached the lines 'all part of the ~~iwh~~ wish to...torment...but not in the least ...not a twinge ...for the moment...ah...for the moment...' (02r), Beckett abandoned the draft near the top of the second page. In the left margin, an address is written in black ink: '231 Mill Rd. / Cambridge' (02r).

ET2 (MS-UoR-1227-7-12-3)

> Untitled typescript, with manuscript additions and corrections. F.1 lettered 'II' and inscribed 'for Reading University Library – Sam. Beckett'. 27 × 21 cm. 5 leaves. (Bryden, Garforth and Mills 1998, 66)

Detailed stage directions are added in black ink in the top and bottom margins of folio 01r. On folio 05r, there is a typed-up version of Addendum A from EM1. This is marked for insertion in the left margin of folio 03r. Folios 04r and 03r contain the insertion marks B and C respectively, referring to the Addenda on EM1 (05v). At the end of the text, there are stage directions outlining how the play should conclude (04r).

ET3 (MS-UoR-1227-7-12-4)

> Untitled typescript with manuscript additions and corrections. F.1 lettered 'III' and inscribed 'for Reading University Library. Samuel Beckett'. 30 × 21 cm. 5 leaves. (Bryden, Garforth and Mills 1998, 66)

The Addenda marked for insertion on ET2 (A, B and C) are typed up as part of the main text of ET3. As well as marking these additions in the margin of the typescript, Beckett added insertion labels for Addenda D–H from EM1 (04v) in the left margin of folios 02r–04r.

Stage directions indicating when the Auditor's four movements happen are added in black ink. On the last recto, Beckett started a note regarding these movements (see chapter 2.2.2).

ET4 (MS-UoR-1227-7-12-5)

> Typescript, with manuscript additions and corrections, headed 'Not I'. F.1 lettered 'IV' and inscribed 'for Reading University Library. Sam. Beckett'. 30 × 21 cm. 5 leaves. (Bryden, Garforth and Mills 1998, 66)

This typescript uses two instead of three ellipsis points, a textual feature that would be carried over into the next two typescripts.[28] Addenda D–H are incorporated into the typed text, indicating that this typescript was composed after these Addenda on EM1 (04v). The title is added for the first time, in red ink. The Auditor's movements are integrated into the typescript.

Croker's Acres, a set of fields used for horse training near Beckett's childhood home in Foxrock, South County Dublin, are mentioned for the first time in this typescript (03r).[29] The note on the Auditor's movements is now typed (05r), with a holograph addition entitling this

28 A copy stored in the Alan Schneider Papers (UCSD, box 26, folder 32) lacks most of Beckett's handwritten additions.

29 As Eoin O'Brien points out, Croker's Acres (or Gallops) are also mentioned elsewhere in Beckett's work (1986, 45–51).

'Note 1'. 'Note 2', on pronunciation, is added in hand (see chapter 2.2.2). In the left margin, Beckett wrote in black ink a word which is not easily legible: 'Greimsmith' (05r).

ET5 (MS-UoR-1227-7-12-6)

> Typescript of *Not* I with manuscript additions and corrections in black ink and red ball pen. F.1 lettered 'V' and inscribed 'for Reading University Library. Samuel Beckett'. 27 × 21 cm. 6 leaves. (Bryden, Garforth and Mills 1998, 67)

This typescript is marked 'corrected' (01r) and the differently coloured inks throughout indicate multiple campaigns of revision. There are three sets of numbers in the left margin: one set runs from 1 to 22, tracking the number of times Mouth says 'what?'. The second set (in the red ballpoint mentioned in the Reading catalogue and in Richard Admussen's 1979 book on Beckett's manuscripts (72), now faded to pink throughout) marks the five interruptions vainly prompting Mouth to say 'I', while the third set runs from B1 to B7, marking the 'buzzing' instances she mentions (see below). On the first page, there are figures in the top margin which give the number of spoken lines up to specific points in the text:

> 89 ← 1. To " words were coming
> 84 ← 2. Thence " something she had to tell
> 50 ← 3.   "   " end (01r)[30]

This corresponds to a subdivision of the text made at the bottom of folio 06r, where there is a list in black ink of seven handwritten lines in which Mouth mentions 'Buzzing'. These lines are then subdivided by square brackets in the left and right margins. The right-margin subdivisions are numbered I–III and correspond to the section divisions made in the calculation of the number of spoken lines at the top of folio 01r. Beckett counts up the number of 'buzzing' instances in each of these three sections using Arabic numerals in round brackets. Higher up the page, the first line of 'Note 2' is now typed,

30 Beckett did not close the speech marks in these three lines.

with two further examples of Mouth's distinctive pronunciation added in hand (see chapter 2.2.2).

There are two lists on folio 06v (see Fig. 5), the first of which is in red ballpoint (now faded to pink). This first list extracts lines from the text, highlighting certain words with underlining. The second list, in black ink, calculates the number of times certain things happen in the text, including the 'buzzing' listed on folio 06r and the interruptions numbered in pink in the left margin of the typescript:

Interruptions Inviting "I"	5
70 to 60	2
Tongue	2
Position (kneeling, lying)	2
tense (had been for was)	1
Nothing to do with (telling, thinking)	2
Girl for thing	1
buzzing	7
	22 (?)[✓] (06v)

The list is ticked to indicate the accuracy of the calculation.

On 30 September 1972, Alan Schneider pointed out an error on Beckett's typescript which he was using to rehearse *Not I* for its world premiere in New York: 'I believe there's typographical [*sic*] error on page 4 near the bottom, three lines from the bottom: after "so far", shouldn't it be "then thinking ..."? We've assumed so' (*NABS* 280). Beckett's reply of 16 October confirmed Schneider's assumption: '"Then" thinking is correct' (*LSB IV* 312). On ET5, near the bottom of folio 04, 'th~~a~~^{e}n thinking' is edited in black ink.

The Deutsches Literaturarchiv in Marbach holds three copies of this typescript, all of which were made after Beckett had only added a few of his handwritten edits and which therefore can be discounted as possible setting copies for the Suhrkamp 1978 edition (see chapter 1.5.4). For instance, the DLA documents contain none of the numbers in the left margin of ET5. Two of these documents are dated 23 July 1973 and feature the logo of Beckett's agents Curtis Brown on their first pages. However, the most advanced DLA typescript (henceforth DLA TS) – which is undated – does contain the edit 'th~~a~~^{e}n thinking' in Beckett's hand, indicating that it postdates Beckett's letter to Schneider of 16 October 1972 (DLA TS, 04r).[31] Aside from the addition of new handwritten edits on ET5, there are no variants between it and the DLA typescripts. The only discrepancy is with regard to the handwritten addition ‘with hood’; this appears on the DLA TS (01r), but in a different place on the page to ET5 (01r).

ET5' (Not I folder, TA)

An annotated photocopy of the DLA TS, used by Elmar and Erika Tophoven for their German translation of *Not I*, is held in the Tophoven-Archiv, Straelen. It contains the same placement of the marginal addition ‘with hood’ as the DLA TS and the same correction ‘th~~a~~en thinking’ (01r, 04r). Aside from such additions, which were already part of the typescript before it was copied, there is another layer of revisions in blue ink on folios 01r–04r. Many of these handwritten additions match those on ET5 but there are also a number of edits which indicate that this typescript postdates the first layer of revisions on ET5. For instance, ‘..what?..who?..**what?..no**..no!~~"she"~~..<u>she</u>!..’ (ET5, 01r) appears as ‘..what?..who?..~~**what?**~~..~~**no**~~..no!..<u>she</u>!..’ on ET5' (01r), as it does (with three ellipsis points) on later documents such as Faber's setting copy (FSC, 02r–03r; see chapter 1.3.1).

However, there is another layer of revisions on ET5 which shows that Beckett went back and edited it after completing his work on ET5'. Notably, there are no handwritten additions on folios 04r–06r of ET5', so all the additions on this part of ET5 can be presumed to postdate ET5'. In addition, none of the red-pen additions on ET5 (now faded to pink) are included on ET5', so we can be confident they postdate the Tophoven typescript. All of this indicates that ET5 was a document with multiple revision layers, which Beckett returned to after giving the annotated copy of the typescript to the Tophovens.

31 On all three copies of ET5 stored in the Alan Schneider Papers (UCSD, box 26, folder 32), ‘than’ is uncorrected (04r). These copies lack almost all of Beckett's handwritten additions. One copy is keyed to the synopsis on ET8 in a hand other than the author's.

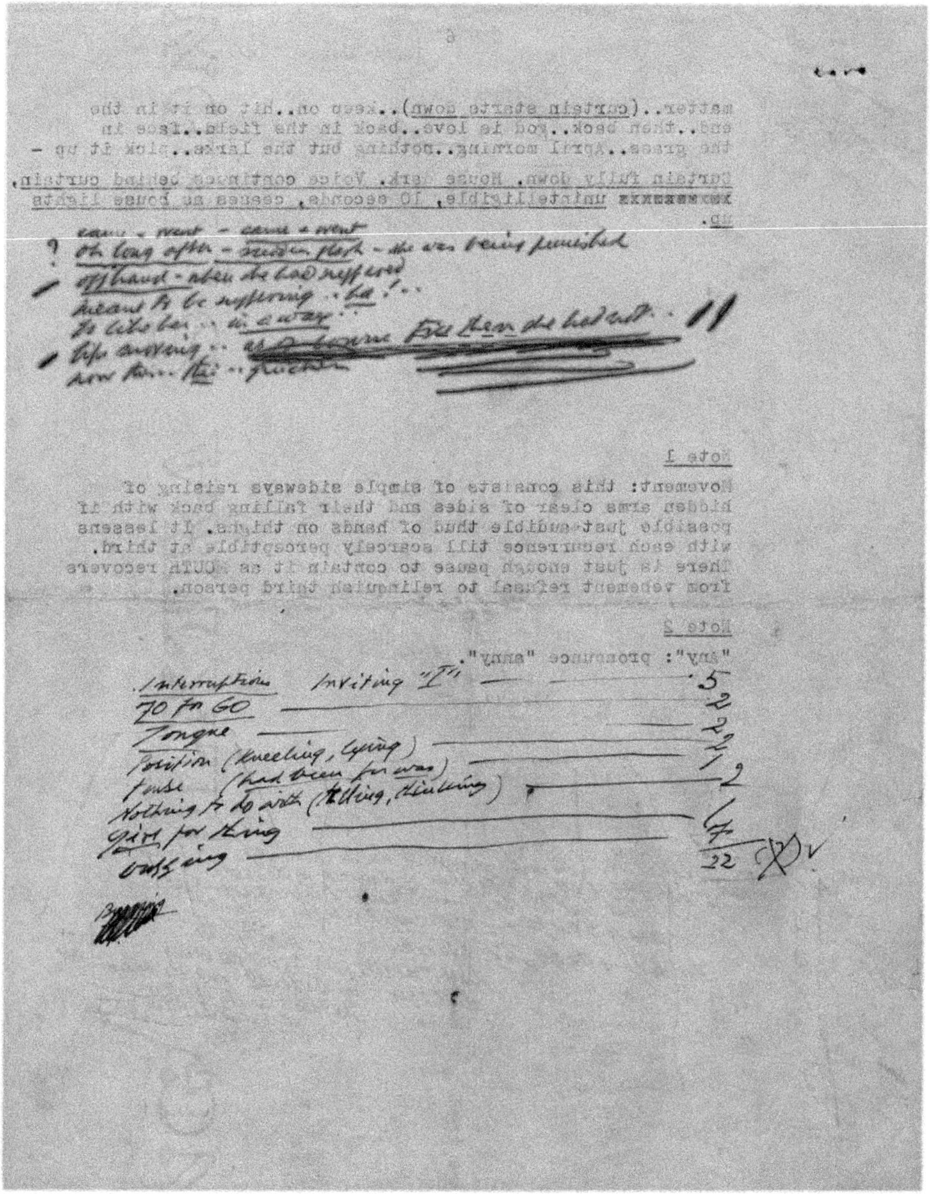

Fig. 5: Beckett's two lists on the fifth typescript of *Not I* (ET5, 06v).

ET6 (MS-UoR-1227-7-12-7)

> Typescript of *Not I* with manuscript additions and corrections in black and red ink and type. F.1 lettered 'VI' and inscribed 'for Reading University Library, Sam. Beckett'. 27 × 21 cm. 6 leaves. (Bryden, Garforth and Mills 1998, 67)

In the top margin of folio 01r, there is a note in black ink:

> Nolan
> gallery
> Wed.
> 10

It is possible this refers to painter Sidney Nolan's exhibition at the Marlborough Gallery in London, which ran while Beckett was rehearsing *Not I* (Anon. 1972, 3).

Throughout the manuscript, the red ink mentioned in the Reading catalogue and by Admussen (1979, 73) is now faded to pink. In this ink, there are 29 pauses inserted in the margin across the manuscript: a lower case 'p' indicates a pause, while a capital 'P' indicates a long pause.

In addition to pink and black ink, folios 04r and 06r contain marginal additions in blue ink. On folio 06r, two letters are rendered illegible by what looks like a cigarette burn. In Note 1, the instruction to make the Auditor's movement audible is deleted (see chapter 2.2.2). Note 2 is now typed, including the handwritten additions made on ET5. However, the entire note is then deleted by a St Andrew's Cross. In pink ink, there is a note regarding further possible pauses:

> consider pause for mouth to stare ~~in space...~~ after "stare into space" – "stop & stare again". – once or throughout. (06r)

This is not integrated into later published editions of the text, so it may be a 'performance variant', written for Whitelaw when rehearsing the play (see Introduction). A suggestion on the same page regarding an ad lib does show up in the version of the text broadcast on BBC television (see chapter 1.6.1), providing a concrete example of how deeply imbricated Beckett's methods of textual composition were with performance practice at this point in his career.

ET7 (MS-UoR-1227-7-12-8)

> Stencilled typescript with minor manuscript additions and corrections. F.1 inscribed 'for Reading University Library with all good wishes, Samuel Beckett, London Jan. 1973'. 33 × 21 cm. 6 leaves. (Bryden, Garforth and Mills 1998, 67)

The changes made on ET7 are fewer than those on previous typescripts. The first four repetitions of 'SHE' are deleted in Mouth's responses to interruptions (01r, 03r, 04r, 05r). This repetition is now only retained for the fifth and final interruption: '...what?...who?...no...SHE!...SHE!..' (06r). Having been reduced to two for the previous three typescripts, the ellipsis points are restored on ET7 to the standard three, barring a few typos where Beckett uses only two dots.

The edits to the two notes at the end of the text are very similar to those on ET6. Both notes are again typed out. Note 2 is again deleted with a large St Andrew's Cross.

ET8 (MS-UoR-1227-7-12-10-synopsis)

> Typescript of synopsis of *Not I*. F.1 inscribed 'for Reading University Library, Sam. Beckett'. 30 × 21 cm. One leaf + carbon copy. Headed 'NOT I – synopsis'. (Bryden, Garforth and Mills 1998, 67)

This typed synopsis divides the play into five sections which are numbered 1 to 5 in the left margin. Sections 1–3 are divided according to the first two interruptions which prompt Mouth's first two renunciations of the first person (and the movements of the Auditor); sections 4 and 5 are structured according to the page breaks 03r–04r and 04r–05r on ET7. As well as summarizing key points in the text, the synopsis mentions five 'life scenes':

> life scene~~1~~ 1 ~~9~~(field) [...]
> Life scene 2 (shopping centre) [...]
> Life scene 3 (Croker's Acres) [...]
> Life scene 4 (courtroom) [...]
> Life scene 5 (rushing out to tell) (01r)

The first is the only life scene mentioned more than once, showing up four times in the synopsis. Two gaps between typed lines are repaired by means of handwritten bows in black ink in the left margin.

CPG (MS-BC-1991001-43-10)

A photocopy of the playscript produced for the UK premiere of *Not I* at the Royal Court (see RC playscript, chapter 1.6.1) is held in the John J. Burns Library, Boston College. Its title page is marked 'Corrected copy for Grove / December 72' and the rest of the document contains edits in Beckett's hand.[32] Further down the title page, Beckett wrote:

> London
> 1. 1. 73
> Dear Barney
> All yours,
> Love
> Sam (01r)

32 This typescript is incorrectly labelled 'Author's corrected / galleys – / included in Ends & / Odds' (01r).

On 1 January 1973, Beckett was in London for rehearsals of the Royal Court production of *Not I*. As was probably also the case with the Faber setting copy (FSC; see chapter 1.3.1), Beckett prepared CPG in light of his rehearsals of the play, though these rehearsals did continue after 1 January 1973. On 20 January 1973, Beckett told Ruby Cohn: 'Sent revised text of Not I to Grove for Evergreen' (*LSB IV* 323), suggesting his work on the corrected playscript continued up to (and possibly beyond) the play's premiere on 16 January. Markings on both the Faber and Grove copies are largely identical, with similar edits made on the same part of the page in most instances. However, there are differences between the two, the most substantial of which is that the note on the Auditor's movement is not yet described as a 'gesture of helpless compassion' in the Grove copy.[33]

1.2.2 French

French typescripts

FT1 (MS-UoR-1396-4-27)

> Untitled typescript with manuscript corrections and additions by Samuel Beckett, of *Pas moi* [...]. Various sizes. (Bryden, Garforth and Mills 1998, 68)

The online catalogue at the University of Reading gives further detail on the pages of different size:

33 Though most of the handwritten edits are made on the same part of the page, some small differences in positioning show that Grove's corrected playscript is not a photocopy of Faber's setting copy.

> Typescript comprises 8 leaves. Leaves 2–7 are 30 cm. First leaf (12 × 21 cm) appears to have been sellotaped to top of leaf 2. Final leaf (9 × 21 cm) appears to have been sellotaped to bottom of leaf 7.[34]

This typescript is undated. It is numbered 2–6 in type in the centre of the top margin (03r–07r). Corrections and additions are made in black ink. Beckett also used pencil for a list of words on folio 01v, another short list on folio 08v and an addition on folio 08r. Throughout the typescript, Beckett made additions in pencil and then erased them; some of these are written over in black ink. There are blue marks on folio 06r; these may have been made by a crayon or an eraser. The typewriter seems to be the same as that used for folios 03r–06r of the first English typescript of *That Time* (see chapter 3.2.1).

FT2 (MS-BnF-4-COL-344-27)

The Fonds Roger Blin at the Bibliothèque nationale de France holds a typescript of *Pas moi*, containing a title page and a typewritten synopsis of the play. The document, nine sheets in total, contains handwritten marks in black ink, blue ink and pencil. Black ink – in Beckett's hand – is used mainly to correct typos, with blue ink – in someone else's hand – for the most part inserting new words and underlining a few others. Pencil is used to underline words and introduces 'Temps' at two points on folio 06r in a similar hand to the blue ink additions. There are staple holes in the top left corner of each page except the synopsis (02r), though the creasing on this page may hide staple holes. All pages of the document show two horizontal fold marks, which indicate it may have been stored in an envelope. A missing ellipsis point on folio 07r suggests the typed material has been copied.

34 http://www.reading.ac.uk/adlib/Details/archiveSpecial/110074974. The printed catalogue supports the view that the pages were sellotaped together at an earlier stage, mentioning a final folio which measures '36 × 21 cm (extended with attached sheet)' and counting a total of '7 leaves' in the document. It also mentions that all leaves measure 21 cm in width (Bryden, Garforth and Mills 1998, 68). Richard Admussen too mentions 'Seven sheets' (1979, 76).

The most striking material aspect of this document is the large tear which goes almost all the way up folio 02r (see Fig. 6). This means that some of the synopsis is missing. The visible text shows that it differs from the corresponding English 'synopsis' (ET8). In the transcription below, square brackets indicate informed guesses of text missing due to the tear:

Naissance
Enfance
Scénette 1 (prairie)
Refus du je 1
Situation dans le noir
Idée-illumination 1 (punition)
" " " 2 (gémir comme si)
Refus du je 2
Arrivée de la voix
Scénette 2 (supermarché)
Mouvement de~~x~~s lèvres
Idé[e-i]llumination 3 (retour de la sensation)
["] " " 4 (impossible continuer)
et cerveau

[Scénette] 3 (vaine pâture)
prairie retrouvée 1
[Refus du j]e 3
[Idée-illumi]nation 5 (chose à dire)
[Scénette 4] (tribunal)
– prairie retrouvée 2
[Idée-illumi]nation 6 et suivantes
[Refus du je] 4
[Scénette 5] (inconnu abordé)

[Refus du je] 5
prairie retrouvée 3 (02r)

FT3 (MS-BnF-4-COL-178-970)

The Fonds Renaud–Barrault at the Bibliothèque nationale de France holds a seven-page photocopy of *Pas moi* with handwritten annotations [‘7 feuillets multigraphiés photocopiés, annotations manuscrites’].[35] This document contains a title page, but it lacks the synopsis and first page of monologue (see FT2, 02r–03r). All black-ink edits in Beckett’s hand on FT3 are also found on FT2, though differences in the handwriting indicate that these edits were not copied, but made separately on each typescript. There is underlining in (now) pink ink, red ink, black ink, blueblack ink and what looks like pencil. Pink ink additions are in Beckett’s hand; one of these is written over in black ink, in what also seems to be his handwriting: ‘durer’ (04r). There is brown, age-related staining throughout and the type has faded substantially. In addition, there are staple marks in the top left corner and a horizontal fold line across the centre of each page.

An addition on folio 04v (not in Beckett’s hand) includes what may be a Paris phone number, possibly relating to some ticket reservations:

> ~~xi~~fournier
> 5 places **548.65-90**
> <u>samedi</u>

35 https://archivesetmanuscrits.bnf.fr/ark:/12148/cc588917/ca1139.

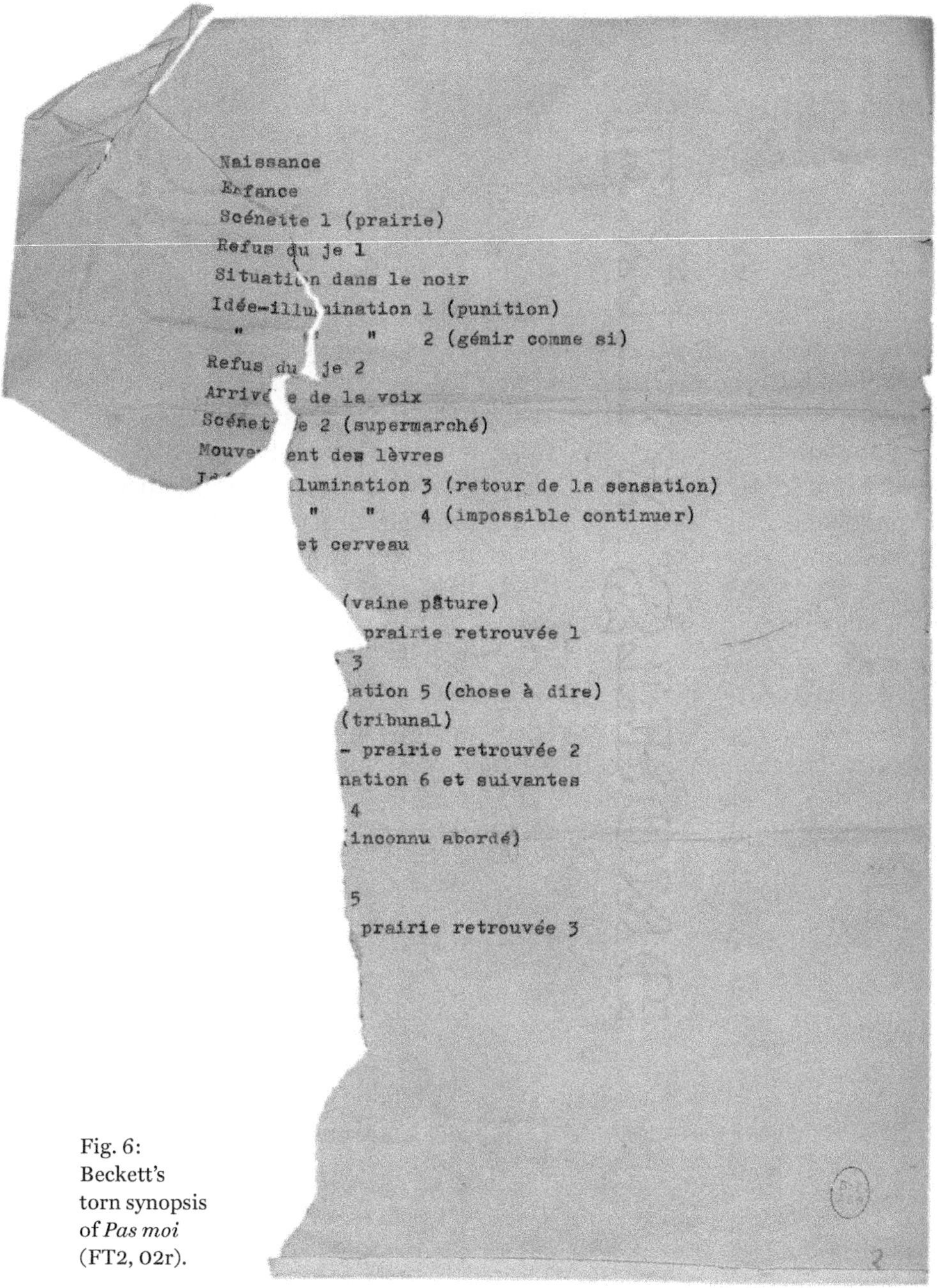
Naissance
Enfance
Scénette 1 (prairie)
Refus du je 1
Situati n dans le noir
Idée-illu ination 1 (punition)
" " " 2 (gémir comme si)
Refus du je 2
Arrivé e de la voix
Scénet e 2 (supermarché)
Mouve ent des lèvres
Id llumination 3 (retour de la sensation)
" " 4 (impossible continuer)
et cerveau
(vaine pâture)
prairie retrouvée 1
3
ation 5 (chose à dire)
(tribunal)
- prairie retrouvée 2
nation 6 et suivantes
4
(inconnu abordé)
5
prairie retrouvée 3

Fig. 6: Beckett's torn synopsis of *Pas moi* (FT2, 02r).

1.3 Setting Copies, Galleys, Proofs and Annotated Copies

1.3.1 English

FSC

This document is marked 'Corrected copy for Faber / December 72' in black ink on its title page (01r) and is a corrected copy of the playscript issued on the occasion of *Not I*'s UK premiere (together with *Krapp's Last Tape*; see chapter 1.6.1). It is stored in the Harry Ransom Center's Samuel Beckett Collection (HRC SB MS 5/3). Beckett was in London for this production from 15 December 1972, returning to Paris on 18 January 1973 after the premiere on 16 January (Pilling 2006, 191). This makes it possible that he corrected this text for Faber after he had begun rehearsing the play, though it is not possible given current available evidence to determine the exact date of correction.[36]

Beckett's correspondence shows that he was keen to rehearse *Not I* before publishing the text. On 7 August 1972, he wrote to head of Grove Press, Barney Rosset, about the play: 'With regard to publication, I prefer to hold it back for the sake of whatever light N.Y. & London rehearsals may shed. I have not yet sent the text to Faber.' On 3 November 1972, Beckett wrote to Rosset again:

36 Further light may be shed on this by Beckett's correspondence to Faber, but at the time of writing, the archive is 'Not currently open to external researchers' (https://discovery.nationalarchives.gov.uk/details/a/A13532968). In an email of 1 February 2016, Faber archivist Robert Brown told Dirk Van Hulle: 'there are no Beckett manuscripts, typescripts or marked proofs here (to the best of my knowledge)' (qtd. in Van Hulle and Verhulst 2017a, 133n46).

> Re. text of Not I, I have already made a number of changes in view of London production (opening Jan. 15) and shall probably make more during rehearsals at Royal Court. So I'd rather hold up publication in Evergreen till I have the final text which I hope to get to you early in the New Year. (CU, Barney Rosset Papers, box 46, folder 5)

Though these letters do not totally rule out the possibility that Beckett sent the text to Faber before the premiere, they do strongly signal his desire to have the play rehearsed before publication. Given that on 20 January Beckett had only very recently sent a similar corrected copy to Grove (see chapter 1.2.1), it seems likely that he also waited for rehearsals to conclude before sending FSC to Faber.

The setting copy is inscribed in black ink 'for John & Evelyn [Kobler] / with love from Sam / Paris Feb. 1973' and the heading '~~ACT ONE~~' is deleted (02r). There are numerous changes and corrections in the margins throughout in blue and blue-black ink, as well as one edit in pencil, all of which are implemented in the first published version (Faber 1973a). Mouth's responses to the 'interruptions' are edited down according to a regular pattern:

> what? ... who? ... ~~what? ... no ...~~ no! ... ~~SHE!~~ she! ... (pause and movement 1) (02r–03r)
>
> what? ... who? ... ~~what? ... no ...~~ no! ... ~~SHE!~~ she! ... (pause and movement 2) (04r)
>
> what? ... who? ~~... what? ... no~~ ... no! ... ~~SHE!~~ she! ... (pause and movement 3) (07r)
>
> what? ... who? ~~... what? ... no~~ ... no! ... ~~SHE!~~ she! ... (pause and movement 4) (07r)
>
> what? ... who? ... ~~what? ... no ...~~ no! ... she! ... ~~SHE!~~ SHE! (08r)

Other changes relate to punctuation and the addition, deletion as well as transposition of words. Stage directions are highlighted for italicization in the published text.[37]

As on ET6 and ET7, the note on the Auditor's movement is edited (see chapter 2.2.2). Also matching ET6 and ET7, Note 2, on pronunciation, is deleted by a large St Andrew's Cross, having caused problems when Beckett assisted Alan Schneider by letter with the 1972 world premiere of the play in New York (see chapter 2.2.1).

GSC

The Grove Press Records at Syracuse University Library contain a setting copy for Grove's 1976 [1977] edition of *Ends and Odds* in a folder marked 'Production – setting copy' (SU, Grove Press Records, box 91). It consists of typescripts and photocopies of previously published editions, annotated by Beckett and by Grove staff members for typesetting. For the setting copy of *Not I*, Grove used a photocopy of the text from *First Love and Other Shorts*. The annotations on this setting copy are all related to matters of house style and there is no evidence of authorial involvement.

On 20 October 1976, Rosset wrote to Beckett: 'Many thanks for GHOST TRIO which we received this morning. Alas, too late, the book is already at the printer' (CU, Barney Rosset Papers, box 46, folder 5). However, the Grove setting copy, the galleys and the published edition all include *Ghost Trio*. A note on an unnumbered loose sheet in the setting copy for *Ghost Trio* confirms that the play was a late addition: 'Ghost Trio was first taped for television by the BBC in October, 1976, directed by D. McWhinnie. **It will be taped again** by the Süddeutscher Rundfunk in May, 1977, directed by Samuel Beckett, with Klaus Herm as F' (SU, Grove Press Records, box 91). The phrase '**will be taped again**' indicates that this part of the setting copy was compiled at some point between October 1976 and February 1977 (when the edition was published).[38]

37 Though Faber used italics for stage directions in later editions of the play, their first published edition uses underlining (1973a).

38 This note seems to have been prepared from a list of information given by Beckett in the galleys (GG, 39r).

GG

The variants between *Not I* as it appears in Grove's *First Love and Other Shorts* and their later *Ends and Odds* can be tracked through the galleys stored in the Syracuse University Library, in a folder marked 'Production – galleys' (SU, Grove Press Records, box 91). The *Ends and Odds* galleys are photocopies which have been annotated by a Grove Press staff member in red ink, with responses and minor edits by Beckett in black ink. However, he missed the two errors in punctuation which went on to appear in Grove's *Ends and Odds* (see chapter 1.5.1).

PPG

The Lilly Library at Indiana University, Bloomington holds an uncorrected proof copy of *First Love and Other Stories*, corrected in black ink to *First Love and Other Shorts*: 'In the Lilly copy, the cover title, half title and title page have been altered in black ink by an editor to read "Shorts" instead of "Stories"' (Mitchell, forthcoming). *Not I* is found on pp. 55–65.

Fac(D)

The DLA archive in Marbach holds a copy of Faber's first edition of *Not I*, featuring a single annotation on page 11: 'all those contortions without ₰ ~~touch~~ which'. The deletion and accompanying deleatur sign in the right margin are both in pencil and it is difficult to decipher the handwriting. However, the change does correspond to the only textual edit on Beckett's annotated copy held in the Harry Ransom Center, Fac(K).

Fac(K)

The copy held in the Harry Ransom Center is inscribed by Beckett to John and Evelyn Kobler:

for
John & Evelyn
with love from Sam
Paris Oct. 1973 (3)

This HRC copy also has the word 'touch' crossed out in black ink: 'all those contortions without ~~touch~~ which' (11). Given that the same ink is used for the dedication to the Koblers, it is safe to assume that this is Beckett's edit. The deleted word does not appear in the 1973 reprint of Faber's first edition, which is unpaginated (1973b, 11).

1.4 Pre-book Publications

1.4.1 French

1975a *Pas moi*, in: *Minuit* 12 (January). 71 pp. [*Pas moi*: pp. 2–9]

In addition to publishing *Pas moi* in a standalone book (see chapter 1.5.2), Jérôme Lindon of Les Éditions de Minuit decided to publish the play in the house journal *Minuit*, which regularly featured Beckett's shorter texts. While published in the same month as the standalone edition, the exact publication date of the *Minuit* journal is not recorded, with the contents page reading simply 'JANVIER 1975', and the legal deposit dated '1er trimestre 1975' (1975a, 1). However, on the Minuit webpage for their combined edition of *Oh les beaux jours suivi de Pas moi*, there is a line regarding *Pas moi* which indicates that the journal came out before the book: '*Pré-publication* de la traduction française par l'auteur dans la revue *Minuit*, n°12, 1975'.[39]

In a letter of 19 September 1974, sent by the same mail as the proofs for the book edition of *Pas moi*, Lindon mentioned that Beckett would be receiving a different set of proofs for the journal publication within a number of days. On 23 September, Beckett duly replied that the *Pas moi* proofs had arrived that day (IMEC, S. Beckett, Correspondance 1969–1972, box 7). This indicates that there were proofs of both the journal and the book edition which I have been unable to locate.[40]

39 http://www.leseditionsdeminuit.fr/livre-Oh_les_beaux_jours-1511-1-1-0-1.html; emphasis added. [Pre-publication of the author's French translation in the periodical *Minuit* 12, 1975].

40 In response to my query as to whether Les Éditions de Minuit hold any manuscripts, typescripts, corrected proofs or annotated editions related to the plays in this module, Irène Lindon wrote: 'Je vous confirme que les manuscrits comme les épreuves sont retournés aux auteurs et c'est le cas pour *Pas moi, Cette fois* et *Pas*' [I confirm to you that manuscripts and proofs alike are returned to the authors and this is the case for *Pas moi, Cette fois* and *Pas*] (email correspondence, 27 January 2020).

1.5. Editions

1.5.1 English (UK)

1973a *Not I*. London: Faber and Faber. 16 pp.

The first edition of *Not I* was published in a slim, 16-page volume. The playtext takes up pages 6–16; pages 1–5 and 16 are unnumbered. The cover is stiff, coloured black white and orange, with a photograph of Mouth on the front cover. The copyright page contains the note:

> The first performance in Great Britain of NOT I was given at the Royal Court Theatre, London, on 16th January 1973. It was directed by Anthony Page, and the décor was by Jocelyn Herbert. The cast was as follows:
>
> Mouth Billie Whitelaw
> Auditor Brian Miller (5)

1977a *Ends and Odds: Plays and Sketches*. London: Faber and Faber. 104 pp. [*Not I*: pp. 11–20]

This edition of *Ends and Odds* seems to postdate Grove 1976d [1977] (see chapter 1.5.2), as it includes ... *but the clouds* ..., which was not included in the Grove edition.[41] Aside from this, the order of plays is the same as Grove's 1976 [1977] *Ends and Odds*, with ... *but the clouds* ... added to the Faber edition as the last of the 'ENDS', after *Ghost Trio*.

Beckett's letters to Faber show that there was some debate regarding the title of this edition. When *Not I* and *That Time* were added to *Rough for Theatre I* and *II* and *Rough for Radio I* and *II* as works for publication,

41 See Beckett's letter to Alan Schneider on 6 January 1977: 'TV piece [... *but the clouds* ...] too late for inclusion in Grove vol., but in time for Faber's due in March' (*NABS* 352). Beckett mentions *Ends and Odds* as being 'due out from Faber & Faber any day now' in a letter to Paul Auster dated 21 March 1977 (*LSB IV* 454).

Beckett began to have misgivings about the title *Roughs for Theatre and Radio*. On 4 October 1975, he wrote to Charles Monteith:

> If Not I & That Time are included with the Roughs we shall have to find another general title. [...] I accept the idea of all 6 together and shall in due course propose another title. (*LSB IV* 410)

On 24 February 1976, Beckett wrote again to Monteith: 'What would you think of Ends and Odds as title for the book of plays, That Time & Footfalls being the "ends", the other four the "odds"?' (*LSB IV* 424). In his response of 1 March, Monteith approved (*LSB IV* 425n1) and, though *Not I* seems to have slipped Beckett's mind when writing his February letter, the play was included when the edition went to press.

Though it has not been possible to locate the setting copy used for *Not I* in this edition, two variants indicate that the base text was Faber's own 1973 standalone edition rather than Grove's more recently published texts. Faber 1977a retains a repeated 'still ...' which was omitted both from Grove's 1974 *First Love and Other Shorts* and their 1976 [1977] *Ends and Odds* (1977a, 14). The Faber edition also features a hyphen in the phrase '... not as much as **good-bye** ...', which also occurs in their 1973 edition (due to a line break) (1973a, 10).

Sentence	Grove 1976d [1977]	Page	Faber 1977a	Page
0009	... but the brain still ... in a way	15	... but the brain still ... **still ...** in a way	14
0019	... not as much as **goodbye** ...	18	... not as much as **good-bye** ...	16
0024	... no idea what she's saying**!** ... imagine! ...	19	... no idea what she's saying ... imagine! ...	17
0027	... what? ... the buzzing ...	20	... what? ... the buzzing**?** ...	18

Faber 1977a does not contain the two errors of punctuation in Grove's earlier *Ends and Odds* (see sentences 0024 and 0027 in the table above). Notably, neither does Faber's 1973 edition, which again supports the idea that Faber used this as their base text rather than the more recent Grove editions.

1984a *Collected Shorter Plays*. London and Boston: Faber and Faber. 316 pp. [*Not I*: pp. 213–23]

This edition contains a text of *Not I* based on Faber's 1977 edition of *Ends and Odds*, but with a reset text. It was published on 13 February 1984 (Mitchell, forthcoming). The edition corrects an error from Faber's *Ends and Odds*, filling in a missing ellipsis point in the line '... now this . .' (Faber 1977a, 20). However, it also introduces three variants of its own, one of which adds a fourth ellipsis point and is almost certainly an error (see table below). The house style of punctuation and formatting of stage directions also differs between the two editions. For instance, three ellipsis points after a question mark or exclamation mark are shortened to two in Faber 1984a.

Sentence	Faber 1977a	Page	Faber 1984a	Page
0004	**...** out ...	13	**....** out ...	216
0012	... as if in actual **...** agony ...	15	... as if in actual agony ...	218
0027	... or grabbing at **the** straw ...	18	... or grabbing at straw ...	221
0033	... now this **. .**	20	... now this **...**	222

In addition to the edition's textual proximity to 1977a, Beckett's correspondence also supports the idea that Faber took the lead on producing this joint edition with Grove.[42] Having met Faber's Charles Monteith, Beckett wrote to Knowlson on 20 May 1981: 'He [Monteith] would like to publish next year all the short plays including Krapp in 1 or 2 vols. (theatre, radio, TV) for which your help wd. be sorely needed' (*LSB IV* 552). This indicates that *Collected Shorter Plays* was planned as a revised edition. However, Beckett soon lost heart, telling Knowlson later the following month: 'I couldn't face adjustment of short plays. As they totter or not at all' (20 June 1981, *LSB IV* 553). In spite of this, Beckett did ask Faber to send him proofs (Beckett to Knowlson, 21 May 1983, *LSB IV* 611), which arrived in June 1983: 'Faber proofs (corrected by them) no doubt in pickle for me in Paris whither reluctantly tomorrow' (Beckett to Knowlson, 20 June 1983, *LSB IV* 615).

42 According to Gontarski, 'both the *Complete Dramatic Works* and *Collected Shorter Plays* were projects initiated by Faber and photo-offset by Grove Press' (1998, 139).

It has not been possible to locate these proofs, though they may be in the Faber archive (which is currently closed to researchers; see chapter 1.3.1).

1986b *The Complete Dramatic Works*. London and Boston: Faber and Faber. 476 pp. [*Not I*: pp. 373–83]

On 25 July 1982, Beckett wrote to Monteith: 'If you are at a loss for an editor of the Collected Shorter Plays I suggest Katharine Worth of Holloway Royal College, Egham, Surrey. She is very competent and knows the work well' (*LSB IV* 586). Monteith replied that the book was already in production: 'But we'll be very glad to bear her name in mind for the future' (Monteith to Beckett, 28 July 1982, *LSB IV* 586n2). It is not clear if Faber followed through on the idea to use Worth as an editor for their 1986 *Complete Dramatic Works*, but the text of *Not I* shows no variants from Faber's 1984 *Collected Shorter Plays*, indicating that it was photographically reproduced.

1.5.2 English (US)

1974 *First Love and Other Shorts*. New York: Grove Press. [*Not I*: pp. 73–87]

Variants between CPG and the copy of the RC playscript Beckett annotated for Faber (FSC; see chapter 1.3.1) prove that Grove's corrected playscript was not used as a setting copy for *First Love and Other Shorts*, which is closer to Faber's 1973 edition than to CPG. It is therefore likely that, having received the playscript from Beckett, and with their plans to publish *Not I* in the *Evergreen Review* abandoned, Grove decided to base their 1974 text on the recently published Faber edition instead. The strongest evidence for this is that of all the variants between Grove's corrected playscript and Grove 1974, the lines that appear in Grove 1974 are all replicated from Faber 1973.[43]

43 All the variants between Grove's corrected playscript and Grove 1974 can also be found on FSC, leaving open the possibility that Grove relied on the latter to set *First Love and Other Shorts*.

The time that elapsed between Rosset's initial suggestion in March 1973 and the eventual publication date of 1974 supports the hypothesis that a document other than Grove's corrected playscript was used as a setting copy by the publisher. Beckett responded to Rosset on 21 March: 'First Love & Not I hardly go together, but I don't suppose it matters if that is what you wish.' Rosset's reply of 18 June indicates he had forgotten in the intervening months that the combination with *First Love* was his idea, not Beckett's: 'Following the suggestion in your letter – yes we would like to publish it [*First Love*] together with NOT I. We think the two will make a fine book.'[44] This letter also suggests the inclusion of 'four more prose pieces which we do not have in book form: From an Abandoned Work, Imagine [*sic*] Dead Imagine, Enough and Ping.' Beckett's next letter on the matter (dated '4.7.73') indicates that *Breath* had meanwhile been suggested as a further addition: 'If you use Breath in your vol. I think it should come at the end, after Not I, though written earlier. ~~You~~ The title could now be Breath & Other Shorts if you prefer. As you like' (all in CU, Barney Rosset Papers, box 46, folder 5).

In the end, the edition was published with all the texts suggested by Rosset: *First Love* (9–36), *From an Abandoned Work* (37–49), *Enough* (51–60), *Imagination Dead Imagine* (61–66), *Ping* (67–72), *Not I* (73–87) and *Breath* (89–96). The title *First Love and Other Shorts* focuses on the more substantial prose work rather than the short theatre text *Breath* suggested as a title piece by Beckett.

There is one interesting textual variant between Faber's 1973 first edition of *Not I* and the text in *First Love and Other Shorts*, involving the deletion of one of Beckett's favourite words, 'still'. The second variant corrects a punctation error in the first edition, while the third may derive from a dropped dash on the reprint of Faber's first edition of *Not I*: 'all ...' (1973b, 11). The fourth variant is almost certainly a printing error, with an extra ellipsis point being added. Aside from the rectified punctuation, none of these changes are to be found on Grove's corrected playscript, confirming (as discussed above) that it was not used as a setting copy for *First Love and Other Shorts*.[45]

44 There may be a missing letter in Beckett which makes this suggestion.
45 All four variants between Faber 1973a and Grove 1974 appear in the same form as the Faber 1973 text on FSC, thus making it impossible on current

Sentence	Faber 1973a	Page	Grove 1974	Page
0009	but the brain still ... **still** ... in a way	7	but the brain still ... in a way	77
0018	then finally had to admit . .[46]	10	then finally had to admit **...**	80
0023	all – ... what? ... the buzzing?	11	all ... what? ... the buzzing?	82
0027	nothing there **...** on to the next	13	nothing there **....** on to the next	83

On 17 June 1974, Alan Schneider wrote to Beckett regarding Grove's *First Love and Other Shorts*:

> One small matter, you may have noticed. Grove accidentally put Hume Cronyn's name in as the Figure in NOT I instead of Henderson Forsythe. I have called it to their attention, and am apologising to Henderson. Had I seen the galleys earlier, I would have noticed it. (*NABS* 317)

This error is corrected on Grove's setting copy for *Ends and Odds* (GSC, see chapter 1.3.1). Not only does Schneider's letter allow us to roughly date the publication of *First Love and Other Shorts* to circa June 1974, it also indicates there were galleys for this volume which I have not been able to locate.[47]

1976d [1977] *Ends and Odds: Eight New Dramatic Pieces*. First Evergreen edition. New York: Grove Press. 128 pp. [*Not I*: pp. 11–23]

A publisher's review slip in a copy of this edition in the Lilly Library, Indiana University, indicates that its publication date was 17 February 1977 (Mitchell, forthcoming), in spite of the verso of the title page stating: 'First Edition 1976'.

evidence to know if FSC or Faber 1973 was used as Grove's setting copy.

46 This punctuation error is not corrected in the Faber reprint I consulted (1973b, 10).

47 Schneider visited Beckett on 11 June in Paris (*NABS* 317n2); by the time he got back to the United States, a copy of Beckett's newly published book was waiting for him there (Schneider to Beckett, 17 June 1974, *NABS* 316).

The edition is divided into two sections: 'ENDS' – comprising the three theatre works *Not I* (11–23), *That Time* (25–37) and *Footfalls* (39–49) as well as the TV play *Ghost Trio* (51–65) – and 'ODDS', subtitled 'Roughs for Theatre and Radio' (7) – featuring *Rough for Theatre I* (here entitled *Theatre I*, 69–80); *Rough for Theatre II* (here entitled *Theatre II*, 81–101); *Rough for Radio I* (here entitled *Radio I*, 103–12); and *Rough for Radio II* (here entitled *Radio II*, 113–28). The bright orange cover features on its back a bio of Beckett below a description of the eight dramatic pieces. The text itself fixes one error in *First Love and Other Shorts*, reinstating the dash in the phrase 'all– ... what?' (19), but introduces two errors of punctuation, as can be seen below.

Sentence	Grove 1974	Page	Grove 1976d [1977]	Page
0023	all ... what?	82	all– ... what?	19
0024	... no idea what she's saying ... imagine!	82	... no idea what she's saying**!** ... imagine!	19
0027	what? ... the buzzing**?** ...	83	what? ... the buzzing ...	20

These changes can be tracked through the galleys for *Ends and Odds* (GG). The late arrival of the text of *Ghost Trio* (see chapter 1.3.1) may explain the discrepancy between the publication date on the copyright page (1976) and the actual publication date (1977).

1981 *Ends and Odds: Nine Dramatic Pieces*. First enlarged edition. New York: Grove Press. 138 pp. [*Not I*: pp. 11–23]

Grove released this enlarged edition in paperback so as to include ... *but the clouds* ..., which was omitted from their previous *Ends and Odds*. The sequence of plays is the same as that in Faber 1977a, with ... *but the clouds* ... following *Ghost Trio* as the last of the 'ENDS'. The text of *Not I* in this edition is a photographic reproduction of Grove 1976d [1977] and contains no variants.

1984b *Collected Shorter Plays*. New York: Grove Press. 316 pp. [*Not I*: pp. 213–23]

This edition contains a photographic reproduction of the text of *Not I* in Faber's *Collected Shorter Plays*, so there are no variants.

1.5.3 French

1975b *Pas moi*. Paris: Les Éditions de Minuit. 24 pp.

According to its front matter, this is a limited edition on vellum running to 242 copies: 150 on *vélin arches* and 92 on *vélin supérieur*. In addition, the front matter mentions a few unnumbered copies *hors commerce*. The pagination runs from 7 to 24. The standalone edition was *achevé d'imprimer* on 17 January 1975.

The text of *Pas moi* in the standalone edition has a different setting to *Minuit* 12. As well as correcting one error in the earlier journal, the book introduces three of its own, omitting a question mark after 'le bourdon' (1975a, 13) and omitting the third ellipsis point on two occasions, as can be seen in the following table.

Sentence	Minuit 1975a	Page	Minuit 1975b	Page
0007	ainsi de suite**...**	3	ainsi de suite**..**	9
0014	quoi ?... le bourdon **? ...**	4	quoi ?... le bourdon**...**	13
0016	**tout** cette clarté...	5	**toute** cette clarté...	13
0024	langue**...**	6	langue**..**	17
0028	un mot par-ci par-là...	7	un mot par ci par là...	19
0029	**pas** d'amour...	7	**point** d'amour...	20
0034	pas entendue...	8	**ou** pas entendue...	23

The book includes two variants which were almost certainly made by the author. While the changes of ellipses, punctuation and correction could very well have been carried out by the publisher, it is extremely unlikely that they would have altered '**pas** d'amour...' to '**point** d'amour...' (1975a, 7; 1975b, 20) or inserted an '**ou**' before 'pas entendue' (1975a, 8; 1975b, 23) without Beckett's involvement. These latter edits may have been made by Beckett on the page proofs for the book edition, but not on those he corrected for the journal. While the text in the journal is more reliable when it comes to punctuation, the book edition is more reliable with regard to the words themselves.

1975c *Oh les beaux jours suivi de Pas moi*. Paris: Les Éditions de Minuit. 95 pp. [*Pas moi*: pp. 79–95]

Lindon's letter to Beckett of 23 September 1974 indicates that he initially planned for *Pas moi* to be included in an expanded edition of *Comédie et actes divers* (IMEC, S. Beckett, Correspondance 1969–1972, box 7). However, it was paired instead with *Oh les beaux jours*, alongside which it continues to appear in the Minuit catalogue. This two-play edition was *achevé d'imprimer* on 3 April 1975 and contains a text that generally follows the words of Minuit's earlier standalone edition. The variants between the two book editions can be seen in the following table.

Sentence	Minuit 1975b	Page	Minuit 1975c	Page
0007	ainsi de suite..	9	ainsi de suite...	82
0007	et la voilà dans le — ...	9	et la voilà dans le —...	82
0009	(*bref rire*)... miséricordieux...	10	(*bref rire*)...miséricordieux...	83
0014	quoi ?... le bourdon...	13	quoi ?... le bourdon **?**...	85
0019	**plus qu'à le donner... avec le cabas...**	14	*	87
0024	**mâchoires**... langue..	17	**mâchoire**... langue...	89
0036	*La voix continue, inintelligible,*	24	*La voix continue inintelligible,*	95

Notably, Minuit 1975c follows the earlier standalone edition with regard to the authorial variants '**point** d'amour' and '**ou** pas entendue' (1975c, 92, 94). While it does insert the missing question mark after 'bourdon' (1975c, 85) and restores missing ellipsis points, the collected edition with *Oh les beaux jours* introduces multiple new errors, including the omission of an entire phrase in the supermart scene (1975c, 87; see table). This means that the first edition is the more reliable of the two *Pas moi* texts published in Minuit books.

1.5.4 Multilingual

1978b *Stücke und Bruchstücke*. Frankfurt am Main: Suhrkamp Verlag. 275 pp. *Not I* (pp. 10–28)

By 1978, Suhrkamp had published two volumes of Beckett's *Dramatische Dichtungen*, containing the original texts (in English or French) with German translation on the facing page and Beckett's own translations (into French or English) after each text. The same format was followed for *Stücke und Bruchstücke*, which contains the same plays as Faber's 1977 *Ends and Odds*. The copyright page of *Stücke und Bruchstücke* features the note:

> Die englischsprachigen Texte wurden mit freundlicher Genehmigung dem 1977 bei Faber and Faber, London, erschienenen Band »Ends and Odds. Plays and Sketches« entnommen.
>
> [The English texts are taken, with kind permission of Faber and Faber, London, from their 1977 volume *Ends and Odds: Plays and Sketches*.]

The text of *Not I* published by Suhrkamp features a fair number of variants with regard to the Faber edition. These variants are all errors of spelling, word choice, spacing and punctuation introduced by Suhrkamp in their text, with one exception – the filling-in of the missing ellipsis point in Faber's '... now this . .' (1977a, 20). None of the changes made by Suhrkamp can be traced to Grove 1976d [1977] and it is unclear which text they used as a setting copy.

There are also changes of house style by Suhrkamp, such as emphasis being indicated by spaces between each letter: 'm e a n t' (1978b, 14).

Sentence	Faber 1977a	Page	Suhrkamp 1978b	Page
0012	... all the time the buzzing **...** so-called	15	... all the time the buzzing so-called	14
0016	... on her part **...** so on ...	16	... on her part **..** so on ...	16
0019	... **supermart** ...	16	... **supermarket** ...	18
0024	... what? ... **tongue**? ...	17	... what? ... **togue**? ...	20
0025	... like maddened **...** all that together ...	17	... like maddened all that together ...	20
0027	... quick grab and on ...	18	...quick grab and on ...	22
0031	... what? ... who**?** ... no! ...	19	... what? ... who ... no! ...	26
0033	... now this **. .** this ...	20	... now this **...** this ...	26

Pas moi (pp. 31–40)

Suhrkamp's French text follows that of Minuit's standalone book edition (1975b). Most of the variants between the two relate to punctuation, with Suhrkamp replacing two individual ellipsis points absent from the earlier text but also erroneously editing entire sets of ellipses – sometimes introducing them, sometimes deleting.

Sentence	Minuit 1975b	Page	Suhrkamp 1978b	Page
0004	— monde...	8	**...** monde ...	31
0005	père mère fantômes...	8	père mère **...** fantômes ...	31
0005	elle pareil...	8	elle **...** pareil ...	32
0007	ainsi de suite..	9	ainsi de suite **...**	32
0024	langue..	17	langue **...**	36
0029	qu'il faut qu'elle... dise**...** si c'était ça...	20	qu'il faut qu'elle ... dise si c'était ça ...	38
0033	affolé... krac ! dans le vide	23	affolé ... krac! **...** dans le vide	39
0034	jusque-là**...** tout ça	23	jusque-là tout ça	39
0036	*derrière le* ***rideau***	24	*derrière le* ***rideaux***	40

The closing error '*derrière le* ***rideaux***' (1978b, 40) means that Suhrkamp's text is unreliable at the level of wording as well as punctuation. On 21 August 1978, Beckett received a copy of this edition from Siegfried Unseld, head of Suhrkamp Verlag (DLA, SUA: Suhrkamp/01 Verlagsleitung/ Autorenkonv./Beckett, Samuel: Briefwechsel Suhrkamp Verlag).[48]

48 I would like to thank Dirk Van Hulle for sharing this information with me.

1.6 Playscripts and Production Notes

1.6.1 English

RC playscript

> *Not I* and *Krapp's Last Tape*. Mimeographed acting versions. London: Royal Court Theatre [1972]. Folio, loose in sheets within red paper covers. (Lake 1984, 155)

This mimeographed playscript of *Not I* is stored in the Harry Ransom Center with a playscript of *Krapp's Last Tape* (HRC SB MS 5/4; see *BDMP3* catalogue). Both were produced for the plays' double bill at the Royal Court, which premiered on 16 January 1973. On 20 January, Beckett told Ruby Cohn: 'Faber are bringing out in haste a "libretto" edition for sale at Royal Court' (*LSB IV* 323), so it was evidently not ready for sale at the premiere.[49] However, Beckett did date his annotated copies for Grove and Faber December 1972 (see CPG and FSC, chapters 1.2.1 and 1.3.1), indicating that the document was already available for its author to use at that point. The playscript is professionally typeset, not typed by Beckett. The title page features the theatre's address: 'Royal Court Theatre, / Sloane Square, / London, S. W. 1' (01r). The playscript is undated and uncorrected.

The deletions of the repeated 'SHE' in the first four interruptions – marked by Beckett on ET7 (see chapter 1.2.1.) – are integrated into the text. However, the final interruption also receives only one 'SHE!' from Mouth (08r), unlike the repetition of this word in Faber's first edition (1973a, 15).

A photostat copy of this playscript is held at the University of Reading (UoR MS 1227/7/12/9), inscribed by Beckett: 'for / Reading University / Library / Sam. Beckett' (01), otherwise uncorrected.

49 This was presumably in response to the commercial success of the production (see 'Box Office Figures' on https://www.reading.ac.uk/staging-beckett/Productions.aspx?p=production-644226808).

RC notes.A[50]

Catalogued under the manuscript number 1227/7/12/11 in the University of Reading's Special Collections, this document is described as follows in *Beckett at Reading*:

> Manuscript note by Samuel Beckett indicating places and lengths of pauses in *Not I*. Inscribed 'for Reading University Library, Sam. Beckett'. 30 × 21 cm. One leaf. (Bryden, Garforth and Mills 1998, 68)

The document is reproduced and transcribed in *TN4* (461–7). This list is written on headed paper from the 'Hyde Park Hotel', where Beckett stayed while attending rehearsals of the UK premiere of *Not I* in the Royal Court (Knowlson 1997, 596). The list of 30 pauses – numbered 1 to 25, with five pauses unnumbered – corresponds to the 29 pauses added in the margin of ET6 (see chapter 1.2.1), suggesting that ET6 was used as part of Beckett's preparation for the Royal Court premiere. However, there is one pause which is unique to this document: pause 20, listed as being added at '"another few –" what (not that)', is not marked on ET6 (05r).

The page and line numbers in the left margin correspond to those on the RC playscript. The page numbers 1 to 6 are deleted; 7 is undeleted. A tick appears after each line number. It seems likely that Beckett used his own ET6 to create the list of pauses, which he then keyed to the page and line numbers of the RC playscript, or to a document with the same foliation as the playscript, such as the performance script used by Whitelaw (BW playscript; see below). In her autobiography, Whitelaw mentions:

> Sam went back to his room at the Hyde Park Hotel and wrote out page after page of notes for me in his immaculately unreadable writing, headed 'Aids to learning'. [...] I threw them into the nearest wastepaper basket. [...] I found one little scrap of paper a couple of years ago. (Whitelaw 1996, 126)

50 In *TN4*, these notes are referred to as 'Samuel Beckett's Production Notes for *Not I*' (xi) and 'THE HYDE PARK HOTEL MANUSCRIPT' (ix, 467).

RC notes.A are just such 'Aids to learning', created to help Whitelaw learn this difficult performance text.

While preparing the play for performance, Beckett created at least one variant which appears in the published text. Below the list of pauses, there is another short list in the left margin of 'Hesitations to point', with page and line numbers again corresponding to the RC playscript and to Whitelaw's performance script. One emendation on this list is implemented on Beckett's setting copy for Faber (FSC): the idea mentioned in the last item of 'omitting "to"' (RC notes.A, 01r) from the line 'sudden urge to ... to tell ...' (RC playscript, 09r) is implemented as 'sudden urge to ... ~~to~~ tell' on FSC (08r) and then appears in the first published edition as 'sudden urge to ... tell' (Faber 1973a, 15). Again, we can see here just how much performance practice helped Beckett shape his texts.

Further to the right of this list, Beckett noted: '~~Further~~ Other breaks possible pp. 4 & 5 if needed'. Underneath this is written: 'p.6 1.8 reinsert something she', referring to the line 'something she – ... something she had to ... what?' (RC playscript, 08r; numbered '1.6' in the top right corner). In ET6, this line appears simply as 'something she had to –' (05r). The words are cut on Whitelaw's working script: '~~something she~~ – ...something she had to – ...' (BW playscript, p. 6).[51] The Faber setting copy and Faber's first published version contain the reinsertion: 'something she – ... something she had to – ...' (FSC, 07r; Faber 1973a, 13). This suggests that Beckett may have been using BW playscript as the text to which this list of edits refers.

RC notes.B

This document is stored in the Billie Whitelaw Collection of University of Reading's Special Collections (BW A/2/3). It consists of three sheets, all of which contain Beckett's directorial notes for the Royal Court production of *Not I* in January 1973. The rectos of all three sheets have the note 'Billie Whitelaw / IMPORTANT' in pencil in the top-right corner. Like RC notes.A, all three sheets of this document are written on headed paper from the Hyde Park Hotel. It is not discussed in *TN4*.

51 I follow the numbering on the script.

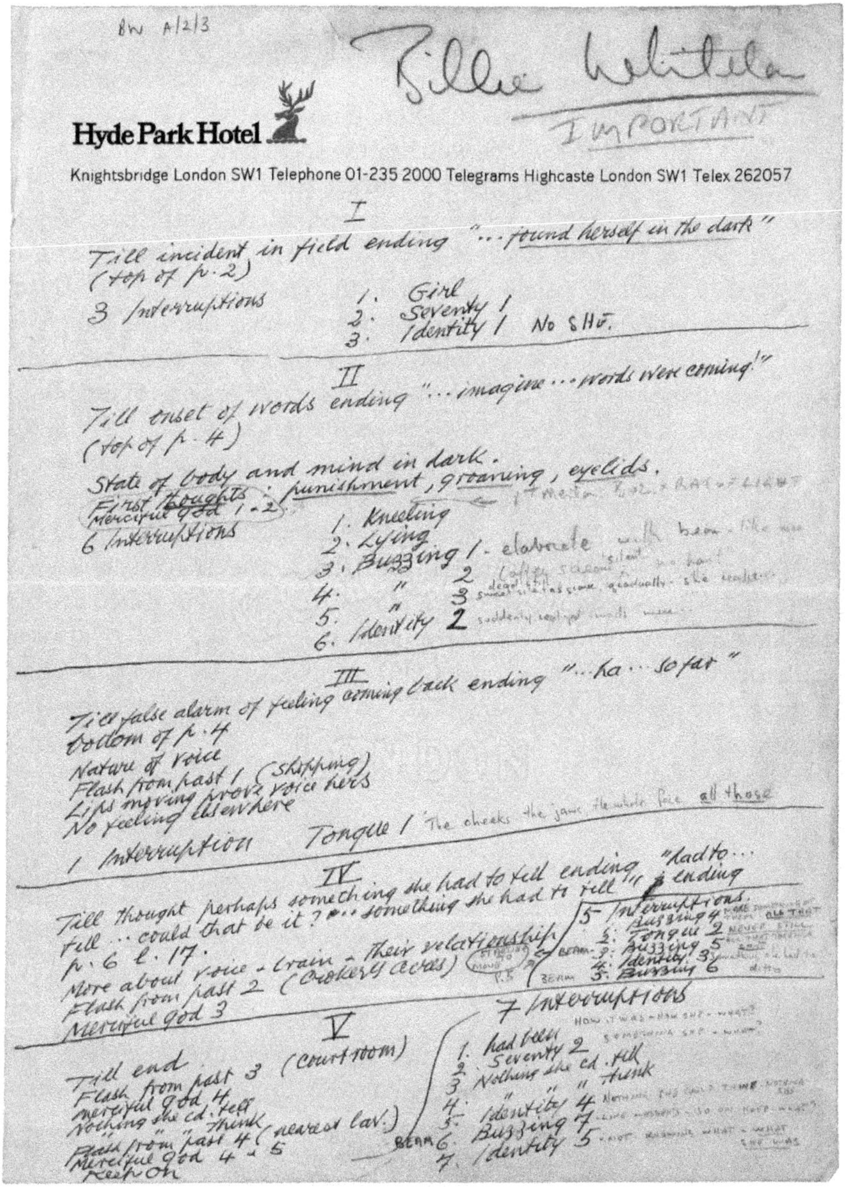
BW A/2/3

Billie Whitelaw

IMPORTANT

Hyde Park Hotel

Knightsbridge London SW1 Telephone 01-235 2000 Telegrams Highcaste London SW1 Telex 262057

I

Till incident in field ending "... found herself in the dark"
(top of p. 2)

3 Interruptions
1. Girl
2. Seventy 1
3. Identity 1 No SHE.

II

Till onset of words ending "... imagine ... words were coming"
(top of p. 4)

State of body and mind in dark.
First thoughts: punishment, groaning, eyelids.
Merciful God 1 - 2

6 Interruptions
1. Kneeling
2. Lying
3. Buzzing 1 - elaborate
4. " 2
5. " 3
6. Identity 2

III

Till false alarm of feeling coming back ending "... ha .. so far"
bottom of p. 4
Nature of voice
Flash from past 1 (shopping)
Lips moving proves voice hers
No feeling elsewhere

1 Interruption Tongue 1 The cheeks the jaws the whole face all those

IV

Till thought perhaps something she had to tell ending "had to ... tell ... could that be it? ... something she had to tell" p. 6 l. 17.
More about voice - brain - their relationship
Flash from past 2 (Croker's Acres)
Merciful God 3

5 Interruptions
1. Buzzing 4
2. Tongue 2
3. Buzzing 5
4. Identity 3
5. Buzzing 6

V

Till end
Flash from past 3 (courtroom)
Merciful God 4
Nothing she cd. tell
" " think
Flash from past 4 (nearest lav.) - 5
Merciful God 4 - 5
Keep on

7 Interruptions
1. had been
2. Seventy 2
3. Nothing she cd. tell
4. " " " think
5. Identity 4
6. Buzzing 7
7. Identity 5

Fig. 7: Beckett's and Whitelaw's notes on RC notes.B (01r).

01r

Folio 01r divides the play into five sections, with lists of notes for each section made in Beckett's hand, and annotations to these lists in Billie Whitelaw's hand (see Fig. 7). Beckett's notes are in blue ink, while Whitelaw's are in pencil. The divisions on the page broadly correspond with the five-part synopsis on ET8; the one exception to this is discussed below. In order to make his lists, Beckett used a copy of the RC playscript, noting page and line numbers which correspond to that document. One extract quoted here indicates that the copy he used may have been the Faber setting copy (FSC, chapter 1.3.1). The quotation '... **imagine ...** words were coming!' (RC notes.B, 01r) contains a word which, in extant versions of the playscript, is only found on FSC: '... imagine! ... words were coming~~!~~' (05r). However, the exclamation marks in this quotation differ and another quotation also differs slightly from FSC: in section IV, Beckett quotes the line 'something she had to tell' (RC notes.B, 01r), which appears on FSC as 'something she had to ... tell' (07r). While all this indicates that Beckett may have used FSC to create his notes before adding this ellipsis by hand, it is difficult to be definitive about which version of the playscript he used.

In each of the five sections, Beckett lists topics from the text, as well as the 'Interruptions' to Mouth's monologue, such as the following list for section II:

1	Kneeling	
2	Lying	
3	Buzzing	1
4	"	2
5	"	3
6	Identity	~~1~~2

After Beckett's note on 'Buzzing 1', there is a note in Whitelaw's hand which suggests the text was further modified in performance: 'elaborate with beam – like moo [*sic*]'. This note is ticked in pencil.

Whitelaw famously described Beckett's textual awareness in the following anecdote, which has its roots in the 1964 *Play* rehearsals: 'I have a memory of him saying: "Billie, will you bring your pencil over here and look at page

2, speech 4, fifth word. Will you make those three dots, two dots"' (1996, 77).[52] In this document, Beckett erases the first ellipsis point in the phrase 'could that be it? ...'. While ET4, ET5 and ET6 feature just two ellipsis points throughout, including those ellipses after question marks and exclamation marks (see chapter 1.2.1), this particular form of punctuation – in which three ellipsis points are used but only two following an exclamation mark or question mark – would only become part of the text in Faber's *Collected Shorter Plays* (1984a).[53]

02r

This page is headed 'Formulae', with four subheadings: 'Buzzing', 'back in the field ..', 'Merciful God', 'Prayer for it to stop'. Aside from the pencilled note in the top-right corner, the writing is in blue ink and in Beckett's hand. The line numbers, page numbers and references to page locations ('foot', 'top') correspond with the RC playscript. Quotations are written throughout with two ellipsis points rather than three. In the right margin of the section on 'Buzzing' are Roman numerals which correspond to the list on folio 01r.

03r–03v

The two sides of this sheet contain notes in Beckett's hand in black ink. At the bottom of the page, in blue pen, not in Beckett's hand, is the note: 'ORIGINAL – DO NOT / LOOSE!! [*sic*]'. The rest of the writing is in black ink. On folio 03r, the Hyde Park Hotel logo is upside down in the bottom-right corner.

Folio 03r is a handwritten version of Beckett's typed 'SYNOPSIS' (ET8). The five-part section divisions (now labelled with Arabic numerals) correspond to those on folio 01r, with one variant to the typewritten list. On ET8, the incidents 'Life scene 1 (field) again / Perhaps something she should

52 In his genetic study of Joyce, Proust and Mann, Van Hulle defines authorial 'textual awareness' in terms of a 'tension between the construction [of a text] and the awareness of its being only a construction' (2007, 157).

53 There are other places in the genesis where two points are used after a question mark or exclamation mark in manuscripts otherwise containing three ellipsis points, but these seem to be errors (EM1, 01r; ET2, 01r, 04r; RC playscript, 04r).

tell? Life scene 4 (courtroom), / life scene 1 (field) and no from within' are listed as being part of section IV (01r). However, according to the section divisions on folio 01r of RC notes.B, the courtroom scene is in section V. This structural discrepancy is also marked on folio 03r, where the line 'Perhaps something she should tell? Life scene 4 (courtroom), life scene 1 (field) and no from within' is bracketed twice, thus included both in section 4 as well as section 5. While there is nothing to confirm the sequencing of ET8 and RC notes.B, the handwritten notes do show Beckett still working to conceptualize the structure of his text as he prepared it for performance in the two months after its November 1972 premiere in New York.

Especially if we consider a text as 'The sequence of words *and pauses* recorded in a document' (Shillingsburg 1999, 171; emphasis added), then Beckett's list of 'pauses' constitutes an important part of his text as it developed in performance. Folio 03v is a fair copy of the list of pauses made on RC notes.A. Yet the heading on this folio is not 'Pauses' but 'BREAKS', which underlines *Not I*'s status as what Roland Barthes termed a *texte brisé*, that is, a text broken up by a reader (in this case the text's own author) into various lexias 'or units of reading, the size of which may vary' (Van Hulle 2009b, 47). This concept of *Not I* as a *texte brisé* will help us navigate Mouth's 'steady stream' in chapter 2.2.2.

BW playscript

The Billie Whitelaw Finding Aid at the University of Reading describes this document (BW A/2/1) as follows:

> Typescript rehearsal script for Not I and Krapp's Last Tape by Samuel Beckett, Royal Court Theatre [...] Inscribed by Samuel Beckett 'For Billie with fond love and gratitude from Sam'. Not I annotated with marks and notes in pencil and coloured inks. [...] Undated [1972–1973][54]

It is not discussed in *TN4*.

54 https://collections.reading.ac.uk/wp-content/uploads/sites/9/2020/04/Billie-Whitelaw_BW-.pdf.

AS playscript

The Alan Schneider Papers at the University of California, San Diego hold a playscript of *Not I* (box 48, folder 24), containing twelve pages including a cover page: '"NOT I" / by Samuel Beckett' (01r).[55] Aside from a handwritten '4' added inline in the opening stage directions (02r), the AS playscript does not contain any handwritten edits. The typewriter is different to any of those used for Beckett's typescripts, or for the other playscripts in this module. However, the system of page numbering does match the RC playscript: 1.1, 1.2, 1.3, etc. Given this evidence, the AS playscript seems not to have been typed by Beckett himself.

Aside from a very few small exceptions, this playscript integrates the handwritten edits Beckett made on CPG (see chapter 1.2.1). This indicates that it is a 'clean copy' of CPG, possibly made by someone at Grove Press, though there is no firm evidence for this. As these two playscripts do not appear to have been the basis for any published edition, they form a sidelined 'dead end' in the Genetic Map.

BBC Not I script

Soon after *Not I* opened at the Royal Court, the BBC approached Beckett regarding a TV adaptation of his play. He replied to producer Bill Morton:

> Though I regard Not I as a specifically stage work and virtually unfilmable you have my permission to present it with Billie Whitelaw on BBC TV after the current run at Royal Court Theatre. (8 February 1973, *LSB IV* 328n2)

As Jonathan Bignell notes, though the contract for broadcast on the BBC's *Second House* programme was drawn up in May 1973, it was eventually broadcast on *The Lively Arts* (2009, 106–7), which was subtitled *Shades* following Beckett's suggestion (Beckett to Tristram Powell, 18 November 1976, *LSB IV* 442). The recording itself took place on 13 February 1975, with

55 A copy of this playscript is held in another folder of the Alan Schneider Papers (UCSD box 26, folder 32).

further delays until the broadcast of April 1977 caused in part by Beckett's composition of *Ghost Trio* for the programme (Knowlson 1997, 620–1, 636).

The BBC holds on microfilm a script for *The Lively Arts: Shades*, which names Tristram Powell as producer and Morton as Executive Producer.[56] Anthony Page is listed as director for *Not I*, though Whitelaw records in her autobiography that 'Page was in America' when the film was shot, and that Powell provided the production's creative impetus (1996, 132). The document is foliated continuously throughout – except for the title pages of each play – with each double page of *Not I* receiving a single number. Melvyn Bragg and Martin Esslin provide scripted introductory material to each piece. While the programme script contains typescripts for *Ghost Trio* and *... but the clouds ...*, the text of *Not I* is a photocopy of a reprint of the first Faber edition, with no handwritten edits to the text. The top right corner of folio 26r (page 11 in the Faber edition) is rendered almost illegible by what looks like another sheet from the script interfering in the copying process. This document is not mentioned in *TN4*.

Variants in the TV broadcast for which Beckett may have been responsible are discussed in chapter 2.2.2. With regard to the script, it is worth noting that it does feature the dash which is missing on the reprint I consulted: 'all ...' (1973b, 11). The presence of this dash in the BBC photocopy indicates that its omission in my copy of the reprint was simply a printing error (26r). The BBC photocopy omits page 16 of the Faber edition, which contains the closing stage directions and the note on the Auditor. Instead, the document ends with Mouth's final scripted words.

The BBC adaptation of *Not I* was included in a 1977 Süddeutscher Rundfunk (SDR) broadcast of Beckett's TV plays in German. Beckett wrote to Reinhart Müller-Freienfels on 13 December 1976:

56 The script was transferred to microfilm and the original document was then destroyed. With many thanks to BBC archivist Katie Ankers for this information.

> The BBB [sic] wil[l] include in their program, together with these two pieces [*Ghost Trio* and ... *but the clouds* ...], a film of Not I. It is a tight close-up of the mouth alone from beginning to end and a quite extraordinary performance by Billie Whitelaw. It occurred to me that you might like to include this piece in your own program, BBC permitting. In English of course. (*LSB IV* 445; first two editorial additions in *LSB*)

This unusual suggestion of broadcasting an Anglophone text to a German audience shows Beckett's admiration for the BBC adaptation. It may also be an indication of the importance given by the author to the play working 'on the nerves of the audience', with Beckett not caring so much about 'intelligibility' (see chapter 2.2.2).[57]

57 Beckett's dissatisfaction with the German translation should also be borne in mind here (see chapter 2.2.2). Citations of the broadcast text refer to the SDR version (Beckett 2008b).

1.7 Genetic Map

1. Before *Not I*

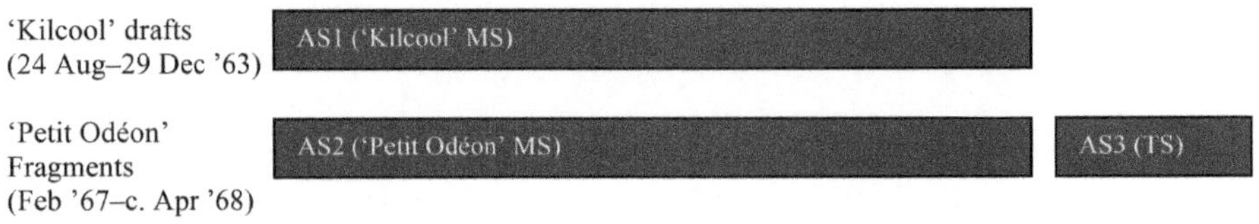

'Kilcool' drafts
(24 Aug–29 Dec '63)
AS1 ('Kilcool' MS)
'Petit Odéon'
Fragments
(Feb '67–c. Apr '68)
AS2 ('Petit Odéon' MS)
AS3 (TS)

2. *Not I*

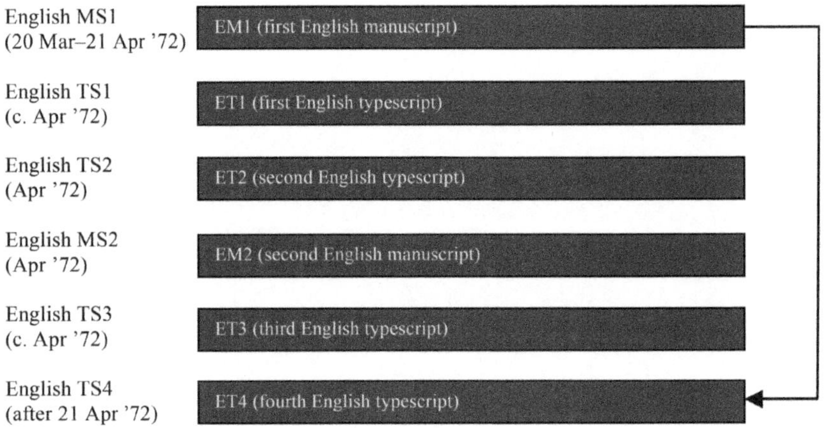

English MS1
(20 Mar–21 Apr '72)
EM1 (first English manuscript)
English TS1
(c. Apr '72)
ET1 (first English typescript)
English TS2
(Apr '72)
ET2 (second English typescript)
English MS2
(Apr '72)
EM2 (second English manuscript)
English TS3
(c. Apr '72)
ET3 (third English typescript)
English TS4
(after 21 Apr '72)
ET4 (fourth English typescript)

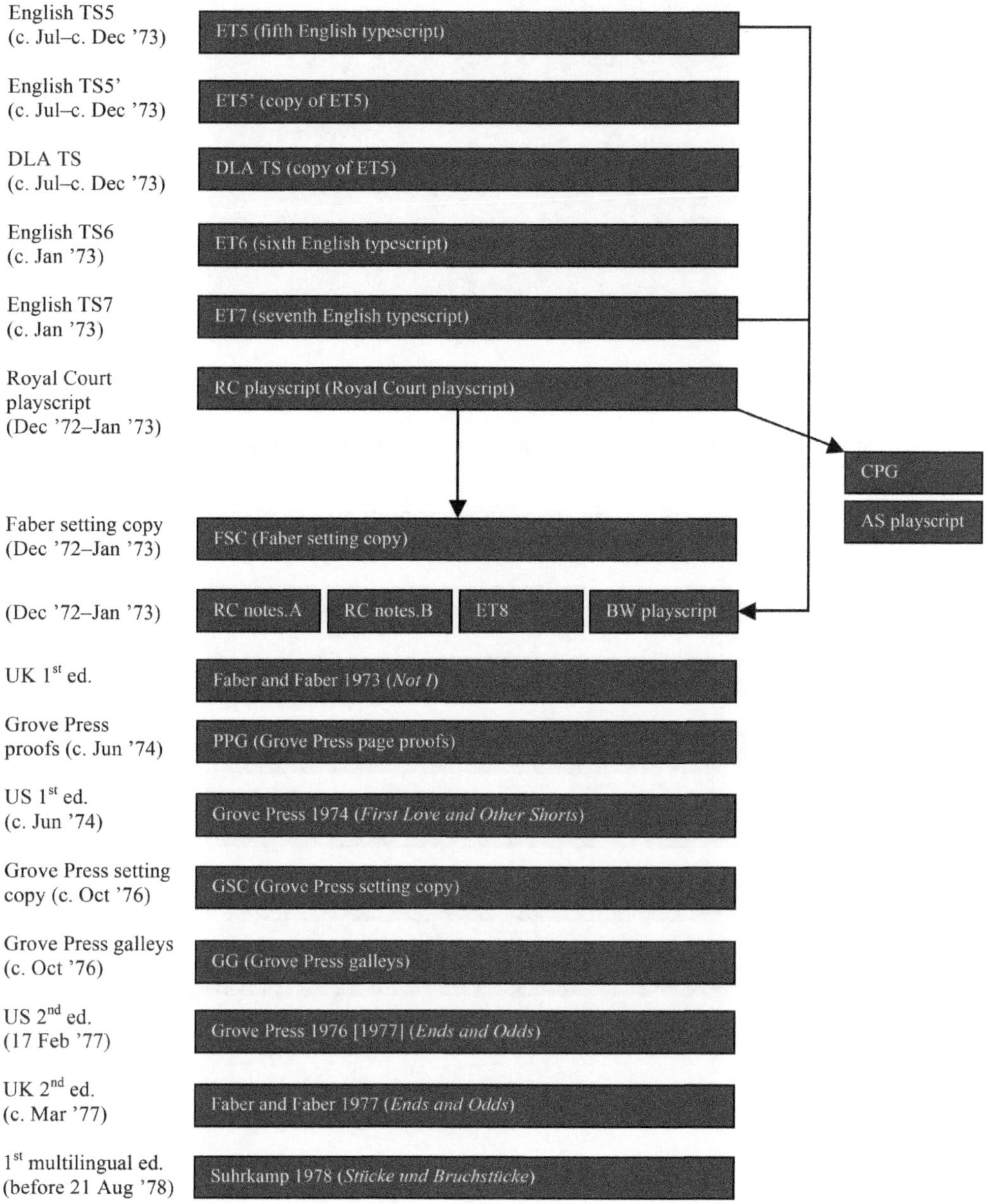
English TS5 (c. Jul–c. Dec '73)
ET5 (fifth English typescript)
English TS5' (c. Jul–c. Dec '73)
ET5' (copy of ET5)
DLA TS (c. Jul–c. Dec '73)
DLA TS (copy of ET5)
English TS6 (c. Jan '73)
ET6 (sixth English typescript)
English TS7 (c. Jan '73)
ET7 (seventh English typescript)
Royal Court playscript (Dec '72–Jan '73)
RC playscript (Royal Court playscript)
CPG
AS playscript
Faber setting copy (Dec '72–Jan '73)
FSC (Faber setting copy)
(Dec '72–Jan '73)
RC notes.A
RC notes.B
ET8
BW playscript
UK 1st ed.
Faber and Faber 1973 (*Not I*)
Grove Press proofs (c. Jun '74)
PPG (Grove Press page proofs)
US 1st ed. (c. Jun '74)
Grove Press 1974 (*First Love and Other Shorts*)
Grove Press setting copy (c. Oct '76)
GSC (Grove Press setting copy)
Grove Press galleys (c. Oct '76)
GG (Grove Press galleys)
US 2nd ed. (17 Feb '77)
Grove Press 1976 [1977] (*Ends and Odds*)
UK 2nd ed. (c. Mar '77)
Faber and Faber 1977 (*Ends and Odds*)
1st multilingual ed. (before 21 Aug '78)
Suhrkamp 1978 (*Stücke und Bruchstücke*)

US enlarged (3rd) ed.	Grove Press 1981 (*Ends and Odds*)
Missing Faber proofs (Jun '83)	[Faber and Faber proofs]
UK 3rd ed. (13 Feb '84)	Faber and Faber 1984 (*Collected Shorter Plays*)
US 4th ed.	Grove Press 1984 (*Collected Shorter Plays*)
UK	Faber and Faber 1986 (*Complete Dramatic Works*)

3. *Pas moi*

French MS1 (1–13 Mar '73)	FM1 (first French manuscript)
French MS2 (2–19 May '74)	FM2 (second French manuscript)
French TS1 (c. May–c. Jun '74)	FT1 (first French typescript)
French TS2 (c. May–11 Jun '74)	FT2 (second French typescript)
French TS3 (c. May–11 Jun '74)	FT3 (third French typescript)
Pre-book publication (Jan '75)	*Minuit* 12
Minuit 1st ed. (17 Jan '75)	Minuit 1975 (*Pas moi*)
Minuit 2nd ed. (3 Apr '75)	Minuit 1975 (*Oh les beaux jours suivi de Pas moi*)

2 The Genesis of *Not I / Pas moi*

2.1 Before *Not I / Pas moi*

The following genetic analyses of the three 'Abandoned Sections' composed before *Not I* incorporate accounts of their respective 'Chronologies', which stand as separate sections in the 'Genesis' chapters on *Not I / Pas moi*, *That Time / Cette fois* and *Footfalls / Pas*.

2.1.1 'Kilcool' (AS1)

Particularly because it is dated some nine years before *Not I* was commenced, it is helpful to briefly outline Beckett's artistic activity the year he wrote 'Kilcool', a year in which his work across different media bore much fruit (see Beloborodova and Verhulst 2020). As was commonly the case at this point in his career, Beckett spent 1963 moving between creative forms: translating the prose pieces *How It Is* and some of the *Texts for Nothing*; correcting proofs of *Watt* (Beckett to John Calder, 12 February 1963, *LSB III* 530); working on the stage play 'J. M. Mime' (see chapter 1.1.1); drafting his only piece for cinema (*Film*); revising the English text of *Play*, translating it into French as *Comédie* and attending the German premiere (*Spiel*); working on the English translation and French page proofs of *Cascando*, whose French recording sessions he also supervised; as well as collaborating on the rehearsals of *Oh les beaux jours* (see chapter 2.1.2).[58] I will return to some of the specific overlaps between 'Kilcool' and these other works below. For the moment, it is worth bearing in mind the multi-faceted creative context in which Beckett wrote these drafts.

As discussed in chapter 1.1.1, there is considerable critical debate about the 'Kilcool' draft material in TCD MS 4664. This is largely due to the difficulty in determining the status of the different drafts contained in this document. While 'the earliest outline to "Kilcool" bears strong similarity to *Not I*' (Gontarski 1985, 133–4), there are also links to other Beckett texts (see below and chapter 1.1.1; Gontarski 1985, 134–42). What seems clear is that the material in the 'Kilcool' Notebook was at one point abandoned. Because of this, its four sections can be regarded as drafts. Peter Shillingsburg

58 Details from Pilling (2006, 161–4) unless noted otherwise.

defines a draft as 'a preliminary form of a version' and includes in this definition 'false starts or experimental forms' (1999, 45). According to Shillingsburg, a version is 'one specific form of the work', which is in turn 'conceptually that which is implied by the authoritative texts' (Shillingsburg 1999, 44, 1; Shillingsburg 2013). Given the links of the 'Kilcool' drafts to multiple published texts, it might be useful to think here of 'the work' as Beckett's entire oeuvre, rather than any single text (see Van Hulle, 2021, 47).

As genetic critics, we have to try and decide what constitute given drafts and versions, even when their connections cannot be limited to a single published text. Van Hulle and Weller explain in their genetic analysis of *Fin de partie*: 'The documents are the physical objects, such as the notebooks containing (sometimes only fragments of) versions of *Fin de partie*. A version is an abstraction, not a physical object. The link between a document and a version is not always a one-to-one relationship' (2018, 41). In the case of TCD MS 4664, there are four different drafts of one version ('Kilcool') within a single document (see Fig. 3, chapter 1.1.1). While these 'Abandoned Sections' are here headed 'Before *Not I*', this does not mean their connections to other Beckett texts should be discounted.

Draft 1: 10r–11r

Under the heading 'KILCOOL', Beckett drafted lines which, as Gontarski points out (1985, 135), contain some of the basic elements of *Not I* and *That Time*, such as a single face lit against a dark background: 'Woman's face alone in constant light. [...] Nothing but fixed lit face & speech' (10r). Like *Not I*, 'Kilcool' also features speech which begins before the houselights are fully up: 'When theatre lights down~~, curtain~~ before curtain up, light on face and speech already' (10r). A note further down the page also indicates there will be speech before the curtain rises, foreshadowing the ad lib in the published text of *Not I* and confirming that this was yet another piece Beckett wrote for the Cartesian Theatre of a proscenium stage: 'Opening: 4 – 5 **lines** ~~text mu~~ **muffled** ~~**text**~~ speech, **curtain up**, conclusion of this speech, ~~long~~ pause. Tears' (10r). Finally, the protagonist's speech is defined in such a way that links her most directly to the pronominal conflict of *Not I*, but which has similarities too with the speaking subjects who refer to themselves in *That Time* and *Footfalls*: 'Talks of herself **in 3rd** person'

(10r). The opening text also recalls *Not I* and especially *That Time* in the way Beckett starts midsentence: '– come ~~then~~ now to Kilcool[e] ~~the~~ ~~that~~ this **time** in Kilcool' (10r).[59] In a letter to James Knowlson, Beckett called *That Time* 'a brother to *Not I*' (24 September 1974, qtd. in Pountney 1988, 92). To extend this metaphor, 'Kilcool' certainly has family resemblances to both plays. At the story level, the main protagonist, like Mouth, is an orphan: '**papa** dead ~~xx~~ we have seen and then **mamma** perhaps of grief' (10r). It is a 'widowed childless' aunt who takes in this orphan girl 'to go on living with her in her humble home in Kilcool[e]' (10r), with Beckett correcting the spelling of the County Wicklow town name in a later revision campaign.

Then follows a prayer, part of which suggests that the speaker is deceased: 'that dark when she dies when she so young so long ago was laid in **Redford by the sea**' (10r). Lying just six kilometres from Kilcool, the coastal townland of Redford is where Beckett's mother May (officially named Mary) was buried following her death on 25 August 1950 (Pilling 2006, 109). Though one of the digits in the dating of Draft 1 is slightly difficult to read, it looks like '24 8 63' (10r), almost thirteen years to the day after the death of Beckett's mother. We know Beckett thought of his parents on their anniversaries, telling Barbara Bray on 26 June 1975: 'This afternoon, 42 years ago, my father died' (qtd. in Van Hulle and Nixon 2013, 109). It is hard to avoid the conclusion that Beckett's mother's death would have crossed his mind while composing 'Kilcool'. While the theme of motherhood is central to *Footfalls* – where the distinction between Mary and May plays an important role in the genesis (see chapter 6.1.2) – throughout the 'Kilcool' drafts it features as a negative image, shadowing the draft material without ever becoming an explicit focus of the text.

A psychoanalytic reading would probably put more emphasis on Beckett's relationship with his mother as a creative source. And such an interpretation would find ample material in the paragraph which follows. Mention of a 'darkened room' followed by the description of tunnels through which the orphaned girl travels by train would all fit a reading of this draft material as part of what Phil Baker calls the 'underlying nomination of the womb as

59 In a list of themes included at the start of Draft 2, Beckett considered marking the tempo of the piece in a manner which foreshadows the ticking clock in the drafts of *That Time* (see chapter 4.1.2): 'Whole text spoken over soft rapid beat only audible in major pauses & during silent weeping (11r).

paradigm' in Beckett's work (11r; Baker 2001, 90). Baker reads the lamplight filtered by a 'pink shade' in the *The End* in connection with the centrality of the womb in Beckett's work (1997, 84); a 'pink shade' is also found in this draft (11r). However, to read Beckett's work as having one psychoanalytic source seems antithetical to the ways in which he spends much of his creative energy in the drafts trying to open up readings beyond a single interpretation (see Little 2020c, 74). It is difficult to know for certain why Beckett gave up on this particular draft, but it may have been something to do with the overt symbology of this passage, which ends with the aunt welcoming the girl, using a line one might expect in the early scenes of a horror movie: 'Don't be fretting pet don't you be fretting you'll be happy with me' (11r).

Draft 2: 09v, 10v, 11r–14r

Having written the word 'Abandoned' and drawn a line under Draft 1 (11r), Beckett listed a set of themes for his play. In the drafts which follow, Beckett tends not to return to the narrative content of his first draft. Instead, he uses similar themes to create new content. One of these, which becomes central to *Footfalls*, is the theme of prayer.

Beckett opens his 1934 review of Thomas MacGreevy's *Poems* with the words: 'All poetry, as discriminated from the various paradigms of prosody, is prayer' (*Dis* 68). Though he goes on to exclude from this definition performative forms such as Meistergesang (a form of German sung poetry from the fifteenth and sixteenth centuries) and vaudeville, Beckett did become increasingly interested in ways of framing a prayer during theatrical performance. Having used a prayer in the first draft of 'Kilcool', Beckett included the following comments in a list of themes which start off the second draft, foreshadowing the main theme of *That Time*:

> Certain **of above prayer** to **time** for dark as light is darkened. This the tear producer. Three times, including curtain (light on weeping face, prayer unanswered).. (11r)

Discussing Beckett's use of prayer in his critical writings of the 1930s, Conor Carville links the figure of the failed prayer to Beckett's interest in the subject–object breakdown, provoking an experience of 'frustration and impossibility' in the beholder of the work of art (2018, 107).[60] By staging his characters' prayers as unanswered, their needs unmet, Beckett recalls the concept of art outlined in his review of Denis Devlin's poetry (1938): 'pure interrogation, rhetorical question less the rhetoric'. In this review, Beckett goes on to declare that the connection between art and 'social reality' has now been cut (*Dis* 91). Beckett's concept of artistic production as a question posed without a clear framing context returns in the enactive environments of his later plays, in which the 'vaguened' stage space – devoid of physical markers of 'social reality' – creates an interpretive environment that encourages multiple interpretations of the text. For instance, Beckett considered giving his protagonist '~~bad enunciation~~' (14r), indicating that he may well have had the social class of this impoverished woman in mind, but then struck it out.[61]

On the verso, Beckett listed his themes again, this time more succinctly:

> 1. Light – dark leading to **prayer** for dark and tears. 3 ~~tim~~ Three times: Opening, midway, end.
>
> **2 Voice imitated**
>
> **3 Thoughts.**
>
> **4 Lover.**
>
> 5 Age.
>
> 6 Never properly seen, heard.

60 We will return to the question of audience perception in chapter 2.2.2.

61 Like Listener in the drafts of *That Time*, the protagonist of Draft 1 carries her belongings in a single 'grip' (11r; see chapter 4.1.2). Mouth too carries a 'bag', though hers is an 'old black shopping bag' (1973a, 10; *KLT* 88). This note on enunciation may have influenced Beckett's notes on pronunciation in the genesis of *Not I* (see chapter 2.2.2).

7 Her body

8 Burial (11v)

In the monologue which follows, Beckett builds on another draft prayer, which outlines the narrator's thoughts and mentions the woman lying on a '**pillow**', foreshadowing the genesis of *That Time* (10v; see chapter 4.1.2). Another, separate paragraph starts by focussing on the position of the woman's body: '… and ~~xxx~~ while it was not clear at first that she was now in **position**' (12r). Mention of what seems to read as her 'entourage' – who fail to grasp her position even though it is clear to her – foreshadows the disconnect between protagonist and those around them in all three plays of this module, however limited the description of these others may be. But it is the '**Lover**' who then receives most attention (11v), in a passage Beckett drafted under another page-dividing line. This monologue again starts in midstream, this time critiquing the male lover's departure: '… leave her like that ~~without~~ in the state she was in'. For the speaker, his excuse is far from satisfactory: 'that he had to go away – meaning a journey – and did not know when he would be back' (12r). After he departs, the woman becomes spectator rather than the observed, 'closing the curtains behind her to shut off the light of the room and see into the street' (12r). After a 'Long pause', the prayer of Draft 1 is returned to, metatheatrically marked 'Conclusion' by the speaker (12r).

The next section focuses on '**The body**', which is again 'On its back' (12r–13r), the position so crucial to Beckett's memory pieces such as *That Time* and *Company*. Having initially included a '~~pillow~~', Beckett struck this out and wrote 'no pillow', again anticipating *That Time* (13r; see chapter 4.1.2). The focus then shifts to the '**Voice**' (11v), which is marked by an abrupt tonal shift: 'Tone of irritated expostulation' (13r). In this new voice, the speaker outlines a familiar litany of encouragement to the bedbound: 'Get up. Draw the – ~~curtains~~ (Pause.) Fling open the curtains, the windows, let in the sun, the breeze, pour in, go out, sun, breeze, flowers, birds, get up, open all up, go out, live! (Pause) Can't you!' (13r). She then returns to a 'Normal tone', in order to announce the next passage: 'The voice' (13r).

The text which follows draws directly on Beckett's manipulation of the voice while rehearsing *Play* in the theatre and recording the radio play

Cascando earlier in 1963. Beloborodova has outlined how a high-speed voice became central to the stage production of *Play* in 1963, particularly after the addition of the repeat or '*da capo*', which turns the text into an infernal repetition (2019, 35). She cites Beckett's letter of 26 November 1963 to director Alan Schneider: 'Everything for the sake of speed if you adopt the da capo' (*LSB III* 584, qtd. in Beloborodova 2019, 202). As Beloborodova and Verhulst point out, this high-speed delivery was influenced by the composition of *Cascando*, which has indications in the early manuscripts that it should be delivered at a fast tempo (2020, 15–16). This high tempo was actualized in the recording of the French version of *Cascando* in June 1963, which Beckett attended between rehearsals of the world premiere of *Spiel* in Ulm. So, there is a 'cross-pollination' between these two plays (Beloborodova and Verhulst 2020, 18), which also feeds into Beckett's work on 'Kilcool' later that same year.

Beloborodova and Verhulst note that the hi-speed tempo indicator '*débit rapide, haletant*' was reduced to simply '*haletant*' in the published version of *Cascando* (2020, 15–16). In Beckett's English translation, this is rendered as '*panting*' (*ATF* 85), which is noteworthy due to the relation it has with *How It Is*, in which the word 'panting' appears repeatedly.[62] Beckett started his translation of *How It Is* in early 1960, preparing part of its opening for Patrick Magee to read on the BBC. In a letter to the actor, he described the work as being 'separated by pauses during which *panting* cordially invited' (26 February 1960, *LSB III* 306; emphasis added). The term would show up again in Beckett's letter to Schneider on 16 October 1972, describing the voice of *Not I*: 'I hear it breathless, urgent, feverish, rhythmic, *panting along*, without undue concern with intelligibility' (*LSB IV* 311; emphasis added).

As all of the above suggests, a rapid, panting voice was on Beckett's mind when composing both prose and dramatic work during the early 1960s and this went on to shape the high-speed voice of *Not I*.[63] In this draft of 'Kilcool', he uses rapid delivery to differentiate the 'normal' voice of the single speaker from the 'assumed' voice, who rejects the advice given by the former

62 The French text most often uses the infinitive 'haleter' (Beckett 2015).

63 As Pountney discusses, Beckett used the differentiation of voices within a single speaker in his 1959 radio play *Embers* (1988, 108). Variation in the vocal tone of a single speaker also features in earlier plays such as *Krapp*, *Endgame* and *Godot*.

to get out and 'live': '(assuming voice, **low, fast, breathless.**) Ah you and your living, will you leave off talking to me about living. (**Panting.**)' (13r). After the 'normal' voice announces 'The thoughts', there is further conflict between the two voices, culminating in an unnamed song by the 'normal' voice, marked by a series of lines containing only spaced dots.

After this song, Beckett wrote a paragraph on the facing verso which ends by mentioning one of his favourite themes – silence: 'I do of course get some **silence**, as just now, when I ~~pause~~ ~~go silent.~~ **pause after a period**' (12v). Back on the recto, Beckett made a rough calculation: '(**Pause** of 1 to 2 seconds every minute or minute & a half at least a week's **silence** in year)' (13r). But the ensuing monologue contains some of the characteristic uncertainty of Beckett's characters when it comes to their mathematical calculations: 'I have reckoned ~~on~~ whilst going along that that one on an average every minute ~~on an average~~ mounts up to a week a year **I think this is accurate**, a ~~week's silence~~ week's silence' (13r). While Beckett was aware from very early on in his career of the value of silence in his aesthetics, his instructions to fill the pauses of *How It Is* with panting shows just how acute this awareness became when he was dealing with single-voice performances of his texts. On the early versos of 'Kilcool', Beckett made calculations of how many days per year a series of short pauses would make up for his speaker. The long list ends with a more precise calculation, suggesting it was composed after the monologue on folio 13r: 'Pause of 2 seconds every minute = ~~xx~~ 12 days silence in year' (09v).

Deleted stage instructions at the end of Draft 2 specify a stage image which once more foreshadows important aspects of *Not I*:

> ~~Old woman's face, 4 ft. above stage level, slightly off centre, lit by strong steady light. Body not visible. Stage in darkness. Nothing visible but face.~~ (14r)

Cohn recalls Beckett asking her in 1971, the year prior to his composition of *Not I*: 'Can you stage a mouth? Just a moving mouth with the rest of the stage in darkness?' (Cohn 2008, 315). But it is important to note that this stage image was on Beckett's mind for some time even before starting the 'Kilcool' drafts. On 10 May 1975, his cousin John Beckett wrote to Rosemary Pountney about an incident he remembered from the 1950s:

'in a conversation with a mutual friend named Desmond Ryan in Paris in 1958, at which I was present, he [Samuel Beckett] said "all I want on the stage is a pair of blubbering lips"' (UoR JEK A/1/1/5, folder 5).[64] So, Beckett seems to have been thinking about such visual concepts for a considerable period. The 'Kilcool' drafts are an important step towards their realization onstage.

Draft 3: 14v–16v

A new draft continues on the theme of silence by developing the meditation on pauses: 'So brief, what is it, it mounts up, it is amazing, I have worked it out, I have worked it out while going along, **one second, two seconds**, every now & ~~then~~ again, a week a year, is it not amazing, this I suppose it is that keeps me going, **one second, two seconds**, every now & ~~then.~~ again' (15r).

There are other gaps thematized aside from those in speech itself, most notably the gaps in memory. Like *That Time*, this draft is a memory play focussed on the loss of memory: '**Memory, gone**, this ~~is~~ too a help ~~too~~, I suppose, **things said before** – (pause) – **things said before**' (16r). This allows for the repetition of speech as if it was new, suggesting one possible backstory for the cyclical structure of Mouth's and Listener's narratives. Nevertheless, the speaker does seem to remember a time 'when there was **dark**', although this could be '~~**pure fancy, pure**~~ mere **fancy**' (16r), a key term in *Footfalls*. She was happy, the speaker tells us, when she was unseen, the memory of which causes tears to flow.

This memory of the '**dark**' leads to a passage which revisits the images of intrauterine confinement found in Beckett's Psychology Notes (see chapters 4.1.2 and 6.1.2):

64 In a letter to Pountney of 27 April 1975, John Beckett recalls 'this remark of Sam's about wanting "only a pair of blubbering lips on the stage"' as having taken place 'in about 1952' (UoR JEK A/1/1/5, folder 5). The editors of Beckett's letters have '1952 or 1953' as possible dates, based on John Beckett's notes (*LSB III* 395n2). He checked the veracity of the story with his cousin Sam, who said that while he did not remember the conversation, it was fine to share the story with Pountney: 'What good or ill can come?' (4 May 1975, *LSB III* 395). I would like to thank Pim Verhulst for bringing this to my attention and sharing his transcriptions with me.

> ~~There is s~~Someone in **me**, trying to get out, saying let me out, let me out, when **I** think of that, inside **me** all ~~xxx~~ dark, someone there, wanting out, into the light, poor creature, sometimes it seems ... it seems true, **I** talk and talk and hear nothing only (assumed voice, low, ~~panting~~ breathless), Let me out! Let me out! (normal voice) Was **I** in someone once, and where is she now, if **I** was in her once, and she let **me** out. (16r)

This passage also breaks the rule sketched in the list of themes at the start of Draft 2: '"I" "me" etc. never spoken outside **assumed voice**' (11r). As the assumed voice is given to the figure trapped inside the main speaker, the lines preceding her appeal, which include both 'me' and 'I', must be attributed to the 'Normal voice' of the speaker. Though pronominal conflict is central to the drafts of 'Kilcool', we can see Beckett here adapting the terms of this conflict as he writes his drafts.

The following verso contains a group of notes on the theme of narrative non-being, including the line '**Nothing speaks** of **nothing**' (16v). This seems to be a reference to *King Lear*, Peter Brook's production of which Beckett attended on 10 May 1963 (*LSB III* 523). Beckett's phrase echoes Lear's lines when his daughter Cordelia refuses to emulate her two sisters in their fawning declarations of love to him, for which they each receive a portion of his kingdom:

LEAR	[...] what can you say to draw
	A third more opulent than your sisters? Speak.
CORDELIA	Nothing, my lord.
LEAR	Nothing?
CORDELIA	Nothing.
LEAR	How, nothing will come of nothing. Speak again.

(I. 1. 85–90)[65]

65 All Shakespeare references are to *The Arden Shakespeare Complete Works* (2001) unless otherwise stated. Beckett's line could also refer to Part II of T. S. Eliot's *The Waste Land*, 'A Game of Chess', which itself echoes *King Lear*: 'Speak to me. Why do you never speak? Speak.' [...] / 'What is that noise now? What is the wind doing?' / Nothing again nothing. / 'Do / You know nothing? Do you see nothing? Do you remember / Nothing?' (2001, 9).

Cordelia refuses to placate her father and Shakespeare gets a whole tragedy out of her 'Nothing'. But in spite of the importance of Shakespeare in his exploration of nothing (see Van Hulle 2010), Beckett went in a different direction. Rather than foregrounding the 'social reality' of the division of a kingdom, with its plots, intrigues and familial conflicts, Beckett chose to focus his study of nothing on the speaking pronoun, particularly the first person. This much is evident in the list of statements which follow:

> There is no **me** and there is no one else, there is no one at all, there was never any me at all.
> My **I**'s are **nothing** and my **mes** are **nothing** and my **my's** are **nothing** and so for all the other persons in the quartet or quintet as may be.
> **I** am **nothing speaking** of **nothing** neither to **myself** nor to **anyone else**. (16v)

Beckett would go on to make the rejection of the first person pronoun a key structuring principle of *Not I* and it also plays an important role in the narrative of *That Time*. But he knew that in order to explore this world – however devoid of kingdoms – he needed a speaking consciousness of some kind. A later note duly states: 'Of things I am less formal, **mind** ~~**is**~~ **being** **the nothing maker**' (16v). Beckett did indeed realize that nothing would come of nothing, so he focussed his later, gap-ridden theatre on the human mind. However, as a later note suggests, staging one mind immediately implies its interaction with others: '**Other minds?** ... oh, quantities' (18v). Beckett may not have focussed on the interpersonal networks which provide the twists and turns of Shakespeare's tragedies, but he knew he could not stage a mind without taking '**Other minds**' into account. However fractured and distorted they might be, there are interpersonal networks in Beckett's late theatre.

Draft 4: 17r–19r

By altering the vocal tone of his single speaker in the 'Kilcool' drafts, Beckett fashions a voice which anticipates the 'polylogic' nature of his later stage monologues (see chapter 2.1.2). But he also considered having multiple characters onstage in a draft that mirrors the stage setup of *Play* (1964), which, by December 1963, had already been staged and published in German, but whose English and French texts were still being edited for publication (see Beloborodova 2019, 129–30). In a stage sketch featuring his favoured rectangular theatre space, Beckett placed two women (B and C) upstage centre and one man (A) downstage right (see Fig. 8). There is no spoken text on this page, but a set of stage directions describe a situation of observed speaking, whereby the two women each give a 'statement', during which their upraised faces are picked out by a spot and the other figures are in darkness (17r). While Beckett would have difficulties with the Auditor of *Not I*, he was also unsure as to how many listeners should be on the stage of this draft play. He added another (silent) female figure (D) to the bottom of his stage directions along with the word 'Possible', and also added her to the diagram, downstage left, accompanied by a question mark.

It is not certain that the monologue on the next page was intended to be one of the statements given by B and C. However, due to their material proximity, the thematic importance of a romance between a man and a woman as well as the presence of two women and one man in the storyworld, I consider this final monologue to be part of the same draft as the stage sketch and stage directions.

The monologue itself is structured as a question-and-answer session, with a single voice asking itself questions in a tone distinct from the rest of the speech, as we can see outlined in the opening stage direction: 'All opening questions in tone of one intoning a question' (18r). The first

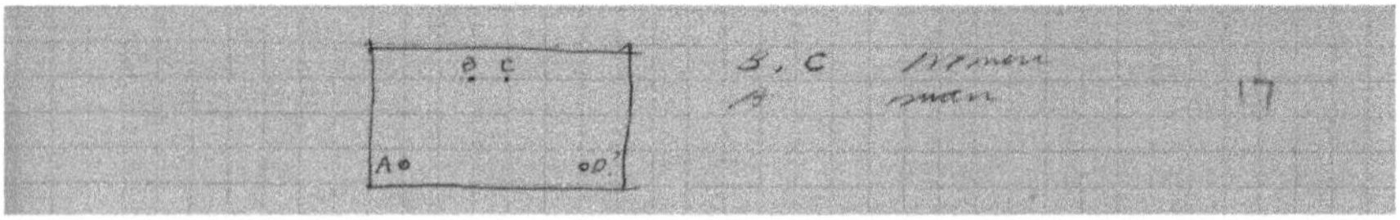

Fig. 8: Beckett's stage sketch in the 'Kilcool' drafts (AS1, 17r).

question returns to a theme familiar from the previous drafts: '**The** time? – (Pause.) Night. (Pause.) He always came at night. (Pause.) They never met by day, (Pause.) He had never seen her, she had never seen him, by the light of day' (18r). The next question prompts an answer which recalls the speaker dictated to in *How It Is*: 'Met in the first place? – (Pause.) **I** hear **told this**' (18r). This is developed in a note on the verso: 'You speak what you hear etc.' (18v). The couple used to meet, we are told, on either side of a pane of glass, pressing their faces against it and smiling. This happened at the house of the physically impaired Mrs Frost, which she shares with the younger woman (whom Mrs Frost calls 'Miss') (18r). The tears of earlier drafts return at intervals, before a remarkable final passage: '(Normal voice.) In the world? – (Pause.) God knows. (Pause.) **Pestilence & famine**. (Irritated.) For God's sake!' (19r). This character does not want to spend time focussing on 'how it is' in the world and the mere suggestion that 'Pestilence & famine' might be a subject worthy of her attention is immediately dismissed. Instead, the monologue ends with her preparing to recount: 'The incident? – (Long pause. Deep breath.) Well … briefly … . (Pause.)' (19r). This ending prefigures the circular structures of *Not I*, *That Time* and *Footfalls*, while also suggesting that the text of the previous drafts – such as the abandonment of the woman in Draft 2 – may have been considered as possible narrative material for this 'incident'. However, Beckett did not develop the draft material further in this notebook, and it was to be almost a decade before he returned to the 'lit face' theme in *Not I*.

2.1.2 'Petit Odéon' Fragments (AS2, AS3)

Between 'Kilcool' and *Not I*, Beckett started his career as a director, which was to have an enormous influence on the making of his later plays. His first directorial credit was for Robert Pinget's *L'Hypothèse*, initially staged in the Musée d'Art Moderne in 1965, then in the Odéon-Théâtre de France in 1966 as part of the Spectacle Beckett–Ionesco–Pinget (Gontarski 2015b, 139; *LSB IV* 9n1). The Odéon was to become a crucial space for Beckett's development as a theatre practitioner in the 1960s. With common acquaintances such as stage designer Charles Henrioud (aka Matias) and the actor–director Roger Blin, Beckett developed a close working relationship with Madeleine Renaud and Jean-Louis Barrault, who started running the Odéon in 1959. Having staged *Godot* there in 1961 (Pilling 2006, 155), they went on to have huge success with Renaud's interpretation of *Oh les beaux jours* (first staged 1963), with Beckett greatly admiring her performance (Knowlson 1997, 510). Over the course of the 1960s, Renaud and Barrault became frequent interpreters of Beckett's work, and would go on to play an important part in the translation process of *Pas moi* and *Pas* (see chapters 2.3.1 and 6.2.1).

Having had a small performance space in one of the Compagnie Renaud–Barrault's earlier theatres (the Petit Marigny), Barrault planned to create a smaller theatre at the Odéon for more experimental work. Beckett was keenly aware of these plans for a space which would accommodate the more confined plays he began creating after *Godot*. On 21 April 1959, Beckett wrote to A. J. Leventhal about a meeting with Barrault: 'His "little theatre" plans still vague, but he said he wants to play Krapp with an Endgame revival, sometime next year I hope' (*LSB III* 226). In fact, it took seven years for Barrault's plans to start materializing, but when they did, he turned to Beckett to open the Petit Odéon, a 'mini-théâtre' located in the converted foyer of the Odéon, with a stage measuring just 3.5 × 4 metres (N. Z. 1967).[66] Beckett told Jocelyn Herbert on 16 June 1966:

> New small theatre (120 seats) in Odéon now also certain. They want to open, round about November, with evening of your humblecumdumble, one half readings, t'other Krapp with [Jean] Martin. Can't get out of it after all their kindness. Never get free from theatre. (*LSB IV* 32–3)

In fact, the theatre would not open until January 1967, and Beckett would not be the first author staged there.[67] Instead, he spent that winter visualizing a piece for the new space, telling Herbert on 27 December 1966:

66 A small platform extended into the audience, giving the stage an 'L' shape. A video of the Petit Odéon is available at https://www.ina.fr/video/CAF89022979/le-petit-theatre-de-l-odeon-video.html.

67 That honour went to Nathalie Sarraute.

> Nothing but further translation – alone & assisted – in view, except a play, if I can, for the Petit Odéon. It is a very strange and interesting little theatre, beautifully adapted from the old gallery, just over 100 seats. But needs to be written for. There was talk of Krapp there, but it seemed to me too difficult. I have a vague idea of what I want to do for it, but I want an hour at least & can't see how to go that long. (*LSB IV* 58)

With AS2 dated February 1967 (AS2, 01r), this letter shows Beckett imagining his play before getting to work on the earliest extant draft, something we will see also with *Not I* (in chapter 2.2.1). This compositional method is clearer still in Beckett's letter to Ruby Cohn of 23 January 1967, in which he tells her of his hope to visit Ussy: 'And try and write for Petit Odéon the little play already shaped' (UoR MS 5100 COH/26). Besides indicating that Beckett composed for the theatre before putting pen to paper, these letters suggest that the shape of the theatre influenced the shape of the play. As a writer now heavily involved in the practice of theatre production, Beckett is cognizant of the spatial and temporal limits for which he is composing, or that the Petit Odéon 'needs to be written for'.[68] These limits, as well as the importance of Renaud as a prompting 'agent' in his compositional process (see chapter 2.3.1), are again clear in Beckett's letter of 8 February 1967 to Alan Schneider: 'Had an idea for a 40 min. play for the *Petit Odéon* (105 seats) and I suppose I could find it again if I looked, but haven't been able to write it. Only the wish to oblige Madeleine in any case, no heart in theatre now' (*NABS* 207; emphasis in original). The second draft scenario in AS2 contains a 45-minute play structure (AS2, 12r), so Beckett may be referencing this in his letter to Schneider. On 28 March 1967, Beckett told Ruby Cohn: 'Little Odéon play down the drain' (qtd. in Cohn 2008, 302n). But this was not the end of the story. According to Nixon, 'Beckett told Cohn that he had been looking at the "Petit Odéon abortion" again with little understanding' on 19 April 1968 (Nixon 2014, 294). Since the latter date on the manuscript is April 1968 (AS2, 16r), Nixon suggests:

68 In 1967, Beckett also became involved in a plan to build a theatre in Oxford (see Tucker 2013). Though this theatre was never built, it shows his deep involvement in the creation of theatre space in the period he was writing the 'Petit Odéon' Fragments.

‘It is possible that the four-page typescript of the play [AS3] dates from around this period’ (2014, 294). As the two drafts contained in the typescript (AS3) are revised versions of material from the notebook (AS2), these typescript drafts are discussed alongside the relevant notebook material in the analysis which follows.

Fragment 1 *(*AS2, flyleafverso)

In a January 1967 TV interview on the opening of the Petit Odéon, Barrault spoke of creating a ‘surgery of human feelings’ [‘la chirurgie des sentiments humains’].[69] Beckett may have taken this metaphor literally in writing fragments which Cohn has called ‘Medical Monologue’ (2008, 302). A female ‘monologue’ is mentioned in the six-paragraph synopsis on flyleafverso, where a man and a woman reduce the space of the stage and give each other medicinal doses with syringes. When the man comes onstage, he has a ‘rouleau’ [roll], probably made of ‘papier’ [paper], with which they carry out their ‘Réduction de l’espace’ (AS2, flyleafverso). This bears a striking resemblance to Barrault’s reduction of space for the 1963 premiere of *Oh les beaux jours* (staged in the main Odéon auditorium):

> By means of a muslin canopy [‘un velum en tissu de verre’] we found a way of altering the volume of the Odéon auditorium quite quickly: all that was left of it was the stalls and the first circle – six hundred and fifty seats. A true ‘royal’ theatre. Its atmosphere was extraordinary. For certain plays that I call ‘easel plays’ [‘certaines œuvres que j’appelle “de chevalet”’] it was ideal. It was in that format that Beckett’s masterpiece, *Oh! les Beaux Jours*, had its first performance. (Barrault 1974, 289; Barrault 1972, 323)

69 https://www.ina.fr/video/CAF89022979/le-petit-theatre-de-l-odeon-video.html.

Interestingly, Barrault used the very same phrase – 'de chevalet' – to describe the kind of work suitable for the Petit Odéon.[70] But Beckett thought that spatial reduction should this time be part of the performance process. All this suggests that he wrote with Barrault's theatre practice in mind while crafting a two-hander that could be played by him and Renaud.

Fragment 2 (AS2, 01r–05r)

The next fragment is also a two-hander, but this time involving two women [femmes], F1 and F2. The decor is suitably bare for the Petit Odéon, with F1 lying on a bed and F2 seated on a stool, reading aloud from a book. She recounts stories in the third person which seem to be about F1. In his direction of Pinget's *L'Hypothèse*, Beckett had already staged a material text (in the form of a typescript) from which the central character, Mortin, reads out his hypotheses in dialogue with a projected image of himself, with Gontarski even going so far as to label this typescript 'a character' (2015b, 129). As Gontarski rightly points out, this setup has similarities with Beckett's later play *Ohio Impromptu* (2015b, 129). But it may also have fed into Beckett's composition of Fragment 2, which in turn foreshadows the emphasis on textuality in the Mrs Winter–Amy dialogue of *Footfalls* (see chapter 6.1.2).

The stage mechanics are referred to frequently, with instructions from F1 causing the light to strengthen and fade (AS2, 01r, 04r). There are also references to 'draperies' (AS2, 01v, 04r), which move when the speech stops. According to the TV report of 10 January 1967, the Petit Odéon stage was without a traditional, front-facing curtain, which would have been quite tricky to fit around its L-shaped platform.[71] With the picture-frame stage being such an important part of Beckett's creative process, this L-shaped

70 https://www.ina.fr/video/CAF89022979/le-petit-theatre-de-l-odeon-video.html. A 'tableau de chevalet' is a small or medium-sized painting which one has worked on and finished with great care ['Petit tableau, ou tableau de moyenne grandeur, qu'on a travaillé et fini avec grand soin'] (https://www.cnrtl.fr/definition/academie8/chevalet). Many thanks to Emilie Morin for her help with this phrase.

71 'La scène est sans rideau' (https://www.ina.fr/video/CAF89022979/le-petit-theatre-de-l-odeon-video.html).

stage may have been another reason why he struggled to complete something for the theatre.

Beckett's interest in staging the breakdown of subjectivity is signalled by the lines in which F1 refers to herself in the third person, such as: 'Elle a une confidante [*for* confidente]' (AS2, 03r). This recalls Beckett's description in his TCD lectures of Racine's confidantes, less highly ranked characters who accompany a central protagonist onstage. Beckett saw these confidantes not as passive auditors but rather active interlocutors, who create a 'polylogue' or 'interior poliloquy' (qtd. in Moorjani 2012, 47) in order to 'express *inner* discussion' of the main character's thoughts (TCD MIC/60/73, qtd. in Van Hulle 2015, 30; emphasis in Van Hulle). In Fragment 2, F1's confidante is the onstage reader, F2. The possibility that F2 may simply be part of F1's mind is raised on the following page, when F1 declares: 'Vous êtes moi' [You are me] (AS2, 04r). Suitably, Beckett here mixed up the speaker directions for F1 and F2, correcting them later, foreshadowing the pronominal confusion of his later plays.

A final element links the fragments strongly to *Footfalls* and to Beckett's creative use of psychoanalysis more generally. F1 mentions early on that she is not ill of an illness: 'Elle n'est pas malade ... de maladie' (AS2, 03r). F2 then suggests, in a passage Beckett deleted, that it is rather a languor of the soul which has troubled F1 since she was a young girl: '~~C'est une sorte de douce langueur qui l'a saisie fillette et ne l'a plus quittée depuis~~' (AS2, 03r). The parallels in this deleted passage with May in *Footfalls* are notable, though Beckett then settled on a shorter phrase: 'Une ~~sorte de~~ langueur de toute l'âme' [A languor of the entire soul] (AS2, 03r). These parallels only increase when F1 returns to this topic:

> F1: Une langueur, vous dites. Alors c'est comme la fille venue au monde sans naître. Ou née sans venir au monde.
>
> [A languor, you say. So, it's like the girl come into the world without being born. Or born without coming into the world.] (AS2, 05r)

As we will see in chapter 6.1.2, this motif preoccupied Beckett throughout his career, and it was on his mind around the time he composed the 'Petit Odéon' Fragments. In a conversation with Charles Juliet on 24 October 1968, he mentioned its Jungian source (Juliet 2009, 13). The phrase comes from a lecture given by Carl Gustav Jung on 2 October 1935, which Beckett attended with his friend Dr Geoffrey Thompson while living in London undergoing psychotherapy. At the end of the lecture, Jung answered questions from the audience, including one from Dr Charles Brunton about some recent dreams had by Brunton's daughter: 'I do not know whether it is fair to ask about the dreams of someone who is not here, but I have a small daughter five and a half years old who has recently had two dreams which awakened her at night' (Jung 2014, 94). Having heard the details of these dreams (which involved a rolling wheel burning the girl and a beetle pinching her), Jung replied: 'You have to consider that it is very difficult and not quite fair to comment on dreams of someone one does not know; but I will tell you as much as one can see from the symbolism' (Jung 2014, 94). Jung then goes on to diagnose an abdominal disorder (symbolized by the beetle) and describes the dream of the wheel as an 'archetypal dream' (2014, 94–5). These archetypal dreams occur, according to Jung, when the child is young enough to be aware of the collective unconscious. He continues:

> Usually at the age of four to six the veil of forgetfulness is drawn upon these experiences. However, I have seen cases of ethereal children, so to speak, who had an extraordinary awareness of these psychic facts and were living their life in archetypal dreams and could not adapt. Recently I saw a case of a little girl of ten who had some most amazing mythological dreams. Her father consulted me about these dreams. I could not tell him what I thought because they contained an uncanny prognosis. The little girl died a year later of an infectious disease. She had never been born entirely. (Jung 2014, 95–6)

In spite of the distinctly Jungian ring to F1's suggestion that the girl is like 'la fille venue au monde sans naître', F2 rejects this comparison: 'Ça n'a pas l'air d'être pareil' [It does not seem to be similar] (AS2, 05r).

Fragment 3 (AS2, 05r–06r)

Spatial reduction again features in the first line of the next fragment: '<u>Réduction de l'espace par draps très légers</u>' [Reduction of space with very light sheets] (AS2, 05r). After this reduction, F1 begins a long monologue in which she expresses her happiness that the space has been reduced – 'Ça ~~d~~c'est de l'espace!' – and looks forward to having an even more confined living area when the women's husbands arrive (AS2, 06r). One husband, Thomas, has prepared a big book from which they will read 'citations incompréhensibles sur **la condition humaine** et sur la vie des animaux' (AS2, 06r). This may be a reference to André Malraux's novel *La condition humaine*, which Beckett cited in his 1938 novel *Murphy* (*Mu* 99). Malraux was appointed Minister of Cultural Affairs by Charles de Gaulle in 1959 and was instrumental in establishing the Odéon-Théâtre de France, supporting Renaud and Barrault's work there with government subventions (see Bonal 2000, 271). But that important relationship was soon to be disrupted, as we will see in chapter 2.3.1.

Fragment 4 (AS2, 06v–07v)

In this short dialogue, B's attempted monologue is interrupted by A: 'Ne ~~me~~ parlez pas dans ~~ce désert~~ cette **immensité**' [Do not speak to me in this **immensity**] (AS2, 07r). This last word is also used in Fragment 6 (see below). The closing interaction switches from A talking about space to A asking about time:

A	~~On a gagné combien de temps~~ Combien déjà?
B	~~Huit minutes.~~ (ayant consulté montre). Huit et demie.
[A	How many already?
B	(having consulted watch). Eight-and-a-half.]

(AS2, 07r)

This may be related to Beckett's letter of 30 January 1967 to Ruby Cohn: 'off to Ussy in a week to look for a way of reducing stage time the way one can stage space' (UoR MS 5100 COH/27). As we will see in *That Time*, staging time itself was a major preoccupation for Beckett.

Fragment 5 (AS2, 07v–11r; AS3, 02r–03r)

Jeantroux notes that this monologue is one of those given by the woman while her husband is drugged asleep (2004, 198). It focuses on medicinal doses, with the speaker remarking that the difference between the levels of her two liquids, A and B, is indistinguishable to the naked eye (AS2, 08r). Each time dose A is used, dose B is also used, which means that the levels remain very similar (AS2, 09r). She also returns to the earlier temporal focus, calling on speech to help her pass the time: 'quinze ou vingt minutes, disons vingt, ce sera plus commode pour les calculs à venir' [15 or 20 minutes, let's say 20, it will be handier for the calculations to come] (AS2, 08r).

The calculations on the following verso show details of Beckett's plan for 'reducing stage time' through pharmacologically induced slumber, with dose A sending a given character to sleep and dose B waking them up. A timetable of doses is given for one hour:

> Lui
> 1 dose A à 0 minutes
> 1 dose B à 20 minutes
> 1 dose A à 30 minutes
> 1 dose B à 50 minutes
>
> Elle
> 1 dose A à 20 minutes
> 1 dose B à 30 minutes
> 1 dose A à 50 minutes
> 1 dose B à 60 minutes (AS2, 08v)

Beckett goes on to note that he ['lui'] will thus reduce his hour awake to 20 minutes, while she ['elle'] will reduce hers to 40 minutes (AS2, 08v).

As for the effect of the calculations on the speaker, she echoes Samuel Johnson's sentiment, later noted in Beckett's 'Super Conquérant' Notebook: 'Nothing amuses more harmlessly than computation' (*BDMP1*, UoR MS 2934, 01r). Her version has more than a ring of salvation about it: 'c'est l'arithmétique qui m'a **sauvée**' (AS2, 09r). What it has 'saved' her from might be the company of other people, such as the halfwit ['demeuré' (AS2, 09v)] who follows her and her male companion. When she declares that two is enough to make a hell ['à deux c'est déjà l'enfer' (AS2, 09v)], Beckett seems to be referencing Garcin's famous line in Jean-Paul Sartre's *Huis clos*: 'l'enfer, c'est les Autres' ['Hell is – other people!'] (Sartre 2000, 93; Sartre 1989, 45). This reference to the most prominent philosopher of mid-century existentialism shows Beckett to be conversant with such currents of thought, albeit he did not embrace Sartre's philosophy, as he told Tom Driver during a conversation which was published in the *Columbia University Forum* in 1961: 'When Heidegger and Sartre speak of a cotrast [*sic*] between being and existence, they may be right, I don't know, but their language is too philosophical for me. I am not a philosopher. One can only speak of what is in front of him, and that now is simply the mess' (qtd. in Driver 2005, 242).

Just as Beckett was by no means a card-carrying existentialist, it is equally reductive to pigeonhole him as a nihilist. Rather, he has 'a taste for the negative' (see chapter 6.2.2), as does this speaker. Following some particularly negation-ridden clauses, she remarks: 's'il y a là trop de négatifs je réponds que pour moi il n'y en a jamais assez' [if there are too many negatives there I say that for me there are never enough] (AS2, 09r). At this point, an 'Avertisseur' [alarm/horn] interrupts the monologue (AS2, 09r).

Fragment 6 (AS2, 11v)

This 'Répliques' section charts the journey of a male and a female character through a landscape of bones, which make the earth white even when there is no moonlight. Many of the phrases are reminiscent of Fragment 4, with one noun in particular linking them together, when E2 recalls imploring her male companion during one of these trips: 'Changeons d'**immensité**, allons dans une autre **immensité**' [Let's change **immensity**, let's go to another **immensity**] (AS2, 11v). Whether these immensities are simply part of the characters' dreamworld is not made clear, foreshadowing the bare contexts of Beckett's late theatre. But there is no escape from time here, as E2 notes: 'Le temps, j'en souffre bien sûr' [Time, I suffer from it of course] (AS2, 11v).

Fragment 7 (AS2, 12r)

This draft synopsis contains four numbered parts. Unlike the earlier synopsis (Fragment 1), this one features the medicinal doses that send a character off to sleep ['expédie'] and bring them back to consciousness ['ramène'], in a pattern of departure and (re-)arrival that will be prominent again in *That Time* and *Pas*.

1 Arrivée femme et inspection. " homme. Réduction espace. Elle l'expédie pour 20 minutes[72]	10 minutes
2. Femme seule	20 minutes
3. Elle le ramène. Il l'expédie. Homme seul.	5 "
4. Il la ramène, ils s'expédient. (AS2, 12r)	10 minutes.

Beckett then notes that part 2, a monologue by the woman alone, is an 'explication de méthode' (AS2, 12r), involving calculations and the management of doses. This describes the narrative material of Fragment 5, suggesting that it makes up the 'Femme seule' section of 'Fragment 7'.

72 These four lines are bracketed on their right-hand side.

Fragment 8 (AS2, 12v–15r, 16r; AS3, 01r–02v)

The first paragraph of monologue on folio 13r is given from the perspective of a lone figure who speaks while their female companion is asleep, mentioning the land of bones and the medical doses. They also recall her mother remarking that this female companion was never properly born: 'elle n'est pas vraiment née' (AS2, 13r), echoing the Jungian motif of Fragment 2. There follows a separate monologue in which a woman recalls asking a doctor why injections only work in the buttocks and when administered by another.[73] The doctor responds that study of the buttocks has been neglected, before making an apocalyptic forecast: 'et **la nuit vient en laquelle personne ne ~~peut travailler~~** pourra les étudier' (AS2, 14r). This is taken from David Martin's translation of the Bible:

> Il me faut faire les œuvres de celui qui m'a envoyé, tandis qu'il est jour ; la nuit vient en laquelle personne ne peut travailler. (Jean 9:4)
>
> [I must work the works of him that sent me, while it is day: the night cometh, when no man can work.] (John 9:4)[74]

But in spite of this brief shift in register, this monologue, in tone, content and form, is a medical farce about the arse. More broadly speaking, it can be seen as part of Beckett's critique of medical discourse, in which the administration of a palliative is scant relief for the suffering subject (see chapter 6.1.2). The monologue incorporates some of the draft material from Fragment 5 (AS2, 08r–09r), before concluding by mentioning the doses and the land of bones (AS2, 15r).

73 This echoes the scene recalled by Henry at the end of *Embers*: 'If it's an injection you want, Bolton, let down your trousers and I'll give you one' (*ATF* 46).

74 All Anglophone Bible references are to the King James Version unless otherwise stated.

Fragment 9 (AS2, 15v)

The calculations on this verso feature a table with the time spent asleep by him and her following their injections:

1. 0-20 lui
2 20-30 elle
3 30-50 lui
4. 50-60 elle (AS2, 15v)

This corresponds to the calculations in Fragment 5 (AS2, 08v), meaning she spends much more time awake than he does. This, in turn, suggests that Renaud would have been the leading light of this play, which makes sense given Beckett's admiration of her acting skills.

Fragment 10 (AS2, 17r)

As Jeantroux points out, this final fragment, which gives a scientific definition of how to calculate the amount of space travelled by a free-falling object, has no real link with those preceding it (2004, 200). Beckett's concern with the relation between space and time in this passage does reflect the thematic material of some other 'Petit Odéon' Fragments, but its status remains provisional until a stronger link can be found. Because of this, it is difficult to see Fragment 10 as belonging to any one line of textual development, 'traditionally [...] visualized as a family tree or a stemma' in textual scholarship (see Van Hulle 2008, 18). Van Hulle and Weller note:

> The term 'stemma', as employed in textual scholarship, denotes the tree-like structure that graphically visualizes the relationships between the extant witnesses of a text. In textual scholarship relating to ancient or medieval texts, the (often lost) 'original' is followed by the 'archetype', the exemplar from which the first split originated. (2018, 136n50)

The 'stemma' model maps the genealogy of a single work, which is not easily identifiable in relation to Fragment 10. In such cases, rather than developing like a tree, Beckett's notebook drafts present a thicket of textual material, with offshoots such as this one not clearly connected to any of his individual works.[75]

75 Though the phrase 'jeu du caillou' (AS2, 17r) may recall the sucking stones episode of *Molloy* (*Mo* 69–75), the material which follows is quite different (see AS2, 17r in the online genetic edition).

2.2 The Genesis of *Not I*

2.2.1 Chronology

Not I was composed amid the aftershocks of a 'catastrophe', as Beckett's wife Suzanne Déchevaux-Dumesnil famously termed his winning the Nobel Prize on 23 October 1969 (Anon. 1969). Among the debris of this catastrophe were works in self-translation (*Mercier and Camier* and *First Love*), original short prose works (*Pour finir encore*, *Still*) and texts he helped others translate (*Watt*), all of which played an important role in the period leading up to *Not I*.

Even before being awarded the Nobel Prize, with some in his circle already aware that he might win it, Beckett had been under pressure from his publishers to allow for editions of previously unpublished works. On 7 January 1969, he told Barbara Bray of contact from his French publisher: 'Lindon dug up Premier Amour I know not where. He wants to publish limited [edition] with Mercier & Camier. Couldn't bring myself to re-read either' (*LSB IV* 144). But the pressure mounted and in a letter to Siegfried Unseld of 22 March, Beckett's determination started to waver:

> Two things are bothering me: the threat of this prize, and the question of the unpublished texts ['cette menace de prix et la question des inédits']. They call for decisions which are very hard to make, and which, I feel very strongly, engage my whole small and problematic future, finishing if not finished, as a writer. If no one but myself were involved, it would be easy. ['Si j'étais seul en cause ce serait facile.'] I do not know yet what I am going to do. I shall of course keep you informed. (*LSB IV* 154–5)

On 21 April, he explained to Unseld that he had given the matter much thought:

> To accept publication of my unpublished texts, with the translation work that that would necessarily mean for me, would be, in view of my age and the state of my carcass, to give up the possibility of writing anything else. No doubt I shall not manage to do that in any case. But I am obliged to go on trying, right to the end. Forgive me on both counts. (*LSB IV* 160)

After the prize was awarded, Beckett finally relented, informing John Calder on 31 January 1970 that Richard Seaver of Grove Press, among others, had pushed him to release previously unpublished work:

> Some days ago I had a letter from Seaver saying 'they could wait no longer to publish M.P.T.K. [*More Pricks Than Kicks*]'. I answered that this was against my wish. But in the last few days pressure on all sides has grown so strong, and I so tired, that I capitulate. You may therefore proceed with trade edition of this juvenilium. I also capitulate for Premier Amour & Mercier et Camier – but NOT for Eleutheria. I consider you control European rights of M.P.T.K. (*LSB IV* 221)

Alluding to the fact that he would now have to translate *Premier amour* and *Mercier et Camier*, Beckett finished: 'I hope you don't realize what this will involve for me' (*LSB IV* 222).

Beckett started translating *Mercier et Camier* on 6 May 1970 and the process would last almost four years, continuing into the spring of 1974 (Pilling 2006, 184–94). From the very start, there were problems, as he told Barbara Bray on 12 May: 'Advance slowly with M. & C. Much left unsolved such as "petite reine" (bicycle)' (*LSB IV* 230). Beckett here refers to a passage in which Mercier speaks of two copulating dogs who, like the bicycle, are under threat by a park ranger: 'Ils contreviennent à l'arrêté, dit Mercier, au même titre que la petite reine' (Beckett 2013b, 19). Eventually, he would cut such passages from the English text, 'amount[ing] at a conservative estimate to a loss of about 12 per cent of the material in the French version. These losses are compensated for only by the addition of a few phrases here and there' (Connor 2007, 101). Steven Connor has pointed to 'the frequent omission of details which might link Mercier and Camier to any realistic world' in the English translation (101). This is in line with Beckett's practice of 'vaguening' his texts in this late period of his career. Advising Raymond Cousse on a draft of his play *Péripéties*, Beckett wrote: 'Principes: Enlever tout le superflu et aller vite' ['remove the superfluous and move fast'] (7 December 1969, *LSB IV* 209–10). Both in this statement and the translation of *Mercier et Camier*, we can see a working process that plays an important role in the stripped back world created in *Not I*.

There is also a more specific way in which Beckett's translation work of this period seems to have influenced the play. This relates to a detail which did not get cut from *Mercier and Camier* – the strange cameo of Watt in its final chapters. *Watt* was on Beckett's mind in the years leading up to *Not I*: shortly before translating *Mercier et Camier*, he helped Elmar Tophoven finish the German translation of the earlier novel (Beckett to Gottfried Büttner, 17 March 1970, *LSB IV* 226). As he sits locked into the waiting room of the train station, waiting for night to fall, Watt hears a female voice which, as Ann Beer has noted (1985, 67), bears a striking resemblance to the yet-to-be created Mouth. This voice speaks of the waiting room:

> Whispering it told, the mouth, a woman's, the thin lips sticking and unsticking, how when empty they could accommodate a larger public than when encumbered with armchairs and divans, and how it was vain to sit, vain to lie, when without the rain beat down, or the sleet, or the snow, with or without wind, or the sun, with greater or lesser perpendicularity. This woman's name had been Price, her person was of an extreme spareness, and some thirty-five years earlier she had shot, with colours flying, the narrows of the menopause. Watt was not displeased to hear her voice again, to watch again the play of the pale bows of mucus. He was not displeased either when it went away. (*W* 202–3)

This voice's being called 'the mouth', its speaking in the dark, the speaker's apparent experience of vagrant nights spent sleeping in the waiting room and the image of bow-like lips: all of these are elements which we again find in the stage image and voice of *Not I*.

Mine is by no means the first reading to link Mouth's genesis to a derelict female voice from Beckett's past. Deirdre Bair, in a much-quoted statement, has Beckett connecting Mouth's monologue to that of itinerant Irish women he had known as a child:

> I knew that woman in Ireland. [...] I knew who she was – not 'she' specifically, one single woman, but there were so many of those old crones, stumbling down the lanes, in the ditches, beside the hedgerows. Ireland is full of them. And I heard 'her' saying what I wrote in *Not I*. I actually heard it. (1990, 622)

But Bair's account is doubtful as she reports Beckett telling the same story, using exactly the same words, to multiple people: 'Alan Schneider, Billie Whitelaw, A. J. Leventhal and others' (1990, 748n59). It is thus unclear if Beckett told precisely this story to all his friends or repeated elements of it which Bair then coalesced into a quotable narrative. While the disembodied voice of Price in *Watt*'s waiting room scene stands as a textual precursor to the protagonist of *Not I*, Mouth's biographical forerunners remain tenuous.[76]

Other translation work from this period shows that derelict women were on Beckett's mind as he composed *Not I*. On 24 April 1972, three days after the last date on EM1, Beckett turned his attention to the translation of *Premier amour*. Love, particularly its absence, is a persistent theme throughout Beckett's play. But it is while writing of a place of death that Beckett seems to have again thought of women on the periphery of social norms. When passing through a graveyard, the narrator tells us, 'with a little luck you hit on a genuine interment, with real live mourners and the odd relict trying to throw herself into the pit' (*ECEF* 62). In *Premier amour*, this was simply a 'veuve' [widow] (Beckett 2012c, 10); the archaic 'relict' in the English text emphasizes the sense of a woman 'left behind', as outlined in the word's etymology.[77] Though there is no evidence of Mouth being a widow,

76 C. J. Ackerley links Price to Miss Carridge in *Murphy*, 'who derives from Beckett's childhood neighbor, Mrs. Coote', also the name of a character in *Company*, on the basis of all three being women who are of slight build (2005, 194).

77 'Relict' derives from the Old French *relicte*, meaning '(woman) left behind' (*OED*a).

she does fit this picture of a woman 'left behind' by the rest of the world, starting with her parents.

The narrator of *First Love* too is left behind by his father and, as a father, he leaves behind his own child as it is being born at the story's end. There are also other elements linking the story to *Not I*, not least the narrator's reference to a 'non-self' ['non-moi'] (*ECEF* 66; 2012c, 21). In translating the narrator's reaction to Loulou/Anna speaking, Beckett further emphasized the disjunction between subject and object which was to become such a key feature of his play. The French reads: 'Quand elle eut fini, et que mon moi à moi, l'apprivoisé, se fut reconstitué à l'aide d'une brève inconscience, **je me trouvai seul**' (2012c, 22). The English translation, rather than concluding with the self-reflexive translation 'I found myself alone', speaks of the narrated self as a separate object to its narrator: 'When she had finished and my self been resumed, mine own, the mitigable, with the help of a brief torpor, **it was alone**' (*ECEF* 67).[78] While foreshadowing Mouth's own self-dissociation, Beckett may have been critiquing here the philosophy of Karl-Leonhard Reinhold, a figure referenced soon after in the novella. Thinking of how he understands his pains better than other people or animals, the narrator of *First Love* tells us: 'Yes, there are moments, particularly in the afternoon, when I go all syncretist, à la Reinhold' (*ECEF* 68). Reinhold held that 'in consciousness, the subject distinguishes the representation from the subject and the object and relates the representation to both' (qtd. and trans. in Breazeale 2018). In contrast to Reinhold's description of a subject able to separate representation from both itself and the world around it, Beckett's characters, from *Premier amour* to *First Love* to *Not I*, cannot get a firm grip on this subject–object distinction.

The breakdown between subject and object is prevalent in the pronouns Beckett used when working on other translations in this period. Having translated Apollinaire's 'Zone' for *Transition* in 1950, he revised the poem for a deluxe edition in January 1972 (see Beckett to Liam Miller, 19 January 1972, *LSB IV* 281). 'Zone' is a self-reflexive description of the physical and imaginative wanderings of a central male figure who refers to himself with both the first- and second-person pronoun, a pronominal disjunction which is central to the self-alienation in the poem. In Beckett's 1950 translation,

78 For more on Beckett's disjunctive use of pronouns, see Little (2020a).

one line reads: 'You dare not look at your hands tears haunt **your eyes**' (Apollinaire 1950, 130). But when the poem was republished in 1972, the final possessive pronoun was changed so that the line ended with '**my eyes**' (Apollinaire 1972, 19). As the owner of a 1967 reprint of the 1965 edition of Apollinaire's *Œuvres poétiques* – which contains editorial notes on the poems' composition – Beckett may have been aware that Apollinaire himself had altered the subject pronoun of the same line when revising the poem at draft stage: 'Je n'ose plus regarder' became 'Tu n'oses plus regarder' (Apollinaire 1956, 43, 1033).[79] In these changes, we can see both poets trying to pin down a set of pronominal forms that will best refer to a self estranged from itself, an important feature of Beckett learning to say 'not I'.[80]

As seen in his letters to Unseld, Beckett's primary concern was that all his translation work would leave him unable to produce anything new. But, as evidenced by *Not I* itself, he did produce remarkably strange and original works in the midst of all this self-translation. Another such is *Pour finir encore*, whose origin John Pilling tentatively dates to letters of 22 April 1969 (2006, 180). Beckett's later letters on the piece demonstrate a focus on the darkness which had already become a feature of his theatre work in *Krapp's Last Tape*, *Play* and *Come and Go*: 'Struggle not to abandon work in absolute dark', Beckett wrote to Barbara Bray on 5 December 1969 (*LSB IV* 206). On 21 December he returned to the theme of darkness when describing his efforts on *Pour finir encore* to Henri and Josette Hayden, in a statement that foreshadows his final poem *Comment dire*: 'How to say black, silence and void? ['Comment dire noir, silence et vide?'] Interesting technical problem' (*LSB IV* 213–14). He was still working on the text on 9 January 1972 and had it with him on the trips to Malta and Morocco where he picked up some of the visual concepts for *Not I* (Pilling 2006, 188–9; see below).

In the published text of *Pour finir encore*, Beckett has 'crâne seul dans le noir', before the narrative shifts to focus on the head's memories (2014d, 9). Both are important features of *Not I*. Though 'crâne' would be translated as the anatomical 'skull' in the English prose piece (*TFN* 151), the French

79 https://www.beckettarchive.org/library/APO-OEU.html.

80 Beckett's interest in the pronominal gymnastics of French poetry is also evident in his allusion to Rimbaud's 'Je est un autre' in *Malone meurt* (see Van Hulle and Verhulst 2017b, 156).

version shows more direct links with the later play. In order to activate the process of imagination from which derives the narrative content of the text, Beckett uses a metaphor of the mind as machine, an image which would again surface in Mouth's monologue, where memories return in sudden flashes: 'Toujours un peu moins noir jusqu'au gris final ou soudain comme au commutateur sable gris à perte de vue sous un ciel même gris sans nuages' (2014d, 9) ['By degrees less dark till final grey or all at once as if switched on grey sand as far as eye can see beneath grey cloudless sky same grey' (*TFN* 151)]. The word 'commutateur' also appears twice in *Le Dépeupleur*, which Beckett translated as *The Lost Ones* from 29 September to 8 November 1971 (Beckett 2013a, 31, 35; Pilling 2006, 188).[81] The second instance is in the description of the two 'storms' of heat and light in the cylinder: 'the two storms have this in common that when one is cut off as though by magic then in the same breath the other also as though again the two were connected somewhere to a single commutator' (*TFN* 113). These descriptions of the imagined environment being controlled by the flick of a switch strongly foreshadows the image of mechanistic thought in *Not I* (see chapter 2.2.2), not to mention the darkened environment of the modern proscenium stage itself.

The process of 'say[ing] black' on the stage was another challenge altogether to saying it just on the page. Beckett directed *Happy Days* in Berlin in 1971, over which he had fretted a decade earlier 'whether this is really a dramatic text or a complete aberration and whether there is justification for trying to push further this kind of theatre' (Beckett to Alan Schneider, 15 September 1961, *LSB III* 435). He saw *Not I* within the same experimental paradigm, noting with relief after the Royal Court production: 'Learnt what I hoped to learn, that in some strange way it's theatre in spite of all' (Beckett to Horace Gregory, 21 January 1973, *LSB IV* 324).[82]

Note the repeated use of the word 'theatre' in these letters. As I have already argued, for Beckett, creating in the theatre meant writing for the

81 The term also occurs (but is deleted) on a typescript of *Pochade radiophonique* (UoR MS 1396/4/43, 01r), which has been dated to 1958 (see Verhulst 2015). I would like to thank Pim Verhulst for this information.

82 Beckett had indeed already pushed his theatre to its minimum in writing *Breath*, the only one of Beckett's stage plays not to present a body, which he translated as *Souffle*, working on the typescripts in January 1971 (Pilling 2006, 186).

proscenium stage. Even as the influence of Antonin Artaud made itself felt globally in the rise of immersive forms of performance (see Schechner 1994), Beckett was still absorbed by works composed for the Cartesian Theatre of proscenium performance space. Particularly on his mind in the year leading up to the composition of *Not I* was Joyce's heavily Ibsenite *Exiles*. Advising Harold Pinter on his 1971 production of the play, Beckett described a spatial and interpersonal scenario which also serves as a good description of the relationship between Mouth and the Auditor:

> I feel the clue to the production is apartness. As much stage as possible as often as possible between the actors [...]. All exiled in one another from one another. [...] All speaking and listening more to themselves than to the others. Similarly for set. Elements isolated apart from one another. (17 September 1970, *LSB IV* 240)

This description of isolated elements demonstrates Beckett's concern with the subject–object breakdown at this point in his career. His interpretation of *Exiles* shows him again identifying this breakdown in the work of previous writers – and spatializing it for the stage. Such framed 'apartness' is also a key feature of one of the most widely discussed influences on *Not I* – Caravaggio's *Beheading of St John the Baptist* (see Fig. 9). On 25 October 1971, Beckett told Avigdor Arikha and Anne Atik that he had seen this 'formidable peinture' in Valletta, while holidaying in Malta (*LSB IV* 270). He later informed James Knowlson: 'Image in *Not I* in part suggested by Caravaggio's Decollation of St. John in Valetta Cathedral' (29 April 1973, *LSB IV* 332). Almost thirteen years later, he wrote to Edith Kern:

> The Caravaggio painting in Valletta shows, outside & beyond the main area, at a safe distance from it, a group of watchers intent on the happening. Before the painting, from another outsidedness, I behold both the horror & its being beheld. This experience had some part in the conception of the Auditor in Not I. (15 March 1986, *LSB IV* 671)

Fig. 9: Caravaggio, *The Beheading of St John the Baptist* (https://commons.wikimedia.org/w/index.php?curid=10475830).

As in his advice on Pinter's production of *Exiles*, Beckett here again stresses distance, with the extra element in the 'experience' being his own viewing perspective, watching the doubly framed watchers. This viewing of another's attentiveness is also evident in another visual source for the Auditor, picked up when watching a woman in a djellaba in Morocco. Returning to a phrase he had used when discussing the 'Kilcool' drafts (see chapters 1.1.1 and 2.1.1), Beckett told Barbara Bray of a play with a 'lit face' on 23 February 1972:

> Vague image for a short play of a lit face (mouth) with ? to say and a cloaked hooded figure, sex unclear, completely still throughout, listening and watching. Latter suggested by an Arab woman all hidden in black absolutely motionless at the gate of a school in Taroudant and by the watching figures in Caravaggio's Malta decollation. Might produce 10 min. strangeness if text found. (*LSB IV* 287)

The phrase 'Vague image' suggests that Beckett had been working on his visual ideas prior to the first date on the earliest extant manuscript, '20.3.72' (EM1, 01r), just as he had done with the 'Petit Odéon' Fragments (see chapter 2.1.2). This would categorize Beckett as one of Siegfried Scheibe's 'mindworkers' (*Kopfarbeiter*), who first develops ideas before writing them down (see Van Hulle 2008, 47). Scheibe opposes such authors to 'paperworkers' (*Papierarbeiter*), who work out their ideas on paper (see Van Hulle 2008, 47). The manuscripts discussed in chapters 1.1.1 and 1.2.1 demonstrate the extent to which the text of *Not I* was also shaped on the page. But the hypothesis that Beckett worked on his stage images before drafting his text is supported by his letter to Mary Hutchinson of 6 April 1972, in which he tells her: 'Began work **last week** on a short play (in English). It may not come to anything but not without hope' (*LSB IV* 299n2). The date of 20 March on EM1 would have him starting this 'paperwork' a week earlier than what he reported to Hutchinson. But this still leaves a significant gap between his February letter to Bray and the first extant manuscript of *Not I*, suggesting that some substantial work did take place away from the writing desk before Beckett drafted the play. This is not the 'écriture à programme' which Beckett critiqued as a young lecturer when speaking of the work of Balzac (Louis Hay qtd. in O'Reilly, Van Hulle and Verhulst 2017, 153; Van Hulle and Verhulst 2017b, 29).[83] However, it does

83 As shown in earlier volumes of the BDMP series, there were tensions between Beckett's preference for 'écriture à processus' as against the Balzacian 'écriture à programme' in his earlier prose, as when he wrote the first paragraph of *Molloy* 'last of all' (O'Reilly, Van Hulle and Verhulst 2017, 33), came up with an ending (which he later changed) while writing *Malone meurt* (Van Hulle and Verhulst 2017b, 190) or confessed to writing the last page of *L'Innommable* before he had finished the novel (Beckett to Georges Duthuit, 1 June 1949, *LSB II* 160). As Van Hulle and Weller explain, this did not in fact

show Beckett using his stage image as scaffolding around which he built his stage speech and (minimal) stage movements, an approach he would again use when composing *That Time* and *Footfalls*.[84]

On 24 April 1972, Beckett told Ruby Cohn: 'Seem to have nearly finished a short play in English (15 min.) Should know by middle of next month. Nice posthumous feel' (*LSB IV* 299n2). This corresponds with the latest date on EM1, which appears to be '21' April 1972 (04v). According to the editors of Beckett's letters, he informed Jocelyn Herbert on 12 June 1972 that he had sent the play to Oscar Lewenstein, Artistic Director of the English Stage Company at the Royal Court (*LSB IV* 299n2). However, though he seems to have had a complete version at this point, Beckett was still weighing up whether or not to stage the text: 'It's a monologue (woman) about 20 mins. But I'm doubtful about it. I replied that if I released it I'd give the Court the first refusal' (Beckett to Herbert, 12 June 1972, *LSB IV* 299n2). Four days later, he wrote teasingly to Cohn: 'The play I think I can do no more with but I feel like packing it up in an old box, with other odds and ends. After a few jars, if you're very nice to me, I might let you have a quick look' (16 June 1972, *LSB IV* 299).[85] By 31 September, Beckett was able to tell Alan Schneider: 'Have seen Ruby Cohn & shown her Not I which she likes' (*LSB IV* 307).

Schneider himself was planning a short season of Beckett plays in 1972 at New York's Forum Theater, starring Hume Cronyn and Jessica Tandy, alternating performances of *Happy Days* and *Act Without Words I* one evening and *Krapp's Last Tape* the next. As this list suggests, Schneider had a gap in his schedule for a play to accompany *Krapp*, and *Not I* arrived at a perfect moment to fill it. On 2 July 1972, Schneider told Beckett that 'we need something at least 15–20 minutes' in order to fill the evening with *Krapp* (*NABS* 272). On 7 July, Beckett replied: 'Think I may have what you need to go with *Krapp*' (*NABS* 273n1). Beckett met Schneider and Tandy along with Rosset on 13–15 July in Paris, discussing the play with them there (*LSB IV* 302n1). Though he told Avigdor Arikha and Anne Atik that Tandy's

end up as the novel's final page (2014, 123). See also Van Hulle and Verhulst's description of the genesis of *Malone meurt* as 'paradigmatic of what Louis Hay (1986–87) dubbed "écriture à processus"' (2017b, 29).

84 As Georgina Nugent-Folan has shown (2021), Beckett used a highly schematic form of 'écriture à programme' in the later prose text *Company*.

85 *Ends and Odds* would be the title, suggested by Beckett, for Grove's and Faber's collected editions of his short plays (see chapter 1.5.1).

were 'Silly questions' ['Questions bêta' [*sic*]] (*LSB IV* 304, 303), Beckett's letter of 19 July to Cronyn suggests that this meeting was instrumental in his decision to 'release' the play for performance:

> Jessica Tandy will have told you about our for me most enjoyable meeting. If this exceptional occasion had not arisen I would not have released Not I before testing it further, both text and image, in a sterner workshop than imagination's. I shall be sending a revised version to Alan before the end of this month. I am not at all sure it is viable but have nothing else to offer. (*LSB IV* 301–2)

Beckett did indeed send Schneider a typescript for performance on 25 July (*NABS* 273), almost certainly a copy of ET5, on which Beckett implemented Schneider's suggested change of 'than thinking' to 'then thinking', made in October 1972 (see chapter 1.2.1).[86] One addition on the annotated copy Beckett sent to Elmar and Erika Tophoven (ET5') helps us roughly date the later revisions on ET5. In the supralinear additions 'this other thought then..oh long after...sudden flash...very foolish really' (ET5', 02r) and '..that she might do well to···groan..', Beckett uses three ellipsis points rather than two. As the typescripts after ET7 include three points, it seems reasonable to assume that Beckett made these additions to ET5' after ET7 was composed, around January 1973. This also suggests that Beckett made his later revisions to ET5 (such as those in red pen, now faded to pink) in view of the UK premiere with Billie Whitelaw in January 1973. We know that Beckett continued to produce typescripts after the play's world premiere in New York on 22 November 1972, up to and including a typed synopsis (ET8) that matches the handwritten synopsis he created while rehearsing for the UK production with Whitelaw (see RC notes.B, chapter 1.6.1).[87] In spite of his deep involvement in the rehearsal process, it is worth noting that Beckett

86 In the same letter, Beckett mentions having sent *Not I* 'by same mail' to the Royal Court (Beckett to Schneider, 25 July 1972, *NABS* 273).

87 There were previews of the play in October, leading up to the November premiere (see Alan Schneider to Beckett, 22 October 1972, *NABS* 286).

was assistant to director Anthony Page at the Royal Court production, and only ever officially directed the play in French (see chapter 2.3.1).[88]

Writing to Schneider before his rehearsals for *Not I*'s US premiere began, Beckett expressed his openness to changing the text: 'Don't hesitate to ask for cuts or consult about difficulties' (25 July 1972, *LSB IV* 302n2). As seen in the analysis of *Not I*'s television adaptation (chapter 1.6.1), this openness to 'cuts' would have ramifications for the text in performance, specifically with regard to the vexed question of how to accommodate the Auditor alongside Mouth. In a letter of 30 September 1972, Schneider reported progress with the challenging process of staging *Not I*. However, he admitted: 'Question of location of Auditor yet to be settled' (*NABS* 279). Schneider wrote again on 22 October, by which point previews had already started: 'We're still working on lighting Figure of Auditor, which is even trickier business [than staging Mouth]. Last night, we couldn't see his arms well enough, better tomorrow, and so on. Problem is to suspend him in space and yet see him' (*NABS* 285). Having already expressed his willingness to change the text, Beckett now proposed a cut of his own: 'The auditor? only answer worth giving: try it without him. The more he disturbs the better' (5 November 1972, *NABS* 287). Beckett would later approve the omission of the Auditor from the BBC television adaptation.[89] However, Schneider decided against this: 'Got your previous card, and thought about cutting Auditor. I don't want to do that' (13 November 1972, *NABS* 288), and he would go on to emphasize the importance of the Auditor's onstage presence (24 and 30 November 1972, *NABS* 290, 292). This incident is further evidence of Beckett's growing awareness throughout the 1960s and 1970s of the importance of staging a play as part of his compositional process. As discussed in chapter 1.3.1, Beckett was unwilling to release *Not I* for publication before seeing it in rehearsal. And the precise role of Auditor would continue to change when he came to stage *Pas moi* in Paris (see chapter 2.3.1).

88 The 1973 Royal Court production was reprised at the same venue in 1975 with Melvyn Hastings as the Auditor instead of Brian Miller.

89 According to Whitelaw, the decision to omit the Auditor onscreen was a joint one between Tristram Powell and Beckett (1996, 132).

2.2.2 Genesis

Like predecessors such as *The Unnamable*, *Cascando* and *Play*, the text of *Not I* can have the effect of an onrushing stream, with little for the reader/listener/spectator to orient themselves aside from the interruptions to Mouth's monologue, marked by the Auditor's movements. But it is possible to read '*Not I* as a *Texte Brisé*', following Beckett's own outline (Van Hulle 2009b, 44). As part of his analysis of Balzac's *Sarrasine*, Roland Barthes suggested breaking texts up 'into a series of brief, contiguous fragments' ['en une suite de courts fragments contigus'] (2002b, 13; 2002a, 13) which he called lexias. As we saw in chapter 1.2.1, Beckett divided the text of *Not I* into five sections on his typewritten synopsis (ET8; see Fig. 10), then using this structure when rehearsing the play with Billie Whitelaw (RC notes.B, see chapter 1.6.1). Within this five-part structure, Beckett subdivided his text into smaller lexias, some of which are marked by one of the five 'life scene[s]' he identified in Mouth's monologue (see Fig. 10). For the purposes of this genetic analysis, I follow these lexias as units of reading Beckett's text.[90] The following schema, based on Beckett's own synopsis, shows the outline of the genetic analysis which follows:

1 Premature birth (ET3, 01r)
Parents unknown (ET3, 01r)
No love at any time (ET3, 01r)
At age of 70 in a field picking cowslips suddenly finds herself in the dark (ET3, 01r)

90 The lexias on ET8 have also been used to structure the segmentation of the text in the online genetic edition of *Not I / Pas moi*. Since ET3 is the first typescript in which all the lexias appear, I have used that to key the lexias in Beckett's list. The only exception to this is 'Note 2', which first appears on ET4 (see 'Note 2' below).

2 No feeling apart from buzzing in her head and awareness of a ray of light (ET3, 01r)
Mind still active in a way (ET3, 01r)
First thought: she is being punished for her sins (ET3, 01r)
Dismissed as she realises she is not suffering (ET3, 01r–02r)
Second thought: perhaps she should groan (to please tormentor) (ET3, 02r)
Failure to utter a sound (ET3, 02r)
All silent but for the buzzing (ET3, 02r)
Motionless but for eyes opening and shutting (ET3, 02r)
Mind questions this in view of life scene~~1~~ 1 ~~9~~(field) (ET3, 02r)
Hears a voice largely unintelligible (ET3, 02r)

3 Accent suggests it is hers (ET3, 02r)
Life scene 2 (shopping centre) (ET3, 02r–03r)
Tries to delude herself voice not hers (ET3, 03r)
Renounces as she feels lips moving (ET3, 03r)
Fear that feeling may come back but for the moment mouth alone (ET3, 03r)

4 Next thought: such distress can't continue (ET3, 03r)
Description of same: unintelligible irrepressible voice, consternation of mind (ET3, 03r)
Prayer for voice to stop: unanswered (ET3, 03r)
Life scene 3 (Croker's Acres) (ET3, 03r)
Brain grabbing at straws (e.g. God's mercy) (ET3, 03r)
Life scene 1 (field) again (ET3, 03r–04r)
Perhaps something she should tell? Life scene 4 (courtroom), (ET3, 04r)
life scene 1 (field) and no from within (ET3, 04r)

5 Something she should think? No as before (ET3, 04r)
Life scene 5 (rushing out to tell) (ET3, 04r)
Distress worse: description of same (ET3, 04r)
Prayer for all to stop: unanswered (ET3, 04r)
Life scene 1 ~~9~~(field) again (ET3, 04r–05r)

NOT I - synopsis

1. Premature birth
Parents unknown
No love at any time
At age of 70 in a field picking cowslips suddenly finds herself in the dark

2. No feeling apart from buzzing in her head and awareness of a ray of light
Mind still active in a way
First thought: she is being punished for her sins
Dismissed as she realises she is not suffering
Second thought: perhaps she should groan (to please tormentor)
Failure to utter a sound
All silent but for the buzzing
Motionless but for eyes opening and shutting
Mind questions this in view of life scene 1 (field)
Hears a voice largely unintelligible

3. Accent suggests it is hers
Life scene 2 (shopping centre)
Tries to delude herself voice not hers
Renounces as she feels lips moving
Fear that feeling may come back but for the moment mouth alone

4. Next thought: such distress can't continue
Description of same: unintelligible irrepressible voice, consternation of mind
Prayer for voice to stop: unanswered
Life scene 3 (Croker's Acres)
Brain grabbing at straws (e.g. God's mercy)
Life scene 1 (field) again
Perhaps something she should tell? Life scene 4 (courtroom), life scene 1 (field) and no from within

5. Something she should think? No as before
Life scene 5 (rushing out to tell)
Distress worse: description of same
Prayer for all to stop: unanswered
Life scene 1 (field) again

Fig. 10: Beckett's 'synopsis' of *Not I* (ET8).

Since Beckett's synopsis is focussed on Mouth's monologue, it does not deal with notes on the text or the stage directions, which is where my analysis begins.

Opening Stage Directions: Mouth (ET3, 01r; 1973a, 6)

The stage directions on the first draft of *Not I* show striking similarities with the 'lit face' in the 'Kilcool' drafts, reinforcing the idea that Beckett had this concept in mind for a considerable period before starting the composition of *Not I* proper. However, their position on the page suggests they were not the first lines written, but rather squeezed in around the existing drafts of Mouth's monologue (see Fig. 11). The first draft has the fundamental concepts of the stage image: 'Stage in darkness but for MOUTH, ~~back~~ up **stage** audience R, convenient level, faintly lit from close up & below, as little as possible of rest of face, invisible microphones' (EM1, 01r). Interestingly, for someone with Beckett's increasing theatre experience, he seems to have first put Mouth '**backstage**', which would have kept her out of sight of the audience altogether. This, as well as his unorthodox manner across many different theatre works of writing all his stage directions from the point of view of the onlooking audience member rather than, as is standard in Anglophone theatre, from the perspective of the performing actor, is in line with Beckett's own assessment, as reported by a theatre practitioner with whom he often worked closely, that 'he was not a theatre man' (Walter Asmus qtd. in Knowlson and Knowlson 2006, 192).[91] Bearing in mind the strong lines of multimedial influence on *Not I*'s composition, there is a strong case to be made that it was Beckett's very interest in forms of art outside the theatre that enabled him to refashion 20th-century theatre space.

91 It is also quite possible that Beckett was influenced here by French theatre practice, in which stage right and left are considered from the point of view of the spectator. Asmus worked with Beckett as production assistant from 1975 onwards, later directing some of Beckett's plays in collaboration with the author.

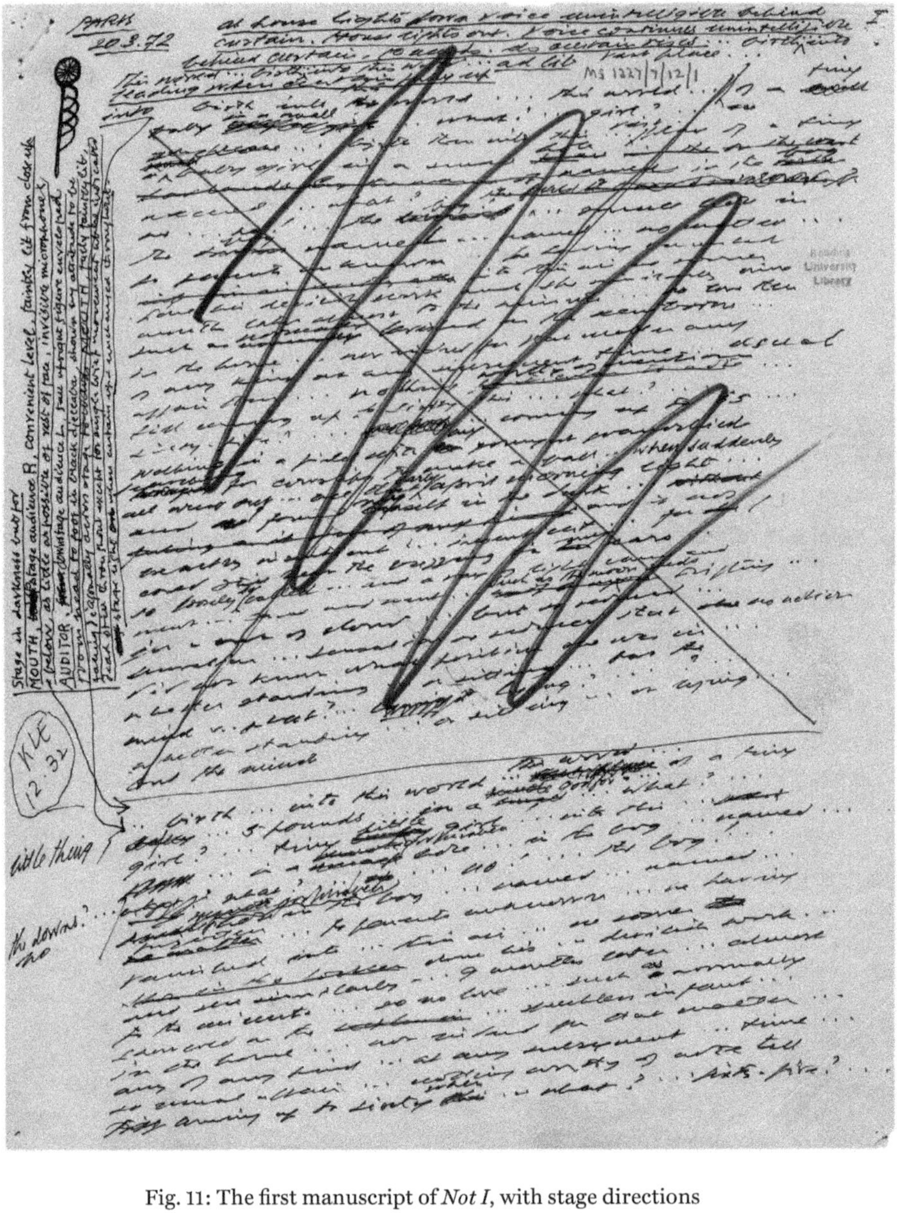

Fig. 11: The first manuscript of *Not I*, with stage directions squeezed into the margins (EM1, 01r).

Opening Stage Directions: Auditor (ET3, 01r; 1973a, 6)

Though the word in question is again hard to read, Beckett's error in the terminology of stage space seems to have been repeated in his first version of the stage directions for the Auditor:

> AUDITOR, ~~front~~**downstage** audience L, tall upright figure enveloped from head to foot in black djellaba, shown by attitude to be facing diagonally across stage towards MOUTH, fully faintly lit, dead still throughout except for single brief movement where indicated[.] ~~Ligh~~ Stage light on when curtain up & unchanged throughout. (EM1, 01r)

On ET5, there is an example of Beckett 'vaguening' his text by adding more detail, a marginal insertion reading 'sex **undeterminable**' (01r). Though this would be clarified somewhat in the translation of the Auditor's name into French (see chapter 2.3.2), here we have an interesting instance of Beckett making his text more vague by addition rather than his more habitual process of 'vaguening' through subtraction.

Opening Stage Directions: Voice (ET3, 01r; 1973a, 6)

First-hand accounts of performing *Not I* have focussed on the physical restraints put on the actor playing Mouth (Whitelaw 1996, 124–5; Dwan 2016), suitably enough for a character who speaks of being 'in control ... under control' (1973a, 16; *KLT* 88). But these stage directions are quite remarkable in that they contain the only ad lib of any Beckett play.[92] While he specified the ad libs in early drafts, ET3 states simply '**ad-libbing as required** leading when curtain fully up, & ~~silence~~ **attention sufficient** into [start of monologue]' (01r). The addition of '**attention sufficient**' here also indicates that Beckett had the audience's response to his play in mind, at least from a functional perspective. On ET5, Beckett added the two words (here in bold)

92 *Play* does feature its voices speaking, '*largely unintelligible*', just after the curtain rises, though this is a reference to the scripted chorus which follows rather than an improvised ad lib (*KLT* 53).

'ad-libbing ^from text^ as required', narrowing the range of options for his actor's improvisation (01r).

The reference to the audience seems to indicate a departure from standard Beckettian performance practice. In his analysis of *Not I* in the context of scientific experiment, Josh Powell has memorably described Beckett's work as follows: 'Beckett is interested in how conditions might be manipulated so as to produce a particular perceptual experience for himself, but not in observing and measuring that experience in others' (2017, 234).[93] But as an observer of his own plays, he did seem to understand the necessity for taking into account the audience's perception and behaviour in the course of his compositional process. In 1958, Beckett spoke disparagingly of the need for a dramatist to shape their work with 'The reactions of the public' in mind (qtd. in *LSB III* 167n2). Later in his career, however, the difficulty of presenting 'Mongrel Mime' (written 1983) to an audience seated in front of his preferred proscenium stage space seems to have been one of the reasons that play was abandoned (see Little 2018, 204–5). In one of his best-known statements about *Not I*, Beckett included the audience when telling Schneider about the intended effect of the 'panting' stage voice: 'Addressed less to the understanding than to the nerves of the audience which should in a sense share her bewilderment' (16 October 1972, *LSB IV* 311; emphasis in original). According to this statement, the audience should *feel* the breakdown as it is staged. He also mentioned the audience to Tandy: 'I am not unduly concerned with intelligibility [...]. I hope the piece may work on the nerves of the audience, not its intellect' (qtd. in Brater 1987, 23). So, it is no surprise that the stage directions of *Not I* show Beckett was considering how his audience would react when confronted with such an unusual protagonist. After the play's previews in New York, Alan Schneider reported to him: 'Business of starting and ending voice muttering with house lights worked perfectly today, some of them even Shhhhing the others to listen to her' (22 October 1972, *NABS* 285). While the phrase 'worked perfectly today' suggests that it had not worked so well on other days, this part of the stage directions shows that audience perception did shape Beckett's conceptualization of his play from a very early stage in the genesis.

93 For more on *Not I* in the context of scientific experiment, see Salisbury (2008, 97).

'1. Premature birth' (ET3, 01r; 1973a, 6)

One of the key themes in Beckett's theatre is birth, which is often closely associated with death. In a Shakespeare play Beckett knew since his schooldays, Macbeth uses 'out' to refer to death, just after he has heard of Lady Macbeth's demise: 'Out, out, brief candle!' (V. 5. 23; see Van Hulle 2019b, 14).[94] In the opening phrase of the main monologue in *Not I*'s published text, Beckett, by contrast, uses 'out' to signify birth: '**out** ... into this world' (1973a, 6; *KLT* 85; see Van Hulle 2019b, 14). But the earlier drafts were more explicit: EM1 contains '~~**birth into the**~~ this ~~**world ...**~~' (01r), only changing to 'out' in ET5: '..~~**birth**~~ out..into this world..' (01r).

From the 'wombtomb' of his early prose to the image of 'giv[ing] birth astride of a grave' in *Godot* (*WfG* 86), the spaces of birth and death are never far apart in Beckett's work. The two are again proximate in the 1979 play *A Piece of Monologue*, which opens: 'Birth was the death of him' (*KLT* 117). But though 'birth' may be 'the rip word' according to the Speaker of *A Piece of Monologue* (*KLT* 121), neither birth nor death have finality for him, as is evident in his metatheatrical reference to performing this opening word 'Night after night the same. Birth' (*KLT* 119). Similarly, though Mouth does not repeat 'out' in precisely the same way in her text – the later version is '... tiny little thing ... **out before its time** ...' (1973a, 14; *KLT* 92) – there is a sense in which her tragic situation is linked to the fact that this story, having begun badly, is not easily ended.

That this was a premature birth is suggested by the fact that the baby has a low birthweight of '**five pounds**' (ET1, 01r). On ET2, this point is made more clearly, before being 'vaguened': '~~five pounds~~ ~~**premature**~~ before ~~her~~ its time' (01r). While the baby is '~~**small**~~ tiny' (EM1, 01), many of Beckett's changes in the first draft emphasized the difference between it and the '~~**vast**~~ ~~place~~' it occupies (EM1, 01r), increasing the sense that this figure does not fit into the world it inhabits.[95] This is something Beckett would emphasize in his later additions to pronunciation (see below).

94 I would like to thank Dirk Van Hulle for sharing the script of this paper with me. I follow the pagination on the script.

95 As outlined in chapter 1.1.1, there are two draft versions of the monologue's opening on EM1 (01r). As well as containing deletions within the body of

Other early edits alter the living environment of the newborn: in the first version, '~~in the **lowlands**~~' became ~~'on the coast'~~, recalling the coastal setting of the first 'Kilcool' draft, before being changed to '~~in the **downs**~~ **bog**' (EM1, 01). As the change from '~~**downs**~~' to '**bog**' shows, before she is even 'properly born' (see chapters 2.1.2 and 6.1.2), the world of Beckett's protagonist is getting worse and worse. Beckett would later publish a poem entitled 'The Downs', which gives a relatively romantic account of a couple walking the countryside together.[96] The opening stanza is representative:

> the downs
> summer days on the downs
> hand in hand
> one loving
> one loved
> back at night
> the hut (*CP* 207)

By contrast, 'bog' has much more negative connotations – unlike the word it replaced, you are unlikely to find this in the listings of a real estate brochure. Whereas 'downs' is associated with the landscape of southern and south-eastern England (*OED*b), 'bog' is often used to describe the peaty countryside of central and western Ireland, so we could read this change as Beckett bringing Mouth's story back closer to the country of his own birth.[97] But it is the pejorative sense that gained prominence as the passage was further edited: the 'hole in the bog' into which the baby has the misfortune of being born is described in the second draft version as '~~**small**~~' (think 'cosy', says the real estate agent), ~~**'remote'**~~ (think 'peaceful', they say, smiling), before becoming the unsellable **'godforsaken'** (EM1, 01r).

If we think of the colloquial sense of 'bog' as 'toilet' (*OED*b), we could also associate this change with Otto Rank's *Trauma of Birth*, in which the

the text, the entire first version is crossed out with a St Andrew's Cross and squiggles.

96 A manuscript of the poem exists which is dated 1977. The poem was first published in 1989 (*CP* 446).

97 To add to the archipelagic resonances, the 'lowlands', used in the first draft version, is the name of a region in Scotland.

prenatal stage is described in terms of being '*inter fæces et urinas*' (1929, 18), copied by Beckett in his Psychology Notes (TCD MS 10971/8/34). For it is here, in this 'godforsaken hole…in the bog', that Mouth has what Molloy would call her 'First taste of the shit' (ET2, 01r; *Mo* 13).[98] Keir Elam puts it plainly: 'As with Molloy, Mouth's begining [*sic*] is in her end' (1997, 176).

Following the discussion of the symbolic importance of faeces in Ernest Jones's *Papers on Psycho-analysis*, there is a description of a monologue by a man with 'flatus complex' which Beckett copied out in his notes:

> A man, habitually reticent in speech, cherished the ambition, largely carried out, of being able so to construct his clauses, on a very German model, as to expel all he might have to say in one massive but superbly finished sentence that could be flung out & the whole matter done with. (TCD MS 10971/8/19; see Jones 1923, 703)

Though Mouth's syntax is much more fragmentary, this passage has some similarities with her own speaking situation. As the Unnamable puts it when talking about defecation and wondering 'whether to fill up the holes or let them fill up of themselves, it's like shit, there we have it at last, there it is at last, the right word, one has only to seek, seek in vain, to be sure of finding in the end, it's a question of elimination' (*Un* 81).[99] In ET4, Beckett turned Mouth's 'godforsaken hole…in the bog' into a textual hole, leaving a gap in the narrative: '..godfor~~..~~^{sa}ken hole~~..in the bog..named – ..what?..what?..no.. no!..the bog..godforsaken hole in the bog..named~~ ^{called}..~~named~~ ^{called}..~~gone~~.. ~~^{called}~~ no matter..' (01r). In a text punctured by ellipses, this writing procedure recalls Beckett's determination to 'drill one hole after another' in the surface of language, as stated in his much-quoted letter to Axel Kaun (9 July 1937, *LSB I* 518). In ET5, Beckett created an information gap by removing the pejorative 'bog': '… godforsaken hole **called … called … no matter …**' (01r),

98 Molloy remembers that his mother 'brought me into the world, through the hole in her arse if my memory is correct' (*Mo* 13). 'Hole' also features as a descriptor of a townland in *Molloy*, though this time as a proper noun.

99 Beckett may also have been thinking of the Jones passage when writing of the constipated Pomeranian dog in *Molloy* (see O'Reilly, Van Hulle and Verhulst 2017, 149–50).

replacing the missing word with ellipses as he did when 'boring holes' in the textual surface of earlier plays like *En attendant Godot* (see Van Hulle and Verhulst 2017a, 221).[100] Such gaps activate the reader's interpretive process, performing a similar function to the darkness which envelops the stage in *Not I* and calls out for interpretation from the audience.

Unlike Jones's man with flatus complex, Mouth can never completely finish what she wants to say. Rather, like the Unnamable, she has to 'go on' repeating her speech from the 'rip word' onwards. The word 'birth' helped Beckett start Mouth's torrential narrative, but, as the subsequent text demonstrates, it fails to eliminate either her or her need to speak.

'Parents unknown' (ET3, 01r; 1973a, 6)

Another 'hole' in Mouth's story concerns the identity of the baby's parents, who disappear almost as soon as they are mentioned in the first draft version: she is born, we are told, '~~to parents unknown ... he having vanished~~ **~~into thin air months after into thin air no sooner done his devilish work~~** ~~and she similarly nine months later~~ **~~almost to the minute~~** ~~...~~' (EM1, 01r). Beckett's deletion of '**~~months after~~**' shortens the time period before the father's departure, with the mother making an equally hasty exit. From a psychoanalytic point of view, the little girl therefore does not develop relationships within the triangular family unit which much early twentieth-century analysis takes as its norm (see Freud 1933, 175–6), but is instead on her own from the start.

The father's '**~~devilish work~~**' suggests an infernal aspect to his role in procreation, but Beckett 'undid' this satanic sex act in ET2, replacing it with a more mundane physical action: '...no sooner ~~done~~...~~his devilish work~~ **~~pulled~~ buttoned up his trousers**...' (01r), reverting to the more alliterative **'breeches'** in ET3 (01r). While this edit emphasizes the laborious nature of the paternal getaway, Beckett must have realized that a nine-month period between conception and delivery would not constitute a premature birth. So, he shortened the time before the mother's flight: '...and she similarly...**~~nine~~** **eight** months later almost ~~t t~~ to the minute...' (ET2, 01r). While the girl is therefore without parents, it does not necessarily mean she is without

100 Van Hulle and Verhulst use the verb 'to bore' when translating the verb 'bohren' in Beckett's letter to Kaun (*LSB I* 514; see also *Dis* 172).

human contact, as emphasized on the same typescript, where Beckett added the fact that the parents were not only 'unknown' but **'unheard of'** (ET2, 01r). As well as indicating that the parents never came back, this change implies another listener who hears whatever information is related about the parents, suggesting more strongly a social group where the family is discussed.

'No love at any time' (ET3, 01r; 1973a, 6)

Karin Stephen's *Wish to Fall Ill* contains a chapter entitled 'Infantile Pleasure-seeking by the Mouth', which is given the running title 'The Mouth Stage' in the text. When reading this chapter, Beckett noted: 'For babies, living in terms of their mouths, the outside world must seem a mouth-world, &, for the angry baby, a biting world' (TCD MS 10971/7/1; see Stephen 1933, 102). However, there are some important differences between Beckett's theatrical 'mouth-world' and the role the mouth plays in Stephen's psycho-analytic work. Elsewhere in the same chapter, Stephen argues: 'In addition to trying to survive, living beings also try to get pleasure' (1933, 94). She goes on to discuss breast-feeding as 'the starting-point of human love' (95), passages from which Beckett took the following notes: 'The act of suckling is the baby's first great physical pleasure, the breast his first love-object' (TCD MS 10971/7/1). But the girl of whom Mouth speaks does not entirely fit such a paradigm, deprived as she is from day one of love and human contact from her biological parents: '... so no love ... spared that ... **no love such as normally vented on the ... speechless infant** ... in the home ...' (1973a, 6; *KLT* 85). Reflecting on his first (and last) encounter with love, the narrator of *Premier amour* makes the point that love is not beholden to one's will: 'Mais l'amour, cela ne se commande pas' (Beckett 2012c, 56). However, even if it is arbitrary, love is usually seen as a positive thing, as in the first verb used to describe it in the *Not I* drafts. In the first draft version, love is '~~**lavished on the newborn**~~' (EM1, 01r), then '**showered**' on her (EM1, 01r), but this later becomes the biblical **'visited'** – suggesting the onset of some kind of retribution from which this particular girl has been '**spared**' (ET4, 01r). In ET5, things get worse for the child, with love being ~~**'inflicted'**~~, before **'vented'** is introduced as an open variant for 'visited' (ET5, 01r). The 'newborn' has meantime (in the second draft version) become a '**speechless** infant'

(EM1, 01r), emphasizing its lack of ability to protest against this imposition of parental affection. In light of these textual changes, one gets the feeling that the small girl in Mouth's story may well be better off without love.

Beckett translated the closing line of *Premier amour* non-literally in *First Love*: 'But there it is, either you love or you don't' (*ECEF* 80). As his title heading for this lexia suggests, the early lack of love continues through this woman's life, making it a 'typical affair' in Mouth's estimation (ET4, 01r).

'At age of 70 in a field picking cowslips suddenly finds herself in the dark'
(ET3, 01r; 1973a, 6–7)

As mentioned in chapter 2.2.1, Beckett was annoyed by Jessica Tandy's questions regarding what happened to the woman in the field. While the manuscripts do not answer such questions, Beckett's earliest version does give a bit more information on the play's first 'life scene':

> ~~till coming up to sixty this ... what? ... sixty-five? ... my God ... coming up to 65 ...~~ ~~**walking in a field with**~~ ~~her~~ my ~~**youngest grandchild**~~ ~~looking~~ searching ~~for cowslips to make a ball ...~~ ~~**when suddenly all went out**~~ ~~... all that~~ early ~~April morning light ... and~~ ~~**she**~~ ~~I found~~ ~~**her**~~my~~self in the dark ...~~ (EM1, 01r)

As well as evoking a change in lighting that happens at the flick of a switch (see chapter 2.2.1), this passage contains an interesting extra detail in the form of the '~~**grandchild**~~', indicating that, in spite of the lack of love, the woman has herself given birth to another, and that this pattern has continued on into the next generation.

The most striking change here is the shift from third to first person, indicating that the figure of whom Mouth speaks is in fact herself. Van Hulle points to Beckett's notetaking from a section of Max Nordau's *Degeneration* in which Nordau argues that the 'I' needs the '"not-I", of an external world' in order to constitute itself (Nordau qtd. in Van Hulle 2008, 134).[101] But unlike

101 Beckett came across a similar conception of the self when reading Aldous Huxley's *Doors of Perception*, though he was less than enthusiastic about it: 'Read the Huxley without much pleasure. Mind-at-large and the Divine not-self of Flannel Bags too much for me' (Beckett to Barbara Bray,

the self which opposes itself to the non-self, Van Hulle argues that from a compositional perspective, 'Beckett first needed an "I" in order to be able to decompose it and compose *Not I*' (2008, 134). As Nixon has shown, Beckett spent quite a lot of energy in the early part of his career as he 'learnt to say "I"' (2011, 35). For Mouth, the struggle is rather *not* to 'say I', as the imperative on the first page of *The Unnamable* has it (*Un* 1). That Beckett chose to negate this 'I' in the second version shows how central this self-decomposition was to his process of composition: '... and ~~she was~~ she ~~in~~ found herself in the **... what? ... I? ... no ... no! ... she ...** found herself in the dark ...' (EM1, 01r). In ET2, the merest suggestion of an 'I', even as interrogative, was deleted: '**...what?...~~I?~~** who?...what? **...no...~~no~~** NO**!...she**' (01r).[102] Then the play does become a 'not-I' work, with the phrase itself first appearing as the title on ET4. As Gontarski puts it, Beckett used the narrative hesitation between first- and third-person voices in order to construct 'the play's principal conflict' (1985, 145). Interestingly, this pronominal conflict also maps onto Beckett's own long effort to 'say I' in his own work, an effort which quickly turns focus onto saying 'not I'. By ET4, the first-person pronoun had been thoroughly decomposed and does not appear in the body of the text. Instead, it is violently rejected by Mouth each time it is suggested by a voice we cannot hear.

'2. No feeling apart from buzzing in her head and awareness of a ray of light' (ET3, 01r; 1973a, 7)

This passage is the first to mention Mouth's 'brain', referred to as a '~~mind~~' in the first draft version, before being given the more physiological term in the second draft version (EM1, 01r), thus moving the text closer to the description of a mind as machine. Interestingly, however, as well as appearing on his typewritten synopsis (ET8; see Fig. 10), the word 'mind' is used when Beckett outlines the separation between Mouth and her mind in a letter to Schneider. Referencing a previous meeting at which the US

27 August 1959, *LSB III* 239). While on mescaline, Huxley is repeatedly fascinated by his flannel trousers (1990).

102 On the supposition that Mouth is speaking of herself, this analysis will henceforth refer to 'her' even when she references herself in the third person.

director remembers him 'distinguishing between the VOICE and the MOUTH' (30 September 1972, *NABS* 280), Beckett states:

> If I made a distinction it can only have been between mind & voice, not between mouth & voice. Her speech a purely buccal phenomenon without mental control or understanding, only half heard. Function running away with organ. The only stage apprehension of text is Auditor's. (16 October 1972, *LSB IV* 311)

While Beckett favoured 'brain' over 'mind' in the text of *Not I*, he still maintained the concept of 'mind' in his later analyses of the play, even when emphasizing the embodied nature of the breakdown of Mouth's subjectivity as in this letter.

Not I's brain/mind perceives both aurally and visually: '~~the **buzzing** in her [my] ears~~ [...] ~~and a ray of light~~' (EM1, 01r), with the former possibly being a reference to William James's 'big blooming **buzzing** confusion', a phrase Beckett noted when reading Woodworth's account of Gestalt psychology and put into the mouth of Neary in *Murphy*:

> 'Murphy, all life is figure and ground.'
> 'But a wandering to find home', said Murphy.
> 'The face', said Neary, 'or system of faces, against **the big blooming buzzing confusion**.' (*Mu* 4; see also 153)

In Woodworth, James's concept is explicitly opposed to the Gestalt concept of figure and ground:

> The figure is typically compact, but at any rate it appears as having form and outline, while the background appears like unlimited space. The figure is more apt to attract attention than the ground. When the baby first opens his eyes upon the world, while he certainly does not see a world of objects such as adults know and see, *he may not, on the other hand, see a mere chaos of miscellaneous points, a 'big, blooming, buzzing confusion', as James thought*. (Woodworth 1931, 107; emphasis added)

Like Woodworth's baby, Mouth struggles to fully interpret information in her sensory field. In this, she is not alone among Beckett's characters. Malone complains

> that the noises of the world, so various in themselves and which I used to be so clever at distinguishing from one another, had been dinning at me for so long, always the same old noises, as gradually to have merged into a single noise, so that all I heard was one vast continuous **buzzing**. (*MD* 33)

Decomposition is for Malone an 'analytical activity' (Van Hulle 2008, 172), separating out the parts of his sound-world in order to make sense of them. In this regard, Mouth has a little more success in decomposing the 'ray of light [which] came and went ... came and went ... such as the moon might cast ...' (1973a, 7; *KLT* 86). The early draft verb '**shed**' (EM1, 01r; ET1, 01r), like its later counterpart '**cast**', suggests the cognitive illumination that is so elusive for Mouth. At the same time, the simile of the moon may be seen to stand as a metatheatrical reference to the theatrical spotlight the audience sees illuminating the speaking protagonist.[103]

Beckett's published conversation with Tom Driver indicates that the Irish author associated the above concept more broadly with the attempt of the artist to give form to what he called 'the mess'. The first instances of direct speech by Beckett come as Driver introduces this topic: 'His talk turns to what he calls "the mess", or sometimes "this buzzing confusion"' (Driver 2005, 242). Having differentiated this 'mess' from the existentialism associated with Heidegger and Sartre (see chapter 2.1.2), Beckett is challenged by Driver about the relationship between this description of chaos and his theatre work. Beckett's stage plays to date – *Godot*, *Endgame* and *Krapp's Last Tape* – are, after all, highly formalized, Driver argues. It is in Beckett's reply that he outlines some of his best-known statements on aesthetic form:

103 Beckett had used a non-naturalistic rising of the moon in *Godot* to highlight the staged nature of the action, a technique that can be traced as far back as to the concluding section of 'Dante and the Lobster': 'Let us call it Winter, that dusk may fall now and a moon rise' (*MPTK* 13).

> What I am saying does not mean that there will henceforth be no form in art. It only means that there will be new form, and that this form will be of such a type that it admits the chaos and does not try to say that the chaos is really something else. The form and the chaos remain separate. The latter is not reduced to the former. That is why the form itself becomes a preoccupation, because it exists as a problem separate from the material it accommodates. To find a form that accommodates the mess, that is the task of the artist now. (Driver 2005, 243)

Beckett's repetition of 'chaos' further ties this statement to his creative use of James's concept: the word appears in the above passage from Woodworth and in the following description of Celia in *Murphy*, where it is associated with James's 'big, blooming, buzzing confusion': 'The beloved features emerging from **chaos** were the face against the **big blooming buzzing confusion** of which Neary had spoken so highly' (*Mu* 21).[104] Based on Driver's notes, we can see that the psychological image of a 'buzzing confusion' gave Beckett ways of thinking about aesthetic form into the 1960s. And Driver's line of argument about formal rigour could be carried further regarding Beckett's later theatre, which is even more formally defined than his early plays. *Not I* – despite its apparently chaotic narrative – is a case in point, divided as it is by Mouth's five renunciations of the first-person pronoun. In this play, we see Beckett trying to accommodate 'the mess' of 'what is in front of him', with Mouth's experience of her own monologue corresponding to the playwright's comments on this chaos: 'it invades our experience at every moment. It is there and it must be allowed in' (Driver 2005, 242–3). Moreover, the very process of giving shape to chaos is thematized in Mouth's reference to the 'buzzing' that she hears, which echoes Beckett's statements to Driver on 'the mess'.

It is notable that the buzzing is described from the very outset as '~~so~~ **~~called~~**' (EM1, 01). So, there must exist some kind of outside authority which has bestowed this name on what Mouth hears. What the phrase '~~so~~ **~~called~~**' further suggests is a narrative distance between Beckett's protagonist and the psychological terms used in the play. This recalls the author's own

104 Indeed, 'chaos' is a key word in *Murphy*, where it is associated via etymology with the gas which kills the eponymous protagonist (*Mu* 110, 158).

ironic attitude towards the psychological and psychoanalytic terminology he took notes on in the 1930s (see Introduction). While the highly sensory description of Mouth's brain function shows Beckett's continuing interest in the physiological aspects of thought, he did not absorb psychological and psychoanalytic terminology uncritically. Evidently, neither does Mouth.

'Mind still active in a way' (ET3, 01r; 1973a, 7)

Beckett again favours 'brain' over 'mind' in this lexia: though the first version mentions a '**~~mind~~**',[105] this was soon replaced with '**brain**' in the second version (EM1, 01r) and stayed like this up to and including the published text (1973a, 7; *KLT* 86).[106] The word 'mind' appears only once in the published text, as part of a phrase where 'brain' would be unusual: '**flashed** through her **mind**' (1973a, 7; *KLT* 86). This preference for 'brain' over 'mind' in the monologue emphasizes the focus on the mechanics of thought in *Not I*, while the use of '**flashed**' echoes modernist descriptions of the mind, such as Virginia Woolf's account of Joyce's fiction: 'he is concerned at all costs to reveal the flickerings of that innermost flame which flashes its messages through the brain' (1966, 107). According to Anne Atik, Beckett never liked to discuss Woolf (2001, 91), but this part of Mouth's monologue does tap into some of the same imagery she used. In stark contrast to the epiphanic resonances of Woolf's text, Mouth's mind stays in the dark, unable to build on flashes of thought.

From early on in the drafting process, Beckett used one of his favourite words, 'still', to portray a mind still active: 'but the brain **still** ... in a way ...' (EM1, 01r). He may have been thinking here of the short prose text *Still*, which he wrote while composing *Not I*. Mental activity became even more lively in ET3, paradoxically through the repetition of a word implying stasis: 'but the ~~barin~~ brain **still**···still...in a way...' (01r). The word 'active' is not itself mentioned; instead, a description of Mouth's thoughts displays her ongoing mental activity. Her 'first thought' derives from her religious upbringing, '... brought up as she had been to believe (<u>laugh</u>)...in **a merciful (<u>laugh</u>)...God (<u>laugh</u>)...**' (ET1, 01r), foreshadowing the importance of religious material later in the text. In ET2, some important social context was added, in a

105 The word 'mind' put an end to Beckett's first draft version on EM1.
106 Beckett also uses '<u>brain</u>' in his handwritten analysis (EM2, 01r).

notable example of Beckett 'adding and redoing' as part of his predominant compositional method of 'undoing' (Van Hulle and Weller 2018, 243; Gontarski 1985): 'brought up as she had been to believe (laugh)...with the other waifs (laugh)...in a ~~merciful (laugh)~~ merciful (laugh)...God (laugh)...' (ET2, 01r). The added mention of 'waifs' suggests Mouth was brought up in an orphanage, evidently a religious one, though neither the institution nor the religious denomination is named.[107]

'First thought: she is being punished for her sins' (ET3, 01r; 1973a, 7)

The religious shaping of Mouth's mind is evident in her immediate association of suffering with sin. This association was also made immediately by her author, in the first draft version: 'first thought was ... **she was being punished ... for her sins ...** ~~x~~ a number of which then ... further proof if proof were needed ... flashed through her mind ...' (EM1, 01r). However, he then decided to introduce another gap, this time temporal, between Mouth's experience in the field and this 'first thought', suggesting a long life without significant mental activity. The text in bold was introduced in ET4: 'first thought was..**oh long after!..**flash in the dark...she was being punished..for her sins..' (01r).

In ET1, Beckett thought about replacing '**sins**' with ~~'iniquities'~~, possibly drawing on the correlation of the two in Psalm 51: 'Wash me thoroughly from mine iniquity, and cleanse me from my sin. [...] Hide thy face from my sins, and blot out all mine iniquities' (Psalms 51:2, 51:9).[108] However, he wrote 'stet' in the left margin to indicate that 'sins' should stay (ET1, 01r). If we bear in mind the harsh treatment often meted out to single mothers and their children, the further association of the two words in Psalm 51 may shed light on Mouth's predicament, particularly given the earlier draft description of her 'devilish' father: 'Behold, I was shapen in iniquity; and in sin did my mother conceive me' (Psalms 51:5). As Katharine Worth points out, God 'is more likely to mean punishment' than love in *Not I* (1986, 171) and this is a theme we can see developed throughout the drafting process.

107 For an analysis of Mouth's situation in light of the coercive confinement of Irish women in Magdalene Laundries, see McTighe (2017).

108 The Psalms are also a central component of *The Book of Common Prayer*, which Beckett was very familiar with (see chapter 6.1.2).

From ET2 onwards, thought and sin both 'flash' through Mouth's mind (01r), repeating the earlier motif of thought as the illumination of a darkened space, echoing again modernist images of the mind. Furthermore, this mechanistic version of the mind recalls Murphy's Cartesian Theatre of memories, in a novel which can be read as a reaction against the 'high' modernism of Joyce and Woolf. In a deeply cinematographic scene, Murphy's memories present themselves 'as though reeled upward off a spool level with his throat' (*Mu* 157). Building on Daniel Dennett's critique of the concept of a Cartesian Theatre (see Introduction), we might term this a Cartesian Movie Theatre, Dennett's principle of an outer image being presented to an inner observer remaining the same. The internal mental showreel of Mouth's sins is not likely to bring enlightenment, but is instead offered by the self to itself as 'further proof if proof were needed' of her suffering being a form of punishment (EM1, 01r). When is proof not needed? Only, presumably, when one is already convinced of guilt. This phrase thus further adds to the idea of a strict social order – now internalized – condemning Mouth from birth.

'Dismissed as she realises she is not suffering' (ET3, 01r–02r; 1973a, 7–8)

The thought that Mouth is being punished for sinning is 'then dismissed' (1973a, 7; *KLT* 86). In the first draft of this sentence, Beckett added the supralinear addition 'then dismissed as foolish' (EM1, 02r), this last word marking Beckett's interest in the long history of writing mental disorder, such as his reading of Robert Burton's *Anatomy of Melancholy*, which states that 'Folly, melancholy, madness, are but one disease' (1938, 31).[109] Beckett even began his final poem *what is the word* with this historically loaded concept:

> folly –

109 Beckett first read Burton's *Anatomy* in the early 1930s and returned to it in the late 1930s, taking notes on both occasions. There is a three-volume edition preserved in Beckett's library, with annotations that may or may not be his: https://www.beckettarchive.org/library/BUR-ANA-1.html; https://www.beckettarchive.org/library/BUR-ANA-2.html; https://www.beckettarchive.org/library/BUR-ANA-3.html. See Van Hulle and Nixon (2013, 119–20).

folly for to –
for to –
what is the word – (*CP* 228)

The poem continues building a sentence from 'folly', arriving in the final lines at

folly for to need to seem to glimpse afaint afar away over there
what –
what –
what is the word –

what is the word (*CP* 229)

While the poem may not find what the word is (or may only end up finding that 'what' is that word), it is notable that its speaker, like Mouth, also labels the search for sense as foolish.

Whether it is the mad Mr Endon in *Murphy* or W in *Rockaby*, 'gone off her head' (*KLT* 132), Mouth here links herself with a series of Beckettian fools. But her ability to self-reflect, to separate her 'foolish' thought from the implied reason of her narrative, would seem to set Mouth apart from these other figures. Only a fool would think this suffering was punishment; Mouth here wants us to believe she is not that foolish. However, further reasoning shows the idea of punishment 'was perhaps not so **foolish** ... after all ...' (EM1, 01r). For all it takes to be punished is for suffering to be willed from without. As Mouth puts it: '... unless of course ... she was **meant** to be suffering ... **thought** to be suffering ... just as so often ... in the past ... when clearly **meant** to be having pleasure ... she was in fact ... having none whatsoever ...' (EM1, 01r). This passage shows similarities to experiments set up to observe psychological behaviour, with the underlined words highlighting the fact that Mouth is aware that she is being observed by another subject. If, as Beckett noted from Woodworth, 'Introspection is subjective observation' (TCD MS 10971/7/7; see Woodworth 1931, 19), then Mouth's introspection here allows her to appreciate the significance of punishment being willed from without.

Having first dismissed the idea that she was being punished 'for some sin or other' as 'foolish', Mouth then revises this revision. The logic seems to be here that if someone is trying to punish Mouth – even if that punishment is not experienced as suffering – then it does indeed make sense to think of this as punishment. However, in a handwritten addition to EM1, Beckett decided to have Mouth undermine both sides of her own argument by suggesting that such thoughts are lacking in value: 'so on ... all that ...' (01r). In ET4, Beckett strengthened this, adding the phrase '**vain reasonings**' to the end of this passage (02r), echoing St Paul's description of the unrighteous in his letter to the Romans: 'because that, knowing God, they glorified him not as God, neither gave thanks; but became vain in their reasonings, and their senseless heart was darkened. Professing themselves to be wise, they became fools' (1:21). Mouth brings such biblical wrath upon her own foolish self.

'Second thought: perhaps she should groan (to please tormentor)' (ET3, 02r; 1973a, 8–9)

Mouth's second thought is, like her first, dismissed, this time as 'very childish' (EM1, 02r), which becomes 'foolish' in ET3: 'till another thought...sudden flash...oh long ag^f^ter...very ~~**childish**~~ foolish really' (02r). This substitution calls to mind a much earlier childish Beckettian fool, the 'Petit Sot' [little fool], subject of 21 short poems and one longer poem entitled 'les joues rouges' (written 1938–9).[110] While Mouth tries to refute her first-person pronoun, the 'Petit Sot' collection is unusual in that 16 of the poems start with the first-person pronoun and four – very unusually for Beckett's poetry – open with the phrase 'je suis' [I am] (UoR MS 5479: 258–63).[111] While studying Beckett's *Not I* drafts may encourage us to see parallels between the 'Petit Sot' and Mouth's self-reproach for her '~~**childish**~~ foolish' thought, there is a difference between the two in that Mouth vigorously refuses to 'say I'. While Beckett undid the first-person pronoun in his poetic oeuvre by simply

110 The authorship of these poems has been contested. They were initially included in an appendix to Beckett's *Collected Poems* which the editors were then obliged to omit before the book went to press (see Pilling 2015; Van Hulle and Verhulst 2017c).

111 The only other published Beckett poem which starts with 'je suis' is 'je suis ce cours de sable qui glisse' (1948), which he translated as 'my way is in the sand flowing' (*CP* 118).

removing any mention of it in the poems composed following the 'Six Poèmes', written, according to their author, between 1947 and 1949 (*CP* 400), Mouth's assault on the first-person pronoun follows the poetics of *The Unnamable* in that it undermines the speaking self as it is being spoken.

Mouth's second description of the buzzing she hears develops the mechanistic version of the mind from earlier in the text: '... all the time the buzzing ... so-called ... in the ears ... though of course actually ... not in the ears at all ... in the skull ... **dull roar in the skull** ...' (1973a, 8; *KLT* 87). Along with this buzzing comes the previously mentioned ray of light:

> ... and ~~the ray~~ all the time this beam or ray ... as before ... **like from a moon** ... but ~~**no doubt**~~ **perhaps** not ... ~~no doubt~~ perhaps all part of the wish to ... torment ... (EM1, 02r)

Beckett here uses '**perhaps**', which he described as the 'key word' of his dramatic work (see chapter 6.1.2). In instances of what Van Hulle and Weller, as part of their analysis of Beckett's translation of *L'Innommable*, call 'pejoration' (or 'worsening'), whereby revisions 'are often characterized by a preference for words with greater pejorative force' (2014, 209), this was then changed to '**no doubt**' on ET1 (02r) before becoming the more certain '**certainly not**' in Addendum D on EM1. In this same addendum, Beckett strengthened the metatheatrical aspects of the light: '... **always the same spot** ... now bright ... now ~~veiled~~ shrouded ... but **always the same spot** ... as no moon could ... no ... no moon ...' (EM1, 04v). This '**same spot**' may be the one we see before us in the theatre. The idea that this spot plays a role in Mouth's suffering, that it is 'just all part of the ~~the~~ same wish to...torment...' (ET3, 02r), suggests a link to the inquisitorial spotlight of *Play*, with the difference being that the 'torment' in *Not I* may be self-imposed.

The observed–observer relationship again comes to the fore when Mouth eventually gets round to describing the 'other thought' with which this lexia opens: '... then this other thought ... very childish really but so like her ... that she might do well to ... groan now and then ... (**writhe she could not**) ... as though in actual ... ~~pain ... excruciating ...~~ agony ...' (EM1, 02r). While we, like Mouth, may not know 'what position she was in' (1973a, 7; *KLT* 86), the phrase in parentheses does confirm that there was something restricting her movement, thus restricting the ways in which she could respond to the outside stimuli.

'Failure to utter a sound' (ET3, 02r; 1973a, 9)

On his handwritten analysis, Beckett wrote a note to 'amplify' Mouth's 'failure to simulate suffering (groan)' (EM2, 01r).[112] The next lexia does just that. The first version suggests Mouth could not deceive her tormentor by performing a false response: 'but could not bring herself ... to as much as try ... some flaw ~~thing~~ in her ~~makeup~~ make-up ... incapable of deceit ...' (EM1, 01r). The text which constitutes Addendum E suggests instead a breakdown in the sensory system:

> or the machine more likely ... so disconnected ... never got the message ... or could not respond ... like numbed ... ~~**paralysed**~~ ... could not make the sound ... not a sound ... no calling for help ... ~~no sound at all ... all dead still silent as the grave ...~~ for example ... should she feel inclined ... ~~xxx at ... no ... all silent as the grave ...~~ call ... then listen ... (~~silence~~ pause) call again ... listen again (~~silence~~ pause) ... no ... all silent as the grave ... (EM1, 04v)

The deletion of the word '~~**paralysed**~~' removes a link with the Joycean word 'paralysis', which, in his short story 'The Sisters', evokes general paralysis of the insane (i.e., syphilis) and hence a kind of moral decay (Joyce 2004, 231, 233). In *Not I*, the word's removal suggests that the sources of Mouth's stillness are psychological rather than physical.[113] But the description of Mouth's sensory system as a 'machine' draws strongly on the idea that the mind can be materially explained, with the phrase 'call again' even suggesting some kind of telephonic system.[114] This was replaced in ET4 by a more dramatic action, first mentioned, then enacted by the actor

112 The underlining is in red ink.

113 Beckett also marked 'numbed' with a (now) pink circle on ET5 (02r), suggesting that he may have considered deleting it too. However, the term remained in subsequent drafts.

114 Beckett also includes a telephone conversation in *Rough for Radio I*, which he returned to in the summer of 1973 having first worked on it over a decade earlier (Pilling 2006, 26). This is an idea also briefly mentioned before being

playing Mouth: '..should she feel so inclined..**scream**..(screams)..then listen.. (pause silence)..**scream again**..(screams again)..listen again..(~~pause~~ silence)..no.. spared that..' (02r).

Beckett's notes on Purposivism – a form of psychology which emphasized the importance of motives in human behaviour – critique the behaviourist idea of the mind as a machine. The latter group argued:

> The duty of a behaviorist is to describe behavior in exactly the same way as the physicist describes the movement of a machine. … This human machine behaves in a certain way because environmental stimulation has forced him to do so. (Z. Y. Kuo, qtd. in Woodworth 1931, 183; ellipsis in original)

By contrast, the purposivists claimed: 'The instincts are not acquired by the individual but handed down to him by heredity. They are the original springs of all his activity. Without them, his intellectual and motor machinery would be like a factory with the power cut off' (Woodwoorth 1931, 189). Beckett duly noted that the mind, for purposivists, 'cannot be mechanistically explained or resolved into mechanistic sequences' (TCD MS 10971/7/17; see Woodworth 1931, 200). But his use of the concept of mind-as-machine in *Not I* reflects a behaviourist bent to Mouth's narrative. By using the concept in this way, Beckett again demonstrates he is not simply absorbing the psychological images he took notes on into his work, but rather adapting them for theatrical effect.

deleted in an early draft of *Cascando*: '~~On me le téléphone~~' (HTC MS THR 70/2, 02r).

'All silent but for the buzzing' (ET3, 02r; 1973a, 9)

Silence is never the same from one instant to the next. The same is true of Beckett's composition of silence in his text. It was referred to as '**dead silence**' in early drafts (EM1, 03r; ET2, 02r; ET3, 02r), before being changed to '**all silent as the grave**' in ET4 (02r) to correspond with the description of silence elsewhere in that draft.[115] The Shakespearean resonances of this phrase are dealt with below.

'Motionless but for eyes opening and shutting' (ET3, 02r; 1973a, 9)

Heightening the sense that Mouth's self-observation is coloured by the terminology that others use to describe her, the text mentions an anonymous 'they', harking back to the third-person plural pronoun which oppresses the first-person narrators of Beckett's postwar novellas and three novels:

> no part of her moving ... ~~but the eyelids ... presumably ...~~ that she could feel ... only the eyelids ... presumably ... now & then ... to ~~keep out~~ rest from the light ... ~~little~~ faint though it was ... **reflex they call it** ... no feeling ~~at all~~ ... of any kind ... but the lids ... even in real life ... who feels them? ... opening ... ~~closing~~ shutting ... all that moisture ... (EM1, 03r)

Pointing to Beckett's notes on the role of the conditioned reflex in Behaviourism (TCD MS 10971/7/8–10971/7/10), Rina Kim notes that Mouth 'uses the word "reflex" in a self-conscious way to indicate the body's automatic response' (2016, 157). The trailing phrase 'reflex **they call it**' again shows Mouth filtering this scientific vocabulary. Mouth is not endorsing uncritically the Behaviourist description of her physical condition; she is saying that others would describe her blinking in this way, but that she might not. Just as Beckett himself did not unquestioningly absorb

115 Beckett used a similar phrase in Ada's description of the sea in *Embers*, another play in which memory features prominently: 'Underneath all is **as quiet as the grave**' (*ATF* 44).

psychological and psychoanalytic terminology, here he shows his character again putting a distance between herself and such language.

Another notable aspect of this lexia is a paring down of the text: ‘even **at the** best of times’ (ET2, 02r) becomes ‘even best of times’ (ET5, 02r); ‘**to** ~~**keep out**~~ rest from the light’ (EM1, 03r) becomes ‘**to rest her** from the light’ (ET2, 02r), before the preposition is deleted and the verb changed: ‘~~**to**~~ **shut** out the light’ (ET3, 02r). Even the two-syllable ‘**only** the eyelids’ (ET4, 02r) is reduced to single-syllable ‘**just** the eyelids’ (ET5, 02r), making the phrase quicker in delivery. Beckett’s practice as a poet made him acutely aware of the rhythmic weight of syllables and he paid close attention to syllable length in his prose works too, even numbering the syllables in the ‘Fancy ~~Dead~~ Dying’ Notebook (1964–5):

> 1 2 3 4 5 6 7 8 9 10 11 12 13 14 15
> Tant de syllabes, tant de virgules, ne pas trop oublier (TCD MS 11223, 04v)[116]

With this in mind, we might see these edits in *Not I* as forms of ‘verbal’ and ‘syllabic undoing’, stripping back the words and syllables of the text in an analogous manner to how other details are stripped away. In the case of syllabic reduction, Beckett also makes the text easier to deliver in performance, something which enhances the sense of a verbal ‘stream’ issuing from Mouth.

‘Mind questions this in view of life scene~~1~~ 1 9(field)’ (ET3, 02r; 1973a, 9–10)

Mouth’s return to the first ‘life scene’ of the play is given a Shakespearean dimension by a marginal note on one of Beckett’s typescripts. In the first draft, Mouth is described ‘fixing with her eye ... **a distant cowslip** ... ~~x~~ as she hastened towards it ...’ (EM, 03r). In ET3, Beckett tried some alternatives: ‘...a distant ~~cowslip~~ ~~flower bloom fxxx~~ bell (in a cowslip bell I lie)...as she hastened towards it...’ (02r). Having first written the words ‘~~flower~~’ and ‘~~bloom~~’, it is hard not to imagine Joyce’s *Ulysses* coming to Beckett’s mind here, specifically the character Leopold Bloom and his penname Henry Flower. But it is another

116 Material in this notebook was used in the genesis of the prose works *Faux départs*, *Imagination morte imaginez* and *All Strange Away*.

writer who influenced the change from '~~cowslip~~' to the less specific 'bell'. In the margin, Beckett wrote a line from one of his most frequently alluded to Shakespeare plays, *The Tempest*, which he had read as a Senior Freshman in Trinity College (Pilling 2006, 9; Gunn 2012, 151). Beckett takes the line 'in a cowslip bell I lie' from Ariel's song of impending freedom, sung in the final act when Ariel is promised by his master Prospero that he will be freed from servitude:

> ARIEL [*Sings and helps to attire him.*]
> Where the bee sucks, there suck I,
> In a cowslip's bell I lie;
> There I couch when owls do cry.
> On the bat's back I do fly
> After summer merrily.
> Merrily, merrily, shall I live now,
> Under the blossom that hangs on the bough. (V. 1. 87–94)

For Worth, Beckett's allusion to Ariel's song 'suggests that the possibility of freedom is always there, even if in the confines of the play Mouth cannot win an Ariel-like release' (1986, 173). But the subject of Mouth's story is not an Ariel-like spirit. If anything, the figure she speaks of is closer to Ariel's former tormentor, the witch Sycorax, whom Prospero repeatedly describes as a 'hag', a word Mouth also uses to describe herself (1973a, 12; *KLT* 90; see below).[117] So, Beckett's notation of this Shakespearean intertext in his manuscripts is not an interpretive key which will tell us exactly what happened on that April morning, but an intertextual echo which may set other bells ringing elsewhere in the text. In other words, it is a text dealing with memory which may in turn trigger other textual memories.

In the nature-laden images of his song, Ariel presumably remembers his freedom before captivity with Prospero and, before that, with Sycorax. So, maybe it is no coincidence that Beckett thought of this passage when Mouth recounts a story of how it was before it all went dark. However, his textual memory seems not to have been entirely accurate in this instance. Neither edition of Shakespeare's *Works* preserved in Beckett's

117 In the French translation, Beckett made this link to witchcraft clear by translating 'hag' as 'sorcière' (1975b, 18).

library have Ariel's song marked.[118] What is more, both these editions have the standard 'cowslip's bell', rather than the 'cowslip bell' of Beckett's typescript note (Shakespeare 1896, 19; Shakespeare 1957, 20).[119] This error suggests that Beckett was recalling the phrase from memory, not copying it from an edition.[120]

Shakespeare was clearly on Beckett's mind as he composed this lexia, as can be seen in another intertextual allusion which follows shortly after. In the first draft, Mouth's 'still' mental process was described as '~~**dead silent** thought~~'. But this phrase was then struck out and replaced by 'thought **silent as the grave**' (EM1, 03r). In ET3, the same typescript in which Beckett made the note on Ariel's 'cowslip bell', this became '**sweet** silent as the grave' (02r). The Shakespearean intertextual reference in this phrase is made explicit in Beckett's interactions with his German translators, Elmar and Erika Tophoven. When Beckett received the Tophovens' draft translation, he felt it needed some work: 'Received Tophoven's [*sic*] text of Not I [*sic*] a few minutes before leaving for Orly. Just finished revising it. A few mistakes and little fire' (Beckett to Barbara Bray, 12 March 1973, *LSB IV* 329). To help out the Tophovens, Beckett made a list of corrections and suggestions, each phrase of the text receiving a number to which these notes were keyed. One such suggestion was another intertextual reference to Shakespeare, this time to Sonnet 30:

> 276 Shakespeare: sonnet commence:
> 'When to the sessions of sweet silent thought
> I summon up remembrance of things past..' (*Not I* folder, TA, loose leaf)[121]

118 https://www.beckettarchive.org/library/SHA-COM-1.html and https://www.beckettarchive.org/library/SHA-WOR.html.

119 The phrase appears in italics in the 1896 edition, as does the entire song.

120 Beckett also alters a quotation from *Hamlet* in 'Dante ... Bruno . Vico .. Joyce', suggesting this may have been a pattern in his recall of Shakespeare (see *Dis* 28). With many thanks to Pim Verhulst for bringing this to my attention. For another instance of Beckett quoting Shakespeare from memory, see Little (2020c, 155n4).

121 I would like to thank Pim Verhulst for sharing this information with me.

On a thematic level, it is interesting that this Shakespearean intertext, like Ariel's song, again features the theme of memory:

> When to the sessions of sweet silent thought
> I summon up remembrance of things past,
> I sigh the lack of many a thing I sought,
> And with old woes new wail my dear time's waste;
> Then can I drown an eye (unused to flow) (Sonnet 30, ll. 1–5)

Memory is here not 'involuntary', which is the most valuable aspect of Proust's 'remembrance of things past' according to Beckett's 1931 analysis of the writer (see *PTD* 14–15, 32), but rather involves an active 'summon[ing]' by the speaker. However, nor is this Proustian 'voluntary memory' as Beckett defines it: he associates this 'monochrome' form of memory with 'intelligence' and compares it to 'the application of a concordance to the Old Testament of the individual' (*PTD* 32). Instead, voluntary memory is for Shakespeare highly emotional, just as it is for Mouth when she tries to recall her past through narrative. Like the sonnet's speaker, Mouth is 'unused to flow', but the memories, once triggered, soon become overpowering.

Another image Beckett took from psychology is its description of thought in terms of depth, evident in a note in his 'Whoroscope' Notebook which is based on Sartre's *L'Imagination*: 'the geology of conscience – Cambrian experience, cainozoic judgements, etc.' (qtd. in Van Hulle and Nixon 2013, 210).[122] Van Hulle and Nixon quote a number of instances in Beckett's writing – in the *Watt* Notebooks, *The Unnamable* and *... but the clouds ...* – where such psychological images of depth are critiqued at the level of narrative (2013, 211). In the *Not I* drafts, the notion of thought containing chasms is introduced in the first version – '... so on it reasoned ... ~~**deeper & deeper**~~ **even deeper down** ... vain questionings ...' (EM1, 03r) – before being struck out in ET2, leaving instead the immediate association between reason and vanity that Beckett earlier took from St Paul's letter to the Romans: '...so on it reasoned...~~**deeper and deeper down**~~**...vain questionings**...' (02r). In this instance, digging into Beckett's compositional depths helps us better understand his development of Mouth's critique of

122 John Pilling points out that Beckett here uses 'conscience' in its French sense (2004, 46), where it means consciousness or awareness.

models of psychological depth, long associated with the work of Freudian psychoanalysis (see Jones 1955, 241–2).

'Hears a voice largely unintelligible' (ET3, 02r; 1973a, 10)

The first draft of this lexia highlights the text's 'autographic' aspect. H. Porter Abbott defines autography as a plurality of forms of self-writing, rather than just the narrative of one's own life (1996). Because of this proximity between the writing and the written self, the theme of autographic writing frequently reflects the compositional process behind it. In this way, autographic writing 'brings the document itself into focus' (Abbott qtd. in Van Hulle and Verhulst 2017b, 25), such as when an interruption in the narrative is mirrored in an interruption of the writing process: 'when suddenly she realized ... words were ~~coming ....~~ **~~WORDS WERE COMING! ...~~ what? ... I? ... ~~I realized? ...~~ no... NO! ... <u>she</u> ...** suddenly ~~she~~ realized ... words were coming ... WORDS WERE COMING!–'. However, this was '**a voice she did not recognize** ... at first ... it was ~~... suddenly she realized ... words were coming~~ so long ... since she had uttered' (EM1, 03r). In other words, the speaker is suddenly active after a long silence, something which is also a key theme in *That Time* (see chapter 4.1.2). On ET2, the interruption is given more detail: 'what?...~~I?~~ who?... what?...no...~~no~~ NO!...<u>she</u>...' (02r). On ET3, a marginal note marks 'movement 2' of the Auditor (02r) and the passage is edited: '...it was so long...since ~~she had uttered~~ ~~heard it~~ it had sounded' (02r), the final verb indicating a more passive relationship between speaker and the words they emit, creating the sense of 'a tongue that is not mine', as the Unnamable puts it (*Un* 17).

'3. Accent suggests it is hers' (ET3, 02r; 1973a, 10)

Mouth, like the speaker of Shakespeare's Sonnet 30, is 'unused to flow', though in her case 'flow' refers to speech rather than tears. Early drafts mention this word, but it is struck out and replaced on ET2: 'an unbroken **~~flow~~** stream...' (02r). The reason Mouth 'had finally to admit ... to herself ...' that this voice 'could be no other ... than her own ...' is that it produces 'certain vowel sounds ... she had never heard ... elsewhere ... so that people would look at her ... uncomprehending' (EM1, 03r). In ET5,

Beckett underlined 'vowel' and put an open variant (probably an instruction for pronunciation) in the left margin: 'vow-ell' (ET5, 03r). Beckett also gave specific indications on pronunciation later in this same typescript, which he at one stage felt were necessary for the actors playing this role, though they were eventually deleted (see 'Note 2' below).

There is another example in this lexia of Beckett 'drill[ing] [...] hole[s]' in the text. On EM1, we find the phrase '... she who had never been ~~**a talker**~~ **... a talker** ... on the contrary ... practically speechless ... all her days ...' (03r). However, there is to be no 'talking cure' for Mouth (see Jones 1953, 246) and on ET3, the words marked above in bold are cut: '...she who had never...on the contrary...practically speechless...all her days...' (02r). Not only is the text studded with ellipses, but even the phrases that remain *between* these ellipsis marks are themselves made more elliptical in the drafts. This adds to the sense of a rushed, speeding stream of words in performance.

'Life scene 2 (shopping centre)' (ET3, 02r–03r; 1973a, 10)

As well as removing words to make the spoken text more elliptical, Beckett added repetitions with slight variations to Mouth's monologue, evident in her second 'life scene'. For instance, the opening phrase of this lexia, **'even shopping'**, is joined by the supralinear addition 'busy shopping centre', further emphasizing the social bustle from which Mouth is detached. This in turn is joined by a synonym in ET2: '...supermart' (02r). Another supralinear addition follows on ET6: '..even shopping..out shopping..busy shopping centre.. supermart..' (03r). Such additions, which come across as efforts to pin down with greater specificity the nature of the place Mouth visits, have the paradoxical effect of increasing the lack of certainty and stability about what has just been said. While not consisting in the proposition–negation dynamic of 'denarration' – defined by Brian Richardson as 'a kind of narrative negation in which a narrator denies significant aspects of his or her narrative that had earlier been presented as given' (2006, 87) – these repetitions-with-a-difference can likewise be seen as a means of creating greater hermeneutic indeterminacy in the text.[123]

123 I draw here on Steven Connor's *Samuel Beckett: Repetition, Theory and Text*, a study structured around Gilles Deleuze's concepts of '"naked" repetition, repetition as faithful and exact copy – which is to say, repetition as the

Mouth's '**flow**' (EM1, 03r) is again changed to a 'stream' on ET2 (passing through another variant slightly later in the text): '~~flood~~ stream' (02r). The terms call to mind the philosophy of Heraclitus, for whom, as Beckett noted: 'All things **flow**. For him it is not possible to step down twice into the same **stream**' (TCD MS 10967/24).[124] The central element in Heraclitus's thought was fire, which again brings to mind *Not I*'s image of a 'mouth on **fire**' (1973a, 11; *KLT* 89). With regard to Heraclitus's notion of being, Beckett noted:

> We 'are and are not' at any given moment. The 'way up' (earth – water – **fire**) and 'way down' (**fire** – water – earth) are one and the same, forever being traversed in opposite directions at once so that everything consists of two parts, one travelling up, the other down. (TCD MS 10967/26.1)[125]

As Van Hulle and Verhulst note, Beckett described Heraclitus and Democritus as 'philosophes muets' in his production notebook for *Krapp's Last Tape*, a concept they link to Fritz Mauthner's notion of an 'un-sayer' through Mauthner's use of the verb 'entsagen' in his *Beiträge zu einer Kritik der Sprache*, which Beckett read and admired (2017a, 27–8). In *Not I*, the stream of words is a fire which burns being up rather than expressing it in any clear sense. It is possibly this correlation between being and non-being, formulated as a constant '**flow**' or '**stream**', that had Heraclitus on Beckett's mind as he composed *Not I*, with the content of Mouth's stream putting the focus firmly on non-being.

Beckett's changes to tense put his readers and audience members in the middle of that stream of thought. On ET5, he changed past tense verbs to the present tense, deleting the past tense suffix in 'hand~~(ed)~~' and introducing

servant of presence – and "clothed repetition" – repetition as reproduction, or repetition-with-difference, which tends to disrupt presence' (2007, 203). As Connor points out, Deleuze abandons any clear distinction between these two forms of repetition (2007, 6–7).

124 Beckett used the latter sentence in the short story *Echo's Bones* (*EB* 3) and the essay 'La peinture des van Velde' (*Dis* 128); the former appears in the manuscripts of *En attendant Godot* (Van Hulle and Verhulst 2017a, 229). See also chapter 4.1.2.

125 I would like to thank Matthew Feldman for sharing with me the appendix of his PhD thesis, containing his transcriptions of Beckett's Philosophy Notes.

present tense open variants for '$_{\text{stood}}$ ^{stand}', '$_{\text{paid}}$ ^{pay}' and '$_{\text{went}}$ ^{go}' (03r), all of which are given present tense forms thereafter. Rather than observing Mouth's words flowing past from the riverbank as observers detached from the speaking subject, such changes encourage us to occupy the same mental space as Beckett's protagonist.[126] If Beckett wanted the piece to 'work on the nerves' of the audience, then these changes of tense were an important means of achieving that.

'Tries to delude herself voice not hers' (ET3, 03r; 1973a, 10–11)

In the first draft version, Mouth's efforts to persuade herself the voice is not hers again make mention of accent:

> till she began trying to persuade herself – self-defence! ... it was not her's [*sic*] at all ... not her voice at all **... in spite of the... ~~peculiarities ... of pronunciation ... and~~ idiosyncrasies ...** and would doubtless have succeeded ... vital she should ... ~~xxx~~ was on the point ... after long efforts ... (EM1, 04r)

However, the text in bold was deleted from the next draft and did not appear in succeeding versions: '...till she began trying to...p~~z~~^{e}rsuade herself...it was not hers at all...not her voice at all...and would doubtless have succeeded... was on the point...after long efforts...' (ET2, 03r). This shows that pronunciation was on Beckett's mind as he created Mouth's voice, but he did not make the voice too specific, perhaps fearing that actors would be hamstrung by an overly idiosyncratic description of the play's central voice. Again, we see the balancing act between specificity and 'vaguening' that is so important to Beckett's poetics.

126 This is heightened further in *Pas moi*, where the historic present often replaces the past (Sardin-Damestoy 2020, 116).

'Renounces as she feels lips moving' (ET3, 03r; 1973a, 11)

This lexia returns to the mechanics of physiological processes, with Mouth having to accept responsibility for her speech: 'give up ... admit she ~~alone was responsible~~ ~~and no other~~ and she alone' (EM1, 04r). Like the sole narrator at the opening of *Company*, Mouth implores her unseen audience to 'Imagine' (*CIWS* 3), encouraging them to enact the breakdown of communication between self and itself that Mouth experiences: 'when gradually she felt...suddenly she felt...her lips moving...imagine...her lips moving!...' (ET2, 03r). Given the dominance of Mouth's stage image, it is quite hard for the audience to imagine anything else.

'Fear that feeling may come back but for the moment mouth alone' (ET3, 03r; 1973a, 11)

On the Faber setting copy, Beckett added another imprecation to 'imagine' Mouth's experience when she thought 'that feeling was coming back ... imagine! ... feeling ~~was~~ coming back! ...' (FSC, 05r). In the first draft, this 'awful thought' was refuted with the words 'but no ... ~~only~~ the face alone ... face & mouth for the moment ... **ah** ... for the moment ...' (EM1, 04r), the supralinear additions once more trying and failing to pin down a specific image, which here again is very close to what we see onstage. These repetitions-with-a-difference were removed on ET2: '...the face alone...for the moment...**ha!**... for the ~~mo~~ moment...' (03r). On ET5, the image became even closer to what we see in performance: '..the ~~face~~ mouth alone..' (03r).

The flipping of '**ah**' to the more aggressive '**ha!**' between EM1 and ET2 in the passages above recalls Beckett's own ironic strategies when researching psychoanalysis. For instance, while reading Rank's *Trauma of Birth*, Beckett took the following notes: 'Inestimable advantage of man over woman, consisting in his being able partially to go back into the mother by means of the penis which **stands – ha!ha!** – for the child' (TCD MS 10971/8/35). Beckett here altered Rank's text to create his own joke. Rank's account tells of 'the inestimable advantage which the man has over the woman, and which consists in his being able partially to go back into the mother, by means of the penis, itself *representing* the child' (1929, 39; emphasis added). While Beckett's alteration of Rank's text creates distance between notetaker and psychoanalytic authority, Mouth uses the interjection '**ha!**' in order to once more distance herself from her own self. Further emphasizing this separation of self from itself in overtly dualist terms, the body is referred to as a '**machine**' from ET4 onwards (03r), having earlier been described by the more neutral word '**frame**' (ET3, 03r). This earlier term may have been influenced by Beckett's translation work on *Premier amour*, where the term '**corps**' is translated as '**frame**' (2012c 25; *ECEF* 68). The 'awful thought' is also described mechanistically on ET4, in terms of a 'sudden flash' (03r), signalling another scene in Mouth's inner Cartesian (Movie) Theatre.

'4. Next thought: such distress can't continue' (ET3, 03r; 1973a, 11)

The text added as part of Addendum A features another plea by Mouth to 'imagine ...' her physiological condition: 'body like gone..' (EM1, 05v).[127] The latter phrase was changed on ET5 to 'whole body like gone' (03r). The sense that her body is a sensory machine on the verge of breakdown is emphasized in an edit made on EM1, where Mouth describes herself as '~~trying~~ straining to hear' (EM1, 04r). Whereas a human being might 'try' to hear, the verb 'straining' is more closely associated with mechanistic processes and objects.

'Description of same: unintelligible irrepressible voice, consternation of mind' (ET3, 03r; 1973a, 11–12)

This lexia appears in two separate parts on EM1. The first part appears within Addendum A:

> only a face ... **lips** ... **jaws** ... **cheeks** ... never still a second ... **mouth on fire** ... words ~~pouring~~ streaming out ... **in her ear** ... **practically in her ear** ... and can't hear the half of them ... not the quarter ... doesn't know what she's saying ... **imagine** ... no idea what she's saying! ... (EM1, 05r)

127 This material from Addendum A was integrated into ET3 (03r).

Elements in this passage such as the enumeration of body parts and the inability of the voice to communicate with itself once more picture Mouth as a machine on the verge of breakdown, yet one which is still able to implore its listener to '**imagine**'. Yet again, we have the idea of a stream of words and a 'mouth on fire', the opposition recalling Heraclitus's notion of being in terms of becoming.

The text itself was also in a state of radical flux after its composition in the early typescripts. Having typed this passage out on ET2 and ET3, Beckett then wrote the following note on his handwritten analysis: '<u>voice</u> ... always <u>stream</u> – not the quarter – first denied as hers – in spite of sounds – then accepted when lips move – no idea what she's saying – can't stop it – <u>amplify</u> ✓' (EM2, 01r).[128] In light of this instruction-to-self, Beckett drafted the second part of the lexia as Addendum F, again using a Heraclitan noun to describe Mouth's speech: 'and can't stop ... no stopping it! ... just as a moment before ... a moment! ... she couldn't make a sound ... no sound of any kind ... now can't stop .. imagine ... can't stop the **flow**! ...' (EM1, 04v). ET5 again zooms in on Mouth's mouth: 'just the ~~face~~ **mouth**' (ET5, 04r), once more emphasizing the metatheatrical aspect of her monologue. Indeed, such repetitions of earlier textual developments become an important part of Mouth's circular, repetitive monologue in later sections of the genesis.

'Prayer for voice to stop: unanswered' (ET3, 03r; 1973a, 12)

This lexia follows a similar compositional pattern to its immediate predecessor. The first part was drafted in Addendum A: 'the brain ... ~~**raving** away on its own ...~~ ... **raving** away on its own ... ~~at something else~~ ... trying to make sense of it ...' (EM1, 04v). This was then typed out on ET2, edited on ET3, before additional material was drafted in Addendum F of EM1: 'the whole **brain** begging ... begging the mouth to shut ... .. pause a moment .. if only for a moment ... and no response ... as though it hadn't heard ... or couldn't ... couldn't pause an instant ... like **maddened** ...' (04v). The '**raving**' brain, begging a '**maddened**' mouth to stop – and failing to do so – clearly presents an abnormal mental state in Mouth's narrative, though the specific state is never named, as is the norm in Beckett's late oeuvre. Again, this lexia presents a mouth '~~trying~~ **straining** to hear' the brain's request, giving yet another psychological

128 The word '<u>amplify</u>' and its underlining are in red ink.

image of a sensory system in a state of breakdown, the verb 'straining' again suggesting a mind-as-machine whose very processes are working against itself (ET5, 04r).

'Life scene 3 (Croker's Acres)' (ET3, 03r; 1973a, 12)

Another instruction to expand the text is found on Beckett's handwritten analysis: 'walking .. walking all her days – stop & stare into space – amplify ✓' (EM2, 01r). The tick in the left margin indicates this amplification was completed as part of the Croker's Acres life scene.

Beckett first wrote a set of loose notes in two separate paragraphs in the top margin of EM1:

> ~~the one time she cried~~
> ~~since~~ ~~she~~ ~~could~~ ~~could remember~~
> ~~all over~~
> ~~all over in a second~~
>
> sitting looking at her hand
> palm down on a xxx
> suddenly saw tears on it
> could only have been hers
> all over in a second
> watched them dry (05v)

This was developed as part of the draft Addendum A on the same page:

> or in the past ... bringing up the past ... willy-nilly ... ~~flashes~~ ~~xxx~~ ~~snatches~~ flashes from all over ... ~~odds & ends of walks ...~~ standing waiting for the bag ... odds & ends of walks ... walking all her ~~life~~ days ... stop and stare into space ... **the one time she cried ... since she could remember** ... ~~sitting~~ old woman already ... **sitting looking at her hand ... palm** ~~down~~ **upward in her lap ...** ~~**suddenly tears**~~ ~~on~~ ~~**in**~~ ~~**it ... could only have been hers ...**~~ ~~no one~~ ~~**no one for miles ...**~~ **suddenly wet ... tears presumably ... hers presumably ... no one else for miles ...** ~~xx~~ **all over in a second** (EM1, 05v)

Having typed out and edited this material on ET2 and ET3, Beckett decided to significantly amplify this section. Such textual amplification is in stark contrast to the procedure of 'undoing' his work is so often associated with. The additional material is drafted as Addendum G on EM1:

> ... a few steps then stop dead ... stare into space ... move on a few more ... stop and stare again ... then the time she cried ... the one time she could remember ... **must have cried as a baby** ... perhaps not ... not ~~indispensable~~ essential to life ... **just the birth cry ~~and then no~~ to get her breathing** ... then no more till this ... (04v)

Here, Mouth's crying is linked to her 'vagitus', or birth cry, which Beckett had dramatized in the wordless *Breath* (1969). In that case, the 'brief cry', which brings up the stage lights, is linked to a responding 'cry', which darkens them, through the two cries being vocalized in a similar manner (*KLT* 79). But in the case of Mouth, a large part of her life has been lived tearless, corresponding to the long silence during which she has not been able to speak. Even after the incorporation of Addendum G, the textual amplification was not over for Beckett. Having instructed himself to '<u>add to</u>', Mouth's memories on EM2 (01r), Beckett amplified this passage further on ET4:

> old ~~woman~~ hag already..sitting looking at her hand..where was it?..**Crokser's** ~~**meadows**~~ acres..one evening on the way ~~back~~ home.. home!....a little mound in ~~**Croker's meadows**..sitting staring at her hand~~ **Croker's** acr'es ~~**meadows**~~.. light failing.. (02r–03r)

This use of the South County Dublin place-name 'Croker's Acres' is a rare moment of autobiographical detail; albeit Beckett is not here creating a narrative of his own life, but drawing on topographical material from near his childhood home to construct Mouth's memory of feeling that she has no home. The very notion that the surrounding area might contain a home for Mouth is refuted in the ironic repetition of the word. Mouth's behaviour is instead reminiscent of someone who is homeless, sitting in a field as darkness falls. This sense of Mouth as an outsider is reinforced by her self-description not as a '~~woman~~' but as a witchlike 'hag' (ET4, 03r).

On ET5, Beckett wrote '**babby**' in the left margin, corresponding with the instructions on pronunciation found at the end of this typescript (see 'Note 2' below): '..then that time she cried..the one time she could remember..since she was a baby babby..must have cried as a baby babby..' (04r).[129] As will be discussed below, this particular pronunciation did crop up in performance, though Beckett, like the Director of *Catastrophe*, may have felt it was too much 'explicitation' to include such an overt instruction on pronunciation in the text (see chapter 2.3.2).

'**Brain grabbing at straws (e.g. God's mercy)**' (ET3, 03r; 1973a, 13)

This lexia is another example of Beckett's amplification of the text. All that exists of it in the main monologue of EM1 is a short phrase: 'can't go on … ~~merciful God~~ God is love … ~~xxx xxx~~ she'll be ~~cleansed~~ **purged** …' (04r), this final verb recalling the notion of purgation in the manuscript draft of *Cascando*, where the term is associated with the sin of being born.[130] Having instructed himself to '(amplify)' the section on the 'brain' in his handwritten analysis (EM2, 01r)[131] and written a marginal note to add Addendum A to the text on ET2 (03r), Beckett then wrote a note in the top margin of EM1: '**dull roar like falls**' (05v). This was further expanded as part of the following passage on the same page:

> **dull roar like falls** … and the ray … flickering on & off … starting to move around … seeming **moonbeam but clearly not** … head ~~can't~~ doesn't move but eyes … oh very much so … hundred degrees at least … (EM1, 05v)

129 This marginal note could be interpreted either as an open variant or a note on pronunciation. In the genetic online edition, it is coded as an open variant since it corresponds with other similar variants elsewhere in the genetic dossier.

130 I would like to thank Pim Verhulst for sharing this information about *Cascando*.

131 This note-to-self on the handwritten analysis is written in red ink and has a black-ink tick in the left margin.

This gives us an excellent example of how Beckett's own creative flow could expand on gnomic and fragmentary material, emphasizing the clear necessity for textual expansion before any contraction could take place in later drafts.

Evidence from this lexia also demonstrates the complex chronology of Beckett's handwritten analysis. As part of the series of notes headed 'insentience', Beckett wrote:

> ... first total – doesn't know what position she's in – only eyelids moving since ray disappears – this questioned with memory of field – then lips moving and whole speaking apparatus – also eyes **100°** – (mention earlier!!)[132] (EM2, 01r)

The fact that the eyes move a '**hundred degrees at least**', having been mentioned in Addendum A on EM1, is then typed up in ET2 (05r) and integrated into that typescript by means of a marginal note (03r).[133] The eyes passing ninety degrees means they face back towards Mouth's skull, presenting a hint of the 'inward turn' often associated with modernist writing (see Herman 2011). However, it is notable that this 'inward turn' does not make it all the way to an inner-vision, prevented as it is by the limits of the body. From another perspective, having the eyeballs turn a '**hundred degrees**' would also show observers the whites of the woman's eyes, suggesting deep distress. Whatever theatrical effect Beckett was aiming for, he abandoned it and this phrase does not appear in the published text.[134] In ET4, the words '..can't go on..' are clarified by immediate repetition: '**it** can't go on..' (04r), thus differentiating the phrase from the Unnamable's famous '**I** can't go on' or Estragon's '**I** can't go on

132 Though the main text is in black ink, the instruction-to-self in parentheses is underlined in black and red pen, suggesting Beckett came back and emphasized this in a later campaign of revision.

133 Beckett may have realized that the eyes are mentioned repeatedly on the typescript page just preceding this insertion (ET2, 02r), which possibly prompted his note on EM2 that their unusual movement should be mentioned earlier.

134 As mentioned in chapter 1.1.1, the word 'cut' is circled in the margin beside the passage quoted above from EM2 (01r) and seems to refer to the text about the eyes.

like this' in *Waiting for Godot* (*Un* 134; *WfG* 91). However, this addition disappears from later drafts. For William James, the simple fact of some kind of consciousness happening is the underlying principle upon which any psychological research must be based: 'The first and foremost concrete fact which everyone will affirm to belong to his inner experience is the fact that *consciousness of some sort goes on*' (1992, 153; emphasis in original). In his deletion of 'it', Beckett constructs ambiguity as to whether Mouth or the experience she is undergoing 'can't go on'.

'Life scene 1 (field) again' (ET3, 03r–04r; 1973a, 13)

The description of the light assailing Mouth undergoes an important change in ET2: '...and the ray...~~on and off...~~ferreting around...' (03r). This gives the light more agency, recalling the interrogative spotlight of *Play*. In *Play*, the spotlight is described in a paratextual note as an 'inquisitor' and the stage protagonists as its 'victims' (*KLT* 65). In a letter to Danish translator and theatre practitioner Christian Ludvigsen, Beckett gave further depth to this inanimate protagonist, describing the light's 'inquisitorial intelligence', mentioning that his characters 'speak to the light as to an animated being' and comparing it to 'an accusing finger' (22 September 1963, *LSB III* 573–4).[135] Likewise, the addition of the verb 'ferreting' to the text of *Not I* suggests a more animate, purposeful light in this play, while also suggesting that the mind contains depths which need to be excavated and searched. Alongside Mouth's descriptions of her own physical and mental processes as machine-like, this anthropomorphization of the light further blurs the line between human and nonhuman subjectivity in the play.

135 For a more detailed discussion of *Play*'s 'Note on light', see Beloborodova (2019, 198–9).

'Perhaps something she should tell? Life scene 4 (courtroom),'[136] (ET3, 04r; 1973a, 13–14)

On his handwritten analysis, Beckett wrote a series of notes on the topic of Mouth being '<u>speechless</u>' (EM2, 01r). While composing this lexia, he added one such example by writing Addendum C at the end of EM1:

> <u>Ex. 2 of speechlessness</u>
> practically speechless ... how she survived **... that time in court ... ~~guilty or not guilty ...~~ ~~what~~ what had she to say for herself ... guilty or not guilty ... speak up woman ...** stood there staring at nothing ... waiting to be led away ... glad of the hand on her arm ... (05v)

In what is a polyvocal monologue, this passage features the only example of direct recorded speech from someone other than Mouth: '**guilty or not guilty**' and '**speak up woman**'. It is notable that this interaction takes place in a court: having started the lexia by suggesting that she might have to say something, it is the voice of the law which (unsuccessfully) commands Mouth to speak as she stands in the dock. With regard to the balance between 'undoing' and 'redoing', it is notable that this institutional scene, relatively detailed by the standards of Mouth's monologue, was not present in the first draft version but added only after ET2 was typed. Nor is there any suggestion in the main text as to what Mouth might have done to deserve her day in court. On his handwritten analysis, the phrases 'shopping centre – **fined**' suggest that Beckett may have had a backstory in mind, even if it was not integrated into the draft monologue (EM2, 01r). Again, this suggests the importance of the social sphere in Beckett's theatre, albeit here only visible in the manuscripts.

In ET2, the words 'merciful God' (Deuteronomy 4:31; Nehemiah 9:31) are joined by two more phrases from the Bible: '...merciful God **...tender mercies... new every morning**...' (03r). On ET5, this changes further: '..~~merciful~~ **God** is love..

136 Though the comma at the end of this phrase and the lower case 'l' for 'life' in the next line of his analysis (see below) shows that Beckett thought of these lexias as one unit, they are divided in two for the purposes of my analysis.

tender mercies..new every morning..' (04r). Van Hulle and Nixon point out that this revised passage is

> a combination of I John 4:8 ('God is Love'), Psalm 25:6 ('Remember, O LORD, thy tender mercies'), and Lamentations 3:22–3 ('his compassions fail not. *They are* new every morning'; Lamentations 3:22–3, King James Version). (2013, 179; emphasis in original)

While the verse numbers of the first and last phrases are annotated by Beckett in his French translation (see chapter 2.3.2), the phrase 'tender mercies' may come from any number of points in the Old Testament – it appears throughout the Psalms (40:11, 51:1, 69:16, 77:9, 79:8, 103:4, 119:77, 119:156, 145:9) and once in Proverbs (12:10).[137] In the context of Mouth thinking 'she was being punished', it is worth noting that the God of these biblical books is a punishing deity, whose mercy consists in withholding His wrath.

'life scene 1 (field) and no from within' (ET3, 04r; 1973a, 14)

Mouth is again interrupted and again emphasizes the temporal gap between her past selves; both these features are included in the first draft: 'another few – **... what?** ~~not that~~ **...** not **that? ... nothing to do with that?** ... all right ... something else ... think of something else ... **long after** ...' (EM1, 05r). On ET2, Beckett added 'nothing to do with that?...nothing she could say?...all right...' (04r), which becomes 'nothing she could ~~**say**~~ tell?' on ET3 (04r), further emphasizing the compulsion Mouth is under to tell a story (not just to spout out words). Though she describes her own mind as mechanical, Mouth is not simply a word machine, which is in line with Dan Gunn's description of Beckett's 'theatre of narration, where not just stories but the *tellings* of stories are staged'. As Gunn goes on to argue, and as we will see in future chapters, this is particularly true of his late work, with *Not I*, *That Time* and *Footfalls* all staging 'the drama of the narrative' in their splitting of self and voice (2012, 165; emphasis in original). In Mouth's case, she is staging

137 According to Gontarski, Beckett once considered 'Tender Mercies' as the title for *Happy Days* (1985, 131).

the story for herself, though her repeated, aggressive refutation of the first person pronoun indicates her unwillingness to fully participate in this self-performance.

'Something she should think? No as before' (ET3, 04r; 1973a, 14)

On ET5, a supralinear addition reintroduces the religious theme so prominent elsewhere in the text: 'then forgiven..' (05r). However, it seems unlikely that Mouth's being forgiven is anything but a prelude to further suffering, which would bring her closer to Beckett's unforgiven characters in *Endgame*, *Rough for Theatre I* and *Footfalls* (see chapter 6.1.2).

On ET4, Mouth's birthplace becomes a '..godforsaken hole ~~in the bog~~..' (04r), echoing its pejorative description in the play's opening lines. Beckett strengthens these textual echoes by adding an altered version of the play's opening words to ET5: '..tiny little thing..out into that..' (06r). This became '..tiny little thing..**out before its time**..' on ET6 (05r). The increasing pattern of repetitions adds to the sense that Mouth has been through this outpouring of words before and will go through it all again.

'Life scene 5 (rushing out to tell)' (ET3, 04r; 1973a, 14–15)

Life scene 5 was initially drafted as part of Addendum B: 'always winter for some reason ... the long ~~evenings~~ evenings ... sudden urge to ... tell ... **then rush out & stop the first person she saw ...** man or woman or child' (EM1, 05v). In ET5, having omitted 'man or woman or child', Beckett made the concluding phrase more elliptical by deleting its conjunction: '**then rush out ~~‹and›~~ stop the first she saw**' (05r). A similar pattern of cutting down on link words – this time a preposition – is seen on ET4, though here Beckett balances the deletion by adding an adjective: 'always winter **~~for~~ some** strange reason' (04r). Again here, Beckettian 'undoing' is balanced by 'redoing', even at a micro-level.

'Distress worse: description of same' (ET3, 04r; 1973a, 15)

Having noted on his handwritten analysis the need to 'amplify' passages dealing with the brain and to add other examples of the 'vowel sounds' emitted on the 'rare occasions' when Mouth spoke, Beckett added, as part of Addendum B: 'wild stuff ... half the vowels wrong . **pine for pain** ... that kind ... no one could follow' (EM1, 05v). On ET4, Beckett 'vaguened' the vowel sounds, leaving it to the reader's imagination (and the performer's interpretation) as to what they might actually be: '..half the vowels wrong..~~**pine for pain..that kind**~~..no one could follow..' (05r). An interesting variant on ET5 thickens the vowelly plot. Where the published text reads '... half the vowels wrong ...' (1973a, 15; *KLT* 92), Beckett seems to have written '..half the vowels ~~**round**~~ **wrong**..' on this typescript (ET5, 05r). Given the prevalence of 'round' vowels in middle- and upper-class varieties of English, and given Mouth's position as a vagrant outsider in her community, it is noteworthy that Beckett here seems briefly to have given her erroneous vowels the status of being 'round' before reverting to the earlier 'wrong'. Since 'round' vowels are associated with RP English, Mouth's accent was briefly 'wrong' to be right in this draft version. Beckett's notes on the pronunciation of 'any', 'baby' and 'either' shorten the vowels (see below), again emphasizing Mouth's position on the margins of society.

'Prayer for all to stop: unanswered' (ET3, 04r; 1973a, 15)

Like the text immediately preceding it, this lexia also contains an addition drafted as part of an addendum written to 'amplify' the description of brain activity in the text (EM2, 01r). As part of this, Beckett added the following in Addendum H: '**begging** it all to stop ... unanswered ... prayer unanswered ... or unheard ... **too faint** ... so on ...' (EM1, 04v). While this repeats material about '**begging**' the mouth to stop talking from earlier in the text, this is the first time that the lack of response might be due to the fact that the voice is '**too faint**'. This strengthens Mouth's connection to the 'long silence' experienced by the central figure of *That Time*. As we will see in chapter 4.1.2, this vocal faintness has a Dantean echo, recalling Virgil's appearance and the beginning of his speech in *The Divine Comedy*. In Mouth's case, rather than trying to listen to the too-faint voice of a guide, she is stuck listening to herself, incapable of hearing her own prayer to stop.

'Life scene 1 9(field) again' (ET3, 04r–05r; 1973a, 15)

Emphasizing the circular nature of Mouth's predicament, Beckett chose to end the text by returning for the fifth time to the first life scene as the '(curtain starts slowly down)', repeating '**back**' three times to emphasize the sense of return: '… trying what … no matter … keep on … hit on it in the end … **~~back in~~ then back … back in the field … back in the grass** … nothing but the larks … pick it up –' (EM1, 05r). In ET3, Beckett added **'God is love'** (04r), which was joined by **'tender mercies..new every morning..'** on ET5, returning to the idea of a divine grace that has long been evacuated from Mouth's life (06r).

Closing Stage Directions (ET3, 05r; 1973a, 16)

The draft stage directions at the end of Mouth's monologue on EM1 are almost identical to the published text (05r; 1973a, 16; *KLT* 93). On ET6, Beckett added an idea for the improvised text which would continue to be spoken after the curtain falls: 'For **ad lib** after curtain down: "**..there.. get on with it from there etc.**'[138] (06r). There is no evidence of this idea anywhere else in the written genesis, though it is used in the BBC television adaptation of the play, where Whitelaw ends the play after the fade-to-black by segueing back into the opening, having grafted on '**… a few more**' from elsewhere in the text: 'pick it up **there … get on with it from there … a few more** … out … into this world … this world … tiny little thing … before its time … in a godfor- … what?' (Beckett 2008b, 12:15–12:23; see 1973a, 15, 14, 7, 6; *KLT* 93, 91, 86, 85). The note is an important reminder that in such a precisely composed text, Beckett still left gaps for performance practitioners to fill by means of the only ad lib in his published corpus.

138 Beckett did not close the double speech mark in this line.

Note 1 (ET3, 05r; 1973a 16)

The note on the Auditor's movement is another good example of Beckett's continuous use of EM1 over the early part of his compositional process. Neither ET1 nor ET2 contain this note. The first typescript on which it appears is ET3, but even there it is only a handwritten placeholder: '~~Note~~ Movement This consists **etc**' (05r). The '**etc**' indicates that by the time he made this handwritten note on ET3, Beckett had already drafted the full note on EM1, squeezed in at the bottom of the page under the final Addendum H:

> Movement (Note) **This consists in simple** sideways **raising of** hidden **arms clear of sides and their falling back with if possible just audible thud of hands on thighs**. It ~~is less at~~ lessens with each recurrence ~~and impere~~ till scarcely perceptible at third. There is just enough ~~silence to~~ pause to contain it as MOUTH recovers from vehement refusal to ~~abandon~~ relinquish third person. (04v)

As Van Hulle and Verhulst note, this gesticulation is prefigured in Mme Louis's gesture in the French text of *Malone meurt*, a gesture which the bystander Sapo finds very difficult to interpret but which, given the context of rural poverty in the surrounding text, seems to signify despair rather than the compassion referred to later on in the drafts of *Not I*: 'Elle les écartait en effet de ses flancs, je dirais brandissais [*for* brandissait] si j'ignorais encore mieux le génie de votre langue' (Beckett 1951, 50, qtd. in Van Hulle and Verhulst 2017b, 189).[139] On ET6, Beckett replaced '~~simple~~' with 'slight' and deleted '~~with if feasible just audible thud of hands on thighs~~' (06r), to be replaced by the more explicitly emotive ', in a gesture of helpless compassion' on the Faber setting copy (FSC, 09r).

Analysing the notes on the text in *Play*, Beloborodova has drawn attention to 'the hermeneutic potential of such notes, as some of them transcend the level of technical aid to the production team and contain an extra interpretative layer' (2019, 338). Compared to Beckett's prickly

139 ['She spread them out, removed them from her flanks, I would say brandished them if I were even better at ignoring the genius of your language'] (trans. in Van Hulle and Verhulst 2017b, 189).

comments regarding Tandy's interpretation of Mouth, this highly interpretive addition to the note on the Auditor's movement contains a remarkable amount of hermeneutic potential. It is worth taking into account the timeline of Beckett's comments and subsequent edits. He edited his Faber setting copy in December 1972–January 1973, in preparation for the Royal Court performance. By that point, the play had already been staged in New York by Schneider, who had had problems lighting and positioning the Auditor. So, by the time he came to revise the Faber setting copy, Beckett may have been aware of the need to provide a note which would clarify to theatre practitioners the way in which the Auditor might be played.

Note 2 (ET4, 05r)

Beckett's clarification of his own text for performers did, at one fairly lengthy stage in the genesis, extend to providing notes on pronunciation. Having drafted handwritten versions of this note on ET4 (05r) and ET5 (06r), then having typed it out in full on ET6 (06r) and ET7 (06r) – but deleting it on these latter two typescripts – Beckett saw it included on the Royal Court playscript:

> Note 2
>
> "Any": pronounce "Anny".
>
> "Baby": pronounce "Babby".
>
> "Either": pronounce "Eether".
>
> (for example) (10r)

On his Faber setting copy, Beckett again deleted the note and it does not appear in the published text. But we should not discount its possible influence on the development of the text in performance. In the BBC television adaptation, Whitelaw uses 'babby' (Beckett 2008b, 08:04–08:05), slipping into her broad, North of England accent to include the piece of dialect which positions Mouth further down the social ladder than a speaker with the 'round' vowels mentioned in the earlier draft (Wright 1898, 107).[140] The note was included – undeleted – on her working script for the play so it is possible that she developed this aspect of pronunciation based on Beckett's draft concept (BW playscript, p. 8). Once again, the text created in performance – inscribed in the BBC recording – shows a fascinating variant with regard to the published editions.

Beckett had had problems with Mouth's pronunciation while supervising the US premiere by letter. In the same letter in which he warns Schneider off trying to give Mouth a backstory in order to quell his actors, Beckett rejects the suggestion that a local context be read into his note on pronunciation: 'Anny. Simply an example of the "certain vowel sounds". No Irishness intended' (16 October 1972, *LSB IV* 311). But the three examples he provides in the note all fit a paradigm of Hiberno-English pronunciation. While Whitelaw adapted 'babby' into her own North of England dialect, Beckett may have realized the danger of putting such potential Irishisms into the hands (and the mouths) of other Anglophone performers. So, 'babby' came through in Whitelaw's recording but the note itself was cut. This is another important piece of proof that Beckett's play does not simply depend on the deletion of detail, but the careful balancing of elements in multiple, minimalist performance scenarios.

140 Whitelaw's repetition 'any ... any' uses standard pronunciation (Beckett 2008b, 4:50–4:51; 1973a, 9; *KLT* 88). She also uses RP for 'either' (Beckett 2008b, 10:26–10:35; 1973a, 14; *KLT* 92).

2.3 The Genesis of *Pas moi*

2.3.1 Chronology

Just days after *Not I*'s UK premiere, Beckett was already turning his thoughts to the difficulties of translating the play into French. He wrote to Ruby Cohn on 20 January 1973: 'Hate the thought of releasing it for translation and massacre but suppose must. Can't imagine it in French' (*LSB IV* 323). Less than a week later, he repeated these sentiments to Sheila Page: 'Have now to pull up to the horrible job of translating it into French and to releasing it for general production, i. e. massacre 9 times out of 10' (26 January 1973, *LSB IV* 325). The next day, he told Alan Schneider that the pressure to translate came from Madeleine Renaud: 'Madeleine & Roger Blin went to see the show in London. Former now lepping for it in French. Can't imagine it working on that ice. But suppose must try' (27 January 1973, *LSB IV* 326).[141]

Having tried and failed to write something for Renaud and Barrault's Petit Odéon Théâtre (see chapter 2.1.2), Beckett continued to offer support to the couple in their turbulent, peripatetic years following the Paris student demonstrations of 1968. After they allowed the demonstrators to occupy the Odéon, Renaud and Barrault were evicted from the building by Minister of Cultural Affairs André Malraux. There followed a lean period for the pair, during which they resorted to selling personal belongings to keep the company going (Renaud 2000, 97). Beckett showed sympathy for the couple in a letter to Alan Schneider: 'They've had a bad deal from Malraux and Ministry of "Culture"' (26 August 1968, *NABS* 215). The following year, Beckett agreed to their cycle of his plays at the Théâtre Récamier, telling Renaud: 'Naturally I shall do everything I can to help you, but that may not be very much' (28 November 1969, *LSB IV* 199n1).[142]

141 Maurice Harmon writes that the reference to ice is 'A pun on the theater's name, Palais de Glace, but it did not play there' (*NABS* 300n4). The Compagnie Renaud–Barrault did not move to the Théâtre du Rond-Point (aka 'le Palais de glace') until 1981 (Bonal 2000, 317).

142 'Je ferai naturellement tout ce que je pourrai pour vous aider, mais ça ne sera peut-être pas grand'chose' (*LSB IV* 199n1).

It is in light of this relationship that we must see the genesis of *Pas moi*. As previous BDMP modules have shown, Beckett's translations were determinedly social events, especially when translating for the inherently social art of the theatre. For instance, Beckett translated *Godot* under pressure from the owner of the US performance rights (Van Hulle and Verhulst 2017a, 269), felt that the translation of *Fin de partie* would be best served by him seeing the play in the theatre first (Van Hulle and Weller 2018, 255), created his own translation of *La Dernière Bande* by completely reworking that of Pierre Leyris (Van Hulle 2015, 124–5), translated *Play* as *Comédie* under the influence of its contemporaneous German staging (Beloborodova 2019, 208) and advised on translations of his work into languages other than English and French (Van Hulle and Verhulst 2017a, 278). Indeed, for someone whose later plays explore the 'breakdown' of communication between subject and object, it is striking just how socially embedded Beckett's translation process was, especially when it came to the theatre.

Critiquing the discipline of sociology, Bruno Latour argues that the social is not a 'material or domain' to be drawn on in order to explain another process, but rather that which is 'glued together' by the actors that make it up (2005, 1, 5). Such actors can be human agents (like writers, theatre performers and translators) or nonhuman agents (such as manuscripts and stage props). In Latour's *Reassembling the Social*, he provides an account of Actor–Network Theory, which spreads agency across different objects that constitute the social, thus challenging the binary of active (human) agents acting upon inert objects. In the field of translation studies, Hélène Buzelin has argued that Actor–Network Theory can provide a model for studies of literary translation and called for a genesis of translations through a 'process-oriented kind of research' (2005, 215). Buzelin's research focuses on the actor-networks involved in translations carried out for contemporary publishing houses, often done by teams of translators (see Buzelin 2007). Though genetic criticism of self-translations such as Beckett's puts the author at the centre of any actor-network, it too is a 'process-oriented' study of translation. Through its emphasis on the importance of material agents such as manuscripts and stage performers in the compositional process, this analysis focuses on the different agents involved in the genesis of *Pas moi* rather than using any one of them as an explanatory backstop. One of the mottos of Actor–Network Theory is that we should 'follow the actors themselves' – by which is meant objects (human or nonhuman) that have agency within a given process (Latour 2005). When carrying out a genetic analysis of Beckett's stage texts, it makes sense to take into account the role of theatre actors for whom he translated his work. In the case of *Pas moi*, the fact that it was being translated for Renaud to perform provided Beckett both with an impetus to do the work and weighed on his mind as he struggled to get the French text written.

Having finished the translation of *Premier amour* in February, and with the translation of *Mercier et Camier* still to be completed, Beckett started a draft of *Pas moi* on 1 March 1973 in Paris (FM1, 01r). He brought the work with him on holidays to El Jadida, Morocco, but he did not get far, as he reported to Barbara Bray: 'Struggling feebly with Not I. Kept going till grabbing at the straw' (16 March 1973, *LSB IV* 330). In FM1 – on the page following the date 'El Jadida 13.3.73' (04r) – Beckett's translation cuts off with the words '~~affaire de quelques secondes~~..~~le tout~~..~~xx~~' (05r), just before the point where 'grabbing at the straw' should be translated (1973a, 13; *KLT* 91). He seems to have had trouble with this idiomatic phrase, which would be given the non-literal translation 'happant à vide' in the published text (1975b, 19).[143] Beckett did report to Ruby Cohn that he was working on the translation on 21 March (in El Jadida) and 19 April (in Paris), which may have involved revisions to FM1, of which there are many (UoR MS COH/088, COH/090). Beckett also told Bray on 27 March 1973: 'Dropped Not I for the moment, wish for ever' (*LSB IV* 331). On or around 17 July, Beckett told Alan Schneider: 'Translation of *Not I* rotting on siding. Madeleine pained – patient' (*NABS* 307). Here again we see Renaud as an agent in the translation process, even if her needs have not yet prompted Beckett to finish the work. Instead, he spent the summer of 1973 working on short prose pieces and finishing his draft translation of *Mercier et Camier* (Pilling 2006, 192–3).

On 20 August 1973, he reported to Jocelyn Herbert that the draft of *Mercier and Camier* was finished and that he could now turn his attention to the play again: 'Have another bash now at French Not I.' In the very next

143 It is worth noting that the question marks beside the mentions of Croker's Acres, which likewise indicate Beckett's difficulties with the translation (see chapter 2.3.2), also occur just before the text cuts off (FM, 05r).

line, he mentions the couple for whom he was translating: 'Saw Madeleine & Jean-Louis. Depressed and nervous, she especially' (*LSB IV* 342). In 1972, the Compagnie Renaud–Barrault had moved to the Théâtre d'Orsay and they were looking for material to establish themselves there. However, on 8 December 1973, Beckett told Alan Schneider: 'Still haven't translated *Not I*' (*NABS* 311). He reported a similar lack of progress to Cohn on 20 March 1974 (UoR MS COH/099) and we have no evidence of any further work on the translation until 2 May 1974, the earliest date on FM2 (01r). On 16 May 1974, Beckett told Herbert Myron: 'At last à la tête ['on top'] of a foul draft of <u>Pas moi (il)</u>' (*LSB IV* 370).[144] This probably refers to his completion of the monologue, which is followed by the date '12.5.74' (FM2, 07r). The stage directions took longer, and are dated (what looks like) '19.5.74' (FM2, 08r). Though all three manuscripts are untitled, Beckett's mention of the title to Myron shows that he had decided on it by the time he had finished FM2.

Beckett's three French typescripts are undated (FT1, FT2 and FT3). It was probably FT3, now preserved in the Fonds Renaud–Barrault at the Bibliothèque nationale de France, that Beckett shared with Renaud on 11 June 1974. The next day, Beckett sent another copy to Blin: 'Here is the text which I gave to Madeleine yesterday. I hope it is not definitive. I hope that you will agree to direct' (12 June 1974, *LSB IV* 371).[145] It seems that this second document is the annotated typescript stored in the Fonds Roger Blin at the BnF (FT2). While it is difficult to be certain about the chronology of additions to these two typescripts, some unique edits in Beckett's hand on FT3 are carried through to published editions, making this the more developed draft: 'abandonnées' (02r; 1975b, 10, 11) '~~pas~~ point' (05r, 06r; 1975b, 20, 22).[146]

In spite of his wish that Blin direct *Pas moi*, Beckett ended up doing so himself in the Théâtre d'Orsay's Petite Salle (Cohn 1980, 294). Here, 'after trying several places for Pierre Chabert as the auditor' (Cohn 1980, 266–7), the figure was cut and Renaud spoke the text solo. However, when Beckett

144 It is possible that with the masculine pronoun 'il', Beckett here casts himself as a male Mouth.

145 'Voici le texte que j'ai donné hier à Madeleine. J'espère qu'il n'est pas définitif. J'espère que tu accepteras de faire la mise en scène' (*LSB IV* 371).

146 *Minuit* 12 contains the two corrected instances of 'abandonnés' (1975a, 3, 4) and the second instance of 'point d'amour' quoted above (1975a, 8), but not the first (see chapter 1.5.3).

directed the play again in the same theatre in 1978 – this time in the Grande Salle (Cohn 1980, 294) – the Auditor was re-introduced. According to Cohn, the Auditor's 'gestures were still unsatisfactory to Beckett' in this production (1980, 267). Knowlson reports that the last of these gestures consisted of 'an actual covering of the ears with the hands, as if the figure were unable to bear any longer the flood of sound issuing from Mouth' (1997, 814n88). This seems to have been an attempt to embody the additional gestures Beckett incorporated into the French text, which is one of the translation aspects discussed in my next chapter.

2.3.2 Genesis

Staging the breakdown between subject and object in *Not I* was a complex task, as we have seen from the English-language genesis. Translating this breakdown into French posed additional challenges for Beckett, but also presented him with opportunities to alter 1) the humanity of the play's central subject as well as 2) the world she describes in her monologue. Having drawn on biblical intertexts when composing *Not I*, Beckett had to decide 3) how they would be translated into another linguistic and cultural context. Other key aspects of this translation concern 4) the stage space Bouche inhabits with the Auditeur and 5) the verbal rhythm and syntax of her speech. Finally, Beckett would use the translation process to address 6) concepts of 'unending', which is especially important for a play that continues to enact the subject–object breakdown for different audiences in more than one language. These six areas structure my analysis below.

Dehumanizing Bouche

Mouth's monologue distances her from the realm of the human, something that it is emphasized further in the French translation. For Jean-Michel Rabaté, Beckett's work is not posthuman, but instead presents us with 'humanity at the limit' (2016, 195). This can be seen in the key role of 'the human' in postwar texts such as 'The Capital of the Ruins' and 'La peinture des van Velde', where Beckett reclaims 'the human' as a valid term, albeit one which must be substantially rethought in the aftermath of the Second

World War (see Little 2020b). From the barely human figure of Lucky in *Waiting for Godot* to the dehumanized figures of later work like *Play* (see Beloborodova and Verhulst 2019), Beckett's theatre pushes the limits of what we might consider humanity to be.

Beckett made Bouche notably less human than Mouth from the very first draft. To translate the opening words of the play – '... out ... into this world ...' (1973a, 6; *KLT* 85), he first used '~~..bas..mis bas..~~' (FM1, 01r). As Van Hulle points out, 'The verb "mettre bas" (to have young/puppies/kittens) is usually only used for animals' (2008, 135). In *Endgame*, Clov refers to himself as having been 'whelped' (*E* 12).[147] Similarly, Mouth's birth is here figured in animalistic terms, with birth and death again in close proximity. Though these opening words would later change to '– monde... mis au monde... ce monde...' (1975b, 8), the world which Mouth inhabits retains some of the animalism of Beckett's opening draft.

Beckett also strengthened animalistic connotations when he translated how Mouth would 'crawl back in' after her periodic outpouring of words (1973a, 15; *KLT* 92). This becomes 'rentrer **dans son trou**...' (1975b, 22), calling to mind the image of an animal seeking refuge in its lair. Even the way Bouche's speech is described has nonhuman overtones, with Mouth's 'mad stuff' (1973a, 15; *KLT* 92) becoming the more animalistic 'sans queue ni tête...' [without head nor tail] (1975b, 22). When Bouche rejects the thought that 'she was being punished' (1973a, 7; *KLT* 86), Beckett first used the verb 'rejeter': '~~puis **rejeté**~~ la rejeta ~~comme sottise~~' (FM1, 01r–02r). But having changed '~~sottise~~' to 'bêtise' (FM1, 02r), which expresses an idea of stupidity associated with the word 'bête' [beast], he then chose to change the corresponding verb to '**chassée**...l'idée **chassée**...' (FM2, 02r), one of whose primary meanings is 'hunted'. Here, the meaning is something closer to 'chased away', but the animalistic connotations remain. Finally, when Beckett translated Mouth 'sitting staring at her hand' in Croker's Acres (1973a, 12; *KLT* 90), he first used the more human '~~**assise** par terre~~' (FM1, 05r) before changing this to '**accroupie** par terre' (FT1, 05r), which is replaced by 'a [*for* à] **croupetons** dans l'herbe' in FT2 (07r). The latter two terms are more animalistic, deriving from the noun 'croupe', which designates the hind quarters of an animal (*PR*).

147 The French original references simply the idea of birth: 'Depuis ma naissance' (https://www.beckettarchive.org/findepartie/comparesentences/0375).

Mouth's 'monde'

Beckett had trouble translating the one place-name mentioned in the published English text. 'Croker's acres(**?**)' is already marked with a question mark upon its first appearance in the French drafts (FM1, 05r), indicating translational difficulty.[148] In FM2, the phrase received a loose pencil jotting on a verso of FT1: 'Croker's Acres / **lice**' (01v). The word '**lice**' denotes an area fenced off for sporting competition.[149] This would bring the reference away from the horse-training fields owned by Boss Croker and closer to the nearby Leopardstown racecourse, which Beckett often used in his work. But, instead, Beckett chose to translate Croker's Acres as **'la vaine pâture'** (FT1, 05r). The phrase 'vaine pâture' or 'droit de (vaine) pâture' refers to grazing rights for villagers' livestock on cultivated land, once reaping has been completed.[150] This would accord with the winter setting mentioned elsewhere in the text, as well as further emphasizing Bouche's marginalized social position by suggesting that she visits the pasture in the months when it is occupied by beasts. As Emilie Morin points out, Beckett thus uses the 'culturally specific' practice of French grazing rights to get over this problem of geographical specificity in translation (2009, 149).

One of the few standalone additions (without accompanying deletions) in FT1 emphasizes the fact that Bouche is 'seule **au monde**' (06r, 07r), returning to the theme of *Pas moi*'s opening words and highlighting the fact that Bouche's isolation takes place as part of a social matrix. We have already seen that the society with which Mouth interacts is harsh and unforgiving. This is emphasized in Beckett's choice of verb to describe how Bouche was '**brought up** [...] to believe [...] in a merciful [...] God' (1973a, 7, 8; *KLT* 86, 87): '**dressée** qu'elle avait été à croire [...] en un Dieu [...] miséricordieux' (1975b, 10, 11). In *Rhythmanalysis*, his study of the rhythms of everyday life, Henri Lefebvre uses the term 'dressage' to describe the ways in which

148 Beckett also struggled with the translation of Croker's Acres in *Compagnie*, eventually setting for 'les pâturages' (Nugent-Folan 2021, 373).

149 'Espace entouré de palissades où se déroulaient les tournois, les joutes au Moyen Âge' (https://www.cnrtl.fr/definition/lice).

150 '*Vaine pâture; droit de (vaine) pâture*. Droit réservé à une communauté de faire paître les troupeaux sur certaines terres cultivées, après que la récolte a été enlevée, et sur certaines prairies après la fauche; ensemble des terres où s'exerce ce droit' (https://www.cnrtl.fr/definition/p%C3%A2ture).

bodies are 'broken-in' to a culture like animals through training based on repetition (2007, 39). Beckett's characters – particularly the female ones – are 'broken-in' to social relationships in precisely these terms, with Molloy subjecting his mother to a 'période de **dressage**' (2012b, 22) ['period of training' (*Mo* 15)] which involves repeatedly hitting her on the head. Though the precise type of 'dressage' to which Bouche is subjected as part of her institutional upbringing is not specified, it would presumably have had the repetitious spiritual training of prayer at its centre. The religious aspect of Bouche's worldview – however reluctantly received – is highlighted when her '**begging**' that the mouth stop talking (1973a, 12, 15; *KLT* 90, 92) becomes a '**prière**' in the French version (1975b, 17, 23). And there is a suggestion that such prayers might be answered, with a change from the legalistic '**pardonnée**' (FM2, 06r) to the more overtly religious '**graciée**' (FT1, 06r) to describe how Bouche is 'forgiven' (1973a, 14; *KLT* 91, 92).

Translating the Bible

There are two sets of marginal annotations to Beckett's translation of biblical passages in FM2. The first marks the translation of 'God is love ... tender mercies ... new every morning ...' (1973a, 14; *KLT* 91). The French version is subject to some important changes: 'Dieu ~~c'~~est ~~l'~~amour.. plein de miséricorde bonté intarissable...**renouvelée chaque matin...**' (FM2, 06r). The first term in the open variant relates to Louis Segond's translation of James 5:11: 'le Seigneur est plein de miséricorde et de compassion'. Beckett wrote '1re Epitre Jean.IV.8' in the left margin to mark the change from 'Dieu c'est l'amour' to the version in Segond's translation: 'Dieu est amour'. But part of the second term in the open variant, 'bonté intarissable...**renouvelée chaque matin...**', is derived from Martin's translation: 'ses compassions ne sont point taries. Elles se renouvellent chaque matin'. On the next page, the same open variant is created and this time it is keyed in the left margin: '(Lamentations.III.22–23)' (FM2, 07r).

As Van Hulle and Nixon state in their analysis of this use of the Segond and Martin translations: 'Beckett's use of his French Bibles is sometimes eclectic' (2013, 179). Iain Bailey has drawn attention to the fact that Beckett's francophone biblical eclecticism goes beyond the two French Bibles contained in his library at the time of his death:

> In the 'Whoroscope' Notebook, he writes out passages from the parable of Lazarus and Dives (that biblical staple of his) in English, Italian and French (21–22). The French corresponds to neither of the library copies, but instead to the eighteenth-century Ostervald translation. Even this is not the final word: Hamm's 'mané, mané' in *Fin de partie* corresponds to none of these editions. (Bailey 2012, 356)

Bailey points out that Hamm's phrase 'can be found in translations by de Sacy and Genoude' (2012, 363n5). There could be yet another edition at play in *Pas moi*. In the typed layer of FT1, Beckett returned to his early version of the text from FM2, before again introducing variants: 'Dieu ~~c~~'est ~~l~~'amour...~~plein de miséricorde~~ bonté intarissable...**chaque matin nouvelle**...' (06r). Though these variants are almost exactly the same as those introduced on FM2, the phrase **'chaque matin nouvelle'** is different. It may be based on the translation of Lamentations by J. N. Darby: 'ses compassions ne cessent pas; elles sont **nouvelles chaque matin**'. Before we add Darby to the ever-growing list of Beckett's French Bibles, it does need to be noted that the word order is different here, as is the number of the adjective 'nouvelle' – referring to the singular 'bonté' in Beckett's text but the plural 'compassions' in Darby's. And it is not a huge leap from FM2's **'renouvelée'** (06r, 07r) to FT1's **'nouvelle'** (06r, 07r), certainly not large enough to locate with certainty its origin in an exogenetic source. Nevertheless, the biblical eclecticism noted above raises the strong possibility of there being other French Bibles – such as Darby's – involved in this passage of *Pas moi*.

Translating Stage Space

As in the first English draft, Beckett had trouble with stage terminology in the first draft of *Pas moi*. Though hard to read, it seems he initially put the Auditeur 'vers ~~le devant~~' before changing this to **'l'avant-scène'** (FM2, 08r). The designation of the Auditeur itself is even more interesting. Firstly, the French noun reveals the figure to be male, in spite of the stage directions stating: '*sexe indéterminé*' (1975b, 7).[151] As he wrote on 16 October 1972 in

151 Albeit the adjective '*indéterminé*' [indeterminate] is itself slightly weaker than the English 'undeterminable' (1973a, 6).

response to Alan Schneider's question as to how anyone knows Auditor is a man: 'It is not stated, though suggested by masculine "auditor", that it is a man' (*LSB IV* 311). This is an example of Beckett's multilingual poetics at work even before he had translated the play, with the author seemingly momentarily forgetting that this English noun is not gendered. When he came to translate the term into French, it was indeed the masculine 'Auditeur' that he chose rather than the feminine 'Auditrice'. However, this choice was not made without hesitation. On FT1, Beckett put the open variant 'TEMOIN' in the left margin (01r). While 'auditeur' is most commonly used to denote a listener, 'témoin' [witness] has more explicitly political connotations.[152] There is a much greater ethical force to witnessing than simply listening, especially when the story is one of suffering like Mouth's. In this case, a witness might be feel obliged to remediate what they have witnessed for another audience.

The ethics of witnessing is a key theme in Beckett's work. In 1952, he wrote a short story, 'On le tortura bien', in which the narrator absents himself from a tent while his colleagues torture somebody because, in addition to being unable to carry out torture himself, he cannot bear to be present and witness another carrying it out (UoR MS 1656/3, 01r). Beckett was also considering the problem of witnessing while he translated *Not I*. In the mid-1980s, he gave advice to Lawrence Shainberg, who was trying to write a novel: 'You need a witness and you need the first person, that's the problem, isn't it? One thing that might help ... you might have a look at an early book of mine, perhaps you know it, Mercier and Camier. I had a similar problem there. It begins, "I know what happened with Mercier and Camier because I was there with them all the time"' (Shainberg 1987). Since Beckett was translating *Mercier et Camier* as he started working on *Pas moi*, this narrative aspect of witnessing would have been on his mind.

Moreover, Beckett was acquainted with the literature of witnessing that developed in the wake of the Second World War.[153] For instance, in September 1959 he purchased Elie Wiesel's *La nuit*, a memoir of life in the concentration camps of Auschwitz and Buchenwald, published by Minuit (Morin 2017, 152). Emilie Morin describes *La nuit* as 'a testimony

152 Beckett would go on to use 'witness' in 'The Voice / Verbatim', a precursor text to *Company* (see Nugent-Folan 2021, 159).

153 For more on testimony in Beckett's work, see Houston Jones (2011).

whose initial Yiddish version had remained largely unnoticed, and which became internationally celebrated following its republication in abbreviated form by Lindon and its English translation [1960]' (2017, 152). Wiesel's book is a continual reflection on the importance of bearing witness to his experiences in the concentration camps, from the opening figure of Moishe the Beadle, who tries unsuccessfully to warn Wiesel's Jewish community of the oncoming Nazi destruction, to the text's narrator himself, who is at every stage aware of the importance of bearing witness. In a preface to a new English translation in 2006, Wiesel stated his reason for writing the book: 'Convinced that this period in history would be judged one day, I knew that I must bear witness' (2006, viii). Beckett would have been well aware of these historical resonances attached to the word 'witness'.[154] It is all the more interesting, therefore, that having strongly considered this term, he decided to go for the more neutral 'Auditeur'. While a witness such as Wiesel usually plays the role of mediator between event and audience, Beckett's Auditor has no such mediating role between Mouth's monologue and the theatre audience. Instead, the Auditor's gestures indicate a bafflement on the same level as our own.

When translating the Auditor's gestures into French, Beckett made an important addition. While the English version only mentions 'a gesture of helpless compassion' (1973a, 16; *KLT* 83), Beckett replaced this on FT1: 'un mouvement ~~**de compassion impuissante**~~ **fait de blâme et de pitié impuissante'** (08r), probably as a result of his experience with staging the play. This replacement of compassion with a mixture of reprimand and pity presents a gestural challenge for the actor. From a textual point of view, what is interesting here is the echo of the 'superb pun' from Dante's *Divine Comedy* which Belacqua puzzles over in 'Dante and the Lobster' (1932): 'Qui vive la pietà quand'è ben morta' (*Inferno*, Canto XX, l. 28; see *MPTK* 11). When Dante sheds tears on seeing the suffering of the damned soothsayers in the eighth circle of hell, Virgil rebukes him with these words, which Robert and

154 While Beckett was translating *Not I*, Alan Schneider was collaborating with Wiesel on a stage version of Wiesel's *Zalmen; or The Madness of God*. The pair worked on a TV version of the play later that year (see Schneider to Beckett, 14 January, 17 February and 17 June 1974, *NABS* 312, 313, 316). In these letters, Schneider kept Beckett abreast of this collaboration, so the Irishman would have been hard-pressed to ignore the ethical implications of using a word like 'témoin' in *Pas moi*.

Jean Hollander translate thus: 'Here piety lives when pity is quite dead'.[155] However, since 'pietà' can be translated as either 'pity' or 'piety', the line draws Belacqua's attention. When he asks his Italian teacher for her advice on how to translate the pun, she asks rhetorically: 'Do you think [...] it is absolutely necessary to translate it?' (*MPTK* 12). In Beckett's case, he did have to translate the Auditor's gesture, and he did so by splitting compassion into 'blâme' and 'pitié'.

Beckett had made a similar translation decision when incorporating divine compassion – or rather, the lack thereof – into his 1931 poem 'Text 3': 'Lo-Ruhama Lo-Ruhama / pity is quick with death' (*CP* 39).[156] As Van Hulle and Nixon point out, Beckett used his Italian Bible to mark the salacious Old Testament passages mentioned in Voltaire's *Troisième lettre du journal d'Amabed* (2013, 181). One of these involved God's instruction to Hosea to marry and impregnate a prostitute, which led to the birth of Lo-Ruhama. The relevant passage in the King James Version reads: 'Call her name Lo-Ruhamah: for I will no more have mercy upon the house of Israel; but I will utterly take them away. But I will have mercy upon the house of Judah' (Hosea 1:6–7).[157] In Beckett's Italian Bible, God's 'mercy' appears as 'compassione', making Beckett's translation decision in *Pas moi* a direct descendent of the similarly split translation of compassion in 'Text 3'.[158]

'Why not piety and pity both, even down below?', asks Belacqua (*MPTK* 13). This question regarding the translation of Dante's pun reverberates in Beckett's own decision to translate 'compassion' as a mixture of 'blâme' and 'pitié' in *Pas moi*. In doing so, he may have been trying to square the circle of creating a critical yet compassionate response on the part of the Auditeur. Beckett would edit this still further when directing *Pas moi* in the theatre, first getting rid of the Auditeur for the 1975 Paris production, then changing the gesture in 1978 (see chapter 2.3.1). The problem of translation puzzled over by Belacqua thus became a gestural problem in the translation of Beckett's later play.

155 All references to *The Divine Comedy* are to Dante Alighieri (1999) unless otherwise stated.

156 This poem was first published as 'Text' but is listed as 'Text 3' in *CP*.

157 Van Hulle and Nixon point out that the spelling of this child's name as found in Beckett's *Sacra Bibbia* is the same as in 'Text 3' (2013, 182).

158 https://www.beckettarchive.org/library/SAC-BIB.html, 1173.

Verbal Rhythm and Syntax

Beckett told Knowlson that he used to recite his texts aloud while composing them (Haynes and Knowlson 2003, 8). And Pascale Sardin-Damestoy points out the ways in which rhythm often took precedence over sense in Beckett's translations (2020, 21). Like the compositional manuscripts of *Not I*, the *Pas moi* manuscripts bear witness to Beckett's attention to detail with regards to verbal rhythm. As a general rule, Beckett tends to cut down on the number of words and syllables in each successive draft. As in my analysis of the English text (see chapter 2.2.2), the former is here termed 'verbal undoing' and the latter 'syllabic undoing'. The deletion of actual words can be seen where Beckett changed '~~pas **trace** d'amour~~..' (FM1, 01r) to 'pas d'amour..' (FM2, 01r), deleted a preposition when editing 'pas seulement **~~au revoir~~** merci' (FT1, 04r) and changed '~~même **dans les** meilleures conditions~~' (FM1, 03r) to become 'même meilleures conditions' (FM2, 03r). A striking example of such 'verbal undoing' occurs in the most onomatopoeic part of Bouche's narrative: **'le cerveau..**~~s'affolant~~ ~~par à coups..~~ ~~saccadé~~ affolé...~~à droite **et à** gauche~~...~~vlan~~ **crrac!**' (FM2, 05r). In FT1, this became **'le cerveau...** affolé... **~~crac!~~** **krak**!' (05r). In the published text, it is shorter again: **'le cerveau... krac !**' (1975b, 19). The genesis of this phrase demonstrates very well Beckett's tendency towards 'verbal undoing'.

Beckett's practice of 'syllabic undoing' is evident in the changes from '**~~bourdonnement~~**' (FM1, 01r) to **'bourdon'** (FM2, 01r), **'raconte'** (FM2, 04r) to **'dit'** (FT1, 04r), '**~~promenades~~**' to **'balades'** (FT1, 05r) and '~~le **bereeau**~~' to **'les langes'** (FT1, 05r). And sometimes both verbal and syllabic 'undoing' are evident in the same instance, as when Beckett cut down '~~aux abords de ses soixante ans~~' (FM1, 01r) to '~~abords **de la soixantaine**~~' and then again to **'bientôt soixante'** (FM2, 01r). Another such example is when Bouche comments on her inability to lie: '**~~un défaut~~** vice de caractère' (FT1, 03r). As these instances show, the general tendency is towards a reduction of spoken material.

There are exceptions to the general rule of 'syllabic undoing', which we might term 'syllabic redoing'. For example, Beckett changed the adjective describing an idea Bouche has from '**~~atroce~~**' to **'effrayante'** on FT1 (05r). Likewise, he first considered '~~grimaces~~' for the movements of Bouche's face but then changed this to '~~contorsions~~' (FM1, 04r). In another instance, 'syllabic redoing' is used when the noun 'scènes' (FM2, 05r) is replaced by 'scénettes' (FT1, 05r) in order to translate the 'flashes' of Mouth's past (1973a, 12; *KLT* 90). The move from 'scènes' to the diminutive 'scénettes' is a reduction of sorts, even though the word gets longer. We have already seen another instance of verbal and syllabic 'redoing' in the move from '~~**assise** par terre~~' (FM1, 05r) to '**à croupetons** dans l'herbe' (1975b, 18). In these two latter cases, it seems Beckett made exceptions to the rule in order to create a particular effect with the added material – either using the diminutive or making Bouche more animalistic. The general rule still holds that Beckett stripped back many phrases in *Pas moi* as he worked on the translation.

With regard to the syntax of Beckett's translation, a comparative analysis of the two published texts shows that the first French version is more broken up than its English counterpart, with Minuit's text containing 788 three-dot ellipses to Faber's 750 (1975b; 1973a). It seems that in order to stage the breakdown of the subject in French, Beckett needed to break *up* his syntactic structure. A phrase which is representative of this general tendency is the English 'when clearly intended to be having pleasure ...' (1973a, 8; *KLT* 86), which becomes 'alors qu'elle était présumée... toute évidence... éprouver du plaisir...' (1975b, 10). Fragmentation was not a rigid rule, however, as can be seen in the translation of the very next phrase 'she was in fact ... having none ...' (1973a, 8; *KLT* 86): 'elle n'en éprouvait aucun...' (1975b, 10–11). While Beckett was pragmatic rather than programmatic in his translation of the text, fragmentation is more common than this kind of syntactic consolidation over the course of the entire translation.

Elsewhere, I have suggested that the Director's forceful rejection of 'explicitation' in Beckett's *Catastrophe* may be related to the translation process of 'rendering information which is only implicit in the source text explicit in the target text' (Frankenberg-Garcia 2004, 1; see Little 2020c, 183–4). Though I have come across no evidence of Beckett using the term in this technical sense, frequent use of the translational practice can be found by comparing *Not I* and *Pas moi*. For example, the phrase 'just hand in the list ...' (1973a, 10; *KLT* 88) becomes '**tout inscrit sur un bout de papier...** plus qu'à le donner...' (1975b, 14), giving us the more explicit description that everything is written on Mouth's piece of paper, so that she only has to hand it in, information which is implicit in the English text. As in many cases of 'explicitation', the above instance involves adding words to the target text, proving again that 'redoing' was important in Beckett's epigenetic textual practice. Two further instances of explicitation foreground Bouche's own presence in the spoken text. The phrase 'as if it hadn't heard ...' (1973a, 12; *KLT* 90) becomes 'comme si elle n'entendait pas... **la bouche**...' (1975b, 17) and '... like maddened ...' (1973a, 12; *KLT* 90) is rendered as 'comme folle... **la bouche** devenue folle...' (1975b, 17), having first been the more compact '~~comme folle furieuse..~~' (FM1, 04r). Beckett also added 'bouche' to a passage in FM2, at the point of the monologue where Mouth lists 'lips ... cheeks ... jaws ... tongue ...' (1973a, 11; *KLT* 89): '**bouche**...lèvres...joues... mâchoires...langue...' (04r). In addition to this foregrounding of the protagonist's name, Beckett also uses 'redoing' to bring out a particular theme in the text. We saw in the English genesis how the term 'so-called' was used to draw attention to the social matrix from which Mouth is alienated. In the French text, there is an additional instance of this term, with the phrase 'all dead still but for the buzzing ...' (1973a, 10; *KLT* 88) translated as 'silence de tombe~~au~~ à part le bourdon...**soi-disant...**' (FT1, 04r).[159] Whether adding body parts, references to society or instances of explicitation, Beckett's 'redoing' in translation demonstrates his felt need to have more textual material in order to stage Bouche's breakdown.

In spite of these instances of 'redoing', there is a strange sense that the text is running out in the French version, which Beckett highlighted in a remarkable way. At one point, Mouth's recollection of speaking '**once** or **twice** a year ...' (1973a, 10; *KLT* 88) becomes the more frequent '**deux trois** fois ~~par~~ l'an...' (FT1, 04r), having been '~~deux fois par an maximum..~~' in the first draft (FM1, 03r). But towards the end of the text, two instances of '**once** or **twice** a year ...' (1973a, 15; *KLT* 92) are translated as the more isomorphic '**une deux** fois ~~par~~ l'an...' (FT1, 07r). This suggests that Bouche's breakdown may be running out of steam by virtue of her instances of speech becoming less frequent. A similar strategy is applied to her body parts, which, as we saw above, are mentioned more frequently in the French text. In one passage, 'the mouth alone ...' (1973a, 11; *KLT* 89) is 'redone' verbally to also include the face: 'que la bouche...**la face...**' (FT1, 05r). However, towards the

159 This translation seems to correct an error in the English text, as the phrase 'so-called' appears in all of Beckett's English manuscript versions, before being omitted in RC playscript (https://www.beckettarchive.org/noti/comparesentences/0016).

end of the text ‘just the mouth …’ (1973a, 15; *KLT* 92) is translated simply as ‘rien que la bouche…’ (1975b, 23). Again, there is a sense that a more detailed picture is being reduced as the text goes on. Does this mean that Bouche stands a better chance than Mouth of her breakdown of subjectivity coming to an end? As we will see in my analysis of the play’s ending, there is also evidence which would counterbalance this hypothesis.

Unending

When translating Mouth’s story of her birth cry, Beckett drew attention to the way in which her breakdown of subjectivity is a continuous process. As discussed in chapter 2.2.2, Mouth’s comparison of her current silence to her birth cry recalls the ‘vagitus’ of *Breath*: ‘just the birth cry to get her going … breathing …’ (1973a, 12; *KLT* 90). Having translated this cry in *Souffle* as ‘un vagissement’ (2014a, 137), Beckett brought *Pas moi* even closer to the earlier play by using ‘~~le~~ un vagissement’ (FT1, 05r) before performing both verbal and syllabic ‘undoing’ by using the verb form ‘vagir’ (FT2, 07r). This passage is also notable for introducing a notion of finality, which is immediately undermined by the text that follows: ‘vagir un point c’est tout… la mettre en route… le souffle en route…’ (1975b, 18). The idiom ‘un point c’est tout’ translates as ‘there is nothing more to say’. But Bouche does have more to say – a lot more – and her recounting of the birth cry serves to kick-start another swathe of narrative. By using this idiom in his translation, Beckett draws further attention to the open-endedness of Bouche’s monologue.

Elsewhere, Beckett considered moving away from a term which stresses the incompletion of Bouche’s monologue, but then doubled back on this choice. At the point where Mouth says she was ‘not completely’ speechless (1973a, 14; *KLT* 92), Beckett first went for the literal translation **‘pas complètement’** (FM2, 06r). He then introduced the open variant ‘pas complètement **vraiment’**, the latter term of which would have taken away from ‘The Sense of “Unending”’ (Van Hulle 2014a, 213) in the initial draft’s negation of completion. In the published text, Beckett uses the alternative ‘pas **entièrement**’ (1975b, 22), again drawing on an adverb of wholeness only to negate it.

A fascinating attempt to keep the text open can be seen in Beckett's translation of the final phrase of *Pas moi*.[160] In his note on the gesture of the Auditeur, Beckett hesitated between two terms when describing Bouche's 'véhément refus **de quitter** **d'abandonner** la troisième personne' (FT1, 08r), the latter alternative recalling Bouche's abandonment by her own parents, which led to her growing up with the other 'abandonnés' in an institution (1975b, 10, 11). It is possible that **'quitter'** and '**abandonner**' were too definitive for use as the final verbs of the playtext. So, Beckett chose '**lâcher**' in the published text (1975b, 24), which translates as 'to let go' or 'to drop'. In doing so, he echoes his translation of Mouth's repeated imperative towards the very end of her monologue to 'keep on' (1973a, 15; *KLT* 92–3), the last words spoken before the curtain starts to fall. He first translated this as '**ne pas lâcher**', before verbally undoing this phrase on FT1: '~~**ne**~~ pas lâcher' (07r). While 'quitter' and 'abandonner' have a greater sense of finality, 'lâcher' serves as a complimentary pairing to the closing spoken word of FM2: 'reprendre –' (07r) ['pick it up –' (1973a, 15; *KLT* 93)]. Beckett added to this in FT1, creating a French ending that, even more so than its English counterpart, refuses to let go: 'reprendre là…**repartir de** –' (07r). This final phrase – which translates as 'start again from' – creates a smoother grammatical transition into the ad lib after the curtain falls, but also points to the potential for Bouche's whole monologue to start up again. This implies that Bouche is not a subject who is broken by a single dramatic event, but one who is rather in a continuous state of breakdown as part of a staged – and re-staged – performative process.

160 While some English-language editions print the note on the Auditor at the start of the text, the French published versions all have it at the end.

Part II

The Making of *That Time* / *Cette fois*

3 Documents

3.1 Autograph Manuscripts

3.1.1 English

English manuscripts (EM)

EM (MS-UoR-1477-1)

The *Beckett at Reading* catalogue describes this manuscript as follows:

> Original manuscript of *That Time.* 30 × 21 cm. 13 leaves. Dated f. 1 Paris, 8 June 1974, last date (f. 9) Ussy, 18 June 1974. Written and corrected in black ink. [...] The sheet headed 'A1' (f. 4), is a photocopy. (Bryden, Garforth and Mills 1998, 89–90)

In addition to the first and last dates on the manuscript – 'Paris 8.6.74' (01r) and 'Ussy / 18.6.74' (09r) – Beckett dated the first page of B's monologue 'Ussy 14.6.74' (06r) and the last 'Ussy / 17.6.74' (08r). These Ussy dates mark an intensive period of work in Beckett's rural bolthole. The manuscript is titled 'THAT TIME' (01r) and since this title does not appear again until ET5, it is possible that it was added at a later stage. However, the phrase 'that time' does appear in one of the very first notes on the play (01r).

According to Bryden, Garforth and Mills, 'The first three leaves are numbered by Beckett in black ink, while the rest are numbered by RUL' (1998, 90). On folio 05r, there is a letter/figure in the top right corner of the page which may have been written by Beckett, but this is deleted and illegible. Folios 12r and 13r seem to have a little squares of lighter-coloured paper stuck in the top right corner by an archivist, with '12?' and '13?' written there respectively with an archivist's pencil. This suggests the document was refoliated at some point, a fact supported by Gontarski's account of this manuscript once containing 15 folios (1985, 154; see also Gontarski 1980, 115).[161] The two 'extra' folios included material from Beckett's production

161 Gontarski's transcriptions indicate that the leaf now foliated '13?' was once foliated as leaf 12 in the Reading archive and that the leaf now foliated as '12?' was once foliated 13 (1985, 155, 157).

notes and are now catalogued as part of a separate document (UoR MS 1639; see EN below and chapter 3.5.1).

01r–03r: Stage directions and notes

According to Pountney, this document starts with 'three pages of notes on the projected play' (1988, 268). It would appear that Beckett first tried to write a version of the stage directions at the top of folio 01r, before breaking off into conceptual notes. While the vast majority of the draft material in EM consists of versions of sentences which appear later in the textual genesis, much of the material in the first three pages consists of the conceptual notes Pountney mentions.

EM starts with a paragraph of stage directions, some of which are underlined:

> Old man (sitting) in dark. ~~Front, a~~ Facing front, a little off centre. Face alone lit~~.~~ faintly. Very white, long white hair standing on end. (01r)

In the margins are two versions of later sentences which also contain authorial commentary regarding their place in the text: 'face about 8' above stage level, problem in consequence.' and 'Head on white pillow?' (01r). The following three paragraphs, each featuring one sentence, are likewise versions of later sentences:

> Faint tick-tack throughout, only just audible in silence.[162]

> No blinking. Eyes ~~wide xx~~ staring ~~front~~ wide ~~open~~ as long as possible, then closed as long or longer. or: eyes open only in silence

> 3-fold text in single voice coming from left (A), right (B), above (C). (01r)

162 This line and the one concerning the pillow are discussed further in chapter 4.1.2.

At this point, Beckett begins to outline concepts for the play, most of which do not relate to any particular sentence in the text. So, my editorial interpretation of the document structure is that Beckett started the drafting process by trying to construct a draft of the play (by sketching out stage directions), before conceptualizing it more broadly in the subsequent notes.

If time is the central theme of *That Time*, Beckett's early notes show the degree to which he also used it as an important structural concept when composing the play. One note shows that Beckett had a 'specific duration in mind' (Pountney 1988, 269) at this early stage of composition: '15 min. @ 200 words/min. = 3000 words, i.e. 3 recordings 1000 words ~~each~~ apiece' (EM, 01r). Most of the other notes focus on the problem of the overlap of voices, outlined above on the same page: 'Overlapping voices, ~~i.e.~~ e.g. A beginning stops B or C, but for a moment 2 together. A may resist, B or C yield & A continue' (EM, 01r). Having introduced the concept of two long silences in the middle of the speeches, Beckett then made a series of notes sketching out how this might be achieved, ending

> How: perhaps only 3 changes of voice by interruption, each interrupted & interrupting only once, the other ~~3~~[2] changes following silences, e.g.
>
> <u>Silence</u>
>
> A 2 ½
> B " → (<u>by interruption</u>)
>
> <u>Silence</u>
>
> C 2 ½ (" ")
> A " ↗
>
> <u>Silence</u>
>
> B 2 ½
> C " → (" ")

Silence (EM, 02r)

The above list breaks up Beckett's initial tripartite structure, giving two-and-a-half minutes to every instance of each monologue. Time is divided up even further in a list directly following this, in which Beckett ticks off in red and black ink the letters marking the monologues:

Silence ~~xx~~

✓A✓ 1 ¼
✓C✓ 1 ¼ → (by interruption)
✓A✓ 1 ¼ → "
✓B✓ 1 ¼ → "

Silence

✓C✓ 1 ¼ →
✓B✓ 1 ¼ → (by interruption)
✓C✓ 1 ¼ → "
✓A✓ 1 ¼ → "

Silence

✓B✓ 1 ¼ →
✓A✓ 1 ¼ → (by interruption)
✓B✓ 1 ¼ → "
✓C 1 ¼ → "

Silence (EM, 02r)

These seven red ticks, which follow the letters in the second and third paragraphs, are the only exception to Beckett's use of black ink in the manuscript. Indicating the extent to which the temporal structure of the play was linked to Beckett's writing process, a note in the left margin reads '1 ¼ = 200 words' (EM, 02r). At the bottom of the page, he considered breaking up these one-and-a-quarter-minute chunks even further: 'instead of 4 × 75 sec.

try 8 × 40 secs = 100 words approx with repeat of above order. Or change 2nd time round' (EM, 02r).

It is likely Beckett wrote his structural plans as he composed his typescripts, not before, given that his second structural plan is only implemented on ET2 (see below). The very short third page of notes certainly shows evidence of being written later in the compositional process, particularly through its use of the term 'overlaps', which features prominently on ET2 (see ET2 below and chapter 3.6). As in the composition of *Not I* and *Footfalls*, then, Beckett returned to his holograph draft at a later stage, using it to add conceptual notes as he was composing his typescripts. This points to the potential problems caused by reading Beckett's manuscripts – particularly his early holographs – in a straightforward, linear manner.

04r–13r: monologues and stage directions

Beckett's manner of breaking down the subject in this play built on *Not I*. But his manner of breaking up the text in composition changed as he wrote *That Time*'s monologues. The 'A' monologues are written in long, unbroken paragraphs, reminiscent of the unbroken paragraphs in the manuscripts of *L'Innommable* (see *BDMP2*, FN1 and FN2). In total, A's monologues number 867 words in this draft. B's monologues are broken up into eighteen paragraphs. Unlike A's monologues, these paragraphs are without punctuation regulating the flow of the text, such as commas and dashes, and also lack 'indentation and grammatical capitalisation', making this textual layout very similar to the manuscripts of *Comment c'est* (O'Reilly 2016, xx). The 'B' paragraphs range in length from 32 to 95 words, with a total word count of 1027 and a mean word count for each paragraph of 57.05. C's monologues total 973 words, showing that, especially in the cases of B and C, Beckett stuck quite strictly to his concept of having three sections of 1,000 words each. In the thirteen paragraphs of C's monologue, there is one unusually long paragraph of 215 words, while the shortest is 28, with a mean of 74.85.[163]

163 Word counts are calculated using the 'Top Layer' transcription tool in the online genetic edition, excluding fragments in the margins.

So, while the general concept of three voices – again reminiscent of *Comment c'est* – is present from the first folio of EM, the complex layering of the voices outlined on folio 02r only begins to be evident in the paragraph structure of monologues B and C. Moreover, while close attention is paid to the overall word count of these later monologues, the paragraph lengths themselves are uneven.

The labelling of the monologues with a number and a letter at the top of each page indicates that Beckett used these combinations as a means of foliation rather than a numbering of sections which would map onto the structural lists of folio 02r. A's monologue is labelled 'A1' (04r) and 'A2' (05r), which does correspond to the breakdown of the text on the first list on folio 02r. However, B's monologue is labelled 'B1' (06r), 'B2' (07r) and 'B3' (08r), a subdivision that corresponds to none of Beckett's lists. This may be why Beckett's own more traditional method of foliating the pages by putting folio numbers in the top right corner stops after the page marked 'A1' (04r), as it would have then become possible for him to order the monologue leaves without these more standard folio numbers. C's monologue is divided into four parts – 'C1' (09r), 'C2' (10r), 'C3' (11r) and 'C4' (12r) – which does correspond to the number of 'C' monologues on the second list of folio 02r. However, as shown in the table below, the word counts for each page are uneven, making it unlikely that Beckett was treating these monologue divisions as discrete sections of the text.

Monologue number	Word count	Folio
A1	510	04r
A2	357	05r
B1	395	06r
B2	271	07r
B3	361	08r
C1	360	09r
C2	185	10r
C3	174	11r
C4	254	12r

This evidence supports the hypothesis that Beckett's structural plans on EM (02r) were made after he composed the monologues.

C's monologue shares space with drafts of the stage directions on folio 12r, while folio 13r contains multiple drafts of these same stage directions. As these are drafts of the stage directions made on ET5, they will be discussed further in chapter 4.1.2.

EN (MS-UoR-1639, 02r)

This loose leaf is stored as part of MS 1639 in the University of Reading's Beckett Collection. However, it was not always catalogued thus. As outlined in the above description of EM, the two leaves of MS 1639 were once catalogued as part of MS-UoR-1477-1. While the material on the first page in MS 1639 is part of the post-publication *après-texte*, as it refers to the first published edition of *That Time* in its page numbers (see chapter 3.5.1), the material on the second page is regarded in the online genetic edition as part of Beckett's compositional *avant-texte*.[164] Both leaves are transcribed and photographically reproduced in the fourth volume of Beckett's *Theatrical Notebooks* (*TN4* 357–66).

Like ET6, EN is composed in red and black ink. It begins with lists of paragraph orders which are similar in their content, layout and red ink colour (Bryden, Garforth and Mills 1998, 96) to those found on ET6 (04r).[165] Indeed, one of the lists at the top of the page matches exactly a version of the paragraph order on the earlier typescript: '~~ACBCABCABCAB~~' (EN; ET6, 04r). Though none of the other lists on EN match those of ET6, they can be seen as a common attempt to reshape the play in serial terms. The last group of lists on EN corresponds to the order found on ET7 after the numbers in the left margin of the typescript had been revised in black pen (see below):

> ACBACBACB~~AC~~^{CA}B
> CBACBACBA~~CB~~^{BC}A
> BACBACBACBAC

164 In genetic criticism, the *avant-texte* is defined as 'the multiple versions preceding the published text', while the *après-texte* is constituted by 'epigenetic transformations' (Van Hulle 2014a, 199, 230).

165 On both documents, this red ink has now faded to pink.

On the bottom half of EN, Beckett writes out the first and last phrases of the play's 36 paragraphs, giving each a number and a numbered letter in the left margin. The paragraph order corresponds to the list just above it on the page, with the same revisions made on both lists:

1 A1 that time .. when was that
2 C1 when you went .. when was that
3 B1 on the stone .. no sound

What is interesting about this list in terms of manuscript chronology is that the lines used are not drawn from ET7, or even ET6, but from an earlier typescript, ET5. Three examples demonstrate this:

- '16 C6 when you **began** .. closing time'
  Though 'when you **began**' is found on ET5 (04r), the line becomes 'when you **started**' on ET6 (05r) and all subsequent typescripts.
- '24 A8 huddled on the **step** .. where none ever came'
  The opening phrase appears as 'huddled on the **~~door~~step**' on ET5 (05r), but becomes 'huddled on the **doorstep**' on ET6 (01r) and thereafter.
- '36 C12 only the old breath .. gone in no time'
  The opening phrase is 'only the old breath' on ET5 (07r) but receives an insertion on ET6 which remains in all later versions: '**not a sound** only the old breath' (ET6, 06r).

Based on this evidence, it would appear that the lists on EN pick up from those on ET6 (04r) and provide the basis for the revised paragraph order on ET7, but that when extracting lines from the text itself, Beckett went back to the earlier typescript ET5 (see Genetic Map for a visualization of this). This could be because at this point in the genesis, ET5 was the most up-to-date 'full' version of the play (with stage directions and the monologues fragmented in paragraphs), whereas ET6 and ET7 are '<u>Continuity</u>' versions, with each monologue written continuously to help Beckett work out the order of the various paragraphs (see chapter 3.2.1).

3.1.2 French

French manuscripts (FM)

FM (MS-UoR-1657-1)

> 10 leaves. 30 × 21 cm. Text written and corrected in black ink. Text divided into three major sections: A, B, and C. Each of these is divided into twelve sub-sections in a manner similar to the technique used in drafting the original English piece: see [ET1], for example. These sections are individually numbered by Beckett, and occupy three leaves each. The last leaf carries a 'Note' relating to the staging of the play. (Bryden, Garforth and Mills 1998, 96)

As Bryden, Garforth and Mills point out, this manuscript of *Cette fois* is 'undated' (1998, 96). In addition to using a thin-nibbed ballpoint for most of the text and corrections, Beckett used a felt-tipped black pen for a very small number of insertions. This has faded to very dark purple on folios 01r–02r and 04r–07r. What appears to be the same pen is used for an insertion and deletion on folio 10r, but this time it has faded to a very dark brown. This suggests that the final page containing the note may have been exposed to different storage conditions than the rest of the manuscript, which led to a different change of colour.

3.2 Typescripts

3.2.1 English

English typescripts

ET1 (MS-UoR-1477-2)

> Untitled typescript, with manuscript additions and corrections by Samuel Beckett, of *That Time*; undated. 30 × 21 cm. 6 leaves; f. 1 headed 'TS 1' in black ink by Beckett. (Bryden, Garforth and Mills 1998, 90)

If the multiple dates on EM show that Beckett generated his text in stages, ET1 also 'represent[s] multiple stages of the play's composition' (Gontarski 1985, 157). Just over two weeks after the latest date on EM, Beckett wrote to Barney Rosset: 'That Time advancing slowly' (3 July 1974, CU, Barney Rosset Papers, box 46, folder 5). Indeed, the change of font size between folios 02r (on which A's monologue ends) and 03r (on which B's begins) indicates that this document 'was typed on two different machines' (Gontarski 1985, 157), while 'the change in variety of paper between sections "B" and "C" suggests a possible second break'. The fading type towards the middle of folio 05r further suggests that Beckett 'changed the ribbon on his typewriter' at this point in the writing process (Bryden, Garforth and Mills 1998, 90). All available evidence thus suggests that this was not a one-sitting typing session.

Beckett continues the numbering of pages using the monologue letter followed by a number in the top margin: 'A1' (01r), 'A2' (02r), 'B1' (03r) and 'B2' (04r) are written in black pen, while 'C1' (05r) and 'C2' (06r) are typed. Edits to the monologues are made in black ink and red ballpoint pen, with the majority of these in black ink. Both black and red ink is used to draw lines down the left margin of each page, 'with chevron indentations to mark the divisions between the sections' (Bryden, Garforth and Mills 1998, 91; see Fig. 12). These divisions match the paragraph breaks on ET2 (see below), with edits to the section markings on folios 02r, 03r and 05r demonstrating that red-pen chevrons took priority over those in black. In a particularly long section at the end of C's monologue, Beckett also used an in-line forward slash to demarcate the break between sections. On the same page (06r), Beckett numbered three paragraphs '6', '7' and '8' in red pen in the left margin and linked together paragraphs 7 and 8 by means of a vertical line (see Fig. 13). This moving of material shows that C's monologue was the least fixed of the three at this stage.

Across this manuscript, words are lightly scored with dots in black pen, indicating that Beckett was counting the words, corresponding with the idea on EM to compose a three-part piece within defined word limits. Beckett initially made rough word counts in the top left corner of each page, with '~~400~~' written in pencil on folios 01r and 02r. This figure is deleted in black ink on folio 01r, with an eraser on folio 02r (though it is still visible) and with black ink again on folio 03r, where it is also written in black ink. However, Beckett then made more accurate calculations, with '860' being his word count for A's monologues (02r) and '1030' for B's (04r), both in the bottom right corner of the page.[166]

There are no dates on this typescript, and no stage directions, the latter only being re-introduced on ET2.

ET2 (MS-UoR-1477-3)

> Untitled typescript, with manuscript additions and corrections by Samuel Beckett, of a revised version of *That Time*; undated. 30 × 21 cm. 9 leaves. Inscribed 'TS 2' by Beckett. (Bryden, Garforth and Mills 1998, 91)

This document is shown to be a copy by the letters cut off at the right edge of the page (see 05r). As noted in the *Beckett at Reading* catalogue, 'Beckett divides his pages into three equal vertical columns, headed "A", "B", and "C"' (Bryden, Garforth and Mills 1998, 91). Within these columns, he types out paragraphs according to the divisions made in the left margin of ET1, with large gaps between each. This creates a page layout which shows clearly the order of the monologues (see Fig. 14), divided into sections according to

166 The word count for the 'Top Layer' transcription of A's monologues is 925; B's is 1,053.

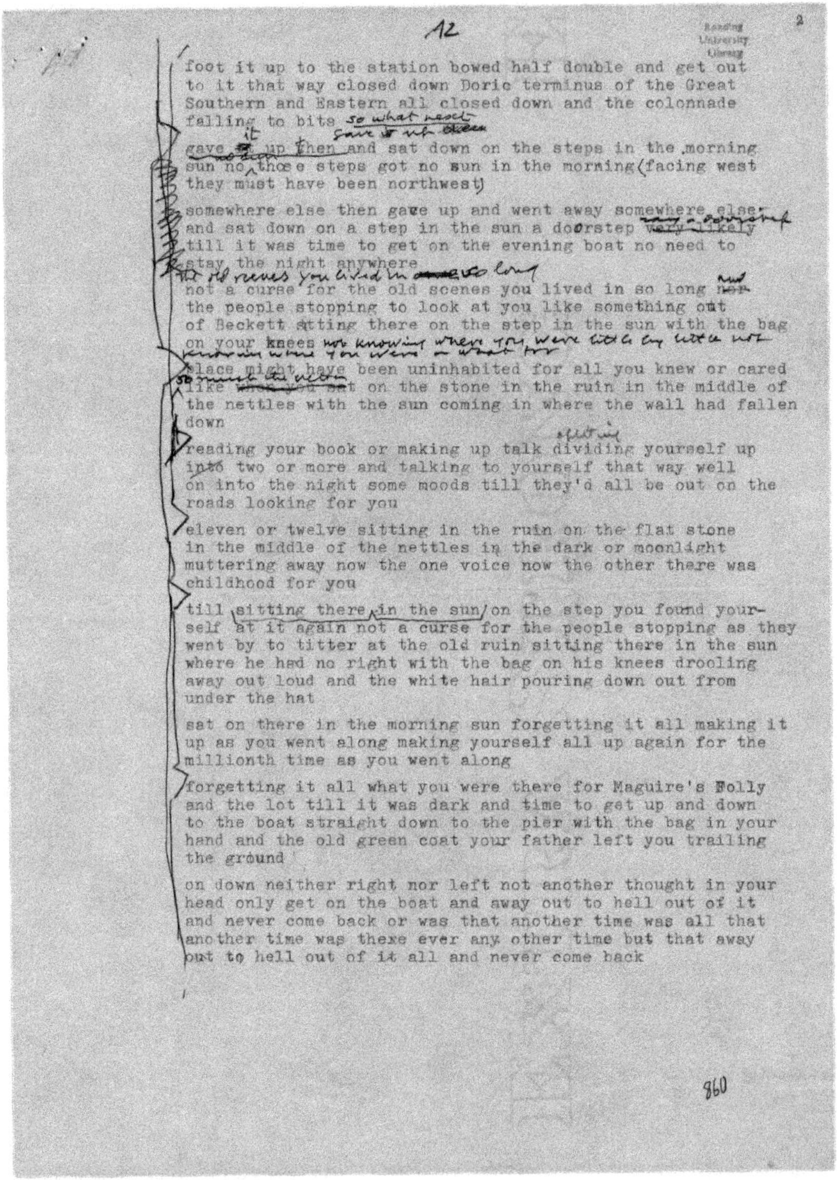
foot it up to the station bowed half double and get out to it that way closed down Doric terminus of the Great Southern and Eastern all closed down and the colonnade falling to bits

gave it up then and sat down on the steps in the morning sun no those steps got no sun in the morning (facing west they must have been northwest)

somewhere else then gave up and went away somewhere else and sat down on a step in the sun a doorstep very likely till it was time to get on the evening boat no need to stay the night anywhere

not a curse for the old scenes you lived in so long nor the people stopping to look at you like something out of Beckett sitting there on the step in the sun with the bag on your knees

place might have been uninhabited for all you knew or cared like when you sat on the stone in the ruin in the middle of the nettles with the sun coming in where the wall had fallen down

reading your book or making up talk dividing yourself up into two or more and talking to yourself that way well on into the night some moods till they'd all be out on the roads looking for you

eleven or twelve sitting in the ruin on the flat stone in the middle of the nettles in the dark or moonlight muttering away now the one voice now the other there was childhood for you

till sitting there in the sun on the step you found yourself at it again not a curse for the people stopping as they went by to titter at the old ruin sitting there in the sun where he had no right with the bag on his knees drooling away out loud and the white hair pouring down out from under the hat

sat on there in the morning sun forgetting it all making it up as you went along making yourself all up again for the millionth time as you went along

forgetting it all what you were there for Maguire's Folly and the lot till it was dark and time to get up and down to the boat straight down to the pier with the bag in your hand and the old green coat your father left you trailing the ground

on down neither right nor left not another thought in your head only get on the boat and away out to hell out of it and never come back or was that another time was all that another time was there ever any other time but that away out to hell out of it all and never come back

Fig. 12: Beckett's edits to the chevron markings in the left margin of his first *That Time* typescript show red-pen indentations taking priority over those in black (ET1, 02r).

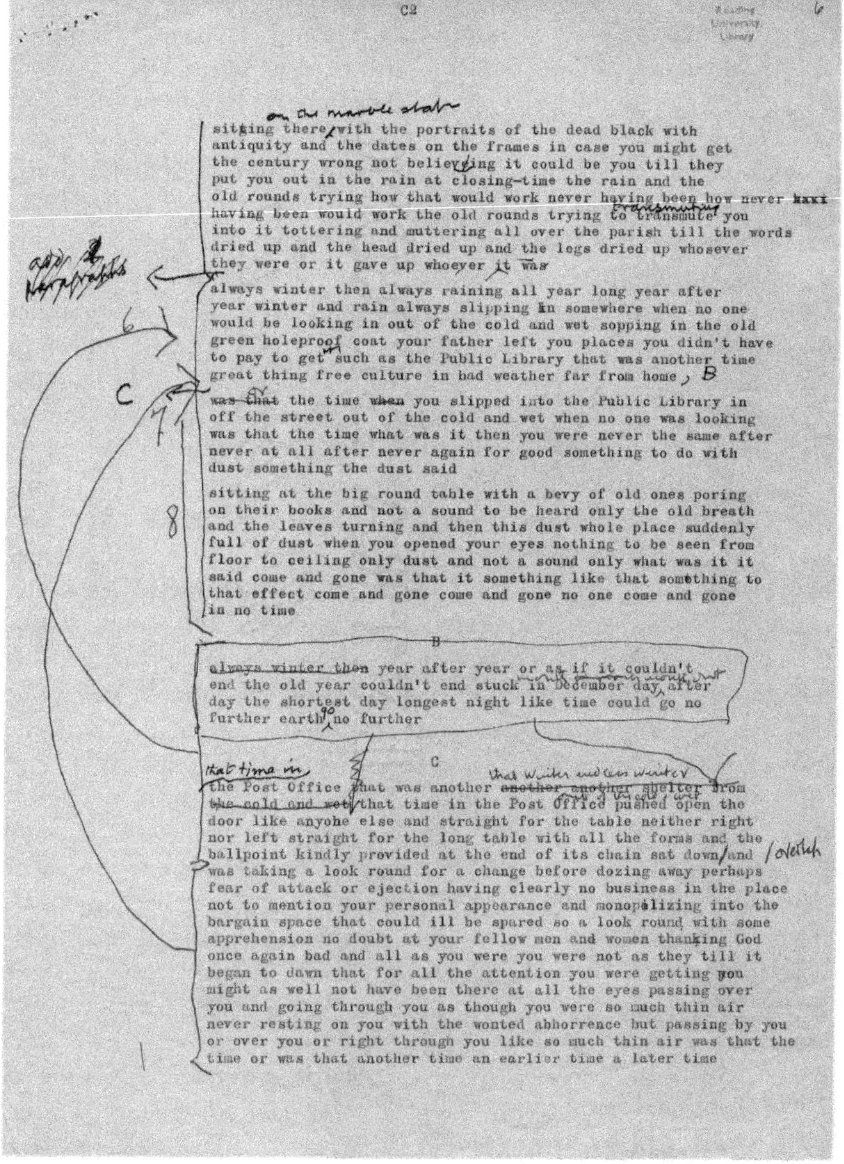

C2

sitting there with the portraits of the dead black with antiquity and the dates on the frames in case you might get the century wrong not believing it could be you till they put you out in the rain at closing-time the rain and the old rounds trying how that would work never having been how never having been would work the old rounds trying to transmute you into it tottering and muttering all over the parish till the words dried up and the head dried up and the legs dried up whosever they were or it gave up whoever it was

always winter then always raining all year long year after year winter and rain always slipping in somewhere when no one would be looking in out of the cold and wet sopping in the old green holeproof coat your father left you places you didn't have to pay to get such as the Public Library that was another time great thing free culture in bad weather far from home

was that the time when you slipped into the Public Library in off the street out of the cold and wet when no one was looking was that the time what was it then you were never the same after never at all after never again for good something to do with dust something the dust said

sitting at the big round table with a bevy of old ones poring on their books and not a sound to be heard only the old breath and the leaves turning and then this dust whole place suddenly full of dust when you opened your eyes nothing to be seen from floor to ceiling only dust and not a sound only what was it it said come and gone was that it something like that something to that effect come and gone come and gone no one come and gone in no time

B

always winter then year after year or as if it couldn't end the old year couldn't end stuck in December day after day the shortest day longest night like time could go no further earth no further

C

the Post Office that was another another another shelter from the cold and wet that time in the Post Office pushed open the door like anyone else and straight for the table neither right nor left straight for the long table with all the forms and the ballpoint kindly provided at the end of its chain sat down and was taking a look round for a change before dozing away perhaps fear of attack or ejection having clearly no business in the place not to mention your personal appearance and monopolizing into the bargain space that could ill be spared so a look round with some apprehension no doubt at your fellow men and women thanking God once again bad and all as you were you were not as they till it began to dawn that for all the attention you were getting you might as well not have been there at all the eyes passing over you and going through you as though you were so much thin air never resting on you with the wonted abhorrence but passing by you or over you or right through you like so much thin air was that the time or was that another time an earlier time a later time

Fig. 13: Beckett's edits to the final page of his first *That Time* typescript (ET1, 06r).

the second structural list on EM (02r): ACAB CBCA BABC. This speaker order is found on folios 01r–05r; it then repeats itself on folios 06r–09r, the '*da capo*' structure echoing the structural arrangement of *Play* (Gontarski 1985, 157; Beloborodova 2019, 186). There are 24 sections in total, with eight for each voice.

Many of the sections have their first and last phrases underlined. Of the underlined opening phrases, almost all are repetitions taken from later in the paragraph. Of the underlined closing phrases, many are drawn from the next paragraph by the same speaker. As Beckett indicates in a repeated note, such verbal echoes create a sense of 'overlap' between sections separated by the interposition of other voices. Beckett typed 'overlap' at the end of all but the final paragraph on folios 07r–09r and at the beginning of all but the first two paragraphs on these folios, but then deleted every instance of the word, replacing it with phrases from the text in black pen. The fact that the same term is found on EM – 'Problem **overlaps**: leave free or write in?'– suggests that Beckett made notes regarding ET2 on EM. Though Beckett headed this short list of notes 'after TS 3 cols', other entries such as 'Short pauses: only once medial p. 4' (EM, 03r) correspond to ET2 where there is one short pause of three seconds on folio 4. As this typescript is numbered 'TS 2' by Beckett (ET2, 01r), it is possible that he simply made a mistake when referring to it as 'TS 3' on EM. It is also possible that Beckett only numbered his typescripts after making the notes on EM and that another typescript (now missing) came before ET2 at an earlier stage of composition.

There is one correction in red ink (ET2, 02r), while the rest of the edits to the text are in black pen. Where a line of text ran on into another column, Beckett often deleted the extra textual material and continued on the next line. The document includes typed stage directions, edited by hand, on folios 04r and 09r. Beckett also added stage directions by hand on folios 01r and 06r and there are handwritten edits in black ink to the spoken text throughout. In the left margin of the opening pages, Beckett numbered the sections for each speaker, subdividing the typed paragraphs anew with black pen in order to do so. However, he stopped this system of numbering on folio 05r – where B is labelled '6' and C '7' – and the subsequent typescripts are subdivided differently.

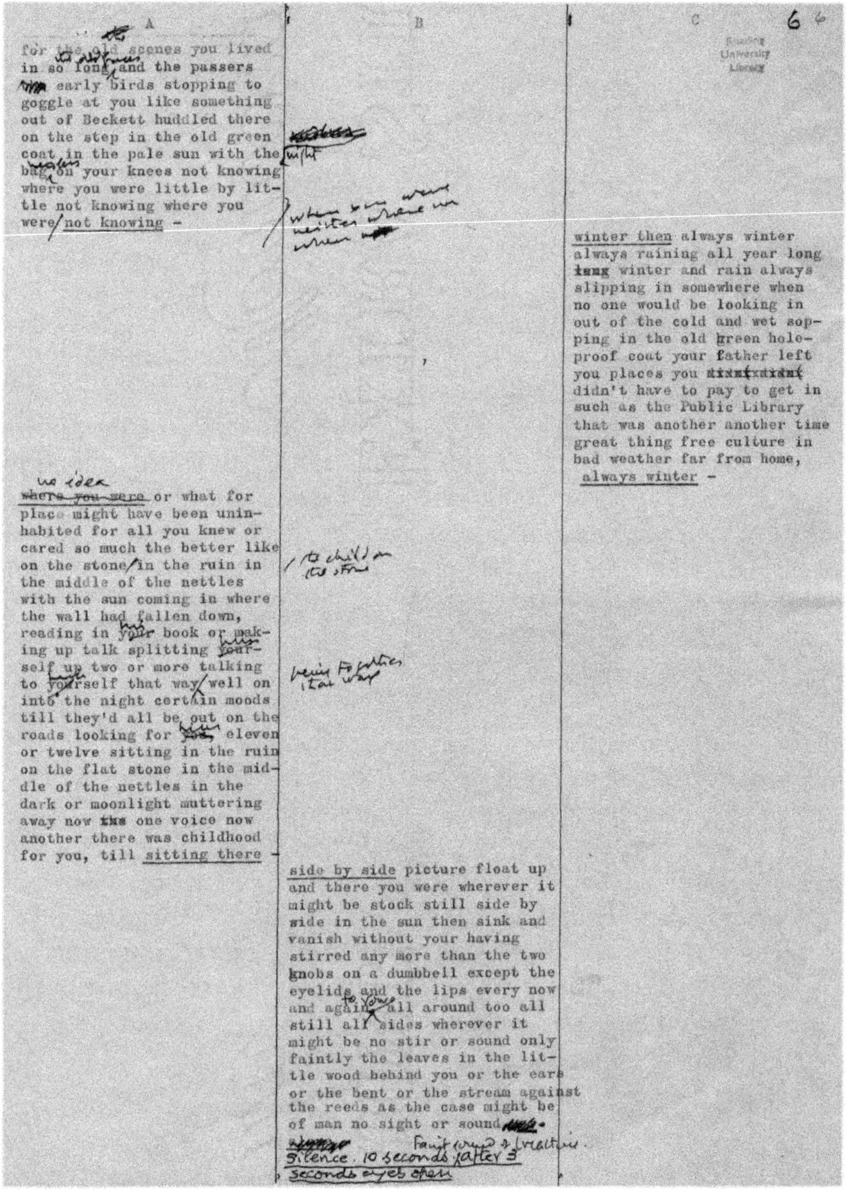

A

for the old scenes you lived in so long and the passers early birds stopping to goggle at you like something out of Beckett huddled there on the step in the old green coat in the pale sun with the bag on your knees not knowing where you were little by little not knowing where you were/ not knowing –

no idea where you were or what for place might have been uninhabited for all you knew or cared so much the better like on the stone/ in the ruin in the middle of the nettles with the sun coming in where the wall had fallen down, reading in your book or making up talk splitting yourself up two or more talking to yourself that way/ well on into the night certain moods till they'd all be out on the roads looking for you, eleven or twelve sitting in the ruin on the flat stone in the middle of the nettles in the dark or moonlight muttering away now the one voice now another there was childhood for you, till sitting there –

B

side by side picture float up and there you were wherever it might be stock still side by side in the sun then sink and vanish without your having stirred any more than the two knobs on a dumbbell except the eyelids and the lips every now and again all around too all still all sides wherever it might be no stir or sound only faintly the leaves in the little wood behind you or the ears or the bent or the stream against the reeds as the case might be of man no sight or sound

Faint wind & breathing. Silence. 10 seconds after 3 seconds eyes open

C 6

winter then always winter always raining all year long long winter and rain always slipping in somewhere when no one would be looking in out of the cold and wet sopping in the old green holeproof coat your father left you places you didn't have to pay to get in such as the Public Library that was another another time great thing free culture in bad weather far from home, always winter –

Fig. 14: Beckett's second typescript of *That Time*, with the text divided into columns (ET2, 06r).

ET3 (MS-UoR-1477-4)

> Untitled typescript with manuscript additions and corrections by Samuel Beckett of a revised version of *That Time*; undated. 3 leaves. 30 × 21 cm. Inscribed on f. 1 'TS 3' by Beckett. (Bryden, Garforth and Mills 1998, 92)

The most notable aspect of ET3 is the markings at the bottom of each recto and top of each verso, showing that Sellotape was used to attach the pages to one another. This could indeed have been done to 'emphasize further [...] the continuity of the individual narratives' (Gontarski 1985, 157), especially given that the monologues are here typed as single block paragraphs. However, these paragraphs run over onto the verso of each page: A (01r–01v), B (02r–02v) and C (03r–03v). This would have created problems in reading the monologues as a continuous roll of text when taped together, with all three sheets having to be turned over each time the reader reached the end of the recto. There is a further point of note with regard to these markings: on folio 01v, the imprint of a block of text from page centre has been transferred to the left margin, where it is faintly visible (see Fig. 15). This was presumably caused by the tape being removed and then stuck on anew.

This document is shown to be a copy by the many letters cut off at the right edge of the page. Corrections are made using black pen and black crayon. Also in black crayon, Beckett divided each monologue into 12 sections and numbered them in the left margin, drawing lines in the text to indicate the boundaries between each section (see Fig. 15). Whereas in ET2 there are 24 sections in total, ET3 contains 36. At the top of each recto, Beckett put the letter of the monologue followed by its number of lines: 'A 71' (01r), 'B – 79' (02r) and 'C 87' (03r). Though the final two calculations are correct, the 'A' monologue contains 73 lines.

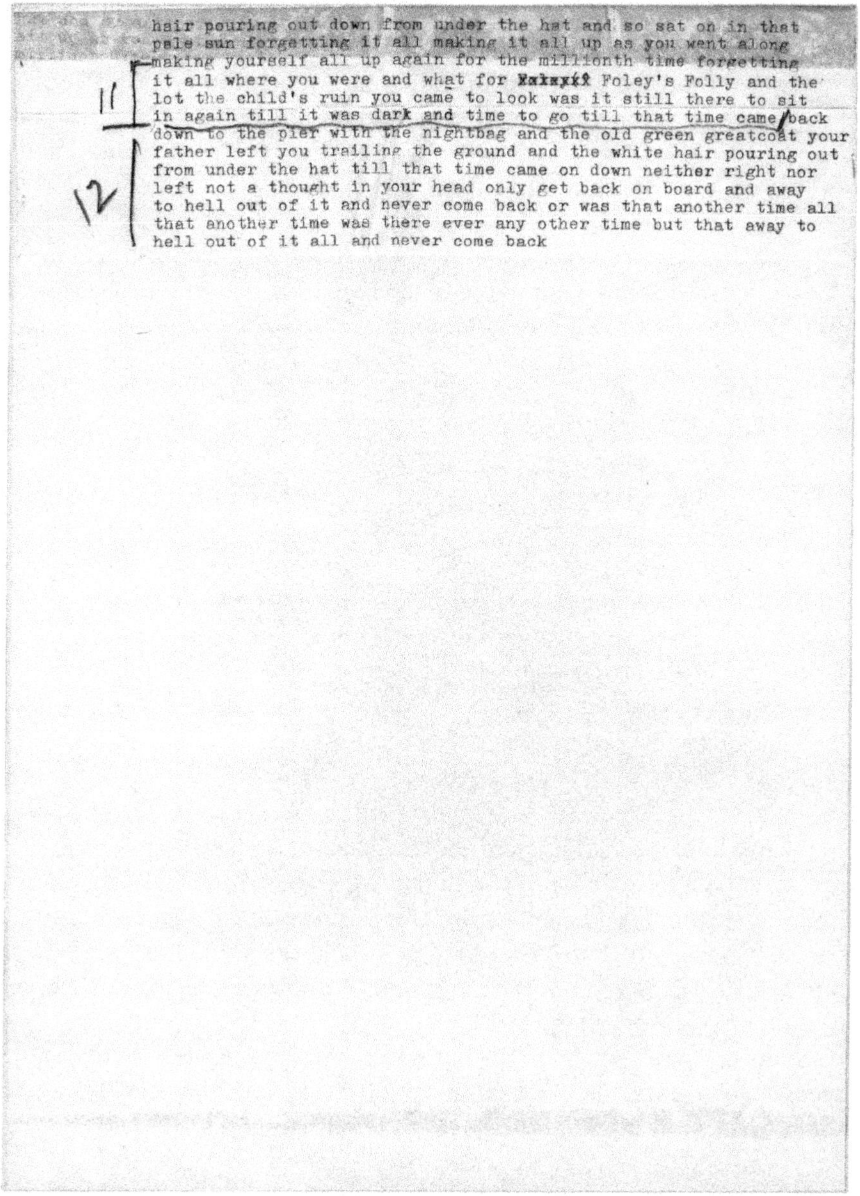
hair pouring out down from under the hat and so sat on in that
pale sun forgetting it all making it all up as you went along
making yourself all up again for the millionth time forgetting
11 it all where you were and what for Foley's Folly and the
lot the child's ruin you came to look was it still there to sit
in again till it was dark and time to go till that time came/back
down to the pier with the nightbag and the old green greatcoat your
father left you trailing the ground and the white hair pouring out
from under the hat till that time came on down neither right nor
12 left not a thought in your head only get back on board and away
to hell out of it and never come back or was that another time all
that another time was there ever any other time but that away to
hell out of it all and never come back

Fig. 15: Sellotape markings on Beckett's third typescript of *That Time* (ET3, 01v).

ET4 (MS-UoR-1477-5)

> Untitled typescript with manuscript additions and corrections by Samuel Beckett of a revised version of *That Time*; undated. 30 × 21 cm. 5 leaves; f. 1 is inscribed 'TS 4' by Beckett. (Bryden, Garforth and Mills 1998, 92)

ET4 contains a typed text of monologues, edited in black ink and pencil. The paragraphs are laid out in the following order, with the various speakers intercutting one another's monologues:

> (S) A1 C1 B1
> C2 A2 B2
> C3 A3 B3
> A4 C4 B4* (S)
> C5 A5 B5*
> C6 A6 C7
> A7 B6 C8
> B7 A8 B8* (S)
> C9 A9 C10*
> A10 B9 A11
> B10 C11 B11
> A12 C12 B12* (S)

In the five lines marked by stars above, the paragraph order has been brought about by changes of position using arrows. In the left margin, Beckett sketched out possible orders for some paragraph groupings (02r, 04r, 05r). Each paragraph is headed by a speaker's initial followed by a number – A1, C1, B1, C2, A2, B2, etc. (01r) – indicating its place in the series of that speaker's monologue.

Silences – marked '(S)' in the list above – are inserted by means of a capital 'S' surrounded by a circle in the left margin of folio 01r (at the start of the text), 02r (after paragraph B4), 04r (after paragraph B8) and 05r (at the end of the text). The stage direction 'eyes close' is inserted in the left margin by means of a capital 'E' surrounded by a circle in paragraphs A1 (01r), B5 (03r) and C9 (04r). Like ET3, ET4 contains 36 paragraphs in total.

ET5 (MS-UoR-1477-6)

> Typescript, with manuscript additions and corrections by Samuel Beckett, of a revised version of *That Time*. [...] 7 leaves. 30 × 21 cm. Titled on f. 1, inscribed 'TS 5'; f. 7 inscribed Paris, 10 July 1974. (Bryden, Garforth and Mills 1998, 93)

This is the first document in the genetic dossier to feature a title page and the first since EM to feature the title 'THAT TIME' (ET5, 01r). The title page suggests that this version 'was apparently designed to be the finished play' (Gontarski 1985, 157), though Beckett would go on to create further drafts. Unlike previous typescripts, ET5 has stage directions before the monologues and a note at the end of the text concerning the differentiation of voices (07r). This note is drafted and redrafted multiple times on the final two pages of EM (12r–13r), which has led to the claim that 'Beckett had from the outset a very clear idea of the appearance and presentation of *That Time*' (Bryden, Garforth and Mills 1998, 93). However, the sheer number of draft versions show what a challenging process it was to create this idea (see chapter 4.1.2).

Five writing tools are used to edit ET5, suggesting at least five campaigns of revision: pencil, black ink, black ballpoint, blue ink and red ink (now faded to pink). The vast majority of the edits made in red ink can be dated after 10 July 1974, the only date on the typescript (07r). The title page of ET5 contains notes in black pen and pencil on textual edits made later in the document as well as an initial note on stage directions:

> are eyes closed
> for A ✓
>
> ~~wangle~~ transmute
> Weather for A – between
> light & dark
> edge – <u>orée</u>
> ~~xxxppers~~
> ~~flipflops~~
> shufflers (ET5, 01r)

Beckett's use of the French term 'orée' may have its roots in Proust's *Recherche*. A paragraph in *La prisonnière* has Proust's narrator Marcel reflecting on the fact that his life with Albertine, as well as preventing him from going to Venice, also prevented him from getting to know the young 'midinettes' in Paris. Before he goes on to describe his annoyance at Albertine, there is a brief description of these young girls being watched by another's eyes:

> Çà et là, entre les arbres, à l'entrée de quelque café, une servante veillait comme une nymphe *à l'orée d'un bois sacré*, tandis qu'au fond trois jeunes filles étaient assises à côté de l'arc immense de leurs bicyclettes posées à côté d'elles, comme trois immortelles accoudées au nuage ou au coursier fabuleux sur lesquels elles accomplissaient leurs voyages mythologiques. (Proust 2011 III, 675; emphasis added)
>
> [Here and there, among the trees, at the entrance to some cafe, a waitress was watching like a nymph on the edge of a sacred grove, while beyond her three girls were seated by the sweeping arc of their bicycles that were stacked beside them, like three immortals leaning against the clouds or the fabulous coursers upon which they perform their mythological journeys.] (Proust 2003 V, 220)

This is not marked in the copy of *À la recherche* in Beckett's library, but the word 'edge' in ET5 (and in the published text) is also associated with a wood:

> °n the stone together in the sun on the stone **at the edge of the little wood** and as far as eye could see the wheat turning yellow vowing every now and again you loved each other (ET5, 02r; see 1976a, 9; *KLT* 99)

The paragraph from which the Proust passage is taken outlines the difficulty of ever knowing the object of one's desire: 'Les yeux qu'on voit ne sont-ils pas tout pénétrés par un regard dont on ne sait pas les images, les souvenirs, les attentes, les dédains qu'il porte et dont on ne peut pas les séparer ?' (Proust 2011 III, 675). In *That Time*, Beckett explores the same theme by using images of spatial separation to portray the two lovers sitting on the stone. So, it could be that Proust's image of interpersonal alienation influenced the spatial metaphors of Beckett's play, especially given that the 'petit bois' of Proust's Balbec seems to have had a formative influence on this particular scene (see chapter 4.1.2).

Having said that, it is also possible that Beckett simply found a word in French denoting more precisely what he was trying to say in English, 'orée' being used primarily in modern French to refer to the edge of a wood or forest (*PR*). While this would make it a simple example of multilingual composition, frequent throughout Beckett's oeuvre, it is not entirely out of the question that the term 'orée' had a Proustian relevance for the Irish author.

In blue ink, further down the page, there is an unfinished calculation of the number of paragraphs in each section:

A 12
B
C 12 (ET5, 01r)

In the rest of the document, each of the 36 paragraphs is numbered in pencil in the left margin, in a similar manner to how Beckett numbered ET6 of *Play* (see Beloborodova 2020, 57). Variations from the paragraph order of the earlier typescript ET4 are marked in bold below:

(S) A C B
C A B
C A B
A C B (S)
C **B** **A***
C A **B***
A **C** C*

B **C A** (S)*
B A C*
A B A
B C B
A **B C** (S)

Starred rows indicate changes to the paragraph order by means of arrows in the left margin. The silences – marked '(S)' above – are in the same position as in ET4, though in the case of the second 'medial' silence, the paragraph after which it occurs has changed from B to A. Each page has two sets of staple marks in the top left corner.

ET5' (WU-MSS008-II-3-68)

A photocopy kept in the University of Washington Special Collections' Samuel Beckett holdings (box 3, folder 68), featuring one set of staple marks in the top left corner and the same date of 10 July 1974 on its final page, lacks a title page as well almost all the red-pen edits made by Beckett to ET5. These include substantial edits to the note on voices at the end of the text, ticks beside the paragraphs' speaker indications, the switching of paragraphs (ET5, 04r–05r) and a few edits to the monologues.[167] For the most part, the WU typescript (ET5') lacks material from ET5 – notably the title page as well as many edits to the text – but there are some left-margin notes to ET5' in pencil which seem to have been made in a hand other than Beckett's: 'when' (01r), '? / building' (02r), 'dried up' (03r) and illegible possible additions to folios 04r, 05r and 06r. The notes 'when' and 'dried up' repeat words from an adjacent paragraph, while there is no obvious place for 'building' in the paragraph next to it, suggesting these are notes on the text rather than additions to the monologues. The word 'shroud' is underlined (06r) and some additional slashes mid-sentence mark the insertion of words (02r), though these mark with greater precision

167 A very small amount of editing in red pen is present on the WU typescript. Another photocopy, with paper-clip marks in the top left corner of each page, is preserved in the Alan Schneider Papers (UCSD, box 49, folder 6). This lacks the extra pencil additions to ET5' as well as most page numbers and the date on folio 06r.

insertions already made in the left margin rather than signalling the insertion of new words. As we will see below, Beckett did share at least one typescript of *That Time* (ET6) with Ruby Cohn while composing, so it is possible he also shared this early copy of ET5 with someone before he finished editing it.[168] A final difference between the two documents is that ET5 has a clear fold mark running horizontally across the middle of its pages, whereas the WU typescript (ET5') does not.

ET6 (MS-UoR-1477-10)

> Untitled typescript, with manuscript additions and corrections by Samuel Beckett, of a revised version of *That Time*; undated. 30 × 21 cm. 6 leaves. (Bryden, Garforth and Mills 1998, 94)

This document presents the three monologues in three continuous blocks: 'Continuity A' (01r–02r), 'Continuity B' (03r–04r) and 'Continuity C' (05r–06r). There are no stage directions. The typescript is edited using two pens: black ink and red ink (now faded to pink). Black ink is used to divide the text up into paragraphs by means of horizontal lines extending into the blocks of text, as Beckett had begun to do in ET2 before abandoning this method.

There is a reordering of the paragraph sequence of ET5, as can be seen in the variants marked with bold below:

A1 C2 B3
C4 A5 B6
C7 A8 B9
A10 C11 B12 (S)
C13 **A~~15~~14 B~~14~~15**
C16 A17 **C18**
A19 **B~~19~~20** C21
B22 **A23 B24** (S)
C25 A26 C27

168 It was common for Beckett to share his typescripts with 'critical readers' in his circle, such as Barbara Bray, Mary Hutchinson, Barney Rosset and Alan Schneider (Beloborodova 2019, 142).

A28 B29 A30
B31 C32 B33
A34 B35 C36

In the bottom half of folio 04r, Beckett sketched numerous possible sequences of the paragraphs. Only one corresponds to the order on this typescript, and this features an open variant: '$\text{ACBCABCAB}_{\text{AC}}{}^{\text{CA}}$B' (ET6, 04r). However, the lists are closely related to EN. The deleted numbers in the above list represent those numbers which Beckett deleted in the left margin, replacing them with alternatives mostly in red pen (now faded to pink). To the left of this column of numbers is another set of figures which details how many paragraphs intervene before the voices restart their monologues. As I will now outline, these two columns of numbers are the best available evidence for this being the typescript that Beckett gave to Ruby Cohn in 1975.

Beckett had spent time with Cohn while directing *Godot* in Berlin and *Not I* in Paris in early 1975. The editors of Beckett's letters presume that Beckett shared a draft with Cohn prior to 20 May 1975, when he wrote to her: 'Have revised order & text very slightly. Shall soon let it go as it totters' (UoR MS 5100, qtd. in *LSB IV* 408n3). She certainly had one by the time she returned to work in Stanford University that summer, where she showed the play to Alan Schneider.

In July 1975, working on a production of *Godot* as part of Stanford University's Beckett Festival and sitting in on Cohn's classes there, Schneider wrote to Beckett:

> Ruby let me see a xeroxed copy of *That Time*, and I am bowled over. It's beautiful, fascinating, difficult and stays with me. Full of questions; which I won't ask – yet. Except that I can't figure out (nor can Ruby) what that first column of figures on left means. Would really appreciate your sending me a copy direct with whatever comments or suggestions you have. The xerox is hard to read, & Ruby won't let me see hers. When I get back

> to NY, with your permission I'd like to explore possibilities for production. Has Barney seen it? I've let *no one* look at the xeroxed version. (27 July 1975, *NABS* 327–8; emphasis in original)[169]

Beckett replied to Schneider's letter on 8 August 1975: 'The text I gave Ruby is not final. The figures in the margin refer to break-down of continuity – order in which fragments recur and number of same intervening before resumptions. This has been reorganized' (*LSB IV* 407). As ET6 and ET7 are the only two surviving typescripts with two columns of numbers in the left margin, it is my hypothesis that Beckett shared ET6 with Cohn before rearranging the paragraph order on ET7 (see below). In the same letter to Schneider, Beckett goes on to describe his struggle with the stage scenario and then outlines the stage directions:

> The delay in parting with it is due to misgivings over disproportion between image (listening face) and speech and much time lost in trying to devise ways of amplifying former. I have now come to accept its remoteness & stillness – apart from certain precise eye movements, breath just audible in silences and final smile – as essential to the piece & dramatically of value. The chief difficulty, A B & C being the same voice, will be to make clear the modulation from one to another, as between attendant keys, without breaking the flow continuous except where silences indicated. I feel that dissimilar contexts and dislocation in space – one coming to him from left, a second

169 The version preserved at Reading is itself a copy, as can be seen from the typed text which runs off the page on folio 04r. It seems Cohn made her own xerox copy, which she showed to Schneider. A copy stored in the Alan Schneider Papers (UCSD, box 28, folder 6) also features the two columns of numbers in the left margin, though they are not identical to those on ET6. For instance, those edited in pink ink on ET6 have not been changed on Schneider's copy. This is unlikely to be the xerox Schneider mentions as it is not 'hard to read'. Though the column to which Schneider refers is 'the first' when read from left to right, it was written later than the figures numbering the paragraphs and is therefore referred to as the second column in the discussion below.

> from above, third from right – should be enough to do it. If not the effect will have to be assisted at level of recording. I do hope we may meet and talk about it – & all the rest. (8 August 1975, *LSB IV* 407–8)

The vocabulary used here is remarkably similar to the note on ET5 (07r) and the drafts towards this note on EM (12r–13r). Beckett presumably would not have written such a detailed description to Schneider were the typescript in question one of those already including stage directions and the note on voices. This reinforces the hypothesis that ET6 was the typescript Beckett gave to Cohn.

ET7 (MS-UoR-1477-9)

> Untitled carbon typescript, with manuscript corrections and additions by Samuel Beckett, of a revised version of *That Time*; undated. 30 × 21 cm.6 [*sic*] leaves. (Bryden, Garforth and Mills 1998, 95)

The typed text of the ET7 is identical to ET6, indicating that they are copies of one another. The fact that the 'r' in 'never' is cut off in ET7 (05r) may suggest that it is a copy of ET6, where the same 'r' is fully visible. However, it is also worth noting that more of the 'e' in '~~scene~~' is cut off in ET6 (04r) than in the corresponding place on ET7 (04r). This indicates that Beckett copied both these documents from another original, before editing them differently in pen.

The paragraph order on ET7 shows further revision from ET6, as can be seen in the variants marked in bold below:

A~~1~~1 C~~2~~2 B~~3~~3
A~~5~~4 **C~~4~~5** B~~6~~6
A~~8~~7 **C~~7~~8** B~~9~~9
C~~11~~10 **A~~10~~11** B~~12~~12 (Silence)
C~~13~~13 **B~~15~~14** **A~~14~~15**
C~~16~~16 **B~~20~~17** **A~~17~~18**
C~~18~~19 B~~22~~20 **A~~19~~21**

B~~24~~22 **C~~21~~23 A~~23~~24** (Silence)
B~~29~~25 A~~26~~26 C~~25~~27
B~~31~~28 A~~28~~29 C~~27~~30
B~~33~~31 **A~~30~~32 C~~32~~33**
B~~35~~34 A~~34~~35 C~~36~~36

The deleted numbers above constitute an initial list made by Beckett in pencil; he then revised this in black pen. Red ink (now faded to pink) is also used on the typescript. A comparison of these deleted numbers with the list on ET6 shows that Beckett first copied the order found on the earlier typescript before devising a new order for the play (see Fig. 16). However, he did not do so directly on ET7. Instead, Beckett used EN as an intermediate document (see chapter 4.1.1).

On the top of the odd-numbered folios, Beckett wrote three sets of figures:

~~2~~1	1~~s~~
8	2s
2	3s (01r)
2	1s
9	2s
0	3s (03r)
1	1
8	2s
2	3s (05r)

These figures represent the total number of ones, twos and threes in the second column of numbers in each monologue.

ET8 (MS-UoR-1477-7)

Untitled typescript, with manuscript additions and corrections by Samuel Beckett, of a revised version of *That Time*; undated. 30 × 21 cm. 5 leaves; f. 1 headed 'TS 6' by Beckett in black ink. (Bryden, Garforth and Mills 1998, 95)

Continuity A

that time you went back that last time to look was the
ruin still there where you hid as a child when was that/grey day
took the eleven to the end of the line and on from there
no no trams then all gone long ago that time you went back
to look was the ruin still there where you hid as a child
not a tram left in the place only the old rails when was
that/straight off the ferry and up with the nightbag to
the high street neither right nor left not a curse for the
old scenes the old names straight up the rise from the wharf
to the high street and there not a wire to be seen only the
old rails all rust when was that was your mother still ah
for God's sake all gone long ago that time you went back to
look was the ruin still there where you hid as a child
someone's folly/Foley was it Foley's Folly bit of a tower
still standing all the rest rubble and nettles where did you
sleep no friend all the homes gone was it that kip on the
front where you xxx no she was with you then still with you
then just the one night in any case off the ferry one morning
and back on her the next to look was the ruin still there
where none ever came where you hid as a child slip off when
no one was looking and hide there all day long on a stone among
the nettles with your picture-book/or talking to yourself
xxxxxxx who else out loud imaginary conversations there was
childhood for you ten or eleven on a stone among the giant
nettles making it up now one voice now another till you were
hoarse and they all sounded the same well on into the night
some moods in the black dark or moonlight and they all out on the
roads looking for you/that time you went back to look was the
ruin still there where you hid as a child straight off the
ferry and up to the high street to catch the eleven neither
right nor left only one thought in your head not a curse for
the old scenes the old names just head down press on up the
rise to the top and stood there waiting with the nightbag
till the truth began to dawn/no getting out to it that way so
what next no question of asking not another word to the living
as long as you lived so foot it up in the end to the station
bowed half double get out to it that way all closed down and
boarded up Doric terminus of the Great Southern and Eastern
all closed down and the colonnade crumbling away so what next/
gave it up gave up and sat down on the steps in the pale
morning sun no those steps got no sun somewhere else then
gave up and off somewhere else and down on a step in the pale
sun a doorstep say someone's doorstep for it to be time to
get on the night ferry and out to hell out of there no need
sleep anywhere not a curse for the old scenes the old names
the passers pausing to gape at you like something out of
Beckett quick gape then pass on pass by on the other side/
huddled on the doorstep in the old green greatcoat in the
pale sun with the nightbag needless on your knees not knowing
where you were little by little not knowing where you were or
when you were or what for place might have been deserted for
all you knew like that time on the stone where none ever came/
none ever came but the child on the stone among the giant
nettles with the light coming in when the wall had ~~fallen~~ crumbled away

Fig. 16: Beckett's revised 'Continuity' typescript of *That Time* (ET7, 01r).

This typescript features the same typeface as folios 03r–06r of ET1 and all of ET2, indicating that these pages were typed on the same typewriter. The layout of paragraphs is similar to that of ET5, with each speaker being given its own paragraph, the three voices thus intercutting one another's monologues. The typescript also contains stage directions and a final note on the voices, written in black pen (05r–05v). Edits to the text are in red ink and two different kinds of black ink.

The paragraph order matches the revised order on ET7 and hence also that on EN:

(S) ACB
ACB
ACB
CAB (S)
CBA
CBA
CBA
BCA (S)
BAC
BAC
BAC
BAC (S)

On the back of the final page, Beckett wrote a list of six addressees in black pen: 'copies to: Schneider / Royal Court / ~~Mc Whinnie~~ / Schroeder / Mc Whinnie / Magee / Herm'. He then wrote a short dash and added in a different black pen (ballpoint): 'Faber / Rosset' (05v). Given that there were further changes made to the next typescript, it seems more likely that the 'copies' here referred to are of ET9.

ET9 (MS-UoR-1477-8)

> Corrected carbon typescript of a revised version of *That Time*. 30 × 21 cm. 7 leaves; f. 1 headed 'TS 7'. Foot of f. 7 dated Paris, August 1975, in Beckett's hand. (Bryden, Garforth and Mills 1998, 95)

The one date on ET9 – 'PARIS / AUGUST 1975' (07r) – indicates that this was the typescript Beckett sent to Alan Schneider and others (see chapter 4.1.1).[170] This is supported by the fact that another copy of this document, made before the date and location was added, is part of the papers of Patrick Magee stored at the Library of Trinity College Dublin (TCD MS 11313/28a). The Trinity and Reading documents contain the same marginal additions in black ink.

The paragraph order of ET9 matches that on ET8, with the note on voices appearing at the end of the text (07r). Though there are minor textual changes between this and the published text, it seems plausible that ET9 was the copy from which Faber set their first published edition (see chapter 3.4.1). In chapter 3.5.1, I will also make the case that this was the copy from which the Royal Court set their playscript.

3.2.2 French

French typescripts

FT1 (MS-UoR-1657-2)

> 9 leaves. 30 × 21 cm. This typescript is corrected in several separate stages, using black ink, pencil, red and green ball-pens and type. All categories of manuscript revision are found in the text and margins [...]. Most of the thirty-six sections are crossed through in a single stroke of artist's pencil.[171] Beckett retains the separate sections A, B, and C, and employs a dual

170 Gontarski points out that the original of this carbon copy has not been located (1985, 154). A photocopy held in the Alan Schneider Papers (UCSD, box 28, folder 6) has the same edits in Beckett's hand, albeit written slightly differently, and lacks page numbers as well as the date on the final page.

171 The only paragraphs Beckett neglected to cross out are the final one of A's monologue (03r), the last one of C's monologue and the closing stage directions (09r). This suggests a simple oversight on his part, rather than any particular difference between these two paragraphs and the rest. None of the paragraphs on ET9 are erased in the text view of the online genetic edition.

> system of numbering: each section is numbered in type 1–12 and also, in ink, according to its position in the sequence. Some handwritten staging directions. Pagination is in type and black felt-tip. (Bryden, Garforth and Mills 1998, 96)

On the first typescript of *Cette fois*, Beckett numbered the folios of each monologue separately, leaving the first page of each (01r, 04r, 07r) unnumbered. The second and third pages of each monologue are numbered '2' and '3' (02r–03r, 05r–06r, 08r–09r). He used type for the foliation of A's monologue, foliating B's and C's in black pen. As in many other documents in this module, the red ink used by Beckett has now faded to pink, which is how it is represented in the 'writing tools' view of the online genetic edition. When numbering the paragraphs, and for some of the edits, Beckett used a black felt-tip pen. This has now faded to a very dark purply brown on FT1 (see 06r).

The typescript is undated. There is the mark of a rusty staple and paper clip on folio 01r, with staple holes on each page of the typescript and a faint rust mark on folio 09r, indicating the document was held together at one stage. At two separate points – first in A's monologue, then in B's monologue – Beckett added cross-references to C's monologue, showing that he was acutely aware of the echoes between speakers (03r, 05r). These will be examined in more detail in chapter 4.2.2.

FT2 (MS-UoR-1657-3)

> 8 leaves. 30 × 21 cm. Titled. Corrections are made in black ink and pencil. [...] Begins with staging directions and concludes with a variant draft of the final 'Note'. First leaf is a title page. [...] Numbering is simple; each section marked A, B or C and 1–12. So the opening trio is marked A1, C1, B1 and this continues to final set: B12, A12, C12. Pagination in type, 2–7 on ff. 3–8. (Bryden, Garforth and Mills 1998, 97)

As on FT1, Beckett used a felt-tip black pen as well as a ballpoint for edits; the former has now faded to very dark purply brown (see 06r). As on the first typescript of *Pas moi* (FT1), Beckett rubbed out some of his marginal additions in pencil (see 07r). These are marked with notes in the online genetic edition. The typescript is again undated.

3.3 Setting Copies and Galleys

3.3.1 English

SSC

The Deutsches Literaturarchiv in Marbach holds two copies of ET9 in its Suhrkamp archive (DLA, SUA: Suhrkamp/03 Lektorate/Theaterverlag) which appear to have been used as setting copies for their 1976 bilingual edition of *That Time / Damals*. The contact details of Spokesmen are on the title pages, 'the media branch' of Beckett's literary agents Curtis Brown (*LSB IV* 361n2), indicating that they posted the typescript to Suhrkamp. Judging by the greater number of letters cut off at the edge of its pages, the first typescript appears to have been copied from the second. Supporting this hypothesis is the fact that the second has two horizontal fold-lines which indicate it was once in a letter-sized DL envelope, whereas the first does not.

Textual evidence strongly suggests that one of the DLA typescripts was used as the setting copy for Suhrkamp's 1976 edition.[172] The note on voices is at the end of the typescript, with 'See note below' (SSC, 02r) appearing in the opening stage directions, as it does in the Suhrkamp edition: '*See note below*' (1976b, 6). The phrase 'wherever it might be' appears in both the typescript (SSC, 05r) and the published text (1976b, 46). However, it is the errors that shed the most important light on this edition's genesis. The table below shows a full list of variants between SSC and Suhrkamp 1976b.

Sentence	SSC	Folio	Suhrkamp 1976b	Page
0025	ten or eleven **on** a stone	04r	ten or eleven **or** a stone	28
0025	and they all **sounded** the same	04r	and they all **sound** the same	28
0031	that time together in the sand	04r	that together in the sand	34
0031	till you could see it **no** more	04r	till you could see it **not** more	34

172 The following analysis uses the second typescript (henceforth SSC) as it appears to be the original.

0033	not knowing who **you** were from Adam	04r	not knowing who were from Adam	38
0039	all still all sides **wherever** it might be	05r	all still all sides **where** it might be	50
0039	or the bent or the **reeds**	05r	or the bent or the **reed**	50
0040	another great thing **free culture**	05r	another great thing **freeculture**	52
0060	After 5 [x] smile	08r	*After 5" smile*	78

The vast majority of the Suhrkamp errors can be explained by the layout of the typescript from which they prepared their edition. In the word 'sounded', the letter 'd' is partially cut off on SSC (04r), which could explain the typo 'sound' in the published text (1976b, 28). The word 'time' in the line 'that time together in the sand' is a handwritten addition in the left margin of the typescript (04r), which may explain why it was missed in the published text (1976b, 34). Furthermore, Suhrkamp's errors 'ten or eleven **or** a stone' (1976b, 28), 'not knowing who were from Adam' (1976b, 38), 'all still all sides **where** it might be' (1976b, 50), 'or the bent or the **reed**' (1976b, 50) and 'another great thing **freeculture**' (1976b, 52) all involve words printed at the end of the line in SSC (04r–05r), making them easy to skip or misread.

GSC

The setting copy for Grove's edition of *Ends and Odds* is stored in the Special Collections Research Center at Syracuse University Libraries (SU), in the Grove Press Records (box 91; see chapter 1.3.1). The *That Time* setting copy is a photocopy of the first Faber edition and shows no textual changes or evidence of Beckett's involvement in annotating it for publication.

GG

The Grove galleys for *Ends and Odds* are also stored in Special Collections Research Center at Syracuse University Libraries (SU), in the Grove Press Records (box 91; see chapter 1.3.1). The *That Time* galleys contain no authorial edits.

3.3.2 French

PPM

The University of Reading holds corrected proofs for Minuit's 1982 edition of *Catastrophe et autres dramaticules: Cette fois, Solo, Berceuse, Impromptu d'Ohio* (MS 3628). Unlike other plays in these proofs, *Cette fois* (05r–22r) is without authorial corrections, featuring instead instructions for the printer in a hand other than Beckett's. The proofs of other plays consist of photocopies, but only the title page of *Cette fois* seems to be a photocopy (05r), suggesting that Beckett may have corrected other, photocopied proofs for *Cette fois*.

On the title page for *Cette fois*, there is a deleted note: '~~à recomposer tel puisque la compo a disparu~~' (05r). The words themselves indicate that a version of the text (the 'compo' or 'composition') was lost, but their deletion may suggest that it was then recovered, and perhaps used instead of these uncorrected proofs.[173] Almost all of the variants between PPM and *Catastrophe et autres dramaticules* match those between Minuit's first edition (1978c) and the 1982 edition, which strengthens the hypothesis that there are corrected proofs which I have been unable to recover. Aside from some punctuation errors – such as a missing *accent grave* in the phrase 'loin de **la**' (PPM, 08r) – the variants largely match those in the table comparing Minuit 1982 to the first printed edition (see chapter 3.4.3).

173 See definition 3(b) at https://www.cnrtl.fr/definition/composition and https://www.cnrtl.fr/definition/compo. The latter link dates the abbreviation 'compo' to 1966.

3.4 Editions

It is unclear as to whether Faber's standalone edition of *That Time* (1976a) was published before or after Suhrkamp's bilingual *That Time / Damals* (1976b). In Siegfried Unseld's account of visiting Paris on 12 April 1976, he mentions bringing Beckett the edition (DLA, SUA: Suhrkamp/01 Verlagsleitung/Autorenkonv./Beckett, Samuel: Briefwechsel Suhrkamp Verlag), indicating that it was published by that date, but it is still unclear as to whether this bilingual edition came out before Faber's edition on 5 April.[174] As the more reliable text – used as the base text for the online genetic edition – Faber's edition comes first in the following list. However, the reader should be aware that this particular ordering is not definitive.

3.4.1 English (UK)

1976a *That Time*. London: Faber and Faber. 16 pp.

According to Robin J. Davis, the publication date of Faber's first edition was '5 April 1976' (qtd. in Mitchell, forthcoming). The first edition is a 16-page standalone paperback volume in stiff black-and-white wrappers. It follows the text of ET9, except for a few variants. The line 'there you were wherever it **might be**' (ET9, 04r) becomes 'there you were wherever it **was**' (1976a, 13). The time markings follow Faber's house style, using the word 'seconds' rather than the punctuation mark " and the final stage direction also differs: 'After 5 s smile' (ET9, 07r) becomes '*After 5* ***seconds*** *smile*' (1976a, 16). These two textual variants suggest authorial involvement and were likely made on authorial proofs or galleys which I have been unable to recover.

174 I would like to thank Dirk Van Hulle for his help in researching this edition.

1977a *Ends and Odds: Plays and Sketches*. London: Faber and Faber. 104 pp. [*That Time*: pp. 21–30]

Demonstrating the remarkable stability of *That Time* as a printed text, the 1977 version in Faber's *Ends and Odds* contains no variants with Grove 1976a [1977] (see below), aside from changes in house style.[175] Its introductory note to *That Time*, however, does contain some extra information, mentioning that the play was 'written specially for Patrick Magee' and the exact date of the Royal Court premiere, '20 May 1976' (1977a, 7).[176]

1984a *Collected Shorter Plays*. London and Boston: Faber and Faber. 316 pp. [*That Time*: pp. 225–35]

Faber's *Collected Shorter Plays* contains a reset text of *That Time*. There are two textual variants between it and Faber's 1977 *Ends and Odds*: 'there **together** on the stone' (1977a, 24) appears in the later edition as 'there on the stone' (1984b, 228) and 'muttering that time together on the stone' (1977a, 26) becomes 'muttering that time **al**together on the stone' (1984b, 230). As discussed in chapter 1.5.1, Beckett mentioned in a letter to James Knowlson of 20 June 1983 that he received proofs for Faber's *Collected Shorter Plays* (*LSB IV* 615), so these variants appear to have had authorial involvement (or at least oversight). The distinction is important as the variant '**al**together' is almost certainly an error, which raises the possibility that Beckett did not introduce it himself, but simply missed it in revision.

175 For more on this edition, see chapter 1.5.1.

176 Previews took place on 18–19 May (Beckett to Alan Schneider, 17 April 1976, *NABS* 337). Though this note is the only explicit reference I have come across to Beckett writing the play for Magee, the actor's involvement in the composition process is signalled in the author's letters and the typescript he sent him (see chapters 3.2.1 and 4.1.1).

1986b *The Complete Dramatic Works*. London and Boston: Faber and Faber. 476 pp. [*That Time*: pp. 385–95]

The text of *That Time* in Faber's *Complete Dramatic Works* is a photographic reproduction of Faber 1984a, so there are no variants.

3.4.2 English (US)

1976d [1977] *Ends and Odds: Eight New Dramatic Pieces*. First Evergreen edition. New York: Grove Press. 128 pp. [*That Time*: pp. 25–37]

On 23 November 1975, Beckett wrote to Schneider: 'Barney did not trouble to acknowledge receipt of *That Time* sent same time as yr. copy. Strange I grant you' (*NABS* 335). While Spokesmen were responsible for sending a typescript to Suhrkamp, the list on ET8 (05v) shows Beckett planning to send one himself to Barney Rosset. However, as a reliable edition was published by Faber in 1976, the typescript ended up not being used when Grove published their first version of *That Time* in *Ends and Odds*.

As discussed in chapter 1.5.1, Grove's *Ends and Odds* was actually published in 1977, in spite of the verso of the title page stating: 'First Edition 1976'. The text of *That Time* is preceded by the same note found in the Faber first edition, with a closing full stop being the sole addition to the Grove edition (1976d [1977], 27). Indeed, the entire text is based on Faber's first edition, with no variants between the two aside from standard alterations in house style.

1981 *Ends and Odds: Nine Dramatic Pieces.* First enlarged edition. New York: Grove Press. 138 pp. [*That Time*: pp. 25–37][177]

The text of *That Time* is a photographic reproduction from Grove's earlier edition of *Ends and Odds,* as is proven by the small black mark that appears between 'the' and 'page' on page 37 of both editions. There are therefore no variants.

1984b *Collected Shorter Plays.* New York: Grove Press. 316 pp. [*That Time*: pp. 225–35][178]

The text of *That Time* in Grove's *Collected Shorter Plays* is a photographic reproduction of Faber 1984a, so there are no variants.

3.4.3 French

1978c *Cette fois.* Paris: Les Éditions de Minuit. 25 pp.

The first French edition is a limited edition on vellum. It is a standalone volume, with page numbers on pp. 7–25. The edition was *achevé d'imprimer* on 28 August 1978, with 100 numbered copies on *vélin d'arches* as well as some unnumbered copies *hors commerce.*

1982 *Catastrophe et autres dramaticules: Cette fois, Solo, Berceuse, Impromptu d'Ohio.* Paris: Les Éditions de Minuit. 81 pp. [*Cette fois*: pp. 7–25]

Minuit republished *Cette fois* as part of a 1982 collection with other '*dramaticules*', printing 100 numbered copies on *vélin supérieur.* The edition was *achevé d'imprimer* on 28 July. The table below shows variants between it and the 1978 edition.

177 For more on this edition, see chapter 1.5.1.
178 For more on this edition, see chapter 1.5.1.

Sentence	Minuit 1978c	Page	Minuit 1982	Page
0009	*du haut* ***respectivement***	7	*du haut* ***recpectivement***	9
0017	pas **une** âme dehors pas un bruit.	9	pas âme dehors **qui vive** pas un bruit	10
0022	**ouvert** les yeux	11	**rouvert** les yeux	12
0033	pour **ne** pas qu'on se trompe	15	pour pas qu'on se trompe	16
0054	pas plus ou guère.	23	pas plus ou guère	24
0055	et ne jamais revenir.	24	et ne jamais revenir	24
0056	en **ouvrant** les yeux	24	en **rouvrant** les yeux	24

Minuit's 1982 edition corrects punctuation errors in their 1978 volume, removing three superfluous full stops. However, one other error is introduced in the opening stage directions. All the other variants appear substantial enough to be authorial, but only one appears on the uncorrected proofs held at the University of Reading (PPM). This is the change from 'pour **ne** pas qu'on se trompe' (1978c, 15) to 'pour pas qu'on se trompe' (1982, 16), which reverts to the variant present not only in these proofs (PPM, 13r), but also in the top layer of Beckett's typescripts (FT1, 08r; FT2, 04r). This raises the strong likelihood that the '**ne**' in the first edition was added by an over-zealous editor. However, without access to proofs or galleys for this edition, it is impossible to be certain. Other changes have a more significant thematic relevance, with the introduction of the abbreviated 're-' prefix in '**rouvert**' (1982, 12) and 'en **rouvrant**' (1982, 24) adding to the sense of the protagonist being stuck in a rut, repeating the same actions over and over again.

1986a *Catastrophe et autres dramaticules: Cette fois, Solo, Berceuse, Impromptu d'Ohio, Quoi où*. Paris: Les Éditions de Minuit. 98 pp. [*Cette fois*, pp. 7–25]

In 1986, Minuit expanded their edition to include Beckett's final stage play *Quoi où* (1983). The edition was *achevé d'imprimer* on 26 March. Though the 1986 text of *Cette fois* is based on that of the 1982 edition, there are two important corrections. Firstly, '*du haut* ***recpectivement***' (1982, 9) is corrected to '*du haut* ***respectivement***' (1986a, 9), bringing the stage directions back in line with the first edition. Secondly, a previously missing participle is inserted into 'tu aurais tout aussi bien **pu** ne pas être' (1986a, 22). The highlighted '**pu**' is missing from both earlier editions (1978c, 21; 1982, 22). Though it is impossible to confirm that this correction is authorial, it does mean that Minuit's 1986 edition is the most reliable published text of *Cette fois*. Two errors occur across all editions: the superfluous accent in 'comme cette fois sur la pierre **où** cette fois dans les dunes' (1978c, 16; 1982, 17; 1986a, 17) and the use of third-person verb conjugation in the second-person phrase 'tu as essayé et **n'a** pas pu' (1978c, 23; 1982, 23; 1986a, 23). These errors appear in none of Beckett's drafts. The role of error in the text will be discussed in chapter 4.2.2.

3.4.4 Multilingual

1976b *That Time / Damals*. Frankfurt am Main: Suhrkamp Verlag. 81 pp.

Though, generally speaking, the English version of *That Time* is a remarkably stable text across editions, Suhrkamp's bilingual edition is riddled with errors. Below is a table of variants between Faber's first edition and Suhrkamp's bilingual edition from the same year:

Sentence	Faber 1976a	Page	Suhrkamp 1976b	Page
0011	*See note.*	9	*See note* ***below.***	6
0025	ten or eleven **on** a stone	11	ten or eleven **or** a stone	28
0025	and they all **sounded** the same	11	and they all **sound** the same	28
0031	that **time** together in the sand	12	that together in the sand	34
0031	till you could see it **no** more	12	till you could see it **not** more	34
0033	not knowing who **you** were from Adam	12	not knowing who were from Adam	38
0037	there you were wherever it **was**	13	there you were wherever it **might be**	46
0039	all still all sides **wherever** it might be	13	all still all sides **where** it might be	50
0039	or the bent or the **reeds**	13	or the bent or the **reed**	50
0040	another great thing **free culture**	14	another great thing **freeculture**	52

These variants provide evidence of ET9 having been used as Suhrkamp's setting copy (see chapter 3.3.1).

1978b *Stücke und Bruchstücke*. Frankfurt am Main: Suhrkamp Verlag. 275 pp. [*That Time*: pp. 42–60]

That Time becomes textually unstable again in Suhrkamp's trilingual edition *Stücke und Bruchstücke*, with errors introduced into the text, albeit not as many as in the 1976 Suhrkamp edition. The general principle of the edition is to print each play in its language of composition with the German translation *en face* and Beckett's own translation in English or French following. However, in the case of *That Time*, no French translation is included, presumably because Beckett had yet to complete it by the time *Stücke und Bruchstücke* went to press (see chapter 4.2.1).

The copyright page of *Stücke und Bruchstücke* indicates that the English texts are based on Faber's 1977 edition of *Ends and Odds* (see chapter 1.5.4), though the text of *That Time* is so stable that this is hard to verify. *That Time* is erroneously given the copyright year of 1974. There are two errors in the text itself: 'to see who it was **was** there at your elbow' (1977a, 25) becomes 'to see who it was there at your elbow' (1978b, 46) and 'look round for once at your fellow **bastards**' (1977a, 29) becomes 'look round for once at your fellow **bastard**' (1978b, 58) in spite of the plural form 'Mitunmenschen' being used in the facing translation (1978b, 59).[179]

179 In the bilingual edition of *That Time / Damals*, 'bastards' is translated as 'Mitmenschen', which means 'fellow human beings' (1976b, 66–7).

3.5 Playscripts and Production Notes

3.5.1 English

Some of the abbreviations in the survey below were coined by S. E. Gontarski in Vol. 4 of *The Theatrical Notebooks of Samuel Beckett* (*TN4*). By analogy, and for the sake of consistency, I have applied the same nomenclature to new documents that have been discovered since the publication of *TN4*.

RC playscript

Along with their playscript of *Footfalls* (see chapter 5.6.1), the Royal Court produced a playscript of *That Time* for their premiere of the two plays on 20 May 1976. It is not discussed in *TN4*. A copy of the *That Time* playscript, signed by Beckett (01r), is held in the Samuel Beckett–Calvin Israel Collection at the Burns Library, Boston College (MS.1991.001, box 13, folder 4).[180] As well as variants with Faber's first edition, which can be explained by the Royal Court's use of ET9 as their setting copy, this playscript introduces multiple errors.[181] Like ET9, of which Beckett intended to post a copy to the Royal Court (see chapter 3.2.1), the Royal Court playscript uses the punctuation mark " to indicate seconds and includes the note on voices at the end of the text, explaining why the stage directions read '<u>See note **below**</u>' (RC playscript, 02r). In addition, the phrase 'there you were wherever it **might be.**' (RC playscript, 06r) appears as 'there you were wherever it **might be**' on ET9 (04r), but as 'there you were wherever it **was**' in Faber's

180 Another copy is held in the Harry Ransom Center's Samuel Beckett Collection (box 5, folder 8). Shared imperfections in the typeface show this and the Burns Library playscript to be copies of one another (or copies of a third, unretrieved original document). Yet another copy is held in the Manuscripts Department of the Wilson Library at the University of North Carolina, Chapel Hill (WL PR6003.E282 T5 1976a). It contains the same errors as the other two copies, as well as the same black mark on folio 03r below the first full paragraph. Neither the Wilson copy nor the HRC copy is signed.

181 All variants can be seen using the 'Compare Sentences' tool of the online genetic edition.

first edition (1976a, 13).[182] This indicates that ET9 was used as a setting copy rather than Faber's edition.

RC ms (UoR MS 1639, 01r)

As noted in chapter 3.2.1, the two leaves of the manuscript UoR MS 1639 are separated for the purposes of this study. Pountney noted that the page references to Faber's first edition on this first leaf show that 'the two sheets comprising MS 1639 were written at different times' (1988, 278). The second leaf, I contend, belongs to the pre-publication *avant-texte*, while the first leaf consists of notes taken in view of the play's premiere at the Royal Court in May 1976, but after Faber's edition was published in April.

The notes on UoR MS 1639 (01r) consist of lighting instructions which Beckett 'prepared [...] for [Donald] McWhinnie', who directed the play's premiere at the Royal Court (*TN4* 357, 365n1). The notes are reproduced in facsimile in *TN4* (355–66), where Gontarski gives a description of them:

> The principle is essentially that the face is established in full light during the pauses, and the lighting fades to half full during the voices, or essentially as Listener's eyes close. Beckett detailed the cues for the fades up and down. (*TN4* 365n2)

As outlined in his letters, Beckett had great difficulty with the visual aspects of *That Time* (see chapter 3.2.1). The opening note addresses these difficulties directly:

> To the objection visual component too small, ~~disproportionate with~~ out of all proportion with aural, answer: make it ~~smaller~~ ~~less, cf.~~ smaller, on the principle that less is more (RC ms)

182 As noted in chapter 3.4.4, the Suhrkamp bilingual edition also has 'there you were wherever it **might be**' (1976b, 46), but it is highly unlikely this was used as a setting copy, given that its manifold errors are not found in the RC playscript.

Beckett may have read the phrase 'less is more' in Robert Browning's poem 'Andrea Del Sarto' (Browning 1979, 186). Like Browning, Beckett was interested in this Florentine artist, referencing his work in *Dream of Fair to Middling Women* when comparing the Smeraldina-Rima to Del Sarto's painting of his wife Lucrezia (*D* 15, 68). But Beckett would not have needed to know Browning's poem in order to use this phrase. By the time Beckett wrote *That Time*, 'less is more' had become widely known as the motto of minimalist architect Ludwig Mies van der Rohe (d. 1969).[183] Though Browning's work appears in plays such as *Happy Days*, I have been unable to find any archival traces with which we could link this intertextual reference to him or van der Rohe, for instance in Beckett's library. Again, this shows this importance of going beyond the written archival record in the study of intertextuality.

3.5.2 Multilingual

German Nb

Beckett's notes for his October 1976 Schiller-Theater Werkstatt production of *Damals* are in the same production notebook as those made for *Footfalls*, *Spiel* and *Tritte* (see chapter 5.6.2), catalogued at the University of Reading as MS 1976.[184] The German Nb is reproduced in facsimile in *TN4* (367–95), where the notebook is described as follows:

> Across the front cover Beckett wrote 'DAMALS' and beneath it 'SPIEL'; on the back cover, overturned, Beckett wrote 'TRITTE' [...]. The notes for Beckett's 1976 Schiller-Theater *Damals* begin on the recto of folio 1 and continue to the recto of folio 6. (*TN4* 367)

183 Google's Ngram viewer – albeit using a selective corpus – shows the phrase 'less is more' taking a sharp upward spike in printed books from the mid-1960s onwards, providing evidence of its growing popularity in this period (https://books.google.com/ngrams).

184 Rehearsals for *Damals* and *Tritte* started on 1 September 1976, with the German-language premieres taking place on 1 October (Asmus 1977, 82).

The first page features notes on the voice, how it should 'falter (slower, fainter)' approaching the silences (01r). When Beckett states that the voice should then 'return to normal débit' (01r), he reuses a French term from the manuscripts of *Cascando*, where the stage directions call for a 'débit rapide, haletant' [rapid delivery, panting] (HL MS Thr 70/1, 06r; HL MS Thr 70/4, 01r; see chapter 2.1.1). As Beloborodova and Verhulst point out, this term 'has the connotation of a flow or an outpouring, reminiscent of logorrhoea' (2020, 16). This shows that Beckett was thinking of the stage voice of *That Time* in the same terms as his earlier radio play (see chapter 4.1.2).[185]

Beckett then outlines the sequence of Listener's reactions to these fades up and down, including a quite remarkable suggestion regarding the stage image: 'If hand allowed in image, holding sheet at neck or collar of shirt, it should tighten hold for silence, relax for listening' (German Nb, 02r). The possibility here of a sheet returns to the idea of a bedbound figure outlined in the early drafts, which Beckett later 'vaguened' with the instruction 'No pillow' (ET5, 02r; see chapter 4.1.2). There is no evidence this idea was used for the Berlin production; however, it does emphasize again Listener's affinity with Beckett's other bedbound memory men, such as Malone in *Malone Dies* or X, the draft character at the beginning of the *Watt* manuscripts (see chapter 4.1.2).

On folios 02v–03r, Beckett wrote out the beginning and the end of lines in each paragraph, numbering them according to the same system used on ET4 (though now with the paragraphs in their published order). Production Assistant Walter Asmus likewise uses this system when discussing the play in his published notes on the Berlin production, numbering the paragraphs 'A1, A2, etc., B1, B2, etc., C1, C2, etc.' (1977, 92). In his production notes, Beckett also makes numerous edits to the text which later appeared in Suhrkamp's 1978 edition of the play. However, the English text was not updated in light of these revisions to the German translation.

185 Beckett also uses '*débit*' in the published texts of *Comédie* and *Dis Joe* (Beckett 2014a, 10, 82), as well as in *Godot* (1966, 37) and *Fin de partie* (2013b, 74). Beloborodova and Verhulst point out that 'the fourth version of the French translation of *Play* (revised in November 1963) has "Débit rapide" as an autograph insertion in the stage directions on the speech tempo' (2020, 16n3); see also Beloborodova (2019, 229); *BDMP8* (FT2, 03r).

On folio 05r, Beckett develops the lighting instructions outlined in his notes to McWhinnie, making the fades approximately the same length as the holds ('approx. 10 "'). On folio 04v, he sketches out an alternative, simpler sequence for the fades up and down.

On the final page of notes, under the heading 'B', there is a quotation from Friedrich Hölderlin's 'Fragment von Hyperion'. Beckett took notes on Hölderlin from the early 1930s onwards and continued to be influenced by the German poet throughout his career. His copy of Hölderlin's *Sämtliche Werke* contains annotations in the novel *Hyperion oder Der Eremit in Griechenland* (almost all in the first book).[186] The poem 'Hyperions Schicksalslied', from the second book of that novel, was extracted by Beckett from J. G. Robertson's *History of German Literature* in 1934 and serves as an important intertext in *Watt*, where it marks Beckett's interest in the disintegration of self in the German poet's work (Van Hulle and Nixon 2013, 93–4; *W* 207).[187] As for the 'Fragment von Hyperion', this was published (suitably enough, considering the theatre in which Beckett directed *Damals*) in Friedrich Schiller's periodical *Die neue Thalia* in 1794. The passage in Beckett's production notebook reads as follows:

> Alles war nun stille. Wir sprachen kein Wort,
> wir berührten uns nicht, wir sahen uns nicht an ...
> Hölderlin
> Hyperion-Fragment (06r)
>
> [Everything was now quiet. We didn't speak a word,
> we didn't touch, we didn't look at each other ...] (*TN4* 391)

Van Hulle and Nixon point out that this passage is 'refracted across the first two utterances made by the figure B' (2013, 93):

186 https://www.beckettarchive.org/library/HOL-SAM.html.

187 In a letter to Arland Ussher, Beckett expressed his interest in 'the terrific fragments of the Spätzeit [late period]', during which Hölderlin suffered from mental illness (14 June [1939], *LSB I* 665; trans. in Van Hulle and Nixon 2013, 94).

> vowing every now and then you loved each other just a murmur *not touching* or anything of that nature you one end of the stone she the other long low stone like millstone no looks just there on the stone in the sun with the little wood behind gazing at the wheat or *eyes closed all still* no sign of life not a soul abroad no sound
>
> ...
>
> *all still* just the leaves and ears and you too still on the stone in a daze no sound *not a word* only every now and then to vow you loved each other (Beckett 1990, 388–9, qtd. in Van Hulle and Nixon 2013, 93; ellipsis and emphasis in Van Hulle and Nixon)

Indeed, such phrases turn up throughout the first two-thirds of B's monologue: '**eyes closed** nothing to be seen', '**no touching** or anything of that nature', '**eyes closed** blue dark blue', '**all still** all sides' (1976a, 11, 12, 13). For Van Hulle and Nixon, 'There is more than a textual echo at work here, but the integration of a textual mood' (2013, 93). Building on this idea, we might consider this Hölderlin annotation in the German Nb to be Beckett's own self-reflection on the 'textual mood' already integrated into his own text, which is of particular note with regard to the theme of memory in the play. Memory is key across Hölderlin's work, as Beckett would have known from his reading: in *Hyperion*; in the third version of the poem 'Mnemosyne', lines from which Beckett extracted in his *Dream* Notebook before using a fragment of them in *Dream of Fair to Middling Women* (Van Hulle and Nixon 2013, 91; see *D* 138); and in 'Ehmals und Jetzt' ['Then and Now'], a poem marked in Beckett's edition of Hölderlin's *Sämtliche Werke*.[188] The monologues of *That Time* focus firmly on the 'then' of memory, with 'now' anchored by the minimalist visual image onstage. It is from this perspective that B recalls what the narrator of *Hyperion* calls 'die lieben Tage meiner Jugend' ['the dear days of my youth'] – a phrase Beckett also marked – as a place of self-refuge.[189] However, as is fitting for a dramatist interested in the breakdown of memory, narrative recollection leads principally to self-fragmentation in *That Time*.

188 https://www.beckettarchive.org/library/HOL-SAM.html, 88.

189 https://www.beckettarchive.org/library/HOL-SAM.html, 441; Hölderlin (2019, 16).

Aside from foregrounding the theme of memory in Beckett's play, the Hölderlin fragment is also noteworthy with regard to his use of intertextuality more generally. When discussing biblical echoes in *That Time*'s phrase 'the passers pausing to gape' with actor Klaus Herm in the Schiller-Theater, Beckett remarked: 'that is from the Bible'. Herm identified the Gospel: 'Yes, from St Luke's Gospel.' Beckett replied: 'I looked it up, but I didn't find it, aha, Luke' (qtd. in Asmus 1977, 93). As Kristin Morrison points out (1983, 92), the reference is to the passers-by looking at Jesus on the cross, which she also identifies in the Gospels of Mark and Matthew, where they 'railed on' (Mark 15:29) and 'reviled him' (Matthew 27:39), 'wagging their heads' (Mark 15:29; Matthew 27:39), thus treating the suffering victim more harshly than in Luke: 'And the people stood beholding' (23:35).[190] An author searching for and identifying intertextual references in his own work provides us with a quite dynamic model of intertextuality. In this case, in spite of a large body of material evidence testifying to Beckett's engagement with Hölderlin's work, we have no evidence that Beckett extracted the 'Fragment von Hyperion' passage as he wrote *That Time* – this particular passage is not marked in Beckett's library, for instance.[191] Instead, the note seems to mark Beckett's own recognition of aspects of Hölderlin's Romantic sensibility in the text, particularly with regard to the key theme of memory, a theme which is strongly evident in the genesis of *That Time*.

190 Luke distinguishes 'the people' from 'the rulers', who 'derided' Jesus on the cross (23:35).

191 In addition to his copy of the *Sämtliche Werke* (Leipzig: Insel-Verlag, [1926]; https://www.beckettarchive.org/library/HOL-SAM.html), Beckett also owned copies of Hölderlin's *Dichtungen und Briefe* (Munich: Winkler-Verlag, 1952; https://www.beckettarchive.org/library/HOL-DIC.html), *Werke, Briefe, Dokumente* (Munich: Winkler Verlag, 1977; https://www.beckettarchive.org/library/HOL-WER.html) and the Menard Press's *In Memoriam Friedrich Hölderlin, March 20 1770–June 7 1843* (London: Menard Press, 1970; https://www.beckettarchive.org/library/HOL-INM.html).

3.6 Genetic Map

1. *That Time*

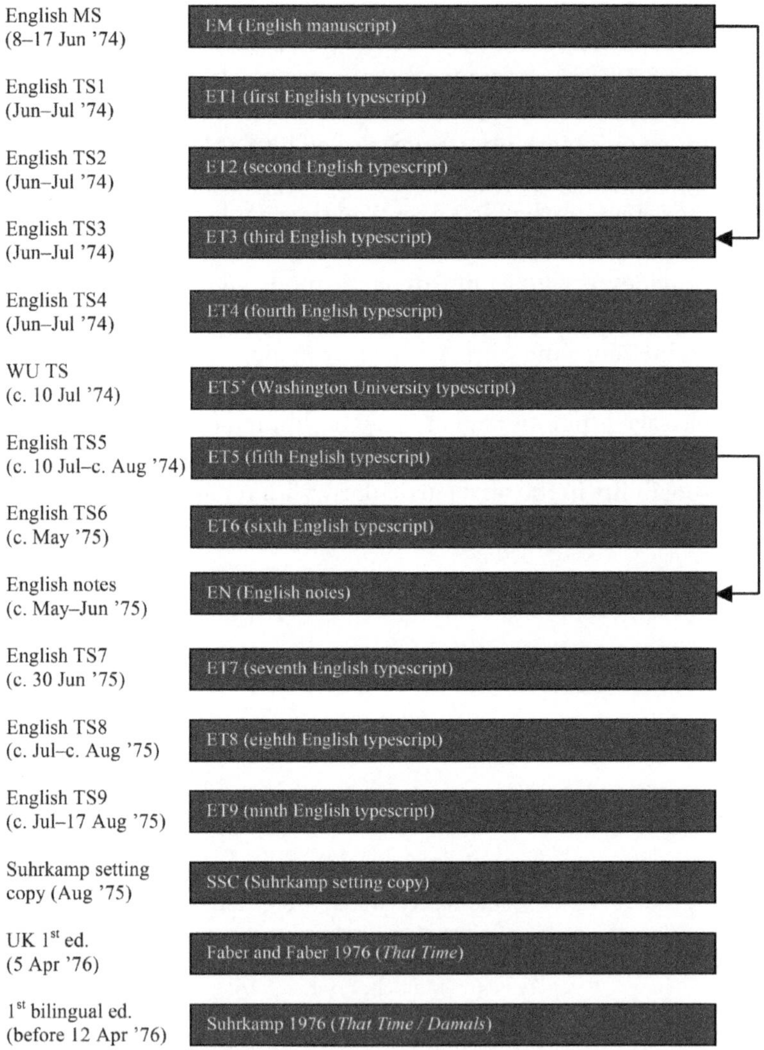
English MS
(8–17 Jun '74)
EM (English manuscript)
English TS1
(Jun–Jul '74)
ET1 (first English typescript)
English TS2
(Jun–Jul '74)
ET2 (second English typescript)
English TS3
(Jun–Jul '74)
ET3 (third English typescript)
English TS4
(Jun–Jul '74)
ET4 (fourth English typescript)
WU TS
(c. 10 Jul '74)
ET5' (Washington University typescript)
English TS5
(c. 10 Jul–c. Aug '74)
ET5 (fifth English typescript)
English TS6
(c. May '75)
ET6 (sixth English typescript)
English notes
(c. May–Jun '75)
EN (English notes)
English TS7
(c. 30 Jun '75)
ET7 (seventh English typescript)
English TS8
(c. Jul–c. Aug '75)
ET8 (eighth English typescript)
English TS9
(c. Jul–17 Aug '75)
ET9 (ninth English typescript)
Suhrkamp setting
copy (Aug '75)
SSC (Suhrkamp setting copy)
UK 1st ed.
(5 Apr '76)
Faber and Faber 1976 (*That Time*)
1st bilingual ed.
(before 12 Apr '76)
Suhrkamp 1976 (*That Time / Damals*)

Royal Court playscript (c. May '76)	RC playscript (Royal Court playscript)
Royal Court notes (c. May '76)	RC ms (Royal Court notes)
Schiller notes (c. Sep '76)	German Nb (Schiller notes)
Grove Press setting copy (c. Oct '76)	GSC (Grove Press setting copy)
Grove Press galleys (c. Oct '76)	GG (Grove Press galleys)
US 1st ed. (17 Feb '77)	Grove Press 1976 [1977] (*Ends and Odds*)
UK 2nd ed. (after 21 Mar '77)	Faber and Faber 1977 (*Ends and Odds*)
2nd bilingual ed. (before 21 Aug '78)	Suhrkamp 1978 (*Stücke und Bruchstücke*)
US enlarged (2nd) ed.	Grove Press 1981 (*Ends and Odds*)
Missing Faber proofs (Jun '83)	[Faber and Faber proofs]
UK 3rd ed. (13 Feb '84)	Faber and Faber 1984 (*Collected Shorter Plays*)
US 3rd ed.	Grove Press 1984 (*Collected Shorter Plays*)
UK	Faber and Faber 1986 (*Complete Dramatic Works*)

2. *Cette fois*

French MS (c. Apr–May '77)	FM (French manuscript)
French TS1 (c. May '77)	FT1 (first French typescript)
French TS2 (c. May '77–c. Aug '78)	FT2 (second French typescript)
Minuit 1st ed. (28 Aug '78)	Minuit 1978 (*Cette fois*)
Minuit proofs (before 28 Jul '82)	PPM (Minuit page proofs)
Minuit 2nd ed. (28 Jul '82)	Minuit 1982 (*Catastrophe et autres dramaticules*)
Minuit 3rd ed. (26 Mar '86)	Minuit 1986 (*Catastrophe et autres dramaticules*)

4 The Genesis of *That Time* / *Cette fois*

4.1 The Genesis of *That Time*

4.1.1 Chronology

Very soon after finishing his draft translation of *Not I* into French, Beckett started work on a new play. The latest date on FM2 of *Pas moi* is 19 May 1974 (see chapter 2.3.1); the earliest date on the first extant manuscript of *That Time* is 8 June 1974, just under three weeks later (EM, 01r). In between times, Beckett worked on a poem which develops the head-in-the-dark motif already familiar from *Not I* as well as prose works such as *Pour finir encore*. The latest extant draft of 'dread nay' is dated 3 June 1974, just five days before the first date on *That Time*'s earliest extant manuscript (*CP* 443). Its description of what seems to be a figure's hair strongly prefigures the central image of the later play, with its '*long flaring white hair as if seen from above outspread*' (1976a, 9; *KLT* 99):

> on face
> of out spread
> vast in
> the highmost
> snow white
> sheeting all
> asylum head
> sole blot (*CP* 203)

All of this suggests that Beckett again conceptualized the main image of his play before writing the text. What is more, 'dread nay' is not the only piece of verse Beckett wrote in 1974 which focuses on a single head. The companion poems 'hors crâne' and 'something there' (both commenced in January 1974) also share this motif (*CP* 441–2). As is evident in the second stanza of 'hors crâne', Beckett had a very specific head in mind when writing these poems:

> crâne abri dernier
> pris dans le dehors

tel Bocca dans la glace (*CP* 201)

The reference is to Bocca degli Abati, whom Dante literally stumbles across in the ninth circle of hell, where the Florentine political traitor is buried up to his neck in ice. Since the Italian word *bocca* translates into English as 'mouth' (Elam 1997, 175), Beckett may well have been thinking of his ongoing translation of *Not I* into French, where Mouth would become 'Bouche' in a draft dated 12 May 1974 (see chapter 2.3.2). In a series of structural notes for 'dread nay' (dated 31 January 1974), 'Bocca is named again and precise reference made to the *Inferno*' (*CP* 442).[192] So, we know Dante was on Beckett's mind as he composed his single-head pieces in 1974, something which may well have influenced the Dantean motifs in *That Time* (see chapter 4.1.2). In the summer of 1975, with the vast majority of the *That Time* already composed, Beckett returned to the *Commedia*, reporting his progress through Dante's text in a series of letters to Barbara Bray (see Van Hulle and Nixon 2013, 109–10). So, it is fair to say Dante was a constant guide for Beckett throughout the compositional process.

The fact that he refers in these cranial poems to the tales told in the *Inferno* raises the question as to whether the memories of *That Time* can likewise be seen as a form of punishment, perhaps even of torture, like the voices which torment the eponymous protagonist of *Eh Joe* (1967). In *As the Story Was Told* (written August 1973), which recycles many details from the unpublished 'On le tortura bien' (see chapter 2.3.2), the narrator refers to 'sessions' in which an unnamed victim is tortured until he dies:

192 As well as referencing lines 44–5 of the canto of the *Inferno* in which Bocca appears (Canto 32), where Dante asks the shades 'who are you?' and they respond by straining their necks and raising their faces, Beckett's notes for 'dread nay' also reference Canto 33 (ll. 1–2), in which Ugolino stops gnawing on the head of Ruggieri to wipe his bloodstained mouth (*CP* 442).

> As the story was told me I never went near the place during **sessions**. I asked what place and a tent was described at length, a small tent the colour of its surroundings. Wearying of this description I asked what **sessions** and these in their turn were described, their object, duration, frequency and harrowing nature. I hope I was not more sensitive than the next man, but finally I had to raise my hand. (*TFN* 159)

In *As the Story Was Told*, the victim is compelled to say something to his torturers, which he fails to do and which is left unstated in the story itself. In *That Time*, the word '**session**' is used twice in Beckett's list of early notes on EM as a way of describing the periods of speech which make up the play (01r). Of course, there is a difference between torture sessions designed to make their victim speak and what might be seen as sessions of torture in which the memories of a character are recounted by himself to himself. We could think of this in terms of a distinction in Beckett's oeuvre between writing which features actual scenes of violent torture, as in texts like *Rough for Radio II*, *How It Is* and – albeit described at a remove – in 'On le tortura bien' and *What Where*, and his texts in which narration itself is a kind of torture, already evident in *The Unnamable* and *Embers*, perhaps most notable in the voice that torments the protagonist of *Eh Joe*. If *That Time* is indeed a 'torture play', it is to this second category that it belongs.

We have already seen another layer of meaning that the word 'sessions' has in Beckett's explicit allusion to Shakespeare's '**sessions** of sweet silent thought' in the text of *Not I* (see chapter 2.2.2). With its 'sigh', 'wail', 'weep' and 'moan', Shakespeare's speaker's memory sessions draw attention to the expressive, emotive nature of what is far from 'silent' thought (Sonnet 30, ll. 3, 4, 7, 8, 11), all of which serves to further enrich our possible readings of the word as a compositional concept in *That Time*. What is certain is that our interpretation of this concept will govern the terms in which we see the play. If we think of Listener's memory sessions as a form of self-torture, then the smile at the end can be read as a sign of relief. If not, then our readings remain more open.

The few manuscripts that are dated point to two bursts of activity on *That Time*: the first clustered around June–August 1974, when Beckett worked on his manuscript (EM) and the first five typescripts (ET1–ET5); the second burst occurring in the summer of 1975, when Beckett reordered the sequence of paragraphs on ET6 and ET7 (working out his ideas on the loose leaf EN), before retyping the play on ET8 and ET9. This delay was largely due to his many other commitments in the theatre: attending rehearsals of *Happy Days* in London (13 October–4 November 1974) and then directing *Warten auf Godot* in Berlin (26 December 1974–9 March 1975) and *La Dernière Bande* and *Pas moi* in Paris (11 March–8 April 1975) (Pilling 2006, 196–7; *LSB IV* 381). He also started composing *Footfalls* during this period (see chapter 6.1.1). He did work on *That Time* 'in the odd spare moment' in March 1975, according to a letter to Alan Schneider in which Beckett also despairs at his lack of free time between (Berlin and Paris) theatre productions: 'One day off when I got back, then at it again in that raileray [*sic*] station' (23 March 1975, *NABS* 324).[193] But, broadly speaking, we can separate the chronology of *That Time* into the summers of 1974 and 1975.

On 10 July 1974, Beckett wrote to Schneider:

> Have been working hard at *That Time*. First draft finished. I had enormous difficulty and must leave it now to cool off. Don't know quite what to think for the moment but not too dissatisfied. (*NABS* 318)

What Beckett refers to here is not the first manuscript draft EM (dated 8–17 June 1974) but the earliest extant typescript to include a title (ET5, dated 10 July 1974). However, as shown in chapter 3.2.1 (see ET5', also dated 10 July 1974), although Beckett felt the draft was 'finished' when writing to Schneider, ET5 was revisited after 10 July. Beckett wrote again to Schneider about the play on 1 September 1974, mentioning his completion of the 'first draft': 'Haven't looked at *That Time* since completing first draft a month ago. Still a little to be done but not much. Hope to get it to you before the year is out' (*NABS* 320). If Beckett is being precise with his dating here, 'a month ago' would refer to the beginning of August – supporting the hypothesis that he went back to work on ET5 after 10 July. Though Beckett told Schneider the typescript was 'finished' on 10 July, the notion of completion is vexed here, as so often in Beckett's work. To borrow Clov's

193 The Théâtre d'Orsay was a converted railway station.

lines in *Endgame*, the typescript on 10 July was only 'nearly finished, it must be nearly finished' (*E* 6), the comparison of ET5 with the WU typescript (ET5') proving that Beckett went back and made further changes to ET5 at some point after this date (see chapter 3.2.1).

The winter of 1974–5 was characterized by numerous delays in the composition of *That Time*: 'Holding up *That Time* for the moment for a number of reasons', Beckett told Schneider on 6 January 1975 (*NABS* 321) – this would become a familiar refrain. In one of many letters communicating the play's slow progress, Beckett told Donald McWhinnie: 'You & Pat are perhaps wondering what has happened to That Time. Simply that it needs revision for which haven't had time with all this effing theatre [...] hope to let you have the piece before the end of April' (19 January 1975, *LSB IV* 386n7; ellipsis in original). Five days later, Beckett wrote to Barney Rosset: 'Have held up That Time for reasons not at all connected with desire & no time to revise, but hope to get it to you & Faber by end of May at latest' (24 January 1975, CU, Barney Rosset Papers, box 46, folder 5). However, it would be later that summer before he did so, explaining to Patrick Magee on 4 May 1975: 'That Time at standstill' (*LSB IV* 398).

It was only when Beckett got to Ussy later in May 1975 that he made any real progress with the play: 'Here [Ussy] past fortnight, faintly flickering. See That Time more clearly & have advanced it a stage. Not much more I can do, but holding it for the moment in case' (Beckett to Jocelyn Herbert, 30 May 1975, *LSB IV* 400). It was around this point that Beckett made significant progress in rearranging the order of paragraphs on ET6, the typescript he had given to Ruby Cohn earlier that year (see chapter 3.2.1). To do so, he worked out the new paragraph order on a loose sheet (EN), where he rearranged the paragraph order on ET6, giving the new order as it would appear in the left margin of ET7. This indicates that EN was used as a sketchpad for Beckett's ideas as he was working out the revised order for ET7.

Though ET7 is undated, a letter from Beckett to Jocelyn Herbert of 30 June 1975 allows us to roughly date his crucial revision of numbers in this typescript's left margin:

> I promised [Royal Court Artistic Co-director Robert] Kidd they wd. have That Time in September at latest. I was barking up a monkey-puzzle of my own making. The remoteness & stillness of listening face is part of the thing & not to be touched. I have simply rearranged the montage of ABC so that none is ever separated from its recurrence by more than 3. Work that out. (*LSB IV* 405)

Indeed, following the revision of paragraph numbers in the left margin of ET7, the second column of figures – indicating the number of paragraphs by another speaker between a given speaker's paragraphs – never exceeds three (see Fig. 16).[194]

As we have seen with regard to the abandoned 1963 piece 'J. M. Mime' (in chapter 1.1.1), such serial permutations and re-combinations have a long history in Beckett's creative process. Indeed, they go back at least as far as the passage in *Murphy* regarding the different possible combinations of the eponymous hero's biscuits (*Mu* 61–2).[195] Harry White has identified the ways in which 'Beckett's later plays constantly draw attention to the idea of a limited series of language, posture, movement, lighting, and sound' and he sees Beckett's dramatic development in terms of 20th-century musical serialism (2008, 189). For White, 'If we adopt the simplest definition of serialism as a compositional technique "in which the twelve notes of the chromatic scale are arranged in a fixed order, the 'series'… which normally remains binding for a whole work" (Paul Griffiths, in *The New Oxford Companion to Music* (Oxford, 1983), ii. 1668), then it is not difficult to

194 It is worth noting that this second column of figures is calculated on ET6 by simple subtraction of successive paragraph numbers, whereas on ET7 it only counts paragraphs by another speaker between paragraphs by a given speaker: e.g., the difference between paragraphs 1 and 5 is calculated as '4' on the 'Continuity A' section of ET6 (01r); on ET7, the difference between paragraphs 1 and 4 is calculated as '2' in the same section (01r). However, despite the difference in calculation methods, Beckett's letter to Herbert still indicates that he was referring to ET7.

195 Beckett conceptualized his extant novelistic oeuvre in serial terms when he described *Watt* to George Reavey as having its 'place in ~~a~~ the series' (14 May 1947, *LSB II* 55, 56n2). He also considered working with serialist composer Humphrey Searle on a BBC production of his translation of *Esquisse radiophonique*, but this never materialized (Verhulst 2017a, 93–5).

see how such a technique provides a paradigm for Beckett's structural procedures in the late plays' (2008, 197n32; ellipsis and reference in original). Though White does not discuss *That Time* in detail, it too is worth considering in the context of serialism.[196]

Having published the combinatory *Come and Go* in 1967, in which the exits of Flo, Vi and Ru are arranged according to an ordered pattern, Beckett returned to experimenting with serial compositional procedures in the prose piece *Lessness* (*Sans*, 1969; translation 1970). Pountney explains the piece's structure as follows:

> *Lessness* is composed of sixty sentences, divided into six sections of ten sentences each. These are lettered by Beckett A 1–10, B 1–10, C 1–10, D 1–10, E 1–10 and F 1–10, but they do not appear in the text in this order. Instead the sentences are shuffled into a completely different order and formed into twelve paragraphs containing varying numbers of sentences. The entire process is then repeated. Each sentence appears once more in a different order and paragraph sequence which forms the second half of the text. The complete work thus consists of 120 sentences divided into 24 paragraphs. (1988, 15)

This labelling of textual fragments is mirrored in the manuscripts of *That Time*, most notably in ET4, where the paragraphs are numbered A 1–12, B 1–12 and C 1–12.[197] As shown in chapter 3.2.1, these paragraphs are rearranged across the genesis of *That Time*, but this does not follow the stochastic procedure reported by Cohn in her account of the composition of *Sans*: 'Beckett wrote each of these sixty sentences on a separate piece of paper, mixed them all in a container, and then drew them out in random order twice. This became the order of the hundred twenty sentences in *Sans*' (1973, 265). Instead, crossovers between *Lessness* and *That Time* can

196 For Beckett's interest in the serialist music of Arnold Schoenberg, see Morin (2009, 128).

197 Beckett would also label sections of *Godot* A1–6 (for the first act) and B1–6 (for the second) when directing the play in 1975 (Van Hulle and Verhulst 2017a, 171).

be more fruitfully explored by looking at an intermedial adaptation which seems to have influenced the composition of Beckett's stage play.

In 1971, Martin Esslin directed a radio production of *Lessness* for the BBC, in which six actors performed the six sections of text, which Esslin termed 'images'. As he explained, 'each group of images was recorded separately by the speaker concerned, so that the actual tapestry of the interweaving images only emerged in the tape cutting room' (qtd. in Stewart 2017, 218). This is reminiscent of the recording procedure for the stage production of *Damals*, during which Herm took pauses for breath that were later cut out by the sound engineer (Asmus 1977, 92; Kalb 1991, 203). Therefore, the continuity of both pieces is guaranteed in post-production, not by the extremely strenuous performance of the actors in a stage work such as *Play*. Indeed, 'continuity' is a technographic term, denoting the linking together of broadcast items by a spoken commentary on the radio as well as a continuous flow of action across scenes of a film.[198] Beckett's use of this word on *That Time* ET6 and ET7 may therefore owe something to his experience as a multimedia artist.

As Paul Stewart sees it, in his account of the BBC Radio *Lessness*, 'The problem was in part a technical one: how to indicate change in image aurally while maintaining some sense of a single consciousness' (2017, 215). Beckett's recommendation to John Calder on vocal delivery recalls not only the voices of *That Time*, but also his other stage and radio voices of the 1960s and 70s: 'As close to one another in pitch and quality as possible. Cold. Low. Monotonous rhythm same for all' (3 July 1970, *LSB IV* 237). However, Beckett was dissatisfied with the result of the BBC production and, though he gave Esslin permission to record the piece again for German radio, he was not happy with that either (see *LSB IV* 258n3). It is Beckett's dissatisfaction with the BBC version that leads Stewart to view *Lessness* as a precursor to the more aesthetically successful *That Time*, where the different voices coalesce around a single stage image: 'Perhaps, then', Stewart contends, 'the solution was ultimately a theatrical, rather than a radiogenic, one' (2017, 215).[199] It seems right to link Beckett's frustrations

198 'A technography is a description of technologies and their application with primary regard to social and cultural context' (Pryor and Trotter 2016, 16).

199 Indeed, Beckett would refuse to grant permission for a radio adaptation of *Damals* (Beckett to Klaus Herm, 8 December 1976, *LSB IV* 443).

with the radio production to the very similar stage piece composed a few years later. But is *That Time* a 'solution' to the problem Stewart identifies? Verhulst highlights the fact that the very wording of *That Time*'s note on the voice raises the prospect that differentiating the three voices may be 'too difficult to execute live' (forthcoming) and many of us may testify to this as audience members without knowledge of the printed text.[200] While this in itself does not render the play a failure, it does at least suggest that the problem of relating different voices to the same mind was still being worked through in *That Time*, rather than being definitively solved. Others have asked the simple question as to why *Not I* – which shares many features with its theatrical 'brother' – has proven so much more successful in its performance history.[201] While one could argue that Beckett's entire aesthetic is invested in failure, it would appear that other works do tend to 'fail better' with their audiences than *That Time* (*CIWS* 81).

Towards the end of the summer of 1975, Beckett finally got around to sending out copies of a play that his letters indicate he was not entirely satisfied with. On 17 August 1975, he wrote to Alan Schneider from Paris:

> Sending you today same mail final That Time as final as I can get it. Could go on fiddling but sense it's time to part. Point of view realisation it's all knife-edge & hair's breadth. Hope we may somehow meet & go through it as we did Not I. If not shall do my best on paper. But not till I have your reactions. Have sent copies to Barney, Royal Court, Pat, Donald, Faber, etc. (*LSB IV* 409)

Again, Beckett describes his theatre texts in terms of incompletion. While the list of addressees on ET8 (05v) is broadly the same as that in Beckett's letter (the only extra names being 'Schroeder' and 'Herm', who could be covered here by 'etc.'), the dating of ET9 – 'PARIS / AUGUST 1975' (07r) – matches the date and place of the letter to Schneider. We can therefore

200 I refer here to my own experience of watching the *Beckett on Film* version of *That Time* without having read the text.

201 I wish to thank Daniela Caselli for raising this question during her Beckett and Dante seminar at the Samuel Beckett Summer School, Trinity College Dublin, 12–16 August 2013.

assume with some degree of certainty that ET9 was the typescript Beckett copied and sent to his collaborators.

4.1.2 Genesis

As with *Not I*, Beckett divided *That Time* up into lexias in order to analyse the play, labelling the different textual units so he could re-arrange them. However, the difference in *That Time* is that these textual chunks are not only units of analysis, but a key aspect of the published text, making visible on the page the interweaving pattern of the three voices that Listener hears. Indeed, as shown in chapter 3.2.1, much of Beckett's compositional activity went into rearranging the sequence of lexias on various typescripts. This reshuffling of lexias thematized the idea of a broken-down system, which is reflected at a narrative level by the failure of memory that runs through the text. As Van Hulle points out, the draft play at one point consisted of 'three sequences of identical triplets' (2009a, 456). Below is the same sequence I quoted in chapter 3.2.1, but this time I have removed Beckett's revisions to give a clearer picture of the structural symmetry he briefly considered:

> ACBACBACBACB
> CBACBACBACBA
> BACBACBACBAC (EN, 02r)

As we have already seen, however, Beckett rearranged the final triplet of these first two lines to '~~AC~~^{CA}B' and '~~CB~~^{BC}A' (EN, 02r), putting a kink in the symmetrical pattern – only to leave the final line itself unchanged. As Gontarski points out (1985, 158), this interest in formal asymmetry is mirrored by positioning Listener's head '*midstage off centre*' (1976a, 9; *KLT* 99). Such asymmetry reinforces the feeling that systems are in a state of breakdown in this play.

In order to provide a clear idea of the play's overall structure, the list below follows the principle of Beckett's English notes (EN), in which he listed the paragraph order with the first and last words of each paragraph. Since EN is a prepublication analysis of the play, I have tweaked Beckett's analysis to create the following list, which is based on the text as it appears in the first printed edition.[202] The line breaks denote silences in the monologues:

1 A1 that time ... when was that (1976a, 9)
2 C1 when you went ... when was that (1976a, 9)
3 B1 on the stone ... no sound (1976a, 9–10)
4 A2 straight off ... someone's folly (1976a, 10)
5 C2 was your mother ... dying away (1976a, 10)
6 B2 all still ... that scene (1976a, 10)
7 A3 Foley was it ... picture-book (1976a, 10)
8 C3 till you hoisted ... at your elbow (1976a, 10–11)
9 B3 on the stone ... long white hair (1976a, 11)
10 C4 never the same ... never the same after that (1976a, 11)
11 A4 or talking ... looking for you (1976a, 11)
12 B4 or by the window ... the shroud (1976a, 11)

13 C5 never the same ... another time (1976a, 11–12)
14 B5 muttering that time ... see it no more (1976a, 12)
15 A5 that time ... began to dawn (1976a, 12)
16 C6 when you started ... closing-time (1976a, 12)
17 B6 no sight ... for the vows (1976a, 12)
18 A6 no getting ... so what next (1976a, 13)
19 C7 the rain ... gave up whoever it was (1976a, 13)
20 B7 stock still ... wherever it was (1976a, 13)
21 A7 gave it up ... by on the other side (1976a, 13)
22 B8 stock still ... no sight or sound (1976a, 13)
23 C8 always winter ... another time (1976a, 13–14)
24 A8 huddled on the doorstep ... where none ever came (1976a, 14)

25 B9 or alone ... all vanished (1976a, 14)
26 A9 none ever came ... none ever came (1976a, 14)
27 C9 always winter ... drowsing away (1976a, 14)
28 B10 or that time alone ... soon after long after (1976a, 15)

202 I have also standardized the ellipses by using three dots instead of Beckett's two.

29 A10 eleven or twelve ... forgetting it all (1976a, 15)
30 C10 perhaps fear ... another place another time (1976a, 15)
31 B11 the glider ... time came in the end (1976a, 15)
32 A11 making it all up ... till that time came (1976a, 15)
33 C11 the Library ... not a sound (1976a, 16)
34 B12 that time ... little or nothing (1976a, 16)
35 A12 back down to the wharf ... never come back (1976a, 16)
36 C12 not a sound ... gone in no time (1976a, 16)

As with *Not I*, Beckett's analysis of *That Time* leaves out the stage directions, which is where my own genetic analysis of the play begins.

Stage Directions: Note on the Voices

Beckett sketched multiple versions of this note towards the end of EM (12r–13r) before he wrote this undeleted version in the left margin:

> The differentiation of A B C as **shades** of the same shd. be sufficiently conveyed by diversity of source & theme. If not it may be indicated by selective recording (12r)

The use of the word 'shades' here is significant. This is the term Dante uses to refer to the dead in *The Divine Comedy*, appearing throughout the English-language translation by Henry Cary of which Beckett owned two copies (Dante 1866).[203] Beckett would later associate the ghostly appearance of Virgil in the *Inferno* with a variation in vocal quality through the use of the line 'per lungo silenzio fioco' [faint/hoarse from long silence] in the manuscripts of *Stirrings Still* (*BDMP1*, UoR MS 2934, 09v). This phrase has been seen 'as a sort of motto for moments of creative *impulse*' across Beckett's writing career, appearing as it does in his early reading notes on Dante as well as later works (Van Hulle 2011, 93; emphasis added). Since it marks the difficulty of translation, we can say that such moments of creative *impulse* arise from creative *impasse*. This is also the case in *That Time*, as the many drafts of the note testify. What seemed to become clear to Beckett

203 See https://www.beckettarchive.org/library/DAN-VIS.html and https://www.beckettarchive.org/library/DAN-DIV-4.html.

while composing these notes was that the audio technology central to his radio and television work would be of equal importance to his stage plays and would therefore need very precise description in the stage directions. Beckett first tried the musical word 'modes' to describe the different voices, before introducing the Dantean 'shades' (13r). However, he then followed his own advice in the notebooks of *Murphy* to 'keep whole Dantesque analogy out of sight', in a further example of his 'vaguening' strategies (UoR MS 3000, 02r).[204] The word '~~shades~~' reverted to 'modes' on ET5 (07r), before giving way to the more temporal 'Moments' on ET8 (05v), which is what appears in the published text (1976a, 8; *KLT* 97).

On ET8, Beckett drafted the lines:

> ABC are one & the same voice and, apart from the two ~~ten-second~~ 10" breaks, ~~xxx~~ relay ~~each~~ one another ~~in unbroken flow~~ **without solution of continuity**. (05r)

As Sardin-Damestoy points out, the final phrase is a Gallicism which directly translates 'sans solution de continuité' (2020, 22). It may also be a Proustian reference. While speaking of the posthumous apparition of his grandmother as he bends to buckle his shoe, Marcel notes that she appears from the past as if time consisted of a series of different and parallel lines 'sans solution de continuité', a phrase Beckett marked in his edition of *Sodome et Gomorrhe*.[205] It is worth pointing out that Beckett's volumes of *À la recherche* seem to have been in the UK by the time he wrote *That Time*, in which case he would not have had them to hand when composing the play.[206] The phrase does recur in Beckett's earlier monograph on Proust (republished by John Calder in 1965), in which he uses it to describe how Marcel's memory of his grandmother invades the present moment 'without

204 I would like to thank Vincent Neyt for his help with this quotation.

205 https://www.beckettarchive.org/library/PRO-ALA-8.html,178. The phrase also appears in a slightly altered form in the short story 'On le tortura bien', in which the narrator promises to pick up his story tomorrow, 'ou après demain au plus tard [...], sans visible solution de continuité' [or the day after at the latest, without visible solution of continuity] (UoR MS 1656/3, 13r).

206 John Pilling recalls consulting these volumes when writing his article 'Beckett's *Proust*', which appeared in the *Journal of Beckett Studies* in winter 1976. With many thanks to John for sharing this information.

any solution of continuity' (*PTD* 41). While there is continuity between the Proustian vocabulary of *That Time* and Beckett's earlier scholarship, this seems not to have been instigated by checking his Proust volumes. It is instead more likely that Beckett had it in mind due to the recent republication of his *Proust* monograph or that his recollection of this phrase is closer in kind to his recollection of *The Tempest* while composing *Not I* (see chapter 2.2.2).

Stage Directions: Listener

Beckett initially had Listener '(sitting) in dark' (EM, 01r), but he also considered presenting him as if in a prone position. In the margin of the same page, Beckett wrote the note: 'Head on white pillow?', suggesting that he considered having an actual pillow onstage (EM, 01r). This idea was developed on the document's penultimate page, where the presence of the pillow as a prop is less certain:

> All in darkness except the Listener's face spotlit about 8' above stage level ~~and~~ midstage off centre. Old face & long flowing white hair as if seen from above spread on a pillows [*sic*]. The voices A B C are his own coming to him from both sides & above (see note)[.] They relay one another without any break in general flow except when ~~pauses &~~ silences indicated (EM, 12r)

Going against Beckett's earlier denunciation of Balzac for using background to explain his characters (see Introduction), the pillow here suggests a background – even if only as part of the 'as if' clause – which would allow the reader, if not the audience, to make sense of Listener's situation and his relationship to the voices that we hear as that of a dying man. On ET5, Beckett made it clear with a handwritten addition that in spite of Listener's head being positioned *as if* on a pillow, there was to be no actual pillow onstage: 'Old white face, long flaring white hair as if seen from above spread on a pillow. No pillow.' (02r).[207] In subsequent drafts, all mention of the pillow is gone. Besides recalling Beckett's own bedridden characters,

207 As this addition does not appear on ET5', which is dated '10.7.74' (06r), it seems to have been added later.

this deleted pillow calls to mind the opening section of *Du côté de chez Swann*, the first book in Proust's *Recherche*, where the narrator recalls his childhood evenings in bed, burying himself in his pillow. Beckett had already based *Krapp's Last Tape* (1958) around the memories of its central character, drawing on a key concept of Proust's novel in order to stage the self as a 'succession of individuals' (*PTD* 19).[208] What is more, he directed *La Dernière Bande* in Paris in April 1975 (Gontarski 2015b, 139), as he was composing *That Time*, so Proustian memory traces were very much in the air during this period.

Indeed, Beckett took a renewed interest in memory plays in the years leading up to the composition of *That Time*, following closely Harold Pinter's progress in adapting Proust's novel for the screen (see Beckett to Barbara Bray, 20 February, 5 March and 16 September 1972; Beckett to Pinter, [? 1 December] 1972, *LSB IV* 283, 288, 309, 315). According to Pinter's co-adapter Barbara Bray, it was Beckett himself who suggested the structure of their screenplay: 'Actually, the basic structural idea came from Sam Beckett. I was talking to him about it and he said that you really ought to start at the end with *Le Temps retrouvé* and so that's what we did' (Billington 2009, 386). Beckett had already started a bedbound memory narrative *near* the end of life in *Malone Dies*, which opens: 'I shall soon be quite dead at last in spite of all' (*MD* 3). A pillowed Listener would have suggested to the audience that they were perceiving the memory process of a dying man, but the published text of *That Time* may be said to have taken this idea one step further, possibly beyond the grave, with the absence of the pillow making his situation indeterminate. Beckett was wary of having his later memory plays interpreted through Proust's work, and disapproved of the appearance of a long passage from *Proust* in the programme for a 1974 production of *Happy Days* (Pilling 2006, 197). It is possibly for this reason, as well as not wishing to provide a realist background for his stage image, that he removed any trace of a pillow from his English drafts.

Beckett started his own monograph on Proust by declaring his interest in 'that double-headed monster of damnation and salvation – **Time**' (*PTD* 11), the last word and principal theme of Proust's novel (Proust 2011 IV, 625).[209] Having spatialized time in the rising, egg-timer-shaped mound of *Happy*

208 For more on this concept in *Krapp's Last Tape*, see Van Hulle (2015, 33–7).
209 Beckett also capitalises 'Time' in the 'Kilcool' drafts (AS1, 10r).

Days, Beckett jotted down the idea of including a '**Faint tick-tack** through[out], only **just audible** in silence' in *That Time* (EM, 01r; see chapter 3.1.1). However, that idea does not appear in any subsequent draft versions, with time instead being embodied in the breathing of Listener, the description of which echoed that of the earlier ticking before becoming '~~**just**~~ **audible**~~.~~ slow & regular' in ET5 (02r). Following Beckett's early note to use the 'element "time" in all 3' monologues (EM, 01r), time is thematized in the spoken text rather than providing an explicit, ticking backdrop.

'1 A1 that time ... when was that' (1976a, 9)

Reflecting a similar structure to Mouth's circular speech in *Not I*, Beckett starts the first monologue of *That Time* in mid-flow. This was even more evident in the first draft version. In music performance, a fragment of melody played before the first beat of the first bar is called a 'pickup'.[210] In EM, Beckett included a small verbal 'pickup' which leads into the main topic of time: '**then there was** that time' (01r). In all subsequent versions, the monologue starts with the play's title, emphasizing the central theme in a similar manner to which Proust did by going from 'Longtemps' to 'Temps' as the first and last words of *À la recherche* (2011 I, 3; 2011 IV, 625). But by prefacing 'time' with the determiner 'that', Beckett immediately raised the question as to *what* point in time is being spoken of, something he would explore at a later point in A's monologue.

The number eleven is important in denoting the separation of two individuals in the play. Like the theme of time itself, this was something present from the first draft description of the tram the protagonist takes: 'took the ~~**eleven**~~ **eleven** to the ~~terminus~~ **end of the line**' (EM, 04r). Beckett may have also chosen the number eleven because it is formed orthographically by two lines, a spatial figure which also turns up in the description of the tramway itself. So, while Proust's narrator sees the coming together of the Guermantes and Swann ways when he meets Gilberte's daughter at the end of the novel (2011 IV, 606), Beckett's spatial figure emphasizes continual separation. Though Beckett initially used 'only the old **rails**' (EM, 04r), this changed in ET3: 'not a tram left in the place all gone only the old **lines**' (01r).

210 In 'Happy Birthday', 'Ha-ppy' is a pickup and the first syllable of 'birthday' marks the first beat of the first bar.

This recalls Beckett's identification of the 'rupture of the **lines** of communication' as the major topic of the modern writer in 'Recent Irish Poetry' (see Introduction). In ET4, Beckett reintroduced 'lines **rails**' as an open variant (ET4, 01r), and 'lines' is absent from subsequent versions. But the theme of broken-down communication between the self and the world of objects is key to what follows.

'2 C1 when you went ... when was that' (1976a, 9)

As in *Not I*, C's memories are always set in winter: 'always winter then always raining' (ET1, 05r). In order to escape this weather, the protagonist takes shelter in 'the portrait gallery' (EM, 09r). From ET1 onwards, '**P**ortrait **G**allery' is capitalized, probably indicating the National Portrait Gallery in London, a city in which Beckett spent much time exploring art galleries in the 1930s (05r; Knowlson 1997, 194–5). It also raises questions about the form of art we see before us in the theatre. Beckett has often been seen as a painterly playwright (see Lloyd 2016) and *That Time* is one in a long line of Beckett plays which presents a striking visual image. In this paradigm, Listener's memories can be said to constitute his self-portrait. Remarking on Beckett's debt towards Joyce in the field of self-writing, Nixon compares Joyce's *Portrait of the Artist as a Young Man* with its predecessor *Stephen Hero*: 'Whereas the more autobiographical *Stephen Hero* could always only be Joyce as he was *becoming*, a "Portrait" by its very nature could frame a development that had found some sort of completion' (2011, 22; emphasis in original). Beckett too 'frames' his theatrical 'portrait' of Listener's face with the rectangle of the proscenium stage. But, just as Joyce increasingly discovered in his later writing, Beckett found out he could only present such portraits in a state of becoming, with the framing of the image offset by the sheer amount of darkness that surrounds it. If this is a portrait, in other words, Beckett is keen to point out that it is not the full picture.

One of the effects of such overwhelmingly dark stages is a breaking down of the categories of inner and outer space. When a stage is darkened in this way, it can be difficult to see where the onstage space ends and the offstage space begins. Beckett points to this when he reduces his text in ET2: '~~shelter from the rain~~ **in out** of the rain' (01r). The clash of adverbs prefigures the style of *Worstward Ho* (1983): 'Stay in. **On in**' (*CIWS* 81). What is also happening here is a form of 'verbal undoing', in which terms are stripped away to produce a more minimalist text. As we can see in the following example, this often involved replacing adverbial phrases with single-syllable adverbs: 'dry off and [get your strength back to get] on out to hell out of there' (ET4, 01r). In ET5, this open variant becomes the simple '**on**' (02r).

'3 B1 on the stone ... no sound' (1976a, 9–10)

The published text also uses 'on' as a link word to start the next lexia (1976a, 9; *KLT* 99). But that is not how the paragraph started life. In the first draft version, Beckett emphasized time in its description of the young couple: '**that time** sitting there together in the sun on the stone at the edge of the little wood' (EM, 06r). In ET1, Beckett added to his text, repeating the phrase '**the little wood**' as a supralinear addition at the start of the line: '**the little wood** that time sitting together in the sun on the stone' (03r). This recalls the 'petit bois' in Proust's Balbec, where Marcel spends time with Albertine (2011 III, 514).[211] But Beckett then replaced this, deciding instead to start with one of his favourite words: '**on the stone** sitting together in the sun on the stone at the edge of the little wood' (ET3, 02r). It is possible this is a reaction to another addition, namely the negative ending added by hand to ET2: '**no sign of life not a soul about**' (02r). In the published text, the opening '**on**' of the paragraph mirrors its penultimate '**no**', just as the two figures mirror one another sitting on either end of the 'long low stone' (1976a, 9–10; *KLT* 99).

'4 A2 straight off ... someone's folly' (1976a, 10)

If the 'lines of communication' no longer operate on the ground, nor do they operate above ground, with the wires used in the old tram system having been dismantled: 'off the boat and up with the grip to main street and **all the ~~xxx~~ wires gone**' (EM, 04r). This adds to a sense of a protagonist cut off from the world, not that he expresses much desire to communicate with the world he once knew: '**not a curse for the old scenes the old faces** straight up the rise to the main street' (ET2, 01r). Beckett's use here of '**scenes**' recalls his analysis of Mouth's monologue

211 Beckett marked this account of the 'petit bois' with a long pencil line in his copy of *Sodome et Gomorrhe* (https://www.beckettarchive.org/library/PRO-ALA-10.html, 235).

in terms of different 'life **scenes**' (see chapter 2.2.2). If, as suggested by recent neurological research, memory structures itself by being divided up into scenes (Baldassano et al. 2017), Listener's apparent rejection of those scenes seems rather to embrace the oblivion of forgetting and non-selfhood. But that rejection itself conjures up another scene, and so the process of memory continues. On the same typescript, the addition of the homonym **'seen'** strengthens the importance of this concept: 'and there not a wire in ~~sigh sight~~ **to be seen'** (ET2, 01r). However, unlike in the maxim describing a child who is 'seen and not heard', the protagonist did not want to be seen as a child, strengthening the picture of a long-standing antagonism with the world around him: 'was the ruin still ~~there~~ standing **where you hid as a child** someone's folly' (ET2, 01r).

'5 **C2 was your mother ... dying away'** (1976a, 10)

Thinking back again to the Portrait Gallery, C calls up a memento which has resonance across Beckett's oeuvre: **'the old green** ~~xxx~~ **greatcoat** ~~trailing~~ with your head on your chest and your arms round you hugging you for a bit of warmth' (EM, 09r). Julie Bates suggests that the clothing of Beckett's characters 'signals their place in the world' (2017, 25) and this passage incontrovertibly locates the protagonist as a down-and-out. Another word in this passage also echoes in the textual memory of Beckett's oeuvre, but in a different manner. Those patrolling the gallery are called '**guardians**' in the first draft (EM, 09r), a term Beckett had used in a more carceral institutional context in his unfinished French-language theatre sketch 'Louis & Blanc' ('gardien'; *BDMP7*, AS3, 02r). But in modern English, the word is not quite appropriate for those who work in a gallery. Perhaps this Gallicism made Beckett think of his Francophone theatrical canon, as the next variant is '**attendants**' (ET1, 05r), recalling the title of *En **attendant** Godot*. Their footwear also had a French resonance at one stage: Beckett first gave them '**slippers**' (EM, 09r) before changing to the archaic '**pantofles**' on ET1 (05r).[212] On ET5, having tried out a list of possible terms on the

212 Beckett uses the French term '*pantoufle*' in *Paroles et musique* and *Dis Joe* (2014a, 64, 77, 81). With many thanks to Pim Verhulst for alerting me to this. It is also used in Ludovic and Agnès Janvier's French translation of *Watt* (1969, 37), which Beckett supervised closely (see Knowlson 1997, 549–50).

opening page (see chapter 3.2.1), he added another variant in the main text of the typescript before striking it out: '~~pantofles~~ ~~galoshes~~ shufflers' (ET5, 02r). As in the 'cowslip bell' passage of *Not I*, Beckett here tries out a Joycean variant before rejecting it in the final text. In Joyce's short story 'The Dead', Gabriel Conroy uses galoshes to protect his shoes from the snow. As his wife Gretta complains to Gabriel's aunts, he has also tried to impose this footwear on her:

> – Goloshes! said Mrs Conroy. That's the latest. Whenever it's wet underfoot I must put on my goloshes. To-night even, he wanted me to put them on, but I wouldn't. The next thing he'll buy me will be a diving suit. (Joyce 2004, 378)

While Beckett wore Joyce's style of narrow shoes, even though they were unsuitable for his feet (Knowlson 1997, 101), there is a sense here that the galoshes do not quite fit Beckett's attendants, who, after all, would be indoors most of the time. Yet again, we see Beckett toying with the idea of including a word that would evoke one of his most important literary influences, but instead leaving it as a trace in his manuscripts.

Gabriel's night with Gretta famously ends with him imagining 'the snow falling faintly through the universe'. 'His soul swooned slowly', the last line of the story begins (Joyce 2004, 412). In *That Time*, Beckett changes focus from the soles of the attendants' feet, a connection evident in the slip he made in ET6: 'not a living ~~sole~~ soul in the place' (05r). In spite of this shift, the 'felt shufflers' that they wear are ultimately what signals the presence of these fellow humans, emphasizing their embodiment (ET6, 05r).

'6 B2 all still ... that scene' (1976a, 10)

Voice B continues to try and call up the memory of being 'still on the stone' (EM, 06r) with his lover. This is termed 'that **picture** of the two of you' in the second draft version on EM (03r). In ET5, this becomes 'that ~~picture~~ scene' (03r), while in ET6, Beckett experimented with another term before rejecting it: 'scene ~~image~~' (ET6, 03r). The concept of a narrative memory floating up as an 'image' is explored in *How It Is*, in which the two terms are equated: 'I've had the image the scene' (*HII* 25).[213] When asked by Mary Hutchinson in 1959 for a piece to publish in the magazine *X*, Beckett sent her a passage composed in the *Comment c'est* notebooks entitled *L'Image* (Pilling 2006, 145). This term features frequently (27 times) in the published text of *Comment c'est* itself (Beckett 2015). Given the similar process of narrative recall in *That Time*, in which a consciousness tries in vain to recall images in their pure state, it is worth asking to what extent the memories that 'floated up' into Listener's consciousness can be considered in the terms of imagism (EM, 06r). In his essay 'Imagisme', Ezra Pound's first two rules regarding imagist poetry outline a poetics one could see as being reflected in Beckett's late minimalist work:

> 1. Direct treatment of the 'thing', whether subjective or objective.
> 2. To use absolutely no word that did not contribute to the presentation. (1913, 199)[214]

In 'La peinture des van Velde' (1945), for instance, Beckett praised Bram van Velde's representation of 'la chose seule' (*Dis* 126), corresponding to Pound's first rule. Moreover, it is by now a critical commonplace that Beckett tries to cut down his own work, as exemplified by the phrase 'less is more' in the lighting instructions for *That Time* (EN, 01r). However, Beckett's final poem, *what is the word*, is about trying and *failing* to create an image, rather than its 'Direct treatment'. The same is true of the memories in *That Time*. Therefore, we can say that it is the failure of the remembering consciousness that became Beckett's focus, rather than the 'Direct treatment' that Pound championed.

213 It is also central to Hölderlin's poem 'Der Spaziergang', which was marked by Beckett in his library (https://www.beckettarchive.org/library/HOL-DIC.html, 250–1) and quoted in his 1938 review of Denis Devlin's poetry (*Dis* 94).

214 The third pertains specifically to verse, so it is not cited here. The essay is published under the pseudonym F. S. Flint.

'7 A3 Foley was it … picture-book' (1976a, 10)

As Eoin O'Brien points out, the original on which Foley's Folly was based is Barrington's Tower, 'situated in the foothills of the Dublin mountains, a mile or so from *Cooldrinagh* [Beckett's childhood home]' (1986, 27; emphasis in original). The name of Beckett's source appears in the first draft version, before it is replaced by a more typically Irish surname: **~~Barrington~~**'Maguire**s** [*sic*] **Folly** ~~nothing left~~ bit of the **tower** still standing' (EM, 04r). Though 'tower' does show up later in the phrase, the folly is specifically a folly from the very first draft version. As well as again indicating Beckett's interest in the concepts of unreason and madness, including 'Folly' in the name itself emphasizes the impracticality of the building from the very start of its existence. In ET2, Beckett tried another name before arriving at the alliterative published version: '**~~Maguire~~** ~~Madden~~ Foley was it **~~Maguire's~~** ~~Madden~~ Foley's Folly' (01r). Madden turns up as a character in *Mercier and Camier*, where he makes the eponymous characters listen to a long monologue about his youth: 'I am old and the only pleasure I have left is to recall, **out loud** in the **noble style** I loathe, the good old days happily gone for ever' (1973c, 34).[215] His brief appearance in the manuscripts of *That Time* is an instance of 'autotextuality' ['autotextualité'], a term used by Raymonde Debray-Genette to describe intertextual self-references (1979, 33).[216] Like *That Time*, Madden's speech evokes Dante, specifically his praise of Virgil, when Dante applauds his guide's 'noble style that has brought me honor' in Canto I of the *Inferno* (l. 87). Madden's recitation of memories also links his own monologue to *That Time*. However, it would be too much to say, as Madden does, that Listener's memories are definitely recited '**out loud**', since the scenography makes it unclear as to whether we are inside or outside his head. The voices strongly suggest that we are hearing Listener's thoughts, but the decontextualized

215 The name would have been on Beckett's mind in the period leading up to the composition of *That Time*, as he gave an early version of his translation *Mercier and Camier*, entitled 'In the Train with Mr. Madden', to David Hayman, who published it in the 1973 *Iowa Review* (Ackerley and Gontarski 2004, 276).

216 Also known as 'intratextuality' (see Martel 2005).

head against a dark background destabilizes any clear gap between interiority and exteriority.

While Beckett spent considerable creative energy choosing the correct name for Foley's Folly, he erased the name of the woman who had a one-night stand with the protagonist on his short return home: '**Dolly** was with you then, ~~no matter, or was it Nelly~~' (EM, 04r). The name is consequential here only to the extent that it must appear inconsequential, with the passage continuing: 'no matter, only one night in any case' (EM, 04r). As Mr Hackett puts it in *Watt*: 'The name is not uncommon [...], even I have known several **Nellies**' (*W* 6). In ET1, Beckett decided it was better still to go with an anonymous pronoun, writing over the previous version: '**~~Dolly~~** She' (01r). Again, in this lexia, we have evidence of Beckett's different strategies of 'vaguening': whereas the replacement of Dolly/Nelly features the removal of a (nondescript) name for a pronoun, the substitution of Barrington for Foley – via Madden – marks a 'vaguening' of biographical and autotextual detail in favour of verbal alliteration.

With the alliteration just described, and also with numerous instances of cutting down on the text while drafting, we see Beckett aware that he is editing a text for performance, just as we did when tracking the genesis of *Not I* and *Pas moi* (see chapters 2.2.2 and 2.3.2). The description of a performance text is also found within A's monologue, when he remembers 'sitting on a stone in the middle of the nettles ~~making it up~~ with ~~a book~~ your picture book' (ET2, 04r). The child's '**play**' – Beckett uses the word in the first draft version – is reflective of Beckett's own plays, involving as it does imaginative creation based on a text (EM, 04r). The only thing missing from this 'play' is an audience, which is probably why the protagonist goes about creating multiple selves. While M desperately asks in *Play*, 'when will all this have been ... just play?' (*KLT* 60), implying that the play he is in will never come to an end, the child's play recalled in *That Time* presents a model of theatrical creation in which the boundaries of the self are questioned and stretched. After the protagonist's juvenile rehearsal, it is this self-multiplication that we see enacted in the stage performance of *That Time*.

'8 C3 till you hoisted ... at your elbow' (1976a, 10–11)

It is not just himself and his former lover that the protagonist has difficulty identifying; even well-known people from the past remain anonymous, as when he remembers seeing a picture in the Portrait Gallery: 'some famous man or woman presumably or even child such as a young prince or princess some young prince or princess of the blood' (EM, 09r).[217] Beckett was very sensitive to the particular way in which paintings were presented in galleries, as we can see in the critical comments about National Gallery of Ireland director George Furlong that he included in a letter of 14 May 1937 to Thomas MacGreevy:

> I was really shocked to see what he [Furlong] had done with the Gallery. [...] The print room is done up a cold dark scientific laboratory or public lavatory green. [...] No matter how one addresses oneself to a picture one has the light in one's eyes. And they are all hung on about a level with the pubic bone. (*LSB I* 496)

Though we must bear in mind when assessing the acerbity of these lines that Beckett's close friend MacGreevy had been Furlong's unsuccessful competitor for the job of director, they do provide insight into the importance the author gave to the framing of an image from very early on in his career. This is all the more reason to see his repeated choice of the proscenium stage for the framing of his own stage image as a central part of his aesthetics.

In 1933, Beckett unsuccessfully applied for a job as an assistant curator at London's National Gallery (Knowlson 1997, 173). His many hours spent in art galleries would have attuned him to the importance of preservation techniques. In *That Time*, the protective covering used for the picture seen in the gallery suggests the protagonist's visit took place during the prewar years:

217 In 'All but I' (1973), Beckett's failed and unpublished attempt to complete *Rough for Radio I*, a voice recalls people from its past 'as if moving through a mental portrait gallery' (Verhulst 2017a, 94). The title – also written as 'all but one' by its author (qtd. in Verhulst 2017a, 94) – calls to mind Beckett's dismantling of the first-person pronoun in his plays of this period.

> **covered with glass** ~~in which~~ in which gradually as you looked trying to make it out **behind the glass & dirt** gradually a ~~**strange**~~ dim face appeared ~~**strange in the** sense **of unfamiliar**~~ that made you twist round to see who ~~it~~ was there in the room ~~with~~ behind you that you hadn't heard come in (EM, 09r)

As Stephen Hackney explains, glazing became popular in London galleries and museums in the late nineteenth century, but was largely done away with after 1945 (2020, 177–8).[218] Since this particular painting is '~~w~~s~~heeted with glass~~ black with age behind the glass (sheet)' (ET5, 03r), we can be reasonably sure this is a prewar memory. But the vocabulary used is typical of Beckett in the 1970s: he toys with the idea of using '~~**strange**~~' – later a 'key word' in *Footfalls* (see chapter 6.1.2) – but then decides against it, the ghostly appearance of someone 'that you hadn't heard come in' evidently being strange enough for this particular play (EM, 09r).

There is a notable revision of verbs of motion in this lexia. The ghostly apparition occurs as he is getting ready to go: '~~**heaving**~~ **levering** yourself up' (EM, 09r), which becomes '**levvying** [*sic*] yourself up' in ET1 (05r). Though not yet a fixed pattern in this particular passage, as the verb was cut in ET5 (03r), the use of the word 'levying' does foreshadow the language of commercial business which becomes prominent later in the monologue (see lexia 30 below).

'9 B3 on the stone ... long white hair' (1976a, 11)

B's next lexia employs the language of psychoanalysis: 'suddenly there you might be back in your boyhood **or the womb that was the worst of all** or wondering wd. it be rice or macaroni for your ~~xx~~ supper' (EM, 06r). Such imagery can be found in Rank's *Trauma of Birth*. While Rank identifies 'a strong unconscious sense of pleasure associated with the return to the mother's womb' and associates coming *out* of the womb as the 'primal trauma' due to the expulsion it signals from 'that primal paradise' (1929, 24, 136), Beckett himself had much less positive memories of his own time in the womb, as he told Knowlson in 1989. He recounted that his sessions with

218 It returned again in the 1980s due to the availability of low reflecting glass (Hackney 2020, 179).

Bion provoked 'extraordinary memories of being in the womb, intra-uterine memories': 'I remember feeling trapped, being imprisoned and unable to escape, of crying to be let out, but no one could hear, no one was listening' (qtd. in Knowlson and Knowlson 2006, 68). In a similar manner, Beckett's narrator departs from Rank's psychoanalytic paradigm by stating that the womb '**was the worst of all**'.

In ET2, Beckett struck out B's final thought and replaced it with something completely different: '~~or merely wondering should it be rice or macaroni for supper~~ ~~xxx~~ **or that old Chinaman born with ~~white~~ long white hair**' (02r). As Ackerley and Gontarski point out, the reference here is to Lao-tzu, traditionally regarded as the founder of the quietist philosophical school of Taoism (2004, 308). This may have chimed with Beckett's own quietist leanings (see Wimbush 2020), though a more likely link here is the legend of Lao-tzu being born already as an old man, a concept which turns up in a jotting for what would become C's last paragraph: '**born** & died in no time at a rather **old age**' (EM, 10r).[219] If Listener can be seen as a figure on the precipice of death, this motif of being 'born late' again links the spaces of birth and death in Beckett's work. While Lao-tzu is reputed to have existed around the 6th century BCE, B's use of language here dates him to a more recent era, possibly the prewar years in which he visited the gallery. Specifically, B's use of the word 'Chinaman' suggests either that he draws his vocabulary from an era where such language was not yet widely recognized as offensive or that he uses it without caring about its derogatory connotations. According to Asmus, Beckett told his German cast and crew: 'The B story has to do with the young man, the C story is the story of the old man and the A story that of the man in middle age', which would fit this interpretation of B using dated vocabulary, widely recognized as offensive by the time Beckett wrote the play (1977, 92).[220] If we accept this interpretation,

219 The same concept shows up in *How It Is*: 'the feeling rather of having been born octogenarian' (*HII* 60).

220 Charlotte Brewer points out the remarkable fact that despite it being widely identified in lexicographical circles as an offensive word from at least the 1960s, 'chinaman' only became labelled as such in the *OED* in 2010 (2016, 496). An avid reader of the *OED*, Beckett also owned a copy of the third edition of *Webster's New International Dictionary of the English Language* (1961; *BDL*). As Brewer notes, 'chinaman' was not marked as offensive in this 1961 printing of *Webster's*, though it was in later printings (2016, 496).

the offensive term definitively punctures the otherwise idyllic mood of B's monologue.

'10 C4 never the same ... never the same after that' (1976a, 11)

The next lexia starts by pointing out that Listener was irrevocably changed by seeing the face in the glass at the Portrait Gallery: 'never quite the same after that' (EM, 09r). However, the words immediately following show that such change was not unique: 'but that was **nothing new**' (EM, 09r), the intertextual reference here emphasizing the point by recalling the first line of *Murphy*: 'The sun shone, having no alternative, on the **nothing new**' (*Mu* 3). In other words, it is no great change to have changed once one has done it so many times. This concept of constant change recalls the Heraclitan 'flow' of words in *Not I* (see chapter 2.2.2). Indeed, Beckett uses '*flow*' to describe the voices of *That Time* in his stage directions (1976a, 9; *KLT* 99), so he may well have been thinking again of Heraclitus – as well as Listener's own theatrical predecessor Mouth – as he composed this play. Having referred to the philosopher explicitly in the manuscripts of *Godot* (see chapter 2.2.2), Beckett alluded to Heraclitus's concept twice in the published text of that play. Both instances refer to the concept of time: 'Everything oozes'; 'Time flows again already' (*WfG* 55, 73). What is more, the second of these Heraclitan references appears very close to an intertextual reference to George Berkeley's *Treatise Concerning the Principles of Human Knowledge*, which Beckett marked with reading traces in his copy of Berkeley's *Works* (see Van Hulle and Verhulst 2017a, 246). Elsewhere in the same *Treatise*, Beckett marked part of a paragraph on time. The text marked by Beckett's pencil is in bold below:

> (For my own part,) whenever I attempt to frame a simple idea of *time*, abstracted from the succession of ideas in my mind, which flows uni**formly, and is participated by all beings, I am lost and embrangled in inextricable difficulties.**[221]

221 https://www.beckettarchive.org/library/BER-NEW, 162; italics in original.

Again we have a concept of time flowing, albeit one which is inaccessible to Berkeley. This struggle to conceptualize the passing of time brings us closer to our struggle as an audience to identify Listener's past through the voices we hear: *That Time* too is 'embrangled in inextricable difficulties' in its attempt to 'frame a simple idea of time' (see also chapter 4.2.2). Indeed, the play's principle theme is the difficulty of recovering past time, an important aspect of Beckett's notes on Winnie for the 1971 production of *Glückliche Tage*: 'her time experience, incomprehensible transport from one inextricable present to the next, **those past unremembered**, those to come inconceivable' (qtd. in Haynes and Knowlson 2003, 142). While *Happy Days* concretises time in the rising mound of Acts I and II, it is Listener's difficulty in recapturing a clear idea of time which is enacted in the scenography of his play, the darkened stage making the relationship between Listener and the voices indeterminate, refusing to provide a clear 'frame' for the temporal relationship between sound and image.

The 'not-I' motif recurs in this lexia as well, with C asking Listener: 'did you ever **say I** to yourself in your life' (EM, 09r). Instead of 'say[ing] I', the three voices Listener hears address him in the second person. However, though it is difficult to read, Beckett may have experimented with the third person in his first draft: '~~he'll~~ you'll never be the same after' (EM, 09r). This would again create a parallel between *Not I* and its later sibling play, this time with regard to the pronominal experimentation in both their geneses.

'11 A4 or talking ... looking for you' (1976a, 11)

A's monologue returns to the model of play which Listener enacted as a child in Foley's Folly: 'or ~~xxx~~ talking to yourself out ~~loxd~~ loud, imaginary conversations, **there was** play **for** you' (EM, 04r). The precise kind of play outlined is a precursor of the performance situation we perceive in the theatre: 'sitting on a stone in a ruin in the middle of the nettles **making it up now the one voice now the other till you were hoarse and they all sounded alike**' (ET1, 01r). The different voice qualities hark back to the difference between 'assumed' and 'normal' voices in the 'Kilcool' drafts (see chapter 2.1.1), another polylogic monologue. At a narrative level, the above passage suggests not only that Listener's performance has been a long time in 'rehearsal', but that the division of selves embodied in the three voices and single stage image is a long-standing part of his identity. As made clear in lexia C4, whatever has happened to Listener is not just a change which has taken place today or yesterday (and which could therefore be attributed to a certain point in time) but rather seems to be present at many of the temporal points he returns to in his memories. This includes his separation from other individuals, which is evoked again in this lexia through the re-use of the number eleven: 'ten ~~years old~~ or eleven' (EM, 04r). Whereas earlier this featured in the description of the broken-down 'lines of communication', here it marks an age at which the protagonist retreated into himself, playing as he did 'well ~~into the nig~~ into the night some moods, **have them all out on the roads looking for you**' (EM, 09r). Though not yet the oppressive 'they' of other Beckett texts, this does establish a clear division between 'I' and 'they' that will be emphasized later in the play.

'12 B4 or by the window ... the shroud' (1976a, 11)

On ET1, Beckett gave B's memory session a moonlit setting: 'or just sitting by the window in the dark or moonlight' (03r). This makes it clear that the recollection of love in a field described in B's previous passages is not just a memory of an event, but a memory of a memory: 'hard to believe harder and harder to believe you ever~~y~~ told anyone you loved ~~g~~them or anyone ever told you' (ET1, 03r). This memory of a memory is linked to A's memory of playing in the ruin, which was described in the first draft version as 'muttering till you were **hoarse**' (EM, 04r), again evoking Dante's 'hoarse/faint' Virgil (see lexia 11 above). In ET5, Beckett introduced the phrase 'went on muttering' to B's monologue, suggesting that these two voices are part of the same cognitive stream, albeit this particular link is only identifiable by studying the manuscripts (03r).

In ET4, Beckett introduces an image to the idea that such memories were used 'to keep the void from pouring in on top of you the still (shroud)' (02r). From ET5 onwards, '**shroud**' becomes the chosen term (03r). In his 1937 letter to Kaun, Beckett wrote of language as a 'Schleier' that 'one has to tear apart in order to get to those things (or the nothingness) lying behind it' (*LSB I* 513, 518). 'Schleier' can be rendered into English as 'veil' (see *LSB I* 518; *Dis* 171), as it is in Judith Norman, Alistair Welchman and Christopher Janaway's translation of Arthur Schopenhauer's 'veil of *mâyâ*', which separates the subject from reality (Schopenhauer 2010, 378).[222] However, the German word can also mean the funereal 'shroud', which again suggests Listener being on the brink of life and death, or possibly beyond it. In B's case, silence itself is a 'shroud' which he tries to stave off with his narrated memories. If we hold B to the young Beckett's (rather high) standards of creating a 'literature of the non-word' (Beckett to Kaun, 9 July 1937, *LSB I* 520), we can see him as another one of Beckett's fictional failed writer figures (such as Krapp), who is here unable to give up on language. However, B is only one part of Listener's identity, and the voices do not last forever in this play.

Silence 1 (1976a, 11)

After this mention of the 'shroud', Beckett enacted what has just been mentioned by B – a silence free from words – by introducing a break from the monologues in ET4 (02r).

'13 C5 never the same ... another time' (1976a, 11–12)

If C's 'turning-point' was not a one-off event but a process, the same can be said of Beckett's composition of the paragraph describing this 'turning-point'. There are two deleted drafts of this passage on EM, as well as a number of shorter notes, before Beckett wrote: '~~**turning-point** that was a great word with you before they **dried up**~~' (10r). If, as Asmus tells us, 'the C story is the story of the old man', this would indicate that the words do eventually cease, having filled the void for many years according to monologue B. This would make Listener someone who has experienced a 'long silence' free from speech, like Mouth in *Not I*, and like Virgil in Dante's *Inferno*. Whether this includes the voices A, B and C is not entirely clear, but it does foreground silence as something distressing (the words having involuntarily 'dried up') which is in line with B's earlier suggestion that language is used to keep out the void.

If language is a *Communication Cord*, as in the title of Brian Friel's 1982 play, then this is yet another 'line of communication' with society which has been cut by C, just as society cut the umbilical cord between him and

222 For Schopenhauer's influence on Beckett, see Pothast (2008).

his mother: ‘**~~you~~** ~~rotating~~ ~~squirming~~ **~~on the same old spit~~** ~~ever since~~ ~~from the moment~~ ~~you saw the light~~ **~~they cut your cord~~**’ (EM, 09r). Rather than B’s negative description of the womb as ‘worst of all’, the drafts of C’s monologue have the womb as a place of respite which is disturbed by this intervention, which echoes Rank’s view of the womb as sanctuary: ‘you lay curled up like **a worm** in slime **in the peace and dark**’ (ET1, 05r). The use of ‘a worm’ here as a metaphor for pre-natal being recalls Beckett’s less than fully human character Worm in *The Unnamable*, also persecuted by those around him. So, the socialization entailed by C’s separation from his mother can be seen as a process of humanization forced by an oppressive third-person plural, ‘when **they** lugged you out and wiped you off and straightened you up’ (ET6, 05r), through which a recalcitrant subject is forced into shape.

‘14 B5 muttering that time ... see it no more’ (1976a, 12)

B’s monologue again echoes A’s description of creative play in Foley’s Folly: ‘**making it up from there** as best you could’ (EM, 06r). Thus, A’s and B’s stories come to be more and more entwined in a model of performativity as the play goes on. One of the memories that B makes up involves being with his lover by a canal: ‘that time together on the **towpath**’ (ET1, 03r). A ‘towpath’ appears in a canal scene in *Mercier and Camier* (*M&C* 15), where it describes a landscape which resembles Beckett’s city of birth. Canals also show up in *Molloy* and *First Love*, where they are an important part of what Gerry Dukes calls a ‘double exposure or montage’ of Irish and French elements in Beckett’s prose (2000, 3). While such ‘double exposure’ is often part of a topographic balancing act in the postwar novellas, a memory play like *That Time* can distribute different geographical elements (Dublin’s canals; London’s Portrait Gallery; the foothills of the Dublin Mountains) among the three voices. Strikingly (when one considers the avant-garde stage image), this makes *That Time* a more topographically realist text, at least in terms of its narrative topography, than either of these two prose predecessors. While *That Time* is very far from being a realist play, it is important to acknowledge the elements of realism that Beckett stages and subverts.

'15 A5 that time ... began to dawn' (1976a, 12)

Part of *That Time*'s topographical palimpsest is the public transport system that A remembers trying, and failing, to use: 'straight off the boat and up on to the main street **to catch the eleven**' (EM, 04r). Until ceasing to operate in 1939, Dublin's number eleven tram terminated on the south side of the city in Clonskeagh, a lengthy two-hour walk to Barrington's Tower (still present – though under erasure – in this early draft version; see lexia 7 above). In an autographical revision to EM, we can see the author (Beckett) remembering that his character (A) should remember that the tram stop no longer existed when he visited: 'just head down straight up from the pier to ~~the old stop,~~ **where the stop** ~~used to be~~ was' (EM, 04r). In ET8, the visit is marked as being the final one the protagonist made with the addition 'that last time' (03r). It is not clear why this is the case, but it could have something to do with the pressure the first-person narrator feels from outsiders. As we saw with *Not I*, Beckett's previous characters are often in dispute with the pronoun 'they' (see chapter 2.2.2), but he does also have precedent in using the first-person plural pronoun 'we' as an aggressive voice, as in the 1938 poem 'Ooftish'.[223] In EM, Beckett tried starting this lexia with a first-person-plural admonition not to keep talking about his childhood: 'well **we**'ve had all that, now that time' (04r). But this was cut from subsequent versions.

'16 C6 when you started ... closing-time' (1976a, 12)

A's monologue moves from psychological to physiological terminology in describing Listener's mental process: 'one thought in your ~~**mind**~~ head' (ET1, 01r). C likewise changes terminology of mind to something more anatomical when wondering 'whose ~~**head**~~ skull it was you were pent up in' (EM, 10r). Though, as Beloborodova has convincingly argued, it is far too simplistic to see Beckett's characters as being trapped in a 'skullscape', she also makes the point that 'both Cartesian and anti-Cartesian (or extended) evocations of the mind coexist in Beckett's fiction' (2018, 119). Similarly,

223 Referring to medical illness, the speaker of 'Ooftish' demands: 'send it along we'll put it in the pot with the rest / [...] get your friends to do the same we'll make use of it / we'll make sense of it we'll put it in the pot with the rest' (*CP* 59).

his plays continue to use dualist imagery of mental confinement, counterbalancing the move towards more enactive models of cognition in his later work. Beckett also medicalizes C's mental state, marking it as an **'infirmity** not to know yourself from Adam' (EM, 10r). However, his very next words show that this mental state was willed: '**began trying** not to know yourself from Adam' (EM, 10r).

In lexia 14 (discussed above), B notes the '**flotsam**' passing by on the nearby waterway (1976a, 12; *KLT* 102). This interest in the detritus carried by the stream of time is also found in Beckett's German Diaries, where he noted in an entry of 15 January 1937 his preference for books focussing on facts rather than narrative interpretation: 'What I want is the straws, **flotsam**, etc., names, dates, births and deaths, because that is all I can know' (qtd. in Nixon 2011, 62). A marginal addition to C's monologue remembers such historical '**flotsam**' on the frames of the paintings in the Portrait Gallery: 'and **the dates on the frame** in case you got the century wrong' (EM, 10r). In his early notes for the play on EM, Beckett noted:

> A: factual, names, dates, places, confusion
> B: mental, confusion of thought.
> C: affective, " " sensation. not inter-exclusive (EM, 01r)[224]

Corresponding to Beckett's marginal note that these traits were 'not inter-exclusive', in this passage it is C who is confused about names and dates: he remembers neither the paintings nor the eras in which they were painted – which is hardly surprising given his decision to deliberately forget his own name.

'17 B6 no sight ... for the vows' (1976a, 12)

Another image of spatial separation turns up in B's description of the imagined lovers 'facing front **like at the two ends of an axle tree**' (EM, 07r), the axle tree being 'The fixed bar or beam, etc., on the rounded ends of which the opposite wheels of a carriage revolve' (*OED*b). As in Beckett's repeated use of the number eleven in *That Time*, this is an image in which

224 The addition 'not inter-exclusive' was made beside a bracket running down the left of the paragraph.

two single figures do not meet: 'always ~~xx xxx~~ space **between** if only a few inches' (EM, 07r). Not only that, the two 'couldn't turn your heads ~~to look at each oth~~ for a look at each other' (EM, 07r), recalling Dante's damned soothsayers in the eighth circle of the *Inferno* (see also *ATF* 24). Though no soothsayer, Listener, like Dante's contorted character Amphiaraus, who must walk in hell with his head twisted to face backwards, is a figure who 'looks behind and treads a backward path' in his stream of memories (*Inferno*, Canto XX, l. 39). This Dantean mood is strengthened by an edit to ET5, in which the lovers are described as being 'no better than ~~figments~~ shades' (04r).

'18 A6 no getting ... so what next' (1976a, 13)

Having realized the tram line no longer operates, A tries the train. Like Mouth, he does not want to interact with anyone: '**no question of** ~~stopping xxx xxx to enquire~~ asking ~~bite your tongue off first~~ **die rather**' (EM, 04r). Instead, he decides to 'foot it up to the ~~railway~~ station get ~~it~~ out to it that way', whereupon he finds that the station is '**closed down**, terminus of the **southern & eastern** all closed down & falling to bits' (EM, 04r). In other Beckett works such as *Watt* and *All That Fall*, the Dublin and South-eastern trainline stands as a marker of a modernized suburban community, albeit one in decline in the radio play.[225] As Nicholas Grene argues, Maddy Rooney's response to the news of her husband's delayed train shows that, for the residents of Boghill, 'the expectation is that the train *will* arrive on time, does normally arrive on time' (2004, 182; emphasis in original). Maddy complains to the stationmaster: 'Even the slowest train on this brief line is not ten minutes and more behind its scheduled time without good cause, one imagines' (*ATF* 18). If the world of *All That Fall* portrays the 'lingering dissolution' of a community which still expects order and stability in its public transport (*ATF* 6), Beckett's use of this trainline in *That Time* focuses on the breakdown of communication between self and the world. Though Harcourt Street Station saw its last train depart in 1958, the station building

225 The same trainline is referred to in the 'Kilcool' drafts by its colloquial name 'the Slow & Easy' (AS1, 11r). For more on the train station in *Watt*, see Little (2020c, 61–5). See also Whelan (forthcoming). I would like to thank Feargal Whelan for sharing his unpublished research with me.

itself still stands today. In *That Time*, the train – like the trams – no longer runs and the station is imagined as being as much a ruin as Foley's Folly.

'19 C7 the rain … gave up whoever it was' (1976a, 13)

C's previous lexia features the juxtaposition of a second-person pronoun with the inanimate third person: 'not believing **it** was **you**' (EM, 10r). This clash of pronouns is further developed in the following paragraph, which begins in the second person and ends by referring to the protagonist as '**it**'. Having been kicked out of the gallery, C recalls, '**you** went the old rounds' of the city (EM, 10r). However, this only goes on 'till the words dried up and the head dried up & the legs dried up ~~up or the~~ whosever they were or ~~they locked~~ **it** gave up ~~whatever~~ whoever **it** was' (EM, 10r). The change of pronoun here might be down to the nature of the protagonist's walks around the city: 'the old rounds ~~turning you into~~ **trying to turn you into it**' (EM, 10r). Though it is not entirely clear what C is referring to here – the verb 'turn' later becomes 'transmute' (ET1, 06r), then the more forceful 'wangle' (ET2, 05r) – it is possible to read this quite literally as the protagonist's effort to turn 'you' into an 'it', much as the same way Mouth turns 'I' into 'she'. Emphasizing the 'it' in his reading of this passage, Beckett told Asmus: 'That is a story of depersonalization – seeing oneself as an object' (Asmus 1977, 93). This is something Beckett focussed on throughout his later work, describing his writing thus to Shainberg in 1984/5: 'It has to do with a fugitive "I" […]. It's an embarrassment of pronouns. I'm searching for the non-pronounial. […] It seems a betrayal to say "he" or "she"' (Shainberg 1987). *That Time* is an important part of this effort. C takes Mouth's self-objectification one step further, as she uses an animate pronoun to refer to herself. In *That Time*, the remembered self becomes merely an inanimate 'it'.

'20 B7 stock still … wherever it was' (1976a, 13)

While the *Inferno* is a key intertext for this piece, Beckett may have been wary of identifying the 'shades' of *That Time* too closely with Dante's figures in the underworld. For instance, he cut an allusion to death in EM, again preferring an alliterative alternative: '~~dead~~ stock **still**' (07r). On the other hand, the importance of the number eleven in the play is hard to overstate.

In this lexia, the two lovers embody that number, 'stretched out parallel in the sun' (EM, 07r), this spatial figure allowing Beckett to represent the communicative 'no-man's-land' between them.

'21 A7 gave it up ... by on the other side' (1976a, 13)

While Beckett carried out a literary demolition order of Harcourt Street Station in order to emphasize the ruined state of A's memory, he seems to momentarily reconstruct it in the following paragraph, where A remembers: 'sat down on the steps in the morning ^{sun}, no, those steps got no sun in the morning, **facing west** they ~~were~~ $^{\text{must have been}}$' (EM, 04r). The steps in front of the old Harcourt Street Station do indeed face west. However, they are immediately subject to an epanorthosis, 'A figure of speech in which something said is corrected or commented on' (Cuddon 1984, 224): '**northwest, somewhere**, went away somewhere else and sat down $^{\text{on a step}}$ in the sun, **a doorstep maybe**' (EM, 04r). What matters here is the memory of sitting in the sun – the city's architecture can be changed to fit that memory.

As Listener waits to get his evening boat, the citizens objectify him, echoing the change of pronouns in lexia 19: '^{and} the people stopping to **look** at you **like something o~~t~~^{u}t of Beckett**' (ET1, 02r).[226] The verb of perception later becomes the more overtly offensive '**goggle**' (ET3, 01r), then '**gape**' (ET4, 03r), recalling the judgemental passers-by regarding Jesus on the cross (see chapter 3.5.2). Beckett's self-reference raises the question of the function of an author's name in their own work. In *Beckett's Dantes*, Daniela Caselli argues that 'Beckett texts read like "something out of Beckett" because the Beckett canon opposes the idea of an authentic voice in a paradoxically coherent manner', a process to which she sees the *auctoritas* of Dante as central. Caselli questions the idea that certain of 'Beckett's Dantes' can be read as more 'successful' than another, challenging the concept of teleological progress in Beckett's different uses of the Florentine poet (Caselli 2005, 201). However, as she also admits, progression of one kind or another is impossible to ignore completely when studying such intertextual

226 As the A monologue was composed first, Beckett may have drawn the change of pronouns in C's monologue from the objectification of the protagonist in A's speech. Beckett first left a gap for the author's name (EM, 05r), before inserting his own on ET1 (02r).

relations. This is evident in A's reference, where the very presence of a canon to which Beckett can autotextually refer makes this a different kind of self-reference to that in his early novel *Dream of Fair to Middling Women*, in which we find '"Mr Beckett" [...] ventriloquising Dante in order to get "the bay about his brow"' (Caselli 2005, 202; see *D* 141). By the 1970s, Beckett had enough of a name for a self-reference to carry weight, his audiences now fully aware what 'something out of Beckett' would look like. But the reference disappears from ET7 (and thereafter) in an instance of 'vaguening' which occurs quite late in the genesis. We can thus see that using his own corpus as an *auctoritas* in *That Time* was a serious consideration for Beckett, albeit one he finally rejected.

'22 B8 stock still ... no sight or sound' (1976a, 13)

Yet another image of spatial separation is introduced in B8, which returns to the lovers by the canal: 'without your having stirred any more than **the two knobs on a dumbbell**' (EM, 07r). In ET1, memory is again presented as something to be actively reconstructed, rather than involuntarily received by the subject. Beckett achieves this through presenting a series of options: 'no stir or sound **only faintly the leaves in the little wood behind you or the ears or the bent or the stream** against the reeds as the case might be **of man no~~r~~ sight or sound**' (ET1, 04r). Having 'remembered' the silence surrounding the couple as they lay on the grass, B then recalls the sounds of the natural world around him. The closing words of the passage quoted are therefore a revision to the original memory of silence, emphasizing the constructed nature of B's memories.

'23 C8 always winter ... another time' (1976a, 13–14)

Having been ejected from the gallery, another public institution is introduced by C, one which is found in most towns or cities: 'that time you took shelter from the rain in the **Public Library**' (EM, 10r). In *The Expelled*, the protagonist asks a cabman to take him to the zoo when unsure of his destination. As he goes on to reflect: 'It is rare for a capital to be without a Zoo' (*ECEF* 9). A similar topographical tactic can be seen in C's monologue, naming institutions which could be anywhere, albeit the location of this memory sequence has already been indicated by the Portrait Gallery. While the location is thus slightly 'vaguened', we can be more certain of the protagonist's social standing. His state of vagrancy is marked by the fact that this library was one of the 'places you **didn't have to pay** to get in' (EM, 11r). And he appears to be a vagrant migrant, as indicated in the phrase 'free culture in bad weather **far from home**' (EM, 11r). As discussed in lexia 5, the nature of this vagrancy is marked by the protagonist's coat, which is identified as a paternal heirloom in ET1: 'the old green holeproof coat **your father left you**' (06r). If we recall Asmus's explanation that the voice of C relates to Listener's experiences as an old man, then the fact that he got this coat from his father and has hung onto it his whole life may further indicate an impoverished position. In sum, this lexia gives us more information on the place of the protagonist in society, even if we do not still know precisely what time frame we are dealing with.

The lexia closes by mentioning another institution: 'the **Post Office** that was another' (ET1, 06r), which will be further explored below (in lexia 27).

'24 A8 huddled on the doorstep ... where none ever came' (1976a, 14)

The coat appears again in A's monologue, where it is first 'the old green **coat**' (ET2, 06r), before becoming 'the old green **greatcoat**' in ET3 (01r). If A is the voice of middle age, then this means the protagonist has spent a long period of his life with the coat in his possession. It is notable that Beckett first included the coat in C's monologue before transferring it into A's, making this an instance where the memories of times recent seeped into the memories of times less recent during the compositional process. Memories start to seep into one another in A's monologue itself, when he compares sitting on the doorstep of one of the buildings of his former hometown to the narratives he used to make up in Foley's Folly: 'that time on the stone **the child on the stone** where none ever came' (ET4, 05r).

All of this adds to a sense that we know less about Listener the more we hear about him, a sense we can see Beckett emphasizing in his edits. For example, the line 'little by little not knowing where you were **when you were neither where nor when**' (ET2, 06r) received a further interrogative phrase in ET3: 'little by little not kn°wing **where** you were **when** you were **or what for**' (01r). Throughout his career, from *Watt* to *What Where*, Beckett used such question words to bring out the fact that his narrators were 'non-knower[s]' (qtd. in Shenker 1956, 3) – as in the opening questions of *The Unnamable*, which never get answered for the reader: '**Where** now? **Who** now? **When** now?' (*Un* 1). Similarly, the audience's hermeneutic response to a play entitled *That Time* will probably be 'what time?'. In the case of *Watt*, questions come at the start of the composition process, a list of interrogative words at the beginning of a set of loose pages stored with the first compositional notebook serving as a catalyst for the narrative genesis: 'who, what, where, by what means, why, in what way, when' (HRC SB MS 6/5/3).[227] Beckett generated from these question words his first draft protagonist: 'X is a man, ~~ignorant~~, 70 years old, ignorant, alone, at evening, in his room, in bed, having pains, listening, remembering' (HRC SB MS 6/5/3).[228] He would go on to create a narrative which is ridden with gaps, especially regarding basic information about its principal figure Watt. In *That Time*, by adding similar question words to A's monologue, Beckett focuses on the state of not-knowing as part of the protagonist's own mental activity. Furthermore, this is a self-interrogation which casts Listener as both subject and object of his own questions, which he then observes from the distance interposed by memory.

Silence 2 (1976a, 14)

Another silence in the monologues follows, marking the end of the second group of lexias.

'25 B9 or alone ... all vanished' (1976a, 14)

The interference of one memory narrative with another is also evident in B's monologue, where he continues to use phrases from A – '**making it up that way** to keep going'; 'alone **on the** edge of the **stone**' (EM, 08r, 04r–05r). When he speaks again about the canal scene, it ends like a movie fade-out: 'and the sun going down till it went down & **you vanished all vanished**' (EM, 08r). In *À la recherche*, Marcel similarly recalls watching the sun

227 I follow the HRC foliation.

228 As well as an erasure across the entire page in blue crayon, both passages are erased using black ink.

go down in his 'petit bois' with Albertine (Proust 2011 III, 514). But that sundown does not have the same obliterating effect on Marcel's memory. In *That Time*, this passage serves as a yet another reminder of the heavily constructed nature of B's memory, with the scene of memory disappearing simultaneously with the self who is remembered. This is made clear at the very start of this lexia: like the narrator of the slightly later prose text *Company* (1977), B recalls coming up with these memories when '**alone**' (EM, 08r; see *CIWS* 42), thus echoing the statement in *Proust*: 'We are **alone**. We cannot know and we cannot be known' (*PTD* 66). In *That Time*, while knowledge of others is off-limits, even self-knowledge has become extremely difficult in a world where the self is isolated and breaking down.

'26 A9 none ever came … none ever came' (1976a, 14)

A's next lexia makes an even clearer link between *That Time*'s theatrical scenario and the memory of Listener performing for himself as a child: '**dividing yourself in two or more** then some moods and **talking to yourself** that way' (EM, 05r). In ET5, this verb changes, recalling Beckett's description of the 'breakdown of the subject' in 'Recent Irish Poetry' (see Introduction): '~~splitting~~ breaking up two or more' (06r). While in Foley's Folly, the protagonist also read, and in the first writing layer Beckett named a Victorian children's book: '**reading ~~Froggy's little brother~~**' (EM, 05r).[229] In ET2, the pronouns change from second to third person, further distancing Listener from his past self: 'reading in **~~your~~** his book or making up talk splitting **~~your~~**himself up' (06r). In ET3, this becomes '**poring** on his book', a verb that will have significance in one of C's later lexias (01r; see lexia 33 below).

229 *Froggy's Little Brother* (1875) tells the tale of two orphaned boys making their way in Victorian London following the deaths of their parents, who run a Punch-and-Judy show. Its themes of performance and vagrancy make it a fitting text for A's remembered reading sessions. Beckett's cousin Sheila Page recalled the author's mother reading the story to them as children (Knowlson and Knowlson 2006, 6). With many thanks to Pim Verhulst for identifying the title.

'27 C9 always winter ... drowsing away' (1976a, 14)

C's monologue returns to the 'Post Office', named '~~another stop~~' in the first draft version (EM, 11r) before becoming more explicitly a sanctuary in the next version: 'another **refuge**' (EM, 12r). If the self-division in the monologues demonstrates that none of the past versions of Listener are very much like himself, neither are they like anyone else. This is emphasized by the way A remembers that he 'pushed open the door **like anyone else**' (EM, 11r), as if doing so was noteworthy of comment. His various selves are represented by **'all the forms** to fill in' (EM, 12r) that he remembers in the Post Office, which are specified as forms related to different types of communication in the first draft version: 'the telegram forms & the postal-order forms & the registered letter forms' (EM, 11r). But the filling-in of these forms is presented in carceral terms, suggesting that constructing the self – and communicating with others – is not as easy as filling a blank page. Indeed, a form typically contains a set of instructions which shape the self according to a set system. No wonder the narrator recalls feeling locked in: 'the **ball**point kindly provided at the end of a **chain**' (EM, 12r). In ET5, this becomes the equally carceral '~~ballpoin~~ts pens' (ET5, 05r), the sense remaining that the creation of a self is constrained by the technology used to construct it, both at the story level in A's monologue as well as at the level of production, with Beckett struggling to differentiate the voices sufficiently.

While we are reminded that it is **'always winter'** in C's memories, a supralinear addition to the third draft version points to the more specific date of the winter solstice, 21 December: 'day after day **the shortest day the longest night**' (EM, 12r). The Post Office itself is 'all **Xmas** bustle' (ET2, 07r), providing the clearest indication yet of what time that time might be in Listener's memories.

'28 B10 or that time alone ... soon after long after' (1976a, 15)

B remembers a time when 'you went back **to** the old scene' (EM, 08r), returning to the scenario imagined with his lover and repeating many details from earlier lexias. The change of preposition in ET1 suggests again that B is a movie character in the showreel of his own life: 'and you back **in** the old scene' (04r), playing a part rehearsed since youth. As the phrase 'before she came or after she went' suggests (EM, 08r), it does not even matter whether he has experienced these scenes with the unnamed woman – he can continue to re-imagine them over and over regardless. One notable addition is the admission that the scene he inserts himself back into only '**might be might have been the same**' (EM, 08r). Is this then really an '**unchanging** scene', as he goes on to claim (EM, 08r)? The mention of many previous elements would seem to suggest that it does not really matter: 'with the **rat** and the **wheat** or whatever it was the **yellowing ears** and that time **in the dunes**', the final element again evoking the seaside trysts of Proust's narrator in Balbec (EM, 08r; see Proust 2011 III, 232). Whereas Marcel's recollection of the past allows him to link one point in time with another, the enhanced substitutability of one incident for another in B's monologue means that they lose their aura. This first draft version ends with the words '**exactly the same**' but this is surely repetition with a difference (EM, 08r), so different indeed that any putative identity that these past experiences may have with one another can be jettisoned in favour of the process of watching these images rush by, as if watching a high-speed spool of one's own past.

'29 A10 eleven or twelve … forgetting it all' (1976a, 15)

Different layers of memory again become interwoven in A's monologue, where he remembers himself sitting on the step, re-enacting the performance of his childhood: 'till sitting there on the step in the sun **you found yourself at it again**' (EM, 05r). Close as this may be to what we see before us onstage, there is one clear difference: A remembers speaking; Listener is listening. So, there may be grounds for interpreting the stage scenario as part of a progression: having learned to tell these stories to himself as a child and having done so throughout his life, Listener is now no longer compelled to speak, but rather able to hear the voices play out until they go silent.

While *That Time* is a memory play, it is as much interested in forgetting as it is in the successful recollection of individual details. For instance, A conceives of the past experience on the step as follows: 'sat there ~~forgetting it~~ in the morning sun **forgetting it all**' (05r). Beckett was well aware of the role of forgetting as part of the process of memory. In *Proust*, he went so far as to claim: 'The man with a good memory does not remember anything because he does not forget anything' (*PTD* 29).[230] Such a man would presumably have been of no interest to Freud, who used techniques such as free association to recover what he understood to be the repressed memories buried deep inside an individual's consciousness. 'Psychoanalysis', Beckett noted when reading Jones's *Papers on Psycho-analysis*, 'is concerned less with the mechanisms & material of remembering than with those of forgetting' (TCD MS 10971/8/8; Jones 1923, 131). And Beckett used Freudian terminology in his 1934 review of Albert Feuillerat's *Comment Proust a composé son roman*, describing 'the uncontrollable agency of unconscious memory' as being central to Proust's aesthetics (*Dis* 65). More recently, Paul Ricœur has identified in narrative a 'selective function [...] consisting from the outset in a strategy of forgetting as much as in a strategy of remembering [*remémoration*]' (2006, 85; 2000, 103).[231] In *That Time*, we see this function of narrative memory-as-forgetting thematized in A's monologue. In the case of A, there seems to be no prospect of re-accessing the material of the past. Instead, he re-enacts the memory of making up stories, which Listener now listens to.

'30 C10 perhaps fear ... another place another time' (1976a, 15)

In a reversal of the instances noted above where the pronouns shift from second- to third-person, the last words of C9 change from '[he] **was** taking a look round for a change before dozing away' (ET2, 07r) to '[you] **were** taking a look round for a change befoe^r^e dozing away' (ET3, 03r). Lexia C10 gives a reason for this inspection, with the opening adverb further emphasizing the dislocation between remembering and remembered self: '**perhaps** just fear of **attack** or ~~expulsion~~ ejection' (EM, 12r). Beckett had clearly considered making Listener one of his canon's 'expelled', as in his earlier novella of that title, before changing his mind. Nevertheless, this

230 In his copy of *Sodome et Gomorrhe*, Beckett marked the line: 'Une mémoire sans défaillance n'est pas un très puissant excitateur à étudier les phénomènes de mémoire' (https://www.beckettarchive.org/library/PRO-ALA-8.html, 32–3).

231 See also Nugent-Folan's analysis of *Company / Compagnie* in terms of 'remémoration' (2021).

protagonist is under threat from a strict social order, as we can see in the change of '**attack**' to '**assault**' in ET3 (03v).

In addition to feeling under threat from those around them, Beckett's characters often reject what the narrator of *Murphy* calls the 'mercantile gehenna' of gainful employment and commercial trade (*Mu* 27). Listener is no different, a fact which is brought into sharp relief by the proliferation of business terms in this lexia: 'having clearly no **business** in the place not to mention your personal appearance & **monopolizing** into the **bargain** ~~xxx~~ space that could ill be **spared**' (EM, 12r). Elsewhere, monologue A describes an earlier version of this same self in moralistic and legalistic terms: 'the **scandal** huddled there in the sun where it had no **warrant**' (ET3, 01r). The religious term **'reprobation'** is used in C's monologue (ET4, 04r). So, it is clear that Listener's voices see the forces of social order and respectability arraigned against him. The fact that such terms are so disdainfully critical suggests that the voices are ventriloquizing the clichés of justice and money in order to emphasize the 'space that intervenes' between Listener's former selves and society (see Introduction). In her study of Beckett and cliché, Elizabeth Barry highlights the ways in which 'Beckett reawakens the images and ideas in familiar figures of speech, revealing in his work the ideological import they contain' (2006, 50). Such undermining of authority through cliché shows that the breakdown of subject and object is not merely psychological, but is experienced by Beckett's characters through a corresponding breakdown in social relations.

'31 B11 the glider ... time came in the end' (1976a, 15)

As in both *Not I* and *Footfalls*, textual repetition is used towards the end of *That Time*'s monologues in order to bring the piece to its conclusion. As B puts it, 'nothing ever changed' (EM, 08r). One small change is the shift from imagining that '**you** loved **each other**' (EM, 06r) to imagining that '**she** loved **you**' (EM, 08r). Note that 'she' never gets to speak here, but only exists insofar as she is part of B's 'scene'. However, this projection of the past is subject to its own break, as signalled in the line 'till the time came in the end' (ET5, 07r), which sets up the crucial, penultimate lexia of C's monologue.

'32 A11 making it all up ... till that time came' (1976a, 15)

Another change of pronouns takes place in the first draft version of A's monologue, going against the trend of a more general shift towards the third person: 'making ~~**himself**~~ yourself all up again' (EM, 05r). The unchanging, repetitive nature of these performances is signalled by a new phrase on EM: '**for the millionth time**' (05r). And as in monologue B, a signal of an impending narrative turning point is added at a later point in the genesis, on the same typescript where Beckett started to arrange the final set of lexias: '**till that time came**' (ET3, 01v).

'33 C11 the Library ... not a sound' (1976a, 16)

C revisits his by now familiar story of that time in 'the Public Library' (EM, 11r), but provides a clue as to what it might have been that caused his irrevocable change: 'something to do with **dust**' (EM, 11r). Beckett memorably described his own creative process in terms of dust when he told Lawrence Harvey that using words was like 'trying to build a snowman with dust' (qtd. in Haynes and Knowlson 2003, 49). And he certainly did think of his characters in these terms, as when he made a note identifying the source of the German line 'Dreck bist du' in Rick Cluchey's bilingual edition of *Eh Joe*: 'Genesis III 19' (UoR MS 3626, qtd. in Van Hulle 2008, 162).[232] As Van Hulle notes, the King James Version of this verse reads: 'for dust thou art, and unto dust shalt thou return' (2008, 162). So, we could certainly see C (and therefore Listener) as part of a long line of Beckett characters who consider themselves to be mere 'dust' or 'Dreck'. But C cannot fully remember what he heard: it is only (he thinks) '**something** to do with dust'. Therefore, his memory of this half-heard phrase serves to remind us of the instability of self-reference, not only in *That Time*, but across Beckett's body of work.

The verb used in ET1 to describe 'a bevy of old ones **poring** on their books' (06r) echoes A's description of the young boy '**poring** on his book' (see lexia 26 above), further emphasizing a continuity of being across different

232 Beckett also noted in the margin of the same edition: 'Den[n] du bist Erde und sollst zu Erde werden (Luther)' (UoR MS 3626, qtd. in Van Hulle 2008, 162; editorial addition in Van Hulle).

individuals. The addition on the same typescript of the phrase 'something **the dust said**' even indicates agency in a seemingly inanimate element of the surrounding environment (06r).

'34 B12 that time ... little or nothing' (1976a, 16)

As outlined throughout this chapter, B keeps himself going by constructing scenes of the past. But he reaches a point where he cannot continue to do so: 'then that time in the end when you tried & couldn't [...] **couldn't** any more no words left to keep it out' (EM, 08r). The language used to describe this change is again reminiscent of Beckett's letter to Kaun, particularly in its description of silence as 'a great white **shroud**' (EM, 08r). There is another echo of that letter in the syntax of the paragraph's closing phrase: '**little or nothing the worse little or nothing**' (ET5, 07r). When writing to Kaun, Beckett expressed his hope that language could be drilled into 'until that which lurks behind, be it **something or nothing**, starts seeping through' (*LSB I* 518). Like Beckett the young letter-writer, B is unsure of the difference between 'something' – however 'little' there may be – and 'nothing'. But a difference there must be, otherwise it would be impossible to distinguish '**worse**' from the worst – or even from the 'worser', as one Beckett's later narrators memorably puts it (*CIWS* 94–7, 100). For Van Hulle, Beckett 'undermines the optimistic streak' in the aesthetics of modernist writers such as Proust (2018, 10). Taken as a standalone narrative, B goes against this general trend, since, for him, things do not get worse once the silence is let in, or, if they do, they only get a 'little' worse. But if we take into account the theatrical context, this optimistic outlook is undercut by the other voices that tell Listener's story. In ET4, Beckett considered ending with the paragraph order ACB, which would have left the audience with a potentially optimistic uplift of 'little or none nothing the worse little or none nothing' (05r). However, from this point on, he put paragraphs A and C at the end. And it is with these voices of middle age and old age – not B's youthful, optimistic outlook – that Beckett decided to end his play.

'35 A12 back down to the wharf ... never come back' (1976a, 16)

A's story too reaches a decisive conclusion, as he remembers going 'back down to the pier with the nightbag and the old green greatcoat your father left you trailing the ground' in order to catch the boat which will take him away from the land of his youth (ET3, 01v). Beckett decided in his very first loose jotting related to this paragraph that this would be the last trip home for A: 'away out to hell out of it & **never come back**' (EM, 05r), and this phrase is retained throughout the genesis. But what C would call this 'turning-point', a sense of dramatic catastrophe that Beckett would again undercut in the structure of *Footfalls* (see chapter 6.1.2), is undermined by the question: 'was there ever any other time than that' (EM, 05r). Beckett interpreted Proust's novel in terms of a 'turning-point' in the life of its narrator, using the term in his monograph on Proust to describe the time at which Marcel decides to start composing his literary oeuvre (*PTD* 38).[233] The use of 'turning-point' as a key term in *That Time* can therefore be seen as another instance of autotextuality. Such a revelation is not granted to Listener's multiple selves in *That Time*. Writing of the characters of Beckett's postwar prose, Barry contends that the memories in these texts 'emphasize the dissonance, the discontinuity, rather than the cumulative picture of themselves that these memories might create' (2006, 79). In this way, she argues, Beckett's work departs from Proust's model of memory, 'emphasizing as it does not only the discontinuity of the self but also the impossibility of mastering the fragmented memories by inserting them into benignly conventional narrative patterns' (Barry 2006, 79). In *That Time*, it is the patterning of memory itself that is brought into focus by the interweaving of the three voices, which comes to a close with C's final lexia.

233 Beckett uses the term when writing of an earlier, 'fugitive precursor' of this moment, when Marcel's reflection on the past is interrupted by the arrival of Robert Saint-Loup: 'But he is not alone, he is interrupted by Saint-Loup, and what might have been the turning-point in his life, the climax that is not to be reached until many years later in the courtyard and library of the Princesse de Guermantes, is nothing more than one of its most fugitive precursors' (*PTD* 38).

'36 C12 not a sound ... gone in no time' (1976a, 16)

From the very first draft version, Beckett linked C's recollection of the pages in the Public Library to the imagery of nature in some of B's earlier lexias: 'only the **leaves** turning and then something to do with dust' (EM, 11r). In case we thought dust was simply a metaphor for being, Beckett literalizes this encounter with the dust of previous generations: 'whole place suddenly full of dust opened your eyes and nothing but dust nothing to be seen from floor to ceiling only dust' (EM, 11r). As well as allowing his play to close with the biblical concept of beginning and ending through the 'dust thou art' motif, this event has the noteworthy consequence of obscuring C's vision, leaving him listening to a voice, the same situation Listener is in onstage: 'not a sound only **come & gone come & gone** no one **come & gone** in no time' (EM, 11r).[234] In *Come and Go*, Beckett ended his play with the cyclical image of rings, which Flo says she can feel on her friends' inter-clasped hands (but which are invisible to the audience) (*KLT* 74–5). In *That Time*, the phrase '**come & gone**' has an interesting resonance with one of Beckett's annotations of Proust's *Temps retrouvé*, where he underlined the phrase 'était venu' and wrote in the margin: 'Fetishes come'.[235] For Beckett, Proust's fetishes were the moments of revelation at which involuntary memory invades the subject. It is notable that Beckett uses this verb at the end of *That Time*. However, Listener's voices may not be 'gone' for good; they may 'come' again. Indeed, by adding the verb 'to go' to the Proustian involuntariness of 'to come', Beckett sets up the opening monologues spoken by A – 'that time you **went** back' – and C – 'when you **went** in' – to start all over again (1976a, 9; *KLT* 99).

234 In ET1, it becomes clear that this is something said by the dust itself: 'what was it it said' (06r).

235 https://www.beckettarchive.org/library/PRO-ALA-15.html, 8.

Silence 3 (1976a, 16)

Listener's closing smile has caused much critical commentary, which Weller helpfully summarizes: for Knowlson, the smile is a 'wry reflection on the insignificance of the individual human existence'; for Pountney, it communicates 'delight in the unbroken silence'; and for Gontarski, it is a response to 'the restoration of order, or at least a formal harmony' (Knowlson and Pilling 1979, 210; Pountney 1988, 41; Gontarski 1985, 158, all qtd. in Weller 2006, 129). Weller himself suggests that it may be read as 'a hermeneutic challenge or trap' which draws us into trying 'to put the play to rest' (2006, 130). At the same time, Listener seems to smile at any such attempt. This would be in line with Beckett's similarly teasing strategies at the conclusion of *Watt* and *What Where*, which end 'no symbols where none intended' and 'Make sense who may' respectively (*W* 223; *KLT* 160). In order to address the relationship between this smile and the ideas of 'worsening' developed earlier in the text, we need to jump forward a little in time.

In November 1977, Beckett worked on a short *mirlitonnade* which brings together the ideas of the worst and laughter:

> en face
> le pire
> jusqu'à ce
> qu'il fasse rire (*CP* 210)

This can be read as a commentary on Edgar's statement in *King Lear*: 'The lamentable change is from the best, / The worst returns to laughter' (IV. 1. 5–6), which Beckett later noted down in his 'Sottisier' Notebook.[236] Just after Edgar says these lines, thinking that the worst has already happened, he sees his blinded father, leading him to revise his previous statement: 'the worst is not / So long as we can say "This is the worst"' (IV. 1. 29–30), also

236 I would like to thank Dirk Van Hulle for drawing my attention to this *mirlitonnade* and its link to these lines in *King Lear*. For further discussion, see *CP* (449).

noted by Beckett in the same notebook.[237] On ET5, Beckett introduced the idea that Listener's smile should be '**toothless for preference**' (07r), thus 'worsening' the stage image we see before us. This change also makes the image more realist, bringing Listener into line with the depictions of vagrant poverty in A's and C's stories. In his volumes of Proust's *Du côté de chez Swann*, Beckett marked the 'Movement from dedans au dehors' that Marcel makes while reading.[238] While this movement from inside to outside was clear for Beckett while reading Proust, it is no longer so in *That Time*, where the stage darkness, decontextualized image and overlapping voices make it very hard to fix our perspective on the narrating consciousness. We could see this as a form of interior monologue, with the audience simply eavesdroppers on Listener's thoughts. But the lack of a clear background also leaves open the possibility of a setting beyond the grave, the voices being part of the *post-mortem* situation. Without a clear dividing line between being inside and outside Listener's thoughts, it is impossible for us to say whether his situation still stands to worsen. In *Eh Joe*, the smile added to the end of the SDR and BBC productions signals Joe's satisfaction at having – seemingly – throttled the voices in his head.[239] Since they are unambiguously internal, Joe at least appears to have some measure of control over his voices. By contrast, Listener faces the prospect that the voices he hears will make that time out of this time the next time they choose to speak.

237 Also in the 'Sottisier' Notebook, Beckett wrote another *mirlitonnade* which ends by echoing Edgar's assertion that the worst gets worse: 'le pis revient / en pire' (*CP* 215).

238 https://www.beckettarchive.org/library/PRO-ALA-1.html, 125. Beckett notes the same movement on pages 128 and 129 of the same volume.

239 'I asked in London and Stuttgart for a smile at the end (oh not a real smile). He "wins" again' (Beckett to Schneider, 7 April 1966, *NABS* 202). See Beckett (2008b); https://www.youtube.com/watch?v=SdWxml9BwgA.

4.2 The Genesis of *Cette fois*

4.2.1 Chronology

The chronology of *Cette fois* is interesting for two principal reasons. Firstly, it spans a very long period, particularly for a short play. Started in the summer of 1976, the French text was first published over two years later, in August 1978, making for an even longer translation process than *Pas moi* (see chapter 2.3.1). During this time, Beckett translated *Footfalls* into French and participated in a host of other projects, giving composer Morton Feldman the short text *neither* to set to music (in October 1976; see *LSB IV* 436–7), completing *Ghost Trio* and *... but the clouds ...* for television (both broadcast April 1977), commencing the prose piece *Company* and the play *A Piece of Monologue* (both in 1977), and writing a number of poems, including many of his short *mirlitonnades*.[240] In the theatre, Beckett directed *Damals* and *Tritte* in German (October 1976), *Krapp's Last Tape* with the San Quentin Drama Workshop (October 1977) as well as *Pas* and *Pas moi* in Paris (April 1978). When considering Beckett's work schedule in the 1970s, nothing could be further from the truth than Estragon's opening line in *Waiting for Godot*: 'Nothing to be done' (*WfG* 5).

The second reason is perhaps even more intriguing: none of the *Cette fois* manuscripts are dated. So, before exploring relevant intertexts for Beckett's translation of *That Time*, I want to use his letters to date these manuscripts as best I can.

Beckett wrote to Herbert Myron on 16 June 1976, indicating that he had already been on the job, having returned from the Royal Court premiere of *That Time*: 'Bit limp after London. Feeble efforts, abandoned, resumed, to translate <u>That Time</u>. Loss at every word. Did you ever hate a conjunction? if so you'll understand my feelings about <u>jusqu'à ce que</u>' (*LSB IV* 429). In the published text, this conjunction first appears in sentence 0033, spoken by C: 'ne pouvant croire que c'était toi **jusqu'à ce qu**'on te flanque dehors sous la pluie à l'heure réglementaire' (1978c, 15). However, for a translation that

240 Beckett referred to *A Piece of Monologue* as 'prose' in a letter to Jocelyn Herbert (2 November 1977, *LSB IV* 471) and did not add stage directions until much later (see Beckett to Martin Esslin, 14 January 1979, *LSB IV* 500).

was giving him such trouble, it seems unlikely Beckett would have got this far in the text by June 1976. An alternative hypothesis is that he considered using 'jusqu'à ce que' as early as C's first paragraph, which reads in English: 'shivering and dripping **till** you found a seat marble slab' (1976a, 9; *KLT* 99). Though '**till**' here acts as a conjunction, Beckett translated it instead with a preposition in the earliest extant manuscript draft: 'transi et ruisselant **jusqu'au** banc dalle de marbre' (FM, 07r).[241] Given the time it took him to complete the translation and his mention of 'abandoned' efforts in his letter to Myron, it is possible that Beckett was struggling with his hated conjunction in this (or another) early paragraph on a document I have been unable to locate.[242] However, since there is no firm evidence of this, I have not included any such missing preliminary document in the Genetic Map (chapter 3.6).

In March 1977 Beckett complained that he was making no progress with self-translation (see Beckett to Herbert Myron, 11 March 1977, *LSB IV* 453; Beckett to Paul Auster, 21 March 1977, *LSB IV* 454), probably a reference to his work on *Cette fois*. Indeed, he was trying to translate *Footfalls* at the same time, as he told Alan Schneider on 10 April: 'Perspiring over French translation of *That Time – Footfalls*. Hopeless thankless chore' (*NABS* 355). But on 3 May 1977, while holidaying in Tangier, he wrote to Ruby Cohn with good news, however tempered: 'Have a rough draft of That Time in French, but loss so great not the heart so far to finalize' (*LSB IV* 457). This 'rough draft' may well be FM, albeit there is no evidence confirming this.

Later that same month, Beckett was struggling again, as he explained to Polish translator Antoni Libera: 'My translation of *That Time* has run into great difficulties ["de grandes difficultés"], and is still not finished. When it is, I shall send it to you' (24 May 1977, *LSB IV* 463). This difficulty is evident in all three of Beckett's drafts, especially FT1, where multiple revision campaigns with different writing tools are proof of the many separate attempts he made to edit the text. Again, there is no firm evidence that Beckett was working on FT1 when he wrote to Libera, but it seems plausible

241 As the 'Compare Sentences' tool in the online edition shows, Beckett used the preposition throughout the drafting process and in the published text (https://www.beckettarchive.org/thattime/comparesentences/0016).

242 As mentioned in the previous chapter (4.1.2), Beckett structured one of his *mirlitonnades* ('en face') around this conjunction.

that, having finished his 'rough draft' by early May, he then moved on to a typescript version later that same month.

What happened to the composition of *Cette fois* after this is something of a mystery, as there appears to be no mention of it in Beckett's letters until August 1978, when he informed Alan Schneider of the piece's impending publication: 'Reedition of French poems in Fall with some recent doggerel [*Poèmes, suivi de mirlitonnades*]. Also my translation at last of That Time (Cette fois)' (5 or 6 August 1978, *LSB IV* 485). Though *Cette fois* was indeed published that August, the precise end-date of Beckett's translation is slightly unclear. This confusion is heightened by another letter to Schneider, of 14 January 1979, in which Beckett again mentions his translation work on the already published *Cette fois*: 'No work apart from translation of *That Time* & some French doggerel' (*NABS* 374). Though Beckett and Schneider exchanged other letters between August 1978 and January 1979, it is most likely that the playwright simply forgot he had already told the US director about *Cette fois*, given he repeats himself regarding the edition of poems containing 'French doggerel' both in this January 1979 letter and in a letter of 24 October 1978 (*NABS* 372). So, though there are no dates on the manuscripts themselves, Beckett's letters indicate that his translation of *That Time* took from c. June 1976 to August 1978.[243]

To return to the terminology used when discussing *Pas moi*, there was in the case of the *Cette fois* translation a significant lack of 'actors' – both in the theatrical sense of that word, but also in terms of Latour's Actor–Network Theory (see chapter 2.3.1) – pressuring Beckett to get it done. Particularly at this point in his career, Beckett often created work in response to various 'actors' within his network. In stark contrast to the pressure Beckett was under to finish *Pas moi*, the first performance of *Cette fois* was not until 15 March 1983, in a production starring David Warrilow at the Théâtre Gérard-Philipe in Paris (Beckett to Alan Mandell, 14 March 1983, *LSB IV* 605).[244] So, Beckett's network was important here too, if only in terms of a lack of 'actors' pushing the translation forward.

243 As Beckett returned from London to Paris on 22 May 1976 (Pilling 2006, 200), it is possible that he got started on the translation before June began.

244 See also http://www.leseditionsdeminuit.fr/auteur-Samuel_Beckett-1377-1-1-0-1.html.

Just before he wrote to Myron about the difficulty of translating *That Time*, Beckett wrote another letter which may also refer to his abortive translation work: 'White page & solitude not easy after the London bustle' (Beckett to Peggy Beckett, 8 June 1976, *LSB IV* 428). Though it may seem strange to speak of a 'White page' when referring to translation, as the source text does at least provide a basis for further work, there are other indications that Beckett thought of *Cette fois* in these terms. The most interesting of these comes in Anne Atik's account of an evening spent with Beckett on 30 December 1977, during which the Irish author spoke of his interest in the work of Stéphane Mallarmé. Earlier in 1977 Beckett had started work on *Company*, which Georgina Nugent-Folan describes as 'an extended investigation into the relationship between self and narrative' (2021, 33), showing in this respect strong similarities to *That Time*. As Nugent-Folan shows, *Company*'s 'precursor text', entitled 'The Voice / Verbatim', fed into the published prose piece much more than scholars have previously presumed (2021, 184). Mary Bryden, Julian Garforth and Peter Mills have noted the similarities between this draft precursor and *That Time*, featuring as it does notes on 'three voices which are simultaneously the same voice' (1998, 108), with the note 'A, B, C, one and the same' showing a remarkable similarity to the initial notes towards *That Time* on folio 01r of EM (qtd. in Bryden, Garforth and Mills 1998, 108). While the above scholars have shown convincingly that *Company* feeds off the concepts of *That Time*, it should also be noted that Beckett was still working on the playtext at this stage, struggling to translate it. The composition of *Company* may have influenced the vocabulary of *Cette fois*, with Beckett using 'pour se tenir **compagnie**' (1978c, 19) to translate 'being together that way' (1976a, 14; *KLT* 104). In light of this 'creative concurrence' between the two texts (see Introduction), it is interesting that, having described to Atik the major problem of his 'new work' (presumably *Company*) in terms of pronouns as '*qui est qui*' [who is who], Beckett used an image which recalls directly one of the final paragraphs in *That Time*:

> One would have to invent a new, a fourth person, then a fifth, a sixth – to talk about *je, tu, il*, never. *Qui est qui*. The logical thing to do would be to look out the window at the void. Mallarmé was near to it in the *livre blanc*. But one can't get over one's dream. (Atik 2001, 95–6)

This image of 'look[ing] out the window at the void' is precisely what ends B's monologue in *That Time*:

> no words left to keep **it** out so gave it up **gave up there by the window in the dark** or moonlight gave up for good and let it in and nothing the worse a great shroud billowing in all over you on top of you and little or nothing the worse little or nothing (1976a, 16; *KLT* 106)

Though the '**it**' that must be 'ke[pt] out' is indeterminate in the English text, Beckett translated this using the French equivalent of 'the void':

> plus de mots pour contenir **le vide** alors plus qu'à renoncer y renoncer là à la fenêtre dans le noir nuit noire ou clair de lune y renoncer pour de bon et le laisser venir et pas plus mal qu'avant vaste suaire venu t'ensevelir et pas plus mal qu'avant ou guère pas plus ou guère. (1978c, 23)

Indeed, though the word 'void' only appears twice in the English text (1976a, 11; *KLT* 101), 'vide' appears four times as a noun in *Cette fois* (1978c, 13, 19, 23) and once as an adjective (1978c, 12). So, as well as conceptualizing his writing process in terms of a 'White page', Beckett also introduced more explicitly the idea of 'the void' into the text itself when translating *That Time*. 'There's no lack of void' in the French text, to borrow another line of Estragon's (*WfG* 61).

It is no surprise Beckett mentioned Mallarmé in his conversation with Atik. Beckett's copy of Mallarmé's *Œuvres complètes* has a ribbon marking the pages of the French poet's *Thèmes anglais* – part of a language instruction course for schoolchildren – which deals with pronouns, so it is not out of the question that Beckett turned to Mallarmé when composing the complex pronominal voices of *That Time* and *Company*.[245] And the final entry in Beckett's 'Sottisier' Notebook – on which he also made notes towards *Company* (Nugent-Folan 2021, 39–41) – is taken from Mallarmé's poem 'Brise marine': '.. la clarté déserte de ma lampe / sur **le vide papier** que la blancheur défend' (UoR MS 2901, 16v, qtd. in Van Hulle and Nixon 2013, 63). Quoting this Mallarmé line to Royal Court lighting engineer Duncan Scott, Beckett said: 'It is that "blancheur" that I wish to attack. I can't wait to get back to the blank paper' (qtd. in Knowlson and Knowlson 2006, 217). It is fair to say that this 'vide papier' was both an important image for Beckett's writing process when translating *That Time* and something that he incorporated into the text of *Cette fois*.

Elsewhere in the same December 1977 conversation with Atik, Beckett spoke of his attempt to find a form for silence: 'All writing is a sin against speechlessness. Trying to find a form for that silence' (Atik 2001, 95, see also 96). Beckett tried to do so with poetic form, as when he structured one of his *mirlitonnades* around a void silence:

> silence vide nue
> ne vous aura jamais
> tant été
>
> vide silence (*CP* 220)[246]

One can see the ending of *That Time* in similar terms: as discussed at the end of the previous chapter (4.1.2), Beckett sets up a pattern of voices to frame and give multiple meanings to a silent gesture at the end of the play. It seems that his struggle to create *Cette fois*, in addition to the fact that he had no immediate pressure to finish it, was due to its being one more 'sin' against this silence.

245 https://www.beckettarchive.org/library/MAL-OEU.html. See Mallarmé (1965 [1945], 1138–9).
246 This poem is dated '21.3.77' (*CP* 467).

4.2.2 Genesis

Beckett's struggles with the translation started with the title's reference to time, as he told Knowlson in conversation: 'There is a problem with the title to begin with [...]. After all *That Time* means both "the time when" and "that Time" in the wider sense. How ever do you render both?' (Haynes and Knowlson 2003, 10–11). This difficulty with how time should be referred to is also evident in Beckett's French manuscript, where one way of referring to a specific time is replaced by another: '~~de ce temps-là~~ que cette heure vienne' (FM, 03r). Yet Beckett used 'temps' to translate the preceding phrase 'every now and then' ['de **temps** en **temps**'] and '**fois**' to translate 'till the **time** came in the end' ['jusqu'à cette dernière **fois** enfin'] (1976a, 15; *KLT* 105; 1978c, 22), demonstrating the different emphases the concept of a moment in time took in his translation from English to French.

At first glance, it is counterintuitive that a self-translation from English into French would *remove* a Proustian element from a Beckett text. Yet this is what happened with *Cette fois*. With regard to the French title, Knowlson notes its lack of double meaning, and the consequent reduction of Proustian resonance:

> For his published French translation, he had to settle on *Cette fois*, thereby missing the wider Proustian allusion to Time as 'that double-headed monster of damnation and salvation', about which he had written in his early study of Proust. (Haynes and Knowlson 2003, 10–11)

From a genetic perspective, it is interesting to note that the title 'CETTE FOIS' only appears on Beckett's second French typescript (FT2, 01r). What is more, it appears in none of the letters before that of 5/6 August 1978 to Alan Schneider (see chapter 4.2.1). So, this introduction of the French title – eschewing Proustian Time – seems to have been a decision made relatively late in the genetic process.

While Proust made way in the French title, the translation of the protagonist's name added to the focus on memory which echoes *À la recherche*. Indeed, Proust's own title almost appears in *Cette fois*, when the group out 'looking for you' (1976a, 11; *KLT* 101) is translated as being 'à **ta** recherche'

(1978c, 12).[247] In the stage directions on the earliest extant draft, Listener's name is already translated as 'Souvenant' (FM, 10r), a term derived from the verb 'souvenir' [to remember] that is not standardly used as a substantive in French.[248] It is possible that, having already expressed his desire not to have the two plays on the same bill, Beckett wanted to differentiate this listening figure from the Auditeur of *Pas moi*. Indeed, Beckett seems to have differentiated his listening figures in different works, using the slightly unusual 'hearer' to describe the protagonist of *Company* (Nugent-Folan 2021, 29), this term harking back to one used in the genesis of *Footfalls* (see chapter 6.1.2). For its part, 'Souvenant' draws attention to the process of remembering at the heart of this play, thereby emphasizing again the Proustian intertext. In addition to focussing on 1) time in *Cette fois*, this chapter will explore Beckett's translation of 2) social order, 3) performativity and 4) stage directions as well as 5) the role of error in the French text.

Time

Through Souvenant's struggle to pin down a moment – 'cette fois' – Beckett's play engages with the broader question of how to define time itself. As Beckett read in Berkeley's *Treatise Concerning the Principles of Human Knowledge*, framing such an idea of time is 'embrangled in inextricable difficulties' (see chapter 4.1.2). This problem becomes even more acute in translation.

Some parts of the French text focus more explicitly on the concept of time: the reference to 'Christmas' (1976a, 14; *KLT* 104) becomes 'fin **d'année**' (1978c, 20), emphasizing the temporal unit of the year; 'not a sound' (1976a, 16; *KLT* 106) becomes '**plus** un seul bruit' (1978c, 23), introducing the idea that there was not a single sound *anymore*. This choice in translation – emphasizing that there is no longer a sound, and thus implying that there may once have been – was developed in the drafts, where 'all the homes gone' (1976a, 10; *KLT* 100) was first translated as 'aucun foyer' (FM, 01r) before becoming '**plus** un ~~foyz~~^ foyer' (FT2, 03r).

At some points Beckett makes temporal references more specific: the '**Doric** terminus of the Great Southern and Eastern' railway (1976a, 13;

247 Later 'à **sa** recherche' (1978c, 19).
248 https://www.cnrtl.fr/definition/souvenant.

KLT 102–3) becomes '**néo-dorique**' in the French text, even as the ensuing 'réseau sud-est' removes the Irish trace of place from the name of the line (1978c, 16). Indeed, this balancing process is also seen in a rare instance of removing a temporal reference from the text, in this case an adverb, when 'what **next**' (1976a, 13; *KLT* 103) became the idiomatic 'quoi faire' (1978c, 15–16).

Overall, however, the trend in translation is toward a more explicit foregrounding of the notion of time, perhaps best exemplified in Beckett's use throughout *Cette fois* of 'moment' (1978c, 8, 10, 11, 18, 20, 22), a word that only appears in the note on the voice in the English text: '**Moments** of one and the same voice' (1976a, 8; *KLT* 97).[249] For instance, 'slipped in when no one was looking' (1976a, 9; *KLT* 99) is translated as 'guetté **le moment** de te faufiler' (1978c, 8) and '**till** you hoisted your head' (1976a, 10; *KLT* 100) becomes '**et là au bout d'un moment** ayant hissé la tête' (1978c, 11), Beckett here finding another way to avoid using 'jusqu'à ce que'.

As well as evoking the recuperated moments of lost time that structure Beckett's analysis in *Proust*, the increased emphasis on time in *Cette fois* brings into focus philosophical concepts of time which he may have come across in the work of Henri Bergson. As Gontarski details, Beckett drew on Bergson when giving his Racine lectures in Trinity College, paying particular attention to the philosopher's distinction between intuition and intelligence: whereas, according to the Burrows lecture notes, 'intuition can obtain a total vision', intelligence can 'apprehend the passage of time but not [the] present moment' (TCD MIC 60/7, qtd. in Gontarski 2015a, 135; editorial addition in Gontarski). This idea, having already been explored in *Krapp* (see Van Hulle 2015, 33), is also central to the dramaturgy of *That Time*, where the distinction between the static visual image and the flowing voices again calls into question the idea of a stable self. Indeed, one could see *Krapp* as a critique of the Bergsonian idea of 'a total vision', with the bombastic recording of Krapp's account of his artistic 'vision at last' held in ironic counterpoint to the decrepit image we see on stage (*KLT* 8).

Beckett's first staged play, performed while he was teaching at Trinity, also saw him drawing on Bergson. *Le Kid* – a pastiche of Corneille's *Le Cid*

249 This is translated as '*Bribes d'une seule et même voix*' (1978c, 7), recalling Beckett's reference to the text of *Play* as 'bribes vocales' (Beckett to Siegfried Unseld, 1 July 1963, *LSB III* 559).

co-written in French with Georges Pelorson – was produced by the TCD Modern Languages Society on 19 February 1931 (McMillan and Fehsenfeld 1988, 17). According to Beckett himself, it was a mix of 'Corneille & Bergson' (Beckett to Thomas MacGreevy, 24 February 1931, *LSB I* 68) and featured two characters with clocks: one, played by Beckett himself, carried an alarm clock onto the stage; the other sat on top of a ladder and moved the hands of a large clock at high speed (Knowlson 1997, 124). In what was possibly a nod to T. S. Eliot's *The Waste Land*, a barman called 'Time, Gentlemen, Time [*sic*]' to get rid of the actors ('Peacock Theatre', 5). Though Pelorson claimed that he wrote most of the piece himself (Knowlson 1997, 123), this is another noteworthy instance of Beckett, Bergson and time operating in close proximity.

It is still unclear whether Beckett actually read Bergson's work or depended on second-hand sources.[250] Whatever the case may be, he would have come across the key idea that time is perceived as an essentially continuous process, which Bergson calls 'durée' ['duration'] (1991, 51), rather than a quantity which can be divided into individual instances. This is part of Bergson's general antipathy towards spatial representations of time and of the perceiving subject. Indeed, one of the impulses in the work of the French philosopher, and one of the reasons Beckett may have been drawn to his work as a young man, is to overcome the problems posed by a dualist distinction between subject and object (see Bergson 1991, 161). For Bergson, this could only be done by avoiding the tendency in Western philosophy to conceptualize subject and object in terms of space. As Bergson puts it in *Matière et mémoire* (1896), '*les questions relatives au sujet et à l'objet, à leur distinction et à leur union, doivent se poser en fonction du temps plutôt que de l'espace*' ['*Questions relating to subject and object, to their distinction and their union, should be put in terms of time rather than of space*'] (1991, 218; 2005, 71; emphasis in originals). However, when Beckett returned to these questions more than four decades after mentioning Bergson in his lectures, he explored them in the spatial art of the theatre. Instead of having the voices represent the overlapping flows of time in something approximating Bergsonian *durée*, the visual image of Souvenant forces us to consider the

250 Gontarski suggests Julien Benda's *La trahison des clercs* as a source for Beckett's use of Bergson (2015a, 135), but that work does not deal in depth with Bergson's philosophy.

relation between the fugitive moments of his recollection and the temporal moment of remembering as it is visualized onstage.

This spatialization of the question of time is a distinctly non-Bergsonian aspect of Beckett's theatre work. It could be argued that, like Krapp before him, Souvenant himself represents an anti-Bergsonian figure of memory, especially given his voices' attempts to capture 'cette fois' in a particular narrative form. In a letter to Thomas MacGreevy of 31 January 1938, Beckett derisively describes 'the kind of people who in the phrase of Bergson can't be happy till they have "solidified the flowing"' (*LSB I* 599). This idea seems to have its source in the following passage from Bergson's *L'évolution créatrice*: '*la forme n'est qu'un instantané pris sur une transition*. Donc, ici encore, notre perception s'arrange pour solidifier en images discontinues la continuité fluide du réel' ['*form is only a snapshot view of a transition*. Therefore, here again, our perception manages to solidify into discontinuous images the fluid continuity of the real'] (1991, 750; 1944, 328; emphasis in originals). Souvenant too is someone trying to 'solidif[y] the flowing' of time, albeit his efforts are unsuccessful. In this light, it is fitting that Beckett had trouble translating the play's title, bringing into focus the difficulty involved in trying to form a coherent idea of time. Had he been around to advise Beckett on this translation quandary, Bergson probably would have said there is no difference between 'That Time' and 'that time when', all time being strictly speaking indivisible (see Bergson 1991, 81). But Beckett, as a self-translator, had to choose.

He may have come across further critique of Bergson's notion of time in Gaston Bachelard's *L'intuition de l'instant*, a 1966 edition of which was preserved in Beckett's library at his death. As against Bergson's central concept of temporal duration, Bachelard's book posits the notion of temporal *discontinuity* as central to experience. Furthermore, he accuses Bergson of falsifying the experience of time by imposing reductive paradigms of memory on what is ineluctably various: 'Sensation is variety. Memory alone confers uniformity' (2013, 50). Souvenant never reaches the epiphanic state of revelation described in Bachelard's account of individual temporal instants as a mode of self-discovery. But he too is far from what Bachelard would describe as the 'uniformity' of a Bergsonian conception of memory.

Social Order

In *L'intuition de l'instant*, Bachelard cites a line from Mallarmé's 'Le tombeau d'Edgar Poe' to argue that the philosopher, like the poet, is obliged 'to give a purer sense to the language of the tribe' ['Donner un sens plus pur aux mots de la tribu'] (2013, 23; Mallarmé 1965 [1945], 70). If he read Bachelard's book prior to translating *That Time*, Beckett would have come across Mallarmé's line, which he may be alluding to in C's description of his former companions in his hometown: 'tous liquidés belle lurette tous poussière toute **la tribu**' (1978c, 9). While in the Post Office, C remembers thanking God 'you were not as **they**' (1976a, 15; *KLT* 105) ['de ne pas être comme **eux**'] (1978c, 21), which recalls the mass 'Eux' who reject Poe's poetry in Mallarmé's 'Tombeau' (1965 [1945], 70). But precisely what kind of 'they' does Souvenant define himself against? In the English text, he refers to the others in the Post Office as 'your fellow bastards' (1976a, 15; *KLT* 105). In *Cette fois*, this becomes 'tes dégueulasses **semblables**' (1978c, 21), recalling Charles Baudelaire's final line of 'Au lecteur': '– Hypocrite lecteur, – mon **semblable**, – mon frère' (1958, 82).[251] As Beckett had already alluded to this line when writing *Malone meurt* (see Van Hulle and Verhulst 2017b, 162), it is hard to believe it did not come to his mind again here.[252]

As so often in Beckett's work, the relationship between central protagonist and outside world is figured in terms of confinement. The '**kip**' where A remembers staying (1976a, 10; *KLT* 100) becomes a '**taule**' (1978c, 10), which can mean 'prison' as well as 'room'. The carceral connotations of 'the pens **on their chains**' (1976a, 14; *KLT* 104; see chapter 4.1.2) are reinforced in the French version: 'les stylos **captifs**' (1978c, 20). Even images of liberation have carceral intertextual echoes. A recurring motif in B's memories is of the 'azur' sky (1978c, 11, 16, 19), a favourite word of Mallarmé's which is key to what Beckett called the French poet's 'Prisoner Poem', entitled 'Les fenêtres' (Beckett to Barbara Bray, 14 May 1964, qtd. in Van Hulle and Nixon 2013, 63). As the central figure of this poem is a dying man in a hospital, the reference casts a shadow of death over B's youthful

251 This phrase may also have been influenced by Elmar Tophoven's German translation: 'deine elenden Mitmenschen' (1976b, 67; see Garforth 1996, 61).

252 This may be another reference to Eliot's *The Waste Land*, which also cites Baudelaire's line (2001, 7).

memories. Indeed, Mallarmé's 'azur bleu' (1965 [1945], 32), which the confined man longs to feed on through the hospital window, becomes the much darker 'azur noir' in B's memory of closing and opening his eyes while lying beside his lover (1978c, 16). Yet again, a potentially transcendent image is significantly darkened in Beckett's text.

Performativity

As we have already seen, *That Time* relies on verbal echoes, which mark it as a text written for performance. These echoes come out even more strongly in translation. For instance, the echo between A's memory of the times he used to '**slip** off' and C's of '**slipping** in' to public buildings (1976a, 10, 13; *KLT* 100, 103) is reinforced in the French text, where they are translated by the same verb – 'guetté' and 'guetter' respectively (1978c, 8, 18). C's memory of '**hugging** you for a bit of warmth' and of being '**curled up**' like a 'worm in slime' (1976a, 10, 12; *KLT* 100, 101) are both translated with '**blotti**' (1978c, 9, 13), strengthening the connection between the two voices. Similarly, B's memory of being 'immobiles comme **marbre**' with his lover harks back to the 'dalle de **marbre**' ['marble slab'] on which C sits to rest in the gallery (1978b, 16–17, 8).

Beckett was keenly aware of these echoes, and sought to emphasize them in his first French typescript. When translating B's recollection of 'making it up that way' (1976a, 14; *KLT* 104), Beckett wrote in the margin 'l'inventant ~~ici~~ **ainsi**', adding a note-to-self on the echo between this and the seventh paragraph of C's monologue: '(cf C. 7)' (FT1, 05r). In the corresponding part of C's monologue, Beckett inserted '**ainsi**' in the margin: 'cherchant à l'inventer **ainsi** t'inventer ainsi' (FT1, 08r). A similar awareness of the echoes between voices can be found elsewhere on the same typescript, in Beckett's translation of A's question: 'was that another time' (1976a, 16; *KLT* 106). Beckett underlined '**est-ce que c'était**', again jotting an alternative in the left margin, which he later deleted: '~~était-ce~~' (FT1, 03r). Further down the same margin, he noted 'cf. C5' (FT1, 03r), referring to the paragraph where C asks himself: '**est-ce que c'étais**^{t} ça une autre fois' (FT1, 07r). Even more than *That Time*, then, *Cette fois* draws on Beckett's extensive experience of writing for performance to create a text which echoes across different monologues.

While the English text already emphasizes the performative nature of A's and B's monologues, *Cette fois* strengthens the sense of performativity in C's monologue. To translate the phrase ‘trying to wangle you into it’ (1976a, 13; *KLT* 103), Beckett left an open variant on FT1, both elements of which have performative connotations: ‘~~cherchant le truquage être en chose~~ ~~s'acharnant à~~ ~~truquer~~ ~~maquiller l'être en chose~~ **passe-passe** **tout au truquage** de l'être en chose’ (08r).[253] Beckett would go for the latter in the published text (1978c, 16). But the rejected element of the open variant, like the published variant, shows that he was thinking of C's monologue in explicitly performative terms.

Stage Directions

Through its references to confinement, the language of *Cette fois* is more explicitly institutional than *That Time*. However, a fascinating edit to the French stage directions suggests a possible institutional framing for the play itself through its reintroduction of an element Beckett had erased in his English-language drafts. As discussed in chapter 4.1.2, he considered, but then removed, a ‘pillow’ behind the head of Listener. On his notes for the German premiere of the play, Beckett thought about using a ‘sheet’, which would have linked Listener to other bedbound figures in his oeuvre (see chapter 3.5.2). In the French translation, the pillow [‘*oreiller*’] is back (1978c, 7), providing an element of realist background which suggests that Souvenant is waiting for death, like Malone in his vaguely defined institution. As discussed in chapter 4.1.2, the pillow was first suggested as an actual stage prop in EM before being incorporated as part of the imagined background of *That Time* (ET5, 02r). The French text is ambiguous as to whether the pillow must be included onstage or is simply part of the ‘as if’ clause: ‘*Vieux visage blême légèrement incliné en arrière, longs cheveux blancs dressés comme vus de haut étalés sur un oreiller*’ (1978c, 7). But the object is nonetheless highly suggestive to the reader of these stage directions. If we consider *Cette fois* as a Proustian memory text, this mention of a pillow would once more connect Souvenant to Marcel in *Du côté de chez Swann* (see chapter 4.1.2). Beckett may have reduced the

253 Both terms are associated with the performance practice of illusionists (https://www.cnrtl.fr/definition/passe-passe and https://www.cnrtl.fr/definition/truquage).

Proustian resonance in his translated title, but this is balanced by the reintroduction of Proustian elements elsewhere in the text. Whatever particular interpretation we may wish to draw from this instance of 'redoing', it again shows Beckett changing key parts of his texts beyond the point of publication, taking into consideration the functioning of the stage image in performance as well as on the page.

Another addition in the French text is to have Souvenant's head leaning slightly backwards [*'légèrement incliné en arrière'*] (1978c, 7). This reinforces the sense of the protagonist as a bedbound figure, given that such figures are normally approached – and therefore viewed – from the foot of the bed. Again, while it is difficult to be certain about Beckett's reasoning behind this instance of 'redoing', it shows him adapting the text based on what he had learned from previous productions. This is also true of the lighting instructions for *Cette fois*: while in the English text, the stage directions within the monologues read only *'eyes close'* (1976a, 9, 11, 14), Beckett added *'légère baisse de l'éclairage'* (1978c, 7–8, 13, 19), drawing on the 'Simpler' version of the lighting instructions in his German Nb while also leaving the necessary wiggle room for lighting technicians by omitting his Berlin instructions on the length of fades (04v–05r).

Beckett finished his monograph on Proust by discussing the importance of music as a phenomenon that is 'apprehended not in Space but in Time only' (*PTD* 92). In *That Time*, Beckett returned to Proustian themes by staging Listener's memory narrative in the spatial art of theatre, though it seems highly doubtful that this protagonist will ever reach the 'Temps retrouvé' of Proust's Marcel. In *Cette fois*, there is the slightest of suggestions that Souvenant may be more satisfied than his English-language counterpart: whereas Listener only smiles for five seconds at the end of his text (1976a, 16; *KLT* 106), Souvenant smiles for seven (1978c, 24). While, again, Beckett's change here was probably governed by the practical stage business of having Souvenant's smile appear clearly visible to the audience for a little bit longer, it does allow us to interpret him as being, if not the best off of Beckett's protagonists, at least 'Less worse' than Listener (*CIWS* 94, 101).

Error

In the 'Scylla and Charybdis' episode of *Ulysses*, Stephen Dedalus reacts aggressively to the suggestion that Shakespeare ever made a mistake: '– Bosh! Stephen said rudely. A man of genius makes no mistakes. His errors are volitional and are the portals of discovery' (1986, 156). As Tim Conley points out, Stephen is often mistakenly considered to be speaking directly for Joyce here (2001, 14), but it is worth noting the gently mocking irony in the narrator's integration of Stephen's phrase as part of the very next line: 'Portals of discovery opened to let in the quaker librarian' (1986, 156). The first French manuscript of *Cette fois* is remarkable for the number of errors Beckett made. Though Beckett did harness the power of error elsewhere in his work, the errors I will discuss here are neither part of what Conley terms a Joycean 'aesthetic of error' (2001, 42, 207), as the portals are firmly slammed shut by Beckett through corrections in subsequent drafts, nor an element in his own aesthetic of 'writing worser' that Georgina Nugent-Folan has analysed in her comparative doctoral study of Beckett and Gertrude Stein (2016, see particularly chapter 5).[254]

Though a detailed genetic examination of Beckettian error requires a larger sample size than the manuscripts currently digitized, a comparison of documents in this module does show the French manuscript of *Cette fois* to be particularly error-strewn. In the online edition, the <choice> element is used 'to encode obvious spelling errors in the documents', which are marked by a note in the text.[255] The table below shows the number of such errors in each of the first full handwritten manuscripts for plays in this module:[256]

	Not I **(EM1)**	***Pas moi*** **(FM2)**[257]	***That Time*** **(EM)**	***Cette fois*** **(FM)**	***Footfalls*** **(EM)**
Errors marked by a <choice> tag	1	7	2	17	0

254 I would like to thank Georgina Nugent-Folan for sharing her unpublished research with me.

255 *BDMP Encoding Manual* (https://bdmpmanual.uantwerpen.be/index.php/the-tags/encoding-text/choice/).

256 Such a document is missing for *Pas*.

257 FM2 is chosen here as FM1 is an incomplete draft.

In this admittedly small sample, it is noteworthy that Beckett makes a greater number of errors in his French translations than in his English texts.[258] This is multiplied in the French manuscript of *Cette fois*, where he makes no fewer than seventeen such errors:

1 un **cable**
for **câble** (01r)

2 autant que tu **sache**
for **saches** (02r)

3 quelles **qu'elle** fussent
for **qu'elles** (04r)

4 la **fênêtre**
for **fenêtre** (04r)

5 jamais un regard vers pour son visage **où** autre partie
for **ou** (05r)

6 que toi tu **disparaisse**
for **disparaisses** (05r)

7 dans les **même** lieux
for **mêmes** (06r)

8 tu ~~tu t'es mis à l'abri de~~ **t'as** fui la pluie
for **as** (07r)

9 une **trainée**
for **traînée** (07r)

10 se **évanouissant**
for **s'évanouissant** (07r)

258 In line with this trend, there are seven such errors in *Pas moi*, FM1.

11 **detortillé**
for **détortillé** (08r)

12 les portraits des morts noirs de crasse et **d'antiquités**
for **d'antiquité** (08r)

13 la **Bibliotèque**
for **Bibliothèque** (08r)

14 le **première** siège
for **premier** (09r)

15 en tant qu'objet de **degoût**
for **dégoût** (09r)

16 la **Bibliotèque**
for **Bibliothèque** (09r)

17 au cas **cas**
for **où** (10r)[259]

Most of these errors are simply errors in gender, number or diacritic usage and have no broader importance in this analysis. However, it is notable that Beckett twice conjugates a verb in the form used for first- and third-person address when the protagonist is speaking to himself in the second person: 'autant que tu **sache**' (02r); 'que toi tu **disparaisse**' (05r).[260] This adds to the sense of Souvenant as a protagonist who is divided across pronouns, trying to psychologically and grammatically realign aspects of his different selves, just as his author struggles to do so in the drafts.

Why did the initial translation of *That Time* produce so many mistakes? Again, without further evidence from other similar texts in the wider oeuvre, it is difficult to say why there are so many errors in this particular short

259 Though it is not marked with a <choice> tag, Beckett also omitted the second 'ni' after 'd'Eve' in 'ni d'Eve d'Adam' (08r).

260 The same happens in the published text, where the form is third-person: 'tu as essayé et **n'a** pas pu' (1978c, 23; see chapter 3.4.3).

text. The chronology showed just how much Beckett struggled to translate the play, and perhaps these errors can be put down to an unusual degree of carelessness related to the difficulty he had with the first French manuscript. But broader conclusions must be withheld until we have a fuller corpus. The question these errors raise is then not simply the question posed of Winnie's situation in *Happy Days*: 'What does it *mean*?' (*HD* 25; emphasis added). Rather, for editors, the question is: what do we *do* with such errors? In his 'Sound-bite against the Restoration' of *Finnegans Wake*, Sam Slote advocates 'the production of something like the verso side of Gabler's synoptic edition [of *Ulysses*] – preferably rendered in a hypertext – but bereft of a corrected recto' (2001). The genetic edition of *That Time / Cette fois* allows us to 'leave ill enough alone' (Slote, 2001), leaving errors visible in the online manuscripts. But what we might term the editorial 'licence to ill' still has to contend with the choices to be made if there are to be critical editions of Beckett's texts.

Beyond Beckett's manuscripts, one of the remaining errors in Minuit's 1986 edition is a superfluous accent that appears on the page, though it would not be heard in performance: 'comme cette fois sur la pierre **où** cette fois dans les dunes' (1986a, 17). Rather than regarding this as a Joycean 'portal of discovery', a genetic analysis shows that this error was absent from all the French manuscripts, and appears first in the 1978 Minuit edition (1978c, 16).[261] So, while leaving such errors visible in the genetic edition, we should (gently) close this door of hermeneutic 'discovery' and try rather to perform an act of *recovery* by publishing Beckett's play in a bilingual critical edition.

261 The error may have been made in proofs or galleys which I have been unable to locate.

Part III

The Making of *Footfalls / Pas*

5 Documents

5.1 Autograph Manuscripts

5.1.1 English

English manuscripts (EM)

EM (MS-UoR-1552-1)

The University of Reading catalogue describes this manuscript as follows:

> Original holograph manuscript of *Footfalls*, entitled *Footfalls / It all?*. 30 × 21 cm. 7 leaves. (Bryden, Garforth and Mills 1998, 38)

The entire text is written in black ink, with dark purple ink (probably faded from black) used for boxes surrounding additions and deletions (07r). As is common in Beckett's plays, left and right are to be considered '~~as from audience~~' (01r; see chapter 2.2.2).

The manuscript is dated 'Berlin / 2.3.75' (01r), 'Paris 1.10.75' (06r) and 'Paris / 25.10.75' (04r). As this indicates, the sequence of composition was complex. Foliation is likewise complex on the manuscript, with Beckett using '1A' to number what in the online genetic edition is folio 02. There is an insertion mark 'A' on folio 01r, indicating that material from 02r (also marked with an 'A') should be inserted there, extending the two women's questioning of one another.

The text is divided into three scenes: '~~One~~' – a word announced by a soon-deleted '~~Speaker~~' (01r) – as well as the headings 'II' (04r) and 'Text for III' (05r), with the third scene initially called 'Appendix' in the text, an addition above a deleted term which looks like '~~Epilogue~~' (05r). Beckett also sketched out a four-scene structure on the last page:

> A Dying mother
> B Mother back

C ~~xxx~~ Appendix
D Empty strip. (07r)

Folio 03r is mainly filled with an initial draft of Scene II, which is struck out with a large St Andrew's Cross. This initial draft does not receive numbering, the scene only being numbered after Beckett re-wrote it on folio 04r. The dating on this folio – '25.10.75' (04r) – indicates that this second version of Scene II was written after Beckett had completed Scene III, which he dated '1.10.75' (06r).

The daughter is called Mary on EM and there are three diagrams of her pacing (see Fig. 17). The first diagram features the same number of steps as the diagram in the play's first edition, with '<u>7 steps</u>' mentioned in the stage directions just preceding it, though Beckett only marked the leading foot for each direction on the manuscript (EM, 01r; see 1976c, 9). The second diagram counts the number of stage lengths Mary paces: starting midstage, she only needs half a length before her first turn; the total number of lengths at the end of the sequence sketched in the diagram is therefore '3 ½' (01r). The third diagram uses whole numbers to label the six stage lengths Mary walks (see chapter 6.1.2). In the dialogue after each numbered diagram, Beckett uses the diagram numbers to indicate where Mary is onstage when certain lines are spoken.

At the bottom of the final recto, there are two lists of calculations, above which is written 'Observed pacing' (07r). The larger list measures the number of paced stage lengths in each of the play's three scenes (here labelled A, B and C):

~~A: 3 ½ + 4~~
A: 3 +   + 4 + 3 approx. = 10+
B: 4 + 3 approx. = 7 approx.
C: 2 + ~~x/x~~ 1 + 3/7 + 4/7 = <u>~~2~~ 4</u>
~~19~~ 21
<u>~~133~~ 149</u> (07r)[262]

262 Beckett left a space in his calculation of lengths in 'A', possibly for another number, but did not fill it in.

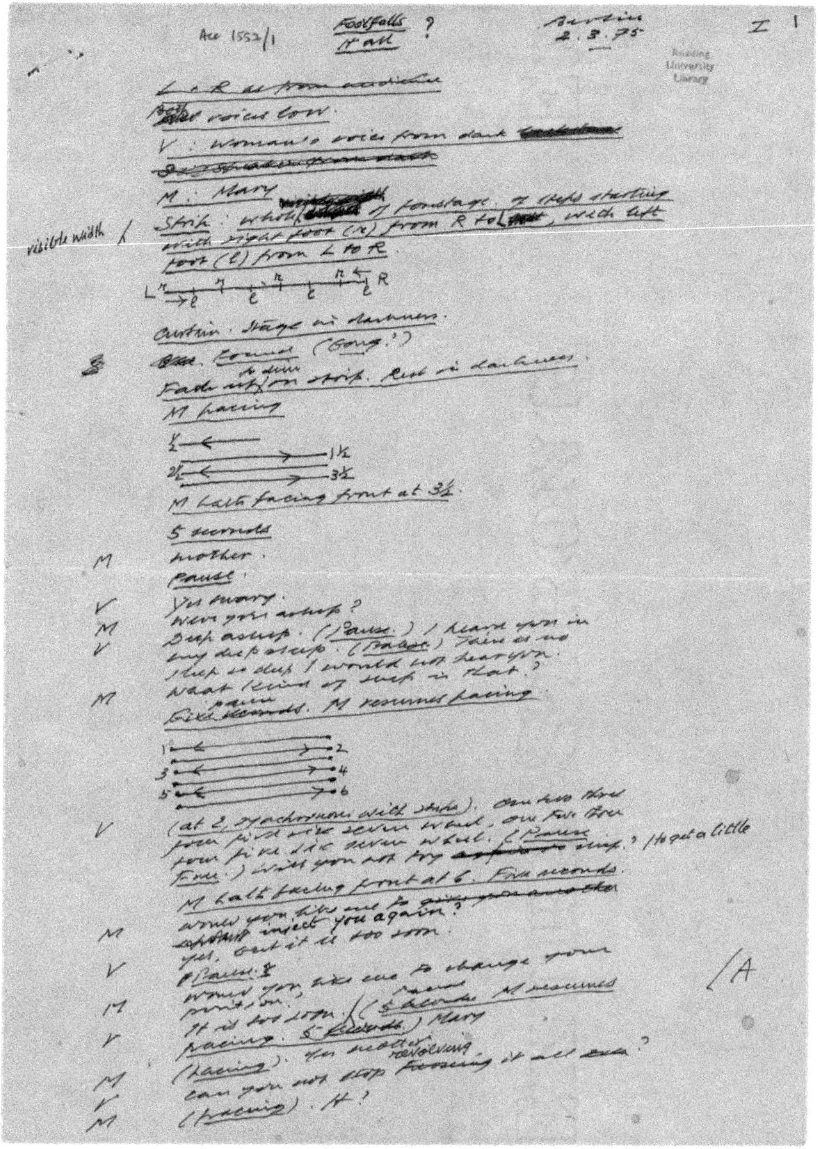
Acc 1552/1 Footfalls / It all ? Berlin 2.3.75 I 1

L & R as from audience

Both voices low.

V: woman's voice from dark

M: Mary

Strip: width of forestage. 7 steps starting with right foot (r) from R to L, with left foot (l) from L to R.

Curtain. Stage in darkness.

Sound (Gong?)

Fade up to dim on strip. Rest in darkness.

M pacing

M halts facing front at 3½.

5 seconds

M mother.

Pause.

V Yes Mary.

Were you asleep?

M Deep asleep. (Pause.) I heard you in my deep sleep. (Pause.) There is no sleep so deep I would not hear you.

V What kind of sleep is that?

Five seconds pause. M resumes pacing

V (at 2, synchronous with steps). One two three four five six seven wheel, one two three four five six seven wheel. (Pause. Free.) Will you not try to get a little sleep?

M halts facing front at 6. Five seconds.

Would you like me to inject you again?

M Yes, but it is too soon.

V (Pause.) Would you like me to change your position?

M It is too soon. (5 seconds pause. M resumes pacing. 5 seconds.) Mary

V (Pacing). You are revolving it all?

M Can you not stop

V (Pacing). It?

Fig. 17: Beckett's first page of his *Footfalls* manuscript, featuring three diagrams of Mary's pacing (EM, 01r).

Beckett multiplied the number of lengths by seven to get the total number of steps, arriving correctly at 133 when his total number of lengths was 19, but erroneously calculating that 21 times 7 equals 149. Beckett's calculations – containing some figures labelled 'approx.' – are not calculated from the text on EM, but from the later ET3 (see below). This is yet another example of the writer adding to his manuscript while working on later typescripts. Indeed, in EM, Scene III has no footsteps and contains a boxed note in the top left corner – 'Punctuated by steps?' (05r) – which suggests that Beckett came up with the idea of inserting the steps into this scene only after writing it. The smaller calculation in the left margin of this manuscript's final page measures what he calls on his later typescript 'bouts of pacing' (ET3, 01r). There are nine in total, a number Beckett revised up from eight:

3
2
~~3~~4
~~8~~ 9 (07r)

5.2 Typescripts

5.2.1 English

English typescripts (ET)

ET1 (MS-UoR-1552-2)

> Untitled typescript, with manuscript additions and corrections by Samuel Beckett, of *Footfalls*; undated. 5 leaves; ff. 1, 2, 4, 5 are 30 × 21 cm; f. 3 is 21 × 20 cm. Lettered top f. 1 'TS 1' by Beckett. Numbered after f. 1 in type. (Bryden, Garforth and Mills 1998, 39)

There is no diagram of the strip on this document, instead, just a blank space after 'Strip' in the opening stage directions (01r). However, Beckett did refer to a diagram as he wrote. The markers 'R' and 'L' are used throughout to indicate audience right and left respectively, while the markers 'l1' (01r) and 'r2' (01r, see also 04r) indicate the place along the strip at which May is positioned according to the first diagram on EM (see Fig. 17). Beckett left such indicators of position blank in the typed material, then filled them in by hand. The instruction 'Say about 3 ½ lengths counting from r2' (01r) shows that he was still thinking spatially in the same terms as on EM, using half-lengths to measure Mary's pacing.

The handwritten additions are most dense around the story of the 'general practitioner named Haddon' (03r). Beckett again uses the insertion mark 'A' on folio 04r, this time for an addition to dialogue in the top margin of the same leaf.

ET2 (MS-UoR-1552-3)

> Untitled typescript, with manuscript additions and corrections by Samuel Beckett, of *Footfalls*; undated. 30 × 21 cm. 5 leaves, f. 1 lettered 'TS 2' in pencil by Beckett. Leaves numbered after '1' in type. (Bryden, Garforth and Mills 1998, 40)

This typescript incorporates the changes on ET1 and contains far fewer edits than its predecessor. There is again a diagram of May's pacing (01r), corresponding to the first diagram on EM (see Fig. 17), but with seven paces now marked on each side of the central line, as in the published text (1976c, 9). The strip is given a width of '1 metre' and other stage directions are likewise more detailed (01r).

The ink used for edits is black. As pointed out in the *Beckett at Reading* catalogue, Beckett uses 'felt-tip for textual deletion, nib and ink for additions' (Bryden, Garforth and Mills 1998, 40). Beckett also uses black nib for transpositions (03r, 05r). Again, in terms of quantity, the most substantial edits are made to the story of the 'general practitioner named Haddon' (03r).

ET3 (MS-UoR-1552-4)

> Untitled typescript, with manuscript corrections and additions by Samuel Beckett, of *Footfalls*; undated. 30 × 21 cm. 5 leaves; f. 1 lettered 'TS 2 A' in pencil by Beckett. (Bryden, Garforth and Mills 1998, 40)

This typescript, labelled 'TS2A', is a photocopy of ET2 (labelled 'TS 2').[263] ET3 contains all the deletions in black felt-tip which appear on ET2 but also features additional edits, having been edited by hand to a far greater degree than its predecessor.[264] As it is a copy, ET3 (01r) also includes the diagram that appears on ET2.

263 Not only is the typed text of both typescripts identical, typing glitches which slightly displace particular letters appear identically on both documents.

264 Though they appear in the same places and delete the same words, there are some discrepancies in the size and shape of the black felt-tip deletions which are found in both typescripts. All the handwritten additions found on

Throughout ET3, pencilled figures in the left margin count up the number of lengths and steps May paces. In the top margin of the opening page, Beckett also used pencil to calculate May's pacing. The first calculation – '8 bouts of pacing (3 + 2 + 3 + 0)' (01r) – counts up the 'bouts' in each of the four scenes outlined on EM (07r). The total number of eight bouts corresponds to the initial result of the shorter calculation on EM (07r), a result Beckett later revised.

A later calculation on ET3 reads 'approx. 19 lengths: 133 steps in all' (01r), corresponding to the initial results of the longer calculation on EM (07r). However, Beckett changed this result on both documents, adding an extra length on ET3 (04r) and rounding up the fractions in two other left margin additions – '~~4/7~~' (ET3, 04r) and '~~3/7~~' (ET3, 05r) both became '1', following handwritten additions to the stage directions which extend May's bouts of pacing on those pages. These edits increase the total number of lengths to '~~19~~[21]' and the total number of steps to '~~133~~[147]', changes which are calculated correctly on ET3 (05r), as is not the case on EM. It is notable that Beckett no longer counts in half-lengths on ET3, using fractions to the base seven and the modifier 'approx.', which also appears in the longer calculation on EM (07r). This supports the hypothesis that the calculations on EM refer to the numbers in the left margin of ET3.

Heavy editing is again found in the story of '~~A general practitioner named Haddon~~' as well as the reference to May's one-time '~~admirer~~' (03r). The opening of M's '~~Appendix~~ [Sequel]' as well as the later exchange regarding the presence of Emily (not yet changed to Amy at all points on this typescript) at Evensong are also heavily edited by hand (04r, 05r).

On folio 05v, written upside down in (now faded) black felt-tip pen, is the number '6330999'.

ET4 (MS-UoR-1552-5)

> Typescript, with manuscript corrections and additions by Samuel Beckett, of *Footfalls*; undated. 30 × 21 cm. 5 leaves; f. 1 lettered 'TS 3' by Beckett. (Bryden, Garforth and Mills 1998, 41)

ET2 can be found on the more heavily edited ET3, but there are some minor differences, such as that between 'fellow[s]hip' (ET2, 05r) and 'fellow[ship]hip [*for* fellowship]' (ET3, 05r). See the online genetic edition for more details.

ET4 contains the standalone title 'FOOTFALLS' for the first time (01r). In addition to using black nib to make edits, many of which are in the margins, Beckett used black nib to write calculations of May's pacing at the end of scenes I, II and IV: '(about 10 lengths)', 'about 7 lengths' and '4 lengths' (02r, 03r, 05r). The deletion of the word '~~Rearrange~~' is in red ink (now faded to pink) as well as black ink (02r). These numbers correspond to the calculations of paces on ET3 and EM.[265] As on previous typescripts, black felt-tip pen is used for deletions. ET4 again features a diagram of May's paces which is seven steps in length (01r).[266]

According to Gontarski, this typescript served as a setting copy for Faber's first edition:

> Eager to make the play available by opening night, Faber and Faber secured a typescript from Beckett before he was finally satisfied with it and set their copy from what, in the sequence of typescripts, Beckett called Ts. 3. (1983, 191)

As explained in chapter 5.5.1, it appears that a document other than ET4 was in fact used as a setting copy. This unretrieved document is labelled 'FSC' in the Genetic Map.

265 The calculation at the end of Scene IV (which features no pacing) relates to the number of lengths in Scene III.

266 The Suhrkamp papers in the Deutsches Literaturarchiv Marbach hold two copies of this typescript; they contain some – but not all – of the handwritten additions Beckett made to the text and so can be discounted as possible setting copies for the 1978 Suhrkamp edition (DLA, SUA: Suhrkamp/03 Lektorate/Theaterverlag). They both feature the address and logo of Spokesmen and one bears the stamp of Suhrkamp Verlag. A letter from Siegfried Unseld to Beckett indicates that he received the text from Spokesmen on 23 February 1976 (DLA, SUA: Suhrkamp/01 Verlagsleitung/Autorenkonv./Beckett, Samuel: Briefwechsel Suhrkamp Verlag). I would like to thank Dirk Van Hulle for sharing this information with me. Another photocopy of this typescript is held in the Alan Schneider Papers (UCSD, box 48, folder 18).

5.2.2 French

French typescripts (FT)

FT1 (MS-BC-1991001-12-24-1)

The Burns Library at Boston College holds two typescripts of *Pas* in a single folder of their Samuel Beckett–Calvin Israel Collection (box 12, folder 24). For the purposes of the online genetic edition, these documents are separated, labelled FT1 and FT2 respectively.

The heavily corrected FT1 comprises five pages, featuring emendations in no fewer than four handwritten inks (red, green, black and brown), black type as well as pencil. The typescript is undated. The typescript is numbered 'I' in black ink (01r) and features the standard inscription made by Beckett when giving manuscripts to Calvin Israel:

> for
> Calvin & Joann
> Sam. Beckett (01r)[267]

In the top left corner of the same page, Beckett wrote the word 'volte' (01r), which he used to translate May's 'wheel' at various points in the typescript (*KLT* 110, 111; FT1, 01r, 03r). However, this was replaced in later revision campaigns (see chapter 6.1.2). There is a rusted staple mark in the top left corner of folio 01r and corresponding staple holes on the other pages, indicating the typescript was once bound together.

The large number of handwritten edits to this document raises the question as to whether it was Beckett's first draft of his translation, going against his usual practice of writing a first draft by hand prior to typing

267 According to the Burns Library finding aid for their Samuel Beckett Collection, Israel was an 'associate professor of English at the State University of New York at Geneseo' to whom Beckett sent 'manuscripts and other materials' from 1976 onwards. 'Israel also began a personal collection of Beckett's work and sent many of his purchases to Beckett to be signed' (http://hdl.handle.net/2345/3248).

it up. The number of errors made in the initial typescript is relatively high, with seventeen spelling errors receiving the <choice> element in the online genetic edition, the same number as the French manuscript of *Cette fois* (FM; see chapter 4.2.2).[268] Though these errors could of course have been made in a second or subsequent draft, Beckett generally made a greater number of errors on his first draft translation than on subsequent typescripts, doing so in the case of both *Pas moi* and *Cette fois*. Given that it has not been possible to locate a holograph manuscript of *Pas*, it is worth bearing in mind the possibility that Beckett's first draft of the translation was typed.[269]

FT2 (MS-BC-1991001-12-24-2)

The second French typescript features fewer emendations than FT1. They are written in black ink, brown ink, type and pencil. The typescript is numbered 'II' and features Beckett's inscription to Calvin and Joann Israel (01r). Folio 01r features a rusted staple mark in the top left corner, with corresponding holes on the other pages indicating FT2 at one point had its own binding, separate from FT1. Like the preceding typescript, FT2 is undated.

As on the typescripts of *Cette fois*, Beckett made emendations in pencil to FT2 of *Pas* which he later erased. These are marked with notes in the online genetic edition.

268 There are also over 50 open variants in FT1, indicating a high degree of uncertainty about the text.

269 This possibility is discussed further in chapter 6.1.2.

5.3 Setting Copies, Galleys and Proofs

5.3.1 English

Some of the abbreviations in the survey below were coined by S. E. Gontarski in Vol. 4 of *The Theatrical Notebooks of Samuel Beckett* (*TN4*). By analogy, and for the sake of consistency, I have applied the same nomenclature to new documents that have been discovered since the publication of *TN4*.

PPF

> Page-proofs, with manuscript corrections by Samuel Beckett, of *Footfalls* (London, Faber and Faber, 1976). 21 × 14 cm. 13 leaves. (Bryden, Garforth and Mills 1998, 42)

These proofs consist of roughly cut, unbound pages. The title 'Footfalls' is written in pencil on the first page (not in Beckett's hand) above a sticker containing instructions for the author from Faber. The list of works published lacks those '*published by Calder and Boyars*' which are listed in the published edition (1976c, 4). However, the proofs do include a very short section of works '*by Samuel Beckett and others*', comprising just one item: 'OUR EXAGMINATION ROUND HIS FACTIFICATION FOR INCAMINATION OF WORK IN PROGRESS' (02v). This item does not appear in the first published edition. PPF also lacks the note on the play's premiere at the Royal Court in May 1976 (see 1976c, 7), probably because the edition itself was 'published to coincide with the play's first production' (Pountney 1988, 287), with the proofs being produced in advance of the premiere.

PPF is corrected almost entirely in black ink, with just one correction in red ink: 'See how still she stands, how ~~firm~~ stark, with her face to the wall' (06r). The few other corrections concern single letters or punctuation; there is also one point at which Beckett spotted an unnecessary re-introduction of the speaker indicator 'M' in M's final speech, resulting in a superfluous line break which he mended with an arrow (07r).

Though numbered 1552/7 in the University of Reading catalogue, Pountney contends that this set of page proofs precedes the typescript numbered 1552/6 (1988, 287), a playscript which this study labels RC playscript.C (see chapter 5.6.1). A comparison of the two documents bears this out, with many (though not all) of the variants between them corresponding to those Beckett would make when preparing the later Grove edition of the play (1976d [1977]).[270]

***Footfalls*(SB)**

> Copy of *Footfalls* (London, Faber and Faber, 1976), corrected by Samuel Beckett. With explanatory note from Professor James Knowlson. (Bryden, Garforth and Mills 1998, 42)

The University of Reading holds the setting copy from which Faber created their 1977 edition of *Ends and Odds* (MS 2828). It is referred to in *TN4* as *Footfalls*(SB). Corrections are in black ink. Knowlson's note explains the provenance of the document:

> This copy was given to me for Reading's Beckett Archive by Frank Pike, editor at Faber and Faber. It is the copy from which Faber's <u>Ends and Odds</u> volume was prepared [...]. It had been retained at Fabers for years after <u>Ends & Odds</u> publ[ication] (*Footfalls*(SB), insert).[271]

Many of the edits made to this document match those made on *Footfalls*(CI); however, others do not. A diagram of the strip with nine steps is pasted onto the verso facing the first page of dialogue (see Fig. 18) and '~~*seven*~~ *nine steps*' are indicated in the opening stage directions, but when V counts May's steps, she only goes up to seven (*Footfalls*(SB), 9; see Fig. 19). Beckett also crossed out the diagram of May's seven steps (*Footfalls*(SB), 9). Significant variants in this setting copy are discussed in chapter 6.1.2. Unique discrepancies in the

270 For more details, see the online genetic edition.

271 This last word is abbreviated due to a lack of page space at the end of the sentence.

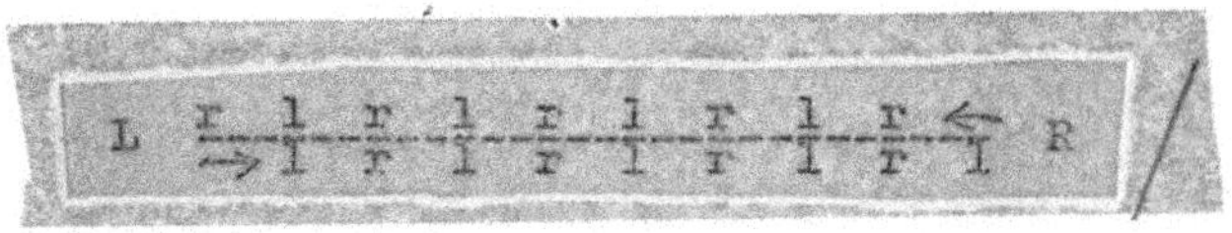

Fig. 18: Beckett's pasted diagram of May's steps in the Faber setting copy of *Footfalls* (*Footfalls*(SB), 8).

printing indicate that the pasted diagram on the verso facing page 9 is a copy of that on RC playscript.C (01r) or the WU playscript (01r).

GSC

The Grove Press Records at the Special Collections Research Center of Syracuse University Libraries (box 91) hold a setting copy for their 1976 [1977] edition of *Ends and Odds* in a folder marked 'Production – setting copy' (see chapter 1.3.1).[272] The *Footfalls* setting copy consists of a marked-up photocopy of Faber's first edition, annotated in black ink and pencil for typesetting. The annotations bring the text in line with Grove's house style. There are no textual changes and no evidence of authorial involvement in the marking-up of this text. Beckett's archaic use of language evidently raised an eyebrow at Grove as there is a question mark beside the encircled word 'feat' in the line 'Watch how feat she wheels' (11).

GG

The Grove Press Records in Syracuse (SU, box 91) also hold a set of galleys for *Ends and Odds* (see chapter 1.3.1), including galleys for *Footfalls*. The printed layer of the text matches that of GSC, with a few small typos which can be categorized as transmissional variants.

272 The same folder contains a typescript which is a copy of ET4 created before every handwritten edit had been made. The only distinguishing features of the typescript in the Grove folder are that there is no title page and the page number '5' is slightly cut off in the top margin. There are two copies of the same typescript, at the same stage of editing, in the DLA archive (DLA, SUA: Suhrkamp/03 Lektorate/Theaterverlag). Both DLA copies contain a title page and one copy features all page numbers fully visible in the top margins.

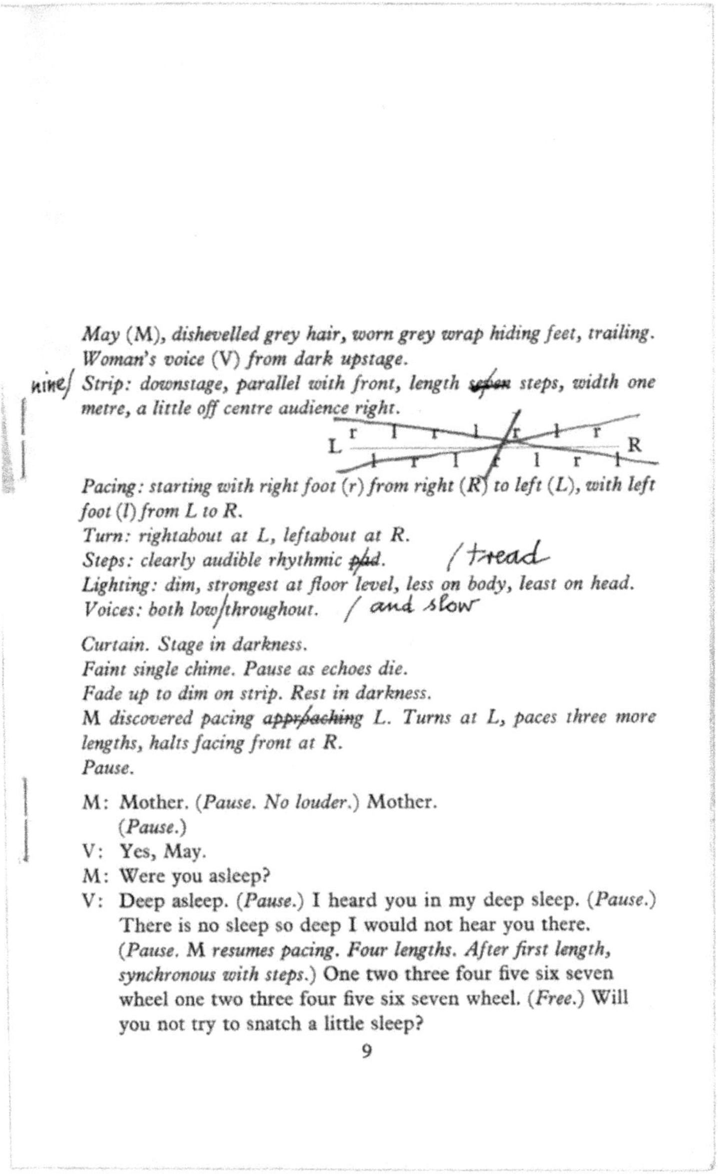

May (M), *dishevelled grey hair, worn grey wrap hiding feet, trailing.*
Woman's voice (V) *from dark upstage.*
nine/ *Strip: downstage, parallel with front, length* ~~*seven*~~ *steps, width one metre, a little off centre audience right.*

L r l r l r l r R
l r l r l r l r

Pacing: starting with right foot (r) *from right* (R) *to left* (L), *with left foot* (l) *from L to R.*
Turn: rightabout at L, leftabout at R.
Steps: clearly audible rhythmic ~~*pad*~~. /tread
Lighting: dim, strongest at floor level, less on body, least on head.
Voices: both low/throughout. / and slow

Curtain. Stage in darkness.
Faint single chime. Pause as echoes die.
Fade up to dim on strip. Rest in darkness.
M *discovered pacing* ~~*approaching*~~ L. *Turns at* L, *paces three more lengths, halts facing front at* R.
Pause.

M: Mother. (*Pause. No louder.*) Mother.
(*Pause.*)
V: Yes, May.
M: Were you asleep?
V: Deep asleep. (*Pause.*) I heard you in my deep sleep. (*Pause.*) There is no sleep so deep I would not hear you there. (*Pause.* M *resumes pacing. Four lengths. After first length, synchronous with steps.*) One two three four five six seven wheel one two three four five six seven wheel. (*Free.*) Will you not try to snatch a little sleep?

9

Fig. 19: In the same setting copy, Beckett extends May's number of steps to nine in the stage directions but not in the dialogue that follows (*Footfalls*(SB), 9).

When marking up the galleys in black ink, Beckett corrected most of these transmissional variants and also incorporated the handwritten edits on his annotated copy of the Faber first edition, changing the number of steps from 7 to 9 and making many changes to the text to bring the galleys in line with his annotated copy *Footfalls*(CI) (see chapter 5.6.1). Indeed, so numerous were the changes made that Beckett wrote at the end of the *Footfalls* galleys: 'Sorry for so / many author's / corrections. / Charge them / to me!' (04r).[273]

The fact that the printed layer of the *Footfalls* Grove galleys follows the text on GSC, added to the fact that the handwritten edits to *Footfalls*(CI) were incorporated into these galleys by hand, proves that *Footfalls*(CI) was not the setting copy for Grove's edition. However, given the close similarity of the handwritten edits on it and the Grove galleys, *Footfalls*(CI) does seem to have played an important part in the production process, probably as the text from which Beckett copied his changes onto the Grove galleys.[274]

5.3.2 French

NRFSC

The Samuel Beckett–Calvin Israel Collection at the Burns Library, Boston College contains a typescript of *Pas* in a subseries named 'Photocopies' (box 18, folder 11).[275] It comprises six leaves, including a title page. Red ink and pencil additions were made after the typescript was photocopied, at which point it seems to have been used as a setting copy for the *Nouvelle*

273 Beckett missed some of the transmissional variants in the Grove galleys but, with one exception, these are all corrected in Grove's first edition of *Ends and Odds*. The exception is where the phrase 'watch her pass before the candelabrum, how its flames' (1976c, 12) is missing its comma in Grove's edition (1976d [1977], 47).

274 The hypothesis that *Footfalls*(CI) preceded the Grove galleys is supported by the fact that deletions within the handwritten additions to *Footfalls*(CI) are incorporated into the galleys. For instance, '(*Pause.*) ~~M resumes pacing, after 1 length halts facing front at L. Pause.~~) M ~~Well~~ What age am I now?' (*Footfalls*(CI), 10) appears simply as '*Pause*. M ~~Well~~ What age am I now?' on the galleys (GG, 12r).

275 http://hdl.handle.net/2345/3248.

Revue Française (*NRF*) text of *Pas*. Some of Beckett's deletions in the text are clearly photocopied, but it is difficult to say whether his black-ink emendations were added before or after the copy was made. The typescript is numbered 'III' on the title page (01r).

The red ink and pencil additions were made by a hand other than Beckett's, probably a typesetter's. On the title page, we find 'Bask. corps 12 1 pt' in red ink (01r), which may refer to the Baskerville font used for the *NRF* issue in which *Pas* appeared. Below this, there is an encircled '2' in pencil (01r). This may refer to the fact that *Pas* was the second item in the September 1977 issue of the journal (not counting Georges Lambrichs's editorial introduction). Pencilled square brackets mark paragraph indents (02r–03r), which again correspond to the *NRF* text (1977b, 9–10).

In addition to this typesetting mark-up, there is also evidence from the text itself that this copied typescript was used as a setting copy for the journal. Namely, a significant majority of variants between the *NRF* edition and Minuit's first published edition can be traced back to this setting copy, where they appear in the form published by the *NRF* (see chapter 5.4.1). The few variants between the typescript and the *NRF*'s published text – excluding those variants due to house style – are listed in the table below.

Sentence	NRFSC	Page	*NRF* 1977b	Page
0001	peignoir gris, dépenaillé	02r	*peignoir gris dépenaillé*	9
0236	Voyez-**le** passer – .	05r	Voyez-**la** passer –.	13
0242	C'est à dire	05r	C'est-à-dire	13

Some of the *NRF* changes in house style are already marked on the setting copy in pencil. For instance, the 'm's in ordinal numbers such as '2me', '3me', '4me', '5me' and '6me', are deleted on the typescript (02r–04r) – these appear as '*2*^{e}', '*3*^{e}' '*4*^{e}', '*5*^{e}' and '*6*^{e}' in the *NRF* text (1977b, 10–12). Likewise, the middle of the word 'Madame' is consistently encircled for deletion on the typescript (05r–06r), appearing as 'Mme' in the *NRF* (1977b, 13–14). Spaced colons in pencil follow the speaker indications (02r–03r), as they do in the journal (1977b, 9–11). At the end of the typescript, Beckett signed the document in black ink (06r), with typesetting marks in pencil corresponding to the way his name appears in the *NRF* text (1977b, 14).

All of the above evidence indicates that the typescript was used by the *NRF* as a setting copy.

5.4 Pre-book Publications

5.4.1 French

1977b *Pas*, in: *La Nouvelle Revue Française* 296 (September). 188 pp. [*Pas*: pp. 9–14]

On 3 May 1977, Beckett told Ruby Cohn that his translation of *Footfalls* would 'appear in the first issue of the N.N.N.R.F., coming Fall, edited by Georges Lambrichs, [Marcel] Arland having withdrawn' (*LSB IV* 457).[276] It was published on 1 September, in an issue featuring writers such as Franz Kafka, Eugène Ionesco and Henri Meschonnic.

In terms of house style, the *NRF* text adds *accents aigus* above initial capitals, except for the first mention of lighting, where this is omitted: '*Eclairage*' (1977b, 9). The *NRF* text also places one space after ellipsis marks (and none before), aside from the phrase 'jouer à ... à ce jeu du ciel et de l'enfer' (1977b, 11), where the spacing is on both sides. Since the omission of the accent on '*Eclairage*' brings the text into line with the subsequent book edition by Minuit, it is omitted from the table of variants below, which compares the *NRF* text to Minuit's first edition.

Sentence	*NRF* 1977b	Page	Minuit 1977c	Page
0002	VOIX DE FEMME	9	VOIX DE FEMME **(V.)**	7
0007|002	*Au fond à gauche un mince rai vertical (R)*	9	*Au fond à gauche, un mince rai vertical (R)*	8
0121	Plutôt j'arrive et je me... poste.	11	Plutôt, j'arrive et je me... poste.	11
0151	à jouer à ... à ce jeu du ciel et de l'enfer	11	à jouer à... à ce jeu du ciel et de l'enfer	12
0236	Voyez-**la** passer –.	13	Voyez-**le** passer —.	15

276 As the editors of Beckett's letters note, his abbreviation here plays on the name of the journal, which for a period in the 1950s was changed to *La Nouvelle Nouvelle Revue Française* (*LSB IV* 458n2). Lambrichs had played a key role in getting Beckett's work published by Les Éditions de Minuit in 1950 (see Van Hulle and Verhulst 2017b, 62). Arland served as editor of the *NRF* until 1977.

0250	à vrai dire plus toute jeune... *(**Voix** brisée.)*...	13	à vrai dire plus toute jeune... *(**voix** brisée)*...	16
0256	nom de baptême de l'enfant comme le lecteur s'en souviendra	13	nom de baptême de l'enfant, comme le lecteur s'en souviendra	16
0286	*Après 5 pas s'immobilise de profil.*	14	*Après cinq pas, s'immobilise de profil.*	18
0301	**Ça?**	14	**Ca ?**	18

Of the nine passages listed here, only 'Voyez-le passer', '(***voix** brisée)*' and 'Ca' show up in the Minuit form on the *NRF* setting copy (NRFSC, 05r–06r).[277] This again supports the hypothesis that the typescript marked up by Beckett was used as a setting copy by the *NRF*.

277 The *NRF*'s use of a capital and a full stop in '*(**Voix** brisée.)*' is a deviation from their house style, which elsewhere on the same page uses lower-case letters for stage directions in mid-sentence (1977b, 13).

5.5 Editions

5.5.1 English (UK)

1976c *Footfalls*. London: Faber and Faber. 13 pp.

Footfalls was first published in a standalone paperback edition by Faber and Faber. It features stiff blue and white wrappers and a photograph of Beckett by Jerry Bauer on its cover.

As noted in chapter 5.2.1, Gontarski states that ET4 served as the setting copy for Faber's first edition. Pountney strikes a slightly more cautious note when positing that ET4 'appears (with further small alterations) to have been the basis for the first Faber text' (1988, 287). Against Pountney's view that Faber's page proofs for their 1976 edition (PPF; see chapter 5.3.1) contain only 'small alterations' from ET4, these changes seem rather substantial, as can be seen in the online genetic edition of the play. This is explained by the fact that Beckett drew up another typescript after ET4 which predates PPF. He later edited this typescript in view of the play's premiere at the Royal Court and the document is therefore discussed in chapter 5.6.1 as RC playscript.B. However, a study of its typed layer reveals it to be an important intermediary stage between ET4 and PPF, which proves that ET4 was not the setting copy for Faber's first edition (see Genetic Map).

While there is some minor textual variation between the typed layer of RC playscript.B and PPF (see chapters 5.3.1 and 5.6.1), all the changes made between ET4 and PPF are carried through to Faber's first edition, which contains no further variants with regard to PPF.

1977a *Ends and Odds: Plays and Sketches*. London: Faber and Faber. 104 pp. [*Footfalls*: pp. 31–7][278]

The preliminary note to this edition mentions that *Footfalls* was 'written specially for Billie Whitelaw' and that the premiere with *That Time* took place at the Royal Court on '20 May 1976' (1977a, 7).

278 For more on this edition, see chapter 1.5.1.

With regard to the text of *Footfalls*, the Faber edition contains many of the changes made in the Grove *Ends and Odds* (see chapter 5.5.2), but not all of them. Most notably, May's number of steps is changed from seven to nine in the opening stage directions, but when V first counts her steps, she only does so up to seven, as in Faber's first edition: 'One two three four five six seven wheel one two three four five six seven wheel' (1977a, 33; 1976c, 9). However, later, during V's monologue, the steps are counted correctly: 'Seven, eight, nine, wheel' (1977a, 35). This is also the case in the Grove edition (though the punctuation differs): 'Seven eight nine wheel' (1976d [1977], 45).

Faber's *Ends and Odds* text also contains its own unique variants with regard to Faber's first edition. The reason for this odd history of textual variants is that Faber did not use a copy of Grove's text as their setting copy, but a copy of the Faber first edition, annotated by Beckett (*Footfalls*(SB); see chapter 5.3.1). When annotating this copy, Beckett overlooked the instance in which May's steps remain at seven, but it is not clear if other variants between the Grove and Faber *Ends and Odds* texts are a result of faulty memory or deliberate authorial revision.[279] The table below lists the variants between the two editions:

Sentence	Faber 1976c	Page	Faber 1977a	Page
0003	*Strip: downstage, parallel with front, length* ***seven*** *steps*	9	*Strip: downstage, parallel with front, length* ***nine*** *steps*	33
0006	*Steps: clearly audible rhythmic* ***pad.***	9	*Steps: clearly audible rhythmic* ***tread.***	33
0008	*Voices: both low throughout.*	9	*Voices: both low* ***and slow*** *throughout.*	33
0015	M *discovered pacing* ***approaching*** L.	9	M *discovered pacing* ***towards*** L.	33
0016	*Turns at L, paces three more lengths, halts facing front at R.*	9	*Turns at L, paces three more lengths, halts, facing front at R.*	33
0042	Would you like me to change your position?	10	Would you like me to change your position **again**?	34
0059–62	Pray with you? (*Pause.*) For you? (*Pause.*)	10	Pray with you? (*Pause.*) For you? (*Pause.*) **Again.** **(*Pause.*)**	34

279 These editions' variants can be tracked in the online edition accompanying this monograph, using the 'Compare Sentences' tool (https://www.beckettarchive.org/).

0081	*(Pause.)*	10	(M ***resumes pacing. After one length halts facing front at L.*** *Pause.)*	34
0082	**Well?**	10	**What age am I now?**	34
0098–9	(***Pacing.***) It?	10	(***Halting.***) It?	34
0107–9	(M ***continues*** *pacing. Five seconds. Fade out on strip.)*	10	*(M* ***resumes*** *pacing. Five seconds. Fade out on strip.)*	34
0110–11	*(All in darkness. Steps* ***silent.****)*	10	*(All in darkness. Steps* ***cease.****)*	34
0112	(***Long pause.***)	10	(***Pause.***)	34
0125–6	**My voice is in her mind. (*Pause.*)**	11	*	35
0135–6	**She hears in her poor mind, She has not been out since girlhood. (*Pause.*)**	11	*	35
0141	**In** the old home, the same where she——	11	**Why, in** the old home, the same where she——	35
0164	**Three four five.**	11	**Seven, eight, nine, wheel.**	35
0193–4	*(All in darkness. Steps* ***silent.****)*	11	*(All in darkness. Steps* ***cease.****)*	35
0195	(***Long pause.***)	12	(***Pause.***)	36
0202|001–06	*	12	(***Pause. Begins pacing. Steps a little slower still. After two lengths halts facing front at R. Pause.***) **Sequel.**	36
0209	Slip out at nightfall and into the little church by the **south** door	12	Slip out at nightfall and into the little church by the **north** door	36
0218–23	The semblance. (*Pause.* ***Begins*** *pacing.* ***Steps a little slower still.*** *After two lengths halts facing front at R. Pause.)*	12	The semblance. (*Pause.* ***Resumes*** *pacing. After two lengths halts facing front at R. Pause.)* **The semblance.**	36
0250	dreadfully——	12	dreadfully **un—— ...**	36
0256	fixing Amy full in the eye she said	13	**raising her head and** fixing Amy full in the eye she said	37
0280	The love of God, and the fellowship of the Holy Ghost, be with us all, evermore.	13	The love of God, and the fellowship of the Holy Ghost, be with us all, **now, and for** evermore.	37
0285	***Begins*** *pacing.*	13	***Resumes*** *pacing.*	37
0318	*(Hold* ***fifteen*** *seconds.)*	13	*(Hold* ***ten*** *seconds.)*	37

Due to Beckett's oversights in preparing the setting copy for Faber's *Ends and Odds*, the version of *Footfalls* in the corresponding Grove edition is the more internally consistent text. Nevertheless, numerous unique variants in Faber's *Ends and Odds* show that Beckett had by no means finished evolving the text by the time it was published in its third edition. These unique variants highlight the continuous nature of Beckett's creative process. So, while Grove's *Ends and Odds* may be the more consistent of the two, the unique variants in Faber's *Ends and Odds* must also be taken into account for any future critical edition of *Footfalls*.

The next table compares Faber's *Ends and Odds* to Grove's 1976 [1977] *Ends and Odds*.[280]

Sentence	Grove 1976d [1977]	Page	Faber 1977a	Page
0015	M *discovered pacing* ***approaching*** *L.*	42	M *discovered pacing* ***towards*** *L.*	33
0016	*Turns at L, paces three more lengths, halts facing front at R.*	42	*Turns at L, paces three more lengths, halts, facing front at R.*	33
0034	**..................** seven **eight nine** wheel **........** seven **eight nine** wheel.	43	**One two three four five six** seven wheel **one two three four five six** seven wheel.	33
0039	Would you like me to inject you **...** again?	43	Would you like me to inject you again?	34
0042	Would you like me to change your position **...** again?	43	Would you like me to change your position again?	34
0064	***Pause.* M *resumes pacing, after one length halts facing front at L.*** *Pause.*	44	(*Pause.*)	34
0077	Forgive me **...** again.	44	Forgive me again.	34
0080	Forgive me **...** again.	44	Forgive me again.	34
0081	*Pause.*	44	**(M *resumes pacing. After one length halts facing front at L.*** *Pause.*)	34
0088	*After first turn at* ***R.***	44	*After first turn at* ***L.***	34
0112	***Long pause.***	44	(***Pause.***)	34

280 Given the complex revision history of the text, readers may wish again to consult the 'Compare Sentences' feature in the online edition which accompanies this monograph (https://www.beckettarchive.org/). There you can easily see which variants are unique to Faber's 1977 *Ends and Odds* and which appeared earlier in the Faber first edition or in Grove's *Ends and Odds*.

0133–4	She has not been out since girlhood.	45	She has not been out since girlhood. (***Pause.***)	35
0164	Seven eight nine wheel.	45	Seven, eight, nine, wheel.	35
0195	***Long pause.***	46	(***Pause.***)	36
0202|001	(**M *begins*** *pacing,* ***after*** *two lengths halts facing front at R.*)	46	(***Pause. Begins*** *pacing.* ***Steps a little slower still. After*** *two lengths halts facing front at R.* ***Pause.***)	36
0209	**His** poor arm	46	**his** poor arm	36
0220–22	*Resumes pacing.* ***Steps a little slower still.*** *After two lengths halts facing front at R.*	47	*Resumes pacing. After two lengths halts facing front at R.*	36
0222|001	*	47	***Pause.***	36
0236	watch her pass before the candelabrum how its flames, their light ... like moon through passing **...** rack.	47	watch her pass before the candelabrum, how its flames, their light ... like moon through passing rack.	36
0250	dreadfully un—	47	dreadfully un—— **...**	36
0256	Amy, did you observe anything ... strange at Evensong?	47	Amy did you observe anything ... strange at Evensong?	37
0286	*After* ***five*** *steps halts without facing front.*	48	*After* **three** *steps halts without facing front.*	37
0318	*Hold* ***fifteen*** *seconds.*	49	(*Hold* **ten** *seconds.*)	37

Many of the published variants unique to Faber's 1977 edition can be found in one of two playscripts edited in view of the play's premiere at the Royal Court (RC playscript.B; RC playscript.C) or in the acting copy stored at Washington University (WU playscript; see chapter 5.6.1). This does not prove that Beckett used one of these playscripts as the basis for his Faber setting copy; indeed, none of the published variants unique to Faber's 1977 *Ends and Odds* appear on all three playscripts. Moreover, there is one extra comma in Faber's *Ends and Odds* text which appears on none of these playscripts: '*Turns at L, paces three more lengths, halts, facing front at R*' (1977a, 33). There is also an extra comma in the sentence 'Amy, did you observe anything...strange at Evensong?', which appears in all three playscripts (RC playscript.B, 04r; RC playscript.C, 04r; WU playscript, 04r) and in Grove's *Ends and Odds* (1976d [1977], 47), but not in Faber's *Ends and Odds* (1977a, 37). So, the playscripts cannot account for all the variants in Faber's *Ends and Odds*, but they do contain a remarkable number of them. This spread of variants across different playscripts shows how post-performance editions of the play were crucially shaped by the epigenesis of the text in performance.

If the trail of textual changes from Faber's first edition to post-performance editions is incomplete, an important missing part of this trail is the development of the text from setting copy to Faber's published text. For instance, the extra comma after '*halts*,' (discussed above) does not appear on Faber's setting copy (*Footfalls*(SB); see chapter 5.3.1). Nor do a couple of other unique published variants in Faber's 1977 *Ends and Odds*:

- '(M *resumes pacing. After one length halts facing front at L.*)' (1977a, 34) is not found on *Footfalls*(SB).
- Two instances of the phrase '***Resumes** pacing.*' (1977a, 36) are still '***Begins** pacing.*' on *Footfalls*(SB) (12).

Furthermore, 'his poor arm' is not capitalized in the published text (1977a, 36), while it appears as '~~h~~^{H}is poor arm' in the setting copy (*Footfalls*(SB), 12; see Fig. 20).[281] While the variants in punctuation and capitalization may be errors, it is unlikely this applies to the other, more substantial, variants, suggesting that Beckett may have made further changes to the text, possibly at proof or galley stage.

1984a *Collected Shorter Plays*. London and Boston: Faber and Faber. 316 pp. [*Footfalls*: pp. 237–43]

This edition contains a reset text of *Footfalls* based on Faber's 1977 *Ends and Odds*. Remarkably, the year after Gontarski castigated Faber's previous editions of the play for textual discrepancies in his article 'Text and Pre-texts of Samuel Beckett's *Footfalls*' (1983, 192), V's first count of May's steps still only goes up to seven, out of line with the rest of the text: 'One two three four five six seven wheel one two three four five six seven wheel' (1984b, 239).

281 Beckett told Antoni Libera that this phrase referred to Christ's arm (4 September 1976, *LSB IV* 433).

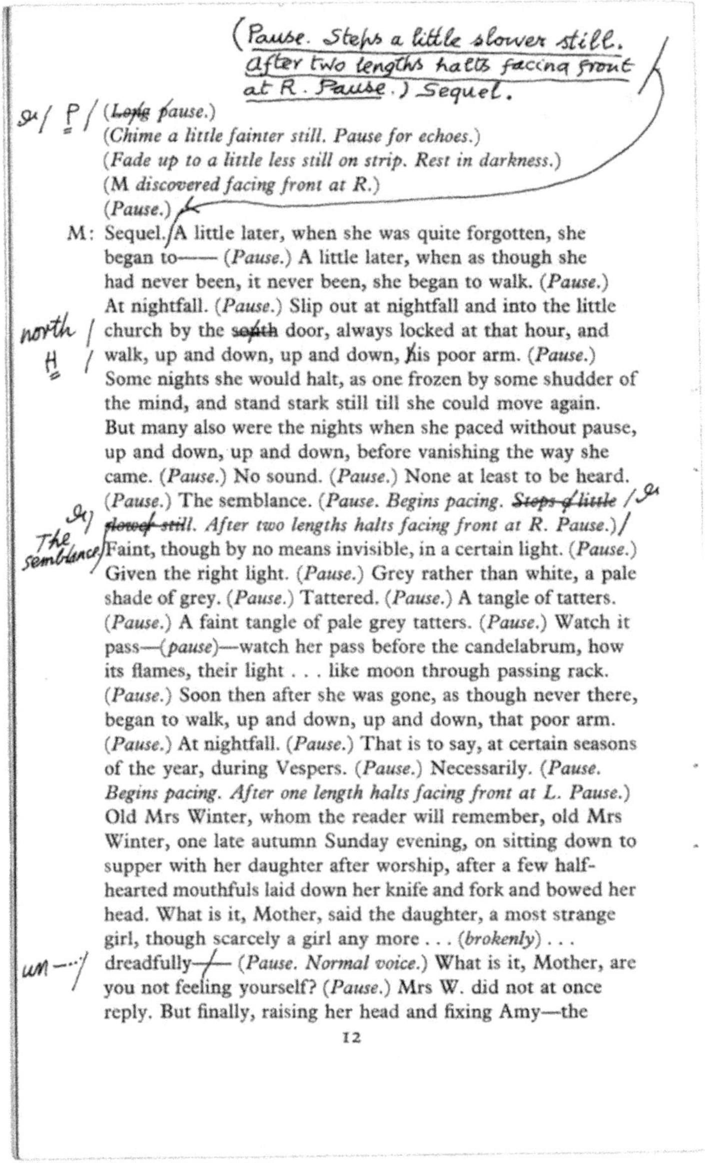

(*Pause. Steps a little slower still. After two lengths halts facing front at R. Pause.*) Sequel.

sy/ P/ (*~~Long~~ pause.*)
(*Chime a little fainter still. Pause for echoes.*)
(*Fade up to a little less still on strip. Rest in darkness.*)
(M *discovered facing front at R.*)
(*Pause.*)

M: Sequel. A little later, when she was quite forgotten, she
began to—— (*Pause.*) A little later, when as though she
had never been, it never been, she began to walk. (*Pause.*)
At nightfall. (*Pause.*) Slip out at nightfall and into the little
north / church by the ~~south~~ door, always locked at that hour, and
H / walk, up and down, up and down, ~~his~~ poor arm. (*Pause.*)
Some nights she would halt, as one frozen by some shudder of
the mind, and stand stark still till she could move again.
But many also were the nights when she paced without pause,
up and down, up and down, before vanishing the way she
came. (*Pause.*) No sound. (*Pause.*) None at least to be heard.
(*Pause.*) The semblance. (*Pause. Begins pacing. ~~Steps a little~~* /sy
sy/ *~~slower still~~. After two lengths halts facing front at R. Pause.*)/
The semblance/ Faint, though by no means invisible, in a certain light. (*Pause.*)
Given the right light. (*Pause.*) Grey rather than white, a pale
shade of grey. (*Pause.*) Tattered. (*Pause.*) A tangle of tatters.
(*Pause.*) A faint tangle of pale grey tatters. (*Pause.*) Watch it
pass—(*pause*)—watch her pass before the candelabrum, how
its flames, their light . . . like moon through passing rack.
(*Pause.*) Soon then after she was gone, as though never there,
began to walk, up and down, up and down, that poor arm.
(*Pause.*) At nightfall. (*Pause.*) That is to say, at certain seasons
of the year, during Vespers. (*Pause.*) Necessarily. (*Pause.*
Begins pacing. After one length halts facing front at L. Pause.)
Old Mrs Winter, whom the reader will remember, old Mrs
Winter, one late autumn Sunday evening, on sitting down to
supper with her daughter after worship, after a few half-
hearted mouthfuls laid down her knife and fork and bowed her
head. What is it, Mother, said the daughter, a most strange
girl, though scarcely a girl any more . . . (*brokenly*) . . .
um—/ dreadfully—/— (*Pause. Normal voice.*) What is it, Mother, are
you not feeling yourself? (*Pause.*) Mrs W. did not at once
reply. But finally, raising her head and fixing Amy—the

12

Fig. 20: Differences from the published text in Beckett's setting copy for Faber (*Footfalls*(SB), 12).

There is also a note preceding *Footfalls* which incorrectly lists Grove as the first publisher of the play.

> Written in English. Begun in March 1975 and substantially completed by November of that year. First published by Grove Press, New York, in 1976. First performed at the Royal Court Theatre, London, on 20 May 1976. (1984b, 238)

That Grove are listed as first publisher is surprising, as this fails to take into account Faber's own first edition of 1976.

There are two variants between the text in Faber's *Collected Shorter Plays* and their 1977 *Ends and Odds*. The first is an error of punctuation, replacing a comma with a full stop in the following sentence: '*Turns at L*. *paces three more lengths, halts, facing front at R*' (1984b, 239). The second is an omission, deleting the line 'A faint tangle of pale grey tatters.' from May's monologue as printed in Faber's *Ends and Odds* (1977a, 36). The fact that this line also appears in Grove's editions of *Ends and Odds* (1976d [1977], 47; 1981, 47), as well as Faber's own first edition (1976c, 12), means it is highly likely this omission is another error, though without having been able to track down Beckett's corrected proofs for *Collected Shorter Plays* it is impossible to be certain about this. As discussed in chapter 1.5.1, in a letter to James Knowlson of 20 June 1983 the author mentioned receiving proofs for Faber's *Collected Shorter Plays* (*LSB IV* 615).

1986b *The Complete Dramatic Works*. London and Boston: Faber and Faber. [*Footfalls*: pp. 397–403]

The Faber edition of Beckett's *Complete Dramatic Works* finally increases May's steps to nine in V's first count: 'One two three four five six seven **eight nine** wheel one two three four five six seven **eight nine** wheel' (1986b, 399). However, it is worth noting that Beckett had inserted ellipses into this phrase when revising the text for publication in Grove's *Ends and Odds* and this may have been his preferred option: '.................... seven eight nine wheel .... seven eight nine wheel' (1976d [1977], 43). In addition, *The Complete Dramatic Works* changes the '**his** poor arm' of Faber's *Collected Shorter Plays* (1984b, 242) and their earlier *Ends and Odds* (1977a, 36) to the '**His** poor arm' of the Grove editions of *Ends and Odds* (1976d [1977], 46; 1981, 46). Nevertheless, *The Complete Dramatic Works* retains the punctuation error from Faber's *Collected Shorter Plays* – '*Turns at L.* **.** *paces three more lengths, halts, facing front at R.*' (1984b, 239; 1986b, 399) – and omits the line 'A faint tangle of pale grey tatters.' (1976d [1977], 47; 1977a, 36; 1981, 47), like the *Collected Shorter Plays*. *The Complete Dramatic Works* also retains the same note preceding the text as Faber's *Collected Shorter Plays* (1984b, 238; 1986b, 398). Thus, though *The Complete Dramatic Works* comes closest to being the most reliable published text, these two editorial errors, added to the fact that we have no documentary evidence of Beckett himself editing May's counting of steps, mean that even this edition is not entirely trustworthy.

5.5.2 English (US)

1976d [1977] *Ends and Odds: Eight New Dramatic Pieces*. First Evergreen edition. New York: Grove Press. 128 pp. [*Footfalls*: pp. 39–49]

A publisher's review slip in a copy of this edition in the Lilly Library, Indiana University, indicates that its publication date was 17 February 1977, in spite of the verso of the title page stating: 'First Edition 1976'.[282] The text of *Footfalls* is preceded by a note: '*Footfalls* was first performed at the Royal Court Theatre in the spring of 1976 during a season mounted to mark the author's seventieth birthday' (1976d [1977], 41).

The text itself features substantial revisions to Faber's 1976 edition: May's steps are changed from seven to nine throughout, including a diagram which now contains nine steps. V's counting of May's steps, which only goes up to 'seven' in the Faber edition (1976c, 9), is likewise extended to 'nine' (and broken up by ellipses) in the Grove (1976d [1977], 43; see table below). In Scene II, V's partial count only reaches 'five' (1976c, 11) while in the Grove it goes up to 'nine' (1976d [1977], 45; see table below). Beckett was here

282 For more on this edition, see chapter 1.5.1.

drawing on his experience of directing the play and the textual variants which resulted (see chapter 5.6.1).

As is evident in the table below, the Grove edition also changes phrases related to May's pacing, inserts extra instances of pacing and changes the stage directions so that they emphasize the continuity of May's pacing episodes. Furthermore, the table features numerous instances in which Beckett inserted ellipses into May's dialogue, breaking up the text. The Grove edition cuts lines relating to May's mind, changes '**south** door' (1976c, 12) to '**north** door' (1976d [1977], 46) and capitalizes '**His** poor arm' (1976d [1977], 46) when referring to Christ. The following table lists the variants between the two editions.

Sentence	Faber 1976c	Page	Grove 1976d [1977]	Page
0003	*Strip: downstage, parallel with front, length* ***seven*** *steps*	9	*Strip: downstage, parallel with front, length* ***nine*** *steps*	42
0006	*Steps: clearly audible rhythmic* ***pad.***	9	*Steps: clearly audible rhythmic* ***tread.***	42
0008	*Voices: both low throughout.*	9	*Voices: both low* ***and slow*** *throughout.*	42
0034	**One two three four five six** seven wheel **one two three four five six** seven wheel.	9	**..................** seven **eight nine** wheel **........** seven **eight nine** wheel.	43
0039	Would you like me to inject you again?	10	Would you like me to inject you **...** again?	43
0042	Would you like me to change your position?	10	Would you like me to change your position **... again**?	43
0059–62	Pray with you? (*Pause.*) For you? (*Pause.*)	10	Pray with you? (*Pause.*) For you? (*Pause.*) **Again. *Pause.***	43
0064	(*Pause.*)	10	*Pause.* **M *resumes pacing, after one length halts facing front at L. Pause.***	44
0077	Forgive me again.	10	Forgive me **...** again.	44
0080	Forgive me again.	10	Forgive me **...** again.	44
0082	**Well**?	10	**What age am I now**?	44
0088	*After first turn at* ***L.***	10	*After first turn at* ***R.***	44
0098–9	(***Pacing.***) It?	10	(***halting***): It?	44
0107	M ***continues*** *pacing.*	10	*M* ***resumes*** *pacing.*	44
0110–11	(*All in darkness. Steps* ***silent.***)	10	*All in darkness. Steps* ***cease.***	44
0125–6	**My voice is in her mind. (*Pause.*)**	11	*	45

0134–6	(***Pause.***) **She hears in her poor mind, She has not been out since girlhood.** (***Pause.***)	11	*	45
0141	**In** the old home, the same where she——	11	**Why, in** the old home, the same where she—	45
0164	**Three four five.**	11	**Seven eight nine wheel.**	45
0193–4	(*All in darkness. Steps* ***silent.***)	11	*All in darkness. Steps* ***cease.***	46
0202|001–02	*	12	**(M *begins pacing, after two lengths halts facing front at R.*) Sequel.**	46
0209	Slip out at nightfall and into the little church by the **south** door, always locked at that hour, and walk, up and down, up and down, **his** poor arm.	12	Slip out at nightfall and into the little church by the **north** door, always locked at that hour, and walk, up and down, up and down, **His** poor arm.	46
0219–23	(*Pause.* ***Begins*** *pacing. Steps a little slower still. After two lengths halts facing front at R.* ***Pause.***)	12	(*Pause.* ***Resumes*** *pacing. Steps a little slower still. After two lengths halts facing front at R.*) **The semblance.**	47
0236	watch her pass before the candelabrum, how its flames, their light ... like moon through passing rack.	12	watch her pass before the candelabrum how its flames, their light ... like moon through passing **...** rack.	47
0246	***Begins*** *pacing.*	12	***Resumes*** *pacing.*	47
0250	dreadfully——	12	dreadfully **un**—	47
0256	fixing Amy full in the eye she said	12–13	**raising her head and** fixing Amy full in the eye she said	47
0280	The love of God, and the fellowship of the Holy Ghost, be with us all, evermore.	13	The love of God, and the fellowship of the Holy Ghost, be with us all, **now, and for** evermore.	48
0285	***Begins*** *pacing.*	13	***Resumes*** *pacing.*	48
0286	*After* ***three*** *steps halts without facing front.*	13	*After* ***five*** *steps halts without facing front.*	48

The most significant of these changes are discussed in chapter 6.1.2.

1981 *Ends and Odds: Nine Dramatic Pieces*. First enlarged edition. New York: Grove Press. 138 pp. [*Footfalls*: pp. 39–49]

The text of *Footfalls* in this edition is a photographic reproduction of Grove 1976d [1977] and therefore contains no variants.

1984b *Collected Shorter Plays*. New York: Grove Press. 316 pp. [*Footfalls*: pp. 237–43]

The text of *Footfalls* in this edition is a photographic reproduction of Faber 1984a, so there are no variants.

5.5.3 French

1977c *Pas*. Paris: Les Éditions de Minuit. 18 pp.

The first book edition of *Pas* was *achevé d'imprimer* on 12 September 1977, just eleven days after the *NRF* published the text in its journal (see chapter 5.4.1). Les Éditions de Minuit published 100 numbered copies of the book on *vélin arches*. In addition, there were 35 numbered copies *hors-commerce*, also on *vélin arches*, as well as 92 numbered copies printed on *bouffant select* paper. As Breon Mitchell notes, this means that 'There was no ordinary trade issue of this separate printing of *Pas*' (forthcoming).

1978a *Pas suivi de quatre esquisses*. Paris: Les Éditions de Minuit. 97 pp. [*Pas*: pp. 7–17]

Minuit republished *Pas* in a collected edition with *Fragment de théâtre I* (19–34), *Fragment de théâtre II* (35–61), *Pochade radiophonique* (63–85) and *Esquisse radiophonique* (87–97).[283] There were 79 numbered copies printed on *pur fil lafuma* – a 'special wove paper' (Mitchell, forthcoming) – as well as seven numbered copies *hors commerce*. The edition was *achevé d'imprimer* on 29 March 1978.

The table below shows the variants between the first Minuit edition (1977c) and the text printed in *Pas suivi de quatre esquisses* (1978a).

283 Pagination from Mitchell (forthcoming).

Sentence	Minuit 1977c	Page	Minuit 1978a	Page
0170	Que veux-tu dire, May, voyons, que peux-tu bien vouloir dire, ne suffit pas ?	13	Que veux-tu dire, May, **ne suffit pas,** voyons, que peux-tu bien vouloir dire, **May,** ne suffit pas ?	12
0244	**Inévitablement.**	15	**Fatalement.**	14
0265	Que veux-tu dire, Amy, voyons, que peux-tu bien vouloir dire, pour en dire le moins ?	17	Que veux-tu dire, Amy, **pour en dire le moins,** voyons, que peux-tu bien vouloir dire, **Amy,** pour en dire le moins ?	15–16
0301	**Ca** ?	18	**Ça** ?	16

The later edition contains what are almost certainly authorial changes, with Beckett accentuating the echo structure of the play in edits to two questions and replacing May's '**Inévitablement**' (1977c, 15) with the more deathly '**Fatalement**' (1978a, 14). In addition, Minuit 1978a corrects a typographic error by adding a cedilla to a question word: '**Ça** ?' (1978a, 16), bringing it into line with Minuit house style. This typographic correction in Minuit 1978a makes it the slightly more reliable edition.

5.5.4 Multilingual

1978b *Stücke und Bruchstücke*. Frankfurt am Main: Suhrkamp Verlag. 275 pp.

Footfalls (pp. 64–74)

The copyright page of this trilingual edition indicates that the English texts are based on Faber's 1977 *Ends and Odds* (see chapter 1.5.1). However, it mistakenly lists the year of copyright for *Footfalls* as 1975. Errors are likewise found in the published text, which, out of all the previously published versions, is indeed closest to Faber 1977a. That said, it contains one variant which, at the time of *Stücke und Bruchstücke*'s publication, had only been previously published in Grove's 1976 [1977] *Ends and Odds*. This is the pronoun pointing to Christ – '**His** poor arm' – which is capitalized in *Stücke und Bruchstücke* (1978b, 70), just as it is in the Grove edition (1976d

[1977], 46). Another variant mixes elements from Grove's and Faber's first editions of *Ends and Odds*. V's first count of May's steps goes up to nine – 'One two three four five six seven eight nine wheel one two three four five six seven eight nine wheel' (1978b, 64, 66) – corresponding to the Grove edition (1976d [1977], 43) rather than the seven steps of the two Faber editions (1976c, 9; 1977a, 33). However, this count is printed without the ellipses substituting the first six numbers in the Grove edition: '.................... seven eight nine wheel .... seven eight nine wheel' (1976d [1977], 43). This error is remarkable as V's counting is printed with ellipses on the relevant facing pages of the German text: '... sieben acht neun kehrt ... sieben acht neun kehrt' (1978b, 65, 67).

Other errors include mistakes in spelling and punctuation and the omission of the final stage direction '(*Curtain.*)' (1977a, 37), meaning that May might indeed go on 'revolving it all' without end in this version of the English text. The full table of variants is listed below.

Sentence	Faber 1977a	Page	Suhrkamp 1978b	Page
0034	One two three four five six seven wheel one two three four five six seven wheel.	33	One two three four five six seven **eight nine** wheel one two three four five six seven **eight nine** wheel.	64–6
0137	Not out since girlhood.	35	Not out since girlhood	68
0160	***Towards** end of second length.*	35	***Toward** end of second length.*	68
0178	some **nights** she does	35	some **night** she does	70
0209	**his** poor arm	36	**His** poor arm	70
0320	**(*Curtain.*)**	37	*	74

Pas (pp. 77–82)

The French text follows the *NRF* journal publication (1977b), even to the point of printing the first instance of '*Eclairage*' without an accent and giving an initial capital to '*Voix brisée*' (1978b, 77, 81). Aside from differences in house style, the one textual variant in the Suhrkamp edition is the omission of '*Rideau*' at the end of the text (1977b, 14), ending instead with '*Noir*' (1978b, 82).

5.6 Playscripts, Production Notes and Annotated Copies

Some of the abbreviations in the survey below were coined by S. E. Gontarski in Vol. 4 of *The Theatrical Notebooks of Samuel Beckett* (*TN4*). By analogy, and for the sake of consistency, I have applied the same nomenclature to new documents that have been discovered since the publication of *TN4*.

5.6.1 English

RC playscript.A

The Samuel Beckett Collection in the Harry Ransom Center (box 3, folder 7) contains an acting copy of *Footfalls*, similar to those produced for the premiere of *Not I* (see chapter 1.6.1). This playscript is not discussed in *TN4*. It was likely made for the Royal Court premiere on 20 May 1976 and contains the theatre's address on folio 01r. A comparison of the two documents indicates that the playscript is a precursor of ET4 (see chapter 5.2.1). For instance, RC playscript.A has a 'Faint gong' (02r), which is changed to 'Faint ~~gong~~ single chime' on ET4 (01r). This playscript thus appears to have preceded the typescript ET4 and therefore also PPF (see Genetic Map).

RC Nb

Two sets of Beckett's production notes for *Footfalls* are catalogued under the same number at the University of Reading (MS 1976). For the purposes of this analysis, they are divided into two documents: RC Nb and German Nb (see below).

Beckett's production notes for the Royal Court premiere of *Footfalls* in 1976 are reproduced in facsimile in *TN4* (289–309). They are stored in a red notebook which Beckett also used to make notes for the German productions of *Spiel* (October 1978), *Damals* and *Tritte* (both October 1976) (see chapter 3.5.2 and Beloborodova 2019, 120–1). It is described in the *Theatrical Notebooks* as 'a red, hard-covered, 90-folio, square-ruled notebook measuring 20.5 × 14.5 cms' (*TN4* 313).

Beckett's production notes for the premiere of *Footfalls* are contained on 'three, loose, double notebook sheets measuring 20.5 × 29.6 cms' (*TN4* 289).[284] According to the *Beckett at Reading* catalogue, they were 'originally inserted into front of book' and are 'headed *Footfalls*' (Bryden, Garforth and Mills 1998, 43). They contain sections headed 'Chime', 'Steps' and 'Turn' (02r) as well as 'Diminuendo' and 'Pacing' (03r). There are six diagrams marking May's position on the strip as she speaks the closing lines of Scene I (01r, 02v) and Scene II (02r–02v, 03r). These are similar to the diagrams on RC playscript.B (06r), RC playscript.C (06r) and the WU playscript (06r); they are also keyed to similar lines. Beckett notes the idea for changing the number of May's steps from seven to nine – '9 rather than 7 per length' (02r) – and a page of diagram sketches is headed '**If** 9 Steps' (02v), suggesting that this was an idea that he was working through as he made these notes.

RC playscript.B

The Burns Library at Boston College holds a typed playscript in their Samuel Beckett–Calvin Israel Collection (box 12, folder 11) with handwritten additions in black and red ink. It is not mentioned in *TN4*. The typed material on this playscript is close to RC playscript.C (see below), though there are differences in the line distribution, so these documents are not copies of one another (the same is true with regard to RC playscript.B's relationship to Beckett's earlier typescripts). The playscript is marked '~~Final~~' in black ink, but, as the strikethrough indicates, this document is in fact just one step in the continuous evolution of the text (01r).[285] It is inscribed 'for /

284 A photocopy of these notes, featuring the stamp of University of Reading Library on each page, is held in the Alan Schneider Papers (UCSD, box 48, folder 18).

285 The non-definitive nature of this word with regard to Beckett's performance texts is highlighted in his letter of 7 December 1963 to Alan Schneider regarding *Play*: 'I shall send you this week the latest "final" text' (*LSB* III 585).

Calvin & / Joann / Sam. Beckett' (01r). On the front of the envelope stored with RC playscript.B is written '6|78 PARIS', indicating that the documents were collected in Paris in June 1978.

The playscript is undated, though it contains changes which confirm it as being a later version than the first Faber edition: the pause of '*fifteen seconds*' at the end of the play (1976c, 13) is reduced to ten seconds by a marginal addition (RC playscript.B, 05r) and, corresponding to the idea sketched out in the RC Nb, May's seven steps (1976c, 9) are increased to nine by hand (RC playscript.B, 01r).

Before the document was edited by hand, however, a version of this typescript was an important intermediary text between ET4 and PPF (see chapter 5.3.1): almost all the variants between these two documents correspond to PPF in the typed layer of RC playscript.B. There are some exceptions: 'Does she still sleep, it may be asked**?**' (PPF, 06r) appears without the question mark on both ET4 (03r) and the typed layer of RC playscript.B (03r). Furthermore, these two typescripts also have '... dreadfully **un** – ...' (ET4, 04r; RC playscript.B, 04r), which appears as '... dreadfully—' in PPF (06v). Therefore, it seems likely that an earlier version of this typescript was sent to Faber as a setting copy, a document I have labelled 'missing' on the *Footfalls* Genetic Map. It is not currently known if Faber produced galleys for Beckett to correct, but if they did, they may provide evidence of the author making changes between the typed layer of RC playscript.B and PPF.

Fac [missing copy sold at Sotheby's]

An annotated Faber first edition, inscribed 'for Barbara [Bray] / with love / from Sam / London May / 1976', was sold at Sotheby's on 13 July 2006. It is not included in *TN4*. The first page of dialogue is available to view online.[286] This page contains edits in black ink, in Beckett's hand, which are similar to those made on the equivalent folio of RC playscript.B: May's steps are

286 See http://www.sothebys.com/fr/auctions/ecatalogue/2006/english-literature-history-fine-bindings-privatepress-and-childrens-books-including-the-first-folio-of-shakespeare-l06404/lot.185.html. This copy is now in private hands. Despite the kind help of Gabriel Heaton at Sotheby's, I have been unable to source further information about this edition. Since, on

changed to nine in the stage directions, there is an encircled note to 'extend' the printed diagram of seven steps, '*rhythmic* ***pad***' becomes '*rhythmic* ~~*pad*~~ *tread*', the voices are both '*low and slow*' according to a handwritten edit and M is '*discovered pacing* ~~*approaching*~~ *towards L*' (Fac, 9), as in the playscript (RC playscript.B, 01r). However, there is also a difference: V's first count of M's steps reads simply 'seven eight nine wheel' (Fac, 9), while the playscript reads: 'One two three four five six seven eight nine wheel one two three four five six seven eight nine wheel' (RC playscript.B, 01r).

RC playscript.C

> Typescript, with manuscript additions and corrections by Samuel Beckett, of *Footfalls*; undated. 30 × 21 cm. 6 leaves; f. 1 lettered 'TS 4' in pencil by Beckett. (Bryden, Garforth and Mills 1998, 42)

A typescript containing manuscript revisions is held at the University of Reading (MS 1552/6). It is not reproduced in *TN4*. All of Beckett's handwritten changes from RC playscript.B are incorporated into this document. Other silent changes are made mainly to punctuation and stage directions, adding or removing pauses. According to Gontarski, Beckett made this typescript 'In preparation for the production' at the Royal Court (1983, 192). As outlined above, it seems rather that RC playscript.B is where Beckett made any such initial changes, then incorporating them into RC playscript.C at a later stage.[287]

RC playscript.C contains lines 'missing in all editions' (Gontarski 1983, 195). These lines are marked in bold below:

current available evidence, it is impossible to say what role this document plays in the epigenesis, I have included it as a 'ghost' document in the *Footfalls* Genetic Map, adjacent to RC playscript.B, but disconnected from the rest of the genesis.

287 According to Pountney, the changes contained in this playscript were 'made during rehearsal of the first production' (1988, 287), while Ruby Cohn reports that the change of steps from seven to nine occurred while Beckett was 'still in Paris' (1980, 270).

> But finally, raising her head and fixing Amy – the daughter's given name, as the reader will remember – raising her head and fixing Amy full in the eye she said – (<u>pause</u>) – she murmured, fixing Amy full in the eye she murmured, **Amy. (<u>Pause. No louder</u>.) Amy. (<u>Pause</u>.) Amy: Yes, Mother. Mrs W:** Amy, did you observe anything...strange at Evensong? (04r; see Fig. 22)

However, these lines do appear in draft form, handwritten in the earlier RC playscript.B:

> But finally, raising her head and fixing Amy – the daughter's given name, as the reader will remember – raising her head and fixing Amy full in the eye she said – (<u>pause</u>) – she murmured, fixing Amy full in the eye she murmured, **Amy.** (**Pause.**) **Amy.** (**P.**) ~~Yes M~~ Amy: Yes M. Mrs W: Amy, did you observe anything...strange at Evensong?' (04r; see Fig. 21).

While these lines do not appear in any of the English-language editions, they were later incorporated into the French translation (see chapter 6.2.2) and also feature in Walter Asmus's TV production starring Billie Whitelaw (see SDR production below).

A set of identical diagrams of May's pacing are found both on RC playscript.B (06r) and RC playscript.C (06r). Significant changes in these two playscripts are discussed in chapter 6.1.2.

WU playscript

The Julian Edison Department of Special Collections, Washington University holds a photocopy of RC playscript.C (MSS008 II, box 2, folder 42). It features all the manuscript emendations of RC playscript.C as well as handwritten edits which do not appear on the document stored at Reading, two of which are in Beckett's hand. After May starts the third scene with the word 'Sequel', Beckett inserted the following line by hand in the bottom margin:

> (<u>Pause. Begins pacing. Steps a little slower still. After 2 lengths halts facing front at R. Pause.</u>) The Sequel.
>
> (03r)

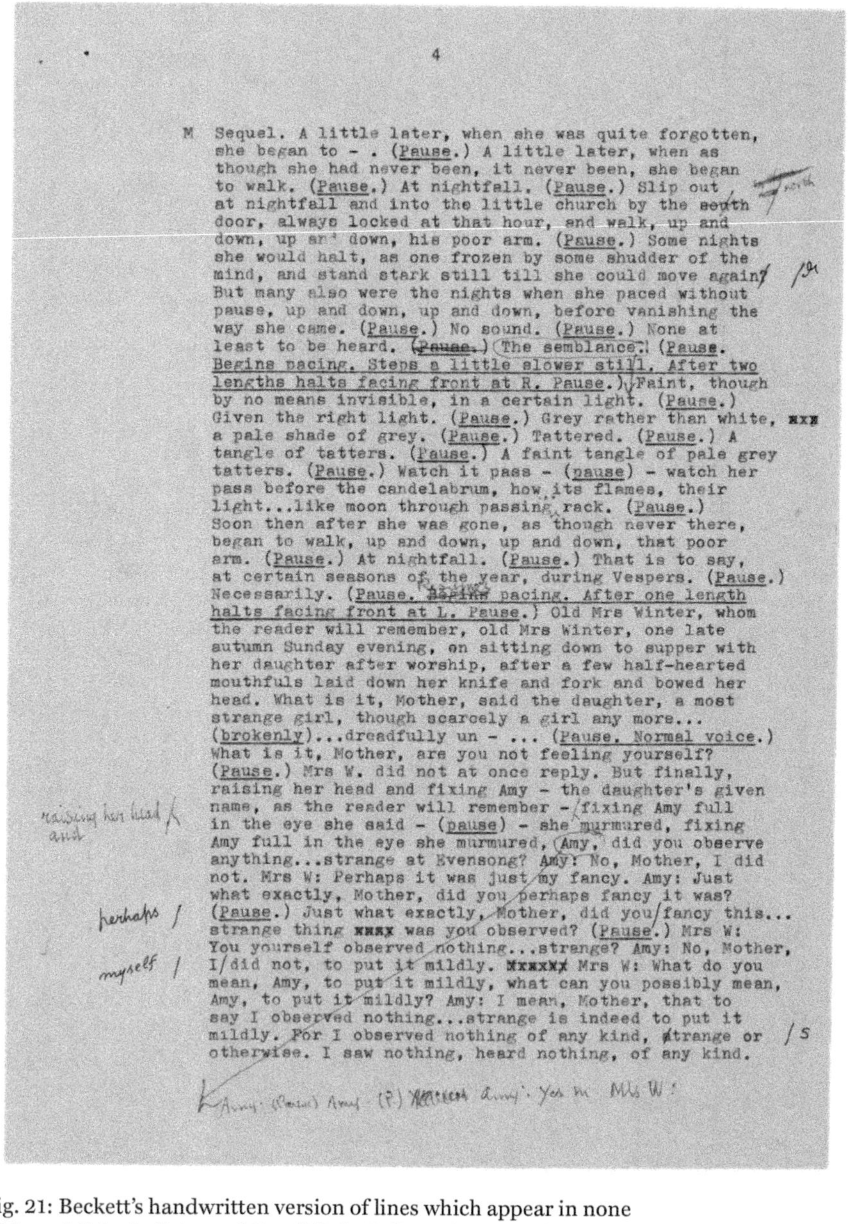
4

M Sequel. A little later, when she was quite forgotten, she began to - . (Pause.) A little later, when as though she had never been, it never been, she began to walk. (Pause.) At nightfall. (Pause.) Slip out at nightfall and into the little church by the south door, always locked at that hour, and walk, up and down, up and down, his poor arm. (Pause.) Some nights she would halt, as one frozen by some shudder of the mind, and stand stark still till she could move again. But many also were the nights when she paced without pause, up and down, up and down, before vanishing the way she came. (Pause.) No sound. (Pause.) None at least to be heard. (Pause.) The semblance. (Pause. Begins pacing. Steps a little slower still. After two lengths halts facing front at R. Pause.) Faint, though by no means invisible, in a certain light. (Pause.) Given the right light. (Pause.) Grey rather than white, xxx a pale shade of grey. (Pause.) Tattered. (Pause.) A tangle of tatters. (Pause.) A faint tangle of pale grey tatters. (Pause.) Watch it pass - (pause) - watch her pass before the candelabrum, how its flames, their light...like moon through passing rack. (Pause.) Soon then after she was gone, as though never there, began to walk, up and down, up and down, that poor arm. (Pause.) At nightfall. (Pause.) That is to say, at certain seasons of the year, during Vespers. (Pause.) Necessarily. (Pause. Begins pacing. After one length halts facing front at L. Pause.) Old Mrs Winter, whom the reader will remember, old Mrs Winter, one late autumn Sunday evening, on sitting down to supper with her daughter after worship, after a few half-hearted mouthfuls laid down her knife and fork and bowed her head. What is it, Mother, said the daughter, a most strange girl, though scarcely a girl any more... (brokenly)...dreadfully un - ... (Pause. Normal voice.) What is it, Mother, are you not feeling yourself? (Pause.) Mrs W. did not at once reply. But finally, raising her head and fixing Amy - the daughter's given name, as the reader will remember - fixing Amy full in the eye she said - (pause) - she murmured, fixing Amy full in the eye she murmured, Amy, did you observe anything...strange at Evensong? Amy: No, Mother, I did not. Mrs W: Perhaps it was just my fancy. Amy: Just what exactly, Mother, did you perhaps fancy it was? (Pause.) Just what exactly, Mother, did you fancy this... strange thing xxxx was you observed? (Pause.) Mrs W: You yourself observed nothing...strange? Amy: No, Mother, I did not, to put it mildly. Mxxxxx Mrs W: What do you mean, Amy, to put it mildly, what can you possibly mean, Amy, to put it mildly? Amy: I mean, Mother, that to say I observed nothing...strange is indeed to put it mildly. For I observed nothing of any kind, strange or otherwise. I saw nothing, heard nothing, of any kind.

raising her head and

perhaps

myself

Fig. 21: Beckett's handwritten version of lines which appear in none of the published editions of *Footfalls* (RC playscript.B, 04r).

M locked at that hour, and walk, up and down, up and
down, His poor arm. (Pause.) Some nights she would
halt, as one frozen by some shudder of the mind,
and stand stark still till she could move again.
(Pause.) But many also were the nights when she paced
without pause, up and down, up and down, before vanishing
the way she came. (Pause.) No sound. (Pause.) None at
least to be heard. (Pause. Begins pacing. Steps a
little slower still. After two lengths halts facing
front at R. Pause.) The semblance. (Pause.) Faint,
though by no means invisible. (Pause.) In a certain
light. (Pause.) Given the right light. (Pause.) Grey
rather than white, a pale shade of grey. (Pause.)
Tattered. (Pause.) A tangle of tatters. (Pause.) A
faint tangle of pale grey tatters. (Pause.) Watch it
pass - (pause) - watch her pass before the candelabrum,
how its flames, their light, like moon through passing
...rack. (Pause.) Soon then after she was gone, as
though never there, began to walk, up and down, up and
down, that poor arm. (Pause.) At nightfall. (Pause.)
That is to say, at certain seasons of the year, during
Vespers. (Pause.) Necessarily. (Pause. Resumes pacing.
After one length halts facing front at L. Pause.) Old
Mrs Winter, whom the reader will remember, old Mrs
Winter, one late autumn Sunday evening, on sitting
down to supper with her daughter after worship, after
a few half-hearted mouthfuls laid down her knife and
fork and bowed her head. What is it, Mother, said the
daughter, a most strange girl, though scarcely a girl
~~xxxxxxxxxxxxxxxxxxxxxxx~~ any more...(brokenly)...
dreadfully un - ... (Pause. Normal voice.) What is
it, Mother, are you not feeling yourself? (Pause.)
Mrs W. did not at once reply. But finally, raising
her head and fixing Amy - the daughter's given name,
as the reader will remember - raising her head and fixing
Amy full in the eye she said - (pause) - she murmured,
fixing Amy full in the eye she murmured, Amy. (Pause.
No louder.) Amy. (Pause.) Amy: Yes, Mother. Mrs W:
Amy, did you observe anything...strange at Evensong?
Amy: No, Mother, I did not. Mrs W: Perhaps it was just
my fancy. Amy: Just what exactly, Mother, did you perhaps
fancy it was? (Pause.) Just what exactly, Mother, did
you perhaps fancy this...strange thing was you observed?
Mrs W: You yourself observed nothing...strange? Amy: No,
myself / Mother, I/did not, to put it mildly. Mrs W: What do you
mean, Amy, to put it mildly, what can you possibly mean,
Amy, to put it mildly? Amy: I mean, Mother, that to say
I observed nothing...strange is indeed to put it mildly,
for I observed nothing of any kind, strange or otherwise.
I saw nothing, heard nothing, of any kind. I was not
there. Mrs W: Not there? Amy: Not there. Mrs W: But I

Fig. 22: Beckett's typed version of the lines which appear in no published edition (RC playscript.C, 04r).

This is quite close – but not identical – to how the lines appear on *Footfalls*(CI) (12) and *Footfalls*(SB) (12), which in turn formed the basis for the Grove and Faber editions of *Ends and Odds* respectively. This addition to the WU playscript version is therefore unique. On the next page, after 'None at least to be heard.', Beckett put an insertion in the left margin and deleted a phrase from the ensuing stage directions: '**(Pause.) The semblance.** (Pause. Begins pacing. ~~**Steps a little slower still.**~~ After two lengths halts facing front at R. Pause.) The semblance' (04r). This again is close – but not identical – to Grove's *Ends and Odds* (1976d [1977], 47).

Further additions are acting directions and do not match Beckett's hand. These were possibly made by one of Beckett's theatrical collaborators, to whom he frequently sent his typescripts. For instance, they may have been made by Alan Schneider.[288] The WU playscript does include the kind of notes a director would make. These notes synchronize steps with speech, as in the note 'Starting on 1 ending about 8', written above 'Will you never have done ... revolving it all? (02r). They also separate lines of speech, as in the note 'beat', written under the final 'It all' on folio 03r. And, like Beckett's own more substantial note at the end of the *Not I* typescripts (see chapter 2.2.2, 'Note 2'), they indicate pronunciation, as in the note 'Awmen', written above 'Amen' (05r).

Footfalls(CI)

> Photocopy of corrected copy of *Footfalls* (London, Faber and Faber, 1976), with manuscript corrections and additions by Samuel Beckett. 5 leaves. (Bryden, Garforth and Mills 1998, 42)

288 Schneider received a typescript from Rosset in late March 1976, but this is probably too early to be the WU playscript (*NABS* 336). It is possible that the director later obtained another typescript, such as the WU playscript, which included Beckett's performance changes.

The University of Reading holds a photocopy (MS 2461) of an annotated edition which seems to have been used by Beckett when he was correcting the galleys for Grove's first edition of *Ends and Odds* (1976d [1977]; see chapter 5.3.1). It is discussed in *TN4* as *Footfalls*(CI). The title page is inscribed:

for
Calvin Israel
Sam. Beckett

Corrections are in black ink throughout. On the versos of pages 12 and 13 is written in pencil (not in Beckett's hand): 'Pres. Dr S E Gontarski, uni Calif. 19/10/82'.

There is an encircled note beside the diagram of May's steps, which measures seven paces: 'Extend to 9' (*Footfalls*(CI), 9; see Fig. 23). Many of the autograph revisions match changes made on RC playscript.B, RC playscript.C and the WU playscript, but not all of them do. Those of significance will be discussed in chapter 6.1.2.

SDR production

Following her other successful performances of *Footfalls* in the 1980s, Billie Whitelaw recorded a TV version of the play. This SDR/Reiner Moritz Associates production (co-produced by Channel Four Television, La Sept and Raidió Teilifís Éireann) was released alongside *Eh Joe* and *Rockaby*, copyright 1988. All three plays were directed by Asmus and starred Billie Whitelaw, with Christine Collins as V in *Footfalls*. As Whitelaw recalls, 'Sam, by now far from well, asked Walter Asmus to direct the play with me for TV in Stuttgart' (Whitelaw 1996, 147). The closing credits read: 'FOOTFALLS is based on the author's original production at the Royal Court Theatre London' (2004). Aside from (significant) performance decisions made regarding lighting, pacing and vocal delivery, the text used is close to that printed in Grove's *Ends and Odds*. The only variants in the dialogue are when May includes the lines added in RC playscript.C (see chapter 5.3.1) and rephrases the question: 'Just what exactly, Mother, **did you perhaps fancy this** ... strange thing was you observed?' (1981, 48). In Whitelaw's

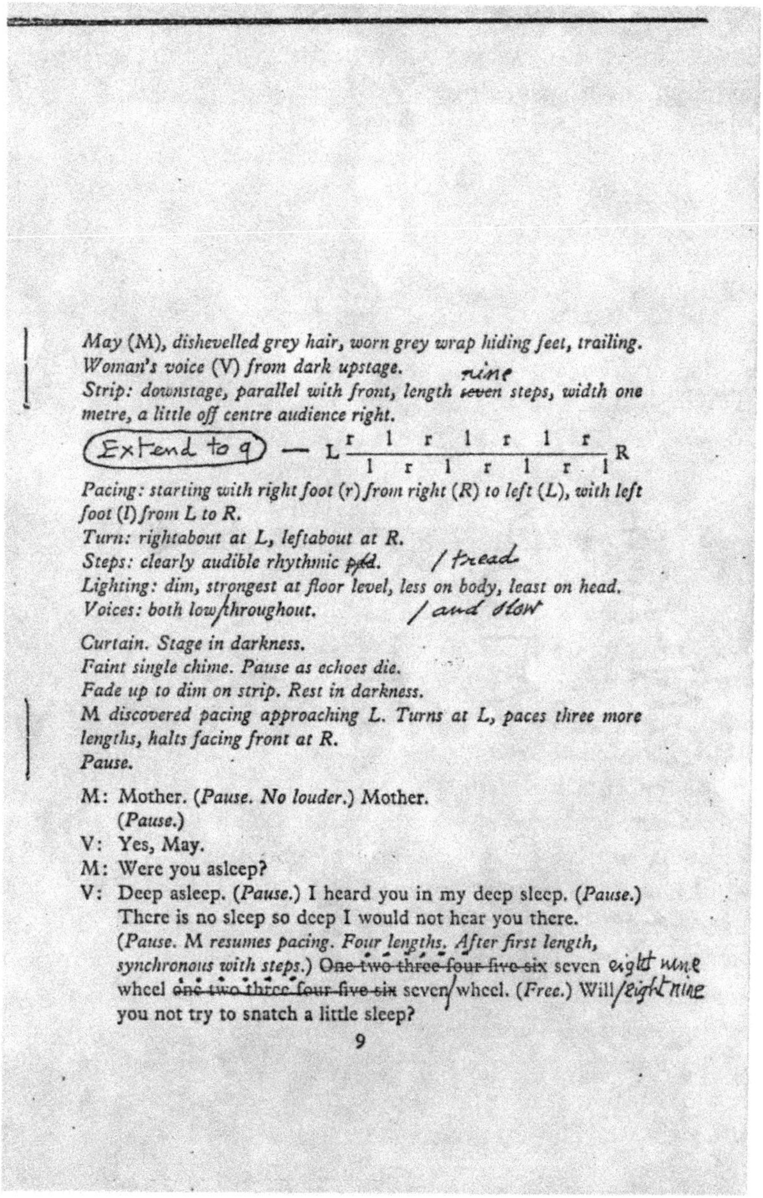

May (M), *dishevelled grey hair, worn grey wrap hiding feet, trailing.*
Woman's voice (V) *from dark upstage.*
Strip: downstage, parallel with front, length ~~*seven*~~ nine *steps, width one metre, a little off centre audience right.*

(Extend to 9) — L r l r l r l r / l r l r l r l R

Pacing: starting with right foot (*r*) *from right* (*R*) *to left* (*L*), *with left foot* (*l*) *from L to R.*
Turn: rightabout at L, leftabout at R.
Steps: clearly audible rhythmic ~~*pad*~~. / tread
Lighting: dim, strongest at floor level, less on body, least on head.
Voices: both low/ *throughout.* / and slow

Curtain. Stage in darkness.
Faint single chime. Pause as echoes die.
Fade up to dim on strip. Rest in darkness.
M discovered pacing approaching L. Turns at L, paces three more lengths, halts facing front at R.
Pause.

M: Mother. (*Pause. No louder.*) Mother.
(*Pause.*)
V: Yes, May.
M: Were you asleep?
V: Deep asleep. (*Pause.*) I heard you in my deep sleep. (*Pause.*) There is no sleep so deep I would not hear you there. (*Pause. M resumes pacing. Four lengths. After first length, synchronous with steps.*) ~~One two three four five six~~ seven eight nine wheel ~~one two three four five six~~ seven/ wheel. (*Free.*) Will/ eight nine you not try to snatch a little sleep?

9

Fig. 23: Beckett's edits on *Footfalls*(CI) (9).

rendition, this becomes: 'Just what exactly, Mother, **did you perhaps fancy it was** ... this strange thing that you observed?' (2004). Given Beckett's involvement in the first edit, it is possible he also made the second, though there is no firm evidence to support this.

5.6.2 Multilingual

German Nb

Beckett's production notes for the October 1976 production of *Tritte* in the Schiller-Theater Werkstatt are reproduced in facsimile in the *Theatrical Notebooks* (*TN4* 313–49). They are contained in the same red notebook which Beckett used to take production notes for the German productions of *Spiel* (October 1978) and *Damals* (October 1976); the notebook also stores his loose-leaf production notes for the Royal Court premiere (see RC Nb above).

The notebook is titled in an unusual manner: 'Across the front cover Beckett wrote "DAMALS" (*That Time*) and beneath it "SPIEL"; on the back cover, overturned, Beckett wrote "TRITTE" (*Footfalls*)' (*TN4* 5). This results in an unusual foliation: 'The *Tritte* notes, counting from the back of the inverted notebook, the way they were written, begin on the recto of folio 1 and continue to the recto of folio 9' (*TN4* 313). The description below follows this foliation, though the reader should be aware that the notes are contained on folios 82v–90v of the notebook.

The notes contain sections on 'Pacing' (03r–04r), 'Standing' (04r), the use of 'Loudspeaker' (06r), 'Light' (07r) and 'Bell' (08r). As in the RC Nb, Beckett sketched diagrams to indicate May's position when speaking specific lines at the end of Scenes I and II (German Nb, 01r, 02r). The diagrams in the German Nb are closer to those on RC playscript.B, RC playscript.C and the WU playscript than any in the RC Nb, suggesting that Beckett copied the diagrams from his playscripts, making minor alternations, when preparing the play for performance in Berlin.

Walter Asmus recalls that Beckett mentioned on the first day of the Berlin rehearsals that periods of lighting should last for seven seconds (1977, 83). In the German Nb, Beckett sketched out lighting patterns of 'approx. 7''' for each scene (07r). Asmus also notes: 'The fade-out at the end of Part I begins with the third step from the left' (1977, 85), which matches how the fade is synchronized with May's steps in Beckett's diagram in the German Nb (01r). On this sketch, V's second 'May' (second length; eighth step) and the beginning of V's final question (fourth length; second step) also correspond with Asmus's description (1977, 83). However, the other lines do not match, indicating that Beckett was still experimenting with this aspect of the text as he directed the play in German.

Two notes on the voices of *Tritte* link Beckett's direction of the play to 'Kilcool' and *That Time*. He suggests the use of an 'assumed' voice for May and Amy (05r), repeating the term used in the 'Kilcool' drafts to distinguish the different voices of a single speaker (see chapter 2.1.1). Cohn discusses these notes and the ensuing performance:

> V, he noted, should use her own voice for the mother but assume a voice for the daughter. Similarly, M should use her own voice for the daughter and assume a voice for old Mrs. Winter. On the facing page [04v] Beckett suggested the possibility of M assuming Amy's voice and V assuming May's 'equating May with Amy'. However, he chose the first plan in performance. (1980, 271)

In his notes on the 'Loudspeaker', Beckett suggests that the 'Delocalized' voice of V in Scene II could be produced using 'one or two of those used for <u>That Time</u>' (06r), showing that the same stage technology shaped the performances of these temporally adjacent plays in Beckett's canon.

5.7 Genetic Map

1. *Footfalls*

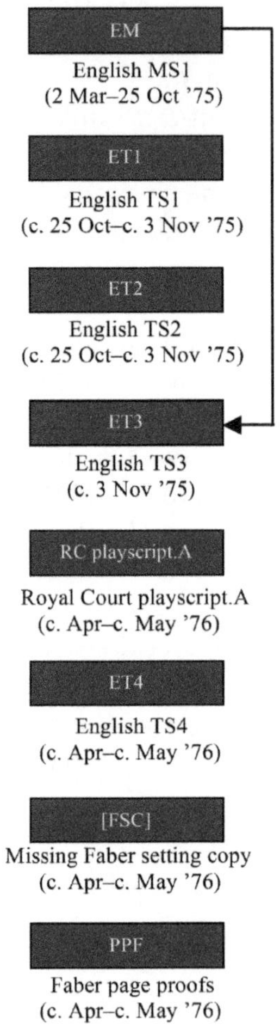
EM
English MS1
(2 Mar–25 Oct ’75)
ET1
English TS1
(c. 25 Oct–c. 3 Nov ’75)
ET2
English TS2
(c. 25 Oct–c. 3 Nov ’75)
ET3
English TS3
(c. 3 Nov ’75)
RC playscript.A
Royal Court playscript.A
(c. Apr–c. May ’76)
ET4
English TS4
(c. Apr–c. May ’76)
[FSC]
Missing Faber setting copy
(c. Apr–c. May ’76)
PPF
Faber page proofs
(c. Apr–c. May ’76)

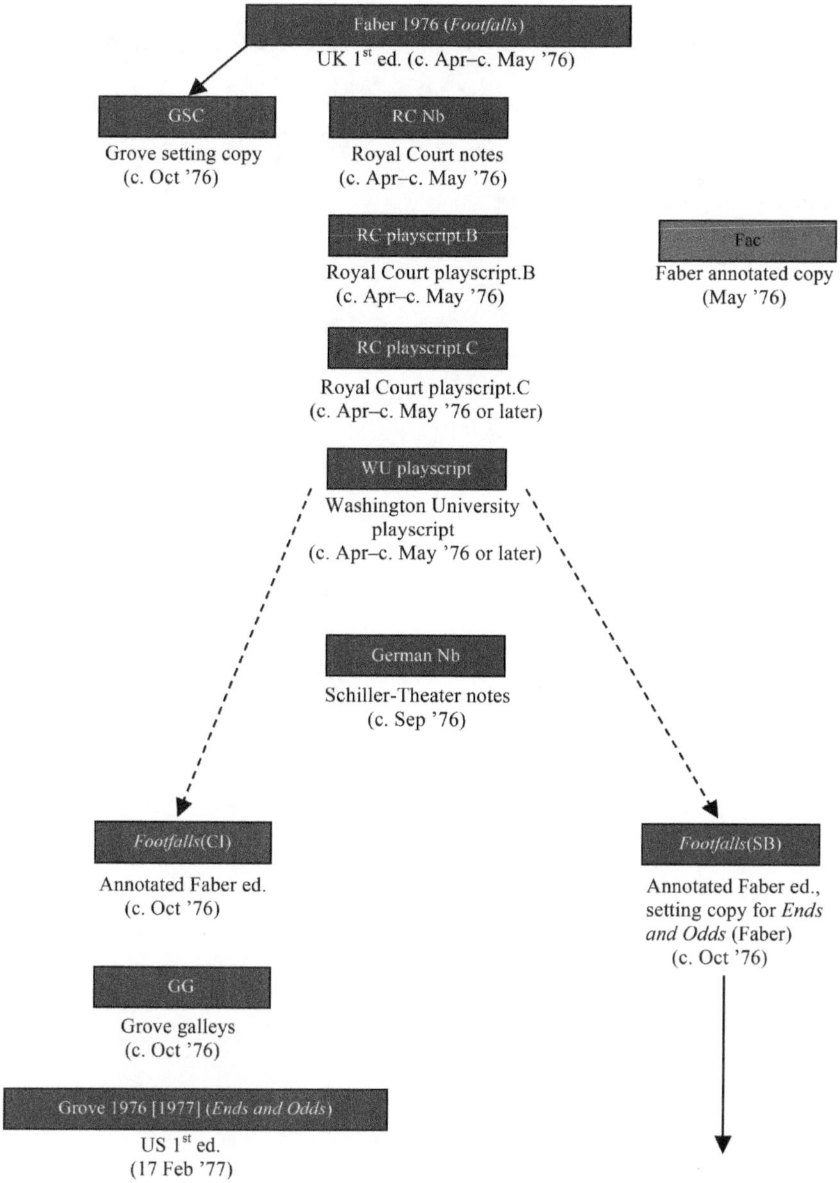

Faber 1976 (*Footfalls*)
UK 1st ed. (c. Apr–c. May '76)
GSC
Grove setting copy (c. Oct '76)
RC Nb
Royal Court notes (c. Apr–c. May '76)
RC playscript.B
Royal Court playscript.B (c. Apr–c. May '76)
Fac
Faber annotated copy (May '76)
RC playscript.C
Royal Court playscript.C (c. Apr–c. May '76 or later)
WU playscript
Washington University playscript (c. Apr–c. May '76 or later)
German Nb
Schiller-Theater notes (c. Sep '76)
Footfalls(CI)
Annotated Faber ed. (c. Oct '76)
Footfalls(SB)
Annotated Faber ed., setting copy for *Ends and Odds* (Faber) (c. Oct '76)
GG
Grove galleys (c. Oct '76)
Grove 1976 [1977] (*Ends and Odds*)
US 1st ed. (17 Feb '77)

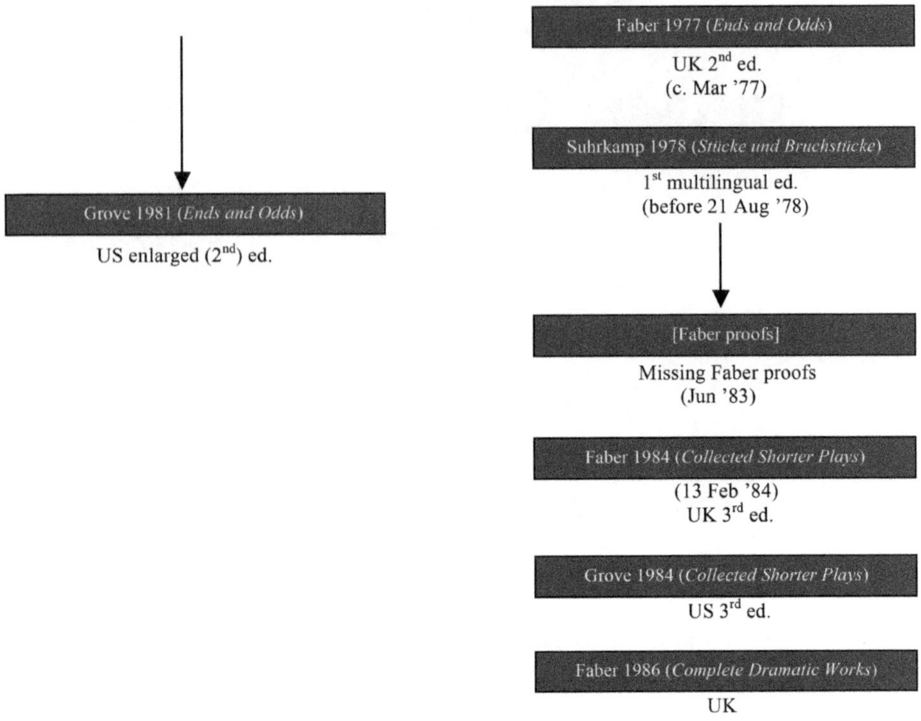
Faber 1977 (*Ends and Odds*)
UK 2nd ed.
(c. Mar '77)
Suhrkamp 1978 (*Stücke und Bruchstücke*)
1st multilingual ed.
(before 21 Aug '78)
Grove 1981 (*Ends and Odds*)
US enlarged (2nd) ed.
[Faber proofs]
Missing Faber proofs
(Jun '83)
Faber 1984 (*Collected Shorter Plays*)
(13 Feb '84)
UK 3rd ed.
Grove 1984 (*Collected Shorter Plays*)
US 3rd ed.
Faber 1986 (*Complete Dramatic Works*)
UK

2. *Pas*

French TS1 (c. May '77)	FT1 (first French typescript)
French TS2 (c. May '77)	FT2 (second French typescript)
NRF setting copy (c. May–c. Aug '77)	NRFSC (*Nouvelle Revue Française* setting copy)
Pre-book publication (1 Sep '77)	*La Nouvelle Revue Française* 296
Minuit 1st ed. (12 Sep '77)	Minuit 1977 (*Pas*)
Minuit 2nd ed. (29 Mar '78)	Minuit 1978 (*Pas suivi de quatre esquisses*)
1st multilingual ed. (before 21 Aug '78)	Suhrkamp 1978 (*Stücke und Bruchstücke*)

6 The Genesis of *Footfalls* / *Pas*

6.1 The Genesis of *Footfalls*

6.1.1 Chronology

The composition of *That Time* overlaps with that of the third play in this module. Beckett started *Footfalls* in early 1975 as he struggled to make progress with the earlier text. While he thought of *Not I* and *That Time* as sibling plays, *Footfalls* could be considered as something of a textual orphan, which is brought into focus by examining the parallels between it and the work of another singular playwright Beckett admired. W. B. Yeats's *At the Hawk's Well* was on his mind on 10 October 1974, when he recited its opening lines for Anne Atik and Avigdor Arikha (Atik 2001, 91), sung in the playtext by three musicians:

> I call to the eye of the mind
> A well long choked up and dry
> And boughs long stripped by the wind,
> And I call to the mind's eye
> Pallor of an ivory face,
> Its lofty dissolute air,
> A man climbing up to a place
> The salt sea wind has swept bare. (Yeats 1989, 399)[289]

Yeats's play tells the story of an old man waiting by a well for its waters to bubble up, so he can drink them and attain eternal life. The three times these waters have appeared during his long life of waiting he has been asleep. We see him miss the waters again, having discussed his need for them with a younger man (the Irish mythical warrior Cuchulain) who enters and waits with him at the well, before this Young Man is drawn offstage by the Guardian of the Well, just prior to the waters appearing.

There is very little in this summary that would link Yeats's play with Beckett's text. Unlike *Happy Days* (*HD* 34), there is no quotation from

289 Beckett recited the same passage to Katharine Worth while rehearsing *Footfalls* at the Royal Court on 30 April 1976 (Worth 2001, 131). He again quoted it while visiting Arikha and Atik on 19 April 1979 (Atik 2001, 100).

At the Hawk's Well in *Footfalls*.[290] But there is a vision of the theatre in this play that might have appealed to Beckett, especially in this part of his career. Or rather, a picture of the theatre as a kind of vision that is difficult to grasp. As Powell argues, *Footfalls* is concerned with 'the qualitative experience of inattention – a feeling of not-quite-there-ness' (2016, 113). This is central to the stories in the play, particularly in Amy's insistence that she was 'not there' at Evensong (*KLT* 113). But as Powell puts it, 'Beckett also attempts to raise this sense in his theatrical audience' (2016, 113). Not only do we have a story in which the ungraspable nature of experience echoes Yeats's elusive magic waters, but *Footfalls* stages a similar idea about the elusive nature of performance: Beckett's May arrives on stage, flickers briefly and is gone, without us ever finding out what her precise relationship is to the disembodied voice that speaks or the characters she summons up in her own story. This adds to the sense of the play as a kind of infinite revolving (see chapter 6.1.2): if May was never really there, in what sense can we say that her story has ended when she disappears in Scene IV? May's flickering presence is in stark contrast to the images of *Not I* and *That Time*, which, however strange they might be, depend on being sharply presented. While May is not quite there, the images of these two earlier plays unmistakably are.

Describing the movements of the Old Man, Yeats's stage directions state: '*His movements, like those of the other persons in the play, suggest a marionette*' (Yeats 1989, 401). We know this kind of performed movement was deeply influential on Beckett, particularly through his engagement with Heinrich Von Kleist's essay 'On the Marionette Theatre', which he referred to during rehearsals of *Ghost Trio* in October 1976 (see Pilling and Knowlson 1979, 277). In spite of Beckett's disavowal of Balzac's 'explicating background' (see Introduction), May's repetitious, almost mechanical movements might be more closely related to an explanatory backstory than those in *At the Hawk's Well*. While May's movements might be put down to her having paced for so long along the same strip, the movements of Yeats's characters all have this machine-like quality. This is the case even for the Young Man – never called Cuchulain in the stage directions – whose very name sets him in direct opposition to his older interlocutor. Yeats's whole theatrical world

290 In October–November 1974, Beckett attended rehearsals of *Happy Days* in London (Pilling 2006, 196).

is thus explicitly stylized, whereas Beckett's functions by virtue of traces of the realist paradigm he was so keen to reject.

At the Hawk's Well, like *Footfalls*, is a play about aging, the treatment of which Beckett admired greatly in Yeats's poetry (Atik 2001, 125). However, there is no suggestion that a young warrior can escape the track of time followed by his older companion. When the Young Man wanders offstage in a daze to follow the Guardian of the Well, the musicians sing:

> He has lost what may not be found
> Till men heap his burial-mound
> And all the history ends. (Yeats 1989, 410)

History here has a destination point, a moment at which youth will have turned to old age and mortality will have caught up with even the hot-blooded Cuchulain. For May, prematurely aged as she is, the linear passing of time is something which only happened in the past, recalled by V's stories of her youth, and all that is left for her is the revolving of a kind of death in life.

In a questionnaire sent to Beckett in 1972, James Knowlson noted Winnie's citation of 'the eye of the mind' from *At the Hawk's Well* and asked if Yeats's theatre was 'consciously in mind as you wrote Waiting for Godot'. Beckett replied briefly: 'No. All theatre is waiting' (JEK 1/2/4), before expanding on his 'wretched answers' in a letter of 11 April:

> I simply know next to nothing about my work in this way, as little as a plumber of the history of hydraulics. There is nothing/nobody with me when I'm writing, only the hellish job in hand. The 'eye of the mind' in H.D. does not refer to Yeats any more that [*for* than] the 'revels ...' in Endgame to The Tempest, they are just bits of pipe I happen to have with me. I suppose all is reminiscence from womb to tomb, all I can say is I have scant information concerning mine – alas. (*LSB IV* 291)[291]

291 Editorial correction in *LSB IV*.

This was not the first time Beckett had used a technical metaphor to describe the act of writing. In *Proust*, he compares the artist who excavates a text from within to the artisan who puts it on the page: 'The artist has acquired his text: the artisan translates it' (*PTD* 84). While disavowing direct reference to Yeats and Shakespeare in his letter to Knowlson, the reference to 'bits of pipe' acknowledges that these intertexts did play a role in the creative process. While their presence in these published texts is clear, Beckett seems to be suggesting that conscious textual extraction is only one aspect of his writing process. Indeed, this paragraph ends by suggesting that the intertexts of his work are indeed remembrances of texts past. Having identified Proust's aesthetic as being based on the rare moments of access to shards of memory which call up an entire world (*PTD* 34), Beckett claims that his own mechanical act of writing calls up only the textual shards of his past reading.

In the questionnaire itself, Knowlson asked which of the many Yeats plays Beckett saw at the Abbey in the 1920s impressed him most and if he considered any of them as having influenced his own plays. Beckett's reply again references the faulty faculty of memory: 'Forget which of his plays I saw. More concerned with them as writing than as theatre' (UoR JEK 1/2/4). This foregrounds a major theme of *Footfalls*: through references to the reader as well as echoes between stage directions and dialogue, the play interrogates the relationship between textuality and theatre performance (see chapter 6.1.2).

The relationship between writing and theatre work was to the fore of Beckett's mind as he rehearsed *Warten auf Godot* in Berlin in 1975. Writing to Jocelyn Herbert on 19 January, he gave an account of the actors in their roles, including a reference to the text of *Happy Days* he had recently worked on in rehearsal: 'Lucky excellent. Bright boy' (*LSB IV* 384; see *HD* 10, 28). He then stated despondently:

> Dear Jocelyn, I have decided I must stop this theatre activity. The way I have to go about it means I can think of nothing else. And the result is quite out of proportion with the efforts I make, so unfitted am I to direct actors. This means that the season of my plays at the Court next year, than which I of course ask

> nothing better, would have to be without my participation.[292] This decision does not proceed from my present weariness & surfeit of theatre, but from the realisation that I owe the little time that remains to the one thing I am a little fitted for. (*LSB IV* 384)

Beckett had announced his retirement from theatre before, and he would do so repeatedly again. Yet two weeks later he was working on a new play. On 2 February 1975, Beckett wrote to Barbara Bray: 'Worked all morning on the footsteps. False start but not unenlightening' (*LSB IV* 387). Beckett had footsteps on his mind while rehearsing *Godot*, during which he 'had made the translation more concise, had made the number of steps taken from the tree to the stone parallel the length of the sentence' (Atik 2001, 93). So, it is possible that this rehearsal process fed into his idea of constructing an entire play around such footsteps (Knowlson 1997, 614–15). While *Footfalls* was his 'pacing play' (see below), Beckett had also quite recently composed what could be considered an instance of 'pacing prose' in the short piece *Sounds*, which he was working on as late as June 1973 – and possibly beyond (Bryden, Garforth and Mills 1998, 171).[293] In this work, the narrator recalls a time when the sole protagonist 'could pace to and fro and no more sound than a ghost or mutter old words once got by heart' (*TFN* 172), foreshadowing May's ghostly recitation of an already composed story in *Footfalls* (see chapter 6.1.2).

The date of Beckett's letter to Bray in which he announces starting work on the play is one month before the date on its first extant manuscript (EM), raising the possibility that he worked on early draft material which no longer exists or is unavailable. It is equally possible that the first date on the manuscript was added only after Beckett had worked on the piece for some time. While the material on the first three folios of EM constitutes a complete draft of Scene I of the play and therefore does not fit Beckett's description of a 'false start', the various diagrams on that page may have been aspects of the play he worked out spatially in his Berlin apartment before attending to the dialogue at a later date. This would be in line with his

292 As discussed below, Beckett participated in the 1976 Royal Court season as planned.

293 The manuscript dated June 1973 is not the final extant draft.

(probable) visualization of the 'Petit Odéon' Fragments, *Not I* and *That Time* before writing them (see chapters 2.1.2, 2.2.1 and 4.1.1). We know he used his Berlin living space for theatrical work, with Cohn reporting that 'he was delighted to find that his Berlin studio was approximately the same width [as the Schiller-Theater's main stage], so that he could physicalize actions when the theatre was not available to him' (1976, 42). Could this domestic rehearsal have given rise to the creative process of a new work? Without definitive evidence, it is difficult to confirm this and the prospect of further manuscript discoveries (or of the existence of an early manuscript which Beckett later lost or destroyed) must equally be kept open.

While the first date on EM reads 'Berlin / 2.3.75' (01r), the next are 'Paris 1.10.75' (06r) and 'Paris / 25.10.75' (04r), indicating a long break during the summer of 1975 as Beckett worked on finishing *That Time* (see chapter 4.1.1). Once he returned to *Footfalls*, he made steady progress and was ready to share the play early in November 1975.

In the meantime, Beckett worked on another piece in which the relationship between 'eye' and 'mind' is crucial. The prose work 'Long Observation of the Ray' was started on 27 October 1975, just weeks after Beckett had returned to work on the text of *Footfalls* (UoR MS 2909/1, 02r). Over the course of two manuscripts and four typescripts, this unfinished text attempts to narrate an observing ray inside a closed sphere. The first draft features a list of nine themes. 'Observation', the first theme on this initial draft (UoR 2909/1, loose sheet), was replaced in a later draft (dated 19 November 1976) by a term which recalls Beckett's favourite lines of *At the Hawk's Well*: 'Eye – Mind' (UoR MS 2909/5, 01r). As Steven Connor puts it, the ensuing text describes an 'observing mind observing itself in the role of the observing ray' (1992, 85).

From the perspective of Beckett's stagings of the human mind, what makes 'Long Observation' interesting is its 'brief struggles of the mind with the observed' (UoR MS 2909/3, 01r; UoR MS 2909/5, 01r). In trying to present an eye–mind observing itself observing, Beckett explores a breakdown between subject and object, but without including an embodied subject. Despite references to a previous observer ('the late Mr Exshaw') (UoR MS 2909/2, 01r)[294] – named 'Mr White' in the first

294 As a boy, Beckett had a teacher called William Ernest Exshaw in Earlsfort House School (*LSB IV* 428n3).

draft (UoR MS 2909/1, 02r) – nowhere in 'Long Observation' is a body described inhabiting the closed space. Nor does the eye–mind ever become anything more than a mechanical means of perception. The lack of anything resembling a perceived or perceiving subject in the text leads to dead-end formulations (even by Beckett's standards), like the following on the final extant draft, in which the eye–mind theme is developed:

> Question where else in order to observe inside of sphere but inside the sphere can the eye be?
>
> Corollary where else in order to communicate with eye inside the sphere but inside the sphere can the mind be?
>
> How given its long past of observation in the light of day ~~can~~ could the eye and its long past of struggles with same the mind get inside the sphere? (UoR MS 2909/6, 01r; see also UoR MS 2909/5, 01r)

This recalls the equivalence of the breakdown of the subject with that of the object in 'Recent Irish Poetry': 'It comes to the same thing' (see Introduction). Like many of Beckett's postwar works, the central problem of 'Long Observation' is a problem of self-reflexivity, taken here to such an extreme that it undermines the very composition of the text in which it is stated. Rather than staging a subject–object relation in which the boundaries between one and the other are open to question, as in *Footfalls*, 'Long Observation' tries (and fails) to do away with the subject altogether.[295]

295 The attempt in 'Long Observation' at self-observation also has similarities with the efforts of the *Texts for Nothing* 'to look inside the head' (*TFN* 21). Elsewhere in the *Texts*, the scientific observation in a closed space of 'Long Observation' is prefigured: 'I bid my head seek, with its probes, within itself' (*TFN* 21). And at various points, the narrators make reference to the possibility of being 'in a head' (*TFN* 8, 41), 'inside an imaginary head' (*TFN* 34) and 'in the head' (*TFN* 8, 45). Beckett attended a BBC recording of the *Texts for Nothing* in October 1974 (Pilling 2006, 196). The *Texts* also prefigure Amy's being 'not there' in *Footfalls*, with the narrator declaring: 'I was not there' (*TFN* 39), 'for the moment I'm not there' (*TFN* 46) and 'I'll have gone on giving up, having had nothing, not being there' (*TFN* 43).

This may be why, in spite of his repeated declarations that he was going to give up theatre, Beckett kept returning to a form in which the embodied perspective of the audience, even in a bodiless play like *Breath*, gave him a relation which he could keep trying to break down.

If the relation between aesthetic object and audience was important to Beckett's staging of the subject–object breakdown, so too were his relationships with his actors. It is well-known that *Footfalls* arose out of Beckett's working relationship with Billie Whitelaw. On 3 November 1975, he wrote to her: 'I have a little play for you that I'd like to put in your fair hand' (UoR BW 1/6). Whether *Footfalls* was started with Whitelaw in mind or not, it became quickly associated with her, Beckett writing to Jocelyn Herbert on 23 November 1975: 'Billie's new piece is finished' (*LSB IV* 412).[296] One week later, he told Ruby Cohn: 'The "pacing play" (Footfalls) is new. Very short. I'm holding it till I see Billie' (30 November 1975, *LSB IV* 413). On 18 December, Beckett explained to Whitelaw: 'I prefer not to show it around till you have seen it and we can talk about it' (*LSB IV* 416n2). On 10 February 1976, he sent Whitelaw the text: 'Herewith playlet. Yours only if you like it & want it. For inclusion in the Court season only if agreeable to you' (UoR BW 1/8).[297] In spite of Whitelaw's concerns at a lack of rehearsal time, the play did indeed premiere at the Royal Court on 20 May 1976, alongside *That Time*, as part of the season of plays celebrating Beckett's 70th birthday.[298]

There is not much correspondence to help us date the chronology of Beckett's setting copies and page proofs. But it is worth briefly explaining the rationale behind the Genetic Map's list of epigenetic documents (chapter 5.7). With Grove already using a copy of Faber's first edition as their setting copy for *Ends and Odds*, Beckett developed the text on a series of playscripts (RC playscript.B, RC playscript.C and WU playscript; see chapter 5.6.1), onto which he incorporated changes made in view of the Royal Court premiere on 20 May 1976. However, having done so, when he

296 On the question of whether *Footfalls* was composed for Whitelaw, see Knowlson (1997, 616).

297 By 13 February 1976, Charles Monteith at Faber also had a copy (Beckett to Martin Esslin, *LSB IV* 422).

298 In a letter to Jocelyn Herbert of 26 December 1975, Beckett denied that he had suggested to Whitelaw that he wanted to direct the play in March 1976: 'So please put her [Whitelaw's] mind at rest. No question of her doing it till she feels quite ready' (*LSB IV* 415).

later annotated two copies of the Faber first edition during the preparation of Grove's and Faber's *Ends and Odds* – using *Footfalls*(CI) when correcting the Grove galleys and the annotated copy *Footfalls*(SB) as setting copy for the Faber edition – Beckett did not incorporate all the changes he had made on these playscript versions. What is more, he made further changes to the annotated editions of which we have no record in typescript form.[299] The relevant textual changes are discussed in chapter 6.1.2. From a chronological perspective, the important thing to note is that the epigenesis of Beckett's text did not develop in one straight line. In the Genetic Map, the geneses of Grove's and Faber's *Ends and Odds* branch off from the main line of prior textual development, while the less than solid connections between the WU playscript and the two annotated editions used to prepare Grove's and Faber's *Ends and Odds* are represented by broken lines.

The epigenetic documents on the Genetic Map therefore demonstrate visually the complex genesis of a play in which birth is itself a crucial theme. In the spoken lines of *At the Hawk's Well* which immediately follow those Beckett liked to recite, this theme is mentioned explicitly, as the musicians deplore the futility of the Old Man's life wasted waiting by the well:

> What were his life soon done!
> Would he lose by that or win?
> A mother that saw her son
> Doubled over a speckled shin,
> Cross-grained with ninety years,
> Would cry, 'How little worth
> Were all my hopes and fears
> And the hard pain of his birth!' (Yeats 1989, 399)

Having revised the translation of 'I Gave up before Birth' in August 1974 and included this same line in the translation of 'Afar a Bird' in March 1975 (Pilling 2006, 194, 197), it is unsurprising that this theme was again on Beckett's mind as he composed *Footfalls* (see chapter 6.1.2).

299 This raises the possibility of there being one or more missing typescripts on which Beckett made further changes before preparing his annotated editions, a hypothesis strengthened by the fact that RC playscript.B, RC playscript.C and the WU playscript are dispersed across three different libraries.

In preparation for the Royal Court premiere, the importance of movement was strongly emphasized. According to Ruby Cohn, Beckett 'had no preconceived idea of posture and walk' (Cohn 1980, 201) when he started London rehearsals on 20 April 1976 (*LSB IV* 417). But he did work on this crucial aspect of the play with Billie Whitelaw before these official rehearsals began. She recalls a memorable evening in a Parisian restaurant:[300]

> What I wanted to know most, at that initial meeting in the bistro, was the exact rhythm of the piece, the tempo. Beckett said: 'Slow, and get slower.' Then he reiterated that the main thing was to get the movements right, the changing of the body's posture as the play progressed, as though the character was slowly turning inward. In the crowded bistro, he now started to show me exactly what he meant, taking seven paces this way and seven paces back, making sure I wouldn't start on the wrong foot. [...] That was our first rehearsal. (1996, 141)

Whitelaw notes further that the production's designer, Jocelyn Herbert, 'put emery boards on the soles of the pumps' she was wearing in order to create the right sound (1996, 144). In the contemporaneous poem 'Roundelay' – first sent to Barbara Bray on 1 February 1976 – we hear footsteps on a strand: 'steps sole sound' (*CP* 445, 205).[301] As Pilling and Lawlor explain, a roundelay is a song 'in which a line or phrase is repeated as a refrain' (*CP* 445). We have already seen Beckett's interest in musical structure in the analysis of *That Time* (see chapter 4.1.1). Indeed, he told Rose Hill, who played V at the Royal Court premiere: 'We are not doing this play realistically or psychologically, we are doing it musically' (qtd. in Haynes and Knowlson 2003, 128). *Footfalls* itself features a musical verbal refrain, which we shall examine in more detail in the next chapter. If, as suggested above, *Footfalls* arose out of Beckett's rehearsal work in the theatre,

300 These unofficial rehearsals took place at some point between 19 February 1976, when Beckett told Whitelaw by letter 'It would be good to see you any time anywhere' (*LSB IV* 424) and 16 April, when he departed for rehearsals in London (*LSB IV* 417).

301 Soon after, Beckett used a similar line in *neither*, sent to Morton Feldman on or around 1 October 1976: 'unheard footfalls only sound' (*LSB IV* 437).

then this verbal repetition was based around the repeated movement of footsteps at the centre of Beckett's play.

6.1.2 Genesis

As in the composition of *That Time* and *Not I*, Beckett returned to the English Manuscript of *Footfalls* as he composed his typescripts, adding passages and notes, such as those at the end of the holograph manuscript (EM, 07r). The reader may wish to refer to the Genetic Map (chapter 5.7), which gives a visual representation of how Beckett continued to use EM as he composed ET1 and ET2, and how it fed into the composition of ET3. Individual instances are discussed in the following analysis, which is structured according to Beckett's four-scene division of the play on EM (07r) and ET3 (01r).[302] Each scene is subdivided into sections, subtitled with material from the text:[303]

Scene I: M–V Dialogue
Scene I, section A: 'Were you asleep?' (1976c, 9)
Scene I, section B: 'Would you like me to inject you again?' (1976c, 10)
Scene I, section C: 'What age am I now?' (1976c, 10)

Scene II: V's Monologue
Scene II, section A: 'I walk here now.' (1976c, 11)
Scene II, section B: 'Where is she, it may be asked.' (1976c, 11)
Scene II, section C: 'But let us watch her move, in silence.' (1976c, 11)
Scene II, section D: Mother–M dialogue (1976c, 11)
Scene II, section E: 'Does she still sleep, it may be asked?' (1976c, 11)

302 Though I have not come across Beckett describing these divisions as 'scenes', the term does fit the standard theatrical practice of defining new scenes by markers such as the blackouts of *Footfalls*.

303 Though the sections are keyed to Faber's first edition, the play's epigenetic instability means that quotations in the analysis itself are taken from the most recent published edition (*KLT*) unless a specific earlier edition is under discussion.

Scene III: M's Monologue
Scene III, section A: 'Sequel.' (1976c, 12)
Scene III, section B: 'No sound.' (1976c, 12)
Scene III, section C: Mrs Winter–Amy dialogue (1976c, 12–13)

Scene IV: *'No trace of May.'* (1976c, 13)

Before analysing the scenes themselves, we need to examine the pacing around which the play was built, and from which it got its name.

Title

In terms of interpretation, *Footfalls* is an ambiguous play, and in the first draft even the title was undecided. 'Footfalls' is written above 'It all' (EM, 01r), with a question mark to their right split evenly between the two titles suggesting that both were considered feasible options. The fact that Beckett included the last spoken line of the play as a possible title indicates this may well have been added after he had drafted the dialogue, which ends with the same words: 'It all' (EM, 06r).

Opening Stage Directions

Footfalls is a polylogue between two voices, but the early stage directions indicate that there was initially going to be at least one extra voice. In the first draft version, we have not only V and Mary, but also the deleted '~~S: Speaker from dark~~' (EM, 01r). It seems the Speaker's role was to announce the start of a new scene, but this was quickly replaced by a sound created via a musical instrument: '~~S~~ ~~One.~~ Sound (Gong?)' (EM, 01r). In ET4, the instrument was changed to something slightly more minimalist: 'Faint ~~gong~~ single chime' (01r). In his German Nb, Beckett has a 'Bell' make the sound (08r), recalling the 'incarnation bell' (Angelus) of the recently composed *Still 3* (*TFN* 173), setting a distinctly religious tone.[304] As Beckett's revision of instrumentation shows, *Footfalls* is a highly musical

304 *Still 3* was written in 1973 and published in 1978.

play, with the steps defined as a 'clearly audible rhythmic pad' by a handwritten addition on ET3 (01r).

The stage direction for V initially had her placed more specifically, using technical theatre terminology, before this was deleted: 'Woman's voice from dark ~~**backstage**~~' (EM, 01r). While it is not inconceivable that Beckett thought of having the voice coming from backstage, it is more likely that this is a simple error, much like the ones made when positioning the Auditor in *Not I / Pas moi* (see chapters 2.2.2 and 2.3.2). This hypothesis is strengthened by the fact that this line features '**upstage**' from ET2 onwards (01r).

V's interlocutor is subject to even more significant alterations. The change of name to '**Ma~~r~~y**' on ET3 (01r) could be read as a self-reference to the importance of ambiguity in Beckett's poetics, given that he told Tom Driver in 1961: 'The key word in my plays is "perhaps"' (Driver 2005, 244), of which 'may' is a synonym.[305] 'Perhaps' is also a 'key word' in Amy's conversation with her mother, who thinks she observed something strange at Evensong:

> Mrs W: **Perhaps** it was just my fancy. Amy: Just what exactly, Mother, did you **perhaps** fancy it was? [*Pause.*] Just what exactly, Mother, did you **perhaps** fancy this ... strange thing was you observed? (*KLT* 113)

Pountney notes that ET3 is a key typescript in the development of the play's ambiguity (1988, 286), and this feature is emphasized by its change of character names from 'Mary', with its associations of religious purity, to 'May', which suggests linguistic indeterminacy.[306] As we will see below, the practice of 'vaguening' is key throughout the composition of *Footfalls*. The name also evokes the theme of birth in its allusion to springtime. In *Cascando*, Opener refers to 'the month of May' as 'the reawakening'

305 According to John Pilling, Beckett also expressed this in a letter to Driver of July 1961 (2006, 155).

306 Both names also suggest Beckett's mother, known generally as May, but whose gravestone has Mary (https://www.findagrave.com/memorial/79270449/mary-jones-beckett).

(*ATF* 90). In *Footfalls*, the emphasis on a seasonal cycle signals a type of tragic rebirth, as May returns yet again to revolve 'it all'.

As in *Not I* and *That Time*, a 'Curtain' in the first draft suggests a proscenium stage (EM, 01r). The audience perspective is emphasized in an addition made to ET3: 'Strip, downstage, parallel with front, length 7 steps, width 1 metre~~.~~ a little off centre **audience right**' (01r).[307] As we have seen in chapters 5.5.1 and 5.5.2, the width of this strip was one of the most notable changes in post-performance versions of the text. The first draft has it taking up the '**Whole** ~~width~~ ~~visible width~~ **visible width of frontstage**'. But in this draft, it still only measures '**7 steps**' (EM, 01r), as it does in the first published edition (1976c, 9; EM, 01r; see Fig. 17, chapter 5.1.1). Beckett would develop the idea of a nine-step strip in his RC Nb (02r) and this is what appeared in post-performance editions of the text, though not without some significant errors in the Faber editions (see chapter 5.5.1).

As well as emphasizing the audience perspective, the idea of the strip – and hence M – being '**a little off centre** audience right' is an important spatial concept in Beckett's theatre. This is all the more relevant when we consider that 'm' is the 13th – or central – letter of the alphabet. In *Endgame*, Hamm repeatedly asks to be placed 'in the centre', demonstrating his egotistical anxiety to be the focal point of attention (*E* 18–19, 45). By contrast, in *That Time* and *Rockaby*, the solitary figures visible onstage are '*off centre*' and '*slightly off centre*' respectively (1976a, 9; *KLT* 127; see McMullan 2005, 109). Spatial theorist Yi-Fu Tuan points out: '"Center" means also "origin" and carries a sense of starting point and beginning' (2001, 126). As Van Hulle notes in his analysis of *Fin de partie*, a draft version of Hamm – suitably called 'A' (*BDMP7*, FT2) – 'epitomizes longevity' with the words 'je suis un exemple de longévité' attributed to him in a list of manuscript notes relating to FT2 (*BDMP7*, FM1, 04r). However, though he is stage 'centre' in the typescript draft (FT2, 01r), the next item on the manuscript list – 'Tous stériles dans notre famille' (*BDMP7*, FM1, 04r) – indicates that A/Hamm is not a central starting point for further generations: 'he does not engender a large family,

307 The audience point of view was re-emphasized in a handwritten addition made to the stage directions of RC playscript.B: 'Pacing: starting with right foot (r) from **audience** right (R)' (01r). This addition is not found in any subsequent versions of the text, including published editions.

for everyone in his family is sterile' (Van Hulle 2019a, 41).[308] If placing a single character centre stage creates visual symmetry, suggesting the order that comes with continuity, then having Beckett's later stage images just a bit 'off centre' puts a kink in this order, which is fitting in an oeuvre that eschews fixed starting points and teleology in favour of 'revolving it all' (*KLT* 110, 114).

For Beckett, the steps were the most important aspect of his play. On 19 February 1976, he told Billie Whitelaw: 'The pacing is the essence of the matter, to be dramatized to the utmost. The text what pharmacists call excipient' (*LSB IV* 424). The pacing was measured precisely in the first draft, with the positions of M's pauses calculated in half-lengths according to the second diagram Beckett included on this manuscript: 'M halts facing front **at 3½**' (EM, 01r) (see Fig. 17, chapter 5.1.1). From ET2 onwards, the measurement of steps becomes more straightforward, measured by whole numbers: '**3** [...] lengths' (01r). In the above letter to Whitelaw, Beckett called the rest of his text 'excipient'. However, in line with an oeuvre that values draff, dregs and refuse, he was equally attentive to other measurements in his text. The opening pause receives the very specific '5 seconds' in his first draft (EM, 01r). This became the more flexible 'Pause' on ET1 (01r), a 'vaguening' of pause length which leaves more wiggle room for those staging the text.

Scene I: M–V Dialogue

While the positioning and stagecraft were altered many times in the play's composition, both before and after publication, the version of the opening dialogue in the first draft is fairly close to the published text. This in itself is a remarkable fact, indicating that this part of the textual 'excipient' was more easily formed than the pacing around which Beckett structured the play.

308 In the published text of *Endgame*, when the curtain lifts on Hamm alone, he is also positioned '*Centre*' (*E* 5).

Scene I, section A: 'Were you asleep?' (1976c, 9)

The question of where one mind ends and another begins is raised in an addition made to ET1. In her answer to M's question 'Were you asleep?', V responds: 'There is no sleep so deep I would not hear you **there**' (ET1, 01r). This final word, which does not appear on EM (01r), suggests that M is on – perhaps even in – her mother's mind when she hears her in her sleep. This sets up a play in which the boundary between one mind and the other is of crucial importance.

The most notable change in this section is again with regard to the number of M's steps. V counts each step of her daughter's walk up to and including ET4: '**One two three four five six seven wheel one two three four five six seven wheel**' (01r). However, post-performance versions of the text extend this pacing, with the following added as handwritten additions on RC playscript.B: 'One two three four five six seven **eight nine** wheel one two three four five six seven **eight nine** wheel' (01r). This demonstrates precisely how 'The pacing is the essence of the matter' for Beckett. It is also further strong evidence that Beckett was a writer for whom work in the theatre was a crucial part of his creative process. Whitelaw has suggested that the dimensions of a given performance space may have governed the play's number of steps: 'He [Beckett] drew diagrams of the seven or nine paces (depending on the size of the stage) the character has to take' (1996, 141).[309] Though there is no evidence of this in the play's genesis, with the steps always changing from seven to nine and never the other way around, it would, if true, be a fascinating example of the degree to which Beckett's performance texts were forged within the spaces where they were performed. As we have seen in chapter 5.5.1, Beckett's oversights in his correction of the Faber *Ends and Odds* proofs meant the steps stay at seven at many points in successive Faber editions.

309 In an interview with Jonathan Kalb, Whitelaw again mentions 'seven or nine paces depending on the size of the stage' (Kalb 1991, 236).

Scene I, section B: 'Would you like me to inject you again?' (1976c, 10)

M's offer of an injection for her mother marks *Footfalls* as one of Beckett's 'painkiller plays' (see Little 2020c, 109) – plays which are structured around a series of medicinal doses. Beckett used such a structural device in 'Mime du rêveur A' [Mime of Dreamer A] (written 1956), the 'Petit Odéon' Fragments and also in *Endgame*, where Hamm asks on six different occasions for his 'calmant' (Beckett 2013b: 19, 24, 38, 50, 65, 91). Beckett even named one of his short stories *The Calmative*, though it is *The End* in which his protagonist takes this form of medicine (*ECEF* 56). In the radio play *Embers* (1959), we hear the story of Holloway, a doctor suggesting to Bolton that he give him an injection to ease his suffering (see chapter 2.1.2). However, as in *Endgame*, the palliative is never administered. In *Footfalls*, the need for relief is present, but the time is wrong: 'Yes, but it is too soon' (*KLT* 110).

The provision of pain relief is dragged out by a handwritten ellipsis on Beckett's galleys for Grove's *Ends and Odds*. There, M asks: 'Would you like me to inject you ··· again? (GG, 12r). The repeated nature of M's offers is signalled by further additions made on post-performance versions of the text: 'Would you like me to change your position again?' (RC playscript.C, 02r), which is also dragged out with an ellipsis on the Grove galleys: '... again' (GG, 12r). A similar addition is made to M's next round of offers:

> Straighten your pillows? (Pause.) Change your drawsheet? (Pause.) Pass you the bedpan? (Pause.) The warming-pan? (Pause.) Dress your sores? (Pause.) Sponge you down? (Pause.) Moisten your poor lips? (Pause.) Pray with you? (Pause.) For you? (Pause) Again. (RC playscript.C, 02r; see GG, 12r)

Such additions make this a play in which M and V are 'revolving it all' from the very start of the text, repeating their routines of refused assistance over and over. This assistance takes on a religious aspect in the same typescript on which the religiously symbolic 'Mary' is pared down to 'May': '**Sponge** you down? (Pause.) **Moisten your lips**? (Pause.) ~~Tell bedtime story?~~ ~~Pray for you?~~ ~~(Pause.)~~ Pray with you? (Pause.) For you?' (ET3, 02r). Rather than having his main character as an embodied religious symbol, Beckett decided to move the play's Christian symbology to within this early dialogue, thus setting up a verbal echo with other key religious motifs later in the text. M's offer of prayer in Scene I adds to the Christian imagery of moistening lips with a sponge, recalling Jesus's suffering on the cross:

> After this, Jesus knowing that all things were now accomplished, that the scripture might be fulfilled, saith, I thirst. Now there was set a vessel full of vinegar: and they filled a spunge with vinegar, and put *it* upon hyssop, and put *it* to his mouth. When Jesus therefore had received the vinegar, he said, It is finished: and he bowed his head, and gave up the ghost. (John 19:28–30; emphasis in original)

Jesus's final words here are echoed in the unending opening of Clov in *Endgame*: 'Finished, it's finished' (*E* 6). For V, the suffering is not ended and she cannot 'give up the ghost', even with the palliative ministrations of her daughter.

An interesting typo has M called 'Ma' in ET1: '~~(Pause. **Ma** resumes pacing~~' (01r). This recalls Molloy's fractious relationship with his mother:

> I called her Mag, when I had to call her something. And I called her Mag because for me, without my knowing why, the letter g abolished the syllable Ma, and as it were spat on it, better than any other letter would have done. And at the same time I satisfied a deep and doubtless unacknowledged need, the need to have a Ma, that is a mother, and to proclaim it, audibly. For before you say mag you say ma, inevitably. (*Mo* 14)

In addition to standing as a colloquial Hiberno-English term for Mother, this (re-)appearance of 'Ma' in the manuscripts of *Footfalls* raises the question as to whether M's relationship may be as aggressively confrontational as Molloy's, perhaps even Oedipal. For Elin Diamond, May's inability to be born is 'a brilliant theatrical metaphor of the paralysis of woman/mother's place in language', through which women are denied full subjectivity by a codification of language within the patriarchal symbolic

(2004, 57).[310] In his analysis of narrative in the manuscripts of *Fin de partie*, Van Hulle has suggested that 'Beckett's rebellion against it is not necessarily Oedipal [...] but directed against "philoprogenitiveness" in general [*CIWS* 33]' (2019a, 41). As will be discussed below, the genesis of *Footfalls* shifts between blame for human suffering being attributed to a particular human being (such as a mother or a doctor) and that suffering being simply part of life, a trauma from which there is no escape.

Scene I, section C: 'What age am I now?' (1976c, 10)

In the first draft, Beckett quickly increased V's age in M's answer to her mother's question 'How old am I now?': 'I suppose ~~coming~~ ~~going~~ getting on ~~to~~ for **$8^{9}0$**' (EM, 02r). In ET4, this answer was simplified considerably: '~~Getting on for~~ ~~Upward of~~ ninety' (02r). Other phrases were also stripped back, such as V's next question on ET3: '~~As much as that~~ **So much**?' (02r). On ET4, Beckett introduced more explicitly the shadow of death hanging over M's birth, splitting up two sentences which were earlier one: 'I had you **late**~~. in life.~~ (Pause. In life.)' (02r). This encourages the actor performing V to lay more emphasis on the double meaning of 'late', adding to the sense that the voices of the play are coming from beyond the grave. On ET2, M responds sardonically: 'Not **late** enough' (02r).

Like Estragon in *Godot*, Hamm in *Endgame* and B in *Rough for Theatre I* (*WfG* 13; *E* 8, 11; *KLT* 18), V asks M to forgive her: '~~I'm sorry~~ **Forgive me again**' (ET1, 02r). But, like Hamm and B, V goes unforgiven, making this another type of failed prayer which signals the breakdown of subject and object (see chapter 2.1.1). V's own plea was created in response to an accusation – '~~Could you not~~ You might have waited' (ET1, 02r) – which elicits more detail on the circumstances of M's conception in the first draft version:

M Could you not have waited?
V **I** ~~lost control of myself~~ **forgot myself** ~~for~~ **a moment**. (EM, 02r)

310 Diamond goes on to interpret the mother–daughter relationship in *Footfalls* through Luce Irigaray's concept of '*parler-femme*', in which there is the possibility of communication between women as subjects, but only between a daughter and an 'engulfing mother' which '*both controls and is subsumed by* May's monologue' (2004, 55, 58–9; emphasis in original).

Though it is absent from later drafts, V's self-reflexive reply does establish a theme according to which the figures of *Footfalls* do not recognize themselves as themselves. This answer, and her failed prayer in later drafts, can be seen as forms of response to the question Hamm asks his own father: 'Why did you engender me?' (*E* 31). In ET3, Beckett deleted the prompting indictment – '~~Not late enough.~~ ~~Better never~~' (02r) – strengthening the force of M's accusation by making it implicit.

V's closing question was originally 'Can you not stop ~~turning~~ revolving it all ~~over~~?', the revision in the first draft pointing to an important move towards the infinite in Beckett's work (EM, 01r). According to Andrew Key, this change in Beckett's manuscripts is exemplary of Hegel's 'bad infinity':

> The bad infinity – infinity imagined as a straight, unending line, rather than a closed circle – is a moment of stagnation in the dialectical movement of thought, an unending oscillation between thesis and antithesis without synthesis, and provides a useful model for understanding moments of stuttering or non-progression in Beckett's texts, as well as questions of closure and finitude. (2015, 1)[311]

Hegel contrasts this 'bad infinity' to that process in which 'something comes together *only with itself* in its transition into something other, and this relation to itself in its transition and in the other is the *true infinity*' (2010, 150; emphasis in original). Safe to say, M and V are not destined to reach such dialectical harmony.

Through etymological analyses of the words 'turn' and 'revolve', Key makes the point that the original ending to V's question is closer to the finite: while 'turn' derives from the Greek word *tornos*, denoting 'lathe', which would finish something off, there is 'an apparent endlessness in revolving: a potentially permanent revolution' (2015, 7). In addition, the deletion of the word 'over' further removes us from the suggestion that this turning is at an end at the end of this sentence. It is this 'permanent revolution' in M's mind that sets up a link between V's question and Hegel's concept of 'bad infinity'. While Hegel sees true infinity as *resolving* the tension between finite

311 I would like to thank Andrew Key for sharing his script of this paper with me. I follow the pagination on the script.

and infinite, Beckett's later drafts of *Footfalls* move definitively towards *revolving*. This potentially endless oscillation between points – May and V; Amy and Mrs W; stage right and stage left; beginning and end – leaves us with a world in which, as Clov puts it in *Endgame*, 'the end is in the beginning and yet you go on' (*E* 41). Beckett creates worlds on stage in which 'bad infinity' predominates – the dramatic tension, such that it is, arises from the fact that these worlds continue to go on revolving.

In ET4, the sense of time is also stretched, with Beckett lengthening the question with repetition and extra ellipsis points: 'Will you never have done? **(Pause.) Will you never have done ...** revolving it all?' (02r). Such mental revolution seems to be given a cranial location in the first version of a sentence on EM, though the deletion makes it hard to read: 'In your poor ~~head~~ mind' (03r). While Mouth's monologue in *Not I* is more focussed on the mechanics of thought – hence the move from 'mind' to the physiological 'brain' in the drafts (see chapter 2.2.2) – this change to V's line suggests that the mind in *Footfalls* is not necessarily confined to the skull, but could also be constituted by other material aspects of May's environment.

Scene II: V's Monologue

As mentioned in chapter 6.1.1, the chronology of Scene II is complex, with the second draft on EM postdating the only draft of Scene III on that document. The following analysis takes into account this distinctive compositional timeline, distinguishing between the first and second draft versions on the English Manuscript. The succeeding typescripts contain one draft version per document.

Scene II, section A: 'I walk here now.' (1976c, 11)

ET1 introduces the idea of the sound marking the end of Scene I being fainter than at the opening: 'Sound a little fainter' (02r). This is in line with Beckett's notes on EM that the play contained

Only regressions: sound
light
~~xxx~~
pacing (07r)

In other words, this is not a revolution that will continue unabated – or, heaven forbid, pick up speed – but which will rather 'shrink and dwindle' in the manner of mankind as described in Lucky's monologue in *Godot*, a monologue that suitably ends with the word 'unfinished …' (*WfG* 41–2), thus prefiguring May's 'revolving'.

The first version emphasizes the sense of death in the opening line of V's monologue: '~~**Now I am one who may not predecease her.** Chilling prospect, for her physical health is fair~~' (EM, 03r).[312] This suggests that V has already passed on and exists only as a figment of M's imagination; therefore, she will only disappear if M does. The mention of '**~~physical~~** ~~health~~' also raises the question as to the state of M's mental health. Could she, for instance, simply be imagining this voice? The idea that V is imagined by M is clearly stated in early drafts. In ET3, this statement is edited, moving from a physiological term to a more overtly mental one: 'My voice is in her **~~head~~** mind' (03r). As discussed in the Introduction, this line was cut from post-publication versions of the text, leaving an important discrepancy between Beckett's models of mind in the *avant-texte* and the *après-texte*, the latter being a product of his rehearsals in the theatre. Even before cutting this line from the text and thus making it less clear as to whether V's voice was in M's mind or not, Beckett had already increased the level of interpretive uncertainty by changing 'She **thinks** she is alone' (ET1, 02r) to 'She **fancies** she is alone' (ET2, 03r). This word choice weakens the mental faculty in question, especially when considered with regard to Beckett's broader engagement with the concept of 'fancy' in the 1960s and 70s (see below).

We can think of Beckett's post-publication editing of May's mind along the lines of Gontarski's concept of 'undoing', in that it moves the evolving play away from being a relatively straightforward psychodrama, with a fairly clear background to the onstage scenario, to something quite different in genre. As we have already seen, there are also examples of 'undoing' in

312 As mentioned in chapter 5.1.1, the entire first version of this monologue is struck out with a large St Andrew's Cross.

which words are simply stripped away. Building on Van Hulle's categorization of different types of 'pentimenti' in Beckett's drafts (2019a), we might call the first kind 'structural undoing' alongside the previously discussed 'verbal undoing' (see chapters 2.2.2, 2.3.2, 4.1.2). The following line is a good example of 'verbal undoing': '~~**See how firm she stands, how clear the**~~ ~~complexion~~ ~~skin~~ ~~**and, when she**~~ ~~moves~~~~**, with what poise**~~' (EM, 03r). In the second version, it becomes much shorter: '~~xxx~~ **See** **~~h~~Hhow** ~~firm~~ **still** **she stands**, **facing the wall**' (EM, 04r). The detail of facing the wall links M to Clov in *Endgame*, who assumes this position in his kitchen as a contrast to Hamm's tyrannical company (*E* 6, 11). In the earlier play, Beckett told his actors to imagine a fourth wall at the footlights (see Van Hulle and Weller 2018, 33). This line in *Footfalls* also references the theatrical fourth wall, which is what May faces when V speaks the line, drawing attention to the fact that the subject–object breakdown is by no means limited to the storyworld. Unlike the bullied Clov, the only company M has is V, who in this version is presented as her own mental projection. On RC playscript.B, Beckett again went for a more alliterative word choice, which was incorporated into subsequent versions: 'See how ~~still~~ ~~stark~~ still she stands, how ~~**firm**~~ ~~**still**~~ **stark**, with her face to the wall' (03r). Other lines are reduced in a similar manner: '**How calm,** **outwardly** ~~**clear, if a little grey, the**~~ ~~complexion~~' (EM, 04r) becomes '**How** ~~**calm,**~~ **outwardly** **unmoved**' (ET1, 02r), with the simplicity of the edited line matching the content of the sentence, which again reduces references to M's physicality.

Another such instance of 'structural undoing' strips back one of the more chilling lines in V's monologue, which in the first version refers to the prospect of M dying: '~~**Yet she never goes abroad, she has not been abroad now for – let me calculate – over 30 years.**~~ **So no** ~~hope from that quarter~~' (EM, 01r). As in their previous exchange, it is clear that death is here a thing to be wished for. But even that hope is denied M (and thus, in this version, the imagined voice of her mother also). This early version of the line also recalls Maddy Rooney's line in *All That Fall*: 'It is suicide to be abroad' (*ATF* 6).[313] As we shall see below, *Footfalls* features strongly the concept that one would be better off not to be born, or to die quickly once one is. In this light, the echo of Maddy Rooney's line takes on an even more sinister twist, in

313 See also the second of the *Texts for Nothing*: 'It was folly to be abroad' (*TFN* 8).

which suicide becomes something denied to M rather than something that confinement at home might protect her from. In the second version, this line becomes shorter and much less detailed: 'She has not been out since girlhood' (EM, 04r). We have no mention here of M's period of seclusion, nor of the idea that going out might lead to her death.

Scene II, section B: 'Where is she, it may be asked.' (1976c, 11)

While there is a shift from the physical term 'head' to the 'mind' in drafts of the play, another change moves from a general verb of speculation to a more specific, material act of communication: '~~Where is she, it may be **wondered**~~' becomes 'Where is she?, it may be **asked**' (EM, 03r, 04r). The first version of V's answer is subject to some of the most extensive revisions in the genesis of *Footfalls*:

> ~~She is in **the old home**, the same where she was **fooled** into this world by the old family physician, a general practitioner named Haddon, **long gone to his account. So much for that** unity. (Pause.) Though on the plain side,~~ as you may see ~~**she has had admirers, male & female**, but none outstanding, as far as~~ that ~~one knows.~~ Indeed that ~~That she is still a maid is almost certain. So no light from that quarter.~~ (EM, 03r)

The 'unity' referred to here can be read as the classical unity of time, with Haddon's death meaning we are no longer anywhere near the same era as when the story involving him took place. Indeed, the second draft mentions that Haddon is 'dead too' (EM, 04r), indicating that M is herself dead. The later mirrorings of May in Amy and V in Mrs Winter also suggest that unity of character is absent. However, V's phrase '~~**the old home**~~' does suggest a unity of place, as emphasized by a handwritten addition to the WU playscript which draws attention to this word: 'Why, ~~I~~in the old home' (03r). Such unity of place is an aspect of theatre famously exemplified in the work of Beckett's favourite French tragedian Jean Racine – it is developed in *Footfalls* to the point of intense confinement, cutting off M's contact with her '~~**admirers**~~'.

The passage was cut down in the second version, where important details nonetheless remain:

> In the old home, the same where she came into the world. (Pause.) **A general practitioner named Haddon**, dead too. (Pause.) Though always on the plain side she once had an admirer. (Pause.) That she is still a maid is almost certain. (EM, 04r)

Note that Haddon is a general practitioner, not a specialist obstetrician, making the trauma of M's birth the responsibility of the flaws of a specific human being, not a general tragic condition.

M's traumatic birth recalls Otto Rank's *Trauma of Birth*, which presents the primary goal of psychoanalysis as an attempt to 'undo' the birth trauma. As Beckett noted when reading Rank's book: 'Whole circle of human creation equals attempt to materialize primal situation, i.e., to undo primal trauma' (TCD MS 10971/8/35; Rank 1929, 103). Beckett's psychological image of birth was certainly influenced by Rank's intrauterine imagery (see lexia 9, chapter 4.1.2). However, as I have argued earlier, he did not absorb this image uncritically into his work. For instance, at the beginning of *The Trauma of Birth*, Rank used an epigraph from Nietzsche's *Birth of Tragedy*, in which King Midas hunts down the woodland deity Silenus in order to ask him: 'What is the very best and the most preferable thing for Man?' Silenus replies:

> Miserable, ephemeral species, children of chance and of hardship, why do you compel me to tell you what is most profitable for you not to hear? The very best is quite unattainable for you: it is, not to be born, not to exist, to be Nothing. But the next best for you is – to die soon. (Rank 1929, v; see Nietzsche 2007, 23)[314]

314 C. J. Ackerley points out that the Latin version of Silenus's statement was transcribed by Beckett in his 'Whoroscope' Notebook: 'Optimum non nasci, aut cito mori', which appears both in Burton's *Anatomy* and Geulincx's *Ethics* (UoR MS 3000, 87v; qtd. in Ackerley 2010, 69). I would like to thank Vincent Neyt for his help with this quotation.

But V does not subscribe to the universalist theory that it is best not to be born in any circumstances. Rather, there is a suggestion in these early drafts that the trauma of M's birth was caused by the failings of a particular human being who could have done a better job. A tension between the suffering of two individuals and the more universal – but never fully defined – 'it', already at this stage the final spoken pronoun of the play, is brought out in the edits made to the Haddon passage on ET2: '~~Made a mess of us~~ ~~**it.**~~ ~~Of us~~ ~~**it**~~ ~~(Pause.)~~ ~~Of~~ **~~us~~** His last mess' (ET2, 03r). The very name Haddon suggests a criticism of the medical profession, or of this particular doctor, who tries to 'have someone on' rather than helping them, something emphasized by the fact that M was '**fooled**' into the world in the first version, this term also standing as yet another indication of Beckett's interest in folly and unreason. The erasure of Haddon from ET3 (03r) moves the play towards a much bleaker perspective on birth and existence: when V asks M to 'forgive me again' for bringing her into the world, it now reads like a more general condemnation of birth.

In a maxim of Nicolas Chamfort's he included in a letter to Kay Boyle on 22 August 1973 (*LSB IV* 343), Beckett addresses directly the problem of tragedy:

> The trouble with tragedy is the fuss it makes
> About life and death and other tuppenny aches
>
> [Le théâtre tragique a le grand inconvénient moral de mettre trop d'importance à la vie et à la mort] (*CP* 197)[315]

Neither Beckett's translation nor Chamfort's original mentions 'birth' specifically, yet in the early drafts of *Footfalls*, birth is seen by V as the cause of the tragic situation of M's life. One could therefore see *Footfalls* as a reply to Chamfort: if tragedy is flawed because it makes too much fuss of life and death, Beckett will redesign tragedy so it focuses instead on birth itself, with living merely a kind of afterlife where one is never fully present. The question then becomes whether there is any relief from this trauma

315 Beckett's draft in the Burns Library, Boston College, has the open variants 'minor' and what looks like 'small' for 'tuppenny' (MS.1991.001, box 11, folder 10).

of birth. While for Rank, psychoanalysis could 'undo' the birth trauma, Beckett's tragedies seem to be closer to Nietzsche's view that we can merely 'learn to tolerate the knowledge' that life is not worth living (Nietzsche 2007, xi; see 115–16). This much can be seen in the structure of his plays.

In his schoolboy copy of *Macbeth*, Beckett copied Gustav Freytag's pyramid, which 'divided tragedies into five main parts (exposition, rising action, climax, falling action, dénouement)' (Van Hulle and Verhulst 2017a, 24).[316] As Van Hulle and Verhulst point out: 'Beckett's drawing offers an interesting variation on the pyramidal image of Freytag's scheme in that it presents the climax not as the high point or pinnacle of the play, but as a flat section or "anti-climax"', which they go on to argue is reflected in the structure of *Godot* and *All That Fall* (2017a, 24). Having used the Freytagian term 'turning-point' as a 'key word' in *That Time* – where it signals the protagonist's repeated, failed resolution to turn over a new leaf (see chapter 4.1.2) – in *Footfalls*, Beckett develops this structure even further. Both the repetitious nature of V's injections and the revolution of 'it all' in M's mind point to a temporal structure which, to quote Beckett's early-career analysis of the purgatorial aspect of Joyce's 'Work in Progress', 'is spherical and excludes culmination' (*Dis* 33). If there is a tragic turning point in *Footfalls*, it is one which has happened long ago and which cannot be retrieved by memory. In this, the play is closer to *Happy Days* and *Not I* than to Beckett's earlier theatre texts.

Enoch Brater has pointed out that the blocking of *Footfalls* turns what seems, from the audience's perspective, to be a linear pacing back and forth into a symbol of infinity when viewed from above. He goes on to link this to Beckett's review of Denis Devlin's poetry, in which Beckett states: 'If only the 8 in the last line had been left on its side. So: ∞' (*Dis* 93). As Brater mentions, the same infinity symbol is found in a draft of Beckett's short prose piece *The Way* in the Harry Ransom Center (1980; HRC CL SB MS 17/3; see Brater 1987, 62). The highly specific stage directions of *Footfalls* mean that this figure of 8 must be paced if they are to be followed:

316 See https://www.beckettarchive.org/library/SHA-MAC.html, tp1.

> *Pacing: starting with right foot (r), from right (R) to left (L), with left foot (l) from L to R. Turn: rightabout at L, leftabout at R.* (*KLT* 109)[317]

Given Beckett's self-proclaimed interest in 'the shape of ideas' (qtd. in Schneider 2005, 191), this infinity symbol can be seen as one of his attempts to find 'a form that accommodates the mess' of human existence through a reshaping of tragic structure (see chapter 2.2.2). If, in classical drama, the turning point of tragedy precipitates some kind of change in behaviour, for M and V the hellish world – like heaven in Beckett's short story 'Ding-Dong' – tends to go 'rowan an' rowan an' rowan' (*MPTK* 39).

Supporting this hypothesis, Ronan McDonald discerns in Beckett's recasting of tragedy the attempt 'to undo its traditional aesthetic consolations in order to come closer to an unmediated tragic condition' (2002, 27). As Burç İdem Dinçel points out, Beckett's tragic imagination is in line with George Steiner's concept of 'absolute tragedy', in which 'substantive truth is assigned to the Sophoclean statement that "it is best never to have been born"' (Steiner 1980, xi, qtd. in Dinçel 2019, 144).[318] Dinçel traces this back to the statement in *Proust* on tragedy:

> Tragedy is not concerned with human justice. Tragedy is the statement of an expiation, but not the miserable expiation of a codified breach of local arrangement, organized by the knaves for the fools. The tragic figure represents the expiation of original sin, of the original and eternal sin of him and all his 'socii malorum', the sin of having been born. (*PTD* 67, qtd. in Dinçel 2019, 148)[319]

317 The best way to understand Brater's argument is to pace the steps oneself.

318 The Sophocles reference is to *Oedipus at Colonus* (ll. 1225–8). I would like to thank Burç İdem Dinçel for sharing his unpublished research with me.

319 Beckett goes on to quote Calderón de la Barca's lines from *La vida es sueño* [*Life is a Dream*]: 'Pues el delito mayor / Del hombre es haber nacido' ['For the greatest crime of man is to have been born'] (*PTD* 67; trans. in Ackerley and Gontarski 2004, 61). The term 'socii malorum' is taken from Schopenhauer's 'Additional Remarks on the Doctrine of the Suffering of the World': 'the really proper address between one man and another should be,

Dinçel identifies this concept in the opening line of *A Piece of Monologue* – 'Birth was the death of him' (see chapter 2.2.2) – and in a line which appears in two of the *Fizzles*: 'I gave up before birth, it is not possible otherwise, but birth there had to be' (*TFN* 143, 145, qtd. in Dinçel 2019, 147).[320]

Drawing on this notion of birth as an 'absolute tragedy', Dinçel links Beckett's use of tragedy to the Jung lecture he attended in 1935 (2019, 148; see chapter 2.1.2). As Davyd Melnyk points out, Beckett's 'creative rewriting' of Jung's phrase 'She had never been born entirely' at different points in his career 'makes the incident his own as much as the phrase' (2005, 355, 357): from the addendum of *Watt* which simply reads 'never been properly born' (*W* 217) to Maddy Rooney's story in *All That Fall* of 'attending a lecture by one of these new mind doctors' (*ATF* 27).[321] Here the phrase becomes, in the mouth of the doctor Maddy heard: 'The trouble with her was she had never really been born!' (*ATF* 28). Maddy recounts that the doctor's young female patient 'did in fact die, shortly after he had washed his hands of her' (*ATF* 28). Maddy's recollection of the doctor standing as Pontius Pilate, washing his hands of the patient recalcitrant to his medical powers, casts the Jung anecdote in a critical light (Melnyk 2005, 358). This is consistent with Beckett's use of 'Haddon' as a punning critique of the medical profession and also with his critical attitude towards psychoanalysis more generally. While Beckett condemned psychoanalysis as a system by the end of his therapy with Bion (see Nixon 2011, 45), he returned to psychoanalytic reading material later in his career, reporting to Barbara Bray on 26 June 1959 that he was reading Ernest Jones's biography of Freud 'with great enjoyment', with special mention for the account of Freud's suffering towards the end

instead of *Sir*, *Monsieur*, and so on, *Leidensgefährte*, *socii malorum*, *compagnon de misères*, *my fellow-sufferer*' (2000, 304).

320 As mentioned in chapter 6.1.1, Beckett worked on both of these *Fizzles* in close proximity to his composition of *Footfalls*.

321 In response to Sighle Kennedy's memo of 30 October 1976 in which she mentioned six of Jung's works as 'interesting background for the "inner world" of Watt' – *On the Psychology of Dementia Praecox*, *Psychological Types*, *Modern Man in Search of a Soul*, 'The Relations between the Ego and the Unconscious', *Psychology of the Unconscious* and 'On the Psychogenesis of Schizophrenia' – Beckett replied: 'I may have dipped into some of the above prior to Watt. My reading of Jung was, to say the least, desultory & unconvinced. There is no trace of his thought in Watt as far as I know' (8 November 1976, *LSB IV* 441).

of his life (qtd. in Van Hulle and Nixon 2013, 212; see Jones 1957). He also accumulated biographical and epistolary works, including *The Freud/Jung Letters*.[322] Though there are no psychoanalytic textbooks preserved in his library, Beckett's interest in the biographical side of psychoanalysis lasted at least until the mid-1970s. Likewise, it is clear that Jung's psychoanalytic phrase stuck with him and proved a key creative impetus as a psychological image in later works like *Footfalls*. While it would be an over-reading to see *Footfalls* as an expression of Jung's psychoanalytic theories, the young girl Amy's awareness of her own lack of existence does resonate with the analyst's description in his lecture of an 'ethereal' child who cannot adapt to the world around her (see chapter 2.1.2).

When pressed during the Berlin rehearsals of *Tritte* by actor Hildegard Schmahl for information which would help her understand her role as May, Beckett responded by referencing Jung's lecture. In Walter Asmus's words, Beckett recounted Jung's 'astonishing explanation. This girl wasn't *living*. She existed but didn't actually live. According to Beckett, this story had impressed him very much at the time' (Asmus 1977, 83–4; emphasis in original).[323] The story came up again when Beckett discussed V's account of May's birth. In the first published edition, V's answer to her question about May's location is simply: 'In the old home, the same where she—— (*Pause.*) The same where she began. (*Pause.*)' (1976c, 11). Beckett stated at the Berlin rehearsals: 'She was going to say: "… the same where she was *born*".' But for Beckett this was not the case: 'It began. There is a difference. She was never born' (qtd. in Asmus 1977, 84; emphasis in original). In ET1, this line read: 'Where it began ~~**for her**~~', the deletion moving the sentence away from the sense of suffering solely belonging to M and putting more focus on the indeterminate 'it' that comes to dominate the

322 As well as Jones's three-volume *Sigmund Freud: Life and Work* (London: Hogarth Press, 1953; https://www.beckettarchive.org/library/JON-SIG.html) and *The Freud/Jung Letters: The Correspondence between Sigmund Freud and C. G. Jung* (Princeton: Princeton University Press, 1974; https://www.beckettarchive.org/library/FRE-FRE.html), Beckett also owned copies of Sigmund Freud, *Briefe, 1873–1939* (Frankfurt am Main: S. Fischer Verlag, 1960; https://www.beckettarchive.org/library/FRE-BRI.html) and Octave Mannoni, *Freud* (Paris: Éditions du Seuil, 1968; *BDL*).

323 Beckett told Whitelaw the same story when rehearsing the play with her (1996, 142).

dialogue (03r). This tension between specificity and 'vaguening' is evident in other edits to the same passage. V's next question is typically wordy in the first version: '~~Let us pass on now and ask, When did this begin?~~ ~~**Shall we say, In girlhood?**~~ ~~xxx~~ ~~**Well before puberty?**~~' (EM, 03r). The second version cuts this down considerably, but does include a reference to what 'this' might be (though the word itself is hard to read): 'When did this ~~behaviour~~ ~~begin~~ ~~start~~ begin?' (EM, 04r). One can see that Beckett struggled with the sentence as he refashioned it on ET3: **'~~But this~~ But this, ~~it may be asked,~~ this,** ~~W~~ when did <u>**this**</u> begin?' (03r). On the Faber page proofs, it appears as: 'But **this, this,** when did this begin?' (PPF, 06r). The repetition of 'this' gets us no closer to the missing referent, standing as another example of additional textual material 'vaguening' the interpretive process (see chapter 2.2.2). In this, it foreshadows the use of the term in *what is the word*:

> what is the word –
> this this –
> this this here –
> all this this here – (*CP* 228)

As we will see in chapter 6.2.2, the translation of this phrase in the manuscripts of *Pas* also has interesting resonances with the French version of this poem, *Comment dire*, with the emphasis put firmly on the inability to express what the pronoun points towards.

V's next question provides a sporting detail which would fit the picture of an upper-middle class upbringing in many Anglophone countries, including Beckett's birthplace of Ireland: '~~And that when other girls of her age were out playing **hockey**, or otherwise revelling in life, she was at this selfsame place where you see her now, now still and outwardly calm, now pacing back & forth, back & forth, with tread more measured than at sentry-go?~~' (EM, 03r). In the second version, another sport is added: 'When other girls of her age were out at hockey **& lacrosse** she was already here' (EM, 04r). By this stage, Beckett had composed Scene III, in which M tells a story about walking along the transept of a Church, comparing this to Christ's arm on the crucifix (see Scene III, section A). Whitelaw recalls Beckett telling her that he included 'lacrosse' 'just because he liked the sound of it and because it conjured up the image of the cross' (qtd. in Brater 1987, 57). On ET3, the first sport is cut and an added ellipsis helps highlight the biblical resonances: '~~at hockey and~~ at … lacrosse' (ET3, 03r).

Beckett often tempered the metatheatrical elements of his plays, removing references to the audience and other metatheatrical features of *Endgame*, both before and after publication (Van Hulle and Weller 2018, 182, 338). However, as Van Hulle and Verhulst point out with regard to the 'vaguening' of *Godot*'s translation, such metatheatre is sometimes 'evoked more subtly' in the later stages of textual development, rather than being erased completely (2017a, 280). We can also see this increasingly subtle approach towards metatheatre in Beckett's development as a playwright, moving as he did from the overt breaking of the fourth wall in *Eleutheria*, with its invading Spectator, to the hints and allusions to the audience in *Godot* and *Endgame*. Metatheatre is still important in Beckett's late theatre, with M in *Play* asking if he is 'being seen' (*KLT* 64) and Mouth in *Not I* referencing stage mechanics such as the spotlight, albeit obliquely (see chapter 2.2.2). Metatheatre is, as we shall see below, still quite prominent in the published text of *Footfalls*, but Beckett did delete a reference to the audience from his early drafts. In the first version, V states: '~~The floor here, now bare **as some** of **you may see**, was once –~~' (EM, 03r). By the second version, the text in bold is gone: 'The floor here, now bare, was once – ' (EM, 04r). In a good example of the centrality of other body sounds over speech in the play, M's steps interrupt the sentence, with their audibility stressed in early drafts: 'Steps **audible** as before' (ET2, 03r).

Scene II, section C: 'But let us watch her move, in silence.' (1976c, 11)

Footfalls may be Beckett's 'pacing play', but he deleted an explicit reference to M's pacing while writing it. The second version of V's monologue reads: 'But let us watch her **pace** in silence' (EM, 04r). In ET1, this becomes: 'But let us watch her **move** in si~~m~~lence' (03r). M's pacing was given a more detailed description in the first version: '~~See with what grace she wheels, **now deasil, now withershins**, and, when she halts, how always facing xxx the wall, to gaze before her with **unseeing eyes**~~' (EM, 03r). In his analysis of Beckett's use of antiquarian language in *How It Is*, Scott Eric Hamilton argues that archaic terms like 'deasil' – which shows up across Beckett's oeuvre to describe clockwise motion – constitute 'a turn against the processional movement of time within any modern linear historical construct' (2018, 173). M's 'unseeing eyes' likewise call to mind Beckett's earlier, novelistic critique of scientific progress in the area of psychiatry. When Murphy comes face to face with Mr Endon in the climactic scene of his eponymous novel, he sees himself reflected in eyes whose unseeing is the marker of madness.[324] While in *Murphy* narrative distance from the main protagonist allows us to see Murphy's hero-worship of Mr Endon's schizophrenia in a critical light, *Footfalls* gives us no such distance from its narrated subject. Indeed, as we have seen, the narrator V was at this stage of the compositional process clearly a figment of M's imagination, making M and V part of one and the same mind. In the course of the play's genesis, Beckett would 'vaguen' such details, resulting in a critique of the objective narrative position associated with naturalism, famously expressed in Émile Zola's call for an aesthetic of 'scientific investigation' which would produce naturalist novels of 'observation and experiment'. For Zola, 'Determinism dominates everything' (1893, 18). For Beckett, it is indeterminacy which holds sway. Instead of allowing us to diagnose M's 'unseeing eyes' as symptoms of a mental disorder, the genesis of *Footfalls* progressively questions the idea that such details can be read diagnostically.

In the second version, this sentence became: '~~With what grace she wheels~~ ~~See how Watch~~ See **how feat she wheels**' (EM, 04r). Here, Beckett draws on another archaism: the word 'feat' is rare enough as an adjective, but as he noted in a letter to Anne Atik in 1983, it is even rarer in the adverbial form used here:

> Thank you for feat (adj.) examples. Few of adverbial use. My compact OED gives, from The Lover's Complaint, "With slei~~x~~ded (sleaved) silk feat & affectedly enswath'd". ([? 7] November 1983, qtd. in Atik 2001, 56)[325]

324 Murphy goes on to call himself 'a speck in Mr. Endon's unseen' (*Mu* 156).
325 For an alternative dating of this letter, see Van Hulle and Nixon (2013, 194).

Though seemingly not a part of the genesis as Beckett wrote the play, his reference to Shakespeare's *Lover's Complaint* is ironic here, given that it relates the story of a girl who tells the poem's speaker: 'Too early I attended / A youthful suit' (ll. 78–9). Though M, like Shakespeare's woman's lover, 'sexes both enchanted' (l. 128), she is now alone – and may have been for a long time.

In a separation of the spoken text from the stage directions, Beckett changed the stage direction '**~~wheels~~**' to 'turns' in ET1 (04r) so that it no longer mirrored exactly V's preceding spoken lines. In this, the text becomes slightly less oriented towards the reader, removing a repetition only available on the page. Beckett initially had V count each of M's steps: '**~~One two three four five six seven wheel, one two three four five six seven wheel.~~** ~~(Pacing continues)~~ ~~Dix till M halts at same point as at curtainside~~' (EM, 03r).[326] This became shorter in subsequent versions, with the numbers also being changed: '**Two three four five** ...' is what appears in the second version (EM, 04r). ET1 adds a figure: '~~Two~~ **three four five** six ...' (03r). Therefore, Beckett's later edit to RC playscript.B can be seen as a (partial) return to material from his first draft: '~~Three, four, five~~ ~~six seven~~ 7 8 9 wheel' (03r). As discussed in chapter 5.5.1, this is a rare instance in which the counting of the steps in Faber's 1977 *Ends and Odds* reflects Grove's *Ends and Odds*, which incorporates the changes from RC playscript.B.

With the description of the floor that follows, Beckett can be seen to have made his work more metatheatrical in an edit to his first version: '~~Now to return to this~~ ~~strip~~ ~~stretch~~ ~~of floor, once it was carpeted, a deep pile~~' (EM, 03r). Beckett chose 'strip' from the second version onwards (EM, 04r), echoing directly the '***Strip***' mentioned in the stage directions (*KLT* 109). Given this printed stage direction is only available to readers of the text, perhaps 'metafictional' would be the more commonly chosen term here, associated as it is with textual creativity, often set in opposition to performance practice in the theatre. However, as we will shortly see, the textual and the theatrical – though distinct – are deeply intertwined in the genesis of *Footfalls*.

326 Beckett may have started writing 'Ditto' at the start of the last sentence, but stopped at the third letter, which is illegible.

Scene II, section D: Mother–M dialogue (1976c, 11)

The beginning of M's reported dialogue with her mother was initially part of the previous sentence. However, on ET4, Beckett separated it into a sentence of its own: '~~t~~T~~x~~ill one day, while still little more than a child, she called her mother and said, Mother, this is **not enough**' (03r). As in the first draft of Haddon anecdote, the mother's response in the first version mentions the death of one of the characters: '~~What do you mean, Mary, said the mother,~~ ~~**incidentally long gone to her account**~~~~, what can you possibly mean, Mary, not enough?~~' (EM, 03r). This reference to death is removed from the second version (EM, 04r), 'vaguening' V's state of being.

The rest of this section is remarkably close to the published text in all versions, though there is one instance, before Beckett had settled on his title, in which he removed an echo of 'footfalls' from the dialogue. In the first version, M replies: '~~No, mother, she said, I must hear xxx the~~ ~~**feet**~~~~, however faint they~~ ~~**fall**~~' (EM, 03r). However, the second version ends with (what looks like) 'faint they **sound**' (04r), before returning to '**fall**' in ET1 (03r) and subsequent versions. In ET2, Beckett considered – but then deleted – '~~**steps**~~' as a replacement for '**feet**', emphasizing the body in the term eventually used in the published text (03r; *KLT* 111).

Scene II, section E: 'Does she still sleep, it may be asked?' (1976c, 11)

V's answer to her own question provided an opportunity for Beckett to develop echoes between scenes. In the first version, this answer was shorter than it eventually became in the published text, making this an exception to Beckett's general process of 'verbal undoing': '~~Does she ever utter now? still sleep?~~ ~~**In fits & starts,**~~ ~~bows her head till it rests against the wall and~~ ~~**gets**~~ ~~a little light sleep~~' (EM, 03r). In ET1, the answer was changed: '**Yes, in snatches**, bows her head against the wall and **snatches** a little sleep' (03r). This provided the basis for a change on ET2, creating an echo between V's monologue and M and V's earlier dialogue in Scene I: 'Will you not try to **snatch** a little sleep?' (01r). The notable instance of addition comes in ET4, where Beckett made the sentence longer by adding a phrase: 'Yes, some nights she does, in snatches, bows her head against the wall and snatches a little sleep' (03r). V's answer to the next question again shows the concept of fancy being brought into play over the course of the genesis.

The second version reads: 'Still speak? Yes, ~~it is thought~~ some nights she does, when she **thinks** none can hear' (EM, 04r). This is changed on ET2: 'Yes, some nights she does, when she **fancies** none can hear' (03r).[327] The closing stage directions of Scene II were added on the early typescripts, with the only change of note coming when the steps are again stopped altogether on RC playscript.B: 'Steps ~~**silent**~~ cease', with Beckett perhaps having realized in the theatre that 'Steps silent' could be interpreted in multiple ways (03r; see also 02r). Here, Beckett's creation of a 'vaguened' stage image requires specific stage directions.

Scene III: M's Monologue

Scene III, section A: 'Sequel.' (1976c, 12)

When supervising the translation of *Footfalls* into German, Beckett made an interesting decision with regard to the first spoken word of May's monologue. As Walter Asmus reports, 'Beckett says that "Sequel" was first translated by "Epilog" (epilogue) but he found "Folge" (continuation) better' (1977, 85). As Julian Garforth points out, 'This final German version suggests the concept of an unending process – hence Voice's question, "Will you never have done?" The French, "epilogue", and the original German, "Epilog", suggest that the situation has a finite conclusion' (1996, 55). The manuscripts reveal that Beckett had already been through this decision process while drafting the English text. The original word choice in the first version was the more conclusive '~~Epilogue~~', which he then struck out and replaced with 'Appendix', suggesting something which is added on (EM, 05r). Beckett liked the punning capability of 'Sequel' ('seek well') and this may have been why he chose it (Asmus 1977, 85), along with the fact that it also suggests continuation and a move towards infinite 'revolving' rather than simply ending.

M's self-revisions were even more prominent in the first draft, such as when she asked herself this closing question: 'Some 5 years later, when it was as though she had never been, ~~as indeed of course she scarcely had,~~ **but had she? (Pause.)**

327 As 'fancy' comes into prominence in Scene III, it will be discussed in detail below.

Had she? (Pause.)’ (EM, 05r).[328] This question was integrated as a conditional in ET1: ‘Some few years later, when it was all as though she had never been, **if she ever had**, she began to walk’ (04r). The revisions to ET3 perform a delicate pronominal balancing act between ‘it’ and ‘she’: ‘~~Some few years~~ A little later, when **~~it~~** it was ~~all~~ as though **~~it~~** she had never been, **~~she had~~** it never been, **she** began to walk’ (04r). While in EM and ET1 the focus is on M’s liminal state of previous existence, the introduction of ‘it’ in ET3 puts focus on the vagueness of the thing M revolves in her mind. In the genesis of *Not I*, Beckett deleted ‘it’ from the phrase ‘it can’t go on’ to express a sense of ambiguity with regard to Mouth’s suffering. In that instance, I cited William James’s contention that the fundamental fact of psychology is that ‘*consciousness of some sort goes on*’ (see chapter 2.2.2). James goes on to argue: ‘If we could say in English “it thinks”, as we say “it rains” or “it blows”, we should be stating the fact most simply and with the minimum of assumption’ (1992, 153). In the above revisions to *Footfalls*, Beckett seems to be trying to say ‘it goes on’, with all the negative connotations attached to that phrase when spoken in isolation.

An important part of M ‘revolving it all’ involves her revising her text as she speaks it. Beckett addressed this explicitly when advising Schmahl at the Berlin rehearsals: ‘You are composing. It is not a story, but an improvisation. You are looking for the words, you correct yourself constantly’ (Asmus 1977, 86). Diamond contends: ‘Given Beckett’s tight control over his texts, it is amazing that he uses the word “improvisation” even as a directorial suggestion in the privacy of a rehearsal. For to improvise implies not merely access to the symbolic but an ability to play with and in language’ (2004, 55–6). Though Beckett’s ‘you’ is ambiguous in his statement, potentially referring to Schmahl, M or an amalgam of the two, it seems that he wants the monologue to be *played* as if it is being improvised. This would then make the monologue a *performance* of a character accessing the symbolic realm, rather than a performance actually constituted by improvisation.

M is a reviser of her own text in the very first draft: ‘She would enter the little church by the south door, always closed at that hour, and walk slowly up & down – (**Pause.**) **and walk up and down at normal walking pace, neither fast nor slow,** the corresponding transept’

328 As M changes name from Mary to May on ET3, I have decided to use the initialism of both names as it appears on Beckett’s manuscripts.

(EM, 05r). In the first typescript, however, this self-revision is absent, perhaps because M's revision to 'normal pace' goes against the concept of the play containing 'Only **regressions**' (ET1, 04r; see above). On RC playscript.B, Beckett shifted the door's position: 'Slip out at nightfall and into the little church by the ~~**south**~~ ~~by the s~~ ~~xx~~ **north** door, always locked at that hour, and walk, up and down, up and down, his poor arm' (04r). Beckett explained to Schmahl: 'South Door is too warm, North Door is colder. You feel cold. The whole time, in the way you hold your body too. Everything is frost and night' (Asmus 1977, 85). It is worth pointing out that Asmus's text is translated from German, but Beckett's use of 'frost' here (or its German equivalent) is nonetheless relevant given the appearance of Mrs Winter later in the same scene. When we recall that 'M[rs] Frost' makes an appearance in one of the 'Kilcool' drafts (see chapter 2.1.1), the female characters of Beckett's late theatre begin to look decidedly wintery, with the deathlike quality of their lives qualified only by the fact that they will have to do 'it all' again in the seasons yet to come, as the exception of May's own spring-like name suggests.

Even more than *Not I* and *That Time*, *Footfalls* relies heavily on religious imagery. Beckett told Colin Duckworth: 'Christianity is a mythology with which I am perfectly familiar, so naturally I use it' (qtd. in Duckworth 1966, lvii). Beckett's use of the Christian 'mythology', which, like 'the mythology of psychoanalysis' (Baker 2001), he was quite happy to subvert, is evident in an architectural edit to the same sentence of M's monologue. In ET3, Beckett personified the reference to the church layout: '~~the corresponding arm~~ up & down, **His poor arm**' (04r). Beckett had already described the layout of the Magdalen Mental Mercyseat in *Murphy* in 'the terms and orientation of church architecture', even referring to 'transepts' which show up (in singular form) in the first draft of *Footfalls*.[329] Jesus's crucified body, which informs the layout of Christian churches, was therefore present by implication in the early novel. But Beckett makes it more explicit in the later play, drawing attention to the similarities between his female 'M' character and the first in his series of 'M' characters. By also introducing the idea that the door was **'locked'** on the same typescript (ET3, 04r), Beckett gave another glancing allusion to the carceral asylum of *Murphy*. But the primary meaning this

329 'the layout of the ward was that of nave and **transepts**, with nothing east of the crossing' (*Mu* 105).

carceral addition brings to the text is that M is able to pass through locked doors, as a ghost would. In spite of the carceral hints in this passage, there is no indication anywhere in the drafts that M is actually locked up in an institution.

The capital 'H' in '**Him**' disappeared from later drafts, only to reappear on RC playscript.C (04r) and the WU playscript (04r). As Knowlson points out in his cover note to *Footfalls*(SB), stored with the document at the University of Reading, this capital letter is missing from Faber's *Ends and Odds* (1977a, 36), in spite of the fact that Beckett inserted it on the annotated copy he prepared for this edition (*Footfalls*(SB), 12). As the capital 'H' cannot be heard in performance, its inclusion adds an extra layer of meaning for the text's readers (*TN4* 285n136). Van Hulle and Verhulst have identified Beckett's move 'from a text-oriented to a more stage-oriented approach' in the genesis of *Godot* (2017a, 40). As is evident from the significant changes made to the text of *Footfalls* in performance, this 'stage-oriented approach' is central to Beckett's later theatre practice. But the importance here of orthography in the process of interpretation is an indication of the degree to which text-oriented and stage-oriented approaches work in tandem in his later plays.

The imagery of confinement continues in the first draft, where M's physical stasis is imagined using a carceral mental simile: 'Sometimes she would halt, ~~**like**~~ as **one arrested by some thought**, and stand quite still more or less long – (pause) – **longly** – (pause) – quite still more or less **longly** before moving on again, at the same speed. **But not always**' (EM, 05r). The nonstandard 'longly' here draws attention to M as a linguistic relic of times past, while the final qualifying sentence stands as yet another revision to her story. Both were cut from ET1, in which Beckett changed the description of thought from one focussing on an object ('thing') to focussing on an action ('motion'): 'as one frozen by some~~**thing in**~~ motion of the mind' (ET, 04r). In ET3, this '~~**motion**~~' became the more ghostly 'phantom' (04r), while RC playscript.A pairs the wintery '**frozen**' with an equally icy noun, returning to the idea of mental movement within ice-bound physical stasis: 'Sometimes she would halt, as one **frozen** by some **shudder** of the mind and stand **stock** still till she could move again' (05r). In ET4, the adjective describing M's stillness was replaced by one which collocates with madness, something already alluded to in the text: '~~stock~~ stark' (04r). This lack of motion is firmly nailed into the text by the deletion of the propulsive adverb 'on', leaving her 'stock still till she could ~~**move on again**~~ ~~pass on~~ **move again'** from ET3 onwards (04r).[330] While Beckett removed a reference to M's pacing in the genesis of Scene II, he added one to M's own monologue, where the mention of (what looks like) her '~~walk~~' is replaced by **'pacing'** (EM, 05r). On the same draft, the edited description of the pacing which 'continued ~~without interruption~~ **unbroken'** draws attention again to the corporeal image of Christ's broken body on the cross (EM, 05r). However, this was changed again on ET3, where the pacing is subject to another instance of textual expansion: '~~the pacing continued unbroken, till she vanished~~ **she paced without pause up & down, up & down, before vanishing'** (04r). On ET4, M's perambulatory '~~**evenings**~~' darken into **'nights'**, deepening the already wintery atmosphere of the monologue, with M's '**vanishing**' foregrounding her ghostly character (04r).

Scene III, section B: 'No sound.' (1976c, 12)

On ET3, Beckett added a phrase in the margin to describe the kind of light needed to see M: 'Faint, but by no means invisible, in a certain light. (Pause.) ~~**Given**~~ **Granted the right light.** (Pause.)' (04r). The replacement of **'~~given~~'** with **'granted'** here again suggests that M is a ghost, recalling as it does a Christian prayer commonly recited at funerals: 'Rest eternal **grant** unto them, O Lord: and let **light** perpetual shine upon them' (*BCP 1928*, 468).[331] This would indeed be, for Christians, the 'right light' in which to be seen after death, as it represents eternal life in the presence of God. Though this prayer does not appear in the 1926 *Book of Common Prayer* used by the Church of Ireland, to which Beckett's family belonged, it is included in the 1928 *Proposed Book of Common Prayer* of the Church of England, rejected by the UK Parliament but still widely used in the Anglican communion, including by some 'high church' parishes of the Church of Ireland. As the

330 What looks like '~~on~~' is also erased on ET2 (04r), though the erasure is so heavy that it is difficult to read.

331 It is a popular prayer in the Roman Catholic Church, of which many of Beckett's close friends were part, though I have not yet come across any record of Beckett attending Roman Catholic funerals. I would like to thank Andrew Pierce, Kevin Moroney, Ken Mawhinney, James Knowlson, Edward Beckett, Feargal Whelan and Archbishop Michael Jackson for their kind help in researching this prayer and its relation to Church of Ireland liturgy.

printed liturgy of the Church of Ireland strictly excludes prayers for the dead, Beckett would have been very unlikely to hear this prayer at services in Tullow Church, where he and his brother were brought by their devout mother. However, Beckett did later attend services with his father Bill in the more liberal All Saints' Church, Blackrock. As Beckett recalled: 'The All Saints' Church in Blackrock was fairly high. But our own church [Tullow] was fairly low' (qtd. in Knowlson and Knowlson 2006, 16–17), suggesting there may have been 'high church' rituals – such as prayers for the dead – at the church Beckett attended with his father.[332] This is all but confirmed by a tribute to the recently deceased Bill Beckett in the August 1933 edition of *Our Church Review*. Written by his friend the Rev. Henry Dobbs, vicar of All Saints', this text ends with the very prayer Beckett alluded to in his *Footfalls* manuscripts decades later: 'May Light Perpetual shine upon him' (1933, 166).[333] So, if we are to speak of Beckett – as Joyce's Stephen Dedalus is referred to by Buck Mulligan in *Ulysses* – as someone who has a religious strain 'injected the wrong way' (1986, 7), then this strain is not pure, but also contains elements of more liberal Anglican liturgy, performed as part of religious service, which would not have been part of the official, printed Church of Ireland liturgy.

As Erik Tonning puts it, Beckett's 'work remains haunted by the repeating gesture of overcoming-Christianity-by-negation' (2019, 214). But having already had Hamm declare God a 'bastard' who 'doesn't exist' in *Endgame* (*E* 34), it is unlikely that any of the above liturgical nuances influenced Beckett's decision to remove the prayer allusion, reverting to the earlier

332 The quantity surveying firm 'J. and W. Beckett Builders' (Knowlson 1997, 6), part-owned by Beckett's paternal grandfather, built All Saints' Church, which may have contributed to the author's interest in church architecture (http://www.churchnewsireland.org/news/irish-uk-news/irish-news-digest-13/). Beckett returned to All Saints' with his mother in 1948, hearing there of the death of a parishioner called 'Mr Frost', which foreshadows the names of some of his draft stage characters (see below and chapter 2.1.1). On that occasion, there was no prayer for the dead, as Beckett related in a letter to Georges Duthuit: 'The parson announced: "Mr Frost, loved and respected by us all, entered life yesterday morning, funeral tomorrow"' (2 August 1948, *LSB II* 92).

333 I would like to thank Ken Mawhinney for bringing this text to my attention and for sharing it with me.

'**Given**' from RC playscript.A onwards (06r).[334] It is probably rather the allusion to eternal comfort that made the term unsuitable – M is not a character to be granted the respite of eternal salvation. What this example shows is the extent to which liturgical tradition is malleable and multiple in Beckett's works, as much a creative 'mythology' as the psychoanalysis he took notes on in the wake of his father's death.

ET3 also features a change of M's described appearance: '~~**Ragged**~~ Tattered (<u>Pause</u>.) A tangle of ~~**rags**~~ tatters. (<u>Pause</u>.) A faint tangle of pale grey ~~**rags**~~ tatters' (04r). While the terms '**ragged**' and '**rags**' suggest poverty – as in the Ragged Schools for destitute children established in 19th-century Ireland and Britain – Beckett's alternative moves from a term connoting physical destitution to one which alliterates with 'tangle' (ET3, 04r). This may appear to be a rare instance of Beckett moving emphasis away from the body in the drafts of *Footfalls*, reducing emphasis on the destitution of its appearance onstage, a destitution only reinforced by the ragged costume design of Jocelyn Herbert in the play's first production (see Haynes and Knowlson 2003, 44).[335] However, by choosing an alliterative variant, Beckett also brings the text closer to the body, drawing attention to what Mouth in *Not I* calls 'the lips ... the cheeks ... the jaws ... the whole face ... all those – ... what? ... the tongue? ... yes ... the tongue in the mouth ... all those contortions without which ... no speech possible' (*KLT* 89). Instead of using the terms '~~**Ragged**~~' and '~~**rags**~~', which have associations with institutions of material poverty and the bodies they contain, Beckett's use of 'Tattered' and 'tatters' here foregrounds the performing body we hear onstage, reciting the alliterative phrase before us in the theatre.

The next line sees M revising herself, correcting an inanimate pronoun to a personal pronoun: 'Watch **it** – (<u>Pause</u>.) Watch **her** pass before ~~**a**~~ the candelabrum, how ~~**the**~~ its flames, **the**ir light ~~of the flames~~...like moon through passing cloud' (ET3, 04r).[336] In this version from ET3, it is

334 Beckett alluded to his own line in a letter to A. J. Leventhal of 24 September 1978, when he told his friend of smoking and drinking Scotch while rehearsing *Endgame* in a church: 'The bastard took no notice' (*LSB IV* 489).

335 A production note by Beckett in his list of '<u>Diminuendo</u>[s]' seems to indicate his involvement in – or at least approval of – this costume design: 'M's semblance (more tattered)?' (RC Nb, 03r).

336 My use of the phrase 'revising herself' is indebted to S. E. Gontarski's 1998 article: 'Revising Himself: Performance as Text in Samuel Beckett's Theatre'.

notable that articles and pronouns are also revised in Beckett's own drafting process, making this an instance where his characters' attention to such parts of speech – as in the Unnamable's declaration that 'it's the fault of the pronouns' (*Un* 123) – is mirrored by their author's attention to detail in this regard. Rather than referring to M's 'semblance', as the pronoun 'it' would, the personal pronoun 'her' reminds us that we are dealing with a human – or once-human – body described in M's story. Nevertheless, by leaving M's own pronominal revision in the published text of the monologue (*KLT* 112), Beckett reinforces the sense of M 'passing' between embodiment and disembodiment, as does this adjective, added by hand in the draft quoted above. In ET4, '~~**cloud**~~' became 'rack' (04r) and on RC playscript.B Beckett added an ellipsis to draw attention to this final term: 'like moon through passing···**rack**' (04r; see also GG, 13r). Though not an archaism, the old-fashioned 'rack' again gives the sense that M's story, as well as being told *of* the past, is one being told *in* the past. The term also elevates the register to something more poetic. This may be related to the fact that this story is M's 'improvisation', in which she is searching for suitable, sometimes recherché, language. Suitably enough for an oeuvre which ends with a poem entitled *what is the word* – which Beckett marked 'Keep! for end' on one of his compositional manuscripts (*BDMP1*, UoR MS 3316/1, 02r) – Beckett's work is often a search for the 'right word', as in his narrator's snide put-down when Wylie describes Murphy's 'surgical quality': 'It was not quite the right word' (*Mu* 41). Beckett's manuscripts provide insight into the authorial search for the *mot juste*. In an instance such as this one, we can see how he used punctuation to draw attention to M's search for the 'right word'.

A later edit opts for rhythmic repetition over a more technical description of the church building in which M paced: '~~Thus not long~~ soon then ~~h~~afterhaving gone, as though never ~~**been**~~ there, began to walk, ~~**along the south transept, up and down, at nightfall.**~~ up & down, up & down, ~~His~~ that poor arm' (ET3, 04r). However, important as echoes are, the repetition of '~~His~~', already mentioned in the preceding text, was perhaps too clunky here, with Beckett choosing the inanimate pronoun 'that' instead. The change of '~~**been**~~' to 'there' sets up an echo with the later dialogue between Mrs Winter and Amy, in which Amy claims she was 'not **there**' during Evensong (see Scene III, section C). On the same typescript in which 'evensong' was inserted into the Mrs Winter–Amy dialogue, Beckett replaced it with another prayer service in M's earlier monologue:

‘That is to say, at certain seasons of the year, during ~~**evensong**~~ Vespers’ (ET3, 04r).[337] This was presumably done in order to ‘vaguen’ the links between the two stories as well as the characters within them, again going against the general pattern of increasing echoes. The sibilant assonance of ‘**certain** ~~periods~~ seasons’, created by a supralinear addition on ET1 (04r), once more foregrounds the fact that M’s monologue is a performance text within a performance text, written to be spoken by its author and, as discussed below, possibly also written by his character. Indeed, the phrase recalls the Animator’s praise of the ‘sibilant’ text read by Fox in *Rough for Radio II* (*ATF* 63), which Beckett translated in 1975 as he was composing *Footfalls* (Pilling 2006, 198).[338] This assonance is reinforced by the addition of a new, one-word sentence on the same typescript: ‘**Necessarily**’ (ET1, 04r). The section ends with further pacing, introduced as a marginal addition on ET1: ‘**Paces ~~x~~½L+. Halts at r2. P**’ (04r). This movement breaks up the text, setting the scene for its concluding story.

Scene III, section C: Mrs Winter–Amy dialogue (1976c, 12–13)

Female writers are a notable rarity in Beckett’s canon, but *Rough for Radio II* does feature a bullied female Stenographer, under the thumb of her male boss (a situation replayed in *Catastrophe*). In Berlin, Beckett outlined a scenario in which May was a writer oriented towards a future, imagined reader, rather than responding to the misogynist whims of a male authority figure in the storyworld:

> One can suppose that she [M] has written down everything which she has invented up to this, that she will one day find a reader for her story – therefore the address to the reader ‘Mrs Winter, whom the reader will remember …’ (Asmus 1977, 86).

337 I am grateful to Archbishop Michael Jackson for confirming (via his secretary Ruth Burleigh) that the tradition of religious practice in Portora, his Alma Mater, was not High Church, in spite of involving ‘a form of evening prayer for the boarders led by the Head Master’ (email from Ruth Burleigh, 6 May 2020).

338 Like the names May and Mrs Winter, the sibilant passage in *Rough for Radio II* refers to seasons of growth and death: ‘**such summers missed**, such **winters**’ (*ATF* 63).

This reference to the reader was present from the very first draft as a self-correction: Mrs Winter, **whom the reader will remember**, Mrs Winter, one ~~October~~ autumn Sunday evening ~~in October~~, on sitting down to supper ~~with xx~~ with her daughter after worship, after a few half-hearted mouthfuls laid down her knife and fork & ~~gazed before her~~ **bowed her head'** (EM, 05r). In addition to the metatextual reference, it is also worth noting here the **'bowed'** posture of Mrs Winter, familiar from the confined spaces of *All Strange Away* and 'He Is Barehead' ('Il est tête nue', 1972; *TFN* 73–6, 135), later used in the oppressive scenarios of *Catastrophe* (1982) and *What Where* (*Quoi où*, 1983) (*KLT* 143, 153). Here, the bowed head signals Mrs Winter's memory of something she observed at Evensong which will be the undisclosed subject of the ensuing conversation.

In his RC Nb, Beckett considered replacing 'reader': 'Whom as the **hearer** will remember?' (01r), perhaps with his Royal Court audience in mind.[339] However, this variant never made its way into any of the drafts or published editions, leaving the reference to *Footfalls* as a printed text in the published text. Along the continuum from a 'text-oriented' to a 'stage-oriented approach', we might see this as evidence of the theatre being used to play with the boundaries between text and performance. In 1976, with years of avant-garde theatre behind them, the first-run audience of the Royal Court were unlikely to furiously search their copy of RC playscript.A for the preceding reference to Mrs Winter. Rather, M's reference to the reader is an accepted part of the game played between author, theatre practitioners and audience when staging a performance text. If the metatheatrical references to the audience in *Godot* and *Endgame* focussed on stretching the fourth wall between performers and audience, Beckett's late theatre plays with the distinction between text and performance, showing how the two are deeply imbricated without ever collapsing one into another.[340] In this sense, to borrow the title of McMullan's 1993 monograph *Theatre on Trial*, Beckett's later theatre also puts textuality on trial. Consider *Ohio Impromptu*, which

339 'Whom' and 'as' are bracketed together; 'hearer' is underlined twice.

340 In the unperformed *Eleutheria*, these metatheatrical references are even more explicit, with the Spectator referring to the author after he storms the stage: 'Beckett (*il dit*: "*Béquet*") Samuel, Béquet, Béquet, ça doit être un juif groenlandais mâtiné d'Auvergnat' ['he must be a cross between a Jew from Greenland and a peasant from the Auvergne'] (2008a, 136; 1996, 136).

features a printed text onstage, read by a Reader to a Listener. As McMullan notes, the play draws attention to the tension between pairs of elements such as stage and text (2005, 108), deriving its dramatic energy from placing them in opposition. However, it also 'challenges any fixed boundaries which the emphasis on oppositional pairings may at first suggest', particularly through its staging of some of the actions of the monologue, something which also occurs in *Footfalls* (2005, 112). Importantly, the boundaries between the onstage performance event and the performance text which gives rise to it are present in Beckett's plays, otherwise it would make no difference as to whether he chose 'reader' or 'listener' in M's monologue. Her reference to the reader is part of a broader strategy in Beckett's work which undermines such categorical distinctions without ever completely erasing the difference between the two.

M's next line is subject to an instructive instance of 'undoing', which shows that there are limits to what can be stripped away from a Beckett text. The first draft reads: 'What is it, mother, said the daughter, a that very **strange** girl – though hardly a girl any more ... (**Brokenly**) ~~**Terribly**~~ Dreadfully **unhappy ...**' (EM, 05r). This gives us a psychological background worthy of realist theatre, with the proximity of the two terms suggesting that the daughter's '**strange**' nature is connected to her '**unhappy**' state. In ET3, however, Beckett undid this psychological background, leaving M's state of mind undefined: 'Dreadfully **un~~happy~~** -...' (04r). The prefix 'un' is missing on the Faber page proofs Beckett corrected: 'dreadfully––' (PPF, 06v). It is therefore also missing from Faber's first edition (1976c, 12). However, we can presume its omission was an oversight, as Beckett included '**un**' on post-publication versions of the text: it appears in the typed material of RC playscript.B (04r), RC playscript.C (04r) and the WU playscript (04r), while Beckett reintroduced it as a handwritten addition on *Footfalls*(CI) (12) and *Footfalls*(SB) (12). He had to reintroduce it again on Grove's galleys for *Ends and Odds* (GG, 14r), as the printed material of this document does not incorporate his handwritten edits from *Footfalls*(CI) (see chapter 5.3.1). These reintroductions of '**un**' show that while a key part of Beckett's creative practice involved stripping away text, often leaving 'textual scars' which point to more developed passages in the drafts (see Van Hulle 2014b), these scars still needed to be present in the published text for the 'undoing' to have its effect. In *Footfalls*, you cannot have 'undoing' without the '**un**'.

The stage direction '**Brokenly**' in the line quoted above echoes M's description of her own 'unbroken' pacing earlier in the same draft, again providing an extra layer of meaning for the reader. Since this pacing description was changed in ET3, the link is now only available to a genetic reader, making this yet another way in which the published text interacts with its *avant-texte*. The stage directions then have M returning to her '**Normal voice**' (EM, 05r), emphasizing again the importance of different types of vocal delivery for Beckett's late plays.

On the first typescript, the daughter's opening question to her mother was changed to hint at a loss of identity, using a reflexive pronoun to create an idiomatic phrase which foregrounds the self's loss of itself in place of a more straightforwardly medical adjective: 'What ~~is~~ is it, Mother, are you not feeling **~~well~~** yourself?' (ET1, 04r). This recalls the mirrored and split selves throughout the play. Another such instance of mirroring is created by shortening the mother's name on the same typescript: '**Mrs W~~inter~~** did not at once reply' (04r). The sole initial 'W' now stands much more clearly as an inversion of 'M', again something which a reader of the stage directions might notice more readily. Harking back to the instructions on pronunciation he included in drafts of *Not I* (see chapter 2.2.2), Beckett at one point inserted '~~doubleyoe~~' in the margin beside this sentence (ET3, 04r). However, as in *Not I*, he deleted this instruction and it did not appear in later versions. While Beckett was very precise in his stage directions and was concerned with the vocal delivery of his late plays, he did not go so far as to give pronunciation tips in the published text of *Footfalls*, recalling his deletion of the note on pronunciation in *Not I* (see chapter 2.2.2.). In spite of Beckett's well-earned reputation as a meticulously detailed writer for the stage, this is evidence of his awareness there were limits to the level of detail that could be provided for a performance process which would have to be worked out in rehearsal.

In early drafts, the daughter was called Emily, though this was immediately questioned by the inline insertion of a question mark in the first draft: 'Then finally, raising her head and fixing **Emily** (**?**) – the daughter's given name, **as the reader will remember** – fixing Emily full in the eye, she said~~.~~ – (Pause.) she murmured Did you **~~notice~~** ~~see~~ notice anything **unusual** in church this evening?' (EM, 05r). Beckett may have chosen this name for its opening 'em' sound, while links Emily to M (in this draft still called Mary).

However, on ET3, he changed '~~**Emily**~~' to 'Amy' (04r), creating an anagram with the '**Mary**' of the opening stage directions on the same draft (01r). Since May and Amy can be spelled in different ways, this also is a mirroring which is even more clear to the reader – again mentioned here in M's monologue – though the names also create aural crossovers in performance, with the name /'eɪ.mi/ adding just one sound and one syllable to the shorter /meɪ/.

Beckett changed the terms relating to both *what* Mrs W '**notice[d]**' in church as well as to *how* she noticed it. On EM, Beckett moved from a general verb of perception to a verb of vision – 'see' – before reverting back again. On RC playscript.A, this became '**observe**' (06r), suggesting a more active role in *how* the thing was perceived. This phrasing was possibly influenced by Beckett's translation of *Rough for Theatre I*, in which the blind A asks B: 'Have you **observed** nothing?' (*KLT* 17).[341] With regard to *what* Amy perceived, the drafts also changed, with Beckett inserting an open variant on ET1: ' unusual strange' (04r). On ET3, he switched between the two: '~~**strange**~~ ~~unusual~~ strange' (04r). For Beckett in the 1970s, 'strange' was a term loaded with meaning. In 1976, the same year as the premiere of *Footfalls*, he published *All Strange Away*, in which 'strange' denotes the foreignness of objects which the narrator attempts – and fails – to exclude from a confined space.[342] In *Footfalls*, 'strange' refers to an experience which is always kept out of sight, not only from Amy herself, but also from the person reading the text or hearing it performed. The religious service Mrs W and Amy attended also changed on ET3, with Beckett inserting a term which was deleted from an earlier part of the text: '~~in church this evening~~ at evensong' (04r).

Another key concept from *All Strange Away* is mentioned in M's next line: 'Mrs Winter: Perhaps it was just my ~~**imaginati**~~ **fancy**' (EM, 05r). As we can see here, Beckett started writing 'imagination' in his first draft, but then struck it out and replaced it with 'fancy'. This recalls the title of the

341 The first of three drafts of the translation of *Rough for Theatre I* is dated 7 September 1975 (Bryden, Garforth and Mills 1998, 88); it was first published in 1976. There is also an earlier English draft entitled 'The Gloaming' on the first French manuscript of *Fragment de Théâtre I* (Bryden, Garforth and Mills 1998, 87).

342 Beckett sent the text of *All Strange Away* to publisher Andreas Brown on 27 June 1973, so it may have been on his mind as he composed *Footfalls* two years later (Pilling 2006, 192). For more on the use of 'strange' in *All Strange Away*, see Little (2020c, 157–60).

'**Fancy** ~~Dead~~ Dying' Notebook in which Beckett composed the text that would eventually become *All Strange Away* and which also produced the shorter text ***Imagination*** *Dead Imagine*, derived from the same notebook material and published in French as ***Imagination*** *morte imaginez* (1965). In these two related prose texts, there is a play between the title of ***Imagination*** *Dead Imagine* and *All Strange Away*'s repeated references to the protagonists in a confined rotunda murmuring that '**Fancy** is' 'his' or 'her' 'only hope' (*TFN* 74, 76–8). But 'fancy' and 'imagination' are not equivalent in *All Strange Away*. While 'imagine' serves as the narrative impetus, prompting the reader to call up images, fancy is repeatedly referred to as being 'dead'. Moreover, while the phrase 'Imagination dead imagine', which opens *All Strange Away*, contains the paradoxical instruction to imagine the death of the imagination, the phrase 'fancy [...] dead', which ends it, is terminal (*TFN* 73, 84). This downplaying of fancy is also found in *Still 3*, where the sound of the 'incarnation bell' is dismissed as 'perhaps mere **fancy**' (*TFN* 173). It is in this light that we should understand the replacement of '~~**imaginati**~~' with '**fancy**' in the first draft of *Footfalls*. The imagination here evidently still has some of the power granted to it by Romantics such as Samuel Taylor Coleridge, whose tripartite distinction between primary imagination, secondary imagination and fancy Beckett came across while reading his *Biographia Literaria* 'without much pleasure' in 1962, two years before starting work on the 'Fancy ~~Dead~~ Dying' Notebook (Beckett to Mary Hutchinson, 11 June 1962, qtd. in Van Hulle and Nixon 2013, 35).[343] There is no evidence that Beckett was trying to implement Coleridge's tripartite definition when writing his prose or theatre works of the 1970s, but there is a difference between 'fancy' and 'imagination' in these works, making it even more dismissive for Mrs W to say it was 'just my **fancy**' in *Footfalls* (*KLT* 113).

In ET1, Beckett increased the direct repetitions of Mrs W's words in Emily's response: 'Emily: Just what exactly, Mother, did you **perhaps** **fancy** it was?

343 For Coleridge, the primary imagination underpins all perception by repeating 'in the finite mind [...] the eternal act of creation in the infinite I AM' and the secondary imagination 'struggles to idealize and to unify' impressions given to the mind. Fancy is a lower creative faculty which arranges 'fixities and definites' according to their associative qualities (1907, 202). For more on the distinction between 'fancy' and 'imagination' in *Imagination Dead Imagine* and *All Strange Away*, see Little (2020c, 160–3).

(Pause.) Just what exactly, Mother, did you perhaps **fancy** it was you saw?' (04r), setting up some of the many echoes which are so important to this closing section. In Berlin, Beckett spoke of the importance of such verbal and tonal parallels:

> At the end of the rehearsals – Beckett already in his coat – he again points out the similarity between daughter and mother. 'The daughter only knows the voice of the mother.' One can recognize the similarity between the two from the sentences in their narratives, from the expression. The strange voice of the daughter comes from the mother. The 'Not enough?' in the mother's story must sound just like the 'Not there?' of Mrs W in Amy's story, for example. These parallelisms are extremely important for the understanding of the play, he says. (Asmus 1977, 86)

Such echoing was not a new technique in Beckett's theatre. While helping Elmar Tophoven with the German translation of *Godot* in 1953, he pointed to the importance of 'echoes' (Erika Tophoven qtd. in Van Hulle and Verhulst 2017a, 135) and he ensured the precision of verbal echoes when translating the play himself into English (Van Hulle and Verhulst 2017a, 298). He told the actors during his 1967 production of *Endspiel*: 'The play is full of echoes; they all answer each other' (McMillan and Fehsenfeld 1988, 208). And indeed, he had already aimed for these echo effects when translating the play into English in 1957, with Van Hulle and Weller arguing: 'The sense of the characters' confinement within a limited linguistic universe is significantly increased through this kind of revision, complementing the sense of physical confinement' (2018, 279). In *Footfalls*, Beckett also creates linguistic confinement through the repetition of words between characters, often in the same tone. But that confinement is never complete and the dramatic tension in the play derives from our inability to precisely identify May, V, Mrs W and Amy with one another, in spite of their manifold echoes.

In ET3, Mrs W repeats the term '**strange**': 'Mrs W: You noticed nothing ~~**unusual**~~ strange?' (04r). On RC playscript.A, Beckett introduced an ellipsis, giving further emphasis to this term: 'Mrs. W: You observed nothing ... strange?' (06r). Having introduced such an ellipsis before the word's first mention on the preceding ET3, Beckett put it before most instances of 'strange' on RC playscript.A (06r), further highlighting the term's importance in the text. On PPF, Beckett introduced a reflexive pronoun into this line, which he then echoed in Amy's response: 'Mrs W: You **yourself** observed nothing … strange? Amy: No, Mother, I **myself** did not, to put it mildly' (07r). What Michael Haerdter terms Beckett's 'echo principle' in his rehearsal diary for *Endspiel* (qtd. in McMillan and Fehsenfeld 1988, 208) becomes a veritable echo chamber in the closing passages of *Footfalls*. The following lines substantially build up this echo chamber effect, cited here from the version on ET1, where Beckett developed them in handwritten additions:

> Mrs W~~inter~~: You **noticed nothing** strange? Emily: No~~thing whatever~~, Mother, I did not, **to put it mildly**. [...] Mrs W: What do you mean, Emily, **to put it mildly**, what can you possibly mean, Emily, **to put it mildly**? Emily: I mean, mother, that to say I **noticed nothing strange** is **to put it mildly**. For I noticed nothing **of any kind**~~.~~ unusual or otherwise[.] I saw nothing, heard nothing, **of any kind**. **I was not there.** (04r)

This passage could be seen in terms of Julia Kristeva's well-known claim (originally published in French in 1969) that 'any text is constructed as a mosaic of quotations; any text is the absorption and transformation of another' (1982, 66). Mrs W starts this passage by echoing her own preceding phrase: '**noticed nothing** strange'. Her next line echoes Emily's '**to put it mildly**' before going on to echo herself. Emily then echoes her mother and herself, before closing with a line that might sum up the linguistic disorientation caused by all these echoes: 'I was not there'. Throughout, the names of both characters are echoed in M's statement of them preceding each part of dialogue, as well as their repetition in similar parts of Mrs W's and Emily's sentences. Since these lines are all being spoken by the same actor onstage, there is a tension set up between the linguistic confinement caused by the repetition of terms and the feeling that none of these terms are coming from either of the characters identified in the dialogue. When Emily ends with 'I was not there', we could interpret this as M saying 'I'm not here', given that the lines she has just spoken undermine any sense we might have of her as a coherent onstage character.

This echoed dialogue culminates in a line Beckett erased from ET3:

> Mrs W: **Not there**? Emily: **Not there.** Mrs W: But **I heard** you respond. (Pause.) **I heard** you say Amen. (Pause.) **How could you** have responded if you were **not there**? ~~(Pause.)~~ **~~H~~h ow could you** possibly have said Amen if, as you claim, you ~~werr~~ were **not there**? **~~Emily – (Pause.) Emily: At the end? (Pause.) The very end? Mrs W: Well yes I suppose if you like, what difference does that make?~~**' (05r).

For Beckett, it clearly did make a difference as to whether Emily was there at the '**~~very end~~**' of the service or not, as this line did not reappear in later versions. Instead, the repetition now led directly into Mrs W's climactic prayer: '"... the love of God, and the fellowship of the Holy Ghost, be with **us** ~~you~~ all, **~~now & for~~** evermore. Amen"' (EM, 06r). This prayer, taken from the closing lines of St Paul's second letter to the Corinthians (13:14), would have been heard by Beckett at the end of church services when attending worship with his family as a young man in Dublin.[344] He first considered '**you**' as an open variant, which would have corresponded with the biblical text, but then replaced this with the pronoun that appears in the prayer as spoken in church: '**THE grace of our Lord Jesus Christ**, and the love of God, and the fellowship of the Holy Ghost, be with **us** all evermore. *Amen*' (*BCP 1926*, 30; emphasis in original).[345] This passage, combined with the allusion to the prayer for eternal rest on ET3, makes *Footfalls* a distinctly funereal text, in which rituals of death mark not an ending, nor a rest before eternal life, but incessant revolving in the mind(s) of its character(s). Notably, Beckett omits Christ's grace from Mrs W's prayer, making this a rare reduction of Christ's presence in the text. For Christians, grace is a key element in salvation, particularly for the Protestant tradition Beckett was raised in. So, here again, Beckett is not simply returning to the religion of his youth, he is textually editing it as he does so.

344 In the 1926 *Book of Common Prayer* of the Church of Ireland, this prayer closes Morning Prayer, Evening Prayer, The Litany, An Order for the Burial of Children Who Have Been Baptized and the part of The Order for the Burial of the Dead said within the church (*BCP 1926*, 18, 30, 37, 493, 489). It is also used in The Solemnization of Matrimony (*BCP 1926*, 460).

345 Note the deletion of '**~~now & for~~**' in the first draft version, which Beckett reinserted as 'now, and for' on RC playscript.B (05r).

On ET3, after Mrs W insists, 'I heard you distinctly', Beckett deleted Emily's response: '~~**I was there at the very end**~~', again raising doubt as to the line between presence and absence (05r). While M then '*Begins pacing*' in the first published edition of the text (1976c, 13), Beckett changed this on RC playscript.B: '~~**Begins**~~ Resumes **pacing**' (05r; see also GG, 14r). This underlines M's unity of character, however precarious this may be, by linking her final bout of pacing to those she has done earlier. But while this unity might be clearer *within* versions of the text after Beckett's revision, it is not clear *across* different textual versions, as these differ in the number of steps she takes. Faber's first edition has '*three steps*' (1976c, 13), while RC playscript.B introduces the open variant 'three **four**' (05r). *Footfalls*(CI) revises the number to '~~*three*~~ **five**' (13), and this is what appears in Grove's first edition of *Ends and Odds* (1976d [1977], 48), with Faber's including just three (1977a, 37). If M's pacing were, as Beckett told Whitelaw, 'the essence of the matter', then it is notable that this essence was not stable, but changed significantly over the course of the epigenesis.

In the first draft, Mrs W's closing question was modal: **'Can you not stop** revolving it all?' (EM, 06r). However, echoing the future-oriented 'evermore' in her preceding prayer, Beckett changed this to the future perfect on ET2: **'Will you never have done** revolving it all?' (05r). In ET4, Beckett introduced an ellipsis, letting this verb hang before the question's final phrase: 'Will you never have done ~~revolving it all~~... revolving it all?' (05r). He also introduced extra pauses into the final lines of dialogue on ET3 (05r), making this a text which matches Beckett's description in his July 1937 letter to Axel Kaun of Beethoven's Seventh Symphony as 'devoured by huge black pauses', the increasingly gap-ridden text providing an apt counterpart to the stage image of May surrounded by darkness (*LSB I* 518–19).[346]

346 See also the narrator's description in *Dream* of Beethoven's compositions 'eaten away with terrible silences' (*D* 138). Beckett's letter to Kaun probably refers to the rests in the symphony's second movement which follow the opening repetitions of its ostinato. In January 1975, just before he started writing *Footfalls*, Ruby Cohn saw the score of Beethoven's *Ghost Trio* on Beckett's desk (Pilling 2006, 196).

Scene IV: *'No trace of May.'* (1976c, 13)

While Beckett had his closing stage directions almost completed in his first draft, *Footfalls* is not an easy play to end in performance. The fade-out on May, followed by a fade-up to reveal an empty strip in the play's crucial fourth scene, risks creating the impression that the play has already ended before the final fade-out:

> *Pause. Fade out on strip. All in darkness.*
> *Pause.*
> *Chime even a little fainter still. Pause for echoes.*
> ***Fade up to even a little less still on strip.***
> ***No trace of* MAY.**
> *Hold ten seconds.*
> *Fade out.*
> CURTAIN (*KLT* 114)

In his RC Nb, Beckett outlined this problem and attempted to come up with a solution:

> How avoid end of play audience reaction after 3rd fade-out before last chime, fade-up & final fade-out? By reducing to minimum (in all 3 cases) pause after fade-out. Scarcely dark (and steps silent I & II) when chime preventing reaction. Correct 'long' to 'brief' in script. (02r)

In RC playscript.B, Beckett did indeed reduce the pauses between scenes, writing ~~'Brief'~~ in the left margin before scratching this idea out in all three cases (02r, 03r, 05r). Nevertheless, he did reduce the final scene on the empty strip: 'Hold ~~fu'fteen~~ ten seconds' (RC playscript.B, 05r), probably again in view of a potential premature reaction from his audience.[347]

347 This reduction is also made on Beckett's annotated copy for Faber (*Footfalls*(SB), 13), leading to a shorter final scene in Faber's *Ends and Odds* (1977a, 37), but not in the Grove edition (1976d [1977], 49), where the hold was still '*fifteen seconds*', as it is on *Footfalls*(CI) (13) and the Grove galleys (GG, 14r).

In his German Nb, Beckett considered leaving a 'blur' of light between each scene in order to make it clear that the play was not over when May disappeared after the penultimate fade-out (07r). Without the blur, he was concerned that the audience would think the play was over when the lights came up to reveal an empty strip at the beginning of Scene IV (Asmus 1977, 88). This minimal shard of light was problematic, however, with Ruby Cohn noting critically: 'Against his [Beckett's] unshaping intention [...], this looked like a door into the unknown. The vertical lightline joins the illuminated horizontal strip to suggest a frame' (1980, 271). It is perhaps fitting that a text so concerned with May's difficulty in putting an end to 'revolving it all' should continue to pose a significant challenge for its director–author trying to stage May's 'absent presence' in its final scene (Gontarski 1985, 162). As we shall see in chapter 6.2.2, this challenge is also evident in the text's French translation.

6.2 The Genesis of *Pas*

6.2.1 Chronology

Though Beckett started translating *Footfalls* after he had already commenced his translation of *That Time*, *Pas* was finished before *Cette fois*. As we have already seen in chapter 4.2.1, Beckett mentioned the two plays together when complaining to Alan Schneider on 10 April 1977 that he was 'Perspiring' over their respective translations. Yet, just two weeks later, on 24 April, he wrote to Jocelyn Herbert from Tangier that he had a satisfactory translation of *Footfalls* (Pilling 2006, 203).[348] So, unlike *That Time*, Beckett's perspiration over *Footfalls* quite quickly turned into actual translation. Why so? The latter is of course a shorter text, but another reason may be that, as he mentioned in a letter to Ruby Cohn of 5 May 1977, Beckett already had a place of publication in mind for *Pas* – the *NRF* (*LSB IV* 457; see chapter 5.4.1). In the very next line of the letter, he reveals that he was also thinking of a particular theatre group for the play, his favoured Compagnie Renaud–Barrault: 'And I'll offer it to Orsay to refresh Madeleine's revival of Pas moi coming season' (*LSB IV* 457). As in the case of *Pas moi*, we can see actors in Beckett's network providing an impetus for pushing the translation process forward – here a publisher as well as actual theatre practitioners. This is in stark contrast to the long translation period of *That Time*.

Just like the translation documents of *Cette fois*, none of the *Pas* typescripts are dated. Indeed, unusually for Beckett's translation process, there is no holograph manuscript of *Pas*, raising the question as to whether FT1 is a first draft (see chapter 5.2.2). Though Beckett labelled his first French typescript 'I' (FT1, 01r), he did the same with the first English typescript of *Not I* (ET1, 01r), even though this is preceded by a holograph, also numbered 'I' (EM1, 01r). So, the numbering of the *Pas* typescript does not rule out the possibility of a preceding holograph.[349] It may be important that Beckett was in Tangier when he told Herbert he had a translation of

348 On 3 May, while still in Tangier, he also told Ruby Cohn: 'Have translated Footfalls at last' (*LSB IV* 457).

349 There is also the possibility that the 'I' on *Pas* FT1 (01r) is a folio number.

Footfalls, as he seems to have completed the *Cette fois* holograph while on the same trip (FM; see chapter 4.2.1).[350] If Beckett did not have access to a typewriter while on holidays, he may have completed a holograph draft in Tangier which is now lost or inaccessible, only typing up the text when he returned home to France. On the envelope stored with RC playscript.B in the Burns Library, Boston College, Beckett wrote:

> Footfalls 1TS
> Pas 3 ” ~~+ MS~~
> ~~Corrected typescripts~~
> ~~MS~~ Pas (RC playscript.B, front cover)

Whether this crossing out of ‘~~MS~~’ suggests that there may have been a holograph of *Pas* which Beckett was at one stage planning to give to Calvin Israel, or that Beckett simply made a mistake, is impossible to confirm without further evidence. I have therefore not included this ‘virtual’ manuscript in my Genetic Map.

On returning from Tangier, Beckett must have worked further on the text, for he had sent copies – presumably typescripts – to Lindon, Blin and Lambrichs by 23 May (Beckett to Barbara Bray, 23 May 1977, *LSB IV* 462). Beckett left for Tangier again on 25 July, holidaying there for a month (Pilling 2006, 204). On 16 August, he mentioned the title of his translation in a letter to Schneider: ‘Back Paris late September. Then I hope Paris/ Ussy for a spell, apart from a hop to Stuttgart early October for a TV detail. Unless I’m landed with *Footfalls* (*Pas*) at Théâtre d’Orsay’ (*NABS* 356). Since the only typescript to feature a title is NRFSC (01r), we can assume this was composed in the summer of 1977. Indeed, given that the typed layer of NRFSC shows signs of having been photocopied, it seems likely that a version of this typescript was what Beckett sent to his publishers and Blin. Though the precise dates of translation are still uncertain, we can infer that an initial holograph may have been created in April, the two typescripts (and the typed layer of the *NRF* setting copy) in May, with the setting copy itself being further annotated by hands other than Beckett’s sometime later that summer (see Genetic Map, chapter 5.7).

350 The draft of *Pas moi* he worked on while holidaying in El Jadida four years earlier is also a holograph (FM; see chapter 2.3.1)

In the same letter to Schneider in which he complained of 'Perspiring' over his translation of *Footfalls*, Beckett mentioned his desire to write another play: 'Wish I could do an Atropos in black – with her scissors' (*NABS* 355). As Beckett may have read in his *Classical Dictionary*, Atropos was one of the three Fates, 'and her duty among the three sisters is to cut the thread of life without regard to sex, age, or quality' (Lemprière 1833, 103). Though Beckett did not write a play about Atropos, he did compose a poem about her while in Tangier, dated 21 April 1977 (*CP* 463):

> noire sœur
> qui es aux enfers
> à tort tranchant
> et à travers
> qu'est-ce que tu attends (*CP* 218)[351]

The version of 'noire sœur' in Beckett's 'Sottisier' Notebook is followed by a series of notes about the three Fates which seem to have been taken from Lemprière's *Dictionary*:

> Clotho (youngest) – birth – distaff
> Lachesis – life – spindle
> Atropos – death – scissors
> dressed in black[352]
> ministers of Pluto, sitting
> at foot of his throne
> a clew of thread (yarn)[353]
> Prosperine (qtd. in *CP* 463)

351 In David Wheatley's translation: 'dark sister / who art in hell / laying about you / everywhere / what are you waiting for' (*SP* 185).

352 'An arrow links Atropos to the line "dressed in black"' (*CP* 463).

353 The edition I consulted has '**clues** of thread' (1833, 480).

Almost all these phrases can be traced to the section of Lemprière's *Dictionary* dealing with the Fates, though he does not mention Pluto by name here, instead referring to him as 'the king of hell' (1833, 480).[354] This may have led to the infernal imprecation in Beckett's poem: 'noire sœur / qui es aux **enfers**'. Beckett's interest in the Fates, and its temporal overlap with the translation of *Footfalls*, may also be the reason for a darkening of tone in one of *Pas*'s variants. When revising the play for Minuit's collected edition, Beckett changed one word of May's 'Epilogue', in which she speaks of herself in the third person, traversing the transept of a church:

> La voilà donc, à peine en allée, en train de rôder, allant et venant, allant et venant, le long de ce pauvre bras. (*Un temps.*) La nuit venue. (*Un temps.*) C'est-à-dire, en certaines saisons de l'année, à l'heure des vêpres. (*Un temps.*) **Fatalement**. (1978a, 13, 14)

Though this revision was made well after Beckett's initial translation in April 1977, it seems that his interest in the Fates took adverbial form in the later version of the text. Certainly, the use of 'Fatalement' instead of the earlier 'Inévitablement' (1977c, 15) calls Atropos to mind. Lemprière notes that the Roman name of the Fates, Parcæ, 'is derived [from] *a partu* or *parturiendo*, because they presided over the birth of men' (1833, 480). May's own tragedy is that there is no one to cut her thread of life – having not being properly born, she cannot seem to definitively die, so she too may have wanted to ask Atropos: 'what are you waiting for[?]'.

The revisions of *Pas* for the 1978 edition probably arose from Beckett's memorization of the text in preparation for its premiere. He was not thrilled to be directing again and his letters find him once more complaining to his friends of theatre obligations. On 11 December 1977, Beckett wrote to Kay Boyle: 'Landed with a production for the Schiller next Sept., no theatre till then thank God, unless perhaps Footfalls in Paris at the Little Orsay. The shaky French version' (*LSB IV* 475). *Pas* premiered in the Petit théâtre d'Orsay on 11 April 1978 alongside Beckett's revival of *Pas moi*, with Madeleine Renaud as V and Delphine Seyrig as May (Bonal 2000, 348). Beckett's comments to Barbara Bray suggest an in-depth learning of the

354 For other instances of Beckett altering Lemprière's text while taking notes from it, see Verhulst (2019, 117–18).

script typical of his directorial preparations: 'Done work on Pas. Not much to be done but see the problems clearer' (12 February 1978, *LSB IV* 481). On 16 February, he wrote again to Bray: 'Pas learnt and rehearsed daily with growing distaste' (*LSB IV* 482). Interestingly, Beckett describes this process of memorizing the text as a rehearsal, even though he was on holidays in Tangier, far from the actors set to perform *Pas* in Paris. On 18 February, Beckett told Schneider: 'Have *Pas* in my head well in advance. Look forward to working with Delphine Seyrig' (*NABS* 365). Clearly, working with a network of actors and theatre practitioners made Beckett revisit his texts in detail, frequently resulting in significant alterations.

Beckett greatly enjoyed working with Seyrig (Knowlson 1997, 657) and praised her performance to Schneider on 13 April (*NABS* 366). However, the rehearsal process itself was not without hitches, as Seyrig related to her son, musician Duncan Youngerman:

> I am in rehearsal with Sam Beckett and Madeleine Renaud – very difficult – you would be very interested because Sam is like an orchestra leader trying to get rhythms into us. He wants Madeleine to talk to the beat of my footsteps and my footsteps to be like a base – it's difficult for both of us and he suffers from our lack of ability. But he has directed the play in London and Berlin and he now is a little too impatient – Madeleine is quite bewildered and feels like a child with a teacher à l'école primaire. But we shall overcome. (24 March 1978, *LSB IV* 484–5n3)

In a 1986 interview with Pierre Chabert, Seyrig returned to musical terminology to describe Beckett's directing:

> He is like an orchestra conductor: he sets the tempo. Actors, it seems to me, are ever less inclined, or no longer inclined at all, to respect rhythms, and French actors no longer take into account the metrical structure as they used to. When you work with Beckett, you find yourself regretting not having this almost musical education. (Seyrig 1992, 20)

It is important to note that Renaud did have this classical training – indeed, she was one of its prime exponents – but it appears she struggled with the play nonetheless. According to Seyrig, performing May onstage with Renaud offstage was equivalent to playing a sonata with the pianist in the wings, invisible to the violinist (1992, 19–20). This again demonstrates how closely linked Beckett's rhythmic, repetitive texts are to the performance process, especially at this stage of his career.

For Beckett, the premiere of *Pas* was 'satisfactory – but cd. have gone further' (Beckett to Ruby Cohn, 27 April 1978, *LSB IV* 484). Beckett himself did not go much further with this particular network of actors. This was the last time he directed the Compagnie Renaud–Barrault, with whom he had a falling out in 1982 after expressing his preference for Seyrig over Renaud for the part of W in *Rockaby* (see Knowlson 1997, 689). The Compagnie would continue to produce Beckett works onstage, but their direct influence on his composition and editing of texts for performance was over.

6.2.2 Genesis

Title

The title of *Pas* demonstrates what Weller, in the title of his book on Beckett and nihilism, calls 'a taste for the negative' (2005). At the level of narrative, as we have seen, Beckett negates the staged subject: 'Like Mouth in *Not I*', Weller writes, 'May will avoid the first-person pronoun' (2005, 173). This sense of negation is even more pronounced in the French title, which can be considered a form of translational 'unwording', a term used by Van Hulle and Weller to track the different kinds of negation in Beckett's translation of *L'Innommable* (2014, 190–220). By translating *Footfalls* as *Pas*, Beckett produces a title which echoes the French version of his earlier play *Pas moi*, barring the personal pronoun 'moi'. But the homonym 'pas' – in its primary meaning – also describes May's footsteps, making this title as much of a pun as the main character's name. If the 'key word' in Beckett's plays is 'perhaps' (see chapter 6.1.2), a very important word in his French-language plays of this period is 'pas'.

Footsteps were (again) on Beckett's mind just before he translated *Footfalls*, as we can see in two *mirlitonnades*: 'écoute-les' mentions '**les pas** / **aux pas** / un à / un' (*CP* 211) and the very title of '**pas à pas**' recalls May's movement along the strip (*CP* 216).[355] But negation is never far away here either. One could see the latter as a heroic account of the little footsteps that refuse to give up:

pas à pas
nulle part
nul seul
ne sait comment
petits pas
nulle part
obstinément (*CP* 216)

However, the three negations which directly follow the opening line cancel out any idea of a straightforward line of progress: indeed, the only heroism is that the steps keep going, 'stubbornly' ['obstinément'], in spite of the fact that they are going 'nowhere' ['nulle part'] (Beckett and Marcuse 2007, 200).[356] Elmar Tophoven, discussing the title of his German translation of *Footfalls*, said: 'Beckett's first suggestion was "Schritte" (Steps), but that has overtones of "Fortschritte" (progress)' – making it unsuitable for Beckett's play (qtd. in Garforth 1996, 50). Likewise, Beckett's choice of *Pas* for his title reinforces the idea of his oeuvre as a 'work in regress' (Beckett to Jocelyn Herbert, 16 June 1966, *LSB IV* 32; Beckett to Ruby Cohn, 9 January 1972, *LSB IV* 279–81), stripping away the first person, further exacerbating the breakdown of the subject on stage.[357]

355 'écoute-les' is dated '20.2.77'; 'pas à pas' is dated '6.7.77' (*CP* 452, 459).

356 Beckett dedicated 'pas à pas' to the Frankfurt School philosopher Herbert Marcuse on the occasion of his eightieth birthday. The translation cited here is by Édith Fournier.

357 For an analysis of Beckett's oeuvre as a 'work in regress', see Van Hulle (2008, 115–94).

Pacing

It is important that May's is a theatrical, staged breakdown, with Beckett again taking into account his directorial experience when translating one of his plays. For instance, the pacing area of *Pas* matches the nine-step strip of the Grove edition (1977c, 7; 1976d [1977], 42), rather than the earlier, seven-step version. *Pas*'s description of the strip as an '*Aire du va-et-vient*' (1977c, 7) recalls the French title of *Come and Go* (*Va-et-vient*), in which the movement of the characters to exit (and re-enter) the playing area determines the social dynamic of their interactions. Between May, V, Amy and Mrs Winter, there is no clear separation of self, nor is there a clear division between the inside and outside of May's mind, making this strip a much more liminal space of subjectivity. In the first typescript of *Pas*, Beckett went for 'Piste' (FT1, 01r), but this was deleted on FT2, to be replaced by the more ambivalent term (01r). Indeed, this ambivalence resonates with a series of late Beckett works which centre around the movement 'to and fro' of an indeterminate subject. In the short prose piece *neither*, this self is alternately stated and negated in the opening lines: 'to and fro in shadow from inner to outershadow / from impenetrable self to impenetrable unself by way of neither' (*TFN* 167). Beckett returned to this sense of the self being undone when translating May's third-person description of her own movement: 'up and down, up and down' (1976d [1977], 46; *KLT* 112) becomes 'allant et venant, allant et venant' and, soon after, 'allait et venait, allait et venait' (1977c, 14).[358] As in the 'come and gone' ending of *That Time* (1976a, 16; see chapter 4.1.2), May's cyclical movement suggests continued revolving rather than the more standard dramatic peripeteia outlined in Freytag's classical model (see chapter 6.1.2).

The stage directions for pacing are also the result of Beckett's directorial work, with each segment of dialogue matched to a particular length of May's walk. So, for instance, the generic '*pacing*' (1976d [1977], 44) becomes '*avec la troisième longueur*', telling the actor where she should be when speaking a specific line: 'Oui, mère' (1977c, 10). This degree of specification is based on the diagrams Beckett sketched for the London and Berlin premieres of the

358 English lines are cited from the first Grove *Ends and Odds* as this is most likely the edition Beckett used when translating *Footfalls*.

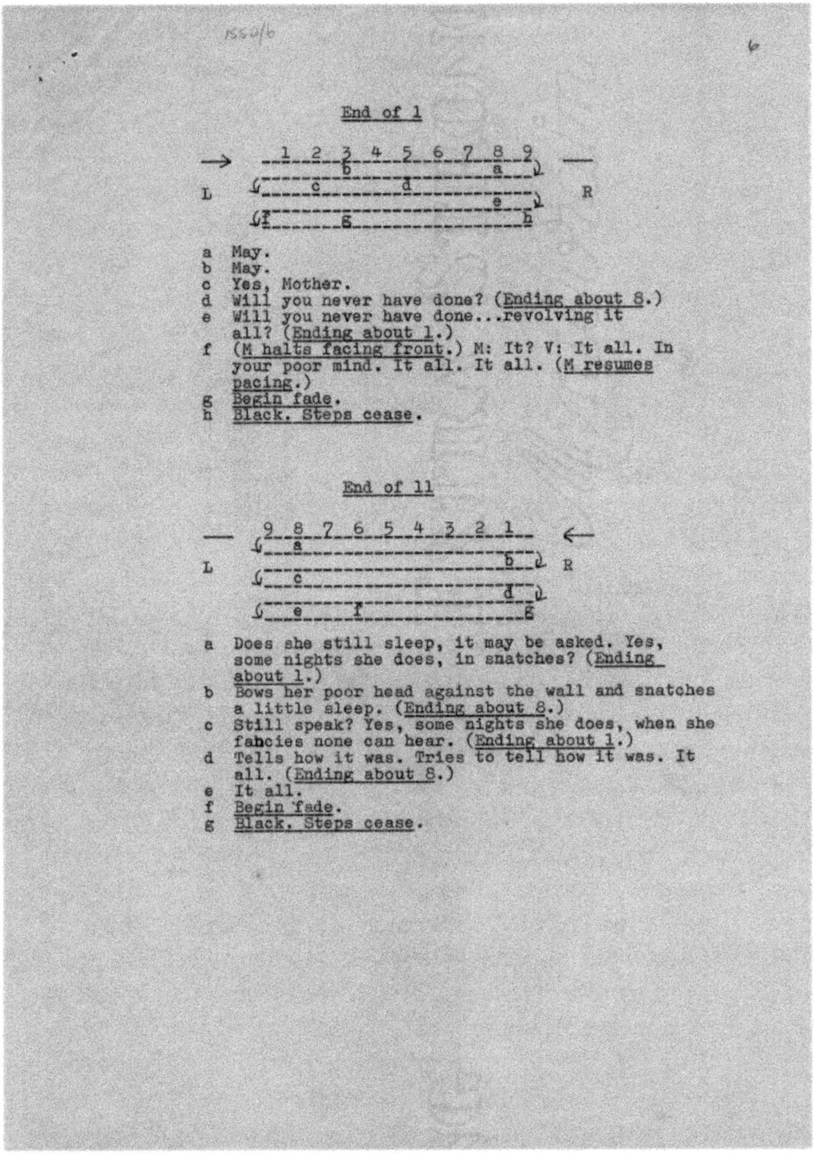

1550/6

6

End of 1

L 1 2 3 4 5 6 7 8 9 R

a May.
b May.
c Yes, Mother.
d Will you never have done? (Ending about 8.)
e Will you never have done...revolving it all? (Ending about 1.)
f (M halts facing front.) M: It? V: It all. In your poor mind. It all. It all. (M resumes pacing.)
g Begin fade.
h Black. Steps cease.

End of 11

L 9 8 7 6 5 4 3 2 1 R

a Does she still sleep, it may be asked. Yes, some nights she does, in snatches? (Ending about 1.)
b Bows her poor head against the wall and snatches a little sleep. (Ending about 8.)
c Still speak? Yes, some nights she does, when she fancies none can hear. (Ending about 1.)
d Tells how it was. Tries to tell how it was. It all. (Ending about 8.)
e It all.
f Begin fade.
g Black. Steps cease.

Fig. 24: Beckett's two sketches of dialogue and pacing on an annotated Royal Court playscript of *Footfalls* (RC playscript.C, 06r).

play. Indeed, the pacing directions at the end of Scene I correspond to the sketch on RC playscript.C (06r; see Fig. 24).

> [(]*M. repart.* ***Quatre longueurs. Avec la deuxième longueur.)***
> [V. —] May. *(Un temps. Pas plus fort.)* May.
> M. — ***(avec la troisième longueur).*** Oui, mère.
> V. — ***(avec la troisième longueur).*** N'auras-tu jamais fini ? ***(Avec la quatrième longueur.)*** N'auras-tu jamais fini de ressasser tout ça ?
> *M. s'immobilise de face à G.*
> M. — Ça ?
> V. — Tout ça. *(Un temps.)* Dans ta pauvre tête. *(Un temps.)* Tout ça. *(Un temps.)* Tout ça.
> ***Un temps.*** *M. repart.* ***Une longueur.*** *L'éclairage s'éteint lentement, sauf R. M. s'immobilise à D dans le noir.* (1977c, 10–11)

The lines highlighted in bold have no direct equivalent in the English text, showing just how much Beckett added to his French stage directions, making them more specific.[359] The pacing directions at end of Scene II correspond with the second part of the same sketch, with one exception: in the French text, Beckett gives a whole length to 'Si elle dort encore, peut-on se demander ?' (1977c, 13), whereas in the English this length includes a second sentence: 'Does she still sleep, it may be asked. **Yes, some nights she does, in snatches?** [*sic*] (<u>Ending about 1</u>.)' (RC playscript.C, 06r).[360]

> [(]*M. repart.* ***Six longueurs. Avec la deuxième longueur.)***
> [V — .] Si elle dort encore, peut-on se demander. ***(Avec la troisième longueur.)*** Oui, certaines nuits, un petit somme, appuie sa pauvre tête au mur et fait un petit somme. ***(Avec***

359 He also removed a few lines (see the 'Compare Sentences' tool in the online genetic edition).

360 This is probably because this second sentence runs on in the French text: '**Oui, certaines nuits, un petit somme**, appuie sa pauvre tête au mur et fait un petit somme' (1977c, 13). The sentences are split in the way they appear in the French text in the sketch on RC Nb (03r).

la quatrième longueur.) Parle encore ? Oui, certaines nuits, quand elle croit que nul n'entend. ***(Avec la cinquième longueur.)*** Dit comment c'était, tâche de dire comment c'était. Tout ça. ***(Début de la sixième longueur.)*** Tout ça.
L'éclairage s'éteint lentement, sauf R.
M. s'immobilise à D dans le noir.
Un temps long. (1977c, 13)

Again, the bold marks the additions in the French text, emphasizing the importance of Beckett's directorial experience in the translation process. He also added another instruction to the opening stage directions, which again corresponds with the sketch on RC playscript.C: '*Texte avec va-et-vient : comme indiqué, demi-tour toujours en silence*' (1977c, 7). This idea can be found in Beckett's RC Nb, where he separates speech and movement in a manner common to his late dramaturgy: 'No speech with turn' (02r). Having already staged May's pacing in English and German, Beckett had a much clearer idea of how he wanted her movements to function in the French text. Nevertheless, he did not carry the specification of steps over from his notes, leaving some room for the actor's own movements.

Lighting

In his Psychology Notes on the Behaviourism of Max Meyer, Beckett noted the strategy of Behaviourist experiments: 'Typical psychological situation becomes, not P faced by universe, but P studying O faced by universe' (TCD MS 10971/7/9; see Woodworth 1931, 79). Whereas this was a strategy for *scientific* experiments, Beckett used the image of a protagonist studying another protagonist who is facing the theatrical 'universe' in an end-stage performance (i.e., the audience) as a form of *theatrical* experimentation: in *Not I*, the Auditor observes Mouth who faces the audience in the auditorium; likewise, V observes May facing the audience in *Footfalls*.[361] Beckett's breakdown of the subject occurs when a protagonist starts observing themself: both Mouth and Listener are presented as being

361 See also the strategies of observation between E and O in Beckett's *Film*.

separated from their staged selves; the brain-twisting moments of *Footfalls* come when May starts talking about herself in the third person.

In most modern theatres, this situation of the audience observing an observer is made possible by lighting. The lighting instructions of *Pas* shape our interpretation of the play by guiding our gaze. For example, Beckett added the line '*Faible spot sur le visage le temps des haltes à D et G*' (1977c, 8). This may have been done to highlight an idea sketched in the RC Nb: 'M's lips sometimes move silently as she walks (or stands)' (03v). Beckett also outlined this in his German Nb: 'M mutters silently, on & off, pacing & standing' (04r). For Ruby Cohn, this extra piece of stage business clarified the division between May and her mother, emphasizing the reality of the mother's voice:

> New to the Berlin production was the daughter's muffled muttering 'on and off' while pacing and standing. Thus, her mother's voice is no longer 'in her mind'. Intent on her own thoughts, the daughter does not hear the mother's words. (1980, 271)

The French text does not go so far as to prescribe lines during May's pacing or standing, in which case it would presumably differentiate between the silent muttering in Beckett's notebooks and the 'muffled muttering' that Cohn records. But *Pas* does direct the audience's attention to May's face during the pauses, opening the possibility of this device being used again in performance.

Beckett also added a lighting direction in an attempt to fix one of the most problematic aspects of staging the play. As we saw in chapter 6.1.2, he had tried inserting a 'blur' of light in the Berlin production to let the audience know that the play was not over at the end of Scene III. This is formalized in the French text: '*Au fond à gauche, un mince rai vertical (R) 3 mètres de haut*' (1977c, 8). While 'Long Observation of the Ray' uses a ray of light to explore the breakdown of subject and object (see chapter 6.1.1), in *Pas*, the slender ray is used throughout in order to clarify the dramatic framing of such a breakdown. It is worth noting that the lighting is described as '*froid*' in the French text (1977c, 8). This builds on what we might call Beckett's 'wintering' of the text, from his decision to name Amy's mother 'Mrs Winter' to his decision to change the 'south door' of the church to a more wintery 'north door' (see chapter 6.1.2). By describing the lighting as cold, Beckett further drains the energy from his French translation.

Weakening

In *Pas*, Beckett not only further 'winters' his text in translation, he also weakens it, a process that is in line with his statement to Herbert Blau that the French language 'had the right weakening effect' (qtd. in Mooney 2010, 196). So, the light returning '*a little less on strip*' (1976d [1977], 45) at the start of Scene II is '*un peu plus **faible*** [weak]' and the same adjective is used to describe the ringing of the bell: '*Cloche un peu plus **faible***' (1977c, 11). This recalls Beckett's description of the need in modern writing for a 'syntax of weakness' (qtd. in Harvey 1970, 249), though here it is the vocabulary rather than the syntax which expresses this weakness. In *Pas*, he foregrounds weakness in the dialogue as well as the stage directions, adding to the sense of a character in a state of breakdown. Having already used the adjective to describe the lighting, Beckett revised his first French typescript to figure the voices of his play as 'weak': 'Voix: ~~bas~~ **faibles**, lentes' (FT1, 01r). He then used it for young May's description of footsteps (FT1, 03r), before revising this on FT2: 'Je veux dire, mère, qu'il me faut ~~entendre les pas, si légers soient-ils~~ la chute des pas, si ~~légère~~ **faible** soit-elle' (03r). Though another term was considered, it was evidently important that the footsteps May hears are **'faible'**.

This is not the first time in Beckett's writing that form and content intertwine. In his early essay 'Dante ... Bruno . Vico .. Joyce', he describes Joyce's 'Work in Progress' in the following terms: 'Here form *is* content, content *is* form [...]. The language is drunk' (*Dis* 27; emphasis in original). Replacing 'drunk' with 'weak' provides a good description of *Pas*. But of course, *Pas* is more than a verbal text. It is a text written to be enacted in the spatial art of the theatre. While Beckett's novel *Molloy* (written in May 1947) has been rightly seen as a crucial transition point in the author's turn from 'representation ("aboutness") to enactment ("isness")' (Beloborodova 2018, 186), it may also be significant that Beckett wrote a full-length play just months before commencing *Molloy*, the posthumously published

Eleutheria.[362] In terms of its narrative content, *Eleutheria* does not have too much in common with the three novels that followed: *Molloy*, *Malone Dies* and *The Unnamable*. But, as the multiple diagrams in its compositional notebooks show, writing *Eleutheria* did make Beckett seriously consider how his writing might come to life in the spatial environment of a theatre. In this way, it may have been an important influence on a shift in approach with regard to the materiality of the creative process in his subsequent prose works. Studying the manuscripts of *Pas*, we can see that the theatre continued to give Beckett an important arena in which to develop his enactive aesthetics.

With all this in mind, we might reconsider Beckett's statement that the French version of his play is 'shaky' (see chapter 6.2.1). In other words, *Pas* could be seen as 'shaky' not because it is worse than *Footfalls*, but because weakness is built into the text. We might further note the marking of the subjunctive mood in the above passage – 'si faible **soit-elle**' (1977c, 13) – which remains unmarked in the English: 'however faint **they fall**' (1976d [1977], 46; *KLT* 111). The favourite Beckettian verb 'fall' echoes throughout the English text of *Footfalls*, recalling Beckett's own comparison of his work to that of Franz Kafka: 'The Kafka hero has a coherence of purpose. He's lost but he's not spiritually precarious, *he's not falling to bits. My people seem to be falling to bits*' (qtd. in Shenker 1956, 1; emphasis added). But it might be argued that it is the French translation in which Beckett's 'people' are even more 'precarious'. Perhaps that is why May leans her head against the wall ['**appuie** sa pauvre tête au mur' (1977c, 13)] in *Pas*, whereas in *Footfalls* she simply '**bows** her poor head against the wall' (1976d [1977], 46; *KLT* 112). Beckett's use of the verb 'appuyer', with its etymology in the idea of physical support, suggests that May needs the wall to hold her up, that she might collapse without it.[363]

There is an important exception to Beckett's 'weakening' of the text in translation: whereas the echoes of the chime '*die*' in *Footfalls* (1976d [1977], 42; *KLT* 109), the corresponding line in *Pas* reads simply: '*Echo*' (1977c, 8).

362 Beloborodova borrows the terms 'aboutness' and 'isness' from H. Porter Abbott (2013, 82, 92). The two *Eleutheria* manuscript notebooks are dated 18 January and 24 February 1947 (HRC SB MS 3/2).

363 https://www.cnrtl.fr/etymologie/Appuyer.

I now turn to Beckett's translation of echoes to understand how he deals with this key aspect of the play.

Echoes, Sound and Rhythm

Just as the echoes of the chime do not explicitly '*die*' in *Pas*, so too did Beckett sustain the text's verbal echoes, drawing attention to the way in which the subject is doubled and multiplied. Sardin-Damestoy notes the echoing of '**rôder**' with its past tense homonym '**rôdait**' in May's 'Epilogue' (2020, 35):

> Un peu plus tard, lorsque c'était comme si elle n'avait jamais été, ça jamais été, elle se mit à **rôder**. (*Un temps.*) La nuit venue. (*Un temps.*) Se glissait dehors, la nuit venue, et dans la petite église, par la porte nord, toujours verrouillée à cette heure, et **rôdait**, allant et venant, allant et venant, le long du pauvre bras sauveur. (1977c, 14)

The same word occurs again soon after, in the phrase 'en train de **rôder**' (1977c, 15). All three instances of the verb translate 'walk' (1976d [1977], 46–7; *KLT* 112), so this is a case of Beckett reproducing the echoing structure of the English text, rather than increasing it. But the manuscripts show that Beckett underlined '**rôder**' on FT1 (04r), marking the importance of this word. Moreover, he did consider alternatives for the same verb at the start of Scene II: 'Je rôde **déambule rodaille** [*for* rôdaille] ici à présent' (FT1, 03r). But in the end, it was '**rôde**' that appeared in the published text (1977c, 11), maintaining the echo with the other lines.

In epigenetic revisions made for *Pas suivi de quatre esquisses*, Beckett again returns the French text to the patterned echoes of its English predecessor. In *Footfalls*, the mother asks May: 'What do you mean, May, not enough, what can you possibly mean, May, not enough?' (1976d [1977], 45; *KLT* 111). The text in bold shows phrases missing from the first French edition (1977c, 13) which Beckett later added: 'Que veux-tu dire, May, **ne suffit pas,** voyons, que peux-tu bien vouloir dire, **May,** ne suffit pas ?' (1978a, 12). The same thing happened with Mrs W's later question to Amy: 'What do you mean, Amy, to put it mildly, what can you possibly mean, Amy, to put it mildly?' (1976d [1977], 48; *KLT* 113). Again, bold denotes text added for *Pas suivi de quatre esquisses*: 'Que veux-tu dire, Amy, **pour en dire le moins,** voyons, que peux-tu bien vouloir dire, **Amy,** pour en dire le moins ?' (1978a, 15–16; see 1977c, 17). In all this, we can see Beckett's acute awareness of the importance of echoes in *Pas*.

Another echo was introduced to the French text in an interesting example of Beckettian epanorthosis, in the part of Scene II where V recounts May's words: 'Till one night, while still little more than a child, she called her mother and said, Mother, this is not enough' (1976d [1977], 45; *KLT* 111). This is translated as follows: '**Jusqu'au jour où, la nuit plutôt, jusqu'à la nuit où,** à peine sortie de l'enfance, elle appela sa mère et lui dit, Mère, ceci ne suffit pas' (1977c, 12). V's self-correction of '**jour**' to '**nuit**' recalls the genesis of *Footfalls*, which had the following as late as ET4: '**~~t~~T~~x~~ill one day,** while still little more than a child, she called her mother and said, Mother, this is not enough' (03r). So, V's use of the phrase 'Jusq'au jour' creates a further, bilingual echo, albeit one which is only perceptible via the compositional manuscripts.

In the *NRF* journal publication of the text, there is an error which creates an inadvertent echo, one which again reverberates back through the genesis of the play. This occurs in May's monologue, when she describes her own pacing in the third person: 'Voyez-**la** passer –. *(Un temps.)* Voyez-**la** passer devant le candélabre' (1977b, 13). In this version, the two pronouns in bold refer to May. But the first pronoun should read 'le' ['it'], referring as it does to 'A faint tangle of pale grey tatters' (1976d [1977], 47). This description of her appearance is a masculine noun phrase in *Pas*: '**Un** blême fouillis de haillons gris blanc' (1977b, 13). The *NRF* error does not appear on the setting copy for that edition (NRFSC, 05r) and is corrected in the Minuit text, in which May corrects herself: 'Voyez-**le** passer —. (*Un temps.*) Voyez-**la** passer devant le candélabre' (1977c, 15). So, it is probably an editorial error. However, it is worth noting that similar pronominal confusion is found in FT1, where Beckett briefly considered using 'her' instead of 'it': 'Voyez-**le**~~a~~e passer –' (04r). On the same page of typescript, he erroneously called Old Mrs Winter '**le** [*for* la] vieille Madame Winter', and on the next page he mixed up May and Amy: '~~**May**: Pas là.~~ **Amy**: Pas là' (FT1, 04r, 05r). Even for its author, the shifting pronominal referents of *Footfalls / Pas* caused trouble in translation, showing just how deeply the breakdown of subjectivity is embedded in this text.

With regard to the rhythm of the piece, a notable addition marks the increased rhythmicity of May's pacing in the French version. In *Footfalls*, this aspect is already important, as we can see in the opening stage directions: '*Steps: clearly audible rhythmic tread*' (1976d [1977], 42; *KLT* 109). But in *Pas*, this rhythmical quality is emphasized further: '*Pas : nettement audibles,* ***très*** *rythmés*' (1977c, 7). Beckett also changed the rhythm of the text itself, inserting and removing pauses in the dialogue. Since these changes were made after he directed performances of the play in English and German, they again draw attention to the fact that a staged breakdown is very different to one outlined only on the page.

Supporting the point that the aural qualities of the text are crucial to the dynamics of Beckett's theatre, one of the most interesting new lines in *Pas* is the introduction of the stage direction '*Psalmodié*' (1977c, 18), just before Mrs W says her closing prayer. The same verb is used in *Comment c'est*, where it also depicts a mother saying her prayers:

> ce n'est pas fini elle ferme les yeux et **psalmodie**
> une bribe du crédo dit apostolique je fixe furtif
> ses lèvres (2015, 23)
>
> [that's not all she closes her eyes and drones a snatch of the so-called Apostles' Creed I steal a look at her lips] (*HII* 11)

As Barry points out, the verb 'psalmodier' 'has two senses, "chant psalms or prayers" and "recite in monotonous fashion"' (2006, 147). Barry links this concept of recitation to the 'depersonalizing' effect of religious discourse in Beckett's work, a depersonalization that is paradoxically deeply personal because of Beckett's own childhood experience of liturgical texts, learning them as he did through repetition (2006, 146). We have already seen how liturgy shadows the text of *Footfalls*, especially its closing passages. In *Pas*, it becomes further integrated into the soundscape of the play through Beckett's instructions on Mrs W's prayer.

Beckett's textual awareness – and his authorial irony with regard to the 'mythology' of religion – is in evidence in the passage from *How It Is*, with the '**so-called** Apostles' Creed' drawing attention to the fact that, as scholars of Christianity have noted, 'the formula itself is not of apostolic origin' (Cross and Livingstone 1993, 75). It is with such authorial textual awareness in mind that I turn to the translation of religion in *Pas*.

Religion and the Bible

The first thing to note about religious imagery in *Pas* is that it is more explicit to the listening ear than in the English text. Consider the image of Christ's cross when May paces in the church, 'up and down, up and down, **His poor arm**' (1976d [1977], 46; *KLT* 112). While in English this is only explicit when one reads the text, the French translation makes it clear in performance that this is the Saviour's arm: 'allant et venant, allant et venant, le long du **pauvre bras sauveur**' (1977c, 14). In his drafts, Beckett experimented with a different adjective, before rejecting it on FT2: '(tout) le long du pauvre bras ~~**divin**~~ sauveur' (04r). In both cases, the arm is unmistakably Christ's.

We have already seen the prominence of the word 'cross' in the English text, Beckett choosing 'lacrosse' as the game that other girls played when a young May was already pacing (see chapter 6.1.2). Elmar Tophoven duly notes: 'the word "Cross" is prominent in the English', though his German translation – 'zum... La Crosse-Spiel' – was altered by Beckett to 'zum Himmel und Hölle-Spiel [hopscotch]' (qtd. in Garforth 1996, 60). So, Beckett decided to remove the 'cross' from the wording, but he alludes to it again in the spatial structure of hopscotch, which often features the shape of a cross in the outline traced on the ground. As Garforth points out, Beckett 'turned to this revised German version' while creating his French translation (1996, 60). On FT1, he tried '**la marelle**', the cruciform imagery of which would have matched May's later description of the church layout. But then two different open variants were added: 'Ciel et enfer' and 'au jeu du ciel et de l'enfer' (FT1, 03r), with the latter appearing in the published text: 'à ce jeu du ciel et de l'enfer' (1977c, 12). So, having considered using the French term for hopscotch, Beckett instead went for a literal translation of the German term, thereby foregrounding the presence of heaven and hell in *Pas*.

The French translation of Mrs W's prayer again demonstrates Beckett's eclectic use of his Bibles (see chapter 2.3.2). In FT1, we find the following:

'~~La~~ Que la **charité de Dieu, et la communication du Saint-Esprit, soient avec** nous, maintenant, et à jamais. Amen' (05r). As the highlighted text shows, this largely maps onto the Martin translation of 2 Corinthiens (13:13): '**Que** la grâce du Seigneur Jésus-Christ, et **la charité de Dieu, et la communication du Saint Esprit soient avec** vous tous! Amen.'[364] But Beckett underlined his FT1 version in red pen, marking it for later attention. When he redrafted the prayer on FT2, Beckett drew on another biblical source: '**L'amour** de Dieu, et la **communion** du Saint-Esprit, soient avec nous, **dès maintenant, et à jamais**' (05r). The closing phrase is not from Corinthiens, but it is biblical, particularly prevalent in the Psaumes. For instance, the Segond translation of Psaume 121 concludes: '**Dès maintenant et à jamais**'. In this case, as well as drawing on religious texts for use in his play, Beckett created his own translation of a liturgical text, grafting the psalmic phrase onto the end of Mrs W's prayer in order to provide a literal equivalent for the conclusion of the English benediction: 'now, and for evermore' (1976d [1977], 48; *KLT* 113; see chapter 6.1.2). In the published version, Beckett removed '**dès**', creating an even more literal word-for-word translation (1977c, 18).

Another variant in the above passage foregrounds what has been the central theme in my analysis of all three Beckett plays in this monograph. In using Martin's translation in FT1, Beckett translated the 'fellowship' of the Holy Spirit (1976d [1977], 48; *KLT* 113) as '**communication**'. However, from FT2 onwards, this becomes '**communion**' (05r). The latter wording can be found in Darby's Bible (Corinthiens 13:13), which also matches another variant in the above passage: Darby's translation includes '**l'amour**' instead of Martin's '**la charité**', again providing a more literal translation of the '**love** of God' in *Footfalls* (*KLT* 113) – and it seems Beckett favoured a literal translation in this particular case.[365] In a part of the play which exemplifies the 'rupture of the lines of **communication**' between staged subjects – with May voicing the prayer of Mrs W, who in turn mirrors her own mother – thus creating a breakdown of interpretation between audience and aesthetic object, Beckett chose not to use that particular word,

364 The verse numbers are slightly different in the English and the French translations.

365 Interestingly, '**communion**' is also found in the *English* text of 2 Corinthians (13:14), in the King James Version.

instead choosing something shorter, perhaps better suited to spoken delivery in the theatre.

10971/7 6

Id, Ego & Superego.

The philosopher Kant once declared that nothing proved to him the greatness of God more convincingly than the starry heavens and the moral conscience within us. The stars are unquestionably superb...

Super-ego: heir to Oedipus complex. A special function within the ego representing demand for restriction & rejection. Acute case of over-severity of super-ego towards ego appears in the melancholic attack. Cp. delusions of observation of certain psychotics, whose observing function (super-ego) has become sharply separated from the ego & projected into external reality.

The Ego, (including super-ego), not coextensive with xxxx the conscious (since patient is frequently unconscious of his resistances), just as the repressed is not coextensive with the unconscious.

Id: Instinctual cathexes seeking discharge - that in our view is all that the id contains.

The ego is that part of the id which has been modified by contact with the external world. It borrows its energy from the id. The means by which it has separated itself off from one part of the id were repressions & resistances. Repressed material merges into the id. The poor ego has to serve three harsh masters & do its best to reconcile claims of all three. The three tyrants are: The external world, the super-ego & the id. Goaded on by the id, hemmed in by the xxxxxx super-ego, rebuffed by reality, the ego struggles with its economic task of reducing forces & influences working in it & upon it to some kind of unity. When it fails it breaks out into anxiety. Reality anxiety in face of the outer world, moral anxiety in face of the super-ego, neurotic anxiety in face of the id.

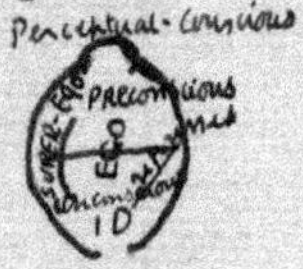

The object of psychoanalysis is to strengthen the ego, make it more independent of the super-ego, widen its field of vision & so extend its organisation that it can take over new portions of the id. Where id was, there shall ego be. It is reclamation work, like the draining of the Zuyder Zee.

Fig. 25: A page of Beckett's notes on Freud's 'Anatomy of the Mental Personality' (TCD MS 10971/7/6).

Conclusion: Beckett's 'dark matter'

When taking notes on Freud's essay 'The Anatomy of the Mental Personality' in 1934–5, Beckett came across a passage outlining how difficult it can be to represent the human mind clearly:

> We cannot do justice to the characteristics of the mind by means of linear contours, such as occur in a drawing or in a primitive painting, but we need rather the areas of colour shading off into one another that are to be found in modern pictures. After we have made our separations, we must allow what we have separated to merge again. Do not judge too harshly of a first attempt at picturing a thing so elusive as the human mind. (Freud 1933, 110)

Having already warned his readers that 'The danger is in the neatness of identifications' in his 1929 essay 'Dante ... Bruno . Vico .. Joyce' (*Dis* 19), Beckett may have been sympathetic to Freud's statement about the difficulty of drawing a precise portrait of the mind. The Irish writer did not transcribe this passage, but he did sketch Freud's diagram of the mind which follows immediately afterwards (TCD MS 10971/7/6; see Fig. 25 and Freud 1933, 111). Thus, long before staging the mind in the spatial art of the theatre, Beckett was interested in the spatial presentation of the human mind, albeit his own compositional procedures took a very different route to the scientific paradigm with which Freud aligned psychoanalysis.[366] In Beckett's staging of the mind, the lack of clarity, or 'shading' of which Freud speaks, would become an aesthetic instrument, key to staging the breakdown between subject and object.

In staging this subject–object breakdown in *Not I / Pas moi*, *That Time / Cette fois* and *Footfalls / Pas*, Beckett revisited the models of the self he had

366 See the repeated use of 'scientific' throughout Freud and Jung (1974).

researched as a young man, writing back against the 'mythologies' of psychoanalysis, psychology, Proustian memory and Protestant liturgy. Particularly pertinent here is Beckett's critique of medicine and its associated discourses: doctors such as Haddon in the *Footfalls* drafts are bringers of pain rather than relief, while the scientific jargon used to describe Mouth's experience is put at a firm distance from the speaking subject. At an authorial level, Beckett's filtering of scientific discourse resulted in a creative adaptation of 'images' in his plays, rather than a straightforward staging of psychoanalytic concepts. What emerged was a form of theatre that was barely theatre, at least according to its author. With regard to *Not I*, Beckett was relieved that the experimental form of his play was well received, that 'it's theatre in spite of all', as he remarked just after its 1973 performance at the Royal Court (see chapter 2.2.1). Beckett repeated these sentiments to his cousin Sheila Page on 26 January 1973:

> Astonished by reactions to Not I which I thought would be damned with faint praise by even the most open-minded as anti-theatre and unintelligible. Let's say they couldn't resist Billie! (*LSB IV* 325)

In using 'anti-theatre' here, Beckett may have been thinking of critic L. Estang's review of *Godot* in *La Croix* on 8 January 1953, where he used the very same word to describe Beckett's first staged play (see Pavis 1998, 26). According to Patrice Pavis, the term itself probably derives from Eugène Ionesco's subtitling of *La cantatrice chauve* as an 'ANTI-PIÈCE' ['anti-play'] (2002, title page; Pavis 1998, 26), marking Ionesco's self-estimation as a theatrical iconoclast. Like Beckett's, however, Ionesco's plays have long been associated with the traditional proscenium setup, reshaping that frame from the inside. Indeed, the two playwrights' work even shared the same performance spaces, as during the 1966 Spectacle Beckett–Ionesco–Pinget at the Odéon-Théâtre de France which started Beckett's directorial career (see chapter 2.1.2). What this genetic study has shown is that if Beckett's staging of the subject–object breakdown tended towards 'anti-theatre', it did so by remaking a firmly established set of theatrical conventions, particularly those regarding stage space.

Despite creating models of the mind that were increasingly enactive in the *storyworld* of his plays – as seen in the epigenetic revisions to *Footfalls* – Beckett consistently opted for the Cartesian Theatre of front-facing prosceniums when staging his work. In this, he was going against the contemporary trend in theatre practice, involving 'the rejection of frontal staging which had dominated Western theatre since the Renaissance' (Aronson 2019, 211), thus redefining the audience–performer relationship in a more explicitly enactive performance ecology. In 1965, the same year that Beckett directed his first play, Jerzy Grotowski published the article 'Ku teatrowi ubogiemu', which would later give its title to his famous collection of translated essays *Towards a Poor Theatre* (1968), an account of the environmental stagings of his Polish Laboratory Theatre.[367] In 1973, Richard Schechner's *Environmental Theatre* was published, charting his non-frontal performance environments with the Performance Group (founded 1967), in which audience and performer often mingled. Prototypical of this reaction against proscenium theatre space is the work – particularly the writings – of Antonin Artaud (Aronson 2019, 66). Beckett was familiar with Artaud's work, admitting to James Knowlson that he had read the French theatre maker 'for the odd blaze' (Beckett to Knowlson, 11 April 1972, *LSB IV* 292n1), and owned an English-language translation of *The Theatre and Its Double* (1958), a hugely influential text for models of post-proscenium theatre space.[368] Yet, in his own theatre practice, rather than opting to challenge the proscenium by creating a non-frontal performance space, Beckett opted for 'a subversion or an overstatement of the principles of the proscenium-arch theatre' (Pavis 1998, 134), overstating the proscenium by foregrounding the fourth wall in earlier work such as *Endgame* and subverting it in the darkened stages of his later plays. While others were exploring more enactive performance spaces in which the line between audience and performer was blurred, Beckett stuck with the Cartesian

367 Grotowski's essay appeared in a French translation in the *Cahiers Renaud-Barrault* in 1966 (Grotowski, 2002, 15). Given Beckett's close contact with Renaud and Barrault, it is likely he would have been aware of Grotowski's scenographic concepts circulating at the time. In her 1978 biography, Deirdre Bair quoted Beckett's forceful rejection of the Polish artist: 'Not for me these Grotowskis and Methods' (qtd. in Uhlmann 2013, 174).

368 https://www.beckettarchive.org/library/ART-THE.html.

Theatre as a means of exploring the 'no-man's-land' between viewing subject and aesthetic object.

In this light, it is notable that Beckett's admiration of Bram van Velde was of a painter who reshaped the rules of aesthetic perception from *within* the boundaries of the picture frame (see Introduction). So, it is perhaps unsurprising that Beckett chose to reshape the relationship between subject and object within the limits of the proscenium rather than opting for a more explicitly enactive performance space. After all, this is where the modern theatre subject was forged, with the depth implied by the proscenium stage being a key part of Ibsen's detailed psychological representations of middle-class life. As a young man in Dublin, Beckett admired Ibsen's work, seeing *An Enemy of the People* in 1931 and *The Wild Duck* in 1932 (Pilling 2006, 35, 40; Morin 2009, 24). Van Hulle and Nixon provide evidence that this interest in Ibsen was long-lasting: 'Beckett's correspondence with Barbara Bray reveals that he was reading a book by or about Ibsen in December 1978' (2013, 243n17). All of this might temper our interpretation of Beckett's most famous Ibsen statement, given in response to Alan Schneider's enquiry about the situation of Mouth in *Not I*: 'We're assuming she's in some sort of limbo. Death? After-life? Whatever you want to call it. OK?' (30 September 1972, *NABS* 279). The dominant interpretation is to read Beckett's reply as a forceful rejection of Ibsen's aesthetic (see Gontarski 2015, 138). Having compared Schneider's questions to actor Ralph Richardson's enquiries into Pozzo's backstory (see Beckett to Barney Rosset, 18 October 1954, *LSB II* 507), Beckett continued: 'I no more know where she is or why thus than she does. All I know is in the text. "She" is purely a stage entity, part of a stage image and purveyor of a stage text. The rest is Ibsen' (16 October 1972, *LSB IV* 311).[369] Yet, the same year, Beckett told David Gullette that *An Enemy of the People* was a great play (Van Hulle and Nixon 2013, 127). While Beckett's theatre works are far removed from the stage realism of cause-and-effect created by his Norwegian predecessor, he did create them with the same form of theatre space in mind. In doing so, he may have been influenced by James Joyce's laudatory review of Ibsen's

369 Beckett used a very similar phrase (albeit in English) to describe Richardson's queries as he would almost two decades later when Jessica Tandy asked him about *Not I*: 'stupid questions' (Beckett to Susan Manning, 18 October 1954, *LSB II* 508n1; see chapter 2.2.1).

When We Dead Awaken. 'Ibsen's New Drama' (1900) praises the playwright for activating the audience's interpretive faculties, arguing that the 'scroll' of protagonist Rubek's life is not 'read out to us', but that instead we read it 'for ourselves, piecing the various parts, and going closer to see wherever the writing on the parchment is fainter or less legible' (Joyce 1999, 25). Later in the same review, Joyce declares that 'the surroundings are nothing to Ibsen. The play is the thing' (1999, 55), which may have shaped Beckett's analysis of background in his TCD lectures on Racine (see Introduction), and hence his own interest in just how little could constitute the stage background of his later plays. In terms that foreshadow Beckett's praise of Racine's work as 'modern' due to his refusal to explain away his characters' psychological states (TCD MIC 60), Joyce's review figures Ibsen as a modern playwright who encourages his audiences to actively interpret.[370] Unlike Beckett's late plays, *When We Dead Awaken* does have a realist backstory: Irene has become a psychotic murderer because she gave the sculptor Rubek her 'living soul' by letting him use her as a model for his art (1978, 1055). Beckett's own characters never get such a backstory, and this may be why he sought to distance his late theatre from Ibsen's work. But he does draw on the same spatial paradigm, radically repurposed in the darkness of these later plays. As Erik Tonning points out, Beckett's letter to Schneider 'will not prevent any audience [...] from reconstructing what they can' of Mouth's story (2007, 117). As in *Not I*, what we can interpret in *Footfalls* and *That Time* depends heavily on the role of the darkened stage behind the visible stage image.

370 In Burrows' notes on Beckett's suggested outline for an essay on the character of Oreste in Andromaque, she writes: 'Modernité psichologique [*sic*] (inaccessible mind – stays complex – can't be analysed)' (TCD MIC 60/93). References to Racine as a 'modern' playwright are found throughout these notes.

'Dark matter'

'It is there at last that one finally begins to see, in the dark' ['C'est là qu'on commence enfin à voir, dans le noir'] (*Dis* 126, trans. in Carville 2018, 198). So Beckett wrote in 1945 of Bram van Velde's art. In going on to stage versions of the mind in which darkness engulfs the speaking protagonist, Beckett became an exemplary exponent of what Andrew Sofer terms 'dark matter', 'the invisible dimension of theater that escapes visual detection, even though its effects are felt everywhere in performance' (2016, 3). Using as one of his examples Beckett's offstage character Godot, Sofer argues for what he calls a 'phenomenology of the unseen' which would take into account '*whatever is materially unrepresented onstage but un-ignorable*' (2016, 6, 4; emphasis in original):

> If theater necessarily traffics in corporeal stuff (bodies, fluids, gases, objects), it also incorporates the incorporeal: offstage spaces and actions, absent characters, the narrated past, hallucination, blindness, obscenity, godhead, and so on. No less than physical actors and objects, such invisible presences matter very much indeed, even if spectators, characters, and performers cannot put their hands on them. (2016, 3)

Sofer tracks this performance technique as far back as medieval liturgical drama, in which the 'revelation of Jesus' Resurrection at the empty tomb' brought to a dramatic climax an expression of communal faith based on corporeal absence: 'The real presence of Christ is paradoxically guaranteed by his felt absence – an absence designed to move the crowd from theatrical wonder to reaffirmed faith' (2016, 1–2). When analysing the 'absent presence' of figures such as May (see chapter 6.1.2), material such as manuscript drafts, which are not immediately visible to most readers and audience members, can lead to an enrichment of our interpretive experience.

Building on the idea of the incompletion of the theatre text (see Introduction), the genetic critic Jean-Loup Rivière uses the same metaphor of 'dark matter' ['la matière noire'] to describe the invisible material that theatre practitioners draw on when constructing their performance.[371] Such genetic dark matter becomes evident when we explore an author's archive, gaining knowledge of authorial revisions ['repentirs'] (Rivière 2005, 12). Rivière cites the example of Anton Chekhov ordering his director Konstantin Stanislavsky to condense a two-page monologue of *The Three Sisters* into one line, recalling the 'textual scar' discussed in *Footfalls*, whereby Beckett's 'Dreadfully unhappy' character becomes 'dreadfully un—' (see chapter 6.1.2). So, in the case of manuscripts, unlike the invisible performance elements of Sofer's description, we can 'put [our] hands on' genetic 'dark matter' in the archive, and explore it with digital tools in online environments like the BDMP. Doing so will probably not solve the questions asked by these works – Who is Godot? What happened to Mouth in the field? Is May alive or dead? – but it can help us better understand how these questions are posed. Beckett described his aesthetics as 'a form that accommodates the mess' (see chapter 2.2.2), and while it is experiences of uncertainty and ambiguity that often characterize the reception of these plays, the highly formalized work of his late theatre – evident in Beckett's structural analyses of *Not I*, *That Time* and *Footfalls* – repays close attention to how these texts were crafted.

The 'dark matter' of Beckett's manuscripts continues to reveal many different forms of authorial craft used in the creation of his minimalist stage works. For example, we have seen evidence of Beckett employing additive modes of 'redoing' alongside his predominant method of textual 'undoing' (chapters 2.2.2, 2.3.2 and 4.2.2). Even within this 'undoing', Beckett's methods vary, comprising 'syllabic undoing'– the removal of syllables in revision, making the text smoother to deliver in performance (chapters 2.2.2, 2.3.2), 'verbal undoing' – the deletion of individual words in revision (chapters 2.2.2, 2.3.2, 4.1.2, 6.1.2), 'structural undoing' – the deletion of elements of a realist backstory which would explain the character's abnormal state of mind (chapter 6.1.2), as well as the 'textual scars' mentioned above. Like Rivière's theatre text, the delineation of Beckett's

371 Rivière defines theatrical dark matter in terms very similar to Sofer's: 'matière invisible, mais repérable et descriptible par ses effets sur le sensible' [matter which is invisible, but which can be spotted and described through its effects on what is perceptible] (2005, 12).

poetics is far from complete, but will be expanded upon, nuanced and challenged in future research, including volumes of this BDMP series.

What makes the metaphor of 'dark matter' particularly suggestive for Beckett's later stagings of the mind – both in terms of Rivière's focus on manuscripts as the invisible material of theatrical composition and Sofer's model of invisible elements in performance – is that *Not I / Pas moi*, *That Time / Cette fois* and *Footfalls / Pas* are dominated by actual darkness. Indeed, this encroaching gloom signals the changing nature of Beckett's use of performative 'dark matter' over the course of his theatre career. Darkness starts to make its presence felt on the Beckettian stage with *Krapp's Last Tape*, which features a spotlit protagonist in a pool of light set against a darkened backdrop. The human figure was further reduced in *Play*, where only the heads remain against an obscure background, a motif developed in 'Kilcool' at the same time Beckett was working on *Play*. While Krapp can visit the darkened recesses of his den for a drink, *Play* and 'Kilcool' can be said to have inaugurated a new, anti-representationalist use of 'dark matter', in which the darkened stage suggests but does not reveal, even in the form of a clinking glass or popping cork. The plays analysed in this volume see Beckett's theatrical 'dark matter' becoming even more ontologically uncertain. In *Not I*, *That Time* and *Footfalls*, Beckett hones his creative use of darkness as a means of heightening interpretive ambiguity, casting doubt on who is speaking, whether we are inside or outside a character's mind, or whether the protagonist is alive or dead. This creative use of 'dark matter' would continue to be a key feature of Beckett's theatre work: *Rockaby*'s dark stage makes it unclear as to whether or not W is in the domestic setting to which her monologue refers; the darkness that engulfs the Listener and Reader of *Ohio Impromptu* casts doubt on their situation, and hence the precise nature of the relationship between them; while the background darkness of *What Where* keeps the audience in the dark as to 'where' the stage figures actually are.

In these ways, varied yet consistent in his ever-deepening exploration of the darkened stage, Beckett's creative 'activation of darkness' (Lennon 2018, 57) materializes his statement to Tom Driver that the 'key word' in his theatre was 'perhaps' (see chapter 6.1.2). But of course, some light does remain on the Beckettian stage, however faint this may be. It may therefore be of importance that Beckett preceded his famous comment to

Driver with an analysis of Racine's *Phèdre*, which he outlines in terms of light and darkness:

> The destiny of Racine's *Phèdre* is sealed from the beginning: she will proceed into the dark. As she goes, she herself will be illuminated. At the beginning of the play she has partial illumination and at the end she has complete illumination, but there has been no question but that she moves toward the dark. That is the play. Within this notion clarity is possible, but for us who are neither Greek nor Jansenist there is not such clarity. The question would also be removed if we believed in the contrary – total salvation. But where we have both dark and light we have also the inexplicable. The key word in my plays is 'perhaps'. (qtd. in Driver 2005, 244)[372]

While, in this interpretation, Phèdre's recognition of her illicit love for her stepson Hippolyte, combined with her husband's return and Hippolyte's tragic death, constitutes a form of cognitive illumination set against the darkness of her eventual suicide, Mouth, May and Listener are unable to attain even this level of painful self-knowledge. Instead, the literal darkness that surrounds their partially lit figures makes interpretive clarity regarding the mind that is staged extremely difficult. Rather than staging a representation of a tragic situation or a named pathology, the plays work 'on the nerves' of their audiences, drawing our attention to the mind that tries – and fails – to interpret the play. In this way, the darkened, hollowed-out performance spaces of *Not I*, *That Time* and *Footfalls* play a key role in staging the breakdown of subject and object explored in Beckett's earlier writing. For it is there, 'in the dark', that his audiences finally see the complexity of psychological experience in interpreting a playtext.

Darkness is by no means a new phenomenon in the theatre, but the modern staging technology that Beckett employed did allow for new possibilities in stagings of the human mind that would accommodate psychological 'shading', creating an important material environment for Beckett's enactment of the subject–object breakdown. While emphasizing

372 For more on the key importance of light in Racine's play, see Revely-Calder (2016, 228–9).

its long heritage in the theatre (going back at least as far as Renaissance Italy), Scott Palmer sees the advent of modern lighting technologies as an important step in creating the material environment for turn-of-the-century stage naturalism (2017, 41) – the very theatre Beckett saw as a student at Dublin's Abbey Theatre. It was in this performance environment that Ibsen was able to create what Sofer calls '"speaking" objects' (2016, 107), drawing attention to the materiality of objects such as Hedda Gabler's gun to make the plot move towards its inexorable conclusion. Though Beckett would flaunt such catalysing objects to his audience in the blazing light of *Happy Days* (*HD* 29), in his later theatre he turns off the lights in order to turn his speakers into objects, whether it be the sepulchral images of Mouth and Listener or the near-lifeless figure of May. What this genetic study has done is to show how the 'dark matter' of manuscript material can shed light on Beckett's creation of his theatrical and psychological 'no-man's-land'.

Texts and Performance

Introducing the edited collection *Navigating Ireland's Theatre Archive*, Barry Houlihan has noted a shift in scholarly focus away from 'a singular text equating "performance to/as document"' (2019, 11). In my Introduction, I suggested an alternative to the idea of 'performance as text', instead considering the theatre text in discrete – yet inextricable – relation to the performance process. Over the course of this analysis, we have seen how text and performance were deeply intertwined in Beckett's theatre, particularly in the epigenetic transformations that are such a key part of the making of *Footfalls*. In this play, references to the reader thematize the interdependency of text and performance, playing with the line between the two without ever obliterating it. And these epigenetic transformations crossed languages, with the lighting directions of *Pas* showing just how much Beckett depended on his work in the theatre environment to develop his texts in translation. Rather than trying to establish one definitive version of the playtext ('performance as document' / 'text as performance'), genetic criticism draws on extant compositional documents in order to leave multiple versions open to the reader, foregrounding the dynamics of creativity rather than a 'singular text' 'to rule them all'. The sheer variety of Beckett's theatrical creativity in the making of *Not I / Pas moi, That Time /*

Cette fois and *Footfalls / Pas* should prove a rich source for those interested in interpreting his work, whether reading it on the page or performing it onstage. While 'the making of' his theatre texts began long before he staged them, it was there, on the almost complete darkness of the proscenium stage, that Beckett made his plays come to life, again and again, in spite of his repeated commitment to give up the theatre.

Works Cited

Works by Beckett

- (1951), *Malone meurt* (Paris: Les Éditions de Minuit).
- (1966), *En attendant Godot: pièce en deux actes*, ed. by Colin Duckworth (London: Harrap).
- (1969), *Watt*, trans. by Ludovic and Agnès Janvier in collaboration with the author (Paris: Les Éditions de Minuit).
- (1973a), *Not I* (London: Faber and Faber).
- (1973b), *Not I*, reprint (London: Faber and Faber).
- (1973c), 'In the Train with Mr. Madden', in: *The Iowa Review* 4.3: 33–5.
- (1974), *First Love and Other Shorts* (New York: Grove Press).
- (1975a), 'Pas moi', in: *Minuit* 12 (January): 2–9.
- (1975b), *Pas moi* (Paris: Les Éditions de Minuit).
- (1975c), *Oh les beaux jours suivi de Pas moi* (Paris: Les Éditions de Minuit).
- (1976a), *That Time* (London: Faber and Faber).
- (1976b), *That Time / Damals* (Frankfurt am Main: Suhrkamp Verlag).
- (1976c), *Footfalls* (London: Faber and Faber).
- (1976d [1977]), *Ends and Odds: Eight New Dramatic Pieces* (New York: Grove Press).
- (1976e), *Proust and Three Dialogues with Georges Duthuit* (London: John Calder).
- (1977a), *Ends and Odds: Plays and Sketches* (London: Faber and Faber).
- (1977b), 'Pas', in: *La Nouvelle Revue Française* 296 (September): 9–14.
- (1977c), *Pas* (Paris: Les Éditions de Minuit).
- (1978a), *Pas suivi de quatre esquisses* (Paris: Les Éditions de Minuit).
- (1978b), *Stücke und Bruchstücke* (Frankfurt am Main: Suhrkamp Verlag).
- (1978c), *Cette fois* (Paris: Les Éditions de Minuit).
- (1981), *Ends and Odds: Nine Dramatic Pieces*, enlarged ed. (New York: Grove Press).
- (1982), *Catastrophe et autres dramaticules: Cette fois, Solo, Berceuse, Impromptu d'Ohio* (Paris: Les Éditions de Minuit).

- (1984a), *Collected Shorter Plays* (London and Boston: Faber and Faber).
- (1984b), *Collected Shorter Plays* (New York: Grove Press).
- (1986a), *Catastrophe et autres dramaticules: Cette fois, Solo, Berceuse, Impromptu d'Ohio, Quoi où* (Paris: Les Éditions de Minuit).
- (1986b), *The Complete Dramatic Works* (London and Boston: Faber and Faber).
- (1990), *The Complete Dramatic Works* (London: Faber and Faber).
- (1992), *Dream of Fair to Middling Women*, ed. by Eoin O'Brien and Edith Fournier (Dublin: Black Cat Press).
- (1996), *Eleutheria*, trans. by Barbara Wright (London and Boston: Faber and Faber).
- (1999), *The Theatrical Notebooks of Samuel Beckett, vol. IV, The Shorter Plays*, ed. by S. E. Gontarski (London and New York: Faber and Faber; Grove Press).
- (2001), *Disjecta: Miscellaneous Writings and a Dramatic Fragment*, ed. by Ruby Cohn (London: Calder Publications).
- (2004), *Three Plays by Beckett*, DVD, dir. by Walter D. Asmus (Princeton: Films for the Humanities and Sciences).
- (2008a), *Eleutheria* (Paris: Les Éditions de Minuit).
- (2008b), *Filme für den SDR*, DVD (Frankfurt am Main: Suhrkamp).
- (2009a), *All That Fall and Other Plays for Radio and Screen*, pref. by Everett Frost (London: Faber and Faber).
- (2009b), *Company / Ill Seen Ill Said / Worstward Ho / Stirrings Still*, ed. by Dirk Van Hulle (London: Faber and Faber).
- (2009c), *Endgame*, pref. by Rónán McDonald (London: Faber and Faber).
- (2009d), *The Expelled / The Calmative / The End / First Love*, ed. by Christopher Ricks (London: Faber and Faber).
- (2009e), *How It Is*, ed. by Édouard Magessa O'Reilly (London: Faber and Faber).
- (2009f), *Krapp's Last Tape and Other Shorter Plays*, pref. by S. E. Gontarski (London: Faber and Faber).
- (2009g), *The Letters of Samuel Beckett, vol. I, 1929–1940*, ed. by George Craig, Martha Dow Fehsenfeld, Dan Gunn and Lois More Overbeck (Cambridge: Cambridge University Press).
- (2009h), *Molloy*, ed. by Shane Weller (London: Faber and Faber).
- (2009i), *Murphy*, ed. by J. C. C. Mays (London: Faber and Faber).
- (2009j), *Selected Poems, 1930–1989*, ed. by David Wheatley (London: Faber and Faber).
- (2009k), *Watt*, ed. by C. J. Ackerley (London: Faber and Faber).

- (2010a), *Happy Days: A Play in Two Acts*, pref. by James Knowlson (London: Faber and Faber).
- (2010b), *Malone Dies*, ed. by Peter Boxall (London: Faber and Faber).
- (2010c), *Mercier and Camier*, ed. by Seán Kennedy (London: Faber and Faber).
- (2010d), *More Pricks than Kicks*, ed. by Cassandra Nelson (London: Faber and Faber).
- (2010e), *Texts for Nothing and Other Shorter Prose, 1950–1976*, ed. by Mark Nixon (London: Faber and Faber).
- (2010f), *The Unnamable*, ed. by Steven Connor (London: Faber and Faber).
- (2010g), *Waiting for Godot*, pref. by Mary Bryden (London: Faber and Faber).
- (2011), *The Letters of Samuel Beckett, vol. II, 1941–1956*, ed. by George Craig, Martha Dow Fehsenfeld, Dan Gunn and Lois More Overbeck (Cambridge: Cambridge University Press).
- (2012a), *The Collected Poems of Samuel Beckett*, ed. by Seán Lawlor and John Pilling (London: Faber and Faber).
- (2012b), *Molloy* (Paris: Les Éditions de Minuit).
- (2012c), *Premier amour* (Paris: Les Éditions de Minuit).
- (2013a), *Le Dépeupleur* (Paris: Les Éditions de Minuit).
- (2013b), *Fin de partie* (Paris: Les Éditions de Minuit).
- (2013c), *Mercier et Camier* (Paris: Les Éditions de Minuit).
- (2013d), *Murphy* (Paris: Les Éditions de Minuit).
- (2014a), *Comédie et actes divers: Va-et-vient, Cascando, Paroles et musique, Dis Joe, Actes sans paroles I et II, Film, Souffle* (Paris: Les Éditions de Minuit).
- (2014b), *Echo's Bones*, ed. by Mark Nixon (London: Faber and Faber).
- (2014c), *The Letters of Samuel Beckett, vol. III, 1957–1965*, ed. by George Craig, Martha Dow Fehsenfeld, Dan Gunn and Lois More Overbeck (Cambridge: Cambridge University Press).
- (2014d), *Pour finir encore et autres foirades* (Paris: Les Éditions de Minuit).
- (2015), *Comment c'est* (Paris: Les Éditions de Minuit).
- (2016), *The Letters of Samuel Beckett, vol. IV, 1966–1989*, ed. by George Craig, Martha Dow Fehsenfeld, Dan Gunn and Lois More Overbeck (Cambridge: Cambridge University Press).

— Beckett, Samuel, and Alan Schneider (1998), *No Author Better Served: The Correspondence of Samuel Beckett & Alan Schneider*, ed. by Maurice Harmon (Cambridge, MA and London: Harvard University Press).

— Beckett, Samuel, and Herbert Marcuse (2007), 'Samuel Beckett's Poem for Herbert Marcuse and an Exchange of Letters', in: *Collected Papers of Herbert Marcuse, vol. IV, Art and Liberation*, ed. by Douglas Kellner (Abingdon and New York: Routledge), 200–2.

Other Works Cited or Consulted

— Abbott, H. Porter (1996), *Beckett Writing Beckett: The Author in the Autograph* (Ithaca, NY: Cornell University Press).
  · (2013), *Real Mysteries: Narrative and the Unknowable* (Columbus: Ohio State University Press).
— Ackerley, C. J. (2005), 'Obscure Locks, Simple Keys: The Annotated *Watt*', in: *Journal of Beckett Studies* 14.1–2: 1–6, 8–213, 215–91.
  · (2010), *Demented Particulars: The Annotated 'Murphy'* (Edinburgh: Edinburgh University Press).
— Ackerley, C. J., and S. E. Gontarski (2004), *The Grove Companion to Samuel Beckett: A Reader's Guide to his Works, Life, and Thought* (New York: Grove Press).
— Admussen, Richard L. (1979), *The Samuel Beckett Manuscripts: A Study* (Boston: G. K. Hall).
— Anon. (1969), 'Samuel Beckett Goes into Hiding', *The Times*, 25 October: 3.
— Anon. (1972), 'Art Exhibitions', *The Times*, 23 December: 3.
— Apollinaire, Guillaume (1950), 'Zone', trans. by Samuel Beckett, in: *Transition* 50.6: 126–31.
  · (1956), *Œuvres poétiques*, ed. by Marcel Adéma and Michel Décaudin (Paris: Gallimard).
  · (1972), *Zone*, trans. by Samuel Beckett (Dublin: Dolmen Press).
— Aronson, Arnold (2019), *The History and Theory of Environmental Scenography*, 2nd ed. (London: Methuen Drama).
— Asmus, Walter D. (1977), 'Practical Aspects of Theatre, Radio and Television: Rehearsal Notes for the German Premiere of Beckett's *That Time* and *Footfalls* at the Schiller-Theater Werkstatt, Berlin', trans. by Helen Watanabe, in: *Journal of Beckett Studies* 2: 82–95.
— Atik, Anne (2001), *How It Was: A Memoir of Samuel Beckett* (London: Faber and Faber).

— Bachelard, Gaston (2013), *Intuition of the Instant*, trans. by Eileen Rizo-Patron (Evanston, IL: Northwestern University Press).
— Bailey, Iain (2010), 'Samuel Beckett, Intertextuality, and the Bible' (PhD thesis, University of Manchester).
  · (2012), 'Beckett, Bilingualism and the Bible', in: *Samuel Beckett Today/Aujourd'hui* 24: 353–65.
— Bair, Deirdre (1990), *Samuel Beckett: A Biography*, rev. ed. (New York: Touchstone).
— Baker, Phil (2001), *Beckett and the Mythology of Psychoanalysis* (Basingstoke and New York: Palgrave).
— Baldassano, Christopher, Janice Chen, Asieh Zadbood, Jonathan W. Pillow, Uri Hasson, and Kenneth A. Norman (2017), 'Discovering Event Structure in Continuous Narrative Perception and Memory', in: *Neuron* 95: 709–21.
— Barrault, Jean-Louis (1972), *Souvenirs pour demain* (Paris: Éditions du Seuil).
  · (1974), *The Memoirs of Jean-Louis Barrault: Memories for Tomorrow*, trans. by Jonathan Griffin (New York: E. P. Dutton & Co.).
— Barry, Elizabeth (2006), *Beckett and Authority: The Uses of Cliché* (Basingstoke and New York: Palgrave Macmillan).
  · (ed.) (2008), 'Beckett, Language and the Mind', special issue of the *Journal of Beckett Studies* 17.1–2.
— Barry, Elizabeth, Ulrika Maude, and Laura Salisbury (eds) (2016), 'Beckett, Medicine and the Brain', special issue of the *Journal of Medical Humanities* 37.2.
— Barthes, Roland (2002a), *S/Z* (Paris: Éditions du Seuil).
  · (2002b), *S/Z*, trans. by Richard Miller (Malden, MA: Blackwell).
— Bates, Julie (2017), *Beckett's Art of Salvage: Writing and Material Imagination, 1932–1987* (Cambridge: Cambridge University Press).
— Baudelaire, Charles (1958), *Œuvres complètes*, ed. by Y.-G. Le Dantec (Paris: Gallimard).
— Beer, Ann (1985), '*Watt*, Knott and Beckett's Bilingualism', in: *Journal of Beckett Studies* 10: 37–75.
— Beloborodova, Olga (2018), 'The "Inward Turn" of Modernism in Samuel Beckett's Work: A Postcognitivist Reassessment' (PhD thesis, University of Antwerp).
  · (2019), *The Making of Samuel Beckett's 'Play' / 'Comédie' and 'Film'* (Brussels and London: University Press Antwerp and Bloomsbury).
— Beloborodova, Olga, and James Little (forthcoming), 'Staging Beckettian Minds: *Umwelt* and Cartesian Stage Space in Beckett's Plays', in: *Contemporary Theatre Review*.

— Beloborodova, Olga, and Pim Verhulst (2019), 'Human Machines Petrified: *Play*'s Mineral Mechanics and *Les statues meurent aussi*', in: *Journal of Beckett Studies* 28.2: 179–196.
· (2020), '"Mixing Media", or the Bee and the Bonnet: *Play* between Radio, Theatre, Television and Film', in: *Samuel Beckett Today/Aujourd'hui* 32.1: 9–24.
— Benda, Julien (1946), *La trahison des clercs*, rev. ed. (Paris: Éditions Bernard Grasset).
— Bergson, Henri (1944), *Creative Evolution*, trans. by Arthur Mitchell (New York: Modern Library).
· (1991), *Œuvres* (Paris: Presses universitaires de France).
· (2005), *Matter and Memory*, trans. by Nancy Margaret Paul and W. Scott Palmer (New York: Zone Books).
— (2008), *The Bible: Authorized King James Version* (Oxford: Oxford University Press).
— Bignell, Jonathan (2009), *Beckett on Screen: The Television Plays* (Manchester and New York: Manchester University Press).
— Billington, Michael (2009), *Harold Pinter*, rev. ed. (London: Faber and Faber).
— Bonal, Gérard (2000), *Les Renaud-Barrault*, ed. by Hervé Hamon (Paris: Éditions du Seuil).
— (1926), *The Book of Common Prayer and Administration of the Sacraments and Other Rites and Ceremonies of the Church According to the Use of the Church of Ireland* (Dublin: Association for Promoting Christian Knowledge).
— (1928), *The Book of Common Prayer, with the Additions and Deviations Proposed in 1928* (London: Society for Promoting Christian Knowledge).
— Brater, Enoch (1987), *Beyond Minimalism: Beckett's Late Style in the Theater* (New York and Oxford: Oxford University Press).
— Breazeale, Dan (2018), 'Karl Leonhard Reinhold', *The Stanford Encyclopedia of Philosophy*, ed. by Edward N. Zalta, https://plato.stanford.edu/archives/spr2018/entries/karl-reinhold/.
— Brenda ([1875] 2011), *Froggy's Little Brother*, Kindle ed. (n. p.: Read Books).
— Brewer, Charlotte (2016), 'Labelling and Metalanguage', in: *The Oxford Handbook of Lexicography*, ed. by Philip Durkin (Oxford: Oxford University Press), 488–500.
— Browning, Robert (1979), *Robert Browning's Poetry: Authoritative Texts, Criticism*, ed. by James F. Loucks (New York and London: W. W. Norton).
— Bryden, Mary, Julian Garforth, and Peter Mills (1998), *Beckett at Reading: Catalogue of the Beckett Manuscript Collection at the University of Reading* (Reading: Whiteknights Press and the Beckett International Foundation).

— Burton, Robert (1938), *The Anatomy of Melancholy*, ed. by Floyd Dell and Paul Jordan-Smith (New York: Tudor Publishing Company).
— Buzelin, Hélène (2005), 'Unexpected Allies: How Latour's Network Theory Could Complement Bourdieusian Analyses in Translation Studies', in: *The Translator* 11.2: 193–218.
· (2007), 'Translations "in the Making"', in: *Constructing a Sociology of Translation*, ed. by Michaela Wolf and Alexandra Fukari (Amsterdam; Philadelphia: John Benjamins Publishing Company), 135–69.
— Camp, Pannill (2007), 'Theatre Optics: Enlightenment Theatre Architecture in France and the Architectonics of Husserl's Phenomenology', in: *Theatre Journal* 59.4: 615–33.
— Carville, Conor (2018), *Samuel Beckett and the Visual Arts* (Cambridge: Cambridge University Press).
— Caselli, Daniela (2005), *Beckett's Dantes: Intertextuality in the Fiction and Criticism* (Manchester and New York: Manchester University Press).
— Clark, Andy, and David J. Chalmers (2010), 'The Extended Mind', in: *The Extended Mind*, ed. by Richard Menary (Cambridge, MA and London: MIT Press), 27–42.
— Cohn, Ruby (1973), *Back to Beckett* (Princeton: Princeton University Press).
· (1976), 'Beckett's German *Godot*', in: *Journal of Beckett Studies* 1: 41–9.
· (1980), *Just Play: Beckett's Theater* (Princeton: Princeton University Press).
· (2008), *A Beckett Canon* (Ann Arbor: University of Michigan Press).
— Coleridge, Samuel Taylor (1907), *Biographia Literaria, vol. 1*, ed. by John Shawcross (Oxford: Clarendon Press).
— Conley, Tim (2001), 'Joyces Mistakes: Problems of Intention, Irony, and Interpretation' (PhD thesis, Queen's University, Kingston, ON).
— Connor, Steven (1992), 'Between Theatre and Theory: *Long Observation of the Ray*' in: *The Ideal Core of the Onion: Reading Beckett Archives*, ed. by John Pilling and Mary Bryden (Reading: Beckett International Foundation), 79–98.
· (2007), *Samuel Beckett: Repetition, Theory and Text*, rev. ed. (Aurora, CO: Davies Group).
— Cross, F. L., and E. A. Livingstone (eds) (1993), *The Oxford Dictionary of the Christian Church*, rev. ed. (Oxford: Oxford University Press).
— Cuddon, J. A. (1984), *A Dictionary of Literary Terms*, rev. ed. (Harmondsworth: Penguin Books).
— Dante Alighieri (1866), *The Vision; Or, Hell, Purgatory, and Paradise*, trans. by Henry Francis Cary (London: Bell and Daldy).

· (1999), *The Divine Comedy*, bilingual ed., ed. by Robert Hollander, trans. by Robert Hollander and Jean Hollander, http://etcweb.princeton.edu/dante/pdp/.

— Debray-Genette, Raymonde (1979), 'Génétique et poétique: le cas Flaubert', in: *Essais de critique génétique*, ed. by Louis Hay (Paris: Flammarion), 21–67.

— De Compagnon, Antoine (1997), '*À la recherche du temps perdu*, de Marcel Proust', in: *Les lieux de mémoire, vol. 3, Les France, 2, Traditions*, ed. by Pierre Nora (Paris: Gallimard), http://www.college-de-france.fr/media/antoine-compagnon/UPL18784_1_A.Compagnon_Lieu_de_m_moire.pdf.

— Dennett, Daniel C. (1991), *Consciousness Explained* (New York, Boston and London: Back Bay Books).

— Diamond, Elin (2004), 'Feminist Readings of Beckett', in: *Palgrave Advances in Samuel Beckett Studies*, ed. by Lois Oppenheim (London: Palgrave Macmillan), 45–67.

— Dinçel, Burç İdem (2019), 'Translating the Tragic: Mimetic Transformation of Attic Tragedies on the Contemporary Stage' (PhD thesis, Trinity College Dublin).

— Di Paolo, Ezequiel A., Marieke Rohde, and Hanne De Jaegher (2010), 'Horizons for the Enactive Mind: Values, Social Interaction, and Play', in: *Enaction: Toward a New Paradigm for Cognitive Science*, ed. by John Stewart, Olivier Gapenne and Ezequiel A. Di Paolo (Cambridge, MA and London: MIT Press), 33–87.

— Dobbs, Henry (1933), 'All Saints', Blackrock', *Our Church Review*, August ed.: 165–6.

— Driver, Tom (2005), 'Tom Driver in *Columbia University Forum*', in: *Samuel Beckett: The Critical Heritage*, ed. by Lawrence Graver and Raymond Federman (London and New York: Routledge and Kegan Paul), 241–7.

— Dukes, Gerry (2000), 'Introduction', in: Samuel Beckett, *First Love and Other Novellas*, ed. by Gerry Dukes (London: Penguin Books), 1–8.

— Dwan, Lisa (2016), 'Mouth Almighty: How Billie Whitelaw Helped Me Find Beckett and *Not I*', in: *American Theatre*, 12 April, http://www.americantheatre.org/2016/04/12/mouth-almighty-how-billie-whitelaw-helped-me-find-beckett-and-not-i/.

— Elam, Keir (1997), 'World's End: West Brompton, Turdy and Other Godforsaken Holes', in: *Samuel Beckett Today/Aujourd'hui* 6: 165–80.

— Eliot, T. S. (2001), *The Waste Land*, ed. by Michael North (New York and London: W. W. Norton & Company).

— Favorini, Attilio (2008), *Memory in Play: From Aeschylus to Sam Shepard* (New York: Palgrave Macmillan).

— Feldman, Matthew (2006), *Beckett's Books: A Cultural History of Samuel Beckett's 'Interwar Notes'* (New York and London: Continuum).

— Fludernik, Monika (2005), *Towards a 'Natural' Narratology* (London and New York: Routledge).
— Frankenberg-Garcia, Ana (2004), 'Are Translations Longer than Source Texts? A Corpus-based Study of Explicitation', paper presented at CULT (Corpus Use and Learning to Translate) Conference, Barcelona, 22–4 January: 1–8, http://hdl.handle.net/10400.26/253.
— Freud, Sigmund (1933), *New Introductory Lectures on Psycho-analysis* (New York: Carlton House).
— Freud, Sigmund, and C. G. Jung (1974), *The Freud/Jung Letters: The Correspondence between Sigmund Freud and C. G. Jung*, ed. by William McGuire, trans. by Ralph Manheim and R. F. C. Hull (Princeton: Princeton University Press).
— Frost, Everett C., and Jane Maxwell (2006), 'Catalogue of "Notes Diverse Holo[graph]"', in: *Samuel Beckett Today/Aujourd'hui* 16: 15–181.
— Garforth, Julian A. (1996), 'Translating Beckett's Translations', in: *Journal of Beckett Studies* 6.1: 49–70.
— Gontarski, S. E. (1980), '"Making Yourself All Up Again": The Composition of Samuel Beckett's *That Time*', in: *Modern Drama* 23.2: 112–20.
  · (1983), 'Text and Pre-texts of Samuel Beckett's *'Footfalls*', in: *The Papers of the Bibliographical Society of America* 77.2: 191–5.
  · (1985), *The Intent of 'Undoing' in Samuel Beckett's Dramatic Texts* (Bloomington: Indiana University Press).
  · (1998), 'Revising Himself: Performance as Text in Samuel Beckett's Theatre', in: *Journal of Modern Literature* 22.1: 131–45.
  · (2006), 'Greying the Canon: Beckett in Performance', in: *Beckett after Beckett*, ed. by S. E. Gontarski and Anthony Uhlmann (Gainesville: University Press of Florida), 141–57.
  · (2015a), *Creative Involution: Bergson, Beckett, Deleuze* (Edinburgh: Edinburgh University Press).
  · (2015b), 'Samuel Beckett and the "Idea" of Theatre: Performance through Artaud and Deleuze', in: *The New Cambridge Companion to Samuel Beckett*, ed. by Dirk Van Hulle (Cambridge: Cambridge University Press), 126–41.
— Grene, Nicholas (2004), *The Politics of Irish Drama: Plays in Context from Boucicault to Friel* (Cambridge: Cambridge University Press).
— Grésillon, Almuth (1994), *Éléments de critique génétique: lire les manuscrits modernes* (Paris: Presses universitaires de France).

— Grotowski, Jerzy (2002), *Towards a Poor Theatre*, ed. by Eugenio Barba (New York: Routledge).
— Gunn, Dan (2012), 'Samuel Beckett', in: *Great Shakespeareans, vol. 12: Joyce, T. S. Eliot, Auden, Beckett*, ed. by Adrian Poole (London: Continuum), 149–97.
— Habibi, Reza (2018), 'Samuel Beckett's "Psychology Notes" and *The Unnamable*', in: *Journal of Beckett Studies* 27.2: 211–27.
— Hackney, Stephen (2020), *On Canvas: Preserving the Structure of Paintings* (Los Angeles: Getty Conservation Institute).
— Hamilton, Scott Eric (2018), 'Antiquarianism, Archaeology, and Aporetic Immanence in Beckett's Prose', in: *Irish Studies Review* 26.2: 163–80.
— Harvey, Lawrence E. (1970), *Samuel Beckett: Poet & Critic* (Princeton: Princeton University Press).
— Haynes, John, and James Knowlson (2003), *Images of Beckett* (Cambridge: Cambridge University Press).
— Hegel, Georg Wilhelm Friedrich (2010), *Encyclopedia of the Philosophical Sciences in Basic Outline, Part I: Science of Logic*, ed. and trans. by Klaus Brinkmann and Daniel O. Dahlstrom (Cambridge: Cambridge University Press).
— Herman, David (2011), 'Re-minding Modernism', in: *The Emergence of Mind: Representations of Consciousness in Narrative Discourse in English*, ed. by David Herman (Lincoln, NE and London: University of Nebraska Press), 243–72.
— Hölderlin, Friedrich (2019), *Hyperion, or the Hermit in Greece*, trans. by Howard Gaskill (Cambridge: Open Book Publishers).
— Houlihan, Barry (2019), 'Introduction: The Potential of the Archive', in: *Navigating Ireland's Theatre Archive: Theory, Practice, Performance* (Oxford and New York: Peter Lang), 9–27.
— Houston Jones, David (2011), *Samuel Beckett and Testimony* (Basingstoke and New York: Palgrave Macmillan).
— Hutto, Daniel D., and Erik Myin (2013), *Radicalizing Enactivism: Basic Minds without Content* (Cambridge, MA and London: MIT Press).
  · (2017), *Evolving Enactivism: Basic Minds Meet Content* (Cambridge, MA and London: MIT Press).
— Huxley, Aldous (1990), *The Doors of Perception*, in: *The Doors of Perception and Heaven and Hell* (New York; San Francisco; Toronto: Perennial Library), 7–79.
— Ibsen, Henrik (1978), *The Complete Major Prose Plays*, trans. by Rolf Fjelde (New York: Plume).

— Ionesco, Eugène (2002), *La cantatrice chauve, anti-pièce, suivi de La leçon, drame comique* (Paris: Gallimard).
— Iser, Wolfgang (1980), *The Implied Reader: Patterns of Communication in Prose Fiction from Bunyan to Beckett* (Baltimore, MD and London: Johns Hopkins University Press).
— James, William (1992), 'The Stream of Consciousness', in: *Writings: 1878–1899* (New York: Library of America), 152–73.
— Jeantroux, Myriam (2004), 'La structure du huis clos dans le théâtre de Samuel Beckett: un "art d'incarcération"' (PhD thesis, University of Franche-Comté).
— Jones, Ernest (1920), *Treatment of the Neuroses* (London: Baillière, Tindall and Cox).
· (1923), *Papers on Psycho-analysis* (London: Baillière, Tindall and Cox).
· (1953), *Sigmund Freud: Life and Work, vol. 1, The Young Freud, 1856–1900* (London: Hogarth Press)
· (1955), *Sigmund Freud: Life and Work, vol. 2, Years of Maturity, 1901–1919* (London: Hogarth Press).
· (1957), *Sigmund Freud: Life and Work, vol. 3, The Last Phase, 1919–1939* (London: Hogarth Press).
— Joyce, James (1986), *Ulysses*, ed. by Hans Walter Gabler, Wolfhard Steppe and Claus Melchior (New York: Vintage Books).
· (1999), *On Ibsen*, ed. by Dennis Phillips (Copenhagen and Los Angeles: Green Integer Books).
· (2004), *A Portrait of the Artist as a Young Man and Dubliners* (New York: Barnes and Noble Classics).
— Juliet, Charles (2009), *Conversations with Samuel Beckett and Bram van Velde*, trans. by Tracy Cooke, Aude Jeanson, Axel Nesme, Morgaine Reinl and Janey Tucker (Champaign, IL and London: Dalkey Archive Press).
— Jung, C. G. (2014), *The Collected Works of C. G. Jung, vol. 18, The Symbolic Life: Miscellaneous Writings*, rev. ed., ed. by Herbert Read, Michael Fordham, Gerhard Adler and William McGuire, trans. by R. F. C. Hull (London and New York: Routledge).
— Kalb, Jonathan (1991), *Beckett in Performance* (Cambridge: Cambridge University Press).
— Key, Andrew (2015), '"Will You Never Have Done Turning It All Over?" Doubt, Dialectics and Bad Infinity in the *Footfalls* Manuscripts', paper presented at The Inaugural Conference of the Samuel Beckett Society, Phoenix, AZ, 19–20 February.

- Kim, Rina (2016), '"[G]azing into the Synaptic Chasm": the Brain in Beckett's Writing', in: *Journal of Medical Humanities* 37: 149–160.
- Knowlson, James (1997), *Damned to Fame: The Life of Samuel Beckett* (London: Bloomsbury).
- Knowlson, James, and Elizabeth Knowlson (eds) (2006), *Beckett Remembering, Remembering Beckett: Uncollected Interviews with Samuel Beckett and Memories of Those Who Knew Him* (London: Bloomsbury).
- Knowlson, James, and John Pilling (1979), *Frescoes of the Skull: The Later Prose and Drama of Samuel Beckett* (London: John Calder).
- Kristeva, Julia (1982), *Desire in Language: A Semiotic Approach to Literature and Art*, ed. by Leon S. Roudiez, trans. by Thomas Gora, Alice Jardine and Leon S. Roudiez (New York: Columbia University Press).
- Lake, Carlton (1984), *No Symbols Where None Intended: A Catalogue of Books, Manuscripts, and Other Material Relating to Samuel Beckett in the Collections of the Humanities Research Center* (Austin: Humanities Research Center, University of Texas at Austin).
- Latour, Bruno (2005), *Reassembling the Social: An Introduction to Actor-Network-Theory* (Oxford: Oxford University Press).
- Lefebvre, Henri (2007), *Rhythmanalysis: Space, Time and Everyday Life*, trans. by Stuart Elden and Gerald Moore (London: Continuum).
- Lemprière, John (1833), *A Classical Dictionary*, rev. ed., ed. by T. Smith (London: printed for T. Allman).
- Lennon, Andrew (2018), 'Beckett and Darkness: The Drive to and the Flight from…', in: *Contemporary Theatre Review* 28.1: 54–67.
- Little, James (2017), 'Closed Spaces: Beckett and Confinement' (PhD thesis, Trinity College Dublin).
  - (2018), 'Beckett's "Mongrel Mime": Politics and Poetics', in: *Journal of Beckett Studies* 27.2: 193–210.
  - (2020a), '"First the Place, Then I'll Find Me in It": *The Unnamable*'s Pronouns and the Politics of Confinement', in: *Beckett and Politics*, ed. by William Davies and Helen Bailey (London: Palgrave Macmillan).
  - (2020b), 'Inhuman Habitations: Samuel Beckett's *Imagination Dead Imagine* and *All Strange Away*', in: *Samuel Beckett Today/Aujourd'hui* 32.2: 239–54.
  - (2020c), *Samuel Beckett in Confinement: The Politics of Closed Space* (London: Bloomsbury Academic).

- Lloyd, David (2016), *Beckett's Thing: Painting and Theatre* (Edinburgh: Edinburgh University Press).
- Mackintosh, Iain (2005), *Architecture, Actor and Audience* (London and New York: Routledge).
- Malafouris, Lambros (2013), *How Things Shape the Mind: A Theory of Material Engagement* (Cambridge, MA and London: MIT Press).
- Mallarmé, Stéphane (1965 [1945]), *Œuvres complètes*, ed. by Henri Mondor and G. Jean-Aubry (Paris: Gallimard).
- Martel, Kareen (2005), 'Les notions d'intertextualité et d'intratextualité dans les théories de la réception', in: *Protée* 33.1 (2005): 93–102.
- Maude, Ulrika (2015), 'Beckett, Body and Mind', in: *The New Cambridge Companion to Samuel Beckett*, ed. by Dirk Van Hulle (Cambridge: Cambridge University Press), 170–84.
- Maxwell, Jane (2006), 'The Samuel Beckett Manuscripts at Trinity College Library Dublin', in: *Samuel Beckett Today/Aujourd'hui* 16: 183–99.
- McConachie, Bruce (2001), 'Doing Things with Image Schemas: The Cognitive Turn in Theatre Studies and the Problem of Experience for Historians', in: *Theatre Journal* 53.4: 569–94.
- McDonald, Ronan (2002), *Tragedy and Irish Literature: Synge, O'Casey, Beckett* (Basingstoke and New York: Palgrave).
- McKinley, Grace (2006), 'Appendix: Beckett on Racine', in: *Beckett Remembering, Remembering Beckett: Uncollected Interviews with Samuel Beckett and Memories of Those Who Knew Him*, ed. by James and Elizabeth Knowlson (London: Bloomsbury), 306–13.
- McMillan, Dougald, and Martha Fehsenfeld (1988), *Beckett in the Theatre: The Author as Practical Playwright and Director, from 'Waiting for Godot' to 'Krapp's Last Tape'* (London and New York: Riverrun Press and John Calder).
- McMullan, Anna (2005), *Theatre on Trial: Samuel Beckett's Later Drama* (London and New York: Routledge).
  - (2006), 'Samuel Beckett's "J. M. Mime": Generic Mutations of a Dramatic Fragment', in: *Samuel Beckett Today/Aujourd'hui* 16: 333–45.
- McNaughton, James (2018), *Samuel Beckett and the Politics of Aftermath* (Oxford: Oxford University Press).
- McTighe, Trish (2017), 'Vessel and Nation: Company SJ's *Beckett in the City: The Women Speak*', in: *Performance Ireland, Special Issue: Gender, Sexuality, and the City*, Kindle ed., ed. by Shonagh Hill and Cormac O'Brien (Dublin: Carysfort Press).

— Melnyk, Davyd (2005), 'Never Been Properly Jung', in: *Samuel Beckett Today/ Aujourd'hui* 15: 355–62.
— Mitchell, Breon (forthcoming), *Samuel Beckett: A Bibliography, Part III: The Final Years, 1970–1989*, https://www.beckettarchive.org/.
— Mooney, Sinéad (2010), 'Beckett in French and English', in: *A Companion to Samuel Beckett*, ed. by S. E. Gontarski (Chichester: Wiley-Blackwell), 196–208.
— Moorjani, Angela (2012), 'Beckett's Racinian Fictions: "Racine and the Modern Novel" Revisited', in: *Samuel Beckett Today/Aujourd'hui* 24: 41–56.
— Morin, Emilie (2009), *Samuel Beckett and the Problem of Irishness* (Basingstoke and New York: Palgrave Macmillan).
  · (2017), *Beckett's Political Imagination* (Cambridge: Cambridge University Press).
— Morrison, Kristin (1983), 'Neglected Biblical Allusions in Beckett's Plays: "Mother Pegg" Once More', in: *Samuel Beckett: Humanistic Perspectives*, ed. by Morris Beja, S. E. Gontarski and Pierre Astier (Columbus: Ohio State University Press), 91–8.
— Nietzsche, Friedrich (2007), *The Birth of Tragedy and Other Writings*, ed. by Raymond Geuss and Ronald Speirs, trans. by Ronald Speirs (Cambridge: Cambridge University Press).
— Nixon, Mark (2010), 'Preface', in: *Texts for Nothing and Other Shorter Prose, 1950–1976*, ed. by Mark Nixon (London: Faber and Faber), vii–xxiv.
  · (2011), *Samuel Beckett's German Diaries, 1936–1937* (London: Continuum).
  · (2014), 'Beckett's Unpublished Canon', in: *The Edinburgh Companion to Samuel Beckett and the Arts*, ed. by S. E. Gontarski (Edinburgh: Edinburgh University Press), 282–305.
— Nugent-Folan, Georgina (2016), '"Say it Simply [...] Say it Simplier": Samuel Beckett and Gertrude Stein's Aesthetics of Writing Worser' (PhD thesis, Trinity College Dublin).
  · (2021), *The Making of Samuel Beckett's 'Company' / 'Compagnie'* (Brussels and London: University Press Antwerp and Bloomsbury).
— N. Z. (1967), 'Inauguration de deux "secondes salles" dans les subventionnés: le "Petit-Odéon" et le "Théâtre Firmin-Gémier", *Le Monde*, 11 January, https://www.lemonde.fr/archives/article/1967/01/11/inauguration-de-deux-secondes-salles-dans-les-subventionnes-le-petit-odeon-et-le-theatre-firmin-gemier_2609132_1819218.html.
— O'Brien, Eoin (1986), *The Beckett Country: Samuel Beckett's Ireland* (Monkstown: Black Cat Press).

— O'Reilly, Édouard Magessa (2016), 'English Introduction: How to Use this Edition', in: Samuel Beckett, *Comment c'est / How It Is and / et L'image: A Critical-genetic Edition / Une édition critico-génétique*, ed. by Édouard Magessa O'Reilly (New York and London: Routledge), ix–xxxv.
— O'Reilly, Édouard Magessa, Dirk Van Hulle, and Pim Verhulst (2017), *The Making of Samuel Beckett's 'Molloy'* (Brussels and London: University Press Antwerp and Bloomsbury).
— Paavolainen, Teemu (2016), 'Textures of Thought: Theatricality, Performativity and the Extended/Enactive Debate', in: *The Cognitive Humanities: Embodied Mind in Literature and Culture*, ed. by Peter Garratt (London: Palgrave Macmillan), 71–92.
— Palmer, Scott (2017), 'Harnessing Shadows: A Historical Perspective on the Role of Darkness in the Theatre', in: *Theatre in the Dark: Shadow, Gloom and Blackout in Contemporary Theatre*, ed. by Adam Alston and Martin Welton (London: Bloomsbury Methuen Drama), 37–63.
— Pavis, Patrice (1998), *Dictionary of the Theatre: Terms, Concepts, and Analysis*, trans. by Christine Shantz (Toronto and Buffalo: University of Toronto Press).
— 'Peacock Theatre: Three Foreign Plays' (1931), *Irish Times*, 20 February: 5.
— Pilling, John (1976), 'Beckett's *Proust*', in: *Journal of Beckett Studies* 1: 8–29.
· (2004), 'Dates and Difficulties in Beckett's *Whoroscope* Notebook', in: *Journal of Beckett Studies* 13.2: 39–48.
· (2006), *A Samuel Beckett Chronology* (Basingstoke and New York: Palgrave Macmillan).
· (2015), '"Dead before Morning": How Beckett's "Petit Sot" Never Got Properly Born', in: *Journal of Beckett Studies* 24.2: 198–209.
— Pothast, Ulrich (2008), *The Metaphysical Vision: Arthur Schopenhauer's Philosophy of Art and Life and Samuel Beckett's Own Way to Make Use of It* (New York: Peter Lang).
— Pound, Ezra (1913), 'Imagisme', in: *Poetry: A Magazine of Verse* 1.6: 198–200.
— Pountney, Rosemary (1988), *Theatre of Shadows: Samuel Beckett's Drama, 1956–76* (Gerrards Cross and Totowa, NJ: Colin Smythe; Barnes and Noble Books).
— Powell, Josh (2016), 'Perception, Attention, Imagery: Samuel Beckett and the Psychological Experiment' (PhD thesis, University of Exeter).
· (2017), 'Sharing her Bewilderment: *Not I*, Experimentation and the Perception of Speech', in: *Journal of Beckett Studies* 26.2: 221–38.

— Proust, Marcel (2003), *In Search of Lost Time*, trans. by C. K. Scott Moncrieff, Terence Kilmartin and Andreas Mayor, rev. by D. J. Enright, 6 vols (New York: Modern Library).
  · (2011), *À la recherche du temps perdu*, ed. by Jean-Yves Tadié (gen. ed.), 4 vols (Paris: Gallimard).
— Pryor, Sean and David Trotter (2016), 'Introduction', in: *Writing, Medium, Machine: Modern Technographies*, ed. by Sean Pryor and David Trotter (London: Open Humanities Press), 7–17.
— Rabaté, Jean-Michel (2016), *Think, Pig! Beckett at the Limit of the Human* (New York: Fordham University Press).
— Rank, Otto (1929), *The Trauma of Birth* (London: Kegan Paul, Trench, Trubner and Co.; New York: Harcourt, Brace and Company).
— Renaud, Madeleine (2000), *La déclaration d'amour: rencontres avec André Coutin* (Paris: Éditions du Rocher).
— Revely-Calder, Cal (2016), 'Racine Lighting Beckett', in: *Journal of Beckett Studies* 25.2: 225–42.
— Richardson, Brian (2006), *Unnatural Voices: Extreme Narration in Modern and Contemporary Fiction* (Columbus: Ohio State University Press).
— Ricœur, Paul (2000), *La mémoire, l'histoire, l'oubli* (Paris: Éditions de Seuil).
  · (2006), *Memory, History, Forgetting*, trans. by Kathleen Blamey and David Pellauer (Chicago and London: University of Chicago Press).
— Rivière, Jean-Loup (2005), 'La matière noire. Génétique et théâtralité', in: *Genesis* 26: 11–17.
— (1885–8), *La Sainte Bible, qui comprend l'ancien et le nouveau testament*, trans. by J. N. Darby (La Haye: Imprimerie C. Blommendaal, C. H. Voorhoeve, successeur; Pau: Édouard Laügt; Vevey: Guignard).
— (1899), *La Sainte Bible, qui comprend l'ancien et le nouveau testament*, trans. by Louis Segond (Paris: Delessert).
— (1887), *La Sainte Bible, qui contient l'ancien et le nouveau testament: version d'Ostervald* (Paris: Société Biblique Britannique et Étrangère).
— (1852), *La Sainte Bible, qui contient le vieux et le nouveau testament*, trans. by David Martin (New York: Société Biblique Américaine).
— Salisbury, Laura (2008), '"What Is the Word": Beckett's Aphasic Modernism', in: *Journal of Beckett Studies* 17.1–2: 78–126.
— Sardin-Damestoy, Pascale (2020), *Samuel Beckett: auto-traducteur ou l'art de l''empêchement'*, eBook (Arras: Artois Presses Université).

— Sartre, Jean-Paul (1989), *No Exit and Three Other Plays*, trans. by S. Gilbert and I. Abel (New York: Vintage International).
  · (2000), *Huis clos suivi de Les mouches* (Paris: Gallimard).
— Schechner, Richard (1994), *Environmental Theater*, rev. ed. (Montclair, NJ: Applause).
— Schneider, Alan (2005), 'Alan Schneider in *Chelsea Review*', in: *Samuel Beckett: The Critical Heritage*, ed. by Lawrence Graver and Raymond Federman (London and New York: Routledge and Kegan Paul), 191–206.
— Schopenhauer, Arthur (2000), 'Additional Remarks on the Doctrine of the Suffering of the World', in: Arthur Schopenhauer, *Parerga and Paralipomena: Short Philosophical Essays, vol. 2*, trans. by E. F. J. Payne (Oxford: Clarendon Press), 291–305.
  · (2010), *The World as Will and Representation, vol. 1*, ed. and trans. by Judith Norman, Alistair Welchman and Christopher Janaway (Cambridge: Cambridge University Press).
— Seyrig, Delphine (1992), 'Interviewed by Pierre Chabert', trans. by Elizabeth Berwanger, in: *Women in Beckett: Performance and Critical Perspectives*, ed. by Linda Ben-Zvi (Urbana and Chicago: University of Illinois Press), 18–21.
— Shainberg, Lawrence (1987), 'Exorcizing Beckett', *Paris Review* 104, https://static1.squarespace.com/static/5a7122dbedaed808205d5ada/t/5a7d089624a6949ae9e1c132/1518143639829/Exorcizing_Beckett_by_Lawrence_Shainberg.pdf.
— Shakespeare, William (1896), *The Works of William Shakspeare* (London and New York: Frederick Warne).
  · (1957), *The Complete Works of William Shakespeare*, ed. by W. J. Craig (London: Oxford University Press).
  · (2001), *The Arden Shakespeare Complete Works*, rev. ed., ed. by Richard Proudfoot, Ann Thompson and David Scott Kastan (London: Arden Shakespeare).
— Shenker, Israel (1956), 'Moody Man of Letters: A Portrait of Samuel Beckett, Author of the Puzzling *Waiting for Godot*', *New York Times*, 6 May, 'Section 2': 1, 3.
— Shillingsburg, Peter L. (1999), *Scholarly Editing in the Computer Age: Theory and Practice*, 3rd ed. (Ann Arbor: University of Michigan Press).
  · (2013), 'Literary Documents, Texts, and Works Represented Digitally', in: *Center for Textual Studies and Digital Humanities Publications* 3, http://ecommons.luc.edu/ctsdh_pubs/3.
— Slote, Sam (2001), 'Sound-bite against the Restoration', in: *Genetic Joyce Studies* 1, https://www.geneticjoycestudies.org/articles/GJS1/Soundbite.
— Sofer, Andrew (2016), *Dark Matter: Invisibility in Drama, Theater, & Performance* (Ann Arbor: University of Michigan Press).

— Sophocles (1912), *Sophocles in Two Volumes, vol. I, Oedipus the King, Oedipus at Colonus, Antigone*, trans. by F. Storr (London and New York: William Heinemann and The Macmillan Co.).
— Steiner, George (1980), *The Death of Tragedy* (New York: Oxford University Press).
— Stephen, Karin (1933), *Psychoanalysis & Medicine: A Study of The Wish to Fall Ill* (New York and Cambridge: Macmillan and Cambridge University Press).
— Stewart, Paul (2017), 'Fitting the Prose to Radio: The Case of *Lessness*', in: *Samuel Beckett and BBC Radio: A Reassessment*, ed. by David Addyman, Matthew Feldman and Erik Tonning (New York: Palgrave Macmillan), 211–27.
— Tonning, Erik (2007), *Samuel Beckett's Abstract Drama: Works for Stage and Screen, 1962–1985* (Bern: Peter Lang).
 · (2019), 'Modernism, Tragedy, and Christianity: Beckett and the Theatre of Racine', in: *The Transformations of Tragedy: Christian Influences from Early Modern to Modern*, ed. by Fionnuala O'Neill Tonning, Erik Tonning and Jolyon Mitchell (Leiden and Boston: Brill), 199–216.
— Tuan, Yi-Fu (2001), *Space and Place: The Perspective of Experience* (Minneapolis: University of Minnesota Press).
— Tucker, David (2013), *A Dream and Its Legacies: The Samuel Beckett Theatre Project, Oxford, c. 1967–76* (Gerrards Cross: Colin Smythe).
— Ubersfeld, Anne (1999), *Reading Theatre*, ed. by Paul Perron and Patrick Debbèche, trans. by Frank Collins (Toronto, Buffalo and London: University of Toronto Press).
— Uhlmann, Anthony (2006), *Samuel Beckett and the Philosophical Image* (Cambridge and New York: Cambridge University Press).
 · (2013), 'Staging Plays', in: *Samuel Beckett in Context*, ed. by Anthony Uhlmann (New York: Cambridge University Press), 173–82.
— Van Hulle, Dirk (2007), *Textual Awareness: A Genetic Study of Late Manuscripts by Joyce, Proust, and Mann* (Ann Arbor: University of Michigan Press).
 · (2008), *Manuscript Genetics, Joyce's Know-how, Beckett's Nohow* (Gainesville: University Press of Florida).
 · (2009a), 'The Dynamics of Incompletion: Multilingual Manuscript Genetics and Digital Philology', in: *Neohelicon* 36: 451–61.
 · (2009b), 'The Urge to Tell: Samuel Beckett's *Not I* as a *Texte Brisé* for Television', in: *Journal of Beckett Studies* 18:1–2: 44–56.
 · (2010), 'Beckett and Shakespeare on Nothing, or, Whatever Lurks behind the Veil', in: *Limit(e) Beckett* 1: 123–36, http://www.limitebeckett.paris-sorbonne.fr/one/vanhulle.pdf.

- (2011), *The Making of Samuel Beckett's 'Stirrings Still' / 'Soubresauts' and 'Comment dire' / 'what is the word'* (Brussels: University Press Antwerp).
- (2014a), *Modern Manuscripts: The Extended Mind and Creative Undoing from Darwin to Beckett and Beyond* (London: Bloomsbury Academic).
- (2014b), 'Textual Scars: Beckett, Genetic Criticism and Textual Scholarship', in: *The Edinburgh Companion to Samuel Beckett and the Arts*, ed. by S. E. Gontarski (Edinburgh: Edinburgh University Press), 306–19.
- (2015), *The Making of Samuel Beckett's 'Krapp's Last Tape' / 'La Dernière Bande'* (Brussels and London: University Press Antwerp and Bloomsbury).
- (2018), 'Introduction – Negative Modernism: Beckett's Poetics of Pejorism and Literary Enactment', in: *Beckett and Modernism*, ed. by Olga Beloborodova, Dirk Van Hulle and Pim Verhulst (Cham: Palgrave Macmillan), 1–18.
- (2019a), 'The Pentimenti Principle: The Draft and the Draff in Beckett's Critique of Narrative Reason', in: *Samuel Beckett Today/Aujourd'hui* 31.1: 37–52.
- (2019b), 'Shakespeare in Beckett's Library', paper presented at Beckett International Foundation Seminar, Reading, 8 November.
- (2021), 'Creative Concurrence. Gearing Genetic Criticism for the Sociology of Writing', in: *Variants* 15–16: 45–62.

— Van Hulle, Dirk, and Mark Nixon (2013), *Samuel Beckett's Library* (Cambridge: Cambridge University Press).

— Van Hulle, Dirk, and Pim Verhulst (2017a), *The Making of Samuel Beckett's 'En attendant Godot' / 'Waiting for Godot'* (Brussels and London: University Press Antwerp and Bloomsbury).
- (2017b), *The Making of Samuel Beckett's 'Malone meurt' / 'Malone Dies'* (Brussels and London: University Press Antwerp and Bloomsbury).
- (2017c), 'Notes on a Newly Discovered Draft of the Poem "Le Petit Sot"', in: *Journal of Beckett Studies* 26.2: 206–20.

— Van Hulle, Dirk, and Shane Weller (2014), *The Making of Samuel Beckett's 'L'Innommable' / 'The Unnamable'* (Brussels and London: University Press Antwerp and Bloomsbury).
- (2018), *The Making of Samuel Beckett's 'Fin de partie' / 'Endgame'* (Brussels and London: University Press Antwerp and Bloomsbury).

— Verhulst, Pim (2015), '"Just Howls From Time to Time': Dating *Pochade radiophonique*', in: *Samuel Beckett Today/Aujourd'hui* 27: 143–58.

· (2017a), 'The BBC as "Commissioner" of Beckett's Radio Plays', in: *Samuel Beckett and BBC Radio: A Reassessment*, ed. by David Addyman, Matthew Feldman and Erik Tonning (New York: Palgrave Macmillan), 81–102.
· (2019), '"A Thing I Carry About with Me": The Myth(s) of Sisyphus in Beckett's Radio Play *All That Fall*', in: *Samuel Beckett Today/Aujourd'hui* 31.1: 114–29.
· (forthcoming), 'Beckett's Technography: Traces of Radio in the Later Prose', in: *Samuel Beckett and Technology*, ed. by Galina Kiryushina, Einat Adar and Mark Nixon (Edinburgh: Edinburgh University Press).
— *A Wake for Sam* (1990), TV programme, BBC2, 7 February, https://www.youtube.com/watch?v=M4LDwfKxr-M.
— Weller, Shane (2005), *A Taste for the Negative: Beckett and Nihilism* (London: Legenda).
· (2006), *Beckett, Literature, and the Ethics of Alterity* (Basingstoke and New York: Palgrave Macmillan).
· (2008), '"Some Experience of the Schizoid Voice": Samuel Beckett and the Language of Derangement', advance access publication, in: *Forum for Modern Language Studies* 45.1: 32–50.
— Whelan, Feargal (forthcoming), 'The Permanent Way: Movement and Stasis in Beckett's Railways', in: *Samuel Beckett and Technology*, ed. by Galina Kiryushina, Einat Adar and Mark Nixon (Edinburgh: Edinburgh University Press).
— White, Harry (2008), *Music and the Irish Literary Imagination* (Oxford: Oxford University Press).
— Whitelaw, Billie (1996), *Billie Whitelaw ... Who He? An Autobiography* (London: Sceptre).
— Wiesel, Elie (2006), *Night*, trans. by Marion Wiesel (New York: Hill and Wang).
— Wiles, David (2007), *A Short History of Western Performance Space* (Cambridge and New York: Cambridge University Press).
— Wimbush, Andy (2020), *Still: Samuel Beckett's Quietism* (Stuttgart: ibidem-Verlag).
— Woodworth, Robert S. (1931), *Contemporary Schools of Psychology* (New York: Roland Press Company).
— Woolf, Virginia (1966), *Collected Essays, vol. 2* (London: Hogarth Press).
— Worth, Katharine (1986), 'Beckett's Auditors: *Not I* to *Ohio Impromptu*', in: *Beckett at 80 / Beckett in Context*, ed. by Enoch Brater (New York: Oxford University Press), 168–92.
· (2001), *Samuel Beckett's Theatre: Life Journeys* (Oxford: Oxford University Press)

– Wright, Joseph (ed.) (1898), *The English Dialect Dictionary, vol. I* (London: Henry Frowde; New York: G. P. Putnam's Sons).
– Yeats, W. B. (1989), *The Variorum Edition of the Plays of W. B. Yeats*, ed. by Russell K. Alspach (Basingstoke and London: Macmillan).
– Zola, Émile (1893), *The Experimental Novel and Other Essays*, trans. by Belle M. Sherman (New York: Cassell Publishing).

Index

Abbott, H. Porter 38, 184, 469
Ackerley, C. J. 144, 300, 304, 425, 428
Adler, Alfred 27
Admussen, Richard 70, 74, 78
Ankers, Katie 108
Apollinaire, Guillaume 145–146
Arikha, Avigdor 148, 151, 401
Arland, Marcel 368
Aronson, Arnold 479
Artaud, Antonin 148, 479
Asmus, Walter 157, 269–270, 273, 286, 304, 308, 313, 316, 388, 392, 394–395, 430, 436–438, 444, 450, 455
Atik, Anne 148, 151, 171, 332–334, 401, 403, 405, 433
Auster, Paul 88, 330

Bachelard, Gaston 339–340
Bailey, Iain 41, 211–212
Bair, Deirdre 144, 479
Baker, Phil 117–118, 438
Baldassano, Christopher 297
Balzac, Honoré de 36, 150, 154, 292, 402
Barrault, Jean-Louis 128, 130–131, 134, 204, 207, 479
Barry, Elizabeth 30, 322, 325, 472
Barthes, Roland 106, 154
Bates, Julie 297
Baudelaire, Charles 340
Bauer, Jerry 370
Beckett, Edward 440
Beckett, John 122–123
Beckett, Mary (May) Roe 117, 318, 413, 441
Beckett, Peggy 332
Beckett, Samuel
· *Acte sans paroles I / Act Without Words I* 151
· 'Afar a Bird' 409
· 'All but I' 302
· *All Strange Away* 180, 445, 448–449
· *All That Fall / Tous ceux qui tombent* 30, 312, 423, 427, 429
· *A Piece of Monologue / Solo* 31, 161, 259, 263–264, 329, 429
· *Assez / Enough* 92
· *As the Story Was Told* 280–281
· *Bing / Ping* 92
· *Breath / Souffle* 92, 147, 192, 219, 408
· *... but the clouds ...* 54, 88, 94, 108–109, 183, 329
· *Cascando* 115, 121, 154, 178, 193, 270, 413
· *Catastrophe* 193, 217, 259, 263–264, 444–445
· *Ceiling / Plafond* 59
· *Come and Go / Va-et-vient* 42, 146, 285, 326, 463
· *Comment c'est / How It Is* 115, 121–122, 127, 229–230, 281, 298–299, 304, 432, 472
· *Comment dire / what is the word* 146, 173–174, 299, 431, 443
· *Company / Compagnie* 120, 144, 151, 188, 210, 213, 318, 321, 329, 332, 334, 336
· 'Dante and the Lobster' 169, 214
· 'Dante ... Bruno . Vico .. Joyce' 182, 468, 477
· 'Ding-Dong' 428
· 'dread nay' 279–280
· *Dream* Notebook 272
· *Dream of Fair to Middling Women* 269, 272, 315, 453
· *Echo's Bones* 186
· 'écoute-les' 462
· *Eh Joe / Dis Joe* 270, 280–281, 297, 323, 328, 392
· *Eleutheria* 30, 34, 142, 432, 445, 469
· *Embers / Cendres* 121, 138, 179, 281, 417
· *En attendant Godot / Waiting for Godot* 43, 121, 128, 161, 164, 169, 186, 195, 205, 209, 248, 270, 282, 285, 297, 305, 329, 403–405, 419, 422, 427, 432, 439, 445, 450, 478
· 'en face' 327, 330

- *Esquisse radiophonique / Rough for Radio I* 44, 88–89, 94, 177, 284, 302, 381
- 'Fancy ~~Dead~~ Dying' Notebook 180, 449
- *Faux départs* 180
- *Film* 115, 466
- *Fin de partie / Endgame* 116, 121, 128, 169, 198, 205, 209, 212, 270, 283, 403, 414–415, 417–419, 421, 423, 432, 441–442, 445, 450–451, 479
- *Foirades / Fizzles* 429
- *Fragment de théâtre I / Rough for Theatre I* 44, 88–89, 94, 198, 381, 419, 448
- *Fragment de théâtre II / Rough for Theatre II* 44, 88–89, 94, 381
- *From an Abandoned Work / D'un ouvrage abandonné* 92
- 'German Diaries' 29, 311
- *Ghost Trio* 84, 88, 94, 108–109, 329, 402, 453
- *Happy Days / Oh les beaux jours* 42, 87, 96–97, 115, 128, 130, 147, 151, 197, 269, 282, 293–294, 306, 347, 401–404, 427, 486
- 'Horn Came Always at Night' / 'Horn venait la nuit' 54–55
- 'hors crâne' 279
- 'I Gave up before Birth' 409
- *Imagination morte imaginez / Imagination Dead Imagine* 37, 92, 180, 449
- 'J. M. Mime' 49–51, 53, 56, 115, 284
- 'Kilcool' 39, 49, 54–56, 115–118, 121–124, 126–127, 149, 157, 162, 293, 306, 312, 395, 438, 484
- *Krapp's Last Tape / La Dernière Bande* 82, 90, 100, 106, 121, 128–129, 146, 151, 169, 186, 205, 282, 293, 329, 337, 484
- *La Fin / The End* 118, 417
- 'La peinture des van Velde ou le monde et le pantalon' 186, 208, 299
- *Le Calmant / The Calmative* 417
- *Le Dépeupleur / The Lost Ones* 147
- *Le Kid* 337
- 'le pis revient' 328
- 'les joues rouges' 175
- *L'Expulsé / The Expelled* 315, 321
- *L'Image* 299
- *L'Innommable / The Unnamable* 37, 39, 53, 150, 154, 167, 176, 183, 229, 281, 309, 317, 461, 469
- 'Long Observation of the Ray' 406–407, 467
- 'Louis & Blanc' 297
- *Malone meurt / Malone Dies* 146, 150–151, 201, 270, 293, 340, 469
- *Mercier et Camier / Mercier and Camier* 141–143, 206, 213, 300, 309
- 'Mime du rêveur A' 417
- *mirlitonnades* 327–331, 334, 462
- *Molloy* 140, 150, 163, 309, 468–469
- 'Mongrel Mime' 160
- *More Pricks Than Kicks* 142
- *Murphy* 30, 134, 144, 168, 170, 174, 284, 291, 305, 322, 433, 438
- *neither* 329, 410, 463
- 'noire sœur' 458–459
- *Ohio Impromptu / Impromptu d'Ohio* 131, 259, 263–264, 445, 484
- 'On le tortura bien' 213, 280–281, 291
- 'Ooftish' 310
- 'pas à pas' 462
- 'Petit Odéon' Fragments 39, 56–57, 59, 127, 129, 133, 139, 150, 406, 417
- 'Petit Sot' poems 175
- 'Philosophy Notes' 186
- *Play / Comédie* 33, 42, 96, 104, 115, 120–121, 126, 146, 154, 159, 176, 195, 201, 205, 209, 238, 245, 269–270, 286, 301, 337, 385, 394, 432, 484
- *Pochade radiophonique / Rough for Radio II* 44, 88, 94, 147, 281, 381, 444

· *Pour finir encore / For to End Yet Again* 141, 146, 279
· *Premier amour / First Love* 84–85, 89, 91–94, 141–142, 144–145, 165–166, 189, 206, 309
· *Proust* 183, 291–293, 318, 320, 325, 335, 337, 343, 404, 428
· 'Psychology Notes' 27, 29–30, 37, 39, 123, 163, 466
· *Quad* 50
· *Quoi où / What Where* 264, 281, 316, 327, 445, 484
· 'Recent Irish Poetry' 28–29, 295, 318, 407
· *Rockaby / Berceuse* 30–31, 174, 259, 263–264, 392, 414, 461, 484
· 'Roundelay' 410
· *Sans / Lessness* 285–286
· 'silence vide nue' 334
· 'Six Poèmes' 176
· 'something there' 279
· 'Sottisier' Notebook 327–328, 334, 458
· *Sounds* 405
· *Still* 141, 171
· *Still 3* 412, 449
· *Stirrings Still / Soubresauts* 290
· 'Text 3' 215
· *Textes pour rien / Texts for Nothing* 115, 407, 423
· 'The Capital of the Ruins' 208
· 'The Downs' 162
· 'The Gloaming' 448
· 'The Voice / Verbatim' 213, 332
· *The Way* 427
· *Watt* 37, 115, 141, 143–144, 183, 270–271, 284, 297, 301, 312, 316–317, 327, 429
· 'Whoroscope' Notebook 183, 212, 425
· *Words and Music / Paroles et musique* 49, 55–56, 297
· *Worstward Ho* 295

Beckett, William (Bill) Frank 117, 441–442
Beer, Ann 143
Beethoven, Ludwig van 453
Beloborodova, Olga 33–34, 54, 115, 121, 126, 195, 201, 205, 209, 238, 245, 247, 270, 310, 385, 468–469
Benda, Julia 338
Bergson, Henri 337–339
Berkeley, George 305–306, 336
Bignell, Jonathan 107
Billington, Michael 293
Bion, Wilfred 27, 304, 429
Blau, Herbert 468
Blin, Roger 127, 204, 207, 457
Bonal, Gérard 134, 204, 459
Bourdelle, Émile-Antoine 49
Boyle, Kay 426, 459
Bragg, Melvyn 108
Brater, Enoch 160, 427–428, 431
Bray, Barbara 54, 56, 117, 141–142, 146, 149–150, 166, 182, 206, 247, 280, 293, 340, 386, 405, 410, 429, 457, 459–460, 480
Breuer, Josef 31
Brewer, Charlotte 304
Brook, Peter 124
Brown, Andreas 448
Brown, Robert 82
Browning, Robert 269
Brunton, Charles 133
Bryden, Mary 57, 59, 61, 66, 68–70, 74–75, 77–78, 101, 225, 231, 233–235, 240, 242–243, 247, 250–251, 253, 255, 332, 351, 355–357, 361–362, 385, 387, 391, 405, 448
Burleigh, Ruth 444
Burrows, Rachel 36, 337, 481
Burton, Robert 173, 425
Büttner, Gottfried 143
Buzelin, Hélène 205

Calder, John 55, 115, 142, 286, 291
Calderón de la Barca, Pedro 428
Camp, Pannill 35
Caravaggio 148–150
Carville, Conor 119, 482
Cary, Henry 290
Caselli, Daniela 287, 314–315
Chabert, Pierre 207, 460
Chalmers, David 32
Chamfort, Nicolas 426
Chekhov, Anton 483
Clark, Andy 32
Cluchey, Rick 323
Cohn, Ruby 77, 100, 122, 129–130, 135, 151, 204, 206–208, 247–250, 283, 285, 330, 368, 387, 395, 406, 408, 410, 453, 455–456, 461–462, 467
Coleridge, Samuel Taylor 449
Collins, Christine 392
Conley, Tim 344
Connor, Steven 142, 185–186, 406
Corneille, Pierre 337–338
Cousse, Raymond 143
Cronyn, Hume 93, 151–152
Cross, F. L. 473

Dante Alighieri 199, 214–215, 280, 287, 290, 300, 307–308, 312–315
Darby, J. N. 212, 474
Davis, Robin J. 260
Debray-Genette, Raymonde 300
Déchevaux-Dumesnil, Suzanne 141
de Compagnon, Antoine 40
de Gaulle, Charles 134
Deleuze, Gilles 185–186
Dennett, Daniel 33–34, 173
Descartes, René 33
Devlin, Denis 119, 299, 427
Diamond, Elin 418–419, 437
Dinçel, Burç İdem 428–429
Di Paolo, Ezequiel A. 38
Dobbs, Henry 441
Driver, Tom 136, 169–170, 413, 484–485
Duckworth, Colin 438
Dukes, Gerry 309
Duthuit, Georges 35, 150, 441
Dwan, Lisa 159

Elam, Keir 163, 280
Eliot, T. S. 124, 338, 340
Esslin, Martin 108, 286, 329, 408
Estang, L. 478
Exshaw, William Ernest 406

Favorini, Attilio 40
Fehsenfeld, Martha 338, 450–451
Feldman, Matthew 27, 186
Feldman, Morton 329, 410
Feuillerat, Albert 321
Fludernik, Monika 37
Forsythe, Henderson 93
Frankenberg-Garcia, Ana 217
Freud, Sigmund 27, 29, 31, 164, 321, 429–430, 476–477
Freytag, Gustav 427, 463
Friel, Brian 308
Frost, Everett 30
Furlong, George 302

Gabler, Hans Walter 347
Garforth, Julian 57, 59, 61, 66, 68–70, 74–75, 77–78, 101, 225, 231, 233–235, 240, 242–243, 247, 250–251, 253, 255, 332, 340, 351, 355–357, 361–362, 385, 387, 391, 405, 436, 448, 462, 473
Geulincx, Arnold 425

Gontarski, S. E. 41–44, 50, 54, 61, 63, 65, 90, 115–116, 127, 131, 167, 172, 197, 225, 234, 238, 240, 243, 254, 267–268, 288, 293, 300, 304, 327, 337–338, 358, 361, 370, 375, 384, 387, 392, 422, 428, 442, 455, 480
Gregory, Horace 147
Grene, Nicholas 312
Grésillon, Almuth 39, 41
Griffiths, Paul 284
Grotowski, Jerzy 479
Gullette, David 480
Gunn, Dan 181, 197

Habibi, Reza 39
Hackney, Stephen 303
Haerdter, Michael 451
Hamilton, Scott Eric 432
Harmon, Maurice 204
Harvey, Lawrence 323, 468
Hastings, Melvyn 153
Hay, Louis 150–151
Hayden, Henri 146
Hayden, Josette 146
Hayman, David 300
Haynes, John 216, 306, 323, 335, 410, 442
Heaton, Gabriel 386
Hegel, Georg Wilhelm Friedrich 420
Heidegger, Martin 136, 169
Henrioud, Charles (aka Matias) 127
Heraclitus of Ephesus 186, 190, 305
Herbert, Jocelyn 88, 128, 151, 206, 283–284, 329, 404, 408, 410, 442, 456, 462
Herm, Klaus 84, 253, 273, 286–287
Herman, David 194
Hill, Rose 410
Hölderlin, Friedrich 271–273, 299
Hollander, Jean 215
Hollander, Robert 214
Houlihan, Barry 486
Houston Jones, David 213
Hutchinson, Mary 150, 247, 299, 449
Hutto, Daniel D. 32
Huxley, Aldous 166–167

Ibsen, Henrik 480–481, 486
Ionesco, Eugène 127, 368, 478
Irigaray, Luce 419
Iser, Wolfgang 37–38
Israel, Calvin 359–360, 386, 392, 457
Israel, Joann 359–360, 386

Jackson, Michael 440, 444
Jaegher, Hanne De 38
James, William 168, 170, 195, 437
Janaway, Christopher 307
Janet, Pierre 31
Janvier, Agnès 297
Janvier, Ludovic 297
Jeantroux, Myriam 57, 135, 139
Jesus Christ 273, 314, 375, 379, 382, 418, 431, 438, 440, 452, 473–474, 482
Johnson, Samuel 136
Jones, Ernest 27, 29–31, 163–164, 184–185, 321, 429–430
Joyce, James 105, 148, 171, 173, 177, 180, 182, 295, 298, 344, 347, 427, 441, 468, 477, 480–481
Juliet, Charles 133
Jung, Carl Gustav 133, 138, 429–430, 477

Kafka, Franz 368, 469
Kalb, Jonathan 286, 416
Kaun, Axel 163–164, 307–308, 324, 453
Kennedy, Sighle 429
Kern, Edith 148

Key, Andrew 420
Kidd, Robert 284
Kim, Rina 179
Knowlson, Elizabeth 157, 304, 318, 334, 441
Knowlson, James 59–60, 90, 101, 108, 117, 128, 148, 157, 208, 216, 261, 295, 297–298, 302–304, 306, 318, 323, 327, 334–335, 338, 362, 377, 402–405, 408, 410, 439–442, 460–461, 479
Kobler, Evelyn 83, 85–86
Kobler, John 83, 85–86
Kristeva, Julia 451
Kuo, Z. Y. 178

Lambrichs, Georges 366, 368, 457
Lao-tzu 304
Latour, Bruno 44, 205–206, 331
Lawlor, Séan 410
Lefebvre, Henri 210
Lemprière, John 458–459
Lennon, Andrew 484
Leventhal, A. J. (Con) 128, 144, 442
Lewenstein, Oscar 151
Leyris, Pierre 205
Libera, Antoni 330, 375
Lindon, Irène 87
Lindon, Jérôme 87, 96, 141, 214, 457
Little, James 34, 42, 118, 145, 160, 182, 209, 217, 312, 417, 448–449
Livingstone, E. A. 473
Lloyd, David 295
Ludvigsen, Christian 195

MacGowran, Jack 50
MacGreevy, Thomas 27–28, 118, 302, 338–339
Mackintosh, Iain 35
Magee, Patrick 121, 253–254, 261, 283, 287
Malafouris, Lambros 32–33
Mallarmé, Stéphane 332–334, 340–341
Malraux, André 134, 204
Mandell, Alan 331
Mann, Thomas 105
Marc, Franz 29
Marcuse, Herbert 462
Martel, Kareen 300
Martin, David 41, 138, 211, 474
Martin, Jean 128
Maude, Ulrika 30
Mauthner, Fritz 186
Mawhinney, Ken 440–441
Maxwell, Jane 30, 49
McConachie, Bruce 34–35
McDonald, Ronan 428
McKinley, Grace 37
McMillan, Dougald 338, 450–451
McMullan, Anna 50, 52–53, 414, 445–446
McNaughton, James 42
McTighe, Trish 172
McWhinnie, Donald 84, 253, 268, 271, 283, 287
Melnyk, Davyd 429
Meschonnic, Henri 368
Meyer, Max 466
Miller, Brian 88, 153
Miller, Liam 145
Mills, Peter 57, 59, 61, 66, 68–70, 74–75, 77–78, 101, 225, 231, 233–235, 240, 242–243, 247, 250–251, 253, 255, 332, 351, 355–357, 361–362, 385, 387, 391, 405, 448
Mitchell, Breon 85, 90, 93, 260, 381
Monteith, Charles 44, 89–91, 408
Mooney, Sinéad 468
Moorjani, Angela 132
Morin, Emilie 131, 210, 213, 285, 480
Moroney, Kevin 440
Morrison, Kristin 273

Morton, Bill 107–108
Müller-Freienfels, Reinhart 108
Myin, Erik 32
Myron, Herbert 207, 329–330, 332

Neyt, Vincent 59, 291, 425
Nietzsche, Friedrich 425, 427
Nixon, Mark 28–29, 50, 55, 117, 129, 167, 173, 183, 197, 211, 215, 271–272, 280, 295, 311, 334, 340, 429–430, 433, 449, 480
Nolan, Sidney 74
Nordau, Max 166
Norman, Judith 307
Nugent-Folan, Georgina 151, 210, 213, 321, 332, 334, 336, 344

O'Brien, Eoin 69, 300
O'Reilly, Édouard Magessa 150, 163, 229

Paavolainen, Teemu 33
Page, Anthony 88, 108, 153
Page, Sheila 204, 318, 478
Palmer, Scott 486
Pavis, Patrice 478–479
Pelorson, Georges 338
Picasso, Pablo 29
Pierce, Andrew 440
Pike, Frank 362
Pilling, John 50, 82, 115, 117, 128, 142, 146–147, 175, 177, 181, 183, 206, 282, 291, 293, 299, 327, 331, 402, 407, 409–410, 413, 444, 448, 453, 456–457, 480
Pinget, Robert 127, 131, 478
Pinter, Harold 148–149, 293
Poe, Edgar Allan 340
Pothast, Ulrich 308
Pound, Ezra 299
Pountney, Rosemary 41–43, 54, 117, 121–123, 226–227, 268, 285, 327, 361–362, 370, 387, 413
Powell, Josh 160, 402
Powell, Tristram 107–108, 153
Proust, Marcel 40, 105, 183, 244–245, 291–294, 296, 318, 320–321, 324–326, 328, 335, 342–343, 404
Pryor, Sean 286

Rabaté, Jean-Michel 208
Racine, Jean 36–37, 132, 337, 424, 481, 485
Rank, Otto 27, 162, 188, 303–304, 309, 425, 427
Reavey, George 284
Reinhold, Karl-Leonhard 145
Renaud, Madeleine 128–129, 131, 134, 139, 204, 206–207, 456, 459–461, 479
Revely-Calder, Cal 485
Richardson, Brian 185
Richardson, Ralph 480
Ricœur, Paul 321
Rimbaud, Arthur 146
Rivière, Jean-Loup 44, 482–484
Robertson, J. G. 271
Rohde, Marieke 38
Rosset, Barney 76, 82–84, 92, 151, 234, 247, 249, 253, 262, 283, 287, 391, 480
Ryan, Desmond 123

Saint John 148–149
Saint Luke 273
Saint Paul 175, 183, 452
Salisbury, Laura 30, 160
Sardin-Damestoy, Pascale 187, 216, 291, 470
Sarraute, Nathalie 128
Sartre, Jean-Paul 136, 169, 183
Schechner, Richard 148, 479
Scheibe, Siegfried 150
Schiller, Friedrich 271

Schmahl, Hildegard 430, 437–438
Schneider, Alan 50, 54, 71–72, 84, 88, 93, 121, 129, 144, 147, 151–153, 160, 167, 202–204, 206–207, 213–214, 247–250, 253–254, 261–262, 282–283, 287, 328, 330–331, 335, 385, 391, 428, 456–458, 460, 480–481
Schoenberg, Arnold 285
Schopenhauer, Arthur 307–308, 428
Schroeder, Ernst 253, 287
Scott, Duncan 334
Searle, Humphrey 284
Seaver, Richard 142
Segond, Louis 41, 211, 474
Seyrig, Delphine 459–461
Shainberg, Lawrence 27, 213, 313
Shakespeare, William 40, 124–125, 161, 181–184, 281, 344, 403–404, 434
Shenker, Israel 317, 469
Shillingsburg, Peter L. 106, 115–116
Slote, Sam 347
Sofer, Andrew 482–484, 486
Sophocles 428
Stanislavsky, Konstantin 483
Stein, Gertrude 344
Steiner, George 428
Stekel, Wilhelm 27
Stephen, Karin 27, 165
Stewart, Paul 286–287

Tandy, Jessica 151–152, 160, 166, 202, 480
Thompson, Geoffrey 133
Tonning, Erik 42, 441, 481
Tophoven, Elmar 72, 143, 152, 182, 340, 450, 462, 473
Tophoven, Erika 72, 152, 182, 450
Trotter, David 286
Tuan, Yi-Fu 414
Tucker, David 129

Ubersfeld, Anne 43
Uhlmann, Anthony 30, 479
Unseld, Siegfried 99, 141, 146, 260, 337, 358
Ussher, Arland 271

van der Rohe, Ludwig Mies 269
Van Hulle, Dirk 31, 33, 39, 42–43, 82, 99, 105–106, 116–117, 125, 132, 139, 146, 150–151, 154, 161, 163–164, 166–167, 169, 172–173, 175–176, 183–184, 186, 197, 201, 205, 209, 211, 215, 219, 231, 260, 271–272, 280, 285, 288, 290, 293, 305, 323–324, 327, 334, 337, 340, 358, 368, 414–415, 419, 423, 427, 430, 432–433, 439, 446, 449–450, 461–462, 480
van Velde, Bram 35, 208, 299, 480, 482
Verhulst, Pim 43, 54, 56, 82, 115, 121, 123, 146–147, 150–151, 163–164, 175, 182, 184, 186, 193, 201, 205, 209, 270, 284–285, 287, 297, 302, 305, 318, 340, 368, 427, 432, 439, 450, 459
Virgil 199, 214, 290, 300, 307–308
Voltaire 215
Von Kleist, Heinrich 402

Warrilow, David 331
Welchman, Alistair 307
Weller, Shane 30–31, 42, 116, 139, 150, 172, 176, 205, 327, 423, 432, 450, 461
Wheatley, David 458
Whelan, Feargal 312, 440
White, Harry 284–285
Whitelaw, Billie 42, 75, 88, 101–104, 106–109, 144, 152–154, 159, 200, 202–203, 370, 388, 392, 408, 410, 415–416, 430–431, 453, 478
Wiesel, Elie 213–214

Wiles, David 34
Wimbush, Andy 304
Woodworth, Robert S. 27, 29, 37, 168–170, 174, 178, 466
Woolf, Virginia 171, 173
Worth, Katharine 91, 172, 181, 401
Wright, Joseph 203

Yeats, W. B. 28, 401–404, 409
Youngerman, Duncan 460

Zola, Émile 433